Charles Annandale, Thomas Thomson

A History of the Scottish People From the Earliest Times

Charles Annandale, Thomas Thomson

A History of the Scottish People From the Earliest Times

ISBN/EAN: 9783337008437

Printed in Europe, USA, Canada, Australia, Japan

Cover: Foto ©ninafisch / pixelio.de

More available books at **www.hansebooks.com**

A HISTORY

OF THE

SCOTTISH PEOPLE

FROM THE EARLIEST TIMES.

BY THE

REV. THOMAS THOMSON,

EDITOR OF "THE COMPREHENSIVE HISTORY OF ENGLAND;" ETC.

WITH

A CONTINUATION TO THE JUBILEE YEAR OF HER MAJESTY
QUEEN VICTORIA (1887), AND AN

INTRODUCTION

GIVING AN ACCOUNT OF THE COUNTRY AND ITS INHABITANTS IN THE
PERIOD PRECEDING THE INVASION OF THE ROMANS.

BY

CHARLES ANNANDALE, M.A., LL.D.

EDITOR OF "THE IMPERIAL ENGLISH DICTIONARY;" "THE MODERN CYCLOPEDIA;" ETC.

DIVISIONAL-VOLUME I.
EARLIEST TIMES TILL DEATH OF ROBERT BRUCE, 1329.

BLACKIE & SON, LIMITED,
LONDON, GLASGOW, EDINBURGH, AND DUBLIN.
1895.

CONTENTS OF DIVISIONAL-VOL. I.

LIST OF PLATES AND MAPS.

	Page
BRUCE SLAYS HENRY DE BOUNE BEFORE THE BATTLE OF BANNOCKBURN: A.D. 1314, *Frontis.*	236
DEFEAT OF THE DANES AT LUNCARTY NEAR PERTH: A.D. 973, *to face*	80
JOCELYN, BISHOP OF GLASGOW, REPUDIATES THE JURISDICTION OF THE ARCHBISHOP OF YORK, ,,	118
THE COUNTESS OF CARRICK CARRIES ROBERT DE BRUCE OFF TO TURNBERRY CASTLE, - ,,	138
WALLACE ATTACKED BY LORD PERCY'S FOLLOWERS WHILE FISHING IN IRVINE WATER. ,,	182
LINLITHGOW CASTLE CAPTURED FROM THE ENGLISH: A.D. 1313, ,,	232
MAP I.—SCOTLAND ABOUT A.D. 850, ,,	74
MAP II.—SCOTLAND ABOUT A.D. 1066, ,,	,,

INTRODUCTION. SCOTLAND IN THE PERIOD ANTERIOR TO THE ROMAN INVASION.—Earliest notices of the Country—The Greek navigator Pytheas circa 350 B.C.—Successive geological changes—Scotland a glacier country—River-drift men—Cave-men—The Stone Age—Bronze Age—Iron Age—Lake dwellings or crannogs—Hill-forts—Picts' houses—Burghs or brochs—Early races, - 1

PERIOD I. FROM THE EARLIEST TIMES TO THE UNION OF THE PICTS AND SCOTS. A.D. 843.

CHAP.   Page
I. Mythic and Legendary History of Scotland.—Origin of the Scots—Gathelus—The Picts—King Fergus—Scots and Picts oppose the Romans—Donald, the first Christian King, · · · · · 31
II. From the Invasion of the Romans to the Settlement of the Dalriad Scots: A.D. 80-503.—Invasion by Agricola—Battle of the Grampians—Hadrian's Wall—Invasion by Severus—The ancient Caledonians—Settlement of the Dalriad Scots, 41
III. The Picts and the Scots.—History of the Picts—Their territory, kings, and wars—History of the Scots—Kenneth succeeds to the Pictish throne—The Picts incorporated with the Scots, · · · · · 50
IV. History of Religion.—The Druids—Their costume, places of worship, and creed—Christianity introduced—Ninian, Palladius, Kentigern, Columba—The Culdees, 56
V. History of Society.—Government among the Caledonians—Their weapons, costume, and ornaments—Their strongholds—Their houses, domestic life, and occupations, · · · · · 66

PERIOD II. FROM A.D. 843-1097.

I. From Kenneth Macalpin to Death of Malcolm II.: A.D. 843-1034.—Wars of Kenneth Macalpin—Malcolm I. and II.—Danes defeated at Luncarty—Canute's Invasion, · · · · · 74
II. From Accession of Duncan to Accession of Edgar: A.D. 1034-97.—Reign of Duncan —Macbeth becomes king—Malcolm Canmore—Queen Margaret—Donald Bane, 83
III. History of Society during the Period, A.D. 843-1097.—Divisions of Celtic Scotland—Life of the Norwegian population in Scotland—Account of the Scoto-Celtic population, · · · · · 94

PERIOD III. FROM THE ACCESSION OF EDGAR TO THE DEATH OF ALEXANDER III. A.D. 1097-1286.

I. Reigns of Edgar, Alexander I., David I.: A.D. 1097-1153.—Edgar's tranquil reign—Alexander I.'s contests with the English hierarchy—David I.—Battle of the Standard—David's grants to the Church, 101
II. Reigns of Malcolm IV. and William the Lion: A.D. 1153-1214.—Minority of Malcolm IV.—Revolt of Somerled—William the Lion invades England, and is taken prisoner—His controversy with the Pope —Independence of the Scottish Church proclaimed, · · · · · 113
III. Reign of Alexander II.: A.D. 1214-1249.—Scotland invaded by King John—Rebellions in Caithness, Moray, and Galloway—Feuds between families of Athole and Bisset—Rebellion in Argyle, 123
IV. Reign of Alexander III.: A.D. 1249-1286.—Difficulties about Alexander's coronation—Alan Durward—Haco's Invasion

CHAP.	Page	CHAP.	Page
—Battle of Largs—Resistance to the Pope—Romantic marriage of Robert de Bruce to Countess of Carrick,	129	tish Church—The kingdom laid under interdict,	141
V. History of Religion: A.D. 650-1286.—The Culdee Church—Council at Whitby—Adamnan, abbot of Iona—Gradual suppression of the Culdees—Ascendency attained by Church of Rome—Archbishop of York claims homage from Scot-		VI. History of Society: A.D. 1097-1286.—Feudal system established—Administration of justice—Slavery in the kingdom—Commercial condition—Style of living—State of clerical society—Architecture—Schools—Michael Scot—Thomas Rymer,	154

PERIOD IV. FROM THE DEATH OF ALEXANDER III. TO THE DEATH OF ROBERT BRUCE. A.D. 1286-1329.

CHAP.	Page	CHAP.	Page
I. The Interregnum from the Death of Alexander III. to the Crowning of Baliol: A.D. 1286-1292.—Troubles on death of Alexander III.—Plots and intrigues of Edward I.—Death of Margaret of Norway—Competitors for the crown—Edward claims right of decision—Claims of Baliol declared superior,	166	VII. War of Independence (continued): A.D. 1312-1314.—Capture of Scottish fortresses by Bruce—Edward Bruce besieges Stirling Castle—Preparations for a decisive conflict—BATTLE OF BANNOCKBURN—Consequences of the victory—Death of John Baliol,	229
II. Reign of John Baliol: A.D. 1292-1296.—Troubles of the Scottish king—Despotic conduct of Edward—War commences—Scots defeated at Dunbar—Baliol's submission and deposition,	175	VIII. Reign of Robert Bruce: A.D. 1314-1318.—Bruce's cares as a legislator—His invasions of England—Edward Bruce in Ireland—His misfortunes, defeat, and death—The Scots retreat from Ireland,	241
III. Resistance to Edward I. under William Wallace: A.D. 1296-1298.—Sir William Wallace begins his patriotic career—His successful exploits—Defeats the English at Stirling—Appointed Guardian of Scotland—Edward invades Scotland—Battle of Falkirk,	182	IX. Reign of Robert Bruce (continued): A.D. 1318-1326.—Succession to the throne arranged—Invasions and counter-invasions—Conspiracy against Bruce—He defeats Edward at Biland—Is reconciled to the Pope—Birth of Bruce's son, afterwards David II.,	252
IV. War of Independence: A.D. 1298-1305.—Repeated invasions of Scotland by Edward I.—Baliol's conduct—Wallace resigns the guardianship—Claims of the Pope on Scotland—English defeated at Roslin—Wallace outlawed—He is betrayed—His trial and execution,	193	X. Reign of Robert Bruce (concluded): A.D. 1326-1329.—Edward III.'s fruitless attempts against Scotland—Peace at last established—Bruce's secluded life at Cardross—His death—His dying charge to Sir James Douglas,	262
V. War of Independence (continued): A.D. 1305-1307.—Robert Bruce's early career—Assassination of Comyn—Coronation of Bruce—He is defeated at Methven Wood and by the Lord of Lorn—Edward's merciless proceedings—Execution of Nigel Bruce,	206	XI. History of Religion: A.D. 1286-1329.—Jealousy of the Scots for their religious liberty—Restrictions imposed on the power of the clergy—The Pope's claim upon Scotland—Bruce's successful resistance,	274
VI. War of Independence (continued): A.D. 1307-1312.—Bruce lands in Ayrshire and renews the war—Edward I.'s last attempt at invasion—Imbecile proceedings of Edward II.—Bruce's invasions of England,	217	XII. History of Society: A.D. 1286-1329.—Condition of Scotland at this period—Its means of defence—Knights and common soldiers—Revenue—Administration of justice—State of commerce and agriculture—Free peasantry, slaves, and bond men—Sports of the people—John Duns Scotus—John Bassol,	280

A HISTORY

OF

THE SCOTTISH PEOPLE

FROM THE EARLIEST TIMES.

INTRODUCTION.

SCOTLAND IN THE PERIOD ANTERIOR TO THE ROMAN INVASION.

Written history of Scotland begins with Agricola's invasion, that of England with invasion by Julius Cæsar—Civilization in Scotland and England at the beginning of their history—Britain visited in the fourth century B.C. by the Greek navigator Pytheas—State of civilization at this time—History can tell us nothing of Scotland or England previous to this, but archæology helps us to go much further back—Geology shows us both countries in ages vastly more remote—Various successive periods distinguished by geologists—Great changes in former times in the geographical features, and the animal and plant life of the British Islands—Early land connection between Britain, the European continent, and North America—Climate of Britain then tropical, with plants and animals corresponding—Scotland and England inhabited by great monsters long extinct—Active volcanoes in Scotland—Connection with America ceases, and Britain becomes a peninsula of Europe—Change of climate to extreme cold, and Scotland smothered up in ice and snow—Effect of glacier action on Scottish scenery—Britain becomes an archipelago by sinking into the sea, but again rises and forms a large peninsula—First appearance of man in Europe and in Britain, in England earlier than in Scotland—The river-drift men—The cave-men—The prehistoric period proper, previous to which Britain separated from the Continent—The inhabitants of Scotland in the Stone Age and their civilization—Probably belonged to the Iberian race—The Stone Age followed by the Bronze Age: Celts now inhabit Britain—Civilization of Scotland in the Bronze Age—Great skill in metal working, articles of gold plentiful—The Iron Age succeeds the Bronze, leading down to the beginnings of written history—The lake-dwellings or crannogs—The hill-forts—The earth-houses or Picts' houses—The burghs or brochs—With what races are the early inhabitants of Scotland to be connected—The Celts akin to the Anglo-Saxons, Germans, Greeks, Romans, and other Aryan peoples—Early civilization of the Aryans and their primitive seat and migrations—The Pictish question in its most recent phases.

IN the present chapter we purpose to set forth briefly the main facts that inquirers have been able to glean regarding the condition of Scotland in times anterior to the point at which the written history of the country begins.[1] This point may be fixed at the year 80 of the Christian era, when the Romans invaded the country under Agricola, and endeavoured to add it to their already overgrown empire. The campaigns of Agricola are described in the contemporary narrative of the Roman historian Tacitus, and it is with this that the authentic history of Scotland begins, though, as we may remind the reader, neither the name Scotland nor the designation Scots existed for centuries afterwards. At this period, as duly narrated in a subsequent chapter, we find Scotland inhabited by a fairly numerous and decidedly warlike

---

[1] For the statements in this chapter the following are the chief authorities: *Early Man in Britain and his Place in the Tertiary Period*, by Prof. W. Boyd Dawkins (Macmillan & Co., 1880); *Cave-hunting*, by same author (Macmillan & Co., 1874); *Origins of English History*, by Charles J. Elton, F.S.A. (Bernard Quaritch, 1890); *Scotland in Pagan Times: The Bronze and Stone Ages*, by Dr. Joseph Anderson (David Douglas, 1886); *Scotland in Pagan Times: The Iron Age*, by same author (David Douglas, 1883); *Prehistoric Annals of Scotland*, by (Sir) Daniel Wilson, LL.D. (Macmillan, 1863, 2 vols.); *The Ancient Stone Implements of Great Britain*, by John Evans, F.R.S., F.S.A. (Longmans, 1872); *Prehistoric Times*, by Sir John Lubbock (Williams & Norgate, 1878); *The Lake-Dwellings of Europe*, by Robert Munro, M.D. (Cassel & Co., 1890); *Celtic Scotland*, by W. F. Skene (David Douglas, 1876-80, 3 vols.); *Celtic Britain*, by Prof. John Rhys (S. P. C. K., 1884); *The Early Ethnology of the British Isles*, by same author (the Rhind Lectures in Archæology for 1889); *Prehistoric Antiquities of the Aryan Peoples*, by Dr. O. Schrader, translated by F. B. Jevons, M.A. (Charles Griffin & Co., 1890); *The Origin of the Aryans*, by Dr. Isaac Taylor (Walter Scott, 1890); *The Scenery of Scotland*, by Sir Archibald Geikie (Macmillan & Co., 1887); *The Physical Geology and Geography of Great Britain*, by (Sir) A. C. Ramsay, LL.D., F.R.S. (Stanford, 5th edition, 1878); *Proceedings of the Soc. of Antiquaries of Scotland*, &c.

people, whom Agricola found to be stubborn opponents, though he at last defeated them in a great and well-contested battle, the leader opposed to him being an able chief or prince named Galgacus.

We thus see that Scotland makes its appearance in history at a much more recent period than many other countries. Not to speak of Greece, Rome, and other celebrated nations of antiquity, Scotland is even behind England in respect to the time at which history first deals with its fortunes, since England was visited about a hundred and thirty-five years earlier by Julius Cæsar, who has left us an account of southern Britain and its inhabitants written by his own hand. In B.C. 55 and 54 he twice crossed over from Gaul with a considerable force and gained some successes against the warlike Britons, though he did not stay to permanently subjugate the country. This, however, the Romans accomplished about a century later under the Emperor Claudius, and the whole of Britain south of the Clyde and Forth was ultimately incorporated in the Roman Empire. Julius Cæsar found a tolerably advanced state of civilization existing among the Britons of the south-east, more advanced, probably, than that which prevailed among the Caledonians in the time of Tacitus. He represents the country as thickly inhabited, the houses numerous, the people as cultivating corn, and as possessing great numbers of cattle. They were governed by petty kings or chiefs, employed war-chariots armed with scythes, possessed ships which could take part in a sea-fight; and altogether were found by the Romans to be no mean antagonists. One practice was very characteristic of them, namely that of painting or staining themselves of a blue colour with woad to render their appearance more terrible to their enemies in battle. Some of the tribes or peoples were so far advanced as to have provided themselves with coined money, and gold pieces of British coinage still exist that are believed to belong to a date as early as from 200 to 150 B.C. Tin was an important article of export, bronze was imported in return, and iron was moderately plentiful, perhaps even smelted from native ores. Away from the south and south-east of the island a more primitive state of matters seems to have existed, since according to Cæsar most of the inland people grew no corn, but lived on meat and milk, and clothed themselves with skins. Only a small part of the country, however, came under Cæsar's own observation, and it must have been difficult for him to get trustworthy information regarding the rest.

Such was the civilization of southern Britain at a period not long before the beginning of the Christian era, and from this time onward the light of history may be said to shine on the country with more or less brightness. Accordingly the line between historic and prehistoric Britain might be drawn here, though we are favoured with a brief glimpse of the country at a period nearly three centuries earlier, when a state of matters is revealed that quite agrees with the more detailed picture presented to us in Cæsar's narrative. The observer to whom we are indebted in this case was a Greek voyager of Marseilles named Pytheas, who about the middle of the fourth century B.C. made a voyage of exploration to the seas and coasts of northern Europe, then almost entirely unknown to the civilized communities dwelling around the Mediterranean Sea. Marseilles, anciently called Massilia or Massalia, had been founded by Greek colonists long previously, and was then a great trading centre; and Pytheas was sent out by some enterprising merchants on a voyage of discovery which, it was hoped, would result in an extension of the commerce of their city. The particulars that have come down to us regarding this voyage are very fragmentary and imperfect, and only reported at second hand, but as far as they relate to Britain are most interesting and valuable. Mr. Elton, who has carefully studied the subject of Pytheas and his voyage, states that Pytheas remained for some time in Britain, and appears to have visited many parts of the island, and to have coasted along the whole length of its eastern side. "He appears to have arrived in Kent in the early summer, and to have remained in this country till after the harvest, returning for a second visit after his voyage to the north. . . . In the southern districts he saw an abundance of wheat in the fields, and observed the necessity of thrashing it out in covered barns instead of using the unroofed floors to which he was accustomed in the sunny climate of Marseilles. 'The natives,' he said, 'collect the sheaves in great barns and thrash out the corn there, because they have so little sunshine that our open thrashing places would be of little use in that land of clouds and rain.' He added that they made a drink by mixing wheat and honey, which is still known as 'metheglin' in some of our country districts; and he is probably the first authority for the description of the British beer, which the Greek physicians knew by a Welsh name, and against which they warned their patients as a 'drink producing pain in the head and injury to the nerves.' . . . Pytheas appears to have known the eastern coasts from the Shetland Isles to the North Foreland, but not to have visited Ireland or even the western region of Britain."

Previous to the time of Pytheas the knowledge of Britain shown by ancient writers is of the vaguest character. Aristotle, however, who wrote probably before the time at which the celebrated voyage was made, knows of the existence of two large islands in this quarter, and refers to them as follows: "Beyond the Pillars of Hercules the ocean flows round the earth; in this ocean, however, are two islands, and those very large, *Albion* and *Ierne*, which are larger than those before mentioned, and lie beyond the Kelti." Britain itself is dimly referred to by the Greek writer Hecatæus of Miletus, about five centuries before the Christian era, as a large island lying off the coast of Gaul, inhabited by the sacred race of the Hyperboreans. At a somewhat later date Herodotus—"the father of history"—appears to refer to the British Islands under the name of the Cassiterides, a remote and rarely visited region known only as an important source whence tin was derived. But in the age of the Greek historian the Alps constituted a wall of separation scarcely less effectual in shutting out all beyond it from the influence and even the knowledge of the nations around the Mediterranean, than the broad waters of the Atlantic in holding apart the New World from the Old. Herodotus, accordingly, not only expressly states his own lack of direct knowledge "of any islands called Cassiterides from which the tin is wont to be brought," but he adds still further: "I am not able, though paying much attention to this matter, to hear of any one that has been an eye-witness that a sea exists on that side of Europe. But doubtless the tin and the amber are wont to come from the extreme parts of Europe." The Cassiterides are usually identified with the Scilly Islands, or with these and part of Cornwall; but they are often spoken of as closely connected with Spain, and their real identity is doubtful. The geographical notions of the ancients were so far from the truth that south-western England and Ireland were frequently represented as coming within a short distance of Spain, while Scotland on the other hand, instead of forming a northern continuation of England, was turned round to the east so as to lie at right angles to it, Ireland being also placed to the north of both.

Of the notices of Britain previous to the time of Cæsar that of Pytheas is by far the most important, the particulars given by him being not only exceedingly interesting, but also highly valuable for the light they throw on the early condition of southern Britain. It is much to be regretted on behalf of Scottish history that similar information has not come down to us regarding the state of matters which Pytheas found prevailing among the inhabitants of the northern portion of the island. This, however, is denied us, and as already stated, Scotland first emerges from the darkness of the prehistoric ages in the narrative of Tacitus and in the first century of the Christian era.

From the account given by the Roman historian we can perceive that the inhabitants—"the Britanni" as he calls them, or "the peoples inhabiting Caledonia"—were not mere savages, that they had made some advances in civilization, and were foemen not unworthy to meet in arms the Roman invaders. Hence we naturally reflect that, as *Vixere fortes ante Agamemnona*—as brave men lived before Agamemnon—so brave leaders may have distinguished themselves before Galgacus encountered the Roman legionaries, and may also have performed exploits worthy of celebration by poet or historian. When we think of "the dark backward and abysm of time" preceding the invasion of Agricola, we are led to speculate also as to the race-connections and the original home of the first inhabitants, and as to the stages of culture through which they had passed previous to the time at which we find them fighting for hearth and home against the Roman soldiers. At one time such speculations would have seemed hopeless and fruitless enough, but at the present day it is remarkable how much knowledge we have acquired of Scotland in the prehistoric period, and how detailed a picture can be drawn of the civilization of its inhabitants in times long before any historical date can be fixed, or any series of events chronologically established. This knowledge we mainly owe to the modern science of archæology, which endeavours to reconstruct the past from unwritten records, from the relics that peoples of former ages have left behind them, from the implements, weapons, and ornaments that they made and used, and from the graves in which their dead were buried. By drawing from these such evidence as they are capable of furnishing, archæologists have come to the conclusion that in Scotland and many other countries three successive stages of civilization must have existed in the past—stages that have now become well known and familiarly spoken of under the respective designations of the Stone Age, the Bronze Age, and the Iron Age—from the materials employed in the successive periods for the making of implements, weapons, and articles of various kinds. The last of those ages had begun by the time that the Scotland of history is presented to our view. The other two had begun and ended long before Scotland was known to the outside world.

It would be impossible, as will be shown in a little, to exaggerate the services that archæology has rendered in enabling us to reconstruct the past; but there is another science, geology, by which it may be supplemented, and which enables us to go further back still, if we desire. Archæology can tell us nothing of Scotland previous to its becoming the abode of man; if we wish to learn something of the country at a more remote period we must put ourselves under the guidance of the geologist. He can carry us with him to a time more distant by countless ages than that during which the archæologist finds any material to work on, and can give us an idea of what our country was long before it had any human inhabitants, when its climate and geography were very different from what they now are, and when it was roamed over by huge animals that have long ago disappeared from the earth, or are now only to be met with in localities far removed from Scotland. The wonderful changes that geology tells of are now well enough known: the substitution of land for sea and sea for land; the upheaval of mountains and their disintegration and remodelling by rain, frost, and other agencies; the appearance of strange types of animals and plants, and their subsequent disappearance, the fact that they once lived being known to us only from "the testimony of the rocks" and their occurrence in the form of fossils. These are all familiar to our minds as phenomena belonging to the past history of the earth, so that the words of Tennyson readily appeal to us as a vivid and picturesque presentation of actual and ascertained fact:

"There rolls the deep where grew the tree.
  Oh, earth, what changes hast thou seen!
There where the long street roars hath been
  The stillness of the central sea.

The hills are shadows, and they flow
  From form to form, and nothing stands;
  They melt like mists, the solid lands,
Like clouds they shape themselves and go."
          —*In Memoriam*, cxxiii.

Of such changes Scotland and the British Islands as a whole have had their full share, and we need not here attempt to trace them in any detail. It will be interesting, however, to go back for a short time to the last of the great periods which geologists have recognized as belonging to the earth's past history, since it was during this period that our planet was prepared for the abode of man. The periods here referred to are called life-periods, being based on the general character of the living forms that successively prevailed. The first of the periods has been named the Primary or Palæozoic period (that is, period of "ancient life"); the second the Secondary or Mesozoic period (the period of "middle life"); the third the Tertiary or Cainozoic period (the period of "recent life"). Some authorities regard the last period as continuing down to the present time, though many others recognize a Post-tertiary or Quaternary period as coming after the Tertiary.

The most noteworthy animals of the first period were fishes and amphibians, while among the most remarkable vegetable forms were pines, tree-ferns, and gigantic trees akin to club-mosses. The Secondary period was characterized by the prevalence of huge reptiles — some herbivorous others carnivorous, some living on land others living in the water, while others again disported themselves in the air like monstrous bats. Birds first appear in this period, and a few insignificant mammals. In the next or Tertiary period mammals reach their highest development, and we become acquainted with the mastodon, mammoth, and other gigantic creatures now extinct, the whole series of animal life being latterly crowned by the appearance of man, in company with the numerous species of animals that still inhabit the earth.

The Tertiary period, regarded as a whole, and as continuing down to the present time, has been divided into six well-defined stages,[1] each marked by its own special characteristics, and named respectively and in order of downward succession Eocene, Meiocene, Pleiocene, Pleistocene, Prehistoric, Historic. It is not till the fourth of these stages or epochs that we find evidence of the existence of man in Britain, but the changes through which the British Islands passed from the Eocene epoch downwards were so remarkable that they deserve to be briefly passed in review.

In the first or Eocene epoch of the Tertiary period, literally in the "dawn" of this period (Greek *ēōs*, dawn; *kainos*, recent), the land that now belongs to the British Islands formed part of the continent of Europe, being joined to Scandinavia on the north-east, as also to France on the south-west, while part of south-eastern England was covered with sea. North-westward from the British area ran a comparatively narrow stretch of land connecting Europe with America, by way of the Faroes, Iceland, and Greenland, and separating the Atlantic from the North Sea, which latter again was separated from the Arctic Ocean by land extending from Scandinavia to Spitzbergen and Greenland. This land connection with America offered a means of migration for plants and animals from America to Europe, and from Europe to America, and thus we find at the period of which we are now speaking an opossum and other animals common both to Britain and America, while the alligator that still remains a denizen of America then haunted the rivers of the south of England. Among the animals belonging to the Britain of this period were also huge turtles and crocodiles, quadrupeds like the tapir of tropical America and Asia, and others somewhat similar to the hippopotamus, a beast of prey resembling the hyæna, and another as large as a bear. The vegetation was to a great extent tropical in character, including evergreen fruit-trees, palms, and cacti, besides oaks, elms, beeches, and other forest trees. That the climate must have been tropical is clear from the evidence both of the plants and the animals, and a mean temperature of 70° has been estimated for Britain in the middle of this period. As regards the physical features of the country, the chief mountain masses were in the same relative positions as at present, but the elevations were higher and more precipitous, and active volcanoes probably existed in the Western Highlands of Scotland.

In the second or Meiocene stage of the Tertiary period (the name means "less recent"

---

[1] By Prof. Boyd Dawkins, in his work, *Early Man in Britain and his Place in the Tertiary Period.*

—as compared with the following stages) the British area was still united to the continent of Europe and to America, but the southern seaboard of England was now washed by a very small portion of sea, the greater part, if not the whole of the English Channel being latterly dry land. The principal mountains were in the same positions as at present, but were very much higher. In the western and northern parts of the island they rose to an estimated height of 6000 or 7000 feet, and as the general level of the land was probably higher by 3000 feet, the actual height of some of the mountains above the sea would be not less than 10,000 feet. At this time there were active volcanoes in the north and west of the British Isles, some of them of remarkable size. In Mull there was a great volcano, now represented by Ben More, which is a mere fragment of the original mass. The original Ben More is calculated to have been 10,000 or 11,000 feet in height at least; and there was a volcano in Skye of like dimensions. At this time, indeed, along a line of 400 miles in the British area, there rose a chain of active volcanoes, comparable in magnitude to those of the Andes, and overwhelming from time to time with lava and ashes the adjacent forests. The plants of the British Islands at this period included an evergreen oak, a huge conifer resembling the mammoth-tree of California, plane-trees, cinnamon-trees, gum-trees, a rattan palm, and various other plants equally strange to modern Scotland. On the continental area grew palms and other plants, all testifying to the mildness of the climate at this period. Among mammals may be mentioned rhinoceroses, tapirs, the giraffe, the dinotherium—a huge quadruped with a proboscis and with tusks in the lower jaw curving downward; the mastodon—a sort of elephant with tusks in both the upper and the lower jaw; a great carnivorous animal called the sabre-toothed lion, and numerous apes. Both Iceland and Spitzbergen had then a temperate climate, and that of West Greenland was such as to allow magnolias, chestnuts, oaks, planes, and vines to flourish.

The succeeding or third period, that is, the Pleiocene or "more recent" stage of the Tertiary, exhibits as regards the geography of Britain several important changes from the two preceding epochs. A great sinking of land had by this time taken place, and where there was formerly a continuous land-surface between the British area and Scandinavia there was now a southward prolongation of the North Sea. The Atlantic and North Sea were now also connected, owing to the sinking and disappearance of the tract of land which had previously extended north-westward to Iceland and Greenland. Accordingly the British Islands now formed a solid peninsula, whose western coast-line lay beyond the present entrance to the English Channel or Cape Clear, beyond the west coast of Ireland and the Hebrides, and ran north-eastwards so as to take in the Shetland Islands; while dry land entirely occupied the place of the English Channel, and afforded a more continuous connection with the Continent than formerly existed in this quarter. The mountains as before were similar in position to those with which we are still familiar, but much higher. The volcanoes were probably active at the beginning of the period, but gradually became extinct. The rivers flowed generally in courses similar to those they still possess, but those in particular that emptied themselves into the Atlantic were very much longer, since the land then extended so much further to the west. The climate, though warmer than that of modern Britain, was colder than formerly, and continued getting colder to the end of the period. Among British animals of this time we find a mastodon, an elephant, a hyæna, a bear, and a beast of prey allied to the leopard. The mammalia, both of Britain and the Continent, are seen to be by this time very closely akin to those that still inhabit the earth.

We now reach the Pleistocene or "most recent" period, the fourth of the epochs or stages mentioned above, otherwise regarded as the first stage of the Quaternary or Post-tertiary division of geologic time. This period is exceedingly interesting for various reasons, but especially for the climatic, geographical, and other revolutions that it witnessed, and because in it, as already stated, we find for the first time indubitable evidence of the existence of man in Britain. During this period, or part of it at least, the British area still formed a portion of the mainland of Europe, but extended much further to the west, north, and east than at present; Ireland, the Hebrides, the Orkneys and Shetlands being all embraced within its limits, and the bed of the North Sea being

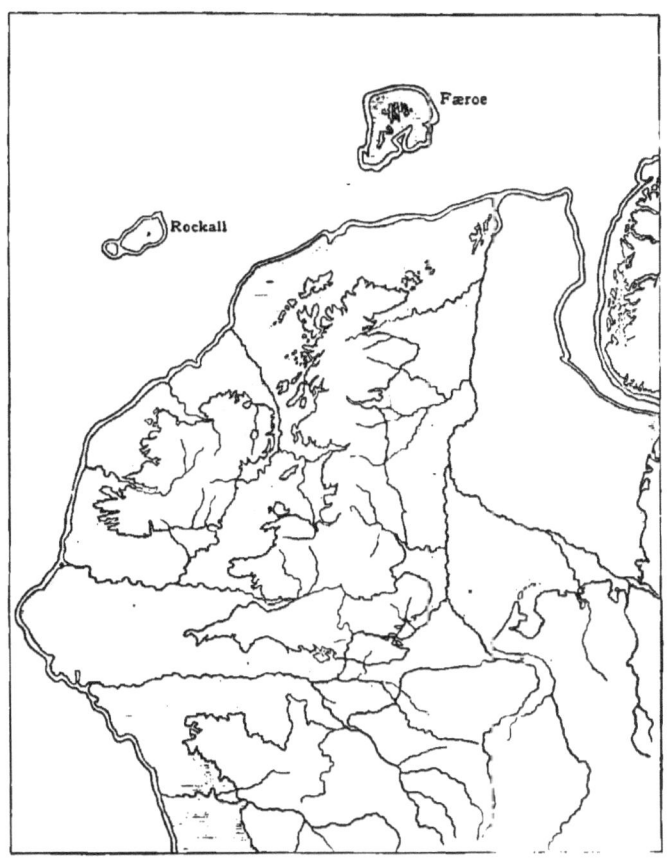

MAP SHOWING BRITAIN IN THE PLEISTOCENE AGE. (By permission of Messrs. Macmillan & Co.)

then dry land. Generally speaking it appears that the climate of Europe during this epoch showed great extremes between the north and the south, there being a middle zone, comprising France, Germany, and great part of Britain, in which the winters were cold and the summers warm, as in middle Asia and North America. Besides this there were one or more periods during which the climate as a whole, after getting colder and colder, reached so great a degree of severity that vast tracts were wrapped up in a permanent covering of ice and snow, such as may still be seen in the interior of Greenland. The greater part of Britain, and Scotland in particular, must have then formed a scene of awful solitude and desolation, being entirely smothered up in glaciers, which slowly and resistlessly moved onwards from the higher grounds to the sea as their mass was continually being augmented by the fall of snow. In some places these icy masses are estimated to have reached a thickness of 2500 or 3000 feet. The effect of glacier action on the scenery of Scotland has been powerful and enduring, as is pointed out by Sir Archibald Geikie in particular.

"The surface of Scotland," he remarks, "like that of Ireland and of the northern half of England, as well as the whole of Scandinavia and northern Europe, is distinguished from more southern countries by a peculiar contour, visible almost everywhere, irrespective of the nature of the rock. This contour consists in a rounding and smoothing of the hills and valleys into long flowing outlines. What were no doubt once prominent crags have been ground down into undulating or pillow-shaped knolls, while deep hollows and gentler depressions have been worn in the solid rock. It may seem paradoxical to speak of the well-known rugged Highland mountains as showing traces of a general smoothing of their surface. But such is really the case . . . . Even in the wildest Highland scenery, where the casual tourist may see nothing but thunder-riven crags and precipices, and glens blocked up with their ruins—

'Precipitous black jagged rocks,
For ever shattered and the same for ever'—

an eye trained to observe it can detect the same universal smoothing and moulding."

With regard to the movements and mass of the Scottish glaciers the same authority writes as follows:—

"It is quite possible to realize the main movements of the Scottish ice-sheet as it crept seaward. From Cape Wrath to the south-west of Ireland one vast glacier pushed out into the Atlantic, where it broke up into icebergs that probably drifted away to the north with the prevalent winds and currents. The Firth of Clyde was choked with deep ice which moved steadily southward, and, joined by the mass that drained from the uplands of Galloway, the Lake Country and Wales, filled up the basin of the Irish Sea. From the southern Highlands the ice marched south-eastwards across the chain of the Ochil Hills, and uniting with that which streamed away from the hills of Lothian and Peebles went out into the basin of the North Sea. There the Scottish ice-sheet appears to have met with that which descended from Scandinavia, and to have marched southward along the east of England. From the eastern Grampians the drainage was towards the sea and north-east, while a vast thickness of ice streamed northwards into the Moray Firth, passing northwards across the low plains of Caithness and the Orkney and Shetland Islands, and forming with the Norwegian ice-sheet a vast glacier that stretched probably in one unbroken wall of ice for some 1500 miles from Cape Clear to beyond the North Cape. Among the many contrasts which geology reveals between the present and the past there is surely none that appeals more vividly to the imagination than that which the records of the Ice Age bring before us."

There is one feature of the surface of Scotland and certain other regions which we should not readily associate with the Ice Age, and which yet such an eminent authority as Sir Andrew C. Ramsay maintains to have had its origin in that period, and to be directly due to the action of glaciers. We refer to the numerous lakes which form such a common and attractive feature of Scotland. . These mostly lie in rock-bound hollows or depressions, and Sir Andrew Ramsay believes that such rocky basins have been scooped out by the action of glacier-ice, though of course he does not attribute the existence of all the lakes to this cause. He first worked out his theory in connection with the Lake of Geneva and the other Swiss lakes, but he applies it equally to the Scottish lakes, such as Loch Lomond, Loch Katrine, and Loch Doon, insisting that the features of the hollows in which these lakes lie can only be explained on the hypothesis of ice action, abundant evidence of which can yet be pointed out. Many of the fiords or sea-lochs so common on the west coasts of Scotland and Norway he believes to have been originally rock-basins formed in this way, though now arms of the sea; and one proof of this origin is the well-known fact that they are generally shallower at their entrance than farther inward.

Authorities are not agreed as to the cause or causes that produced the glacial period here spoken of, but one cause to which the severity of the climate was probably due in part was the greater elevation of the land at this time. A period of subsidence, however, now followed, and a large portion of the surface of the country disappeared beneath the sea, leaving the present British area to be represented by an archipelago of islands formed of the higher mountain masses. These continued to be still covered with glaciers, which, when they reached the sea, gave off great masses of ice to float away as icebergs. As evidence of this submergence we still find sea-shells in Scotland at elevations of more than 500 feet above the present level of the sea, while the well-known "raised beaches" are witnesses of the same fact. The land again emerged, however, and Britain and Ireland became once more united to the rest of Europe. The climate also became less severe, though snow-fields and glaciers still continued to clothe the mountains and to creep downwards into the valleys. By degrees the annual temperature rose higher and higher, becoming at last similar to what it now is. The glaciers thus entirely disappeared from the British area, though not from the higher elevations of Europe, where they are still represented in the Alps, in Scandinavia, and even in the Pyrenees.

That man can hardly have been an inhabitant of Scotland during the rigorous period of ice and glaciers just described is obvious. When we first find evidence of his existence in Europe, it is not in Scotland that he appears, but in England and on the Continent, his presence being attested by the discovery of rude flint implements which must have been fashioned by his hands. These tools, made of stone, have a distinctive character of their own, and as they want the polish and finish of stone implements belonging to a later age, they are classed, in contradistinction to those, as *palæolithic*, the others being known as *neolithic* (from Greek *palaios*, ancient, *neos*, new, and *lithos*, a stone). These early implements are found covered up in certain gravelly deposits laid down by rivers, and hence the men who must have used them are known as the "men of the river-drift." So far these river-drift men are known to have inhabited a part of England only, namely the south-eastern portion, and especially the valley of the Thames, and the implements bearing witness to their presence are chiefly found towards the close of the period now dealt with. The implements belong to a very few types, such as flakes with sharp edges intended for cutting or scraping, pointed instruments of various kinds, some of them similar to lance-heads or spear-heads, others perhaps serving as digging or boring tools, hatchets, &c. Along with these objects made of stone, no doubt others made of wood, bone, or horn may have been used, but of this evidence is wanting. The river-drift men, whatever may have been their natural endowments, mental or physical, were evidently in a very low stage of culture judged by our standards. No doubt they were a race of hunters living entirely on the products of the chase; they had no tillage and no domestic animals, and probably resembled in manner of life more the aboriginal natives of Australia than any other people with whom we are acquainted. Besides Britain the river-drift men inhabited France, Spain, Greece, North Africa, Western Asia, and India.

As contemporaries these nomadic hunters had in Britain the grisly bear, now found only in North America; the cave-bear, another large carnivorous animal making its abode in caves; the lion, the leopard, the horse, the stag, the Irish elk, the reindeer, the urus, the bison, the hippopotamus, the rhinoceros, the mammoth, the elephant; so that if they had plenty of animals to supply them with food they had others to contend with as formidable foes. Only two of these animals, the mammoth and the Irish elk, have become altogether extinct. The mammoth was an inhabitant of Scotland as well as England and Ireland. It lived also in France and other parts of Europe, and its remains have been found in Siberia and North America. In parts of Siberia these remains are so plentiful that the tusks have long formed a commercial source of supply for ivory. In more than one instance specimens of the mammoth, which was simply a kind of large elephant, have been found embedded in the ice-bound soil of the tundras or morasses of Siberia, having been preserved almost entire by the cold. One such specimen was found to be clothed with furry wool of a reddish colour interspersed with black hairs, and no doubt all those that inhabited the more northern parts were protected by a natural covering of the same kind. The tusks were of immense size, being 9 or 10 feet in length measured along the outer curve, and they had something of a spiral form, being directed first downward and outward, then upwards and inwards. The great Irish elk was found most abundantly in the country from which it gets its designation, but was also a denizen, though much rarer, of Scotland and England.

Since Britain then formed part of a large continental expansion of north-western Europe, these animals and others had free access to the country, and could then also roam through the forests that grew in what is now the bed of the North Sea. The rivers of eastern Britain at this time, including both those of Scotland and those of England, had their upper courses much the same as now; in their lower courses they joined with the Rhine, the Weser, and the Elbe to form a great stream flowing northwards and emptying itself into the ocean in the vicinity of the Shetlands. So also the rivers of the south of England and of northern France formed a great river flowing west into the Atlantic; the Severn united its waters with the rivers of the south of Ireland; while those of the east of Ireland joined the Dee, Mersey, and other streams of England and western Scotland, their waters ultimately reaching the Atlantic at a point beyond the Hebrides.

Another race of men, who also made use of rude flint implements of the palæolithic type, appear to have followed the river-drift men in Britain. This new race are known by the name of "cave-men," from the fact that the evidences of their existence in England and on the Continent have been obtained from the natural caves which formed their habitations, though it is also known that certain caves were inhabited by the river-drift men, as indeed has been the case with savage peoples down to the present day. And of course we need not suppose that the cave-men lived perpetually in caves, though they found these to be convenient abodes, and used them as such generation after generation. It seems doubtful if these cave-men extended as far north as Scotland, though the absence of evidence to show this may be partly owing to the rarity of caves in the country, and that again may be explained by the scarcity of limestone rock in Scotland, this being the kind of rock in which caves most abound.

The cave-men seem to have been less widely spread than the men of the river-drift, since, though they inhabited France, Belgium, Switzerland, and Germany, they are not known to have ranged far north or far south in Europe. One of the most famous English caverns inhabited by the cave-men is Kent's Hole near Torquay, another being the Wookey Hole near Wells, while others are situated in Wales, in Yorkshire, and elsewhere. The implements of the cave-men were similar on the whole to those of the river-drift men, but more varied in character, including, besides flint instruments of the kinds already described, also bone needles and pins, bone awls or borers, barbed harpoon-heads of the antlers of deer, flint arrow-heads and javelin-heads, &c. The animal remains found along with such implements prove that in England the cave-man had as his contemporaries the same species of animals that occupied the country along with the men of the river-drift. Some of these animals furnished the cave-men with food, being objects of the chase, and the weapons with which they were attacked were no doubt spears tipped with bone or flint.

Strange to say, spirited though slight sketches of hunting scenes, executed by artists of this remote era, still remain to challenge our surprise and admiration. One of these sketches, incised on a piece of deer's antler, depicts a hunter in the act of throwing a spear at a huge bison or urus which he has been successful in stalking. Another scene, engraved on a piece of the same material, shows a hunter in the act of felling a horse; while two bisons' heads drawn with remarkable spirit adorn the other side of this piece of antler. A striking group of reindeer, a drawing of a single reindeer feeding with some herbage shown near him,

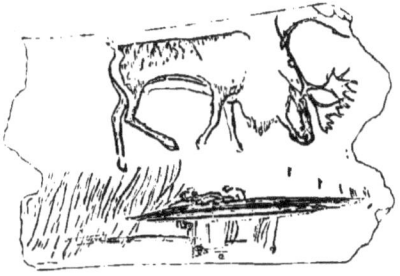

REINDEER INCISED ON ANTLER. (By permission of Messrs. Macmillan & Co.)

an accurate outline of the cave-bear, the figure of a seal and another of a pike, both drawn on the canine of a bear, are also among the most interesting of those early works of art. Nor should we omit to mention the drawing of a mammoth on a piece of ivory, giving a very good idea of this huge beast. Human figures are less frequently presented than those of animals, and are less successfully treated. Among the cave-men there were also skilful carvers, one of the best specimens of their work in this branch of art being the handle of a dagger made of a reindeer's antler cleverly carved into the shape of the animal itself. Such artistic productions, if they do not presuppose any very high state of culture, at least argue the existence of a certain taste and leisure among the cave-men, and show that the struggle for existence did not constantly make itself felt.[1] The general manner of living of these people must have been rude enough, however. For one thing, it is evident that they had no articles of pottery, or fragments at least of this almost imperishable material would have survived. Their vessels would therefore most naturally be made of horn, skin, or wood. The only knives they had must have been made of flint, pieces of which, as also sea-shells, may have served as spoons, though the latter might also be shaped from wood. Their clothes were no doubt made of furs and skins sewed together with sinews by means of bone needles. That they wore gloves is proved by still extant drawings of these articles executed by them. Besides quadrupeds, birds formed part of their food, being probably caught in snares, and no doubt obtained also otherwise; and fish — salmon, trout, carp, pike, and others — were also eaten. They had no domestic animals. Fire was probably obtained by friction as among savages of the present day.

When we ask what were the ethnological relationships of the cave-men, or with what race in the modern world they may be connected, the answer is not very clear. Some authorities do not think they differed ethnologically from the river-drift men, whatever the affinities of these may have been; others have suggested that they were ancestors of the Laplanders. Professor Boyd Dawkins thinks they were not ethnologically related to the river-drift men, and believes that there is no race or people in Europe at the present day which can be considered to represent them. His opinion is that there is only one people with whom the cave-men can be looked upon as closely connected in their manners and customs, their artistic gifts, and in their implements generally, this people being the Eskimos, who now inhabit Greenland and the extreme north of North America, as well as part of north-eastern Siberia. He also draws attention to the fact, which at least forms an interesting coincidence, that as the musk-sheep or musk-ox was a contemporary of the cave-men in Europe, so it is only in the country of the Eskimos, their supposed descendants, that it is to be found at the present time.

Having endeavoured to give some idea of what may have been the condition of Scotland during the later geological periods, we now come to treat of the prehistoric period more strictly so-called. This period, however distant its beginning may have been if measured by years, is yet modern when compared with the periods that have been already passed under review, and leads

---

[1] In regard to this point Sir John Lubbock remarks: "The appreciation of art is to be regarded rather as an ethnological characteristic than as an indication of any particular stage in civilization." — *Prehistoric Times*, p. 502.

us down without any notable gap to the beginnings of actual history. How far back it extended is a question upon which chronology can throw little or no light, any attempt at fixing dates being mere guesswork. In this period man comes to have a prominence that he did not possess in any former epoch; and the progress then made by him in civilization and the arts and occupations that ameliorate life has been continued onwards to our own day. During this period we find him to have advanced from the precarious life of the hunter to that of the herdsman and the farmer. He now appears also as the trader and the handicraftsman, the dweller in fixed abodes constructed by himself, the lord and master of animals reduced by him to a state of dependence and subjection, grain and fruits being also reclaimed by him from their natural wild state. In the earliest portion of the period stone is still the material from which he fashions his tools and weapons, metal being unknown, or at least unworked; but the flint implements we now find in use are of the neolithic type, polished and finely finished, very different from the palæolithic implements of which we have already spoken. After the lapse of ages bronze becomes known and utilized, and subsequently iron, the introduction of bronze, and then that of the more widely useful metal, having led to corresponding changes in the arts and civilization of the peoples among whom they took place.

These successive changes have formed a basis for the division of the prehistoric period, both in Scotland and in other countries, into the three subdivisions or ages formerly mentioned, the Stone Age, the Bronze Age, and the Iron Age. This classification must not be understood to imply any chronology in the proper sense, much less one that would be applicable to all countries alike; it is only to be regarded as emphasizing the fact that there has been a succession of different stages of civilization. It is evident, indeed, that at the time when, for instance, in a country such as Italy or Greece, the Iron Age may have commenced, some of the more northern countries of Europe may have been in their Bronze Age and others again still in their Stone Age. As proof of this we may point to the fact that the Peruvians were in their Bronze Age when they became known to Europeans, while the Polynesians and others, when they first became known to us, were in their Stone Age. Moreover this classification into three periods does not imply that in the Bronze Age of any country stone implements fell entirely out of use (more especially in the early portion of the period), nor even that in the Iron Age both bronze and stone were completely superseded by iron for all cutting purposes.

In treating successively of the Stone, the Bronze, and the Iron Age, we have to trust almost entirely to the guidance of the archæologist, and require comparatively little aid from the geologist, since during the period covered by the three ages geological changes have been comparatively few and unimportant. Before the Stone Age began, however, great changes must have taken place, and Britain, as we have just seen it in the latter part of the Pleistocene period, was very different from the Britain of the age which we have now reached, when the country, so far as concerned geography, differed comparatively little from the Britain of to-day. Before Britain assumed even approximately its present configuration, however, there must have been a great sinking of land and submergence of low-lying tracts, the result of which was that the British Islands became separated from the Continent and from each other by sea, and the North Sea, the English Channel, and the Irish Sea came to occupy the areas that they now respectively cover. The sinking of the land continued even into the prehistoric period, and portions of the present British coast have thus been submerged, as is proved in particular by the fact that in certain places the sea has overflowed forests which can be shown to be of prehistoric age. In like manner the forests which are known to have formerly existed in Orkney and Shetland, Caithness, and elsewhere in Scotland, are believed to have belonged to a period before the sinking of the land finally ceased, the trees having then, it is supposed, been able to flourish in the localities referred to owing to the greater elevation of the surface and the consequent distance of the sea and its blighting influence. The climate of the country generally in the prehistoric period, especially in the earlier portion of it, would probably be damper than in the historic, owing to the greater prevalence of forests and morasses; while, from the somewhat larger area of land existing, there would probably also be a greater difference between the temperature of summer and that of winter. The presence of the reindeer, and the moose or elk, as far south as the valley of the Thames, is regarded as evidence of the same climatic conditions.

Among the animals of the Stone Age of Britain the two just mentioned seem to have been more abundant in Scotland than in England, and no doubt served the inhabitants as an important source of food. Another animal, rare in Scotland, but remarkably abundant in Ireland, was the Irish elk, a splendid specimen of the deer tribe, with huge antlers measuring ten or eleven feet in extent from side to side. Of all the animals that survived from the former period into this it is the only one that has since become entirely extinct. Other animals, however, that were its contemporaries have become extinct so far as Britain is concerned, such as the grisly bear, the brown bear, the wolf, the wild boar, the elk, the reindeer, the beaver, and the great wild ox, the urus. The domestic animals belonging to the inhabitants included the dog, the ox, of the variety known as the Celtic shorthorn, the sheep, the goat, and the hog.

The people of the Stone Age in Scotland are the first inhabitants of this country regarding whom we know anything definite. As they were in the neolithic stage of civilization, possessing implements and weapons of polished stone, they are often spoken of as the neolithic people, a term that does not imply any theory as to the race to which they may have belonged. That they belonged, however, to a homogeneous race spread over the whole of Britain is proved both by the similarity in the weapons, implements, and ornaments in use throughout the island during the Stone Age, and also, and more especially, by the character of the barrows or grave-mounds constructed by them for the interment of their dead alike in Scotland and in England.

These barrows are so important as to require some special notice. They are structures of considerable magnitude, the materials being mostly loose stones piled up, and others of large size regularly laid in position. They are constructed with a definite external form and regular ground plan, and all contain a chamber or series of connected chambers for receiving the remains of the dead, who were in many cases cremated, but in others not. The most remarkable of these sepulchres, on account of their magnitude, are those known as "long barrows," which are believed to be older than another class designated "round barrows." The long barrows are often of what is known as the "horned" type, having projecting horn-like extensions at either end. These grave-mounds or cairns usually lie in a direction from east to west, being higher in the east, and diminishing in height westwards, and they are often surrounded by a single or double retaining wall, as it may be called, rising to a certain height. One of these cairns in Caithness-shire, examined by Dr. Joseph Anderson, was found to be 240 feet in length, the breadth at the base at the eastern end being 66 feet, at the western end 36 feet. The distance between the tips of the eastern horns or projections was 92 feet, of the western 53 feet, while the extreme height was not more than 12. Some of those in England are larger than this, extending to 300 or 400 feet in length. In this Caithness example there was found to be a chamber in the eastern end, entered by a narrow passage between the horns, and of very small dimensions compared with the size of the whole structure, the length being only about 12 feet from front to back, the width 6, and the height 7. Some insignificant pieces of human bone, chips of flint, and two fragments of dark-coloured pottery were all that the chamber contained. Other cairns on being examined gave similar results. Some of the horned cairns are very much shorter, so short indeed that the ground-plan has somewhat the form of a four-pointed star. Perhaps the most remarkable cairns of the period are in the Orkneys, the most famous of these being known as Maeshowe, near the Loch of Stennis. It forms a mound 92 feet in diameter and 36 feet in height, and is surrounded by a trench 40 feet wide, and in some parts 8 feet deep. There is an inter-

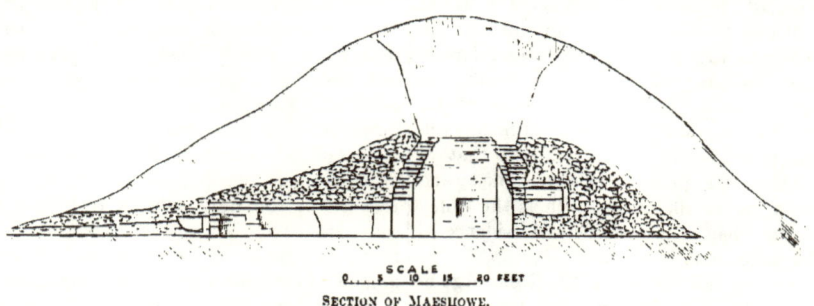

SECTION OF MAESHOWE.

nal chamber, now open to the sky, about 15 feet square, to which a passage 54 feet long gives entrance. Maeshowe appears to have been broken into by the Norsemen in the twelfth century, in the expectation of finding treasure, and it yielded nothing of value to modern explorers. Not a great deal of light, indeed, has been thrown on the life of the neolithic people of Scotland by the relics obtained from these barrows. The samples of pottery found in such circumstances consist of vessels made by hand

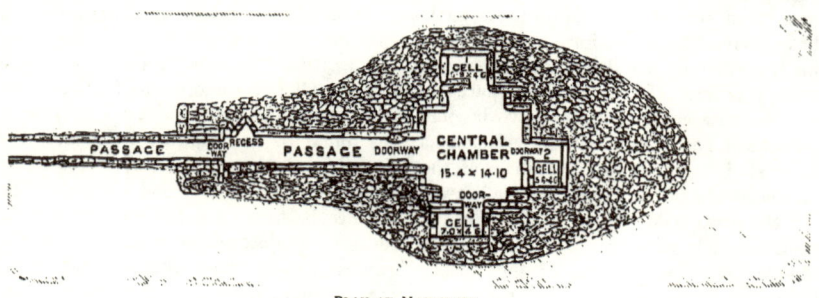

PLAN OF MAESHOWE.

with wide mouths, round bottoms, and thick lips, well-shaped and ornamented with flutings and scorings in straight lines. The barrows have also yielded flint arrow-heads and polished stone axes.

Though comparatively few relics of the Stone Age have been found in connection with the burials of the people, numerous examples of their stone implements, weapons, and ornaments have been obtained in other circumstances. Many have made their appearance in the operations of ploughing, cutting drains, digging peats, or the like, or have been picked up on the surface of the ground. The whole may be divided into various classes according to their shapes and the main uses for which they must have been intended. Thus besides axes and arrow-heads we have stone adzes and hammers, spear-heads, knives, saws, borers, and scrapers. The stone axes and hammers, again, are either pierced with a hole for the shaft or more commonly have no such hole, being thus fixed in some other manner to the shaft. Those having a shaft-hole are characterized by greater variety of form than the others, and are seldom made of flint, but commonly of granite, gneiss, porphyry, basalt, or other hard stone. They vary greatly in size, and while some have an edge at both ends, thus forming a double axe, a far greater number have but one edge, while still others have both ends blunt. Some again have the edge in the same direction as the shaft-hole; others have it at right angles, or belong to the adze type of tool—if indeed they are to be called tools, and not weapons, as some of them at least probably were. The larger specimens are from 7 to 10 or 11 inches in length, the smaller not more than 3½. Some of them are ornamented by incised lines, and one Scottish specimen, probably a war hammer, made of whitish flint and highly polished, has the surface adorned by lozenge-shaped facets, though the pattern has been left incomplete. Another specimen of the same kind found in Wales, with the ornamentation complete, shows what this one might have turned out if the maker of it had fully carried out his design.

The Welsh example is beautifully polished and finished, and the labour and skill spent upon it must have been enormous. The surface is covered with a sort of network of separate facets or compartments, upwards of two hundred in number, and mostly lozenge-shaped in outline. All these are hollowed out to a uniform depth in the centre and rise towards the edges so regularly as to be bounded by ridges of exactly the same height, and all running accurately in the direction intended. Though the stone is so hard that steel will not scratch it, yet all the details of the ornament are perfectly finished, and the polish of the whole surface is admirable.

Among the imperforated axes or celts there are also very beautiful specimens of workmanship, the materials used being flint, porphyry, serpentine, or other hard stone, and the size extending to upwards of 15 inches in length, and 5 inches across the cutting face. Some of those made of flint exhibit a polish and finish equal to anything that the modern lapidary with all his tools and appliances could turn out. The finer specimens are believed to have been weapons rather than tools; others less highly finished, such as also exist, would probably be made for purposes of everyday life. As to the manner in which the imperforated axes were fitted with handles, there is but little evidence, but we know that the rude or uncivilized peoples of the present day who use stone implements have various ways of getting over this difficulty.

Among the articles of flint perhaps the arrow-heads, the "fairies' arrows" or "elf-arrows" of the country people of Scotland, are the most interesting and remarkable, especially those of the well-known barbed form, which must have required extraordinary dexterity in their fabrication. These arrowheads are usually furnished with a stem or tang, which was no doubt intended to be inserted in the cleft end of the shaft. Indeed this has been proved by the discovery of a specimen so attached in an Aberdeenshire moss, the preservative qualities of the peat having prevented the hard wooden shaft from complete decay.

Some of the other flint implements display their character less openly, and those designated knives, or saws, or borers, for instance, would hardly strike us at first sight as being likely tools for their purposes. The knives are flakes of various shapes, worked so as to present a sharp edge, and they seem in many cases to have been intended equally for scraping and for cut-

INTERIOR OF MAESHOWE.

ting, though there are also implements that no doubt were definitely intended for scraping, and were probably used in the preparation of skins. Some of the knives present much more of a knife-like form than

STONE HATCHETS AND FLINT ARROW-HEADS.
From the Hunterian Museum, Glasgow.

others, having the edge ground sharp and the back rounded. Poor tools as they may seem, it has been found by actual experiment that astonishing results may be produced by them with a little skilful manipulation, and in the hands of the trained workmen of the neolithic age of course the results would be out of all comparison superior, both as regards quantity and quality. As to the methods by which the implements themselves were fashioned, in all their perfection of form and finish, these or many of them seem to be among the category of lost arts.

From the character of these implements and weapons, combined with that of the grave-mounds described above, we may fairly come to the conclusion that the people from whom they proceeded were at a much more advanced stage of culture than the palæolithic people, and were far removed from the condition of mere savages, however destitute of the many appliances that we deem essential to civilization. The perfection of workmanship attained by them over so refractory a material as flint, though it may have been the result of ages of practice and training, and the beauty of form imparted to the manufactured articles, seem almost to argue a greater amount of natural capacity than if they had taught themselves how to smelt ores and fashioned their implements of metal. And if they were so skilful in the manipulation of stone we may also suppose that they were equally so in regard to other materials that all nations have made more or less use of—wood, bone, and horn—though of this we have comparatively little evidence. The rearing of such massive structures as the barrows tends to prove that they must have lived in settled communities and carried out their greater works by combined effort, and this again suggests that probably agriculture, and not merely the keeping of flocks and herds, was to some extent practised. The civilization of the Stone Age of the Continent may be adduced as favouring this conclusion, and also as helping otherwise to complete the picture of neolithic life. If we know, for instance, that spinning and weaving, as well as agriculture, were practised among the neolithic people of Switzerland, we may suppose that they were equally so in Britain.

In Scotland during the Stone Age the state of civilization must have been the same as in England, judging from the relics discovered in various localities in the latter country. At one or two places in England the manufacture of flint implements on a large scale seems to have been actively carried on by neolithic artificers, and strange to say, one of those places, Brandon in Suffolk, is still a seat of the flint manufacture, gun-flints being made there, and nowhere else in Britain. The flints are found in the chalk of this locality, the best at a depth of nearly 40 feet, and pits have been dug by the ancient miners so as to reach these, horizontal galleries being excavated when the pit was made deep enough. The implements used in the digging operations were made of deer's horns, and numbers of them have been found, some worn out, others still serviceable. In one case two deer's-horn picks were found in a gallery, the roof of which had evidently fallen in while the miners were absent, and the tools had never been recovered. The handle of one of these was coated with chalk-dust, on which the print of the miner's hand was quite distinctly visible. "It was a most impressive sight," remarks Mr. Greenwell the discoverer, "and one never to be forgotten, to look after a lapse, it may be, of 3000 years upon a piece of work unfinished with the tools of the workmen still lying where they had been placed so many centuries ago." According to the flint-workers still engaged at this place further excavation continued in the same direction would have been unsafe. Another centre of the flint manufacture was at Cissbury in Sussex, where is a well-known ancient encampment, and where great numbers of flint implements in all stages of manufacture have been found, though it appears they did not receive their final polish here.

Since these implements after being made were distributed throughout the country from the place of manufacture, it is evident that commerce, no doubt in the form of barter, was to some extent carried on. That navigation also was more or less practised is evident from the fact that the neolithic inhabitants of Britain — unlike those of earlier times who could make the passage by land — must have crossed over from the Continent in boats. These were no doubt of the "dug-out" kind, being hollowed out of a single trunk by fire or the axe. In Scotland a canoe of this kind, made of oak, was discovered at a depth of 25 feet in digging the foundations for St. Enoch's Church, Glasgow, in the last century. Inside it was a well-finished stone celt, doubtless one of the axes of the ancient Clyde ship-builders, with which they were wont to fashion the oaks of Strathclyde into their primitive craft. Of the dwellings of the neolithic people we know nothing, but we may conjecture that they were mostly slight structures of wood, and probably wattle-work formed part of their materials. Possibly natural caves may have been used as dwellings, where they were available, and for winter-abodes excavations may have been made in the earth.

An excellent idea of what we may conceive to have been the picture presented in many parts of Britain during this age will be obtained from the following imaginative sketch of the neolithic homestead, by Prof. Boyd Dawkins:—"If we could in imagination take a stand on the summit of a hill commanding an extensive view of almost any part of Great Britain or Ireland in the neolithic period, we should look upon a landscape somewhat of this kind. Thin lines of smoke rising from among the trees of the dense virgin forest at our feet would mark the position of the neolithic homestead, and of the neighbouring stockaded camp which afforded refuge in time of need; while here and there a gleam of gold would show the small patch of ripening wheat. We enter a track in the forest and thread our way to one of the clusters of homesteads, passing herds of goats and flocks of horned sheep, or disturbing a troop of horses or small short-horned oxen, or stumbling upon a swine-herd tending the hogs in their search after roots. We should probably have to defend ourselves against the attack of some of the large dogs, used as guardians of the flock against bears, wolves, and foxes, and for hunting the wild animals. At last on emerging into the clearing, we should see a little plot of flax or small-eared wheat, and near the homestead the inhabitants, clad some in linen and others in skins, and

ANCIENT CANOES, found near Glasgow.
Drawn by A. D. Robertson, from his original sketch.

ornamented with necklaces and pendants of stone, bone or pottery, carrying on their daily occupations. Some are cutting wood with stone axes with a wonderfully sharp edge, fixed in wooden handles, with stone adzes and gouges, or with little saws composed of carefully notched pieces of flint about 3 or 4 inches long, splitting it with stone wedges, scraping it with flint flakes. Some are at work preparing handles for the spears, shafts for the arrows, and wood for the bows or for the broad paddles used for propelling the canoes. Others are busy grinding and sharpening the various stone tools, scraping skins with instruments ground to a circular edge, or carving various implements out of bone and antler with sharp splinters of flint, while the women are preparing the meal with pestles and mortars and grain rubbers, and cooking it on the fire, generally outside the house, or spinning thread with spindle and distaff, or weaving it with a rude loom. We might also have seen them at work at the moulding of rude cups and vessels out of clay which had been carefully prepared."[1]

The question to what race of people these ancient inhabitants of Scotland belonged, and whether they can be assigned to any race still existing or known to have existed is a very difficult one. Some who have closely studied the subject, however, believe that they belonged to a race at one time widely spread in western and south-western Europe—the Iberian race namely, or that of which the Basques are the modern representatives. The Basques or Biscayans, as is well known, dwell at the western extremity of the Pyrenees, partly in France, but chiefly in Spain, in which country they occupy the provinces of Biscay, Alava, and Guipuzcoa. They form a distinct nationality from the Spaniards, and speak a language which stands quite apart from all others so far as philologists have been able to determine. They are considered to be the descendants of the ancient Iberi, who are known to have inhabited the Spanish peninsula long before the beginning of the Christian era, and who were afterwards swamped or supplanted by other incoming peoples, an influx of the Celts, for instance, giving rise to the mixed race known as the Celtiberi, whom the Romans found it so hard to subdue. Ethnologists have arrived at the conclusion that a Basque or Iberian of the genuine type is to be described as a man of low stature, dark in complexion, with black hair and eyes, and having a skull of what is called the *dolichocephalic* form—that is, long when measured from front to back as compared with its breadth in a direction transverse to this. Among the present inhabitants of Spain, France, and Britain, many persons are to be met with whose physical features are said to correspond to those here stated, and this, it is believed, is owing to an Iberian element in the population of the respective countries. A preponderance of the Basque or Iberic element, that is of persons with black hair and eyes and swarthy complexions, may be observed, it appears, in the majority of the French departments

---

[1] It will be instructive to compare the above with the following account of the Andaman islanders, an interesting race of people who were quite recently in their Stone Age, and ignorant of the use of metals. The particulars were brought forward by Prof. Max Müller in an address delivered at the Cardiff meeting of the British Association in 1891, Prof. Müller being president of the anthropological section of the Association, and quoting as his authority an English officer, Mr. Horace Man:—"Before the introduction into the islands of what is called European civilization (says Mr. Man) the inhabitants lived in small villages, their dwellings built of branches and leaves of trees. They were ignorant of agriculture, and kept no poultry or domestic animals. Their pottery was hand-made, their clothing very scanty. They were expert swimmers and divers, and able to manufacture well-made dug-out canoes and outriggers. They were ignorant of metals, ignorant, we are told, of producing fire, though they kept a constant supply of burning and smouldering wood. They made use of shells for their tools, had stone hammers and anvils, bows and arrows, harpoons for killing turtle and fish. Such is the fertility of the island that they have abundance and variety of food all the year round. Their food was invariably cooked, they drank nothing but water, and they did not smoke. People may call this a savage life. I know many a starving labourer who would gladly exchange the benefits of European civilization for the blessings of such savagery." They are decidedly a small race of people, the average height among them being 4 feet 10¾ inches. Bigamy, polygamy, polyandry, and divorce are unknown among them; women are treated with respect and consideration; cannibalism or infanticide are practices never heard of. They are naturally truthful and honest, generous and self-denying, but contact with European civilization has not improved them morally. Their food, before they became acquainted with European customs, used to be of the most miscellaneous character, including roots, fruits, bats, rats, lizards, sea-snakes, molluscs, turtle, fish, wild pig, and the larvæ of beetles. They believe in a Supreme Being who created the whole world (except the powers of evil), who has a house in the sky, knows all things, even the thoughts of the heart, and is displeased with wrong-doing.

lying between the Garonne and Loire, as well as in Brittany; and though the skull is generally broader among the natives of this region than that assigned to the typical Iberian, this is explained by the supposition that there has been an infusion of the Celtic element. A people of similar characteristics have been described as inhabiting the Walloon provinces of Belgium, and also as existing in South Germany. A strong Iberic infusion is said to be observable in Wales, where the small dark-complexioned members of the community may be looked upon as descendants of the ancient Silures, whose resemblance to the Iberians was referred to by Tacitus. Much the same holds good in regard to the south-western counties and some of the midland counties of England; the highlands and islands of Scotland, where the small and dark people of Iberian type live side by side with others of a very different type;[1] and the south-west of Ireland.

That the neolithic inhabitants of Britain belonged to the Iberic race is believed on the evidence of skulls and skeletons which have come down to us from neolithic times. The skulls are of the long or dolichocephalic type, and the skeletons represent a race whose stature varied between 4 feet 9 or 10 inches, and 5 feet 5 or 6 inches; so that as regards shape of skull, a very permanent and important characteristic, and as regards bodily stature there is entire agreement with the Basque type already described. Other physical features characteristic of the neolithic race were: an oval face, an aquiline nose, the ridges over the eyebrows and the cheek-bones not specially prominent, and the upper and lower jaws both small. The evidence of the human remains, and the localities in which they have been found, quite confirm what has been already stated, that the population of our islands was uniform and homogeneous in the neolithic period. Similar remains prove that the same race was widely spread on the Continent, being found in Belgium, France, and Spain, as far south as Gibraltar. Sir Daniel Wilson gives detailed measurements of twenty-two skulls of the neolithic type, half of them found in Scotland, and a certain number being from the chambered cairns already described. One of the skulls, that of a young man found in Banchory Devenick in Kincardineshire in 1822, has a hole nearly circular and upwards of an inch in diameter on the top of the head, "caused, it may be presumed, by the blow of a stone axe which abruptly closed the career of its owner."

The Stone Age, or neolithic period, came to an end only after the lapse of unnumbered ages, ages for the computation of which no trustworthy data are available. The bronze period now began, in which a new phase of civilization prevailed, and implements and ornaments of metal superseded those of stone, the metal employed for useful purposes being bronze, while gold was largely used for ornament, and iron was as yet unknown. By this time we find also that a new race has made its appearance in Britain, if not indeed more than one race. Skulls of a different type from those already described are now to be met with, proving that the population is no longer homogeneous, but made up of more than one element. The skulls here referred to are of what is called the *brachycephalic* type, that is they are relatively shorter or rounder than those of the other type when measured from front to back; and the

---

[1] Elton, in his *Origins of English History* (2d edition, p. 136), gives the following quotation from Campbell's *West Highland Tales* as illustrative of this point, the passage having reference to the people of Barra: "Behind the fire sat a girl with one of those strange foreign faces which are occasionally to be seen in the Western Isles, a face which reminded me of the Nineveh sculptures, and of faces seen in St. Sebastian. Her hair was black as night, and her clear dark eyes glittered through the peat smoke. Her complexion was dark, and her features so unlike those who sat about her, that I asked if she were a native of the island, and learned that she was a Highland girl." A committee of the British Association pronounced in 1883 that the short dark type—otherwise called the long-barrow type—certainly exists in the population at the present time, offering a marked contrast to the other chief types, and agreeing in stature, lightness of frame, narrowness of skull, and fine osseous features generally, with the skeleton remains found in the early barrows. The other chief types distinguished by the committee are the round-barrow type (see below), and the Saxon type, otherwise designated respectively as the brachycephalic or sub-brachycephalic fair type, and the sub-dolichocephal c fair type. Of these the former (which is the taller) includes Belgic, Cymric, and Danish varieties; the latter is the pure German or Teutonic. We may also mention here that a series of measurements carried out under the auspices of the British Association, established the fact that among the inhabitants of the British Islands, the Scotch stand first in height (as also in weight), the Irish second, the English third, the Welsh last (second in weight).

people possessed of this form of skull appear ultimately to have entirely over-mastered or absorbed the earlier long-headed race. These brachycephalic skulls have been found in graves and grave-mounds all over Scotland, but the round sepulchral mounds or cairns of this period, built chiefly of earth, are very different from the chambered mounds or cairns of the preceding period. Some of the skulls show a certain flattening of the occiput or hinder part of the head, which Sir Daniel Wilson attributes to the same cause as that which produces a corresponding feature in the skulls of the North American Indians, namely, the use of a cradle-board, or flat board on which the infants are fastened down to be nursed and carried about by their mothers. As the infant is laid flat on its back upon this board, and somewhat tightly bandaged down in that position, pressure on the soft bones of the skull at last produces a marked and permanent effect on its shape.

According to some authorities the round-headed people who intruded on the long-headed Iberian people previously established in the country belonged to the Celtic race, though others believe that a Finnish people, or a people of uncertain affinities, preceded the Celtic invaders of Britain, and that this early invasion took place towards the end of the Stone Age. Whether this be so or not, it is well known that at a period, for which we can assign no date, Celts crossed over from the Continent to Britain, and finally spread over the whole or at least the greater part of the British Islands. The Celts, unlike the Iberians, are akin to several of the races that have played a great part in the history of the world. Their language marks them as belonging to the Aryan or Indo-European family, and thus allies them to the Germanic or Teutonic peoples, to the ancient Greeks and Romans and their modern descendants, to the Russians and other Slavonians, to the Persians and a certain portion of the native inhabitants of India. The Celts had formerly a much more important position in Europe as a distinct people than they have had since the beginning of the Christian era, the increase and spread of other nationalities having borne so hard upon them that they have been pushed to the most westerly parts of Europe, and are now only found speaking their own national tongues in a small portion of France, in Wales, the Highlands and Western Islands of Scotland, the Isle of Man, and in a small part of Ireland. Where the original home of the Celts was situated we do not know, but at one time they possessed a considerable portion of what is now Germany, spread themselves over France and a great part of Spain, while bodies of them devastated northern Italy, marched into Macedonia and Greece, and even crossed over into Asia Minor. So far as we can trace their history they have always been divided into two sections distinguished from each other by certain linguistic peculiarities. The one section or division is known as the Goidelic, the other as the Brythonic; and while the first now embraces the Gaels or Highlanders of Scotland, the Manx and the Irish Celts, the second includes the Welsh, the Bretons, and the Celts of Cornwall. The corresponding tongues are the Gaelic, Manx, and Irish, between which there are comparatively slight differences, and the Welsh, Breton or Armoric, and Cornish, which share very considerable divergencies among themselves. It is generally believed that the Celts who first entered Britain belonged to the Goidelic group, and that at some succeeding period these were followed by Brythonic Celts, who pushed the earlier settlers into the remoter parts of the island, and perhaps then first brought about the Celtic colonization of Ireland. In regard to the treatment and fate of the aboriginal Iberian population at the hands of the invaders we are entirely in the dark.

The use of bronze and the beginning of the Bronze Age in Scotland probably dates from the Celtic invasion of the country. If the Celts when they arrived were armed with weapons of bronze, an alloy with which they must have become acquainted at an early period by coming in contact with more advanced peoples further to the east or south, the conquest over foes armed only with stone weapons would be comparatively easy. The incomers, doubtless, would also have a superiority in regard to many of the arts and occupations of life, through the use of metal instead of stone; and from the testimony of the remains belonging to the Bronze Age we learn that quite a different phase of culture now prevailed in Scotland.

With regard to the funeral observances of the people of this period, there is one feature that seems invariable, namely, the deposition of some article or instrument of bronze in the grave along with the remains of the dead. These objects of bronze are chiefly flat axes, thin flat knives or dagger-blades, pins and heavy rings, besides which there are such non-metallic objects as beads and necklaces of jet or cannel-coal, arrow-heads and knives of flint, &c. The body

BRONZE AXE AND CELTS (Hunterian Museum, Glasgow).
TWO STONE MOULDS FOR CELTS,
Found on a moor in the parish of Rosskeen, Ross-shire.

The urns associated with those burials are of various shapes and sizes, and though made by hand and not with the wheel, are often elegant in form and pleasingly ornamented with straight and zigzag lines. Some of them are very small, not more than 2 inches in height, while others reach a height of 15 inches or more. In many cases the burials of the Bronze Period are commemorated by a remarkable ring or circle of standing stones surrounding the area in which the interments have been made. Some of these circles consist of huge boulders that have simply been rolled into their places in the circle to which they belong, while others are formed of tall slabs set erect on their ends and firmly fixed in the soil. Some-

THE RING OF BROGAR AND STONES OF STENNIS, Island of Pomona, Orkney.

itself was either burned and the ashes buried in an urn, or it was buried unburned, the grave being a cist or rude coffin formed of rough stones surrounding the body. A cairn was often raised over the urn or cist, being a simple heap of stones or earth, not containing any regularly built chamber as in the neolithic barrows. A natural mound or hillock was often selected as the place of burial, and burned and unburned remains are often found buried in the same mound.

times there is a trench, or a trench and embankment, outside the stone circle, and sometimes the circle is double. Among the most remarkable is the stone circle at Stennis in Orkney, which has a diameter of 36 feet, and is surrounded by a trench 29 feet wide and 6 feet deep, the height of the tallest of the stones still standing being 14 feet. Another remarkable circle and series of monumental stones is at Callernish in the Island of Lewis.

Among the immense numbers of weapons and other articles of bronze which have been found all over Scotland, many of them deposited in a hoard together, we may mention swords, daggers, spear-heads, axes, shields, chisels, gouges, fish-hooks, sickles, caldrons, anvils, buckles, pins, rings, &c. The articles found in hoards, in which they had probably been stowed for concealment, are fine in make, heavier, and altogether more elaborate than those found in the graves, and belong probably to a more advanced period of the age of bronze.

The bronze swords are broadish weapons, of the form called "leaf-shaped," that is they widen out to some extent just before they taper towards the point, the blade having its greater breadth about a third of the total length from the point, and widening out again towards the hilt. They were intended for thrusting, not for cutting and parrying, and they are not furnished with a guard for the hand. The hilt portion is usually pierced with holes, evidently for receiving rivets, by which pieces of bone, horn, or wood were attached so as to give a satisfactory grasp. In size they vary considerably; but the largest known specimen has a length of 28½ inches. They have been made by casting the bronze in moulds, and are all in one piece. The dagger-blades are broad, thick, and heavy, of a somewhat triangular shape, with a stout midrib or ridge running from heel to point. The handle was attached to these blades by rivets, and some of them were probably fitted axe-wise to their handles so as to form a kind of halberd or war-pick. The spear-heads are of considerable size, some of them solid, others formed with loops or openings, and generally they are furnished with a socket to receive the end of the shaft. Like the swords and dagger-blades they were cast in moulds of stone, some of which still exist; and it has been remarked that "the coring of their sockets for the reception of their shafts would do credit to the most skilful modern founder." The shields are circular in form and are made of a thin plate of beaten bronze, being ornamented with concentric ridges having rows of small bosses between them.

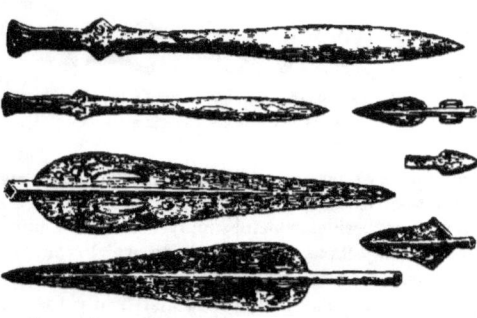

BRONZE SPEAR-HEADS, SWORDS, &c., from different localities in Scotland.

The axes of the Bronze Period vary considerably in their form, but the cutting edge has usually a well-marked convex curve, and is long as compared with the width of the head. The latter is not pierced horizontally with a hole for receiving the helve or haft, as is the case with our axes, other modes of connecting axe and handle being adopted. In some cases the head has a socket sunk perpendicularly into it, this socket being intended no doubt to receive the bent end of a wooden haft, while it is often furnished with a projecting loop through which some kind of cord or fastening went to attach the haft more firmly. In another form of axe-head there are flanges or raised pieces at right angles to the flat of the axe, and the head of the weapon or implement in this case was probably fitted into the split end of the handle, which most likely would have a sharp bend at the extremity to render it suitable for the purpose. A stout branch with a short stump left projecting near the extremity might form a handle for such an axe, the stump being split to receive the thin axe-head. Other axes are quite flat, so that it must have been rather difficult to attach them securely to a handle. As in the case of the spear-heads stone moulds for the casting of axes have been repeatedly found, some of them consisting of two separate halves which could be fastened together in the operation.

The discovery of bronze sickles in Scotland is interesting, as affording undoubted evidence of the cultivation of grain crops at this early period, though how the grain was utilized is not so certain, since no quern or other grinding apparatus undoubtedly of the Bronze Age has as yet been found in Scotland. Perhaps it was parched over the fire and eaten after being crushed or pounded; or it may have been boiled and eaten like rice. Large caldrons made of thin bronze plates riveted together have been discovered in several places, and are among the most noteworthy relics of the period, though it is not known for what purpose they were specially intended. Such vessels, however, would evidently be useful for various purposes, and perhaps more especially as receptacles for grain.

In some respects even more interesting and instructive than any of the above relics are the articles worn for personal adornment by the people of the Bronze Age. Among these the ornaments made of gold

GOLD ARMLET.—Found in the Moor of Rannoch.

deserve the first place, the most numerous class of which are armlets and necklets of the solid metal. They are of several patterns, but are commonly penannular in form, that is, they are bent round into the form of a ring, but the circle is left incomplete, the two ends not being united. While some of these are plain cylindrical hoops, others show ribs or angles, and they may also have small rings or bands of the same precious metal twisted round them. A third class again have been formed of a flat band tapering towards either end, and twisted so as to have much the appearance of the thread of a screw, the two ends being bent so as to hook into each other. One very fine armlet was formed of three gold wires twisted together in the manner of a cord and united into a solid piece at each end, the whole being bent into a spiral, so that four complete coils would encircle the arm. The total length of this beautiful armlet when uncoiled was 4½ feet. Such an ornament as this one would think would of itself stamp the wearer as a person of consequence among his fellows. Gold diadems or lunettes, a class of ornaments of a crescent shape, have also been repeatedly found. They are made of beaten gold and suited for wearing either on the head or on the neck. Very valuable hoards of articles have come to light at various times, and many more have no doubt been discovered and quietly disposed of without the public being any the wiser. Some of the objects made of gold that have come down to us from this period are surprisingly massive. Thus three armlets found in the parish of Kirkurd, Peeblesshire, are said to have weighed about 8½ ounces each, the value of the three being about £110.[1] Rings and armlets of bronze were also worn, as well as necklaces of jet and amber, while buttons of jet, and bronze pins with large flat circular heads, were also in use.

Such were the weapons, implements, and other articles in use among the people of the Bronze Age, and from them we are able to form some idea of the mode of life that then prevailed in Scotland; but it must be remembered that the evidence is naturally very imperfect, and that the absence of many an object from the comparatively meagre list of Bronze Age relics hitherto known does not prove that such objects were not quite common in the period of which we have been discussing. For instance, we possess little actual evidence regarding the clothing or dwellings of the people, yet we can hardly doubt that the rich and powerful at least, those who could afford to wear the ornaments above spoken of, would be dressed in some mode in harmony with those ornaments and with the exigencies of the Scottish climate. We

---

[1] Much more valuable hoards than this have turned up, however, in England, Ireland, and France. In England, for instance, a hoard found in Sussex weighed over 11 lbs., while one found near Newmarket, county Clare, is reported to have been worth £6000.

have evidence to show that in England during the Bronze Period garments of linen and woollen were worn; and as the state of civilization disclosed by the relics was evidently in other respects similar all over Britain, we may assume that the same kinds of clothing were worn in Scotland as in England. Of course skins would also form part of the dress of the people in addition to woven fabrics. As regards dwellings, if there are none extant in Scotland that can definitely be assigned to the Bronze Age, we may be sure that a people possessed of good bronze axes, chisels, gouges, and other tools would be quite competent to construct substantial abodes of timber, while wattle-work, clay, and stone would probably be also more or less employed. Of their pottery we

Urns in different styles belonging to the Bronze Period.

possess numerous examples in the urns or clay-vessels found so commonly in connection with burials, as already mentioned, and also met with in other circumstances. These, we may remark, are rarely provided with handles, but in one case at least a clay mug with a handle has been found in Scotland, while such are not uncommon in England. In another case a horn-spoon was found resting in a clay vessel.

For domestic animals the people of this age had the horse, ox, sheep, and hog, which would yield them a part of their food, another part being furnished by animals of the chase, as the stag, roe, reindeer, wild boar, and hare, while grain, as we have seen, would also serve to diversify their diet. The bronze reaping-hooks already referred to seem to have been of the kind anciently used among the Greeks and Romans for reaping their crops by cutting off the ears of the grain. Oxen were probably used in ploughing, the horse for riding and driving. The use of the bronze axe, besides giving the Bronze Age people many advantages over the neolithic people who had only an axe of stone, in particular would greatly assist in clearing off forest and brushwood to make room for crops or pasture. Fire was obtained by striking a flint against a piece of iron pyrites, though the more primitive method of producing it by friction might also continue to be employed.

The skill of the Bronze Age people in metal-working is sufficiently attested by the character of the objects above noticed, all of which are not only well made so far as mere workmanship is concerned, but are also well-proportioned and graceful in design. And the people were as much at home in the art of casting as in turning out fine hammered work, of which latter branch the bronze caldrons and shields furnish us with admirable specimens.

It has also recently been discovered that the art of soldering metals was not unknown, several hollow gold rings made up of pieces soldered together having been found at Balmashanner, in Forfarshire, in 1892, forming part of a hoard of articles clearly belonging to this period. One of these was a small globular vessel of cast bronze, of a type not elsewhere known in Britain. Such discoveries lead to the hope that much fresh light on the Scotland of the Bronze Age may yet be obtained.

Whence the people obtained their supply of metals is doubtful, though we know, of course, that gold at least is found in Scotland as well as in Wales and Ireland, while tin and copper, the ingredients of bronze, have been worked in England from a remote period. Among the localities in which copper is found in England may be mentioned Cornwall, Devon, Derbyshire, Yorkshire, Cumberland, and Westmoreland; and it is also obtained in several of the counties of Wales. Tin is much less common in the British area, Cornwall, and to a less extent Devonshire, being almost the only localities yielding it. On the Continent copper ore is abundant in various places, and more especially so in Spain, where it has long been smelted. Tin has also been worked from an early period in Spain, France, and several localities of Central Europe. The art of making bronze and articles in bronze first arose, it is believed, in some part of Western Asia, whence it spread to Southern Europe, and then to the rest of the continent and the British Isles. It had no doubt been long in use among the Phœnicians before the tin and copper mines of Spain and Britain were worked. The bronze would probably be introduced into Scotland from the south, at first in the shape of manufactured articles. Subsequently lumps or ingots of the alloy would probably be imported, such as have been discovered in France, Germany, and Scandinavia.

Whether the inhabitants of Scotland themselves fused together the separate metals in the proper proportions for forming the alloy we cannot say, but that they were well acquainted with casting and working bronze, and had among them bronze-smiths as a separate class of craftsmen, there can be no doubt. In reference to this subject Dr. Joseph Anderson remarks: "That these objects were manufactured within the country is apparent from two circumstances: (1) that in many cases they exhibit special varieties of form which are peculiar to Scotland; and (2) that the moulds themselves are found in the soil in which the objects are found. The moulds which have been found are cut in stone. They are skilfully made and can still be used to cast from. Some of them, such as those for rings, knife-blades, and flat axe-heads are open moulds; while others, such as those for spear-heads and looped and socketed axe-heads, are double, closed moulds, made in two moieties, which are dowelled together in casting, and are capable of being fitted with cores. The hammered work of the period was equally skilful. The large globular caldrons formed of plates of bronze beaten almost as thin as sheets of paper, riveted together and ornamented with studs, are really beautiful works of industrial art; and I venture to say that nothing finer than these bronze shields has ever been produced by the hammer."

From whatever source the people of Scotland obtained their bronze, or the copper and tin from which to make it, and whether they got their gold in their own country or from outside its boundaries, it is evident that the existence of metallic articles in such abundance, and spread over such an extensive area as that in which they have been found, implies a considerable traffic and interchange of commodities, and a stage of progress in regard to commercial intercourse quite in keeping with the progress made in the industrial arts. This traffic would almost certainly be by barter, as we can hardly suppose that there would be a circulating medium of any kind in Scotland during the Bronze Age.

That war was equally well known with the arts of peace is sufficiently proved by the abundance of warlike weapons that have come down to us. Probably the people were divided into numerous tribes, between which hostilities were apt to break out. Many of the rude hill-forts so common in Scotland may belong to the Bronze Period, but of this there is no sufficient evidence.

With regard to the religious notions and the general intellectual culture of the people of this age we are naturally quite in the dark. That they had great respect for their dead is clear from the ceremonial and accompaniments with which interments were carried out, from the care with which the deceased were burned and their remains collected in a funeral urn, from the fact that valuable goods were deposited in the grave, and that a cairn and group of monumental stones were in so many cases erected to mark the place of sepulture. Most probably these grave-goods were not deposited along with the remains of the dead without the hope or belief that they would prove useful in a future life to the persons thus honourably interred.

The stone circles or groups of stones accompanying some of the Bronze Age places of burial have often been regarded as connected with some ancient pagan form of worship, especially with that attributed to the Druids; and Professor Boyd Dawkins, among modern authorities, is in favour of the view that these are really heathen temples. Speaking of Stonehenge and Avebury, the two chief monuments of this kind in Britain, he says: "These two great temples of an unknown worship represent the Canterbury Cathedral or Westminster Abbey of the period, while the smaller circles to be found scattered over the moors and hilltops in the south of England, in Wales and Cumberland, as well as in Scotland, are to be looked upon as the parish churches and chapels of ease. It has been urged by Mr. Fergusson, in his interesting work on *Rude Stone Monuments*, that these circles are merely tombs. Even if we allow that they were originally tombs in every case, it does not follow that they have not also been temples, for the religious sentiment has in all ages and in all places tended to centre in tombs which ultimately have become places of worship. Many of our Christian churches have originated in this manner, and it is a most obvious transition from the tomb to the temple."[1] However this may be, there is certainly nothing whatever to connect them with the Druidic rites or worship.

With the conclusion of the Bronze Age we enter upon the Iron Age, and this, though it begins in the prehistoric period, in due course brings us into the historic period. The date at which the Iron Age began in Scotland was probably two or three centuries before the beginning of the written history at the Roman invasion, and was no doubt later than the beginning of the Iron Age in England, and still later than its beginning in France. In Scandinavia the Bronze Age lasted into the Christian era, while in the Grecian world, on the other hand, as depicted in the Homeric poems, we see it dying out eight or nine centuries earlier.[2] Where the knowledge of smelting iron first arose it would be difficult to say, but that it reached Britain from Gaul is certain. The ancient Gauls are spoken of as having swords of iron several centuries before the Christian era, and when Cæsar invaded Britain he found the metal well known in the country, where by this time it was probably smelted. The large swords without points described by Tacitus, as used by the Caledonians, were undoubtedly of iron, and the metal was doubtless also used in the construction of their war-chariots. In Scotland, however, there was no sudden change from bronze to iron. The latter metal must have been rare and expensive at first, and the two metals were employed side by side—as indeed they still are—though the superiority of iron for weapons and cutting-tools would speedily make itself felt, and cause the disuse of bronze for these purposes. The use of iron thus did not introduce any immediate change in the state of civilization in Scotland, and the arts and industries, the burials and other customs, remained much as before, probably till the introduction of Christianity. So far was the use of bronze from being given up, that the most interesting remains of the prehistoric Iron Age in Scotland consist of objects made of this alloy. For iron, it must be remembered, is so readily oxidizable that articles formed of it, unless preserved by specially favourable circumstances, moulder away, and all but disappear in course of time. Hence objects made of iron, and dating from the prehistoric period, are comparatively rare, though a certain number of iron swords, daggers, knives, bosses for the centre of shields, and a few other objects have come down to modern times.

Among the relics belonging to the Iron Age it is often difficult to distinguish those that are strictly prehistoric, but many can at any rate be set down as distinctly pre-Christian, and some as exhibiting artistic

---

[1] Sir Daniel Wilson is inclined to refer Stonehenge to the Iron Age rather than to that of Bronze.

[2] Though the Homeric poems depict Greek life at a time when bronze was being superseded and supplemented by iron, it would no doubt be very hazardous to seek suggestions from Homer as to what may have been the condition of society in Scotland when the Bronze Age was being succeeded by the Iron Age in this country. Nevertheless some of the scenes so vividly set before us in these old poems may very well have been paralleled in prehistoric Scotland. Here, too, might perhaps have been witnessed occasions such as are described in the Odyssey, where, for instance, a boar is taken and felled with a billet of wood, his throat cut, and the carcass singed, the whole being then divided into pieces which are roasted on spits and served up on trenchers. Or where a man is described as roasting a paunch filled with fat and blood (the prototype of the Scotch haggis, shall we say?), and turning it about at a great fire that it may be sufficiently cooked. Or a quarrel may have arisen at a feast, and a choleric Caledonian may have caught up an ox's foot from a dish, and hurled it at the head of a neighbour, as was done to Ulysses by one of the unwelcome wooers of his wife Penelope. The general state of society described in the Homeric poems, however, was no doubt much higher than in Scotland at the period referred to.

features special to the Celtic art in Scotland while paganism still prevailed. It is noteworthy that we now find coloured enamels employed in the ornamentation of articles in bronze, more especially bronze armlets, bridle-bits, and horse-trappings. The Celts of Britain at this period, indeed, seem to have held the foremost place in the art of enamelling, some of their productions being unique in character. Massive bronze armlets, ornamented in a style of art specially Celtic, and specially characteristic of early Scotland, are well known, especially some that have as the basis of their design a coiled double-headed serpent. These in particular possess technical and artistic merit of a rare kind, and would deserve equally high praise though they were the productions of the present day. Among the most curious objects that have come down from this period one is a kind of mask of thin beaten bronze, with two curved cylindrical tapering horns projecting in front, while another is an object evidently intended to represent the head of a boar, and also made of thin plates of beaten bronze.

Hitherto we have not had occasion to describe any structure which may have been employed, either temporarily or permanently, as a residence or shelter by the inhabitants of Scotland. There are certain structures, however, belonging to early Scotland of which we must give some account, more especially as it is only in recent times that they have been investigated with any completeness. Four classes of these are known, namely, Lake-dwellings, Hill-forts, Brochs, and Earth-houses. It is doubtful how far back the origin of some among the examples of each class should be placed. Probably many of the lake-dwellings and hill-forts belong to prehistoric times, and all the four classes of structures may be looked upon as at least dating from the pre-Christian period of Scotland, and as belonging to the unwritten history of the country.

MODERN LAKE-DWELLINGS belonging to New Guinea.

ANCIENT LAKE-DWELLINGS—restored.

The lake-dwellings, or *crannogs* as they are also called, were structures that, for the security of the occupants, were erected in lakes at some distance from the shore, a foundation being first prepared by driving in piles and tying them together with cross-beams, or by heaping up logs, trunks of trees, brushwood, stones, clay, gravel, or other materials, so as to provide a stable support for the dwelling or dwellings to be constructed. In some cases a small natural islet was utilized, if it furnished a surface level with the surface of the water, or nearly so, the labour of adapting it for its intended purpose being then comparatively small. These insular abodes or strongholds were reached either by means of a boat; by a wooden gangway, probably furnished with a kind of drawbridge; or by a stone causeway which, in some cases at least, seems to have been submerged to the depth of several feet.[1] Numerous specimens of such artificial islands have been discovered in

---

[1] These causeways had sometimes also a winding or zigzag direction, so that it would have been dangerous for anyone not familiar with them to attempt to make use of them.

Scotland, as well as in Ireland, while a small number have been found in England, but no examples of the actual dwellings with which they were surmounted are known in Scotland, these, being no doubt constructed of wood, wattle-work, or the like, having naturally long ago disappeared. Many structures of the same kind have been discovered and examined in different parts of Europe, especially in Switzerland, Germany, and Northern Italy; and dwellings of a more or less similar type are in use in Borneo, New Guinea, and other islands of the Malay Archipelago, in the Caroline Islands, and elsewhere, at the present day. It was the discovery of a pile-dwelling in Switzerland in 1854 that led to the systematic investigation of such structures, and was thus the means of bringing to light a whole series of facts hitherto unknown to archæologists.

The general method according to which a crannog was constructed is thus described by Dr. Munro in his comprehensive work, *The Lake-Dwellings of Europe:*—"The construction of a crannog must have been a gigantic operation in those days, requiring in many cases the services of the whole clan. Having fixed on a suitable locality —the topographical requirements of which seemed to be a small mossy lake, with its margin overgrown with weeds and grasses and secluded amidst the thick meshes of the primæval forests—the next consideration was the selection of the materials for constructing the island. In a lake containing soft and yielding sediment of decomposed vegetable matter it is manifest that any heavy substances, such as stones and earth, would be totally inadmissible owing to their weight, so that solid logs of wood, provided there was an abundant supply at hand, would be the best and cheapest material that could be used. The general plan adopted was to make an island of stems of trees and brushwood laid transversely, with which stones and earth were mingled. This mass was pinned together and surrounded by a series of stockades, which were firmly united by intertwining branches, or, in the more artistically constructed crannogs, by horizontal beams with mortised holes to receive the uprights. These horizontal beams were arranged in two ways. One set ran along the circumference and bound together all the uprights in the same circle, while others took a radial direction and connected each circle together. Sometimes the latter were long enough to embrace three circles. The external ends of these radial beams were occasionally observed to be continuous with additional strengthening materials, such as wooden props and large stones, which in some cases appeared also to have acted as a breakwater. The mechanical skill displayed in this structure was specially directed to give stability to the island and to prevent superincumbent pressure from causing the general mass to bulge outwards."

The first person known to have described lake-dwellings is the Greek historian Herodotus, who tells us that the Persians, in their invasion of Thrace and Macedonia, in the beginning of the fifth century B.C., found Lake Prasias inhabited by people who lived in houses constructed on platforms supported on piles driven into the bottom of the lake. His description is worth repeating, as being that of one who was contemporary with the manner of life he describes. The lake, now a marsh, was an expansion of the river Strymon or Struma. The Persians, he tells us, "attempted to conquer those dwelling in the lake, who live in the following manner. Platforms fitted on lofty piles are placed in the middle of the lake, with a narrow access from the shore by one gangway. The piles that support the platforms were originally planted by the whole community in common, but since then they are planted according to the established rule that when a man marries he plants three piles for each wife he takes, bringing them from a mountain called Orbelus; and each has a number of wives. Their way of life is that each owns a hut on the platform and dwells in it, and he has also a trap-door constructed in the platform, and leading down to the lake; and the very young children they tie by the foot with a cord from fear of them rolling into the water. They give fish for fodder to their horses and beasts of burden, and the lake so abounds with these that when a man has opened his trap-door he lets down an empty basket by a cord into the water, and after waiting a short time draws it up full of fish."[1]

Regarding the everyday life of the occupants of the lake-dwellings of Scotland we have no such vivid and informative picture, we can only conjecture what it was from the relics left by them. These include stone querns for grinding their meal, spindle whorls to assist in spinning, iron axe-heads and other articles of iron, dishes and other articles of bronze, combs, pins, needles and borers of bone, canoes and other articles of wood, fragments of pottery, glass beads, and a few flint implements. Probably each crannog was the site of more than one dwelling, and this is all the more likely from the fact above referred to that the formation of such an artificial island would be a work that could only be accomplished by the united labour of a number of persons. Perhaps in some instances they were not intended as permanent abodes, but as places of shelter, to be occupied only on the pressure of sudden danger, and deserted when this had passed away.

By some archæologists a vast antiquity is assigned to the lake-dwellings, but that the majority of those structures in Scotland are not older than the Iron Age seems to be proved by the relics found in connection with them. These, as we have just seen, include implements of flint and bronze as well as others of iron, and thus the three successive ages would appear to be represented; but in most cases, if not in all, these relics are in such juxtaposition that they must have been all in use at the same time. Dr. Munro holds that these dwellings are to be assigned to a comparatively late date, and that the vast majority of the Scottish crannogs were both constructed and inhabited in the Iron Age. If this be so, they are much more recent than many of those on the Continent, which were certainly inhabited, not only in the Bronze Age, but also in the Neolithic or Stone Age. In Switzerland even at the earliest period their inhabitants had made considerable progress in civilization, being acquainted with agriculture, the rearing of cattle, the art of weaving flax, and the making of pottery and basket-work. If the origin of these dwellings in Scotland is later than some have supposed, there is also evidence to show that they continued to be occupied in comparatively recent times. For instance, a crannog in Loch Kinord, Aberdeenshire, was visited by James IV. in 1506, and continued to be a place of strength till 1648, when the Scottish parliament ordered its fortifications to be destroyed; and others are spoken of as places of importance down to a similarly late period both in Scotland and Ireland.

Dr. Munro considers the crannogs to have been especially the work of the Celtic inhabitants of the British Islands, who, he thinks, may have brought with them a knowledge of these lacustrine erections from the Continent. "I believe it probable," he says, "that the early Celts had got this knowledge from contact with the inhabitants of the pile-villages in Central Europe. On this hypothesis it would follow that the Celts had migrated into Britain when these lacustrine abodes were in full vogue in Switzerland, and that they retained their knowledge of the art long after it had fallen into desuetude in Europe. Subsequent immigrants into Britain, such as the Belgæ, Angles, &c., would cultivate new and improved methods of defensive warfare; whilst the first Celtic invaders, still retaining their primary ideas of civilization, when harassed by enemies and obliged to act on the defensive, would have recourse to their inherited system of protection. . . . Though the Anglo-Saxons, in coming from the mouth of the Elbe and the low-lying districts between it and the Rhine, must have been familiar with marine pile-structures, they do not appear to have cultivated the system to any great extent after immigrating into Britain. But this may be accounted for by the fact that very soon they became the conquerors of the country. It is only for defence that lake

---

[1] The modern pile-dwellings have been described by various travellers. They seem generally to be less massive and substantial structures than those of ancient Scotland or Macedonia. The inhabitants in many cases are almost amphibious, and when a child tumbles into the water there is always its mother, grandmother, or some other person to plunge in and pick it out.

and marsh dwellings have been resorted to."[1]

The hill-forts are the most numerous class of ancient structures existing in Scotland, being found in almost all parts of the country. They are erections of earth or stone inclosing an area of greater or less extent, and are usually planted on the summit or slope of some prominent hill. Their essential feature consists in the fact that they have apparently been constructed on the elevated sites they occupy because of the suitability of these for being held as defensive positions. Generally speaking their outline and disposition are more or less dependent upon the nature of the area on which they have been erected. They may be divided into four chief classes: (1) works made of earth, (2) works of commingled earth and stone, (3) works of unbuilt stone, (4) works of dry masonry.[2] The nature of the country, and the ease or difficulty that there might be in procuring stones, would naturally help to determine which mode of construction would

HILL-FORT, called White Caterthun, in Strathmore. - From Roy's Military Antiquities.

be employed in any particular case. Whether made of earth or stone they usually exhibit one or more rings, or lines of circumvallation that inclose an area which is prevailingly of somewhat circular shape. These rings or ramparts may form a more or less complete circuit according to the character of the ground, and may be accompanied by trenches and other works of greater or less magnitude, the defences being stronger on the side that is the weaker owing to the natural features of the site.

The simplest of these forts have been formed by digging trenches and throwing up the excavated earth to form the ramparts. These, as they now exist, are of no great height, perhaps 9 or 10 feet at most, but no doubt the wearing effect of time has greatly reduced their elevation, and perhaps when they were in a serviceable condition they would be crowned with palisades. The works of earth and stone in combination show no specific difference in plan from those of earth alone, nor do those of loosely piled stones—a class which, however, seems to be comparatively rare. Among the most remarkable of the stone forts is that known as the White Caterthun in Menmuir parish, Forfarshire. Here we have three concentric walls or ramparts, the innermost or that nearest the summit inclosing an area of oval outline about 450 feet long by 200 broad. The remains of this wall, which now at least appears to be formed entirely of loose stones, form a mass about 100 feet wide in places, with a height of from 4 to 6 feet above the inclosed area, and a long outer slope. The other walls or ramparts sur-

---

[1] An interesting account of an English crannog recently discovered at Glastonbury was read before the Glastonbury Antiquarian Society in November, 1892. It was stated (according to the report in *The Scotsman*) that "of the dwellings themselves there was nothing left to tell of their size or shape, but there was evidence of their having been constructed of wattle and split timber, the crevices between the wood being filled up with clay. A quantity of this clay had been dug up with the wattle or timber marks on one side, and very distinct impressions of the fingers that had pressed it into position on the other. The clay was probably baked hard when the huts were destroyed by fire, the obvious fate of many of them." Many fragments of pottery were found, and a number of articles in bronze beautifully fashioned, as well as articles of iron. Needles, spindle whorls, loom weights, combs for carding wool, and part of a shuttle were also found. This crannog was probably used as a place of defence against the invading Saxons.

[2] *Proceedings of the Society of Antiquaries of Scotland* for 1888-89, p. 426.

rounding this are much less massive. In the forts with regularly built walls various styles of masonry are employed, and the wall generally varies in strength according to the nature of the ground, the edge of a precipice or a very steep slope naturally requiring little or no defence.

A remarkable feature in connection with these stone forts is that in many cases the walls have been to a greater or less extent vitrified by fire—portions of them being thus consolidated into a somewhat glassy mass; but how this was accomplished, and whether it was intended to give additional strength, is not clearly made out. Some authorities have thought that such forts were constructed originally of wood and stone, and that the vitrification resulted from the structure being set on fire either accidentally or by a besieging enemy. Others have sought to account for the phenomenon on the hypothesis that these forts were the sites of great beacon fires lighted to give warning of the approach of invaders, or they have suggested that great bonfires were kindled on the respective spots in connection with religious or other celebrations, the vitrification in any case being thus accidental rather than intentional. The general belief, however, is that the vitrification was effected intentionally, and with the view of giving increased strength to the structure thus treated, evidence in favour of this being the facts that the vitrified portions of the wall are usually at points least strong by nature, and that in a number of cases stones susceptible of fusion by fire have been carried from some distance to the site selected for a fort, where there was already abundance of rocky material ready to hand, but not of the desired kind. The extent to which fusion has gone varies considerably; when it has reached the highest degree the wall, or a large portion of it, presents the appearance of a solid glassy mass. Vitrified forts have been found in one or two cases in Ireland, and they are also met with in France, Germany, and the Austrian dominions; but no specimens are known to exist in England, Wales, or Scandinavia.

Singularly enough in hardly any instances are the hill-forts provided with a well or other special source of water supply, a feature which gives rise to the belief that they can hardly have been intended to be occupied for any length of time. Altogether they are structures in regard to the origin and use of which little or nothing is definitely known. One might hazard a conjecture that certain of them, instead of being forts, were places intended to be the scene of rites associated with some old-world religion, or of long-forgotten tribal customs or ceremonies.

If we know so little of the hill-forts, we are equally in the dark regarding the works known as "earth-houses" or "yird-houses."[1] These are of so entirely different a character that they are subterranean abodes or receptacles, burrows or excavations, lined with masonry, and completely covered over with the surface soil. They are generally situated in localities where the land is now all under tillage, and have often been discovered in the operation of ploughing. They may be described as long, narrow, underground galleries, entered by a small opening at the surface of the ground, then sloping downwards and widening out till they terminate in a closed and rounded end, the whole being not only lined, but also roofed with stones. They are generally more or less curved in plan, frequently, indeed, exhibiting a very sharp bend in their course at some distance from the entrance. The total length from entrance to extremity, measured along the curve, may vary from 30 feet to more than double this, the greatest width being 8 or 9 feet, and the greatest height of the walls 6 or 7 feet. Some of the roofing stones are rough slabs of great size, as much as 7 or 8 feet in length by 3 in breadth. These earth-houses have been found over the whole length of Scotland, from Berwickshire to the north coast of Sutherland, and thence to the Shetland Islands, and sometimes they occur in considerable numbers together, as in Forfarshire and Aberdeenshire. From the relics found in connection with them they are assigned to a date not earlier than the Roman occupation of southern Scotland,

---

[1] They are also called "Picts' houses" and *weems*, the latter name being from the Gaelic word for a cave.

and to the time when paganism still prevailed in the country, but what precisely was the use to which they were put is not quite clear. Probably they may have served more than one purpose. Many of them might have been used as underground store-houses, or as hiding-places in cases of emergency, while others, perhaps, would be occupied as dwellings during the rigour of a Scottish winter. Somewhat similar structures have been found elsewhere than in Scotland, as in Cornwall and Ireland; but the Scottish earth-houses are so distinct in character as to form a type by themselves.

Much more elaborate and perhaps more interesting structures are those known as

BROCH OF MOUSA, SHETLAND.

"burghs" or "brochs," which form a class of edifices peculiar to Scotland, and to Scotland alone. They occur in by far the largest numbers in the northern counties, including Orkney, Shetland, and the Western Isles, though they are found also in other parts of the country, more than three hundred in all being known. A broch, as described by Dr. Joseph Anderson, is a hollow circular tower of dry-built masonry, rarely more than 70, or less than 40 feet in total diameter, occasionally at least 50 feet high, and inclosing a circular court or area from 25 to 45 feet in diameter. The wall, which may be from 9 to 20 feet thick, is carried up solid for about 10 feet, except where it is pierced by the narrow passage giving entrance to the interior court, or where chambers are hollowed within its thickness and opening off the court. Above this height there are horizontal galleries in the thickness of the wall, each about 6 feet high and 3 feet wide, running completely round the tower, except where they are crossed by the stair that gives access to them, and having peculiarly constructed windows placed above each other, and all looking into the central area. The only external opening is that of the narrow entrance passage, forming a doorway about 5 or 6 feet high, and rarely more than 3 feet wide. The passage itself varies from 9 to 18 feet in length, and about 4 feet from its outer entrance is the place where the door—probably a slab of stone—was placed, and where the masonry presents features intended to enable it to be securely fixed.

Many of the brochs are built in positions naturally strong, such as a precipitous eminence or a promontory projecting into a loch, and they are also defended by ditches and embankments, earthen ramparts, and dry stone walls. Hence it is clear that they were intended to serve as places of shelter and defence. Moreover, as they are generally planted in the neighbourhood of the best land in the districts where they are situated, it is hardly doubtful that they were designed to furnish a refuge for an agricultural population with their cattle and other belongings, when the lives and property of the community were threatened by foreign invaders or by bands of hostile plunderers from any quarter. For this purpose they are admirably contrived, as they form a series of strongholds that could only be reduced by a regular siege. In these fastnesses there was little need for warriors, as the inmates were safe against missiles and even against fire, from the height and strength of the walls, while the only entrance from without was extremely unlikely to be forced, owing to its narrowness and strength. Provided with a sufficiency of food, and obtaining water from a well inside the inclosure, as was often the case in the brochs, the people thus sheltered could hold out for an indefinite time.

The relics found in the brochs, like the structures themselves, are decided by antiquaries to be Celtic in character, and to belong to post-Roman times. The brochs were probably built in most cases as places of refuge from the Scandinavian vikings that for centuries were a scourge to many of the European coasts. They do not therefore strictly belong to the Prehistoric era of Scotland, though little or nothing of their history is known. The relics include swords, spears, knives, axes, and chisels of iron, with rings, bracelets, pins, and other articles of bronze or of brass; and though gold seems to be wanting, silver and lead were now in use, though unknown to Scotland in the Bronze Age. Numerous articles made of the bones and horns of animals are found in the brochs, as also implements made of stone—querns, mortars, pestles, bowls and cups, lamps, &c. Pottery of various kinds was common. Spinning and weaving were evidently practised. Agriculture, hunting, and fishing furnished a subsistence; and the animal food of the people of the brochs was sufficiently varied, being furnished by the stag, the roe, the reindeer, the ox, sheep, goat, and pig, the whale, porpoise, cod, haddock, and other denizens of the sea.

The relics obtained from the brochs, as Dr. Joseph Anderson points out, must have been the product of an advanced stage of culture, civilization, and social organization. We see their occupants, as he says, "planting their defensive habitations thickly over the area of the best arable land, fringing the coasts, and studding the straths with a form of structure perfectly unique in character and conception, and for purposes of defence and passive resistance as admirably devised as anything yet invented. We see that this system of gigantic and laboriously constructed strongholds has been devised and universally adopted with the plain intention of providing for the security of the tillers and the produce of the soil. We find their occupants cultivating grain, keeping flocks and herds, and hunting the forests and fishing the sea for their sustenance. We find them practising arts and industries implying intelligence and technical skill, and apparently also involving commercial relations with distant sources of the raw materials." And when we find all this to be sufficiently substantiated by the evidence, and consider the character of the civilization that we have found prevailing in the preceding periods, we wonder where there is room for the state of rudeness and barbarity that some of the classical writers have depicted as existing in Scotland subsequent to the beginning of the Christian era. Dion Cassius, for instance, a historian of the third century, speaks of the inhabitants of Caledonia as if they were in the habit of going naked and of hiding in marshes for days together, sunk in mud and water up to the neck; and similar statements are made by Herodian, a contemporary writer. If there was any truth at all in such pictures—if they were not based on the proverbial "travellers' tales," current no doubt at this as at other periods, or were not the offspring of an over-lively imagination—these pictures can only have referred to the most miserable and degraded of the inhabitants, possibly to members of an older race reduced to a condition of abject slavery, or to people who, through their misdeeds, had been driven out of the general community, and had become outlaws and Ishmaelites. That the people of Scotland as a whole were living in such a state of utter savagery, is a proposition that can in no way be brought into harmony with the degree of civilization and culture which the indisputable evidence of archæology proves to have existed.[1]

It still remains for us to take into consideration some questions of very great interest regarding the early inhabitants of Scotland, and their relation to other peoples, whether of the present or the past. It has already been stated that the people who appear as the earliest inhabitants of the country in the Neolithic period are believed to have

---

[1] It is possible, however, that there may have been times when numbers of the inhabitants were reduced to great destitution owing to wars, famine, pestilence, or other calamity. This might partly account for the statements of the ancient writers here referred to.

belonged to the Iberian race; and it is also claimed that their descendants still form an element more or less distinct among the Scottish people of the present day. The Iberians seem to have been, as far back as we can trace them, a race of Southern Europe and Northern Africa, who had to make way for stronger, or more able and warlike peoples, and thus were displaced from their ancient seats, or were absorbed by these incomers, and lost their distinctive language and institutions, except perhaps in the Basque country. The peoples who now hold, and have long held the greater part of Europe, speak a series of languages totally different from the Basque; languages which differ indeed among themselves, but yet possess in common such marks of similarity as serve to show that they have all descended from one primitive form of speech, much in the same way as Italian, French, Spanish, and Portuguese have all descended from Latin. All the languages that show this community of descent have been grouped together by philologists into what is known as the Aryan, or Indo-European family of tongues, a family which thus includes not only Greek, Latin, and most of the idioms of modern Europe (excluding, however, Turkish, Hungarian, and Finnish), but also such Asiatic languages as Sanskrit, Persian, and Armenian. That all these languages spread from one centre, or at least from one common area, is tolerably certain; and that a Celtic-speaking people carried their own language with them from this centre over a great part of Western Europe, including the British Isles, is equally certain. It is also highly probable that Celtic thus supplanted an Iberian tongue over a certain area, though that this was the case in Britain we do not know for an actual fact. That Celtic was spoken in Britain, however, long before the beginning of the Christian era, there can be no doubt. The Celtic invaders of Britain, as we have already stated in this chapter, seem to have arrived in two successive waves—with what interval between we know not—the first wave consisting of Celts belonging to the Goidelic or Gaelic division of the Celtic peoples, the second, of Celts belonging to the Cymric or Brythonic division. The subsequent invasion of Britain by Germanic or Teutonic tribes, which has given us the language now almost universally spoken in these islands, belongs, of course, entirely to the historic period.

How remote the period may have been when there was as yet no language in existence that could be called either Celtic, or Teutonic, or Greek, or Latin, or Sanskrit, or Slavonic, but only a language containing within it the germs of all these, we cannot tell; yet there can be little doubt that such a language did exist, and indeed philologists tell us, with some confidence, what consonant and what vowel sounds this Aryan parent-speech must have possessed, what were the forms of its inflections, and what must have been the most important words belonging to its vocabulary, judging from the words that can be traced as forming a common possession of the Aryan tongues, and that are not borrowed from foreign sources. By the method of "linguistic palæontology," as it has been called, by sifting out and collecting such words as can be shown to have belonged to the primitive stock of Aryan vocables; and by reasoning from words to things, philologists have been able to place before us a picture —dim and vague in its outlines, doubtless— of the civilization that existed in the primitive community, and have thus helped in settling where such community must have had its original seat. At one time the primitive home of the Aryans was supposed to have been in Asia, but this view has latterly been almost entirely given up; and the region where the first Aryan-speaking people dwelt is now believed to have been in Eastern Europe, probably in South-eastern Russia, where this country is intersected by the Volga. This view, of course, decides nothing as to the ultimate origin of these primitive Aryans, as to the locality whence they found their way thither—it only decides that here we find the fountain-head of Aryan speech, and further back in this direction we have no means of going.

The civilization that linguistic palæontology reveals to us as existing among the primitive Aryans, presents the following as its chief features:—Our Aryan ancestors, at the stage when they formed as yet a single community or nation,[1] appear to have been a pastoral rather than an agricultural people, being to a large degree nomadic in their habits, though tillage was to some extent practised. They possessed herds of cattle, and flocks of sheep and goats; the dog was then, as now, the faithful companion of man; and they were acquainted with the horse, but whether it was as yet domesticated is uncertain: probably it was kept in a half-wild state to furnish a supply of food. The ass, the mule, the camel, and the cat were animals unknown to the primitive Aryans; and they appear to have had none of the birds belonging to the poultry class. Of wild animals they were acquainted with the wolf, the bear, the otter, the wild boar, the hare, and the beaver; among birds they had names for the owl, the raven and crow, the cuckoo, and some few others. Few names of trees are common to the Aryan languages; and this is one reason that has led to the belief that the primitive seat of the Aryans was a steppe country bare of timber, such as that indicated above. That they recognized only two seasons of the year—winter and summer—is tolerably certain; and this also agrees with the climatic conditions prevailing in South-eastern Russia, where spring and autumn are seasons that form an unimportant portion of the year. The moon was the chief time-measurer in this remote period, and the night, or period of darkness, was regarded as of more importance in computations than the daily period of light—a view still reflected in our *fortnight* and *sennight*. Flesh formed part of the food of the people, being eaten roasted, and probably also raw. The dietary also included milk and vegetable food; but, singularly enough, fish seem to have been entirely neglected, as there is no common Aryan word for fish or for any particular fish. Besides milk, they had also mead as a beverage—so early do men seem to have found out a way to provide themselves with the seductive pleasures of intoxicating liquor. For clothing they had skins, and also some kind of rude woven garments of wool and flax, as well as felted stuffs. As to their dwellings, these appear to have been partly waggons, in which they followed their flocks and herds from place to place; partly rude huts of wood, wattle-work, or clay; and partly excavations in the ground, stone not being used as yet for building houses. Exchange of commodities was carried on by barter; and though navigation was known, it was only effected by boats of the "dug-out" canoe class, and in inland waters, the sea being unknown to the primitive Aryans. As regards family relationships, the husband was lord and master in his household—the wife was not much superior in position to a slave; polygamy and concubinage were practised, and it rested with the father to decide whether children were to be brought up, or exposed and allowed to perish. In regard to religious beliefs or notions, extremely little has been ascertained with any approach to certainty.

The mode of life thus shown by linguistic palæontology to have existed among the Aryans before their dispersion, is on the whole very similar to that which prevails over a considerable portion of Southern Russia at the present day—where the people make flocks and herds their chief care, live in clumsy waggons or dwellings

---

[1] In treating of the peoples speaking Aryan languages, it has been a very common practice with writers to regard them as all of one race—the Aryan or Indo-European race —thus making race and language co-extensive. This is not a very scientific proceeding, however, since the fact that a people or community speaks a certain language is not in itself evidence as to the race to which that people belongs. A people may speak one language at one period of its history, another at another. The Jews as a rule now speak the language of whatever people they happen to live among; the Romans impressed their language upon various peoples, who thus gave up their own tongue in favour of Latin; the negroes of America speak English—or at least a bastard variety of it; and in the present chapter we suppose a change of language on the part of Iberians in Scotland. So the Aryan languages in Europe, it is believed, have been spoken from time immemorial by peoples belonging to more than one race, as is evidenced by the prevalence of the dolichocephalic type of skull in some regions (Scandinavia more especially), of the brachycephalic in others. A controversy has hence arisen as to which type is that of the true primitive Aryan—a question that seems exceedingly difficult of settlement. Dr. Schrader judiciously inclines to the view that the original Aryan community, the community among which the primitive Aryan speech arose, may itself have been of mixed race.

dug in the ground, and use skins at least as part of their clothing. In one respect, however, there is an important difference— the primitive Aryans were unacquainted with the use of metals. In this respect it is important to note, they were on a level with the Neolithic people of Scotland, who also in other respects, as we have already seen, had arrived at a stage of civilization strikingly similar to that which may be predicated of the Aryans in their original home. So that the conclusions at which philologists have arrived by investigations based on language, are in singular accordance with those at which archæologists have arrived by a very different road, namely, by investigations entirely confined to the field of archæology.

Regarding the migration of the Aryans from their ancient home, the evolution of dialects, and ultimately separate languages, from the one ancestral speech, and the contemporaneous evolution of separate nationalities; and regarding the fortunes of the separate peoples up to the time when they reached their final abodes—the Celts as far to the west as the British Islands, the Hindoos as far to the east as India—we can learn little either from history, from archæology, or from philology. Such questions after all, however interesting in themselves, have only, it must be admitted, a somewhat remote bearing on the history of Scotland; but there is an allied question, and one closely connected with Scottish history and ethnology, that still remains involved in almost equal darkness, and that is—Of what race and language were the Picts? This question might be said to belong to the historic rather than to the prehistoric period of Scotland, since we first find the Picts mentioned under this name about three hundred years after the beginning of the Christian era. Still, as they must have entered Scotland in prehistoric times, from whatever quarter they came, it will not be out of place to pass in review some of the most recent conclusions of scholars regarding their race and language, while their history is fully treated in the early chapters of the following work.

The chief reason why there is a Pictish question that has so long been debated, and is so difficult of solution, is that, with the exception of a certain number of proper names, there are hardly any words that can be conclusively shown to be Pictish. The name Pict itself may be said to be equally dark with other matters relating to the people. The first to use it apparently was a Latin writer, Eumenius, in 296 A.D., who speaks of "the Caledonians and other Picts" in connection with the campaigns of the Roman emperor Constantius Chlorus in Britain; and the common view is that "Picts" is a Latin word converted into a proper name, and that it means simply "the painted (or tattooed) people." That the Roman writers so understood it is evident; but this may have arisen from a misunderstanding, and it is by no means certain that the name was not originally Pictish, and from its similarity in sound to the Latin *pictus*, painted, led the Romans to believe that the two words were identical. This is the view to which Professor Rhys and others incline, at anyrate. He points to the similarity between the name of this people of Scotland and the names Pictones and Pictavi occurring among the ancient Gauls, these latter being names that cannot be connected with the Latin *pictus*; and he brings forward other evidence tending in the same direction. It is true that certain ancient writers speak of the Picts or Caledonians as painted or tattooed with figures of animals; so that the name Picti, "the painted men," would thus be justified. Yet it is not altogether certain that such statements were based on actual observation, or that the Picts were more given to ornamenting themselves in this way than other rude peoples. At anyrate, Tacitus, writing in the first century of our era, does not attribute this practice to the Caledonians; and Gildas (writing in the sixth century), as Professor Rhys points out, though he evidently wishes to attribute to the Picts as outlandish an aspect as possible, and refers to their hairy faces and scant clothing, says nothing about painting or tattooing. Indeed, even if they did paint or tattoo themselves, it is allowable to believe that the name was of native origin, and had no reference to this, its similarity to the Latin *pictus* being purely fortuitous.

With regard to the race to which the Picts belonged it will no doubt be deemed probable, from considerations already brought forward, that they were largely of Iberian blood. Whether they still retained their Iberian tongue when we first find them mentioned in history is another question, which Prof. Rhys would answer in the affirmative, especially as regards the more northern Picts. If we take the view that this was so, it will be natural also to take his view that Gaelic spread itself over Northern Scotland owing to the well-known immigration of the Dalriad Scots from Ireland, and the spread of their power and influence; since we know that the Gaelic of Scotland and that of Ireland are practically one and the same language. No doubt Celtic was spoken also south of the Pictish area in early times, but the general belief is that this form of Celtic speech belonged to the Brythonic or British, and not to the Gaelic branch.

As bearing on this subject we may refer to the fact mentioned in Adamnan's *Life of St. Columba*, that the saint (who was himself a Scot from Ireland), though he seems generally to have had no difficulty in understanding, and making himself understood to, the Picts, on one or two occasions required an interpreter. This is hardly consistent with the supposition that Iberian was the prevailing tongue among the Picts, otherwise one would think St. Columba must have generally required an interpreter; but it is quite in harmony with the supposition that it was still spoken in some localities, though the Iberians as a whole had given up their own language and adopted that of the dominant Celts. The state of matters at that time would thus be similar to what we find in the Highlands at the present day, where, though English is the dominant tongue, there are still localities in which a person unacquainted with Gaelic would require the services of an interpreter. As evidence that Iberian, or at least non-Aryan, custom was hard to eradicate we find the rule prevailing in Pictland that succession to the crown went by the mother's side and not by the father's, brothers and sisters' sons succeeding, to the rejection of sons. Such a custom is not known in connection with any of the Aryan peoples. Professor Rhys thinks it probable that Iberian speech lingered longest in the north-east of Scotland, and suggests that the well-known peculiarities of the Aberdeen dialect may be due to Iberian influence. This may possibly be the case, but it is certain that the Scotch of this part of Scotland could not have come directly under the influence of Iberian, since an overwhelming majority of the place-names here are clearly of Gaelic origin, thus showing that Gaelic must have preceded the Lowland Scotch as the speech of the inhabitants.[1]

Dr. Skene on investigating the subject comes to the conclusion that Pictish was a Gaelic tongue in no way very different from the Irish of the same period, though more or less pronounced dialects may have existed locally. Such dialectic differences might account, he thinks, for the fact that Columba on one or two occasions required an interpreter, though generally he found no such difficulty. "There is," he asserts, "almost a concurrent testimony of the Celtic inhabitants of Britain to the Picts having belonged to that branch of the race which the Welsh called Gwyddel, and the Irish Gaedheal. Throughout the whole of the Welsh documents the Picts are usually denominated Gwyddel Ffichti, while the Irish are simply termed Gwyddel. Although this word Gwyddel is generally used to designate a native of Ireland, and is so translated, this is its modern usage only; and it is impossible to examine the older Welsh documents without seeing that it was originally the designation of the Gadhelic race wherever situated, and the Picts are thus clearly assigned to it. . . . The race of the Picts were not, however, confined to Britain. They originally extended over the whole of the north of Ireland, and though eventually

---

[1] There are certain elements in many place-names of this part of Scotland which are commonly regarded as specially Pictish, more particularly the prefixes *Pet* or *Pit*, *Fetter*, *Ar*, and *For*. These do not prove anything as to the prevalence of the Iberian language here, since they can be explained by comparison with the Gaelic or Brythonic. A few place-names do seem to belong to an older stratum of language.

confined to the territory on the east of Ulster called Dalnaraidhe, or Dalaradia, they remained there as a separate people under the name of Cruithnigh till a comparatively late period. Down to the beginning of the seventh century they formed with the Picts of Scotland one nation; but during the whole period of their separate existence the Irish annals do not contain a hint that they spoke a language different from the rest of Ireland." At most he believes that the difference between Pictish and Irish may not have been greater than that between Breton or Cornish and Welsh, and much less than between Welsh and Irish. The Southern Picts he believes may have possessed some differences of idiom from the Northern Picts, and they appear latterly (according to him) to have been incorporated with the Dumnonii of Southern Scotland, who belonged to the Cornish variety of the British race and introduced a British element into the Pictish tongue.

That the Pictish language belonged to the Cymric or Brythonic branch of the Celtic, and was thus more closely akin to the Welsh than to the Irish, has been maintained by other scholars, who find evidence of this in certain of the words and forms that can reasonably be decided to be Pictish. The most recent verdict on this question is given by the distinguished Celtic scholar, Whitley Stokes, who maintains in *The Academy* for June 4, 1892, "that Pictish was a Celtic language retaining several traces of the Old Celtic declensions, but in other respects nearer to Welsh than to Irish."

At one time it was a common theory that the Picts were a "Gothic," that is a Teutonic or Germanic people, and that their language, therefore, was akin to English, German, and the other Teutonic tongues. This opinion was stoutly maintained by Pinkerton, as also by Dr. Jamieson, author of the famous Scottish Dictionary, but it may now be said to be entirely given up. It was never, indeed, supported by very strong evidence, and the arguments that can be brought against it are far too strong to be resisted.

Before closing this chapter we may refer to an argument bearing on the ethnology of Scotland based on the Highland costume. It was brought forward by Professor A. H. Sayce in his address to the British Association in 1887, as president of the Anthropological section of the association. He points out that the dress which has been so commonly identified as "the garb of Old Gaul" is not really such, since the ancient Celtic inhabitants of Gaul, as well as the Celts of Southern Britain, the Germans, and other peoples, wore breeches or trousers. The kilt, on the contrary, is distinctively Scottish, though at one time worn also in Ireland and in Wales, being introduced into the latter country, according to Sayce, by immigrants from Scotland. From this he concludes that the aboriginal inhabitants of Scotland and Ireland were non-Celtic, otherwise there would have been no difference between their dress and that of the Celts elsewhere, since "there are few things about which a population—more especially in an early stage of society—is so conservative as in the matter of dress."

PERIOD I.

FROM THE EARLIEST TIMES TO THE UNION OF THE PICTS AND SCOTS (A.D. 843).

CHAPTER I.

MYTHIC AND LEGENDARY HISTORY OF SCOTLAND.

Origin of the Scots — Gathelus — His departure from Egypt — His landing in Spain and founding the Scottish nation — Migrations of the Scots from Spain to Ireland — Their final arrival and settlement in Scotland — Arrival of the Picts in Scotland — Their wars with the Scots — The Scots send to Ireland for aid — Fergus arrives and conquers the Picts — Early Scottish kings, Fergus, &c. — Reign of Reutha — Arrival of Egyptian envoys at his court — Visit of Spanish priests to Scotland — Effect of their instructions upon the Scots — The Scots unite with the Picts and Britons against Julius Cæsar — They defeat him — Cæsar sends ambassadors to the Scots — Caractacus claimed as a Scottish king — His history according to the Scottish legends — The Scots and Picts continue their resistance to the Romans — Invasion of Agricola as given in the Scottish legends — Its disastrous issue — The Scots drive the Romans back into South Britain — Reign of Galdus [Galgacus] — Worthless reign of Lugtak, his successor — Reign of Ethodius I. — Of Donald, the first Christian king of Scotland — Successive kings — Carausius the Menapian represented as a Scottish prince — War renewed between the Scots and Picts — The Scots defeated and driven out of the island — They are recalled by the Picts — They return under Prince Fergus — His victorious reign as Fergus II. — Death of Fergus — The Romans abandon Britain.

ALTHOUGH the origin of most nations is involved in impenetrable obscurity, there are few that do not claim the distinction of an ancient history. The aim of these early historians is to prove that, instead of having been the savages of yesterday, they have possessed the nationality and the civilization of ages, and that they were among the first who emerged from barbarism into social order and progress. But not content with a remote antiquity, they also assume an illustrious national descent, to vindicate their claims to superiority. It is the common weakness of individual life manifested collectively by a people at large, in which the humble or discreditable sources from which greatness is derived are concealed, and an illustrious ancestry substituted in their room; and thus the old national annals and the old genealogical tree become equally matter of envy, cavil, and controversy. This remark, so applicable to nations in general, peculiarly applies to the Scots, with whom ancestral pride of race as well as family is so especial an attribute, and the destruction of whose earliest national records has left so wide a field for assertion and conjecture.

In this spirit the earliest Scottish historians have derived their countrymen, not from the naked savages of two thousand years ago, who had neither fathers to boast of nor deeds to chronicle, but from the two most renowned nations which sacred and profane history could furnish — from Egypt, the early home of science and civilization, and from Athens, the mother of literature and intellectual refinement. According to this bold statement the origin of the Scots, and the founding of the kingdom of Scotland, occurred in the following manner.

Gathelus, a son of Argus or of Cecrops (for to which of these kings the honour of his paternity belonged has been left unsettled), having made himself notorious by his plundering inroads upon Macedonia and Achaia, which he seems to have conducted in the destructive undiscriminating spirit of his remote descendants, became obnoxious to Greece at large, and was obliged to betake himself to flight. Accompanied by a band of his adventurous followers he arrived in Egypt, during the reign of that Pharaoh who oppressed the Israelites; and having distinguished himself in the service of the king by his gallant deeds against the Moors and Indians, he was enabled to supplant Moses himself in the royal favour, and obtain the princess Scota, the daughter of Pharaoh, for his bride. Dismayed, however, by the coming of the ten plagues, he resolved to leave a land which Heaven had so evidently denounced; and embarking with his wife and family, and his followers Greek and Egyptian, he issued from the mouth of the Nile into the Mediterranean in quest of a new settlement. He first touched at Numidia, but was there refused a landing. His next course was to the coast of Spain; and having landed in Lusitania, thenceforth in honour of him named Portugal (that is, the port of Gathelus), he defeated the natives and obtained from them the surrender of a district, on which he proceeded to found a new colony. The Lusitanians growing weary of such dangerous neighbours, and being not strong enough to eject them, at length bethought themselves of a prophecy: it was to the effect that a strange people should arrive among them and finally settle in the north part of Spain—and Gathelus, to whom they imparted the prediction, was not slow to fulfil it. He passed over with his followers to the province of Galicia, which thenceforth became his home; built the town of Compostella; and imposed upon his people the new national name of Scots, from that of Scota, his beloved Egyptian partner. He also made laws and dispensed justice throughout his new kingdom, while his throne was that memorable stone now inserted in the chair which is still to be seen in the Abbey of Westminster. This slab of black marble, which from its final resting-place has witnessed events and changes that have eclipsed even the marvels of its early history, was the Stone of Destiny of the Scots, as is indicated by the well-known prophecy that accompanies it:—

"Ni fallat fatum, Scoti quocunque locatum
Invenient lapidem, regnare tenentur ibidem."[1]

The Scots being thus a wandering people from the beginning, and finding the bounds of Galicia too narrow for their increasing population, resolved to colonize new settlements; and Gathelus having learned that there was an island opposite Spain, inhabited by a rude people having neither laws nor manners, was desirous to bestow upon it a better population. He accordingly sent out a fleet for the purpose, under the command of his two sons, Hiber and Hemecus, who reached this island; and finding it fertile and the people willing to be "pleasantly subdued," they quietly took possession and called it Hibernia, after the name of the eldest son of Gathelus, who returned to Spain, leaving his brother Hemecus ruler of this future Ireland. After the death of Hemecus a fierce contest broke out between the Scots and the aborigines, as to which of the two races should have the privilege of furnishing a successor; and the old stock of inhabitants being the offspring of giants, were not disposed to concede the point of honour as pleasantly as they had done their superfluous territory. A long war that lasted for several generations was the consequence, and the Scots in Ireland were reduced to such straits that they were obliged to apply to their brethren of Spain for aid. At length the latter sent to them an eminent captain called Symon Brek, by whom this war of succession was ended, and who was himself appointed king, being the first sovereign who ruled in Ireland. Fortunately he had taken care to bring with him from Spain the marble Stone of Destiny, which no doubt secured the promised ascendency to his people, and he reigned forty years in peace and prosperity.

In this manner, our early legendary or mythic history brings the Scots from Greece to Egypt, from Egypt to Spain, and from Spain to Ireland. But their chief exodus had yet to be fulfilled, and this important event occurred only 216 years after the reign of Symon Brek. Why the Scots forsook Ireland for such a country as Scotland must then have been, unless from a restless love of migration and adventure, does not appear. The first places also which they were said to have colonized were Ardgael (Argyle), so called from their original leader Gathelus; the Island of Bute, which was the name of the king then ruling in Ireland; and the Hebrides, thus denominated from Hiber, the son of Gathelus. Thus their choice seems to have fallen upon the poorest parts of the country, although it might have been thought that the whole land lay before them. What people they dispossessed, or whether they found their new wilderness uninhabited, is nowhere told us; and thus, in an age of such violence and forcible occupation, their entrance was effected, as it appears, without a single battle being fought or even a giant overcome. Being thus divided among different localities, they naturally separated into tribes, each having its own district, independent usages, and ruler; and towards these chiefs, who were their judges in peace and captains in war, they acquired such reverential feeling as to swear by their names and invoke them in trouble, as if they had been divinities and not ordinary mortals. In this way, according to the old Scottish annalists, the system of chieftainry was first established among the Scots of North Britain.

The Scots, however, were not to remain the sole occupants of the new country, for not long after their arrival in Scotland the Picts landed upon the coast. And here the old traditions are vague and contradictory about the origin of this new people, some proclaiming them a Ger-

---

[1] Thus translated by Bellenden in his version of Boece's History:—

"The Scottis sall bruke that realme as native ground,
Geif weirdis faill nocht, quhair evir this chiar is found."

man tribe, while others assert that they were the remains of the Huns, who had been driven from their country by the Flemings. At all events, they are described as an erratic people, roaming in quest of a home, who, after being refused a landing in France, South Britain, and Ireland, were fain to steal into the north coasts of our island, from which they spread over Caithness, Ross, Moray, Mearns, Angus, Fife, and Lothian, expelling the original occupants, and establishing themselves in their room. In this summary and unsatisfactory manner their obtaining possession of the best part of the country is accounted for. Being now no longer a landless tribe, they were able to treat with the Scots on equal terms, and their first proposal was for a close alliance with the latter, to be cemented by a marriage with Scottish brides. To this the proud descendants of the Pharaohs and the Cecropidæ demurred; but finding their new neighbours too strong to be contradicted, they submitted with a good grace, and consented to become their fathers and brothers. A strict league was thus established between the Scots and Picts, in which each were to enjoy their own share of the land, and unite as one people against every foreign assailant. In the ticklish question of the royal succession the Scots are also represented as showing a most evident forethought about their own interests: for they secured in this agreement, that as often as the inheritance of the Pictish crown should be matter of question, the controversy should be settled by appointing the nearest of the woman's kindred to succeed to the kingly office.

In this way every precaution had been taken that the two races should have a common interest and in time become one people. A union, however, so advantageous to themselves boded no good to others, and especially to the South Britons, who even thus early began to dread such hungry and formidable neighbours. They set themselves accordingly, only three years after this alliance was formed, to inspire the Picts with jealousy against the Scots, and with such success that war was proclaimed between the two associated races. It was soon evident, however, on mustering their resources, that the Picts, who are described as the more civilized people, being builders of cities and cultivators of the soil, were more powerful than the Scots, who were only hunters and shepherds. The latter accordingly appealed to their brethren of Ireland for aid, who readily responded to the call; and Fergus, the son of Ferquhard, the Scoto-Irish king, was sent to their assistance, bringing with him not only a formidable army, but what was of greater account even—the Stone of Destiny, which would insure a firm footing to their countrymen wherever they were pleased to plant it. This arrival of Fergus in Scotland is stated to have occurred three hundred and thirty years before the commencement of the Christian era. The banner borne before him displayed a red lion rampant on a field of gold, which thenceforth became the cognizance of the Scottish kings. The Scots, who since their arrival in the country had lived in separate tribes that were governed by their own chiefs, soon saw that such a divided rule was insufficient for an encounter with the warlike and united Picts; and therefore they chose Fergus as their king, inaugurated him on the marble slab which was now to find Scotland for its resting-place, and entailed the crown in hereditary succession upon his posterity. As for the war itself, it was only an episode among such important movements. No sooner had Fergus led out his troops against the Picts, than it was discovered by both parties that an army of South Britons was drawn up at no great distance to watch the turn of events, and finally to descend and crush the wearied victors whether they might be Scots or Picts. This flagrant instance of double-dealing brought the latter to a pause, and while the two armies were still in suspense, the Scottish wives of the Picts, in the old Sabine fashion, rushed between them, and implored husband, father, and brother not to imbrue their hands in each other's blood. The appeal prevailed, and the former peace was renewed more firmly than ever. The Picts and Scots, now at one, resolved to turn their arms against the Britons, by whom they had been so perfidiously duped, and who now endeavoured to effect by open manhood what they had failed to accomplish by craft and cunning. For this purpose they invaded Scotland in such numbers that both Scots and Picts were filled with dismay, until Fergus, by a well planned night attack near the Water of Doon, routed their numerous army with great loss, and slew Coyl their king. From the place where the sovereign of the Britons fell the whole district received the name of Kyle, which it retains in our own day. As in many similar cases, the event was probably made for the name rather than the name derived from the event. It may be observed in passing, that among the liberties taken with the memory of King Coyl, Coul, or Cole, this does not happen to be the least.

Having thus delivered the country, Fergus divided that part of it which belonged to the Scots into twelve districts, over which he appointed his principal nobles as lieutenants or viceroys, and established such laws for the preservation of order, that the very cattle were safe in the fields without the trouble of tending them. He also built the castle of Berigon in Lochaber, which became his royal residence. After a reign of peace and prosperity, he had occasion to pass over to Ireland to compose certain troubles that had risen there; but on his return to Scotland he perished by shipwreck on a rock, subsequently called Craigfergus or Carrickfergus, after he had ruled twenty-five years.

As the Scottish chieftains had confirmed the royal authority not only in Fergus but his posterity, they were perplexed at his death upon the question of a successor, his eldest son being still a minor; but they at length solved the difficulty by appointing Ferithais, brother of Fergus, king, with the condition that the children of the late sovereign should succeed him in the throne. This order of succession in the case of royal minors was also established into a law that continued in force more than twelve hundred years. But even already such a rule produced its natural fruits; for, impatient of his inferiority, and conceiving himself defrauded of his right, Ferlegus, the heir apparent, assassinated his uncle, and then fled to South Britain. His younger brother Maynus succeeded to the crown, and after him followed Dornadilla, Nathak, Reuther, and Reutha—all kings in their turn, whose reigns were the usual alternation of good and evil, of fortunate and unfortunate, while even already the chief opposition with which Scottish royalty had to contend arose from the Scottish nobility. The last-mentioned king, Reutha, whose reign was one of peaceful legislation, is noticed as the first king of Scots who had wisdom to devise the commemoration of illustrious men by the honours of a cairn. In these simple erections he ordered that the number of stones should correspond with that of the enemies who had fallen by the hero's prowess; and, as writing was still unknown among the Scots, the nature of his achievements was indicated by the figures of dragons, wolves, and other animals engraved on the stones. During this period, also, certain messengers from Ptolemy, King of Egypt, as we are gravely informed, came into the country to study its condition and the manners of the people. They were delighted to find, it is added, the same language, habits, ceremonies, and religious rites among the Scots, that were prevalent among the Egyptians.[1] This learned deputation, after having surveyed and explored the whole land, wrote a full account of every district which was incorporated into that "richt crafty and proffitable werk" entitled the "Cosmography of Ptolemy," which was afterwards completed in the reign of the emperor Hadrian.

The next kings in succession were Thereus and Josyne, the last of whom was chiefly distinguished as an adept in the healing art and patron of physicians. This reign was marked by a singular visit from two foreigners, who had been shipwrecked upon the coast of Ross, and were brought before the king. They are described as venerable clerks, of pleasant visage and almost naked; but whether this defect in clothing was a distinction of their sect or order, or a consequence of shipwreck, the historian Boetius does not inform us; and it was generally reported that they were priests of Spain who had been wrecked on a voyage from Portugal to Athens. After a short stay at the court of Josyne, they were desired to declare their opinion of the country; and in reply, they stated that Scotland contained more within its recesses than upon its surface, in consequence of the rich metals and minerals with which it abounded. Of this fact their scientific knowledge fully assured them. Their opinion was then demanded about the religion of the people, which they delivered with equal frankness. They declared that the national faith was not to be commended, as it taught the worship of brute forms and images, after the fashion of the Egyptians, instead of the worship of that invisible God who sees and knows all things, and whose likeness it is impossible to represent. They finally advised, that this living and true God alone should be worshipped without any images, and moreover, that purity of life should be cultivated in the hope of a reward hereafter. The people, we are told, were so greatly moved that they complied with the admonition of the strangers; the worship of Isis and Apis was, for a time at least, abandoned, and a simple monotheism set up in its stead. But Fynane, the son of Josyne, who succeeded to the throne, adopted a different course. He caused the deposed images to be replaced in the temples, while he was at the same time so tolerant, that he allowed his subjects to worship what or whomsoever they pleased. He also was the first to institute in Scotland the order of prelates and priests, who, under the name of Druids, superintended the religion of the people, and trained the young nobility in the arts and sciences as they were taught in the schools of Athens. In this quiet and unceremonious way, if we may believe the statement, Druidism was introduced into Scotland, from which it rapidly extended over the island at large.[2] A more creditable

---

[1] Boece in Bellenden.

[2] And yet, a few years after, we have his son and successor swearing to a solemn compact with his nobles in the temple

statement given about this king than even his wonderful religious toleration, is to be found in his just perception of the limits of kingly authority and the proper liberty of the subject; and his decree on this matter was, "that kings should determine or command nothing of great concern or importance without the authority of their great council."

We now pass over a long interval, and not a few reigns, filled with tyrants, heroes, and legislators, and with wars not only against the Picts and Britons but also among the Scots themselves—changes which, though sufficient to have undone most nations, only seem to have made Scotland more civilized and prosperous—and hasten to the great epoch of Britain at large from the hostile entrance of the Romans into the island. It might have been thought that the Scots, confined as they still really were within the narrow limits of Argyle, could have little in common with the distant events that were going on in Kent and Middlesex. But it did not suit our ancient chroniclers to imagine that such a warrior as Cæsar could have entered into Britain without attracting the notice of their countrymen, and even tasting their prowess. Accordingly it happened, that while Edeir, King of Scots, after having "daunted all invaders of his realm," was enjoying his successes in the royal castle of Dunstaffnage, ambassadors arrived to him from Cassivellaunus, King of the Britons, craving aid against "Julius Cæsar, Roman Emperor, whose army was ready with most awful ordinance to come in Albion." No learning was spared on this momentous occasion, for the British ambassadors quoted the downfall of Carthage as an argument for a common resistance to Rome; and the Scottish chieftains, as if they had studied the whole history of the Punic wars, were able to see the force of the appeal. Edeir sent an auxiliary army of ten thousand men to the sorely distressed Cassivellaunus; and besides this, he instigated Gethus, King of the Picts, to contribute a reinforcement for the common defence of the island. Opposed by three such powers, it was not wonderful that Cæsar was "doung out of Albion;" and that after his discomfiture the Britons, Scots, and Picts parted the rich spoil of his tents, and sat down to eat, drink, and be merry. But unfortunately for themselves, the Britons became so arrogant over their victory, which they attributed to their own prowess, that they displeased their brave allies, and refused their offers of aid when Cæsar returned upon his second expedition. The consequence was, that Cassivellaunus was defeated and compelled to submit, and the vain-glorious Britons became tributaries to Rome.

After his conquests in the south Cæsar had full leisure to turn his attention to the Scots and Picts, who had lately fought against him; and having refreshed his army in London, he resolved to direct his march northward and subdue the whole island. But before setting out, he sent ambassadors to the two northern courts to demand complete submission, and threaten war and destruction as the alternative. The ambassadors harangued upon the power of Rome and the hopelessness of resisting it; and to convince their sceptical auditors, they gave a glowing sketch of the Roman conquests and triumphs, from the founding of the Eternal City up to the present period. After having thus dismayed and threatened enough, they changed their style of oratory into the soothing vein, and described the benefits which their rule had conferred upon the conquered, by the excellent laws, order, prosperity, and refinement which they had introduced into all their provinces. It happened, however, that the Scots and Picts were as well acquainted with Roman history as the ambassadors themselves, so that they answered with a counter-statement, setting forth the evils that had everywhere followed the Roman domination; and this they expressed in the good set terms of Grecian rhetoric—evincing the happy effects of the Athenian education established among them by the Druids, and how greatly they had profited by its lessons. Their answers having shown that nothing but war to the uttermost would convince them, Cæsar prepared in earnest for a northern campaign; but before he could commence operations, such tidings arrived from Gaul as compelled him to quit the island. It was perhaps in a happy hour for himself that he did so; for had he persisted in his designs, such was the spirit and valour of the Scots and Picts, that the liberties of Rome, which were afterwards crushed at Pharsalia, might have been saved at the foot of the Grampian Mountains by Cæsar's defeat or death! Even this unfulfilled promise of invasion was still not enough for some of our earliest writers; and Boece informs us of a statement contained in "our vulgare croniclis," that Julius Cæsar did actually enter into Scotland—that he destroyed Camelon, the principal city of the Picts—and that in the neighbourhood of Carron he left a memorial of his invasion in the form of a round house of square stones, twenty-four cubits in height and

---

of Diana! In this way Boece has jumbled together the Egyptian, Classical, and Druidical religions, and the theism of the old philosophers, almost in a single breath. Similar statements occur in the mythic history of South Britain, where Druid circles and the temple of Diana are mixed in most admired disorder.

twelve cubits in breadth. As no common hand could have presumed to destroy the monument of such a man, the infamy was ascribed to Edward I., by whose order, it was said, the tower was demolished.

After this period, and while the Roman conquest of the southern part of the island was continued by the successors of Julius Cæsar, the northern part remained unassailed, with the exception of Orkney, which is represented as having been subdued by the emperor Claudius; and Camelon, the Pictish capital, which was plundered by his general, Vespasian. The latter, following up his successor, is represented as defeating Caratac (Caractacus) near Camelon, and subduing Brigantia (Galloway). This Caractacus, whose renown was so illustrious even in Rome itself, and whom history and romance have equally delighted to honour, was no petty chieftain of North Wales, as has generally been supposed, but a king of Scotland, and as such he is made to occupy a high place in the Scottish chronicles. Neither was he so poor as is generally represented; for we are told that after his coronation he received the "huge treasure" gathered by King Metellane (his predecessor), and exceeded all the people in Albion in riches. Seldom has the faith of a believer in classical history received such a shock as is given by this version of the life of Caractacus. Undismayed by his defeat Caratac ventured a second encounter with the Romans, but was routed by Plautius, the successor of Vespasian in the government of Britain. The bold resistance which he still continued to offer, the treasonable conduct of Cartismandua, or Cartimandua, his step-mother, and her subsequent conduct before the tribunal of the emperor Claudius, are related in the Scottish chronicles, although with several additional circumstances of which the Roman historians seem to have been profoundly ignorant. On being restored to liberty, Caractacus was also re-established in a part of his kingdom comprising Brigantia, Kyle, and Cunningham. The same chroniclers did not forget to mete out a full measure of poetical justice to the treacherous Cartismandua, for she was buried alive by command of Corbred, the brother and successor of Caractacus.

In the meantime the Scots and Picts continued to maintain a gallant resistance to the Roman invaders, in which they were so successful that the latter were all but expelled beyond the North British boundaries. At the same time the great revolt of the Britons occurred in the south, headed by Queen Voada (Boadicea), to whose assistance Corbred her brother arrived, accompanied by the king of the Picts; and thus Suetonius, the Roman governor, had not one but three confederated armies arrayed against him in the field. He was victorious, however, in the engagement that followed, according to the full testimony of Roman history, which our old Scottish chronicles were not hardy enough to contradict; and Corbred after the slaughter returned to Scotland with the remains of his army, and continued to rule undisturbed, for the Romans were too closely occupied in the south to attempt the conquest of the northern part of the island.

After the death of Corbred the wars of the Scots and Picts with the Romans were renewed; the latter invaded Scotland, and battles were fought with scarcely any decisive results, which, however, are recorded with all the circumstantiality of a modern bulletin. Enough, however, has been given not only as a specimen of the tenor of these chronicles, but also to show how unfitted they are as materials for the purposes of veritable history. They assume what indeed was highly probable—that the people of the northern part of the island were alarmed at the Roman invasion of the south, and endeavoured to resist the progress of the conquerors; but this scanty outline they must needs also fill up with the fields on which the battles were fought, the heady changes of every conflict, and the names of the wise leaders and gallant knights, both Scottish and Pictish, by whom victories were won and deeds of prowess achieved.[1]

Of these warlike collisions with the Romans that occasioned by the invasion of Agricola was the chief, and after the full, lucid, rational, and eloquent account of the northern campaigns of that general as they are detailed in the pages of Tacitus, we seem, in turning to the same events unfolded in our old Scottish chronicles, to pass to a new country as well as different actors and achievements. This transformation also has been accomplished not so much by perverting the principal facts, which were too well authenticated to be denied, as by so modifying their character and adding to them, that they assume a new aspect. A slight attention to these

---

[1] From this medley of old traditions and classical history Boece avows that he constructed his record, and values himself upon the combination. His account delivered in the following words (the translation is Bellenden's) shows the manner in which ancient Scottish history was constructed:—"This history, in sa far as we have schawin of Caratak, Corbreid, and Galdus, kingis of Scottis, is drawin, sum part fra vulgar Croniklis, sum part fra Cornelius Tacitus. For we have nocht only writtin his sentence, bot als his wordis; that the redaris, baith of Romane story and Scottis, may understand ilk history concordant with othir, and knaw, be testimoniall of oure cunime, how vailyeantly our nobill elderis hes fochtin, for this realme, aganis Romanis. And to the mair pruffe heirof, we have inserit the eloquent orisonis of Galdus and Agricola, word in word as Cornelius Tacitus rehersis thaim, in this our quhatsumevir werkis."

circumstances is necessary in order to understand the mythic and unsatisfactory character of our early Scottish history.

In turning therefore from Tacitus to Boece and Buchanan, we find that Agricola had other enemies to contend with than a single people, or an army of naked barbarians. According to the latter accounts, the Scots had already been raised to such a state of civilization and refinement as to be scarcely inferior to the Romans themselves, while the Picts were equal if not even superior to their neighbours. But besides the formidable union of two such nations, who were combined against the Roman invaders, ambassadors had been sent from the Scottish and Pictish kings to the courts of Norway, Denmark, and Iceland, to crave assistance; and the application was answered by powerful reinforcements of Danes, Germans, and Norwegians, who arrived for the defence of Scotland. Agricola indeed was victorious at the foot of the Grampians—for how could a fact established by the authority of such a writer as Tacitus be afterwards contradicted? But if we may believe our annalists, who winced at such a consequence, the Romans did not purchase their victory so cheaply, as they lost in it twelve thousand soldiers. In his account of the preparations for battle, also, Boece seems to have sketched the Caledonian army and its equipments from the military musters of his own day in the Borough Muir, near Edinburgh—from that, in fact, which had been summoned for the fearful trial at Flodden. Besides the more swords and bucklers which Tacitus assigns them, the Scottish historian supplies his Caledonian warriors with bills and leaden mells, and arms their foreign auxiliaries with long-bows and "ganyeis," that is missiles of various kinds. Nor does he allow the Roman fleet, after its daring voyage round the island, to return to port in safety; for when the mariners came near the Pentland Firth, they were so dismayed at the dangers of the passage that they arrested certain Scottish fishermen, and gave them tempting promises of reward if they would pilot them through in safety. But these men, it is added, doubtful of the faith of such employers, ran the Roman galleys upon the rocks and quicksands, by which the greater part of the fleet was lost.

But all this is nothing compared with what follows. So little was Galdus (Galgacus) daunted by his losses that he even reappeared on the field, and gave the Romans such a defeat as requited in full his discomfiture at the Grampians. The invaders were driven across the Tay, and finally reduced to such straits by a series of battles, in which Galdus was always victorious, that their ambassadors were fain to crave of him upon their knees, and in abject terms, the favour of an unmolested retreat! And this they obtained, but only on the most humbling conditions. These were, that they should abandon their Scottish fortresses, relinquish their plunder, and pledge themselves to be at peace with the Scots and Picts in all time coming. On these terms a Roman army, originally sixty thousand strong, but now reduced to less than a third of that number, was graciously permitted to retreat. Even in the province, also, an ignominious welcome must have awaited their return; for their authority was at so low an ebb among the Britons of the sorth, that "the young wenchis, gestauris, and commonn pepil sang dailie ballattis, in derisioune and skorne of Romanis."

After a long reign of glory and prosperity, Galdus, the twenty-first king of Scots from the reign of Fergus, died, A.D. 103. He was interred with great pomp, and amidst the lamentations of his people; a stately monument, sculptured with representations of his heroic deeds, and surrounded with tall pillars, was erected over his grave; and by a decree of Parliament (!) the name of the province of Brigantia was changed into Galdia (afterwards corrupted into Galuidia, and finally into Galloway), to perpetuate his memory.

After Galdus, his son Lugtak (Luctacus) succeeded, for whose moral portraiture Nero or Caligula may have been the sitter. In fact the original historian of these periods, whether Boece or some earlier writer, seems to have filled up his outline—if outline he had—with the court of Rome and the twelve Cæsars, whenever it was necessary to describe an event, or limn a character, while, for the purpose of impressing a Scottish stamp upon them, he throws over the whole narrative the manners and characteristics of his own day. Lugtak was succeeded by Mogallus, a beneficent reformer and able warrior, in whose reign the Romans violated the contract of peace into which they had entered with Galdus, by invading Scotland; but they were requited by Mogallus with such a defeat as that of Cannæ could scarcely have equalled. In this battle it is evident that the Scottish chronicles have wholly and gratuitously supplied the unpardonable omission of the Roman historians. This invasion was followed by that of Adrian; but the active enterprising emperor could effect nothing except building the wall which went under his name. Mogallus in the latter part of his reign was so corrupted by the peace he had won, that he became an oppressive tyrant and a wasteful profligate. To him is also attributed the enactment of the law of forfeiture, by which the estates of such as were condemned to death were escheated to the royal treasury, without any portion of them being allotted to the wives and children of the criminals. At length his reign became so obnoxious, that he was slain in an insurrection of his subjects, and succeeded by Conarus his son, who trode in the footsteps of Mogallus until he was deposed and imprisoned. This king also, like his father, owed his downfall to a financial blunder; for having exhausted his revenues in debauchery and riot, he endeavoured to replenish them by the imposition of an income-tax, in which his subjects were to be assessed according to the valuation of their means; and he was told in reply by his nobles in council, that "bawds, parasites, minstrels, and troops of harlots were not fit instruments for kings and kingdoms."

The next king, Ethodius I., of whose reign a long and eulogistic account is given, was chiefly occupied with wars against the Romans, in which he was assisted by the Picts. He was so successful against these powerful enemies that he broke through the wall of Adrian, and defeated the Roman commander, Trebellius. He also subdued the clans of the Isles, who even already are described as having commenced those wars against the Scots of the mainland, which occupied so conspicuous a figure in Scottish history at least a thousand years afterwards. Ethodius is likewise represented as the author of those hunting laws, most of which are still in force, having for their object the preservation of game by the observance of proper seasons in hunting, and the modes of killing them. It was a dexterous device of the fifteenth century to hallow these institutions, otherwise so obnoxious to the common people, by so venerable an antiquity and so illustrious a founder.[1]

Not long after the reign of this king, the invasion of the emperor Severus occurred, which, however, is hastily dismissed with the assertion, that sometimes the Romans and sometimes the Scots were victorious. At this period Donald I. was King of Scots, the twenty-seventh in succession from Fergus, and his reign was distinguished by two important events: the first was the introduction of Christianity into Scotland, to which he became a convert; and the second was the use of *coinage*. It was a singular omission on the part of our chroniclers, who talked of the great riches of the previous kings of Scotland, not to make the slightest mention of *money*.

Donald was succeeded by Ethodius II., an imbecile sovereign who was murdered by his guards. Then followed Athirco, a usurper and tyrant, who slew himself in consequence of a rebellion of his nobles; and he was succeeded by Nathalak, also a usurper and tyrant, who was assassinated by one of his servants. In all these events we seem to see the reigns of the unhappy Stuarts carried back to the second century. As if all these calamities had not been enough, the dissensions of court and kingdom were aggravated by the ambition of the Lords of the Isles, who, not content with the rank of robber chieftains, advanced their pretensions as independent legitimate sovereigns. At last Donald of the Isles was strong enough to usurp the throne of Scotland; but after he had occupied it twelve years he was set aside in the fashion of his predecessors, being slain by Craithlint, the son of a former king, who thus prepared the way for his own succession.

From the time of Fergus I. the Scots and Picts had lived in mutual amity, their chief enemies being the provincial Britons and the Romans, by whose formidable neighbourhood their national jealousy against each other had been held in check. The time had now arrived when they were to be sundered for a war to the uttermost, while previous resentments had so greatly accumulated that a single spark was sufficient to commence the conflagration. And that commencement was nothing more than the theft of a favourite hound belonging to Craithlint, King of Scots, which the Picts had stolen in a hunting-match. A fierce war ensued in which their mutual danger was forgot, until Carausius effected a reconciliation between them for the purpose of driving the Romans out of the island, and establishing an independent sovereignty of his own over Britain and the adjacent province of Gaul. This distinguished personage, commonly called Carausius the Menapian, so justly renowned in Roman as well as British history, was a military adventurer of such uncertain origin, that it is impossible to ascertain whether he had been born in Belgium, Hibernia, South Britain, or the islands of the Rhine, for in all these countries the Menapians had planted their colonies. Boece, thus finding him a waif in history, boldly claims him for his countryman; and calling him Carauce, describes him as a young Scottish prince, who, after having committed the double crime of fratricide and regicide, was obliged to fly from Scotland.

---

[1] The chief of these laws are specified by the historian as follows:—No hare while sitting was to be killed with clubs, arrows, darts, or any such weapons. None were to be taken by nets or gins. No hare was to be killed in any other way than by the chase of hounds. If the hare had outrun the hounds by a great distance it was to be no further pursued. No man was to kill a hind big with young nor yet their calves. No hunting was to be used during the season of winter or warfare, by which the deer were driven down from the mountains to the plains in search of food.

Having thus assigned him a local habitation as well as a name, the historian details the adventurous life of Carauce in Italy, until he had raised himself to high place and renown in the empire, so that the court was compelled to appoint him governor of Britain, which he was resolved to convert into an independent sovereignty. It was not wonderful, therefore, that he was so anxious to reconcile the Scots and Picts; or that, being a Scot himself and connected with the royal family, his mediation was successful.

This union, however, was not fated to be permanent; and after the assassination of Carausius, by whose energetic proceedings the Scots and Picts had been successful against the Romans, these rival peoples were once more at variance, the cause of contest on this occasion being that of the royal succession. The sons of the deceased sovereign being minors, were to be temporarily succeeded, according to the law of Fergus, by the next of kin who was of mature age; and upon this, three relatives of the late king stepped forward, each asserting his claim to the vacant throne. One of these three, named Romak, impatient of the uncertainty and delay of election, gathered a band of Picts, by whose aid he drove his rivals out of Scotland, and placed himself in the royal seat. But his usurpation by such foreign means, as well as his tyrannical rule, was so offensive to the Scottish nobles, that in the third year of his reign they rebelled, and Romak was slain, with many of his Pictish adherents. This was enough for the purposes of a deadly national feud, more especially as Romak was cousin to Nectenus, King of the Picts, and the latter invaded the Scots with a numerous army. The battle that followed was maintained with such rancour, that not only he, but Angusian the Scottish king was slain.

The war thus commenced was attended with such unfavourable results to the Picts, that, in their eagerness for revenge, they endangered their national independence by forming a league with the Romans and Britons for the suppression of their less dangerous rivals. Accordingly a large army of the three confederates entered Annandale, Galloway, and other parts of the Scottish territory, exercising great cruelty on the inhabitants, and garrisoning the places of strength with Roman soldiers. After an indecisive resistance, Eugenius, King of Scots, met the enemy near the Water of Doon with 50,000 soldiers, but was encountered by a still more numerous army composed of Picts, Britons, and Romans, with Maximus the Roman governor of Britain at their head. The King of Scots was slain, and almost all his army cut to pieces. To this disastrous conflict certain particulars are added which give it a character of its own. The aged and feeble of the Scots, who had been left at home as unfit for military service, approached the place of conflict to ascertain the fate of their sons and kindred; but on seeing that all was lost, they rushed upon the weapons of the pursuing enemy and were slain. After them came the women, still more frantic and despairing, who also madly ran forward and met with a similar fate. After this decisive conflict, by which the power of the Scots was utterly broken, the Roman leader, through Pictish instigation, issued a decree, that by a certain day they should quit the country and never return to it. This was in very truth the *væ victis* —the doom of utter expatriation to a people who were defeated beyond the power of resistance. The women indeed, clothed in weeds of mourning, implored for permission to remain, that they might pray for their slaughtered husbands, and be buried in their graves; but even this piteous appeal was unavailing. The Scots thus exiled departed to the Isles and Ireland, others to France, Italy, Norway, and Denmark: they were plucked up and thrown abroad, that they might wither and disappear as a nation among the heaps with which they were mingled. The date of this event is minutely specified in our old chronicles as having occurred in the year of the incarnation 379; from the first residence of the Scots in the island, 712; and in the second year of the reign of the Roman emperor Julian the Apostate.

During the course of this mournful revolution the greatest affliction of the Scots had arisen from their old allies and kindred, the Picts. Not content with enlisting the Romans in their quarrel, and procuring the sentence of banishment to be passed upon their enemies by importunity, and even by bribes, they had carried on the work of extermination to the uttermost, slaying the last lingering remains of the people wherever they could be found, and even though Christians themselves, dislodging the priests and Culdees from their cells, and driving them into banishment with the rest. But their triumph was short, for they soon found that they had exchanged an ancient ally for a new ruler and taskmaster. They were required by the conquerors of the south to pay tribute for a portion of the Scottish territory of which they had taken possession, and to use the Roman laws and none else, under a heavy penalty; and when their king died, they were forbid to acknowledge any other governor than such as was sent to them from Rome. The Picts saw with indignant astonishment that their own fate was worse than that of the exiled Scots, for they were bondmen without having the alternative of banishment; and in this way an old prophecy that had rankled in their minds, and which they had endeavoured to avert, was unexpectedly to be fulfilled, "That the Picts should be destroyed by the Scots." These penitent reflections did not come too late; and they suggested the conclusion that to replace the Scots in their ancient homes would be the best means to avert the displeasure of Heaven, and resist the tyranny of the Romans.

It happened very opportunely for this relenting humour of the Picts, that the season of affliction and trial to the Scots had been maturing a hero for their restoration. This was Fergus, a young prince of the blood royal, who had been conveyed by his uncle to the Danish court, where he was brought up in all kinds of warlike exercises, in which he made great proficiency; and on entering into public life, he was sent by the Danish sovereign to the assistance of Alaric, King of the Goths, who at that time was preparing for his memorable conquest of Rome. Fergus was delighted with an opportunity that brought him into hostile contact with the enemies of his country; and in the siege and storm of the imperial city his services were so valuable, that besides a large share of the spoil in rich jewels, he was rewarded with a chest of choice books, which he brought with him to Germany, and finally to Scotland, where they were deposited in the library of Iona. To him the Picts sent messengers, but secretly, from dread of their watchful masters, explaining their altered minds towards his countrymen, and inviting him to become the leader of both people against their common enemy the Romans. The young hero gladly complied with the summons; and, as soon as he returned to the home of his fathers, accompanied by a multitude of his own countrymen and Danish adherents, his arrival in Argyle was the signal of muster to the banished Scots, who hurried from Ireland to join his standard. In this way the Scottish kingdom in Britain, that seemed to have been utterly annihilated, was suddenly restored to full existence; and Fergus, the national hero, was unanimously elected king, under the title of Fergus II. Our old Scottish writers are delighted with the identity of name in the first and second founders, and are at a loss to decide which of the two should be accounted the most worthy of national commemoration and gratitude. The date of this most seasonable recovery of Scotland is stated to have been A.D. 422, and forty-five years after the expulsion of the Scots from the island.

It was now full time that Fergus should maintain the crown he had so unexpectedly won; and for this, indeed, the Romans were not slow to give him an opportunity, for they soon entered Scotland with a numerous army to chastise both Scots and Picts. The confederates were equally ready to meet them, and with Fergus at their head they encountered the Romans near the Carron. But in the heat of conflict, and while the river ran red with blood, a shower of hail that involved the whole field in darkness, parted the combatants. After this indecisive battle the Romans retired into the province, leaving a part of their army to repair the wall of Severus, which had been breached in many places; and having accomplished this, they garrisoned its forts with British soldiers, being themselves obliged to leave the island for the defence of their own country. Emboldened by their departure, the Scots and Picts assailed the Britons, who made but a feeble resistance, stormed and demolished the wall under the leading of Graham or Græme, a gallant and successful Scottish leader,[1] and committed wild havoc upon the territory of their enemies. But, decayed though the Roman dominion was throughout the province, its last attempts to rally were still characteristic of its former energy, and the advance of the Scots and Picts was checked by more than one severe defeat. In the chief of these, which occurred in Westmoreland, Fergus himself was slain, with his ally Drustus, King of the Picts, and the principal nobility and leaders of both nations. It was evident, however, that this resistance of the Romans must speedily terminate; their hold upon Britain was now but a death-grasp, which was hourly relaxing. The time had come when they must leave it and for ever; and having shut up the Scots and Picts once more within the wall of Severus, and helped the provincials to repair that of Adrian, they bade their last adieu to the island. Then succeeded the memorable "groans" of the Britons, and the arrival of the Saxons, by whom not only the whole history but even the population of Britain was commenced anew.

---

[1] Notwithstanding the renown of this warrior, and the credit he has obtained of founding one of the noblest families of Scotland, Chalmers reasonably doubts whether such a person ever existed. Grime's Dike, he says, was a term given to a strong wall in general, from the word *grym*, which signifies *strength*.

CHAPTER II.

FROM THE INVASION OF THE ROMANS TO THE SETTLEMENT OF THE DALRIAD SCOTS (A.D. 80–503).

Roman accounts of early Scotland — Invasion of Agricola — His campaigns in Scotland — His gradual and steady progress into the country—Co-operation of his fleet with the army—Resistance of the Caledonians — They prepare with Galgacus for a decisive encounter — Speeches of the Caledonian and Roman commanders previous to the battle of the Grampians — Defeat of the Caledonians — Their distresses after the conflict — Supposed site of the engagement — The ships of Agricola sail round the island — Wonders beheld in their voyage — Recall of Agricola to Rome — Hadrian's Wall built — The Roman walls found insufficient for the protection of the south — Invasion of Scotland by the emperor Severus — His death — The invasion abandoned by his son — The inhabitants of Scotland under the titles of Scots and Picts renew their incursions into the south — Distress of the provincial Britons — They are abandoned by the Romans — Their feeble defence of Hadrian's Wall — Their piteous and last appeal to Rome for aid — They call in the Saxons — The Saxons conquer and occupy England — Question as to who were the Picts —Controversies on the subject—Statements of the Roman writers as to the origin of the Picts—Probability that they were Caledonians under a new name—The ancient Caledonians a Celtic people—Arrival of the Scots from Ireland into Scotland—Union of the Scots and Picts in their formidable inroads into the south—Arrival of the Dalriad Scots from Ireland—Their settlement in Scotland.

Having thus briefly glanced at the early and fabulous history of Scotland from the earliest establishment of its people to the downfall of the Roman Empire in Britain, we find it necessary not only to pause but to retrace our steps, and present the record from the Roman point of view. It is true, indeed, that in this case we pass from the partial statements of friends to what might be regarded as the prejudiced account of enemies. And yet who would hesitate between the minute and unimpassioned narrative of the eloquent and philosophic Tacitus and the wild legends of our early chronicles? Tacitus's biography of Agricola, which reduces the condition of the Scots to its primitive simplicity and brings their achievements within their proper dimensions, was also their first introduction to the page of sober and accredited history.

In their progress of conquest it had never been the custom of the Romans to leave one part of a country unsubdued, or to allow a dangerous enemy to remain upon the frontiers of their rule. This of itself is sufficient to account for their invasion of Caledonia or North Britain, irrespective of any resistance offered by the natives to the progress of Roman conquest in the south. Accordingly when Agricola, who was appointed to the government of Britain A.D. 78, had spent two years in the subjugation of his province and the conciliation of the Britons to his rule, he resolved to enlarge the boundaries of the Roman dominion over the whole island, and confirm its stability by carrying his arms northward. On this occasion his progress is described by the great Roman annalist not merely as a conquest but as a discovery of new nations, whose territories he laid waste as far as the estuary now called the Frith of Tay.

In the first northern campaign of Agricola the chief enemy that opposed him was the tempestuous climate, as the natives were struck with such terror at his approach that they did not venture an engagement. It has been contended, however, that the Tay (*Taus*) of Tacitus was not the river known in later times by that name, as Agricola, at the commencement of his invasion, could scarcely have advanced so far; and that the word used by the Roman historian might as well apply to the estuary of the Solway, or any other river. His advance was made with caution and for the purpose of permanent occupation, so that he secured the ground he had gained, with forts and garrisons victualled for a whole year. These strongholds were so advantageously situated that, the historian adds, not one of them that had been fortified by his direction was taken by storm, not one was reduced to capitulate, not one was surrendered or left to the enemy.

In the following year (A.D. 81) the campaign of Agricola in the north was occupied not so much with further aggression, as in securing the acquisitions of the preceding summer. It was necessary to fix a boundary for the Roman dominion in the island, and the place he selected for this purpose was where the waters of the Glotta and Bodotria (the Friths of Clyde and Forth) are prevented from joining by a neck of land, where the two estuaries are now united by the Forth and Clyde Canal. Here he erected a chain of forts, by which the whole country on the south side of the isthmus was secured to the

Romans, and the natives, as Tacitus expresses it, were driven as it were into another island. It was on this site that Lollius Urbicus afterwards erected his famous wall, known by the name of the Wall of Antoninus, or popularly as Graham's Dyke.

In the fifth year of his government, and third of his northern campaigns, Agricola directed his operations against the tribes north of the Clyde, for the purpose of making an impression on the west side of the country. He therefore crossed the estuary at Dumbarton, where Roman ship had never floated before; and after passing through regions till then unknown, and defeating the inhabitants in several skirmishes, he reached the western coast. He now meditated the conquest of Ireland, as he judged that this island would prove a happy medium of communication between the Roman provinces of Spain and Britain.

In the campaign of the following summer (A.D. 83) Agricola, fearing an insurrection of all the tribes beyond the Frith of Forth, which part of the country he had overrun but not conquered, conducted his operations both by land and sea; and therefore while his ships crossed the frith for the purposes of exploration, the army marched along the shore, having crossed the river where it was fordable—probably in the neighbourhood of Stirling. These combined movements on land and water, Tacitus declares, "formed a magnificent spectacle, and added terror to the war." It often happened also that both soldiers and mariners met in the camp at evening, and recounted to each other the wonderful sights they had witnessed during the day. By these bold operations on land and water the war was carried into those districts which now compose the counties of Fife, Perth, and Angus.

During the whole course of these military progresses the Roman march seems to have met with little impediment. The invaders were in such force, their movements were so cautiously conducted, and the tribes in their route were so feeble or disunited, that they appear to have swept onward unmolested except by such encounters as were too insignificant to be recorded. Now, however, the war was to commence in earnest. The invasion had entered their own proper territory, and the Caledonians were in arms to repel it. Their hostility was also of the most daring character; for without waiting to be attacked, they fell upon the Roman forts that had been erected to bridle them, took them by storm, and showed such valour and daring that some of Agricola's officers recommended a retreat. But that skilful leader continued his march; and learning that the Caledonians intended to assail him from various quarters at once, he divided his army into three columns to prevent the risk of being surrounded. On learning these precautions the Caledonians changed their plan, and, uniting their forces, made a furious night attack upon the ninth legion, which was the weakest part of the Roman army. The advanced guard was surprised, the sentinels were put to the sword, and the intrenchments themselves broken through by the onset of the bold barbarians. The din of battle which arose from the camp itself quickened the march of Agricola, who had learned the purpose of the Caledonians; and when the ninth legion had been all but overpowered, their enemies suddenly found themselves inclosed between two armies by the arrival of the Roman general. After a long-contested battle in the very gates of the camp the barbarians were at last defeated; and had it not been for the neighbouring woods and marshes, which favoured their escape, Tacitus declares that this single night encounter might have put an end to the whole war.

The Caledonians, however, were far from being dispirited by this defeat; they had made full trial of the Roman valour, and attributed their discomfiture to chance and better generalship, rather than any superiority of strength and courage; and they resolved to repeat the trial in greater force and with better precautions. Accordingly, while the Romans reposed in winter quarters the Caledonians formed a union of their tribes; chose for their leader Galdus (Galgacus), dignified in the old chronicles with the title of King of Scotland, but who evidently, like Cassivellaunus, was nothing more than a Celtic chieftain raised to the temporary leadership of the clans from his superior military reputation; and having removed their wives and children to a place of safety, they repaired from every quarter to the rendezvous. In consequence of these preparations, when Agricola opened the campaign of the following summer he found an army of 30,000 Caledonians awaiting him upon the acclivity of Mons Grampius, ready to meet him in daylight and upon an open field. Nor were the Romans unequal to such an encounter; for independently of the legions which were drawn up as a reserve in the rear and at the head of the intrenchments, their centre was composed of 8000 auxiliary foot-soldiers and 3000 horse.

Galgacus, who had posted his army with considerable skill, occupied the plain with his first line, consisting probably of his own clan, while the rest were drawn up line behind line on the acclivity of the mountain; and in front of his army, upon the open field, where they had full room to act, were his cavalry, and especially his chariots, which formed so essential an arm in the warfare of all the British tribes. There they are described as rushing to and fro in wild career, and traversing the plain with noise and tumult. Finding all in full spirit for the onset, Galgacus is said to have harangued his troops, an action both probable and proper in such a crisis; and although it is not likely that he used the precise words or ample illustrations put into his mouth by Tacitus, his speech was probably such as the occasion was fitted to inspire. The Roman historian makes him tell his followers, that, living as they did at the extremity of the island, and with nothing but the sea behind them, they occupied the last refuge of British liberty, beyond which it would find no home. He indignantly described the Roman ambition, from which neither poverty nor obscurity could be a protection, and the oppressiveness of Roman bondage that crushed alike every class, sex, and condition; and in proof of this he adverted to the state of their brethren, the Britons of the south. He then spoke of the gallant resistance of the Trinobantes and their queen Boadicea; while to show with what success the example might now be followed, he pointed to the Roman auxiliaries of whom the opposite array was mainly composed—Gauls, Germans, and even Britons—slaves and hirelings, who followed masters whom they detested, and who would be ready to turn against them at the first reverse. And who were the Romans? Men who had no wives in the field to animate their fainting courage, no parents to reproach them if they gave back, no country at hand to kindle their patriotism or witness their shame. All this, and more, the bold Caledonian is said to have expressed in a thunderstorm of eloquent indignation; and when he ended, his speech, the historian tells us, was received "according to the fashion of barbarians, with war-songs, with savage howlings, and a wild uproar of military applause."

Agricola also harangued his troops; for what Roman general could neglect such a duty before he gave the signal of onset? But he had no such theme as that of Galgacus to transport him to the very height of soul-stirring oratory, and therefore his speech was tame in comparison, although his eloquent son-in-law was the reporter. He reminded his soldiers of the dangers they had surmounted, the toils they had endured, the victories they had won. Already they had subdued the bravest of the island; and would they now turn their backs upon these Caledonians, the very scum and refuse of Britain, whom they had lately so signally defeated in a night engagement and chased into their woods and morasses? If they suffered themselves to be discomfited now — now that they had reached the very limits of the earth, which one victory more would make all their own—their dangerous route must be retraced, and the whole work of conquest commenced anew. "Here," he exclaimed in conclusion, "you may end your labours and close a scene of fifty years by one great, one glorious day. Let your country see, and let the commonwealth testify, that if the conquest of Britain has been a lingering work—if the seeds of rebellion have not been crushed—we at least have done our duty."

The Caledonians, who occupied the rising ground, had extended their ranks, probably with the view of outflanking the enemy when they came down into the conflict. Agricola, who apprehended such a consequence, made a correspondent movement of his troops, which caused his officers to fear that he had too much weakened his lines, and they urged him to call up the legionaries to their support. But the general, who was a most skilful strategist, had resolved that the first weight of the conflict should fall upon the auxiliaries, who being themselves barbarians, could best oppose the Caledonian mode of fighting, while the legions were held in reserve till the moment when their heavy simultaneous onset should decide the victory. He therefore dismounted from his horse, which he sent away, and took his station in the front line at the head of the ensigns. The battle commenced with a shower of missiles in which the Caledonians had the advantage, probably from their occupying the higher ground; which Agricola perceiving, ordered three Batavian and two Tungrian cohorts to advance and charge the enemy sword in hand. This judicious movement changed the whole character of the encounter; the unwieldy, pointless, and brittle swords of the Caledonians and their light small targets were no match in close hand-to-hand combat for the short, sharp, well-tempered falchions and broad, strong bucklers of their opponents; and while the successful Tungrians and Batavians pressed forward, overturning and slaying all that stood in their way, and began to ascend the hill, the other cohorts, animated by their example, followed with impetuous ardour, but rather to deepen the confusion than add to the slaughter. In the meantime the fierce onset of the Caledonian chariots had compelled the Roman horse to give way, after which they drove at full speed against the Roman infantry. But although the first shock of these impetuous scythe-armed cars was terrible, the unevenness of the ground and the firm embattled ranks that opposed them broke their career and drove them back upon their own infantry. Still, however, the Caledonians on the hill were undismayed; the bulk of their army was untouched by these disasters, and, confident in their numbers, they slowly descended, intending to wheel round the field of battle and attack the pursuers in the rear. Agricola, who had watched this movement, instantly ordered four squadrons of horse whom he had held in reserve to charge the enemy in front, while his whole cavalry from the wings were directed to assail them in the rear. These skilful movements, executed with a precision and rapidity to which they were unaccustomed, astounded the Caledonians; their manœuvre had been turned upon themselves; and after a gallant but confused and hopeless resistance, they were broken in front, flank, and rear, and chased off the field, while the Romans who followed in close pursuit did not care to encumber themselves with prisoners. The whole ground was covered with broken swords and useless targets, with overturned chariots and struggling entangled horses, with dead bodies and mangled limbs. Even yet, however, the battle was not wholly ended; the gallant barbarians who fled to the neighbouring woods made a desperate attempt to rally, and on several occasions inflicted a severe check upon those pursuers who followed them too eagerly. Agricola, seeing the danger, caused several of his cavalry to dismount and enter the woods on foot where the openings were broadest and safest, while the others guarded the passes or scoured the open country. The Caledonians thus finding themselves hunted into their lair, and with a skill that made resistance hopeless, doggedly awaited their fate or fled to more distant shelters. Ten thousand of their countrymen had fallen, while the Romans, according to their own account, did not lose more than 340 soldiers, among whom was only one officer, the præfect of a cohort.

The Roman army passed the night in triumph. Tacitus adds that they were enriched with plunder; but of what these precious spoils consisted he has not told us, and we are unable to guess. While he records the glee of the victors, he also pauses with generous sympathy over the sorrows and sufferings of the vanquished; and upon that field of death which rang with shouts of military glee were also heard the lamentations of men and women as they searched for the dead or bore away the wounded. Some of the natives set fire to their houses, as they would no longer be homes to shelter them; while others slew their wives and children to save them from the misery of a lingering death, or the oppression and shame of captivity. On the following morning, when the Romans looked abroad, all was silence and desolation; the hills were deserted, the houses were smoking ruins, and not a native was to be seen. Even those whom Agricola sent out to explore the country could discover no trace of the fugitives.

Such was the memorable battle of the Grampians, by which the Caledonians were first introduced, although somewhat rudely, into the notice of the civilized world and the page of accredited history. The precise spot on which it was fought has perplexed the antiquaries both of England and Scotland. This was to be expected not only from the Roman historian's imperfect geographical knowledge of Britain, but from the vagueness of his expression, *Mons Grampius*, which might apply to any particular mountain over the whole range of the Grampians from Dumbarton to Aberdeen. But by attending to the line of march that lay open to Agricola, and comparing it with the statements of Tacitus, the moor of Ardoch, at the roots of the Grampians, has been fixed upon with the strongest probability as the place of the engagement. This conclusion has also been abundantly strengthened from the tokens of an ancient and extensive conflict that have been discovered on the spot. It still shows the traces of a large ditch extending to a considerable distance, such as those with which the Romans were wont to surround their camp. Weapons both Roman and Caledonian, the relics of a mutual encounter, have been disinterred from the soil. On the hill above Ardoch moor are also to be seen two enormous cairns or heaps of stones, the one called Carnlee and the other Carnmochel, which were probably raised by the Caledonians, according to their national custom, to commemorate those who had fallen.

As the armed confederation of the tribes was thus so broken up that they could not easily rally, and the summer so far advanced as to make the continuance of military operations impracticable, Agricola closed the campaign and led his army into the country of the Florestians, probably the modern Fifeshire. He also directed the commander of the fleet to make a coasting voyage round the island—an adventurous exploration which was successfully accomplished; for the Roman galleys, setting out from the Frith of Tay, doubled the promontory of Caithness and Cape Wrath, then went westward as far as the Land's-end in Cornwall, after which, directing their course eastward, they arrived at the Trutulensian harbour, supposed to be the port of Sandwich in Kent. Resuming their periplus from this point and continuing their course along the eastern coast, the fleet reached in safety the river Tay, from which it had first set out, and thus gave full proof that Britain is an island—a fact that hitherto had only been surmised. In this bold voyage of discovery the navigators had also witnessed enough of the wonderful with which to astonish the landsmen at their return. They had caught a glimpse of Thule, that mysterious island of eternal gloom and snow about which their poets had sung as the extreme point where the living earth joins with chaos and nothingness; and perhaps a distant view of the coast of Norway had sufficed as the groundwork of the story. They also not only beheld, but had taken possession of the Orcades (Orkney Islands), although their conquest was probably nothing more than a formal landing. Even the ocean in some parts of their voyage seemed to have almost changed into a new element; for in the neighbourhood of Thule it was "a sluggish mass of stagnated waters that hardly yielded to the stroke of the oar, and was never agitated by winds and tempests."

During this voyage Agricola was leading his army into winter quarters, but by slow marches, to confirm the submission of the natives by seeming to linger in their territory instead of hastily quitting it. Of the place where his army wintered we are not told, but it was probably behind the chain of forts which he had erected on the isthmus between the Friths of Clyde and Forth. But here his Caledonian campaigns were abruptly closed. The tidings of Agricola's victories and conquests had excited the envy of the emperor Domitian, and the successful general was recalled to Rome under the pretext of being honoured with a triumph, but in reality to be displaced from office and thrown aside into private life.

The removal of this able governor and general did not tend to confirm the subjection of the south, and the oppressive rule of his successors roused the provincial Britons to arms, and compelled the arrival of the emperor Hadrian into the island. After he had composed the troubles of the south he directed his attention to the Caledonians, whose incursions during the late commotions had menaced the safety of the province; and, A.D. 120, he attempted to bridle their further aggressions by a new wall much stronger than that of Agricola, but on the same site, extending from the Solway Frith to the German Ocean. In this way the prudent emperor expressed his conviction that the Caledonian conquests beyond this boundary were not worth keeping, and might safely be abandoned. But the arrival of Lollius Urbicus as governor of Britain changed this pacific policy; and after a successful northern campaign in which he is supposed to have advanced the Roman eagles to their old station where the first Roman invasion had planted them, and to have occupied the whole intermediate space within the bounds of the province, he constructed in 138 an immense rampart of earth upon the line of Agricola's forts on the isthmus between the Clyde and the Forth. This rampart, called Antonine's Wall, from the name of the emperor Antoninus Pius, was thirty-one miles in length, and provided with twenty-one forts; while parallel to it was a ditch by which it was protected, and a military highway that kept up the communication between the different forts along the whole length of the wall.

By these strong barriers the tribes of the north living between as well as beyond the two walls appear for a time to have been reduced to a state of forbearance. But their impatience and love of liberty at last rebelled against these restraints, and with such effect, that in the year 170 the Romans of their own accord abandoned the debatable ground between the two walls, and established that of Hadrian as the boundary of their rule. This abandonment produced its natural consequences: the Caledonians, eager to recover their lost territory, broke through or scaled the earthen wall of Antoninus, and invaded the districts between it and Hadrian's Wall, while the Romans and their tributaries, who might easily have driven them back, were uselessly employed in supporting the pretensions of Clodius Albinus to the empire, and waging a war in Gaul in his behalf. The rights of Roman citizenship indeed had been extended to these insurgent tribes by Antoninus Pius; but the bribe was ineffectual with the Caledonians, who were either too ignorant to appreciate or too proud to accept it.

At the commencement of the third century the northern clans, after another interval of peace, renewed their aggressions, being assisted by the Mæatæ, who are supposed to have been a tribe of Caledonians living without the wall of Antoninus in the level country, in contradistinction to the Caledonians proper, who lived at a greater distance in the northern forests of the higher grounds.[1] These invasions roused the spirit of the Emperor Severus, at a time when the extremities of the empire began to be threatened on every side: he was also anxious to drag his two sons, Caracalla and Geta, away from the profligate allurements and political intrigues of Rome. Accordingly he arrived with his family in Britain A.D. 208, and prepared for such a merciless war against the Caledonians that it seemed to have not conquest but extirpation for its object. In the commencement of the following year, he left the wall of Antoninus

---

[1] Chalmers' *Caledonia*, vol. i. p. 184. London, 1807.

behind him, and advanced into the territory of the Mæatæ. His army, indeed, was so numerous that the Caledonians would have been utterly unable to resist it, and they appear to have prudently abstained from the attempt; but the strong natural defences of the country—its swamps, its naked mountains, and its poverty, which so often in after ages repelled the invader, impeded the progress and wasted the legions of the iron-hearted old emperor more effectually than ten such battles as that of the Grampians would have done. He felled woods, constructed roads, built bridges, and drained marshes in his toilsome advance; and after losing fifty thousand soldiers in this desperate war against natural obstacles, he penetrated so far into the north as to be able to notice the length of the days and shortness of the nights, so different from those of Italy, while the tribes, who felt their helplessness, surrendered their arms, and gave up a part of their territory as the price of peace. Scarcely had Severus retired when they broke the treaty, upon which he renewed the war with such merciless vindictiveness, that his orders were to spare neither age nor sex. But Caracalla his son, to whom the conduct of the war was intrusted, was intriguing for the imperial succession, and more eager to keep his forces entire for the approaching struggle than to risk them in a conquest of Caledonia. Accordingly, his campaign in the north was nothing more than a short military promenade, and when Severus died at York, A.D. 211, it was wholly abandoned. It was during this formal expedition, if any faith is to be given to Ossian, or at least his modern translator, that Fingal and the heroes of Selma must have won the most important of their victories. But the only early historical trace of such mythic personages is given in a form that scarcely merits notice. Would such neglect have been possible, if our first historians had possessed but the slightest records upon which to hang a plausible fable, and to show that Fingal and his car-borne chiefs had routed "Caracal, the king of the world," and made him tremble behind the shelter of his heap of stones?[1]

The treaty which Caracalla made with the Caledonians at his abrupt departure from their country seems to have allowed them free range up to the wall of Antoninus, and with this they were so contented that nearly a century of quiet was the consequence. But the wealth of the south, the increasing inability of the Romans to defend it, and the entrance of a new people into the warfare who augmented the strength and resources of the Caledonians, caused their incursions to be renewed with greater frequency and fierceness than ever. The invaders, no longer termed Caledonians, are now for the first time spoken of as two combined nations under the title of Scots and Picts; and during the fourth and fifth centuries their attacks upon the province were so daring, that the walls were but a weak protection for those who had not courage to man them. The Romans indeed endeavoured to retard the downfall of their British possession by the reinforcements they occasionally sent for its defence; but their own growing difficulties at length required every soldier for the protection of Italy, which was as terribly menaced by the barbarians of the north as was Britain itself by the Scots and Picts; and Honorius released the Britons from their allegiance to the empire, and informed them that they must now depend upon themselves both for government and defence. But the long subjection by which they had been enfeebled, and the loss of the best and bravest of their children, who had been carried abroad to fight the battles of pretenders to the dominion of the empire, made the boon of independence little better than a mockery to those who had no longer either hearts to prize or hands to protect it. How small a price, indeed, they set upon it, and how ready they were to be still dependent on their late masters, was evinced by the tenacity with which they clung to Rome when Rome had rejected them; and how utterly helpless they were for self-government, was shown by the feebleness of their resistance to the common foe, by the rancour with which they conducted their wars and feuds against each other, and by the religious dissensions that held them apart from all co-operation even while their nationality was falling to pieces and the enemy thundering at their gates.

In the meantime the Scots and Picts had not been idle. That wall which Agricola had first erected, which Hadrian had so greatly repaired and strengthened, and which Severus had in many places so enlarged and built anew, that it might have protected a people of ordinary spirit for centuries, was first turned by fleets of boats[2] that landed the invaders upon the coast

---

[1] Even Boece gives up the mighty son of Trenmor as a personage either too giantly or too ghostly to be enrolled in a history of mortal men. He therefore introduces and dismisses him with the following unceremonious notice:— "It is said that Fynmakcoule, the son of Coelus, Scottisman, was in thir days; ane man of huge statoure, of xvii cubits of hicht. He was ane gret huntar, and richt terribill, for his huge quantite, to the pepill: of quhome ar mony vulgar fabillis amang us, nocht unlike to thir fabillis that ar rehersit of King Arthure. And becaus his dedis is nocht authorist be autentik authoris, I will rehers na thing thairof."

[2] This mode of invasion is thus particularized by Gildas: "The Roman legions had no sooner returned home in joy and triumph, than their former foes, like hungry and ravening wolves, rushing with greedy jaws upon the fold

within the forts; and afterwards, when such a circuitous route was unnecessary, the invaders boldly stormed the ramparts, which by this time they must have laughed to scorn. The defence, indeed, which was made of them by the Britons, if their own historian, Gildas the Wise, is to be believed, was so puerile or so crazy, that none but children or madmen could have adopted it. Instead of posting sentinels, their whole army kept watch and ward upon the wall; and thus, when they were benumbed with cold and sleeplessness, they were despatched by their assailants almost without resistance.[1] And even yet the Britons—the descendants of those who had fought on equal terms with Cæsar himself —continued to depend upon Roman assistance, and their prayer to "Ætius thrice consul" was the latest as well as the most abject of their appeals. "If the fatal chance of time and destiny," they wrote, "demands that this our realm should be loosed from the unity and friendship of the Romans, compelling us into servitude to a barbarous people, we care not what people have dominion over us, so that we may avoid the tyranny of the Scots and Picts." In describing their sufferings at the hands of the enemy, they added, "they have now beat down the walls and strengths which should have defended us from their inflictions; then they have entered into the Roman province with all manner of cruelty; burned down our towns and castles, razed our ramparts to the ground, and slain our wives, children, and aged people, besides numberless other calamities which we may not write for grief. We, the residue of them, are chased and driven to the seas; and as we cannot pass through them we are again driven into the hands of our enemies."[2]

This application, as is well known, was unavailing, and the Britons began to look for other defenders. If the letter from which we have quoted may be received as genuine, their resolution had been already adopted. It was to risk a future danger, of whatever character or amount, for the benefit of present safety; to submit, if need should be, to any other barbarians rather than to the Scots and Picts. And their choice was soon made.

At this time the people of Northern Germany and the shores of the Baltic, pirates by profession, had, under the name of Saxons, carried the terror of their invasions to every coast. Their friendship had also been as effectual as their hostility was formidable, a fact that was proved by the example of the people of Armorica or Brittany, who had applied to the Saxons in their extremity, and through their aid had been replaced in safety and independence. This case of the Armoricans, who were a colony of South Britons, was enough in the absence of other considerations to turn the scale, and as a small fleet of the Saxons were at present cruising in the British Channel their assistance could be immediate. Animated by these considerations, Vortigern the British king sent an embassy to Hengist and Horsa, the two chiefs of the pirates; and these bold brothers, after having listened favourably to the application, turned their prows to the Isle of Thanet, which was appointed for their future residence. Although this reinforcement consisted of nothing more than the crews of three Saxon warships, such was the valour of these new-comers, and the inspiring influence of their example, that in the first instance the Scots and Picts were checked, and driven back into their own territory. But the work of the Saxons was not yet ended; they had seen the fertility of the country and the weakness of its occupants, and perhaps the idea of a permanent footing on the coast of Britain, from the superior facilities it would afford for piratical expeditions, was the first and only suggestion of their ambition, while that of an entire conquest was the after-thought of favourable circumstances. Be that as it may, they soon created these circumstances by the family alliance which they formed with Vortigern, and by the reinforcements of their countrymen whom they summoned to their aid. They were soon too strong to be dislodged, and they proceeded to occupy as masters the land they had liberated as defenders. Their conquest, indeed, was a work of time, but only the more permanent on that account. From the year 449, when they first landed on the Isle of Thanet, till 647, when they drove the last opposing army of the Britons into the hilly country of Cornwall, the work of the Saxon conquest of England was continued, and not of England alone, but a large portion of that territory which was afterwards to constitute a principal part of the kingdom of Scotland.

In this way the Scots and Picts, by their fierce aggressions upon the southern part of the

---

which is left without a shepherd, are wafted both by the strength of oarsmen and the blowing wind, break through the boundaries, and spread slaughter on every side, and like mowers cutting down the ripe corn they cut up, tread under foot, and overrun the whole country."— Gildas, translated by J. A. Giles, LL.D., Lond. 1841, p. 14.

[1] The following is the account of Gildas:—"To oppose them [the Picts and Scots] there was placed on the heights a garrison equally slow to fight and ill adapted to run away; a useless and panic-struck company, which slumbered away days and nights on their unprofitable watch. Meanwhile the hooked weapons of their enemies were not idle, and our wretched countrymen were dragged from the wall and dashed against the ground."

[2] Bede.

island, had occasioned the introduction of a new people under whose ascendency they were finally to succumb. The Teutonic and not the Celtic race were thenceforth to be the masters of Britain. But before the latter disappear as nations from our view, and become only component parts of the new Scottish population, it becomes necessary to inquire into their real origin and character. Who in reality were these Scots and Picts at whose early history, both native and Roman, we have already glanced, and about whom such learned controversy has been waged? It would be an unprofitable task for the historian to particularize or even to enumerate the theories upon the subject which attempt to solve the question. All we can do is to adopt the most probable answer, without entangling ourselves either among the objections that have assailed it, or the arguments by which it has been confirmed.

As we have already seen, the old Scottish legends make the Scots the prior occupants of the country, into which they entered long before the commencement of the Christian era; and represent the Picts as a wandering people, who arrived at a later period, and took possession of those districts that were still unoccupied by the Scots. By the same authority we are also told that they continued to live as two distinct nations, sometimes at war with each other, and sometimes in close alliance, even prior to the commencement of the Roman invasion of Britain. In turning, however, to the Roman accounts of the inhabitants, from Tacitus who first mentions them, to Dio and Herodian who lived in the third century, we find no mention or hint of any such twofold occupation. On the contrary, Tacitus speaks of those who fought against Agricola under the general name of Caledonians, and describes them as one people; and it is not till the close of the third century that the Picts are spoken of as inhabiting Scotland and invading the Roman province. Had they then stolen into Scotland toward the end of this century, and made so quick a conquest of Pictavia that the Romans were unaware of it, or thought it an event not worth announcing? In this way the difficulty has been attempted to be disposed of by those who consider the Scots as the earliest inhabitants of the country, and the Picts an emigration of a much later period. The idea, however, of such a stealthy entrance and silent location is too absurd to be gravely refuted. Would the Romans, who spent so much in the conquest of Britain, and who valued it so highly, have allowed the intrusion of such rivals without resistance, and even without notice?

In spite, therefore, of the cavils of those theorists who wish to find in the Picts a Teutonic race by whom Scotland was entered after the commencement of the Christian era, we are compelled to rest satisfied with the more natural conclusion that the Picts of the third century were only the Caledonians of the first under a new name. Roman civilization had been introduced into the south of the island, while the north was still unsubdued; and the provincial Britons wore decent attire, while the Caledonians wore little else than their own blue-pictured skins. What more natural, then, than that the latter should be called Picti or painted men by their better-clothed and more polished rivals; and that a name thus given in derision should afterwards become general and permanent, especially when national hatred and warfare had increased with every year.

Supposing, then, that the Picts were no other than the Caledonians, the next question that occurs for solution is, Who were the Caledonians? Their antiquarian remains, their nomenclature of places and objects, their division into tribes, form of government, and other circumstances, all indicate that, in common with the Britons of the south, they were a Celtic people. It is natural in their case to conclude that they were, like their southern brethren, the descendants of those who at some unknown period had emigrated from the opposite coast of Gaul into the island of Britain. The question of settlement and possession would quickly succeed their safe arrival, whether they came in one great torrent of emigration or by successive waves; in this case the stronger would seize the better portion and compel the weaker to be content with the rest. According to this established principle of barbarian conquest, the twenty-one Gaulish tribes or clans that came by the worse had nothing but the cold bleak north for their portion; they were thrust aside or chased into the vast Caledonian forest and the country called by the Roman writers Caledonia proper, comprising the whole peninsula of the island lying northward of the Forth. In this way the original Gaulish emigrants of this portion of Britain lost their first name, and became Caledonians from the new home in which they were settled. Thus the case continued till the close of the third century, when the national appellation was exchanged for a nickname, and that of Pict was heard for the first time. It was bestowed by their enemies, and it was by the same enemies that their deeds were recorded —not favourably, but in wrath and hatred. In this way the Greeks called all men barbarians but themselves, while the Romans made the words *foe* and *foreigner* convertible terms; and as Picts the Caledonians continued to be spoken of long after the practice of tattooing or skin-painting had been abandoned.

It is thus that we have the Pictish kingdom extending over North Britain at the close of the fourth century. And still the Roman writers make no mention of the rival kingdom of the Scots. They indeed allude to a people of that name, but only as the inhabitants of Ireland, not of Britain. In that island their predominance over the native Hibernians had established for it the name of Scotia before the close of the third century, and as Scotia Ireland continued to be exclusively mentioned till the end of the tenth or eleventh. From what country they had emigrated, and how and at what period they entered Ireland, have also been made subjects of controversy; but all that can be clearly ascertained is that they were a branch of the great Celtic family, that they used a dialect of the same language as that of the Britons, and that their government was of the same patriarchal character, being that of separate tribes or families instead of a collective people.

It was not till the latter part of the fourth century that the Scots of Ireland appeared upon the troubled field of Britain, and then only as strangers and marauders. Being of a restless, adventurous, enterprising spirit, like all the nations of the Celtic race, they appear to have allied themselves at an early period with the Saxon pirates, whose love of plunder and adventure was congenial to their own. The first visit of these Scots in Britain appears to have been made A.D. 360, when they invaded the southern province; but although their arrival was by sea, their visits were confounded with those of the Picts by the writers of the period. A few years after they renewed their invasion in still greater force; and having allied themselves on this occasion with the Picts, their united army was able to penetrate into the heart of South Britain and plunder Augusta, the ancient London and capital of the province, until they were defeated by Theodosius, the Roman commander. They repeated their attempt A.D. 398, being joined as before by their new allies the Picts, but were routed with great slaughter by the Roman general, who also repaired the northern wall. But this land-defence, which might protect the province from the Picts, was no safeguard against the Scots, whose invasions were conducted by sea, and who could select those parts of the coast that best favoured their landing. It was after the union of two such formidable and merciless armies as those of the Picts and Scots that the attacks upon the south became more terrible and incessant. It is from this circumstance also that we can better understand the helplessness of the Britons, and the desperate remedy to which they had recourse.

As far as the Scots were concerned, the arrival of the Saxons in the island quickly changed the course of action and adventure. By sea the light curraghs of the invaders from Ireland could scarcely hope to encounter with success the strong well appointed war-galleys of the new champions of Britain, while in battles by land their forces were no match for the disciplined troops that marched under the white-horse banner of Hengist and Horsa. In this strait the Scots appear to have bethought themselves of the country of their friends the Picts, as yet thinly inhabited, and where settlements might be found without difficulty. At this time also there were a people in the province of Ulster to whom a new home was especially desirable; these were the Dalriad Scots, who, having long been at war with the Cruithne of Ulladh, a rival clan, were desirous to end the unprofitable strife by leaving the field of contest for a new country. Accordingly, under the leading of Loarn, Fergus, and Angus, the three sons of Erc, chief of the Dalriads, they landed at the Epidian promontory, to which they gave the name of Caentir (Cantire) or headland; and in the partition of territory that afterwards took place this district was assigned to Fergus, who perhaps was no other than Fergus First and Fergus Second in one person. In this way it has often happened in the mythic history of a people that an individual hero or public benefactor has been reproduced in more forms than one, as well as a series of illustrious personages been concentrated into a glorious unit. This entrance of the Scots appears to have been effected without resistance, but for such a peaceful acquiescence on the part of the Picts several causes may be conjectured. The narrow promontory of Cantire was secluded from Caledonia by a range of lofty hills; it was thinly inhabited by a tribe of Cambro-Britons whom the Pictish clans were likely to regard as aliens, and the Picts themselves were probably too closely occupied in watching the progress of the Saxon conquests in the south to care for what was passing at such a remote and insignificant point as the promontory of Epidium. In the further division of the territory Loarn and Angus acquired for their share the districts that were subsequently impressed with their names, according to the general custom of the Celts, who thus commemorated their leaders in whatever country they settled. As their first entrance had been without conflict, they were probably too few to excite jealousy, and were thus enabled to grow in numbers and extend their occupation by fresh arrivals of their countrymen, until they had grown too strong and obtained too secure a footing on the soil to be easily dislodged.

It was in this manner, as far as can be made out from probable conjecture aided by the testimony of Venerable Bede, that the Scots first became the inhabitants of Scotland. The date of this arrival has been assigned as A.D. 503. If this date is correct the event occurred only fifty-four years after the landing of the Angles in England. Thus a single lifetime of that period had witnessed two of the most important events that have occurred in our national history. These were the entrance of two different peoples almost simultaneously into the island, by whom not only two great kingdoms were to be erected, but the very names of the new occupants to be so indelibly stamped upon them that the old should utterly disappear. North Britain and South Britain, Caledonia, Albion, Pictavia, the Province—these distinctions were to be merged in the two illustrious and distinctive names of ENGLAND and SCOTLAND.

CHAPTER III.

THE PICTS AND THE SCOTS.

History of the PICTS—Their territory—Pictish kings—Their wars with the Scots and Saxons—Danish invasions—History of the SCOTS—Fergus their first king—Successors of Fergus—Reign of Aidan—Reign of Achaius—His alliance with Charlemagne—His marriage with the Pictish princess Urgusia—Reign of Kenneth—His device to induce the nobles to make war upon the Picts—He succeeds to the Pictish throne by his descent from Urgusia—The Picts not exterminated but incorporated with the Scots.

At the beginning of the sixth century two races had obtained possession of Scotland, and the history of the country from this point becomes that of two rival and independent nations lately united in the hour of danger against a common enemy, but now ready to turn their arms against each other, and strive for the exclusive mastery. At this twofold history, which continues from the sixth to the ninth century, we can only bestow a passing glance, not only on account of its essential insignificance, but the contradiction and obscurity in which it is involved. It would be well, indeed, if we had still the light of Roman records to guide us through the perplexing maze, partial and insufficient though we have hitherto found them. But it is here, where they are most needed, that they forsake us; and in their stead we have only the brief notices or contradictory statements of such historians as Gildas, Bede, Nennius, and Paulus Diaconus, who, although they lived while the Pictish kingdom was still in existence, were either too ignorant of its history, or too well aware of its approaching termination, to honour it with a detail.

In turning our attention in the first case to the locality of the Picts, we find an insurmountable difficulty in specifying the limits of the kingdom of Pictavia, and the districts over which it extended. The remoteness of the period at which they are removed from us, and the variety of races by which the different districts of Scotland were occupied, make it often impossible for us to ascertain of this or that particular locality whether it was the home of the Pict or the Scot. This uncertainty is increased by the fluctuating character of the Pictish occupation, which seems to have expanded or diminished with remarkable rapidity during the course of the wars of its people against the encroachments of the Scots on the one hand and the Anglo-Saxons on the other. Speaking in general terms, it appears that during the greater part of this period, commencing with the entrance of the Scots into Argyle, Pictland comprised the whole of that portion of the country which is contained between the boundary of the Frith of Forth to the south and the mountainous barrier that separates the Lowlands from the Highlands of Scotland to the west. To this may be added the kingdom of Cumbria or Strathclyde, comprising the south-west portion of Scotland, which, being a territory inhabited by a Welsh population, is usually considered a province of Pictavia. The Orkney Islands and the Hebrides are also supposed to have formed a part of the Pictish dominions. Other portions to the south of the Forth, and even as far as to the Humber, at one time also were part of Pictavia, until they were wrested from it by the progress of Saxon aggression. Such was Pictland, with Abernethy for its capital. From this general notice it will be seen that the territory still possessed by these descendants of the ancient Caledonians was of large extent and resources, even when the Scots were enabled to establish a rival kingdom upon its border.

Of the Pictish kings who reigned during this period of less than four centuries, forty are enumerated whose names and history have been extracted from the Celto-Scottish and Irish chronicles,[1] a list than which, Chalmers declares, "there is nothing more authentic or satisfactory in the early annals of any country." But be that as it may with regard to their names, and the mere fact of their having actually existed, the history of their achievements is neither sufficiently certain to be accepted, nor yet important enough to be detailed. They seem indeed to have lived for evil or for good, and to have been prosperous or unfortunate according to the pleasure of their historians, who wrote when there were none to contradict them. A brief notice, therefore, of the Pictish kings may be sufficient for our purpose.

The first of these, Drust, the son of Erp, eulogized as the fortunate leader of a hundred battles, is recorded as the hero under whose successful attacks the Roman empire in South Britain passed away. A hundred years succeeded, which were occupied by twelve Pictish sovereigns in the usual quick succession of the time and country; but the silence of the record, except as to their names, indicates that happy state of peace which neither needs a hero to achieve great deeds nor a historian to rehearse them. But even this national blessing was suspicious, as it was occasioned merely by the Saxon conquest of England on the one side of Pictavia, and the consolidation of the Scottish clans on the other. Then succeeded Bridei, A.D. 556, whose reign was of a different character; for he defeated the Scots, whose king Gauran he slew, and was converted to Christianity by the preaching of St. Columba. The demise of Bridei was followed by another long interval of peaceful obscurity, when another Bridei, the son of Bili, after the lapse of a hundred years, succeeded to the Pictish throne, and signalized himself in a war against Egfrid, King of Northumbria. This sovereign invaded Pictland, and advanced as far as Dunnichen, but was there defeated and slain by the Pictish king. Aided by the Britons and Scots, Bridei then carried his successful arms into Northumbria, and inflicted such havoc that this kingdom never afterwards recovered its former ascendency in the heptarchy. This war against Northumbria continued for nearly a quarter of a century; but it was closed with disaster in 710, when Bridei, the son of Dereli, the fourth of the name among the kings of Pictland, was defeated and slain at the battle of Mananfield by the Saxons. But still worse than these contests with a national enemy, was a civil war that occurred among the Picts themselves about the year 724, of which the cause was that fruitful source of Celtic controversy and bloodshed—the royal succession. Into the merits of this warfare it would be unnecessary to enter even if it were intelligible: it exhibits royal pretensions which we are unable to appreciate, and claimants for whom we can feel no interest, while the battles they occasioned were shifted over the whole of Pictland with various fortunes, but disastrous consequences to the kingdom at large. From this strife for the sovereignty Ungus emerged as the most successful of the competitors. On ascending the throne Ungus signalized his long reign of thirty-one years by wars against the Scots, the Northumbrians, and the Britons of Cumbria, and in almost every case with success; and he died a death of peace, with the reputation of having been the greatest and most warlike of all the Pictish kings.

These wars, however, against so many powerful enemies, combined with their own civil dissensions, had weakened the power of the Picts, when a new enemy entered upon the field, as formidable as any they had yet encountered, to accelerate their coming downfall. These were the pirates of the Baltic, the northern Vikingr, who, under the name of Danes, first appeared in England in 832, and afterwards repeated their visits with such terrible effect until near the time of the Norman conquest. Even before this period their war-galleys had cast anchor in the bays of the rugged coast of Scotland, not, however, for the purposes of plunder, of which there was little to be found, but with the design of permanent occupation, and to acquire a more ample seaboard for their vocation of piracy and plunder. During the same century (A.D. 839), after carrying their devastations into the Hebrides, they invaded the mainland of Pictavia, upon which Ueu or Owen, the king, hurried to its defence. But in the conflict which he ventured with these terrible antagonists, who might now be reckoned the most fearless warriors of the age, he fell, along with his brother Brun, and the greater part of his chiefs and soldiers. With this fatal defeat Pictland ceases to have a separate national history, as only four years afterwards Kenneth the Scot occupied its throne, and established upon it a Scottish dynasty.

We now turn to the history of the Dalriad

---

[1] By Father Innes in *Chronica de Origine Antiquorum Pictorum.* See also Chalmers' *Caledonia*, vol. i. p. 206, London, 1807, and Pinkerton's Tables at the end of vol. I. of his *Inquiry into the History of Scotland.*

Scots who accomplished this important change and became the predominant people of the country. From their narrow settlement upon the promontory of Cantire they soon extended themselves over the whole of Ardgael (Argyle), which became the kingdom of Fergus and his sept, while Loarn and Angus, his brothers, in like manner became the sovereigns of Lorn and Islay. Of these three branches of the Dalriad immigration that of Fergus, although he did not possess the right of primogeniture, appears to have obtained the ascendency, and the kings of the Scoto-Irish for the most part belonged to this dominant family. But as we have already seen, the kingly authority over a collection of Celtic tribes was little more than nominal, unless the individual who held it was superior to all his brother chiefs in courage and abilities as well as in title. The right also of the house of Fergus to monopolize this precarious sovereignty was often a ground not only of question but also of quarrel between them and the descendants of Loarn, who is represented as the eldest of the brothers. But this was not the worst, for the race of Fergus was also divided against itself; and between two rival branches that bore the names of the race of Comgal and the race of Gauran wars were frequently occurring, by which the royal succession was shifted from the one family to the other. This brief explanation will suffice to show not only how slight a claim to notice the history of these early Scots possesses, but also how little it is entitled to implicit credence. It will also justify the short notice which we bestow upon the twenty-nine kings who are recorded to have reigned from Fergus, the son of Erc, the first Dalriad sovereign in Scotland, to Kenneth Mac Alpin, by whom the Pictish monarchy was subverted.

The reign of Fergus over his petty dominion continued only three years; but during this brief space he became, in consequence of the death of his two brothers, the sole king or patriarchal chief of his emigrant countrymen in Scotland. He was succeeded by his son Domangurt, who, after a short and obscure reign of five years, died, and left two sons, Comgal and Gauran, who reigned successively, the first for thirty-two and the second for twenty-two years. It was the fate of Gauran, however, to enter into hostilities with the Picts—an event that must sooner or later have occurred between two such neighbours, and of which this seems to have been the commencement; and in the battle that ensued between him and Bridei, the first of the five Pictish kings who bore that name, he was defeated and slain. He was succeeded by Conal, the son of his brother Comgal, to the prejudice of his own family; and thus was laid the groundwork of a war of succession that produced years of confusion and bloodshed. The reign of Conal, which lasted fourteen years, seems to have been either inglorious or positively disastrous, and the chief event that signalized it was the protection he afforded to Columba; but as the saint was of the same royal house as himself, being great-grandson of Loarn, and yet not likely to become a claimant for the throne, which was occupied by himself as the great grandson of Fergus, Conal could well afford to give way to such a strong tie of Celtic relationship, and invest Columba with the island of Iona in perpetual possession. The last years of Conal were clouded by competition from a very different quarter. It came from the rival house of Gauran, whose claims were inherited by Aidan, and who sought by force of arms to supplant Donnacha, the son of Conal. The consequences of this feud were that Donnacha fell before his victorious rival in the battle of Loro, and the tribe of Comgal which he represented was driven into Argyle, while that of Gauran obtained the more desirable portion of Cantire, as well as the Scottish crown, in the person of Aidan, its enterprising chieftain.

The reign of Aidan was not only distinguished by important events, but by superior fulness and clearness in their record; and this last distinction his memory mainly owes to his connection with Saint Columba, who was fortunate in his biographers. His accession occurred A.D. 574, and he was inaugurated at the sacred island of Iona by the saint himself, whose princely birth, high character, and apostolic labours had obtained for him double reverence from the Dalriad Scots. After Aidan had signalized his right to the throne by his victory at Loro, he made war in 577 with the Britons of Strathclyde, but was defeated by Rydderach the Bountiful, their king, on the height of Arderyth. This conflict, however, was so paltry or so indecisive that it is contemptuously styled in the Welsh triads the nugatory battle of Britain. He aided the Britons of Cumbria, and Mulgan their king, against the Saxons, whom he defeated A.D. 584 at Fethanlea on Stanmore. He again defeated them in 590 at the battle of Leitredh, in which two of his sons were slain. His chief conflicts, indeed, were with the Anglo-Saxons of Northumbria under their king Ethelfrid, and the Picts who were allied with them; and although his victories were numerous he also suffered such reverses as were sufficient to hold in check the advancing power of the Scots. It was well for them, however, that against such formidable enemies as the confederate Saxons and Picts they had such a leader as Aidan, by whom they were enabled at least to maintain their ground. During the course of this changeful and protracted warfare Aidan, accompanied by Columba, appeared at the Council of Drumkeat in Ulster (A.D. 590) and obtained the relinquishment of homage which had hitherto been paid by the Scottish kings of Cantire to the sovereigns of the parent kingdom of Dalriada. A reign that was both useful and glorious on the whole, and extended to the unusual length of thirty-four years, was closed amidst sorrow and disaster. Worn out with age, Aidan dragged himself to the field for his last conflict with the merciless and pertinacious Ethelfrid, who had assailed his territory with an army of Northumbrians and Picts; but in the battle which ensued at Dawstane the Scottish hero was utterly defeated and compelled to seek safety in ignominious flight. Soon after his return tidings reached him of the death of the holy Columba, his spiritual father and instructor; and foreseeing the jeopardy to which the infant church would be exposed by such a loss, he soon after expired (A.D. 604), at the age of eighty, and was buried in the church of Kilcheran in Campbelton.

After Aidan a line of kings succeeded whose obscure and contradictory history, even if it could be effectually cleared, would scarcely recompense the trouble. They are dignified with the royal title notwithstanding their limited rule and contested authority; and although their grandeur and political importance are magnified into full-blown regality by Fordun, Boece, and Buchanan, yet in the Ulster Annals and Gaelic Chronicles they shrink into petty dimensions, and are merely reguli or chiefs of the clan that happened for the time to be uppermost. Their wars against their national enemies the Picts and Saxons were intermingled with feuds still more numerous and sanguinary among themselves; and in these heady contests the prize at issue was this barren sceptre or leading-staff, which shifted from the Fergusian branch of Comgal to that of Gauran, and from the family of Fergus itself to that of Loarn, with most bewildering rapidity. And yet these are the ages which antiquarianism has delighted to investigate, and the quarrels which it has endeavoured to explain and reconcile! Compared with this confusion, the perplexing and discordant contemporaneous history of the heptarchy of England becomes both luminous and important. Yet one essential fact is to be deduced from this chaos of names and achievements, which is that the Scottish race, originally so few in numbers and so limited in means, had been growing in importance and power, by which they were enabled at the commencement of the ninth century to hold their own against the utmost efforts of Briton, Pict, and Saxon.

Of all those kings the most distinguished was Eocha', the fourth of that name, and a descendant of the Gauran dynasty, who ascended the throne in 796. His abilities were chiefly occupied by the contentions of the rival clans, which he had the wisdom and good fortune to reconcile as well as rule. But though this was much it was not sufficient for our early Scottish historians, and therefore the name of this Eocha', which is nothing but plain Hugh, they have latinized into the sounding one of Achaius, and aggrandized with a record of which his countrymen might well be proud. For, according to these writers, he quelled the Irish who invaded Scotland, aided the Picts in their successful wars with the Saxons, and founded the chivalrous order of the Thistle, for the encouragement of those gallant knights by whom his august court was adorned and his prosperous reign signalized. His fame in consequence of these achievements was so greatly magnified abroad that Charlemagne himself courted his alliance and sought his aid for the defence of France against the invading Saracens. And here the imagination of Boece absolutely runs riot upon this last portion of the history of Achaius, which Fordun only modestly and briefly touches, and Buchanan passes over in silence. He tells us that William, the brother of Achaius, crossed the seas, not only with a reinforcement of gallant Scottish soldiers to assist the Franks, but with four learned Scottish doctors to enlighten their ignorance. The deeds of William were so chivalrous as to throw those of all the Paladins of France into the shade, so that he obtained the title of the "Knight without Reproach;" and he was so honoured by the fair city of Florence, to which he was a notable benefactor, that the citizens assumed the red lily of the Scottish arms for their civic cognizance, and ordained a certain number of lions to be fed yearly at the public expense, in honour of the supporters of our national blazonry. Nor were the peaceful achievements of the Scottish doctors less illustrious. They became so famous by their teaching that Paris was soon the resort of pupils and learned masters from every country in Europe; and in consequence of this brilliant commencement of a new epoch in the history of France the universities of Paris and Pavia were founded, and two of these erudite strangers placed at their head.

More important events to Scotland, however, were ripening during the reign of Achaius than visionary treaties and chivalric institutions, and these also not to be effected by the sword, but by a peaceful matrimonial alliance. The king espoused the Princess Urguisa, daughter of Urguis, king of the Picts, and thus established hereditary claims in his own house should the royal succession fail in Pictavia, which his descendants were not likely to overlook. On the death of Achaius, which occurred A.D. 826, after a reign of thirty years, he was succeeded by Dungal, of the house of Loarn. After a short reign of seven years, in which it seems there was little or nothing worth commemorating, this king was succeeded by Alpin, son of Achaius by the Pictish princess Urgusia. At this time the crown of Pictavia was contested by Drest, his mother's nephew, against a pretender named Talorgan; and, eager to support the rights of his cousin, Alpin embarked an armament from Cantire, and landing on the coast of Kyle, laid waste the country between the rivers Ayr and Doon, and advanced to the mountain range which separates Kyle from Galloway; but here his career was cut short in a petty skirmish against the Picts. His head, it is added, was cut off, and paraded in triumph before the whole Pictish army, after which it was set up on the most conspicuous place in their capital of Abernethy for the scorn and derision of the rabble. But little did they foresee the reverse that was at hand, or the price they were to pay for their barbarous merriment.

After this tragical close of a short reign of three years Alpin was succeeded by his son Kenneth. His first wish was to revenge the ignominious death of his father; but strangely enough he found his chieftains, especially the elder part of them, exceedingly averse to the performance of this most urgent as well as most congenial of all Celtic moral duties: they alleged that the country was too much weakened by the recent disaster to carry his purpose into effect, and all that he could obtain from them was their consent to a hollow truce instead of an immediate war with their remorseless enemies. The truce continued for three years, and threatened a much longer duration, when Kenneth resolved to break it by an appeal to the superstitious feelings of his loitering and peace-loving nobles. The manner in which it was effected, as first detailed briefly by Fordun, but amplified in the pages of Boece and Buchanan, was sufficiently characteristic of the times and the real condition of the people. Having invited his chiefs to a banquet, Kenneth so successfully plied them with good cheer and hard drinking that the night waxed late, and they were persuaded to remain in the palace till morning—an easy extension of hospitality, where the floor of the banquet-hall served for a bed, and the leaves with which it was bestrewn for pillow and coverlet. When all was silence and sleep the apartment was suddenly lighted up by a glittering apparition; a voice of thunder called the sleepers to awake, and obey the will of Heaven and their king by going instantly to battle against the Picts—and on raising their confused heads the astounded senators beheld a shining form, such as they thought the angels alone should wear, while the tones in which he summoned them could proceed from no mortal organs. Having delivered his mandate the heavenly messenger suddenly vanished, and all was again silence and darkness.[1] But the angel was no other than a young kinsman of Kenneth arrayed in a garment made of the glittering skins of dried codfish, who proclaimed his message through a speaking-trumpet, and then made a harlequin exit by a side door. All this, however, was too much for the brains of these chieftains whether drunk or sober to fathom, and on assembling before the king on the morning they were as loud for war as formerly they had been urgent against it. A merciless campaign followed, in which, if we may believe the historians already mentioned, the whole Pictish nation was utterly swept away.

It is time, however, to turn from this phantasmagoria of war and onset to that cold faint outline which is all that the Scottish history of this period can really present to us for our ready belief. On the death of Alpin not only his kingdom but his new claims of family inheritance descended to his son Kenneth. And that inheritance was not to be a trivial or formal one, as was shown by the result; for the rivalry among the various pretenders to the Pictish throne, and the rapidity with which they successively disappeared, brought him step by step to that enviable eminence as the grandson of the Princess Urgusia. At length, when no one remained between him and the succession but Wred, the last of the Pictish kings, Kenneth speedily overthrew this feeble sovereign and stepped into his room (A.D. 843). He united in his single person the rights of force, good fortune, and hereditary claim; and their combined influence, as might be expected, was irresistible, so that it could hardly be otherwise than that Kenneth, Scot though he was, should become king of Pictavia. As for the Picts, it is also equally probable that they acquiesced, however reluctantly, in this transference of their sceptre, because there was no other nearer, or at least more

---

[1] The three historians evidently adapt the tale to their own sense of what was fittest or likeliest in such an experiment in thaumaturgy, and accordingly each delivers it in a different form. Thus Boece, who furnishes each sleeper with a bedroom, also provides a separate apparition for each of them, and is therefore obliged to enlist not one, but a whole troop of masqueraders for this midnight performance.

powerful claimant; and thus the line of Fergus, the first Scottish king, whose dominion was limited to the petty principality of Cantire, obtained at last the entire sovereignty of the country. This union of the two hostile portions into which Scotland had been divided, and which occurred in the ninth century, was a curious type of that still greater and more unlikely union which took place nearly eight hundred years afterwards, when a similar royal alliance was to unite the two hostile nations of England and Scotland into one people and under the rule of one king.

It is by this peaceful intermarriage between the Scottish and Pictish crowns, and the succession which it originated, that we can satisfactorily account not only for the union of the Scots and Picts into one kingdom, but even their ultimate fusion into a single people. For this last result also, notwithstanding former wars and rivalries, their common origin as Celts, and the similarity of their language, character, and ancient traditions, were an effectual preparative. But a change so gentle and unostentatious as this has found little favour either with the ancient chronicler or the modern antiquary, being too uneventful for the romantic spirit of the former, and too simple and straightforward for the cunning theories of the latter. The supposition of a war of conquest has therefore been assumed in its stead, in which either the Picts vanquished the Scots or the Scots annihilated the Picts. But where are the traces of such a thorough and terrible conquest? Upon what field was it fought, and by what hero was it achieved? In consequence of the Scots having impressed their name upon the country at large, as well as its population, it is generally concluded that they, and not their rivals, were the successful competitors. And what then became of the unfortunate Picts? They were swallowed up, extinguished, annihilated. They are thus got rid of because they stand in the way, and a single drop of ink suffices for the feat. In this arbitrary fashion our old histories have dismissed them, after having crumbled them by a series of defeats commencing with the codfish vision of Kenneth, and ending with the last application of his national extinguisher; and when better evidence is sought for such a wholesale destruction, we are presented with the *Chronicle of the Pictish Kings*, written, as is supposed, about the eleventh century,[1] and the *Register of St. Andrews*, written in the twelfth.

Against such slender testimonies a superior amount of proof has been triumphantly brought forward in favour of the more merciful alternative. It arises from the utter silence respecting such a conquest from those early writers, whether Welsh, Irish, or Saxon, who were more unbiassed witnesses and had better means of information. No allusion to the conquest of Pictland is made by the English historian Nennius, who wrote in the middle of the ninth century and only a few years after the death of Kenneth; nor by Asser, the biographer of Alfred, who wrote about the close of that century; on the contrary, they mention the Picts as still living and possessed of their wonted nationality. In like manner they are announced in the Saxon Chronicle, and by Ethelward and Ingulphus in the tenth and eleventh centuries, who speak of the Picts as a people of their own day. By Tighernac the Irish annalist, by the Welsh annalists, and the Gaelic Duan, Kenneth is simply spoken of as one of the Pictish kings, but in no case as the conqueror of Pictland nor yet the exterminator of the Picts. When with such testimonies we find that people still living and unsubdued, and at the same time ruled over by Kenneth Mac Alpin the Scot, we see in the whole transference nothing more than a case of hereditary succession and the union of the two crowns upon a single head. A common interest and centuries of close union were enough at last to blend the two people into one and impress them with a common name, while the name itself would be naturally chosen from the country of the new dynasty, aided, perhaps, by its greater amount of population or their superior intelligence and enterprise. In this way, without having recourse to a wholesale massacre, we can account for the disappearance of the Picts. As in the case of their ancestors the Caledonians, it was only the name that disappeared; the people still remained.

---

[1] *Chronicon Regum Pictorum*, first published by Father Innes in 1720.

CHAPTER IV.

HISTORY OF RELIGION.

Druidism the religion of the ancient Caledonians—Attested by the Druidical remains in Scotland—Uncertainty about the origin of the Druids—Cæsar's account of them—Classes into which the Druids were divided—Their costume—The ornament of the Druid's egg—Ceremony of cutting the mistletoe—Druidical places of worship—Human sacrifices—Nature and principles of the Druidical creed—Acquirements of the Druids in science—Their teaching—Their influence—Entrance of Christianity into Scotland—Ninian—Palladius—Kentigern—Columba's arrival in Scotland—Successful progress of his mission—The Culdees—Their creed and mode of life—Nature of their ecclesiastical government—Death of Columba—Aidan called to Northumberland—Establishment of the Culdees in England—Their suppression.

In our inquiries into the kind of religion that prevailed among the ancient Caledonians and their descendants, the Picts, before the entrance of Christianity among them, we are justified in concluding that it was the same Druidical system which prevailed among the Britons of the southern division of the island. This is attested by the remains of Druid architecture which are still plentiful in Scotland,[1] They do not, indeed, rival in vastness and architectural skill the imposing temples of Avebury and Stonehenge; but this circumstance is nothing more than might be expected from the poverty of the north, which presented fewer attractions to an ambitious priesthood than the fertility and superior importance of the south. Still the Druidical structures which are to be found over the whole extent of Scotland, and the Druidical observances which the introduction of Christianity failed to obliterate, seem to attest that the Druidical rule was as firmly established in the north as in the south, and maintained by the same superior science, ability, and intelligence.

Few questions in early history have been more perplexing than the origin of this remarkable order. From the manifest intellectual superiority of the Druids and their attainments in science, by which they were equally distinguished beyond, and separated from, the rude tribes among whom they dwelt, it can scarcely be thought that they had originally been Britons or even Gauls. They may, indeed, have been settled in Gaul long before they were known in our island, and have formed an essential part of the Gaulish emigrations by which Britain was originally peopled; but the sciences in which they excelled as well as the creed they promulgated all seem to attest that they originally came from the East—the fountain-head of science as well as religious belief. In this case India has been supposed to have been the native home of the Druids, and that they were a branch of that Brahminical order which has existed from the earliest periods of Indian history or tradition. But in opposition to this theory we find that the Druids were not an exclusive caste, neither did they reserve the priestly office wholly to themselves, which they would have done if they had been Brahmins. May they not rather have been Phœnicians—that homeless disinherited people who, by their superior intelligence and enterprise, were enabled to make every land their country, and assume the leadership wherever they settled? This idea their sun and fire worship, their sanguinary rites, and their favourite haunts of consecrated groves, would appear to sanction. But as to what people they originally were and whence they came antiquity is silent; and thus the Druids are still aggrandised with that mystery by which they awed our earliest ancestry among the deep shades of the Caledonian Forest, or in their Perthshire chief seat and capital in the recesses that bordered upon the range of the Grampians. Even of the doctrines they taught we still know little, and that imperfectly, notwithstanding the numerous notices which have been given of the Druids by some of the most eminent writers of antiquity.[2] But more than all, their very name is a mystery which as yet no philological learning has been able to solve.[3]

Of all the ancient writers who have given an account of the Druids none is so full and distinct, so reasonable and worthy of belief, as Julius Cæsar, who, not only on account of his

---

[1] A different view of the origin and purpose of these so-called Druidical structures is taken by some writers. See introductory chapter.

[2] Of these writers we may mention the names of Cicero, Diodorus Siculus, Strabo, Mela, Suetonius, and Ammianus Marcellinus.

[3] Thus some have derived the name of Druid from the Hebrew word *derussim* or *drussim*, signifying contemplative men; and others from Greek δρυς, an oak, the favourite tree of the Druids. Others, seeking a Celtic or British root, have divided upon the following words, each of which has its partisans:—*Derwyddon*, the lord of the oak; *druthin*, a lord; *drus*, a magician; *dru* or *deriv*, an oak; *trowis*, a teacher of truth. All this only indicates a difficulty that will never find a solution.

clear dispassionate judgment and observant habits, but his long residence in Gaul, had the best opportunities of becoming acquainted with this singular priesthood. For these reasons we quote his description of the Druids, notwithstanding its length, as being the best and most ample account which we can anywhere obtain of the ancient hierarchy of Scotland:—

"They preside over religion, take charge of public and private sacrifices, and interpret religious mysteries. To them a great number of young men resort for the purpose of training, and by these they are held in great honour. For they decide in almost all controversies, both public and private; and if any crime has been committed or any murder perpetrated, or if there is a dispute about birthright or boundaries, they decide the same—they settle rewards and punishments; and if any individual, whether private or public, refuses to abide by their decree, they interdict him from the sacrifices. No punishment among them is more severe than this. Those on whom this interdict is laid are accounted among the unholy and accursed; all forsake them, all shun their approach and conversation lest they should be infected by their touch; nor are the claims of right accorded to them nor any honours conferred on them. Over all these Druids one presides who holds among them the highest authority. On his death, if any one of their number excels the rest in merit, he succeeds him; but if there are several who are equal, the successor is chosen by the votes of the Druids, and sometimes the contest is decided by an appeal to arms. At a certain period of the year they hold a meeting at a consecrated spot in the country of the Carnutes [supposed to be the place now called Dreux in the Orleannais], which is considered to be in the centre of all Gaul. Hither from all quarters repair those who have cases for litigation, and submit themselves to their decision and sentence. It is supposed that the system of Druidism was formed in Britain and from thence carried over into Gaul, and now those who wish to be more completely versed in it generally go thither [to Britain] for the purpose.

"The Druids are not accustomed to engage in war, neither do they pay taxes like the rest of the community; they have exemption from military service and all public burdens. Induced by these advantages, many come of their own accord to be trained by them, and others are sent by their parents and relations. There they are said to learn by heart a number of verses, so that some remain twenty years under this tuition. Nor do the Druids think it proper to commit their instructions to writing, although in almost all other matters, in their accounts both of the public and individuals, the Greek characters are used. They seem to me to have adopted this course for two reasons: they do not wish that the knowledge of their system should be diffused among the common people; nor yet, that their pupils, trusting to written characters, should abate their diligence in cultivating the memory, because, in most cases, it happens, by trusting to the security of written characters, that people become careless both in acquiring knowledge and in retaining it. The chief object of the Druids is to impress the conviction that souls do not perish, but after death pass from one set of bodies to another; and they think that by this belief more than any other men can be roused to courage, and to cast away the fear of dying. They also discuss many points concerning the heavenly bodies and their motion, the extent of the universe and the earth, the nature of things, the influence and power of the immortal gods, and teach these to their young pupils.

"The whole nation of the Gauls is much addicted to religious observances; and for that reason those who are afflicted with the more serious diseases, and those who are involved in the dangers of warfare, either sacrifice men as victims or vow that they will sacrifice them; and in these immolations they use the services of the Druids; for they consider that the immortal gods cannot be propitiated unless the life of one man be offered up for that of another: they also have sacrifices of the same kind appointed for the state at large. Some have images of immense size, the limbs of which they construct of wicker-work, and fill with living men, and setting them on fire, the men are destroyed by the flames. They believe that the torture of those who have been apprehended in the commission of theft, or robbery, or any atrocious crime, is more grateful to the immortal gods; but when there is a deficiency of such kind of criminals they inflict this torture even upon the innocent.

"The god whom they chiefly worship is Mercury: of him they have many images, and they consider him the inventor of all arts, their guide in all their journeys, and the divinity who has the greatest influence in the pursuit of wealth and transactions of merchandise. Next to him they worship Apollo, and Mars, and Jove, and Minerva; and of these gods they hold the same belief that is entertained by other nations—as that Apollo wards off diseases, that Minerva imparts the rudiments of manufactures and manual arts, that Jupiter holds the rule of the celestial beings, and that Mars presides over war. To Mars, when they have resolved to engage in a battle, they usually devote whatever spoil they may take in the war. After the conflict they sacrifice all the live animals they have taken; the rest of the spoil they collect into one place. In many states heaps of these things may be seen piled up in consecrated localities, nor does it often happen, that any one is so negligent about religious sanctions as to conceal at home any part of the spoil, or to take it away when deposited: against this crime a very heavy punishment with torture is denounced.

"The Gauls declare that they are all descended from Father Dis [Pluto], and this they say has been handed down to them by the Druids. For this reason they distinguish every space of time, not by the number of days but of nights; and they so regulate their birthdays, and the commencement of months and years, that the day shall come after the night."

Such is Cæsar's account of the Druids; and although his statements are confined to the order as it existed in Gaul, yet from the pre-eminence which was assigned to Britain, as the great fountain-head of their religion, and the chief school in which it was taught, we are warranted in concluding that his description can equally apply to the Druids of our own island. It is also so comprehensive that succeeding writers have added little to its amount. But even its clearness gives rise to a historical perplexity. Seeing that the Druids were so learned, so superior in science and philosophy, and so careful to indoctrinate their pupils in all they knew as to subject them to a twenty years' course of instruction, how is it that the Britons of the south were still so barbarous at Cæsar's arrival, and those of the north at the time of Agricola's invasion? The only alternative left to us is the conclusion, either that the Druids were not so learned, or their disciples not such savages as they have been represented. But the fact of this Druidical superiority is too well attested by the structures they have left behind them, independently of the testimony of ancient history, to be a subject of cavil or denial; and we are compelled to suspect that both Britons and Caledonians were not so utterly ignorant and uncivilized as the Roman writers have represented them.

The Druidical order according to Strabo consisted of three classes: these were the Bardi or poets, a very essential class in a religion whose precepts were inculcated in verses; the Vates, who were the priests and naturalists; and the Druids proper, who, besides the study of nature, inculcated the doctrines of religion and the laws of morality. These last were the class of highest account; and with their pontifex maximus at their head, they constituted a power in the state which at any time could outweigh that of either king or chieftain. Such, indeed, was their influence that, as Strabo informs us, they could sometimes stop armies on the point of engaging, and persuade them to a mutual accommodation.

The costume of the Druids was particularly imposing. To distinguish themselves from the laity, who wore their hair at full length and shaved their chins, the Druids cropped the hair of their heads, while their beards were allowed to grow in full luxuriance. They wore long garments almost reaching to the ground; and when employed in their public religious ceremonies they were distinguished by a white surplice.

On these occasions also they wore a chaplet of oak, which was likewise done by all the worshippers. It appears from the relics found in their places of sepulture that they also wore gold chains round their necks and bracelets upon their arms and wrists. But the chief ornament, and that to which they attached a high religious importance, was the Druid's egg, of which so many wonderful traditions have been recorded. This egg, the people were taught to believe, had been formed by a great number of serpents interwoven and twined together; and as soon as formed, was raised aloft into the air by the hissing of these serpents, when it had to be caught in a clean white cloth before it fell to the ground. He who caught it was obliged instantly to mount a swift horse, and ride off at full speed, to escape the angry serpents that could only be stopped in their pursuit by a river.[1] To ascertain that the egg had been thus secured so as to warrant its efficacy, it was then encased in gold, and if it was genuine it would swim against the stream. Pliny, who had seen this egg, describes it as being about the bigness of a moderate apple, having a cartilaginous shell full of little cavities. This amulet, on having passed its ordeal, was worn round the Druid's neck as his chief distinctive badge and ornament, and the virtues attributed to it were commensu-

---

[1] The whole process is thus poetically described in Mason's *Caractacus*:—

"Tell me yet,
From the grot of charms and spells,
Where our matron sister dwells,
Brennus, has thy holy hand
Safely brought the Druid wand;
And the potent adder-stone,
Gendered 'fore the autumnal moon,
When in undulating twine,
The foaming snakes prolific join;
When they hiss, and when they bear
Their wondrous egg aloof in air;
Thence, before to earth it fall,
The Druid in his hallow'd pall
Receives the prize,
And instant flies,
Follow'd by the envenom'd brood,
Till he cross the crystal flood?"

rate with its wonderful origin: among other benefits it made him who wore it superior to his adversaries in all disputes and controversies, and attracted to him the favour of the rich and influential. If to these particulars we add a wand, which he usually carried, and to which perhaps a due amount of wonder-working power was attributed, we have a Druid in full costume, whether he stood upon the high altar stone surrounded by the silent multitude, or glided along with phantom-like step among the distant trees of the forest, while the people reverently avoided his path or knelt and worshipped as he passed by.

But a still more important ceremonial, in which not only the Druids but the people at large were personally interested, was the cutting of the mistletoe from their sacred tree the oak. To this parasitical plant such extraordinary virtues were attributed that it was believed to be an especial gift of heaven; and as it was so scarce that it could not easily be found, while the want of it would have foreboded great national calamity, the search for it was a matter of vital importance and anxiety. When the mistletoe was found growing on an oak-tree a procession of priests and people, with the Arch-Druid at their head, went in procession upon an appointed day to cut it, which was done with great solemnity. On assembling round the tree two white bulls were fastened to it by the horns; then a Druid clothed in white mounted the tree, and with a long knife or pruning-hook of gold severed the branch, which was received below in a white mantle or sagum; and after this the whole company united in a festival of sacrifice, feasting, and merry-making. This festival, we are told, was kept as near the 10th of March, which was their New-year's Day, as the age of the moon permitted. Besides this important occasion, other annual festivals were held by the Druids, among which was May-day, in honour of the sun (Bel or Baal), from which practice the Scots derived their Beltane; Midsummer-day, on which the favourable influences of heaven were invoked for their fields; and the first of November, in which thanks were returned for the fruits of the harvest, and the yearly contributions of the people were paid to the Druids.

From the roofless character of their temples it has been supposed that the Druids, like the ancient Germans of the days of Tacitus, thought it unlawful to worship the gods under any other covering than that of their own bright heaven. Their temples were therefore those circles of huge stones, the remains of which still astonish our scientific men on account of the skill and labour that must have been employed both in transporting and setting up such masses. But besides these they had as places for worship their sacred groves, of which the oak was the principal tree; for according to Pliny they held it in such esteem that they believed everything that grew upon it came from heaven, and never performed a religious rite without a garland of its leaves on their heads. These groves were also watered by a consecrated fountain, and surrounded by a ditch or mound to prohibit the entrance of the profane. No worshipper also was permitted to enter them unless he carried with him a chain, in token of his complete dependence on the deity. Such gloomy, mysterious, guarded recesses were well fitted to awe the susceptible imaginative Celtic spirit, and deepen its veneration for the priesthood who presided over it. In the centre of this religious twilight rose the massive Druidical temple for which such an approach was so well fitted. It would have been well, indeed, if no worse rites than mistletoe and midsummer festivals had animated these cheerless recesses; but what shall we say of the human sacrifices by which they were lighted with such fearful conflagrations, and filled with dying groans?[1] And yet the fate of these victims was scarcely to be deplored by those unhappy excommunicated ones upon whom the terrible Druidical ban had been laid—the men who could not even approach the outside of these jealous groves without danger—who were taught to believe that heaven was in the same manner closed against them, while earth had no longer a welcome or a place for them. Perhaps not even the papal excommunication itself, when it was most dreaded and obeyed, could transcend in its fearful consequences the anathema of the Druids upon the forlorn wretch, who had thenceforth neither home, nor country, nor kindred—whose presence was an infliction and whose touch was pollution—whom all might insult without retaliation, and any one slay with impunity. With regard to human sacrifice, it could scarcely fail to be of frequent occurrence, not only from the fierce revengeful spirit of the Celtic character, but its superstitious craving for the knowledge of future events, both of which the institution

---

[1] In the third book of Lucan's *Pharsalia* a Druidical grove is thus described:—

"Lucus erat longo nunquam violatus ab ævo," &c.
—*Pharsal.* lib. iii. v. 399.

"Not far away, for ages past had stood
An old unviolated sacred wood,
Whose gloomy boughs thick interwoven made
A chilly cheerless everlasting shade:
There, nor the rustic gods, nor satyrs sport,
Nor fawns, and sylvans with the nymphs resort;
But barbarous priests some dreadful power adore,
And lustrate every tree with human gore."
—Rowe's *Lucan*.

was well fitted to gratify; and accordingly we find that, in addition to those wholesale sacrifices of human victims which Cæsar has mentioned, the Druids, according to Diodorus Siculus, practised divination by the same rite. When they wished to know the result of any important pending event they slew their victim by the stroke of a sword across the diaphragm, and took the omen from the manner of his falling, the quivering of his members, and the mode in which the blood gushed out. It is probable that investigations of this kind were by no means unfrequent among such a people as the Caledonians, and that they were continued long after the imperial edicts had checked them in South Britain and the capture of Anglesey had effected their downfall.

When we inquire into the nature and principles of the creed over which this singular priesthood presided, we are here compelled to confess our ignorance. They did not intrust their doctrines to writing; they did not symbolize them in images or indicate them in the carved work of their temples, like the other nations of antiquity; and thus when the Druids themselves became extinct, no record remained of the principles of that creed which had once been so widely diffused and so powerful in its agency. Here, also, the Roman writers to whom we turn for instruction are so vague, and withal so contradictory, that we are equally at a loss to ascertain what the Druids believed and whom they worshipped. We are told that they adored the Supreme Being under the title of Esus or Hesus, and hence it has been supposed that their creed was a simple theism; but on the other hand we learn from Cæsar and other writers that they worshipped a plurality of gods, whose names and attributes they have also specified. It is easy to solve this apparent contradiction by supposing that, like the priests and even the sages of antiquity, the Druids had two sets of doctrines—the one exoteric and suited to the popular taste, and the other esoteric or abstract and secret, which they reserved for the initiated. In this way they may have inculcated the refined principles of theism to their favoured pupils amidst the retirement of their groves, and preached polytheism to the community at large. We know, however, the general fate of such a compromise, and how quickly the former system is swallowed up and lost in the latter; so that even the Druids themselves may at last have abandoned the exclusive worship of Hesus for that of gods, oaks, and mistletoes. Our perplexity is deepened at this part of the inquiry by the names which these Roman writers give to the gods of the popular Druidical worship; and at the head of them Cæsar places the Greek god Mercury, after whom came Apollo, Mars, Jupiter, and Minerva. But how, it might be asked, did the Britons learn such names, or when did the Druids become converts to the Greek mythology? We know, however, how careless the Romans were about the nomenclature of every mythology, and how readily they gave the names of their own deities to the analogous gods of other countries; with them a god of battles would be no other than Mars, and of the sun no other than Apollo. In this way the deities of the Britons—Hesus, Teutates, Taranis, and Bel or Bal—received Greek names according to their attributes, irrespective of the Druidical nomenclature.

While we are informed of the contemplative character of the Druids and their diligence in the study of physical sciences, the particular kind as well as the extent of their acquirements has also given rise to much controversy and conjecture. Of their skill in mechanics and geometry there can be no question, as long as Stonehenge and Avebury remain. In astronomy also, to which they were greatly addicted, they must have made considerable proficiency according to the standard of the times, when they were able not only to mark the duration of the different seasons, but to fix with some degree of exactness the return of the days of their annual religious festivals, which were attended by persons not only from remote districts but even foreign countries, who were to assemble at one and the same day upon a particular spot. But whether they were as well acquainted with the motions of the stars and planets as those of the sun and moon — although these also, we are told, were the objects of their most careful observation — may reasonably be doubted. A strange attempt has been made indeed to prove that the Druids knew and used the powers of the telescope; but for this there is no better authority than a vague sentence of Diodorus Siculus, in which he tells us of the Hyperborean island: "They say, moreover, that the moon is seen from that island as if she were but at a short distance from the earth, and having hills and mountains like ours on the surface." To the arts of healing, from which a priesthood often derive their chief influence among a rude people, the Druids were not inattentive; and while they studied the natural qualities of herbs and simples in the cure of diseases, they were careful to identify their efficacy with their own divine authority and wonder-working power. We learn from Pliny that their chief specific was the mistletoe, which they believed to be a cure for all diseases, and therefore called it by a name equivalent in their language to "All-heal." It was especially efficient in the relief of epilepsy or falling sickness—a disease from which even the hardiest of savage tribes are by no means exempted. He also specifies their use of a kind of plant called selago, which was a sovereign remedy for all diseases of the eyes; and mentions also other herbs and plants which were of similar application and use. It was not wonderful, indeed, that the Druids, living so much in the woods, should have had their attention turned to the medicinal properties of such objects and have become skilful herbalists. But as the faith of their patients as well as the intrinsic power of their specific were to be enlisted in the process of curing, the life-giving balm had to be sought in a propitious manner and season, and applied with due religious ceremonial. From Pliny's account we also learn that the Druids were skilful pharmacists as well as excellent herb-doctors. This was shown in their potions and decoctions, their fumigations and powders, their salves and ointments, in which forms they often administered the simples whose various qualities in the cure of diseases and restoration of health they must have very carefully studied.

But as the chief influence of the Druids was founded upon their schools, where the children of kings and nobles were their pupils, and through whom they could direct the whole community at pleasure, it was necessary to fit the young aristocracy for their purpose not only by superior knowledge, but by full power to embody and impress it. Hence, in addition to the twenty thousand verses which the young students were required to commit to memory, and which, no doubt, composed a complete encyclopedia of Druidical knowledge, the study of eloquence occupied a chief portion of their time and attention. It is by this great instrument that the savage mind in general and the Celtic in particular is most effectually moved and controlled, and without the possession of this faculty a chief or king would have been deprived of more than half his influence. The future leaders of the Britons were therefore trained to be orators, and no battle could be fought without what Tacitus calls the *incitamenta belli*—the speeches with which they inflamed the courage, increased the hopes, and dispelled the fears of their countrymen, as they flew from rank to rank before the signal of onset was given. Nor was the power of eloquence less needed among the British chiefs to preside over a turbulent council, and control the manifold changes and aberrations of a popular debate. But even in such an education as this, and so superior to that of almost every barbarous, or even semi-civilized state of society, we see that the Druids still retained the means of ascendency in their own hands, and possessed the power of ruling and directing their pupils to the last. This is evident from the fact, that although they possessed the knowledge of writing and used the Greek character, they carefully confined it to themselves. Had they but taught their pupils to read and write, the whole laborious task of education would have been both simplified and abbreviated; but it did not suit them that these pupils in after-life should be able to consult their note-books when judgment or memory was at fault, instead of applying to their preceptors, whose award would be final and decisive.

In short, we recognize in the whole history of the Druids a very able and also a very ambitious priesthood. They kept the key of knowledge wholly in their own hands, and thus retained the obedience of the people to the last. And not content with their priestly influence as the hierarchs of a despotic creed, they were also the legislators, senators, judges, statists, physicians, and schoolmasters of the community: they thus barred up every possible outlet, whether religious, civil, or political, by which the mind could escape, so that not a thought could go forth without finding a Druid in the way. It was a tremendous power whether for good or evil; but unfortunately an imperfect knowledge of the society over which it was exercised prevents us from ascertaining the amount of either, and judging whether the good or the evil predominated. At all events it was well fitted to raise a community from the savage state to a certain degree of civilization; or, finding it in this condition, to prevent its relapse into utter barbarism. It would also be a check at any time upon the despotism of kings whose regal power had no specified limits, or the wild feuds of the people when royal authority was unable to control them. Even at the worst, too, this Druidical power, so unlimited and irresponsible in other respects, must have conceded largely to the popular weal, and what was generally felt to be just and right, otherwise it could not have long maintained its own standing and ascendency. We know at any rate that in South Britain it was the greatest obstacle to Roman ambition, so that the country could not be fully subdued until Druidism itself was broken and destroyed at Anglesey. We also know that when the Druids were proscribed and massacred, or compelled to flee to Ireland, Caledonia, or the neighbouring isles, the theology they had planted was still inwoven among the national habits of the people, and could not be eradicated from their creed even long after Christianity had been planted in its room, so that Canute in the eleventh century was obliged to resume the war against Druidism by enacting a strict law prohibiting all his subjects "from worshipping the gods of the Gentiles; that is to say, the sun, moon, fires, rivers, fountains, hills, or trees, and woods of any kind."

From the existence of the Druidical remains in Scotland we are warranted, notwithstanding the absence of any historical testimony, to adopt this account of the Druidism of Gaul and South Britain as applicable to the Caledonians and Picts. Its practices may have been affected by the greater barbarism and poverty of the north; but still its general principles must have been the same that were taught to the Briton and the Gaul. Even when Druidism was suppressed in the south by the edicts of the Roman emperors and the early introduction of Christianity, we can also conclude that it still continued to flourish with undiminished vigour in Scotland, where Roman laws had no access, and into which no Christian missionary had as yet entered. At what period this last happy event occurred it is difficult to determine. Fordun and Boece, who, like other national historians, are eager to secure this advantage for their country as near the fountain-head of the apostolic age as may be consistent with probability, assert that it occurred A.D. 203. According to their account Donald, whom they represent as king of the whole country, at that period applied to Pope Victor for Roman missionaries to convert and civilize his heathen subjects; upon which the latter sent a band of Christian ministers, by whose pious labours Scotland was converted to the Christian faith. But this account of the early entrance of religious truth has been abandoned for one that makes it to have occurred two centuries later. This was occasioned by the ministry of Ninian, a Briton, but educated as a priest at Rome, who came to Valentia, the country of the southern Picts, as Bede calls them, at the end of the fourth century (A.D. 397), and founded the monastery and church of Whithern (or Whitborn), called otherwise Candida Casa. He died there A.D. 432, after a course of successful apostolic labour, in which he is supposed to have had the Romanized province of Valentia for his diocese, and at a later period he was enrolled in the hagiology of North Britain.

Next to Ninian in the list of the early Christian instructors of Scotland was Palladius. England, having been overrun about the middle of the fifth century with the Pelagian heresy, Celestine at that time Bishop of Rome, sent Palladius, who was distinguished by his great learning as well as piety, to confute and suppress it. This important mission he discharged so effectually that the Britons were recalled from their errors; and on hearing of his fame Eugenius II., son of that Fergus II. who is said to have restored the Scottish nation to the island, entreated Palladius to come and settle among his subjects, who had also been infected with the prevailing Pelagianism. The successful missionary complied with the invitation, in which he was sanctioned by Celestine, who, according to Bede, "sent him to the Scots who believed in Christ as their first bishop." It would appear from this circumstance that Christianity had previously prevailed among the Scoto-Irish, and that at their emigration into Scotland they had brought it with them as an essential part of their national polity. It has been supposed, however, and with some show of probability, that Ireland, at that time called the land of the Scots, rather than the northern portion of our island, was the real diocese assigned to Palladius.

The little kingdom of Cumbria, which is usually considered a part of Pictavia, was the chief scene of the labours of Kentigern, better known in the west of Scotland by the name of St. Mungo, which signifies the "gentle" or the "courteous," bestowed upon him by the affection of his people. His labours, which extended over the latter part of the sixth century, were closed by his death, A.D. 601; and during this time he is alleged to have converted many of the Cumbrians to Christianity, and founded the diocese of Glasgow, the memorable cathedral of which, on being built in after ages, was dedicated to his memory.

In this way the southern Picts received the light of religious truth chiefly from Ireland, which during these dark ages became renowned as an island of saints and missionaries. The histories of Kentigern and Ninian, with the labours they underwent, the dangers they encountered, and the miracles they wrought, have been fully written and distinctly detailed; but these we may well pass over as unsuitable to impartial history. All that can be accurately ascertained is the fact of the existence of the early reformers and the efficiency of their labours among a people whose authentic records have descended to our own day only in the form of a few fragments. From this obscurity, however, we may except Columba, the illustrious apostle of the northern Picts, who may be said not only to have taught Christianity to Scotland at large, but to have impressed upon its polity that peculiar form which was to outlast whole ages of Roman Catholic ascendency, and finally to reappear and triumph when the season of religious reformation had arrived.

Columba was a native of Ireland and a descendant of the kings of Ulster: by this origin, as has been formerly mentioned, he was closely connected with the house of Fergus, and half cousin to Conal, king of the Dalriad Scots of Cantire. He was born about the year 521. Many miraculous incidents are related of his birth and early life by his biographers Adamnan and Cummin; but they are too much tinctured with the superstition of the seventh century to merit repetition. He is supposed not only to have founded several monasteries in Ireland, but also to have travelled in foreign countries before he visited Scotland. To this important mission he addressed himself at the mature age of forty-two, being probably influenced in his choice by the example of one of his preceptors, St. Ciaran, who had become a missionary to the Scots of Cantire. Columba, however, directed his attention in the first instance not to his countrymen of Scotland, but the northern Picts, among whom Druidism was still the prevalent religion. Accordingly he embarked, A.D. 563, accompanied by twelve faithful followers in a light boat made of wicker work covered with skin, and furnished with a single sail, and reached in safety the island of Hy, or more classically termed afterwards Iona, a convenient spot for his purpose, as it not only preserved his communication with Ireland, but was situated on the borders of the Pictish and Scottish kingdoms.

Having made his perilous voyage in safety, it was on land that the greatest dangers of Columba were to commence, and these were as many and alarming as those which a modern missionary might be expected to encounter among the most remote tribes of India or Africa. The king shut his doors against his entrance; the common people repeatedly made attempts on his life; the wild beasts with which the country abounded endangered his journeys, while the Druids, who must already have taken the alarm at the progress of Christianity, exerted all their influence to defeat or injure him. But the intrepid self-denying preacher persevered in his purpose, and was finally victorious. For this, indeed, he was eminently fitted; for, besides his illustrious descent, we are told that he had a cheerful pleasant countenance and winning address, with a voice so powerful that when raised it was like peals of thunder, and could be heard in its distinct articulations at the distance of a mile, when he was employed in singing psalms. To these natural advantages he also added such skill in healing diseases, that his cures were often thought to be miraculous. All these endowments soon produced their natural effect: the kings of Pictland and Scotland became his warmest friends and supporters; the people followed the example of their sovereigns; and at length Columba was recognized both by Scot and Pict as a sacred teacher, whose instructions were to be cordially received and followed.[1] His public influence, indeed, was well attested not only by the numerous conversions with which his preaching was accompanied, but the readiness with which the kings and chiefs repaired to him for counsel, and the efficacy of his mediations in composing the sanguinary feuds of the little kingdoms into which the country was parcelled. The brotherly intercourse which he maintained with his distinguished contemporaries is also indicated by the touching account of a visit which he paid to St. Kentigern, when he left Iona for that purpose. They met in procession near the monastery of the latter at Glasgow, each accompanied by monks, who alternately sang verses of psalms and hallelujahs; and at their parting, after much religious intercourse and amicable discussion, the two missionaries exchanged staves in token of their mutual affection and esteem.

The island of Iona, at which Columba first landed, was bestowed upon him as the site on which to erect a monastery; but whether the investiture was made by Conal king of Scots, or Bridei king of the Picts, has been a matter of question. This, indeed, was scarcely worthy of being mooted about a little barren island, two miles in length and one in breadth, and which, perhaps, at the time could support no inhabitants. On obtaining possession Columba proceeded to found his monastery; but this, in the first instance, must have been nothing better than a few huts or tabernacles, of which the walls were chiefly constructed of wattles, for the shelter of himself and his twelve companions, and the performance of their devotions. "They neither sought nor loved anything of this world," says Bede of them; and their whole lives and proceedings confirmed the truth of his declaration. Two years were spent in the erection of these humble fabrics, which they built with their own hands. Having thus found a home for them, Columba proceeded to form them into a regular ecclesiastical body, which, under the name of Culdees, was soon to overspread the whole country, and become the representative of the Christian church in Scotland.

This institution partook of the monastic character, but without the stern restriction of celibacy; and in drawing up its rules Columba could be at no loss, as he had founded many such monasteries in Ireland before he became the apostle of Scotland. A scholar himself ac-

---

[1] The peace-loving spirit of Columba was once expressed in the following characteristic manner:—A man had the boldness to request him to bless his dagger. The saint complied in the following words: "May God grant that it may never shed a drop of the blood of either man or beast!"

cording to the learning of the age, he was anxious that his monasteries should be schools of industrial education as well as religious instruction; and as a long education was necessary for his monks before they could be fitted for such an office as that of national teachers, he was careful to select the young, that there might be the promise of time, and vigour, and docility for the work of training. They must learn to read and write, and employ themselves in studying and transcribing the Scriptures—not indeed in the original Greek and Hebrew, which languages were beyond the scholarship of the times, but in the Latin translation, which was the language of religion over the whole of Christendom. In this way every Culdee monastery became a school, of which the parent university was at Iona. But besides being instructors as well as conservators of the learning of the age, the Culdees were also the teachers of every handicraft occupation. This is attested in the works of Cummin and Adamnan, where we find these monks employed in building, carpentry, husbandry, and horticulture. In this way Columba had well-stored granaries out of which he supplied his neighbours with grain to sow their fields, and a Saxon baker in his monastery, who perhaps was the only one in the country. Orchards also appear to have been planted round the earliest monasteries, and apple-trees are mentioned among their other possessions. If to these we add the clerical labours of the Culdee in visiting, preaching, and administering the rites of religion throughout his district, we have a very different picture of monastic labour, intelligence, and usefulness, compared with that which the life of a monk presented in other countries even so early as the beginning of the eighth century.

The purity and simplicity of Christian doctrine, as professed and taught by the Culdees, appears to have been in full harmony with their character, habits, and mode of life. Their Christianity had little connection with that of Rome; and when Roman innovations in doctrine and ceremonial began to increase, these found in the Culdees their most determined opponents. Instead of the Western church, they seem to have rather followed the Eastern, as established by St. John and his disciples; and thus they were obnoxious to those who had begun to receive, as an essential part of Christianity, the untrustworthy traditions of Rome. This is indicated by the Venerable Bede, where, while he speaks of them as schismatics because they followed uncertain rules in the observation of the great festival (Easter), he also declares that "they only practised such works of charity and piety as they could learn from the prophetical, evangelical, and apostolic writings." This strict adherence indeed to the written word, and utter abnegation of all other authority in religion, was the head and front of their offending.

Few questions connected with these early ages have excited more keen debate among modern British writers than that of the kind of ecclesiastical polity which was established among these primitive scriptural Culdees. Had they bishops? or did they at least invest their abbots with episcopal authority? or was their abbot merely a *primus inter pares*, like the moderator of a Presbyterian church court? For more than two centuries has this debate continued between the churches of England and Scotland, and been urged not only with all the ardour of a national, but of a religious controversy; it has been felt indeed both by Presbyterianism and Episcopacy that the distinct testimony of so early a period, and from such a people as the Culdees, was well worth contending for. Into so wide a field of controversy it cannot be expected that history should enter; leaving the arguments to theologians, it can only state the leading facts or briefly announce the result. So far, then, as investigation has gone, it cannot be found that a bishop was recognized among the Culdees, according to the authoritative meaning of the term. Bede, who is the chief authority on this point, expressly informs us that "the island [Iona] is wont to have always for its ruler a presbyter-abbot, to whose authority the whole province, and even the bishops themselves, after an unwonted manner, are bound to be subject, according to the example of its first teacher, who was not a bishop, but a presbyter and monk."[1] In the seventh century also, when King Oswald applied to Iona for a bishop to instruct the heathen people of Northumbria, the abbot and his brethren appointed first one and afterwards another of their number to the important office of the bishopric. What else could this mean, it has been triumphantly asked, than that presbyters themselves ordained bishops, and acted in this case, as in all inferior matters of church rule, upon the principle of Presbyterian parity? To get out of this difficulty it has been assumed on the other side that a bishop was kept at Iona expressly for the purpose of such consecrations; but this is merely an assumption, as no name or trace of any such episcopal resident can be discovered. As freely might an archbishop himself have been assumed for the little island of Iona, with his whole staff of episcopal subordinates, down to the acolyth who held the taper and the ostiary who kept the door.

---

[1] *Bedæ Histor.* lib. iii. c. 4.

The death of Columba occurred on the 9th of June, 597, when he was in the seventy-seventh year of his age. The account of that event forms a mild and beautiful episode which falls like a passing ray of sunshine upon that dark and stormy age. The saint had been premonished that the day of his departure had arrived; but still, diligent to the last, he was intent upon those duties on which the welfare of the brotherhood depended. One of these was to repair to the barn or storehouse of Iona to take account of the provisions laid up for the monastery, and invoke a blessing upon them. As he returned to the monastery he was obliged to rest by the way; and while he sat, an old white horse that used to carry the milk-vessels from the fold to the building reclined its head upon the good man's breast, and, as if sensible of his approaching death, it uttered piteous groans, and even began to shed tears. One of the monks attempted to lead the animal away, when he was checked by his master, who said, "Let him alone, for he loves me. To thee God has given reason; but, behold, that they might not be despised, he has also planted affection in brutes, and in this case also even something like a foreknowledge of my departure." Then turning to the animal he said, "Now go away, my faithful, affectionate friend, and may you be kindly cared for by Him who made you!" On returning to his closet he resumed the pen, which was seldom out of his hand during his intervals of leisure, and employed himself in transcribing the psalter, until he came to that passage in the thirty-fourth Psalm, "They that seek the Lord shall not want any good thing." "Here," he said, "I have come to the end of a page, where it will be proper for me to stop; for the verse that follows, 'Come, ye children, hearken unto me; I will teach you the fear of the Lord,' will better suit my successor than me: I will therefore leave it to Baithen to transcribe it." He went to the evening service, and at his return delivered his parting charge to the brethren, and lay down to die; but afterwards, on hearing the bell ringing for the midnight vigil, he hastily dressed himself and hurried to the church, where he was the first who arrived. But it was the last effort of nature, the final gleam of the lamp that had burned so brightly, for on the arrival of the monks they found Columba lying dead before the altar in the attitude of prayer.

During the thirty-four years of this eminent reformer's life in Scotland his labours had extended not only over northern Pictland and the territory of the Scots, but over the Western Islands; and although it would be difficult to settle the number of churches and monasteries which he founded, yet the numerous names of places in Scotland with which his own or that of his followers is identified, show how widely and with what popular favour the principles of the Culdees had been extended. After his death Columba was considered not only as the patron saint of Scotland, but of Ireland also, in which last country he shared the distinction with St. Patrick and St. Bridget; and both countries were so eager for the possession of his relics, that while the Pictish Chronicle alleges his remains to have been transported by Kenneth Macalpin to a church which he built for the purpose, the Irish writers declare that they were carried to Down in Ireland, and deposited in the same grave with those of St. Bridget and St. Patrick.[1]

In the meantime the monastery of Iona or Icolmkill continued to enjoy a prominence over the similar institutions both of Scotland and Ireland, which made it be regarded as their metropolitan head; and its abbot as primate enjoyed the privilege of exercising his jurisdiction over all the other bishops.[2] So high also was its reputation for sanctity that kings and princes, both Pictish and Scottish, both Saxon and Norwegian, coveted a last home in its cemetery, as if there, above all other places, the wicked would cease from troubling and the weary be at rest. But living kings as well as dead were fain to seek the shelter of Iona, and a case of this nature gave the opportunity of extending its principles over a large portion of England. Oswald, prince of Northumberland, having been compelled in early youth to fly from the pursuit of Edwin, betook himself to Iona, where he was instructed in the Christian faith, and trained in the learning for which the island had now become illustrious. The course of revolution in 634 summoned Oswald from his cell to ascend the throne of Northumberland. Anxious for the conversion of his heathen subjects, he looked out for Christian teachers; but in this case, instead of applying to the clergy of the neighbouring kingdoms of the Heptarchy, who followed the Latin rule of faith and doctrine, he addressed himself, as was natural, to his old friends and instructors, the monks of Iona. They gladly responded to his call by sending to him Corman, the most learned and accomplished of their brethren, whom they

---

[1] In confirmation of this last statement Giraldus Cambrensis quotes the following old leonine couplet:—
Hi tres in Duno, tumulo tumulantur in uno,
Brigida, Patricius, atque Columba pius.

[2] "Pictorum et Scotorum Primas"—"Omnium Hiberniensium Episcoporum Primas," are among the titles bestowed by several ancient writers upon St. Columba, while the authority implied by these titles was enjoyed by his successors until it was thought that abbots were unfit to confer the episcopal office.

appointed bishops for the purpose; but Corman was speedily disgusted with the barbarism of the Northumbrians, and abandoned his charge in despair. On returning home he was describing the hopeless nature of such a mission to the assembled monks, when he was checked by a voice of Christian reproof: "Brother, you should have remembered the apostolic injunction to feed them with milk; afterwards they would have become fitted for stronger food." The speaker was Aidan, one of their number, and judging him well qualified for the task they sent him to succeed the fastidious and disappointed Corman. Their choice was a happy one; but still an almost insuperable difficulty remained: Aidan was ignorant of the Anglo-Saxon tongue, and was therefore unintelligible to the people. But in a singular manner this obstacle was surmounted, for Oswald accompanied him in his missionary journeys, and while the monk preached in the Celtic language, the king translated his sentences into Saxon. The good work so earnestly prosecuted could scarcely fail to be successful, and the result was the conversion of the kingdom of Northumberland to the Christian faith.

On his arrival in England Aidan selected for the seat of his bishopric the bleak island of Lindisfarne, being probably influenced in the choice by its resemblance to the parent seat of Iona. This soon became a diocese of large extent, for it not only comprised Northumberland, but extended over the greater part of Roxburgh and Lothian. To this episcopate also the monasteries of Melrose, Coldingham, Tyningham, and Abercorn are supposed to have owed their origin. It would be difficult indeed to define how far the kingdom of Northumberland extended into the Lowlands of Scotland, and thus to ascertain the bounds of this Culdee bishopric of Lindisfarne, as established by Oswald and presided over by Aidan. The troubles that ensued after it had maintained its supremacy for thirty years, the controversies that were waged against it on the questions of the proper period of observing Easter and the right form of shaving the head into what was deemed the orthodox clerical tonsure, and the manner in which Culdee simplicity was finally overthrown in England under the ascendency of Latin refinements and innovations, belong more properly to English ecclesiastical history. It is enough to state, that eighty years after the mission of Aidan the Northumbrians had fully recognized the authority of the Roman Church by adopting its period for the celebration of the Easter festival.

CHAPTER V.

HISTORY OF SOCIETY.

Causes of our limited knowledge of the Caledonians—Form of government among the Caledonians—Their military character—Their weapons—Their war-chariots—Their costume—Their skin-painting—Their personal ornaments—Buildings of the Caledonians—Druidical temples—Burial-places and modes of burial—Caledonian strongholds—Hill-forts—Houses of the Caledonians—Their domestic life—Their strange marriage institutions—Food of the Caledonians—Handicraft occupations of the Caledonians—Their boat-building—Our ignorance of the progress of Caledonian civilization.

While the accounts which the Roman historians have left us of the ancient Britons in the southern part of the island are so brief, those which they have given of the inhabitants of the north, or the Caledonians, are still more scanty. A few sentences indeed, and those of a very vague character, are all that they have condescended to bestow upon the unconquered Caledonians. But for this omission some apology may be found. The Romans were more intent upon conquering a people than investigating their previous history. Their conquests were so numerous that an historical account of the different countries they subdued would have been a history of the world at large rather than of two or three kingdoms. Hence the latest of their victorious acquisitions—that of South Britain—has been dismissed in so summary a manner. They have devoted merely a few pages to the people whom they reduced the last of all to the common standard of Roman provincialism. It was not therefore to be expected that their narrative would have afforded any particular space to the Caledonians, whom they despised, with whom their warfare had been confined to a few hasty inroads, and who only remained unconquered because Rome herself was on the eve of being conquered in her turn. In such poverty of intelligence our only remedy in attempting to describe the primitive inhabitants of Scotland is to amplify these scanty notices by analogies derived from the condition of the Britons of the south, and by referring to the relics of these early ages which have survived to our own day.

The form of government which prevailed among the Caledonians as among the South Britons attested their common Celtic origin. It was the ancient patriarchal system of the East rather than the elective form of the North, and to this the Celts have pertinaciously clung whatever might be the country to which they migrated. The father of the family, invested with unlimited discretionary power over his own household, imparted this authority to his eldest son when the family had swelled into a tribe; and as each tribe had thus its own distinctive ruler, a country of very limited dimensions might have as many different independent sovereigns as there were family names. In this way we can understand how so many kings were banded against Julius Cæsar at his invasion of the south, and against Agricola at his entrance into the northern part of the island. To their disunion Tacitus chiefly attributes the easy conquest of the south by the Romans. "A confederation of two or more states," he says, "to repel the common danger is seldom known: they fight in parties, and the nation is subdued." Such was the case in his own day; but at an earlier period he acknowledges it was different: "the Britons," he says, "were *formerly* governed by a race of kings." This no doubt referred to their practice of assigning a certain pre-eminence or leadership to the chief who had the greatest number of followers or amount of warlike reputation, and to whom their obedience was chiefly ensured by the presence of some danger that threatened all the other kings alike; as in the case of Cassivellaunus, who was their leader against Cæsar's formidable legions. At a later period also than that of Tacitus, when the Britons were in a great measure abandoned by their conquerors and left to their own resources, they naturally resumed this early form of government by electing a chief of chiefs, who, under the name of Pendragon, was usually recognized as their paramount king, until a stronger than he arose and displaced him. All this we can also dimly trace in the form of government that prevailed among the Caledonians. When Agricola invaded them, Tacitus tells us that "among their many chiefs (*duces*), one called Galgacus excelled the rest in ancestry and courage." He was not therefore king of Caledonia, but merely a chief of superior character and influence, who probably on that account was elected Pendragon either at an earlier period or when the invasion of their country had been commenced. In this way, also, the seven or eight states of England under the Heptarchy were afterwards ruled by a Bretwalda, who figures as King of England in our histories, although he was but the real sovereign of a seventh part of the kingdom. An office so established must have been of uncertain tenure, and the mark of many candidates; and while in some cases it may have been hereditary in a single family, in others it may have depended upon an election, or even a usurpation. This perhaps will explain the diversity apparent in the rule of succession among the Scots and Picts. With the former, whatever might be the contentions of rival branches, the sceptre was always retained in the line of Fergus; but among the Picts, who seem to have had no such predominant family among their tribes, or no such hereditary claims of gratitude to bind them to a single family, an absolutely fixed line is not perceptible. Perhaps the chief of the chiefs, who for the time being held the principal rule, and was dignified with the royal title, was elected from among the nobles themselves, either for that the rest could not oppose his ambition, or because some enemy was at their gates.

Such appears to have been the nature of the government by which the Caledonians were led in war and ruled in peace. It was as a warlike people, however, and in the hour of battle, that they were best known to the Romans; and here, therefore, our knowledge of them assumes a more definite aspect. In the record of Tacitus we have a favourable account of their military enterprise, courage, and skill. Instead of waiting to be attacked, they emerged from their forests, carried the Roman forts and castles of Agricola by storm, and so dismayed his officers by their boldness that they counselled a retreat. The night surprise of the ninth legion by the Caledonians, in which they would have been successful had not Agricola been warned of their motions and come to its relief, was as wisely and skilfully planned as it was daringly executed. The manner in which their army was drawn up on the slope of the Grampians exhibited great natural sagacity in strategy, while the energy and perseverance with which they contested the battle to the last, and only yielded when resistance would have been useless, was creditable to their valour and love of liberty. The manner also in which they gave way before the irresistible inundation of the hosts of Severus, only to reunite and return when the tide had rolled back, reminds us of similar movements during the brightest periods of the wars of Scottish independence against England, and which more than once saved the liberty of the country from ruin. All these events indicate strong arms, fearless hearts, and an amount of knowledge and reflectiveness seldom exhibited by untaught barbarians. In what military school, or by what training, had they so learned the art of war? Feuds among themselves, or occasional forays into the south, could scarcely have imparted to the Caledonian chieftains such sagacity and scientific judgment in warlike leadership; and to account for it, we are compelled to bethink ourselves of the Druids, and the course of education in which they trained the young aristocracy.

This allusion to the military spirit of the Caledonians naturally leads to an inquiry about the weapons with which they fought. Of defensive armour they had almost none. Their chief article of this kind was the shield, either small and round, or of an oblong shape, and with this every combatant seems to have been armed, and a helmet, which, however, was a distinction usually confined to their chiefs. Herodian declares that the Caledonians considered helmets and coats of mail as incumbrances; but perhaps a stronger reason for their scanty armouries may be found in their inability either to forge or purchase defensive armour. Of offensive weapons, however, they had good store, and of the simple kind that are common to most barbarous nations. First of these was the sword, which, however, was constructed more for the application of strength than skill, being a long heavy iron weapon with an edge, but no point, and only suitable for a downright blow. Such, indeed, was the *glaymore*, or two-handed sword, with which the Islesmen and Highlanders in after ages dealt such perilous strokes upon the crests and steel corslets of the Norman and Lowland chivalry. Swords, however, of a lighter description, leaf-shaped, and made of bronze, have been dug up from the ancient Scottish tumuli, indicating that these were also used by the Caledonians.[1] A still earlier and ruder weapon was the stone celt, also found among the relics of the barrows, which seems to have been used like a battle-axe, by having a wooden handle inserted into a hole made for the purpose, or one made of pliant oziers twisted round it. Besides these stone celts, hatchets of bronze have been found in the same receptacles. But some of these weapons may have fallen into disuse before the historical period. Another weapon of the Caledonians was the lance or spear, which was of considerable length, and furnished at the blunt extremity with a hollow ball of brass, which was used as a rattle to frighten the horses of the enemy. If the account of Gildas is to be literally received they also must have used spears that had a hook at the extremity for pulling down an antagonist; and in this way they seem to have cleared the Roman wall of its defenders, when they stormed it. But, besides the sword and spear, the Caledonians used daggers or dirks, of which several still continue to be dug up. The use of the bow was common among them, as we learn from Tacitus in his account of the battle of the Grampians. With these weapons the Caledonians made a gallant stand, and an equal fight of hours against the steady discipline and well-forged panoply of the legionaries; and if anything could have equalized such a fearful disparity it must have been the great stature and strength of these barbarians compared with the Romans. From the bones that have been dug up, it is evident that six feet and upwards was no unusual height among the Caledonians. A skeleton that measured seven feet, the remains of one who probably had fallen in battle against the soldiers of Agricola, was exhumed at what has been reckoned the site of the engagement on Ardoch Moor.

Besides their foot-soldiers, the Caledonians made use of cavalry, but still more of chariots, for the purposes of warfare. This arm was common to all the inhabitants of Britain, and was one of the chief tokens which they presented of their Asiatic derivation as a Celtic people. These chariots, called *essedæ* and *covvini* by the Roman writers, are frequently mentioned in their accounts of the wars in our island, while the cars themselves were sometimes exhibited upon the Roman race-course or arena. The Roman soldiers, who, in the days of Cæsar, had forgot this disused instrument of eastern warfare, were astonished to encounter it in so remote a country as Britain; and the first attacks of these chariots, the confusion they produced, and the havoc they occasioned, were perhaps one of the chief causes of the indecisive result of his first British campaign. In the south also these chariots must have constituted a large portion of their armies, as Cassivellaunus, after dismissing his forces, and betaking himself to a flying warfare of skirmishes and surprises, could still retain four thousand of these with their drivers and fighting men. Tacitus mentions the Caledonian army as being provided with the same means of annoyance, the chariots being drawn up by Galgacus upon the level ground between the two armies. It is evident, however, from the nature of their country, so much intersected by forests, mountains, and morasses, that the Britons of the north could not be so well supplied with these armed chariots as their kinsmen of the

---

[1] See introductory chapter, where figures of such swords are given.

south, who had better scope for their free and effectual action, and therefore their appearance at Ardoch Moor was probably more for show than real service. It was after they were swept off the field that the real tug of war commenced, and we hear no more of the chariots. The fact, however, of the Caledonians being able to construct vehicles that could be used in such a mountainous country, seems to indicate the possession of better tools and more skilful workmanship, and consequently of a higher degree of civilization, than the Roman historians were willing to accord to them. We also learn from Tacitus that the chief guided the reins and drove the horses, while the squire occupied the car. How long the Caledonians may have used it in their own international warfare after it had been laid aside in the south, we are unable to conjecture; but that it was used among the Picts as an article of luxury and for the purposes of comfortable travelling during the sixth century, is evident from Adamnan's *Life of Saint Columba*.

In passing from the warlike weapons to the every-day costume of the Caledonians we are startled by the Roman accounts, which are our only authority on the subject. Dio tells us that they went naked, and wore no shoes; but Herodian is more explicit, and gives us a full-length portrait: "These barbarians," he says, "are strangers to the use of clothes; but they adorn their bellies and necks with iron trappings, having a belief that iron is ornamental, and a sign of wealth, in the same manner that gold is esteemed by other nations. They mark their bodies with a variety of figures resembling many different animals. For this reason they are careful not to cover their bodies for fear of concealing these figures." Here we are brought to an awkward pause. Were these Caledonians, who could construct a war-chariot and all its trappings, unable to fabricate the most simple personal covering? Or were they so impatient of the burden and restraint of clothing, that they agreed to dispense with it? Either way the dilemma is a serious one. The truth, however, as often happens in such cases, may lie midway. We can imagine, for instance, that in summer, or before strangers, the Caledonian may have thrown aside his mantle, and this chiefly for the purpose of soliciting admiration towards the gay picturing upon his tattooed skin. Such is vanity even among the rudest, and we cannot imagine that he would undergo such a painful and laborious process without giving it the benefit of a full display. In war, also, the same impatient independent spirit that made him indifferent to defensive armour, might induce him to throw aside his cloak; and thus the astonished Romans, who saw themselves confronted by an army of naked giants, established the report that these northern tribes were utterly without clothing. As the visits of the invaders were only summer campaigns, and as they only saw the Caledonians when drawn up for conflict, their conclusion though a hasty was a natural one. On this principle, perhaps, we can get rid of the stigma that deprives our barbarian ancestors of even a single fig-leaf. But when the cold frosts and blasts of a Scottish winter succeeded, the aspect of affairs must have been completely altered. No merely mortal undefended skin could have weathered out such a season; and accordingly the Caledonians must have betaken themselves to those defences, however coarse or simple, by which the natural warmth might be retained, and the freezing blast excluded, otherwise the whole nation must have perished in the course of a single winter. As for the clothing, in such a case, it may have been of the most primitive description, and requiring little art or industry to prepare it; but we know that as long as sheep have wool, or deer and oxen hides, the rudest savage can find a mantle. In this way the wardrobe of the Caledonian must have been supplied in spite of the declarations of Dio and Herodian. It was natural also that the upper classes should have worn skins of better appearance and more elaborate workmanship than the common people, and that the latter must have improved their apparel from the example of the former, as well as from the general progress of society. But this course of improvement in costume must have been slow compared with that of their brethren of the south, who had the Romans to instruct them, and who paid dearly for the use of the *sagum*. Accordingly we find that even so late as the sixth century the Scots and Picts, when they stormed the Roman wall, were so scantily attired as to excite the wrathful contempt of Gildas, who says of them, "All were more eager to shroud their villanous faces in bushy hair than to cover with decent clothing those parts of their body which required it." Yet we are warranted in concluding that even already the common people habitually wore leathern coats or jerkins, from a passage in the *Life of Columba*.

In the personal ornaments of the Caledonians Herodian mentions the iron trappings (probably of chain-work) which they wore round their waists and necks. It is fortunate, however, that their places of sepulture have exhibited better articles of adornment, indicating a higher state of civilization than the Roman has vouchsafed to assign them. These are formed of bone or horn in the shape of rude pins and necklaces, of jet, cannel coal, and ivory, and of glass and pebble. Fibulæ of bronze have been discovered—a sure proof that to such fastenings a mantle must have been attached. Amber also was used in the fabrication of necklaces. But besides these types of a better state than mere naked barbarism, rings, bracelets, and torques of gold and silver have been found in various stages of artistic ingenuity, some of them evincing a very considerable degree of taste and skilful workmanship. So numerous, indeed, are these relics of ancient Caledonia, and so varying in material and fabrication, that an attempt has been made to educe from them the progress that civilization must have made among the people during the Primitive, Roman, and Pictish periods of our history. At all events, we are able to recognize in these disinterred specimens—attested as their antiquity is by the places of their deposition—a love of ornament and an ability to gratify it superior to that which the Roman historians have recorded. Numerous illustrations of these ornamental articles are given in works treating of Scottish antiquities.

It is generally in their public buildings that the character, talents, and resources of a departed people are most distinctly and permanently inscribed; and to these, therefore, we gladly turn our attention. As might be expected in a country where the priesthood were so influential, the chief relics of this kind left to us by the Caledonians are supposed to be Druidical and connected with the services of religion. Of these some account has already been given. It is worthy of notice that these vast but rude erections exhibit no token of a building or graving tool, and must have had their origin in a very rude and primitive state of society. But how, in spite of these impediments, the stones were torn from their native beds, transported for miles across marsh and mountain, and borne up the hill, on the top of which they are sometimes planted, has greatly perplexed the philosophical inquirer. It seems an unaccountable combination of utter destitution and helplessness with an amount of power, science, and skill which the most refined and intellectual states of society cannot always furnish.[1]

More important still were the barrows of the primitive inhabitants of Scotland, to our previous descriptions of which we also refer the reader. The contents of the coffins, kistvaens, and urns discovered in these places of interment, show that the Caledonians sometimes deposited the body entire, and at other times the ashes only, after having consumed the corpse upon a funeral pile. The practice of cremation, however, at whatever time it may have been prevalent in Scotland, must have disappeared there, as elsewhere, with the general diffusion of Christianity, under which society has always preferred that the human body should return as dust to dust by the slow and simple process of nature. When the body was interred without being subjected to the process of cremation, it was sometimes laid at full length, but more frequently in a sitting posture, with the knees drawn up to the breast. The Caledonians, in common with most rude tribes, were profuse in their burial observances, and appear to have buried with their dead the articles they valued most while living—such as the horse and arms of the warrior, the dog of the hunter, the rich ornaments of the man of rank, and the trinkets and industrial utensils of women. From the common practice of the earliest antiquity the history of a nation that has been buried for thousands of years may be read more fully and accurately in the recesses of its tombs than in its written record; and from these data of the grave we learn to doubt the stinted measure that has been assigned by Roman pride to Caledonian civilization.[2]

From the early sepulchres of Scotland we pass to its strongholds; and here we find full indications not only of a warlike, restless spirit, but of considerable skill and industry both in the offensive and defensive appliances of war. Of these strongholds the most remarkable are the *hill-forts*, with the traces of which the country abounds. These were often of a somewhat elaborate and artificial construction, and exhibit a remarkable amount of skill in castrametation and military architecture among a people otherwise considered so barbarous. (See introductory chapter.) They are to be found over the whole range of Scotland. But they are especially abundant along the southern declivities of the Kilsyth and Campsie hills, where the greatest danger was to be apprehended; and from these strong inclosures the gallant Caledonians could keep watch upon the Roman wall, or make a sally upon some exposed portion of the garrison. Such a fort as the White Caterthun, manned by such defenders, must have been a desperate task in besieging even for the resistless legions. Its rampart of large loose stones, upwards of 100 feet thick at the base and 25 at the top, formed a barricade that would have altogether set at defiance the ancient battering-ram; and such a fort must have been taken by storm, the assailants clambering up its sloping

---

[1] As might be expected, the *Statistical Account of Scotland* abounds with descriptions of these architectural remains of the Druidical period.

[2] Hoare's *Ancient Wiltshire*, Chalmers' *Caledonia*, Gough's *Sepulchral Remains of Britain*, Wilson's *Prehistoric Annals*.

sides. "The vast labour it must have cost," observes General Roy, "to amass so incredible a quantity of stones, and carry them to such a height, surpasses all description."

It is unfortunate that to these temples, tombs, and fortresses we cannot add a description of the houses which the Caledonians inhabited. But while the first of these places are the homes of man's undying hopes and fears, or unextinguishable hatreds, his house is but the dwelling of a day, and this especially when law is unknown or little cared for. The Caledonian, therefore, who had aided in erecting whole mountains of granite, would scarcely bestow a single stone upon the edifice in which he was merely to eat or sleep, and which he was obliged to fire with his own hand at the coming of an enemy. In the absence of other sources of intelligence respecting the houses of the Caledonians, we are left to conjecture that, like the natives of South Britain in the days of Cæsar, they inhabited dwellings similar to those of their ancestors the Gauls. In this case a Caledonian dwelling would be nothing better than a hut of timber covered with straw, or of upright poles interwoven with wattled work in the form of a cone, terminating at the top either in a rounded semicircular roof or sharp point. Such were commonly the houses of the Gauls; and such, even at the best, were probably the dwellings of the Caledonians. But as homes like these were little fitted to withstand the inclemency of a northern winter, it has also been conjectured with some probability that they converted the natural caves with which the country abounds into permanent dwelling-places; and the idea has been confirmed by the remains of hand-querns for grinding meal which have been found in such places. Similar tokens also indicate, that, like the savages of other inclement regions, the Caledonians frequently dwelt in pit-houses, which were slight excavations in the ground, roofed over with the boughs of trees or sods of turf. The traces of some of these, constructed in a more permanent fashion, are still to be found in various parts of Scotland, composed of large flat stones laid together without any cement. In some cases an accumulation of eight or ten feet of moss has gathered over them; and on being laid open to view, they have exhibited a rough uncemented stone floor about six feet in diameter that had been surrounded with a palisade. We can scarcely imagine a combination of such houses into a township; and accordingly, if Cæsar could find nothing like a regular town in South Britain, we need not wonder if no mention is made of any in the north, in the account which Tacitus has left us of the campaigns of Agricola.

Though we cannot describe any of the structures inhabited by the Caledonians as their everyday dwellings, there are certain subterranean retreats met with here and there that seem to have served as places at least of temporary abode and also of concealment. These underground dwellings are either wholly or in part artificial. Of the first description are those subterranean buildings called *weems*, composed of large rough stones without any kind of cement, consisting of two or more apartments, each not above five feet in width and four in height. Their remote origin is fully attested by the fragments of human bones and coarse utensils of iron and stone which have been occasionally found in them. Those other underground retreats, which are only artificial in part, are the natural caves that have been enlarged and made more commodious by the labours of their inmates; and in these obscure haunts many ages afterwards Wallace, Bruce, and the other champions of Scottish independence are said to have concealed themselves when their fortunes were at the lowest. Of these places the principal are the caves of Hawthornden and those of the island of Arran.

As a matter of course the domestic life of a people who were limited to such narrow accommodations could present little worthy of mention. The chief relics of the furniture belonging to these houses are coarse specimens of pottery, clumsily shaped in most cases, and of fragile construction, and the hand-quern, with which every family was probably provided. Other specimens, however, of Caledonian pottery, either of a later period or that belonged to persons of rank, indicate a knowledge of the potter's wheel as well as considerable taste and artistic skill. These superior pieces of workmanship seem, in most cases, to have been devoted to the purposes of sepulture or the rites of religion, instead of common use. Of the other articles of furniture which these cottages must have possessed we are wholly ignorant.

In the history of the members of an ancient British household, nothing has been more perplexing to the philosopher and historian than the account which Cæsar gives of the marriage institutions of the Britons. According to his statement ten or twelve families used to dwell under the same roof, the husbands having the wives in common, while previous relationship, instead of being a check upon such unions, was rather an encouragement, so that brothers joined with brothers, and parents with sons, in those strange matrimonial associations. He adds that the question of paternity in such cases was settled by the affiliation of the child upon the husband to whom the mother had been first married. It has been asserted that Cæsar must have been strangely mistaken; and that he hastily drew this revolting picture from observing whole families dwelling together in one house, and even. it may be, in one apartment. But no such mistake was made about the Germans, who also lived in whole families under a single roof. Besides, the charge does not rest with Cæsar alone, but was repeated by Xiphilinus at a much later period, and when Britain was better known to the world, so that the affair itself had become a standing joke at the profligate court of Rome. This we learn from a conversation which the same writer reports between the empress Julia and the wife of a Caledonian prince. The latter on being taunted about the plurality of husbands which the usages of her country allowed, frankly acknowledged the fact; but she stated in defence of her countrywomen that they acted avowedly and according to established rule, and were faithful to their mates, while the Roman matrons indulged secretly in unlimited license in violation of their national laws. Next comes St. Jerome, who speaks of the practice as still prevailing in the northern parts of Britain; that is to say, so late as the fifth century. The same strange absence of marital exclusiveness, which was common to the Caledonians with their brethren of the south, appears to have extended as far as the Hebrides, if we may believe the testimony of Solinus. "These islands," he says, "being only separated from each other by narrow firths or arms of the sea, constitute one kingdom. The sovereign of this kingdom has nothing which he can properly call his own; but he has the free use of all the possessions of all his subjects. The reason of this regulation is, that he may not be tempted to acts of oppression and injustice by the desire or hope of increasing his possessions, since he knows that he can possess nothing. This prince is not even allowed to have a wife of his own; but he has free access to the wives of all his subjects, that, having no children which he can properly call his own, he may not be prompted to encroach on the privileges of his subjects in order to aggrandize his family." If this instance is not entirely mythic, it shows that, in the institutions of marriage among the early Britons and Caledonians, a toleration had prevailed which was allowed in no other country. We can only hope that, like the polygamy of the East, it was mainly confined to the powerful, and that the common people for the most part were contented with a single and exclusive helpmate. We also know that the practice itself was banished by the entrance of Christianity into the country.

In the every-day life of the ancient Caledonians, the food they used, and the means by which they procured it, are matters of the highest importance. But here our information is so limited that we have little else than conjecture. When Cæsar arrived in South Britain he found the country inhabited by two different races, the Belgæ and the Celts, of whom the formed lived chiefly on the produce of agriculture, and the latter on that of their flocks and hunting. Such was also the case with the Caledonians, the Celts of North Britain, who are described as not sufficiently advanced in intelligence to be an agricultural people. The wild boar, the mountain bull, and venison must therefore have supplied the principal materials of their flesh-feasts, along with their flocks and herds of tame cattle, as was the case in the south, although, perhaps, in more scanty measure, from the greater barrenness of the soil. The existence of harpoons and fish-hooks of coarse manufacture, which have been found among their earliest relics, show that the Caledonians did not wholly abstain from fish as an article of diet, although it may have been only used in cases of necessity. Solinus, indeed, informs us that the inhabitants of the Hebrides lived solely on milk and fish. As famine must have been no unusual circumstance among a people whose means of subsistence were so precarious as those of the Caledonians, they are stated to have adopted, in common with many other savages, an artificial remedy to deaden the gnawings of hunger. It is Xiphilinus who informs us that they used for this purpose a certain composition, of which, when they had eaten about the size of a bean, their spirits were so greatly supported that they no longer felt hunger or thirst.

As the handicraft occupations of the ancient Caledonians were of the simplest and most limited character, such was also the case with their tools, the earliest of which seem to have been nothing better than knives, chisels, and adzes of flint. Such in all countries has been the first step of mechanical art. When metals were introduced into the country their immense superiority to the hardest flint would be at once recognized; and a piece of rusty iron would constitute a man's treasure, because out of it he could fashion a knife, axe, or spear that would make him superior to all his fellows. Hence the bronze axe-heads that are so frequently found buried among the remains of the primitive period of Scotland, but fashioned and even ornamented in a superior style to that of the clumsy stone celt or wedge. Of the same material have also been found certain utensils supposed from their appearance to have been reaping or pruning-hooks. But as iron is so much superior to bronze in ductility and hardness, the former metal must have soon superseded the latter, whether for the forging of warlike weapons or industrial implements. And that this superior metal had obtained the preference among the Caledonians so early as the second century is evident from the remains which have been dug up from the site of the battle of Mons Grampius. It is unfortunate, however, that with all the zeal of antiquarian research, so little should still be known of the instruments used in Caledonian workmanship. A sword or dagger is carefully preserved because its antiquity is at once recognized and its character understood. But a spade, a chisel, or a knife-blade turned up accidentally by the plough, or disinterred by a treasure-seeker, is only a shapeless piece of corroded iron, and as such is thrown aside without further inquiry.

The earliest stages of British ship-building will always be a subject of national interest, and in this case the vessels which the Caledonians used in their rivers and seas are worthy of close attention. But here we are compelled to confess that the Celtic portion of our ancestry were by no means famed for their nautical activity and enterprise. The whole race in general, however daring on land, seem to have avoided the ocean, where skill, patience, and perseverance are still more needed than courage; and in these first-mentioned qualities the Celt of every age and country has been confessedly deficient. An exception to this appeared in the case of the Scoto-Hibernians when they united with the Saxon rovers, and afterwards not only took possession of a part of Scotland, but visited most of the countries of Europe; this, however, was merely a temporary effort which was soon replaced by the national dislike to the sea. As mentioned in the introductory chapter, the earliest vessels of the Caledonians were canoes formed from a single tree, hollowed with fire in the manner of Indian canoes, and like them impelled with paddles. Of these many specimens have been found buried at the bottom of lakes and marshes. Such vessels as these could be of little use except for inland navigation.

Such is the scanty and unsatisfactory account that has been given to us of the ancient inhabitants of Caledonia at their earliest introduction into the page of history. Indeed, it is little more than the primitive barbarism of every country, whether of ancient or more modern periods—diversified, it may be, by a few of those particular features which afterwards became national characteristics. But for this paucity of information we have already endeavoured to account. It might have been expected, however, that when the country increased in importance and the rude tribes grew into a nation, our information would have been increased with the growth, so that we should have been able to trace the progress, and sum up the amount of civilization, under which the Caledonians had become Picts and a portion of the great family of Christendom. But here, strange, and sad as well as strange to tell, our information becomes more limited than ever. We know more of the infancy of the nation than even of its more important boyhood. The Picts became at last a decently-attired people, and they built towns, and churches, and monasteries; but this we learn only inferentially, and as it were by the course of accident. Even of the Scots, too, we only know that they were of the same race and kindred character with the people to whom they were finally united. There is a void between the periods of Galgacus and Kenneth Macalpin which history has neglected to fill up.

PERIOD II.

FROM A.D. 843 TO A.D. 1097.

CHAPTER I.

FROM KENNETH MACALPIN TO DEATH OF MALCOLM II. (843-1034).

Reign of Kenneth Macalpin—His wars—Reigns of Donald III., Constantine II., and Hugh—Of Gregory the Great, and his fabulous history—Reigns of Donald IV. and Constantine III.—Constantine's victory over the Danes at Tinmore—Constantine's alliance with the Northumbrians—Battle of Brunanburgh—Reign of Malcolm I.—Cumberland ceded to Scotland—Malcolm's invasion of Northumberland—Reign of Indulf—Edinburgh left by England to the Scots—Reigns of Duff and Culen—Reign of Kenneth III.—His connection with Edgar, King of England—The Danes invade Scotland—Their defeat at Luncarty—Kenneth's successes—He sets aside the law of royal succession—His remorse and death—Reigns of Constantine IV. and Grim—Reign of Malcolm II.—His wars with Sweyn, King of Denmark—Victories of the Scots over the Danes—Canute's invasion of Scotland—Doubtful termination of Malcolm's reign.

KENNETH, the son of Alpin, better known in history by his Celtic patronymic of Kenneth Macalpin, ascended the throne of Pictavia, A.D. 843, after he had reigned two years over the Dalriad Scots. It was fortunate that the union of the two people occurred under a chief who seems to have possessed no ordinary share of talent both for peace and war, as enemies were arrayed against the Scots and Picts under whom, if disunited, they would finally have fallen. We know little of the martial exploits of Kenneth, but that little indicates an active and not unsuccessful reign. Six times he invaded Lothian, still a part of England, in consequence of the aggressions of the Northumbrians, and burned Dunbar and Melrose, of which they had taken possession. But, besides the English or Danes of Northumberland, he was obliged to resist the invasion of the terrible Norse pirate Ragnar Lodbrog, who penetrated through the country as far as Clunie and Dunkeld. The Britons of Strathclyde also, alarmed perhaps at the formidable neighbourhood of such a united kingdom as that which Scotland now presented, invaded the territory, and burned Dumblane. It was much, indeed, that against so many and such powerful enemies Kenneth was able to preserve entire a kingdom occupied by such discordant races, and as yet unaccustomed to a single rule.

The other deeds of Kenneth were those of a just sovereign and wise politician. He removed the palladium of the Scots, their Stone of Destiny, from Argyle to Scone, and thus confirmed their rule there by the assurance of infallible prophecy. He removed the venerated relics of Saint Columba from their grave at Iona to a church which he built for the purpose at Dunkeld, and thus attested his zeal for the faith that was now professed equally by Scot and Pict. He is also said to have been the author of the ancient legislative code called the Macalpin Laws, but upon very uncertain evidence. It is not unlikely, however, that the regulations which he must have formed for the purpose of uniting his lately discordant subjects under a common government may have been the basis and groundwork of the code which goes under his name. After a reign of sixteen years Kenneth died on the 6th of February, 859, at Forteviot, the royal residence of the kings of Pictavia.

To Kenneth succeeded, not his son Constantine, but Donald III., the son of Alpin, and brother of Kenneth, a Celtic form of succession that was in accordance with the Tanist law. He is called Donald V. by Boece and Buchanan, who describe him not only as an imbecile king but an unprincipled epicure, wasting his time in riot and sensuality while the country was invaded by the English. To this, however, there are counter-statements, also alluded to by Buchanan, which describe him as a brave and enterprising prince. After a reign of four years he died A.D. 863, and was succeeded by his nephew, Constantine II., the son of Kenneth Macalpin.

The accession of Constantine occurred at a dangerous and unfortunate period for Scotland, the country being exposed to the ravages of the

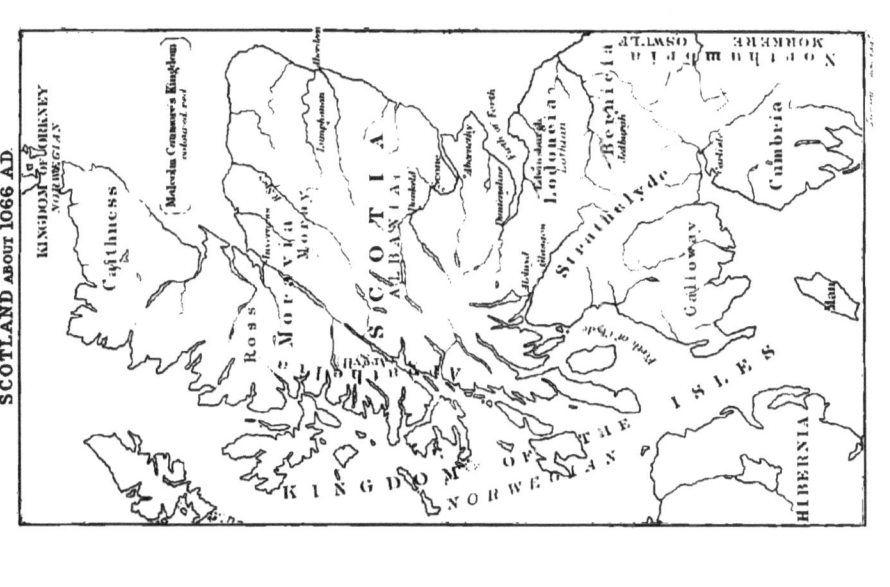

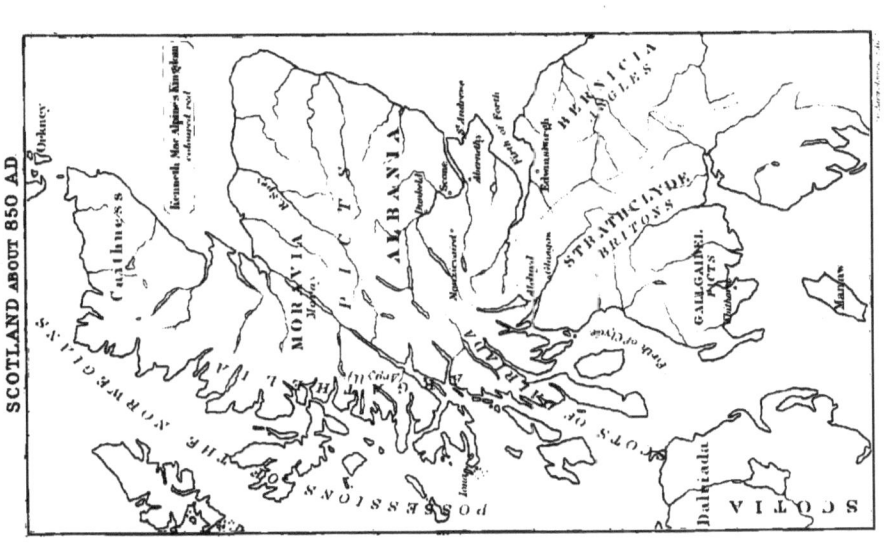

Danish pirates, the enemies of every country and plunderers of every coast. Having secured a footing upon the shores of Ireland after half a century of conflict, they turned their attention to Scotland, which they now found worth plundering. From Dublin, which was their chief mart and harbour, successive fleets of these Ostmen, as the Danes of Ireland were called, entered the Moray Frith and those of the Clyde, the Tay, and the Forth, wherever plunder could most abundantly be found; and during the interval from 866 to 881 a series of these wasteful visits had occurred, in which the whole extent of the coast of North Britain was ravaged without mercy or limit. It was against such formidable invaders that Constantine had to contend during a troubled and disastrous reign of eighteen years; while his subjects, long unused to a foreign enemy, were inferior to the Danes, whose enterprise and military skill had been improved by constant practice. At length his last battle was fought in 881 near the town of Crail, where, on falling into the hands of the enemy, he was dragged into a neighbouring cave, and there barbarously put to death. In the parish of Crail, the supposed site of the engagement, the remains of a rampart, called the Danes' Dyke, are still pointed out by the inhabitants.

To Constantine II. succeeded his brother Aodh or Hugh, whose brief reign of one year was brought to a bloody termination by an insurrection of his own subjects, headed by Grig, the powerful Mormaor of the country between the rivers Dee and Spey. He was wounded in an engagement which took place at Strathallan, and died two months afterwards at Inverary.

Grig, the successful rebel, who succeeded by his victory to the throne, has such a twofold and contradictory history as makes his reign one of the most perplexing in the whole range of Scottish annals. By the monks of St. Andrews,[1] who were careful to register his glorious deeds, he is expanded into Gregory the Great, and made the conqueror of Picts, Britons, English, Irish, and Danes—the very Arthur of Scottish romantic history, who triumphed and subdued wherever he fought. But to these monks, it appears, he was a most liberal benefactor; and in return they gave him lands which he never visited, and conquests over enemies whom he never saw. It was a cheap quittance for the substantial possessions with which he endowed them. And yet he is utterly unnoticed in the annals of England and Ireland, where he might have been allowed to shine if even with a malignant lustre! The truth seems to be, that he was mormaor or chief of Aberdeen and Banff; and that, ambitious of becoming a king, he rebelled against his master, and was successful. To colour his usurpation he is also stated to have associated a grandson of Kenneth Macalpin with himself in the government. After they had thus ruled conjointly eleven years, a rebellion of their subjects drove Grig and his partner from their throne, and the former is stated to have died in peace in his own castle of Dunnideer in Aberdeenshire four years after his deposition. Such is all the reality that can be gleaned of the history of this Gregory the Great, the contemporary of Alfred of England.

To Gregory succeeded Donald IV., son of Constantine II. The Danes, having landed on the shores of the Tay, were encountered by Donald at Collin, in the vicinity of Scone, and totally defeated. In 904 the Danes of Ireland also invaded the western coast, and had penetrated nearly as far as Forteviot, the new capital of Scotland, when Donald engaged and defeated them, but fell in the conflict, after having reigned eleven years.

The next king was Constantine III., son of that Aodh or Hugh whom Grig deposed. His reign was chiefly signalized by Danish invasions, which still continued to be the principal events both of English and Scottish history. It was from the Danes of Ireland that the peril to Scotland was chiefly to be apprehended, as they seemed to meditate nothing less than an entire and permanent conquest of the latter country. In the eighteenth year of Constantine's reign they entered the Clyde, but were met by the Scottish king at Tinmore, having under his banner not only an army of his own subjects, but a strong reinforcement of Anglo-Danes from the Danelagh of Northumberland. Thus Dane was opposed to kindred Dane as well as the Scot to the foreign invader; but for the alliance which produced such an arrangement there was an adequate political cause in the fierce national hostility which still subsisted between the inhabitants of the Danelagh and the Saxons of the rest of England. Of the battle which took place at Tinmore the *Annals of Ulster*, contrary to their usual practice, give a full and minute account. The Danish and Norwegian invaders from Ireland, under the command of Reginald, were drawn up by that practised leader into four divisions, the last of which he placed in ambush, with the purpose of charging at its head when some opportune moment arrived. The Scottish onset was made with such vigour that the three Danish divisions were broken through; but while the victors were probably disordered by their own success

---

[1] Chronicle in the Register of St. Andrews, in Innes's Appendix.

they were suddenly assailed in the rear by Reginald, while the fugitive Danes rallied and returned to the charge. The battle thus renewed was continued upon equal terms till night; but the retreat of the invaders, and the comparatively small loss which the Scots had sustained, left all the advantages of victory to the latter. This was tacitly acknowledged by the Danes themselves, as many years elapsed before they repeated their hostile visits to Scotland.

But although Constantine had been aided in this successful resistance by his efficient allies of Northumbria, the league offensive and defensive which he had made with the men of the Danelagh was to be accompanied with its correspondent disadvantages. These Danish rovers had not yet subsided either into an industrious settled population or true lieges of the English crown; on the contrary, they kept up their communication with their piratical brethren of the north, obeyed no sovereign but their own princes, and were always ready to promote every revolution or invasion that might place the English crown upon a Danish head. Through this cause the alliance of Scotland with Northumbria brought the former into hostile contact with the formidable power of England, and was an early prelude to those contests between the two rival nations which five centuries were scarcely sufficient to assuage. The first-fruits of this alliance with the Danelagh, by which England and Scotland were brought into such undesirable collision, occurred in 924. Edward, who had succeeded to the throne of his father Alfred and successfully repressed the revolts of the Danelagh, now turned his attention to Scotland; and although we read neither of an invasion made nor battle fought, the English chroniclers bestow upon him all the advantages of both, for they tell us that the Welsh, the Scots, the inhabitants of Strathclyde and Cumbria, and the people of Galloway did homage to his superiority, and accepted him as their "lord, father, and protector." In the absence of other history these loose monkish statements were dangerous documents in the hands of Edward Longshanks at a time when it was not easy to meet them with denial or refutation.

The next event that arose from this alliance with Northumbria was of a more intelligible character, and was signalized by woe and disaster to Scotland. Athelstane, the son of Edward, had succeeded to the English crown, and having signalized his reign by reducing the greater part of Wales and Cornwall to subjection, he also attempted an invasion of Scotland both by land and sea. This event is dated A.D. 934. The old English records of course magnify this inroad into an eventful and victorious progress, in which Constantine was so effectually humbled that he was obliged to purchase peace with valuable presents, and by giving his son as a hostage for its observance. It is probable, however, that the King of Scots stood wholly on the defensive, as no battle appears to have been fought; and that Athelstane returned to England with the empty glory of having made an invasion and met with no resistance. Still the event was enough to irritate if it did not dismay the heart of Constantine, and for the purpose of making reprisals with effect he established the most formidable league that had ever as yet been combined against England. Its members, besides himself as head, consisted of Olave or Anlaf, the Danish King of Dublin, his son-in-law; another Anlaf, the Danish King of Northumbria; the Danish Prince of the Hebrides; Owen, King of Cumberland; and a large array of Danish and Norwegian princes and jarls, each of whom ruled as an independent sovereign in his own bay or islet, and could bring a formidable troop to the general rendezvous. The combined army, conveyed in a fleet of six hundred and fifteen ships, entered the Humber and landed at Brunanburgh.[1] But the vigilant and energetic Athelstane was prepared for the emergency; and having collected a numerous army, he came down upon the invaders before they could commence operations either for the reduction of Northumbria or a hostile advance into England. The battle that ensued lasted a whole day, and with various fortunes, until at sunset victory declared in favour of Athelstane. It was perhaps the greatest and most sanguinary conflict that as yet had been fought in England; and while men in after ages talked of the victory, it was doubtless coupled with the remembrance that the invasion had come from Scotland. Five Danish vikings and seven northern jarls lay dead on the field; and Constantine himself, after seeing his valiant son numbered with the slain, escaped with Anlaf to his ships and hoisted sail for Scotland.

The rest of the long reign of Constantine III. may be briefly told. When the battle of Brunanburgh occurred, which bereaved him of a son as well as the better part of his army, he was an old man; and perhaps the dreams of royal and military ambition which had been so rudely disturbed could no longer be recalled. In the

---

[1] The place so designated cannot now be ascertained, and various localities have been conjectured as the ancient Brunanburgh—such as Burn in the south, and Burgh in the north of Lincolnshire. All that can be decided is that it was not far from the Humber, and upon its southern shore.

fortieth year of his reign he adopted the expedient so frequent among the English sovereigns; he laid aside his crown for a monk's cowl, retired to the monastery of St. Andrews, and there became a Culdee abbot, while he was succeeded in his throne and his cares by Malcolm I., son of Donald IV.

As this voluntary abdication appears to have been an unwonted event in Scotland, it was the signal of popular commotion; and the accession of Malcolm was opposed by Kelach, Mormaor of Moray, who at the head of his turbulent clansmen, known in ancient Scottish history as the Moray-men, excited a formidable rebellion. This was suppressed by a victory obtained by Malcolm over the insurgents, in which Kelach himself was slain.

A more important event than the suppression of a dangerous subject was the acquisition of territory to the Scottish crown which occurred at this period, and through an alliance more politic and profitable than that which had been made with the Norsemen. This was with England, whose king, Edmund the Atheling, was involved in such troubles with the Danes of Northumbria under Anlaf, who had returned from Ireland to the Danelagh, that he was glad to purchase the neutrality of Scotland by an important concession. Accordingly, having conquered Cumbria, which had rebelled against him, and driven out its king, Dunmail, he presented the sovereignty of this district, of which he could not easily retain possession, to Malcolm of Scotland, within whose reach it was more conveniently placed, upon the condition of defending the north of the island against Danish invasion and becoming the ally of the English king. Upon these easy terms Cumberland became a part of the growing kingdom of Scotland.

Events soon occurred that summoned Malcolm to discharge his debt, and this he did faithfully and bravely. In the reign of Edred, the brother and successor of Edmund the Atheling, the Danes of Northumbria, aided by swarms of their countrymen from Denmark, Norway, and Ireland, and from the Orkneys and Hebrides, in which they had obtained a settlement, now broke out into their wonted rebellion, and endeavoured to set up an independent kingdom of their own. Several battles ensued, in which the English were victorious, and Northumberland was in consequence incorporated with England, and placed under the government of an earl appointed by the English sovereign. During this dangerous revolt the promised aid of Malcolm was demanded; and, true to his promise, he entered Lothian— at that time a portion of the English territory —which he overran, and proceeded to invade Northumberland. There he was not slow to imitate the merciless proceedings of the English armies, for he wasted the devoted province with fire and sword, and carried off many prisoners and abundance of cattle—acquisitions of vital importance to a country so poor and so thinly peopled as Scotland. The reign of Malcolm was closed in disaster. The Moray-men having renewed their rebellion, the king marched to the Mearns to encounter them, and was killed at Fetteresso. Report adds that his death was not in the battle, but from conspiracy and by the stroke of an assassin.

On the death of Malcolm I., Indulf, the son of Constantine III., ascended the Scottish throne, A.D. 953. The chief events of his reign occurred in the form of Danish invasions. These terrible marauders, who were kept at bay upon the coasts of England by the formidable fleet which Edgar its king had raised, turned their prows to the weaker shores of Scotland, although its barren harvests could scarcely equal the gleanings of the rich fields of the south. Having effected a landing at Gamrie in Buchan, they were proceeding to their wonted occupation of plunder when they were encountered and defeated by the mormaor of the district. This event is still commemorated by the people of that locality as the battle of the Bloody Pots. It only served as the prelude to a more serious invasion, which was made A.D. 961, the Danes being incensed not only at their late defeat, but the recession of Scotland from the Danish alliance. They landed in the bay of Cullen in Banffshire, and were encountered by Indulf upon a moor to the westward of that town. The traditions of this conflict have an air of reality that is entitled to respect. According to these the battle was maintained on both sides with great spirit and equal fortune until an ambush suddenly fell upon the rear of the Danish troops, who were broken in consequence and pursued to their ships. Indulf joined in the chase; but having fallen at unawares upon a band of the enemy who had withdrawn themselves under cover in a valley, he was encountered, overpowered, and slain, after a short reign of eight years.

During this period an event occurred of greater importance to Scotland than such obscure victories over Danish rovers and pirates. "At this time," says the Pictish Chronicle, "the town of Edwin was abandoned and left to the Scots, even until the present day." It is supposed that Athelstane, when he invaded Scotland in 934, had established a garrison in this place, which was subsequently recalled in consequence of the troubles in England, and that the town of Edwin remained thus unclaimed until Scotland had means as well as right to enter and occupy it. This was afterwards done when Lothian was formally ceded to the Scottish crown; and thus Edwin's town became the capital not only of the new province, but at last of the kingdom at large—the Edinburgh of Scottish history and the Athens of modern ages.

Indulf was succeeded by Oda, son of Malcolm I., whose Celtic distinction of Duff, or the Black (probably from the darkness of his complexion), has been adopted by our annalists as his real name, and it is by this that he is known in history. In his case the Tanist rule of succession imported by Fergus from Ireland, and which supplanted the unintelligible Pictish order of kingly appointments at the accession of Kenneth Macalpin, was now to receive a rude shock. This originated in the ambition of Culen, the son of Indulf, who was displeased with the ancient and venerated Celtic rule by which brother succeeded brother instead of a son the father. His discontent in this case was inflamed into actual rebellion through the pernicious counsels of Duncha, the Abbot of Dunkeld, an ambitious ecclesiastic who perhaps hoped to found a priestly government of his own through the influence of his royal pupil. The rivals encountered at Duncrub in Perthshire, and in the battle Culen was defeated, and his counsellor Duncha slain. But Culen was still sufficiently powerful to keep the field, and Duff was defeated in turn and compelled to seek safety in flight. After a troubled reign of four years and a half he was assassinated at Forres, A.D. 965, and with circumstances so like those of the assassination of the "gracious Duncan" by Macbeth, as to warrant us in believing that, if true, they belong wholly to Duff instead of his descendant.

Culen obtained the throne which he coveted; but his short reign, which was without honour, was closed by a disgraceful death. Since the reign of Constantine III. the Britons of Strathclyde, who had accepted his brother Domnal for their king, had lived in close amity with the Scots, when Culen broke this fair union by violating the daughter of Andarch their king, the son of Domnal. The men of Strathclyde, indignant at this insult to their prince, adopted it as a cause for national quarrel; and in a conflict which ensued between them and the Scots in Lothian, Culen was slain, after he had reigned only four years and six months.

The Scottish crown now devolved upon Kenneth III., son of Malcolm I., who succeeded A.D. 970. He continued that war with the Britons of Strathclyde which his unworthy predecessor had occasioned, and prosecuted it with such success that the kingdom of Strathclyde was subdued and annexed to Scotland. By some of the old English chroniclers the intercourse which occurred between Kenneth III. of Scotland and Edgar, King of England, who assumed the lofty titles of "Emperor of Albion, King of the English, and of all the nations and islands around," is made to assume the relationship of a dependent sovereign to his feudal superior. According to these accounts six crowned kings (in one statement the number is raised to eight) rowed the barge of Edgar to the monastery of St. John's on the river Dee, in North Wales, thus acknowledging their vassalage, while Edgar himself guided the helm, and it is stated that one of these kings was Kenneth, King of Scotland. But if this aquatic exploit was anything more than a frolicsome boating excursion, it was probably a meeting of the allied potentates among whom Britain was still divided, for the purpose of concocting a plan of common defence against the Danish invasions, which now threatened the subjugation of the whole island. One fact of a more certain character is that, A.D. 973, Edgar required of Kenneth the fulfilment of those terms on which Cumberland had been ceded to Scotland, and that the Scottish king accordingly conducted an invasion against the Northumbrians, by whom the peace of England still continued to be disturbed. He ravaged the Danelagh and carried off the son of its earl prisoner.

A still more important part of Kenneth's obligation in this compact with England was to guard the northern coasts against the Danes, and prevent their entrance through his own dominions into the English territories. His ability for this important task was now to be fully proved. After several attempts on the north-eastern coast of Scotland, which were attended with indecisive results, the Danes concentrated their force, entered the Tay with a numerous fleet, and advanced with the purpose of commencing operations by plundering Dunkeld. With such troops as he could muster on so hasty a notice Kenneth advanced to the encounter, which took place upon the famous field of Luncarty, near the town of Perth, and on the southern side of the Tay. The right wing of the Scottish army was headed by Malcolm, Prince of Cumberland, and therefore heir-apparent to the crown; the left by Duncan, Mormaor of Athol; while Kenneth himself took charge of the centre. As he foresaw the prospect of a terrible onset from the Danes, he encouraged his troops by promising to absolve them from their wonted military service during the term of five years, and by offering ten pounds, or an equivalent value in land, to every man who would bring him the head of a Dane.

After this the battle joined with equal fierceness on either side; the Danes, who had entered the country chiefly for the purpose of reaching the tempting plunder of England, were animated with double fury when they saw the eagerness of the Scots to obtain their heads, and fought with the desperation of men who expected no quarter. At last both the right and left wings of the Scottish army were driven off the field, so that none were left to resist the Danes but the centre, under the command of Kenneth, which was assailed in front, flank, and rear. At this moment, when all seemed to be lost, the tide of fortune was suddenly turned by one of those wonderful incidents with which the warfare of all ages and countries abounds. A strong stalwart peasant named Hay, with his two sons, who had hastily armed themselves with plough-yokes and come down to take share in the common danger, entered a narrow lane through which their countrymen were flying. Here they closed up the pass, and, not content with exhorting the fugitives to return and fight bravely, they plied their heavy weapons indifferently upon pursuers and pursued. The foremost gave back and turned; a new impulse was imparted to the tide; and the hundreds who a few moments before had been in headlong flight, wheeled round with fresh alacrity upon the astounded Danes and commenced the battle anew. This unexpected charge, that was mistaken for the onset of a new army, paralysed the Danes, and their victory was quickly turned into a defeat so fatal that few escaped to their ships. Such was the battle of Luncarty, whose memory formed a guiding-star to Scottish courage until its light was eclipsed in the superior brightness of Bannockburn; and in this manner England as well as Scotland was delivered for the time from a formidable enemy. But what shall we say of the peasant-patriot and his sons, to whom the glory was attributed? We are told that the Hays were a Norman family, and that they did not come into Scotland until the middle of the twelfth century— and this because their names do not appear in the subscriptions of any charters prior to that period. It is upon such an uncertain argument that we are required to forego an incident as creditable and certainly as pleasing as any of those in which so many of the noble houses of Europe have originated.

Although Kenneth III. was one of the ablest, he was certainly also one of the most unscrupulous rulers of his day. This he evinced by the manner in which he annexed the kingdom of Strathclyde to his own, and thus made the Dalriad sovereignty paramount over the northern division of the island. The same proceeding had been going on in the south, where the successors of Alfred had been employed in reducing the discordant portions of the Heptarchy into a compact government; and thus at the present period there were only two lords paramount over the whole of Britain, and these were Edgar of England and Kenneth of Scotland. Another aim which Kenneth sought to accomplish during the latter part of his reign was of a more personal but also of a more difficult character— it was to set aside the Tanist law of succession in favour of his own son Malcolm, at that time a mere stripling, between whom and the crown stood another Malcolm, son of Duff, who as Tanist of the kingdom held the rank of Prince of Cumberland. Not long after he of Cumberland suddenly and mysteriously died, and men did not scruple to assert that he had been poisoned at the instigation of the king. These evil reports were strengthened after Kenneth had called a council and urged its members to alter the ancient Celtic rule, so that a son might succeed the father in the throne, and have the affairs of the kingdom, if a minor, superintended till he came of age by a regency. His nobles, overcome by his energy and alarmed at his remorseless mode of silencing opposition, gave a reluctant assent, and his son Malcolm was installed in the principality of Cumberland as a preparative to his wearing the royal crown. But able and cunning though Kenneth was, and sanctioned as was his aim by the example of every dynasty of Europe, the tenacity of a Celtic habit was not thus to be rooted up in a day or by a single hand, and two reigns followed before Malcolm became King of Scotland.

After this the soul of Kenneth appears to have been troubled with remorse; his sleep was scared with visions; and when he woke in the night he thought he heard a voice from heaven denouncing his crimes, and assuring him that his posterity, for which he had sinned so deeply, would occupy a troubled and uncertain throne. In despair he betook himself to the counsel of monks and priests, and they, in conformity with the religious spirit of the age, directed him to found churches and monasteries, to submit himself to the guidance of the clergy, and make pilgrimages to sacred shrines and relics. He complied by endowing the church with rich gifts[1] and humbling himself to the prescribed observances. But these acts only accelerated the judgment which they sought to avert. Having wandered in the remorse of his pilgrimages to the Mearns, where the bones of

---

[1] The chief of these was Brechin. In the Pictish Chronicle this king is characterized as "he who gave the great city of Brechin to the Lord."

St. Palladius were preserved, he turned aside to visit the castle of Fettercairn, and thus came within reach of its owner, Fenella, a lady whose son, Crathilinth, governor of Mearns, he had formerly executed for rebellion. Bent upon revenge, she caused the doating pilgrim-king to be assassinated, but in what manner does not clearly appear. In this inglorious manner Kenneth's life was closed after a brilliant and prosperous reign of twenty-four years.

The arrangements of Kenneth III., instead of effecting the abrogation of the Tanist law of succession, only seem to have complicated it with new difficulties; for not only were the claims of his son Malcolm to immediate possession set aside, but two pretenders raised up for the vacant throne. These were Constantine surnamed the Bald, the son of the infamous Culen, and Kenneth surnamed Grim, the son of Duff. The former under the title of Constantine IV. enjoyed the crown little more than a year, when he was defeated and slain by his successful rival near the river Almond, in Perthshire.

On the death of Constantine the throne of Scotland was occupied by Kenneth IV., surnamed Grim, on account of his great strength, which was combined with a stately person and ingratiating manners. He was not, however, to reign in peace; for Malcolm, son of Kenneth III., now stepped into the field, and asserted his double claim to royalty both by Tanist law and the agreement of the nobles with his father. The kingdom was on the eve of being rent by a civil war, when Fothadus, a bishop of great influence, mediated between the contending princes, and persuaded them to a compromise, by which Grim was to retain the title of king during life, and Malcolm, Prince of Cumberland, to succeed him, while the succession thereafter was to devolve upon the children of the latter according to the law established by Kenneth. But this compact fared as such agreements usually do when a crown is at stake in more civilized communities and better governments than those of Scotland. Grim, who was thus reduced to a mere life-tenant of the kingly office, was resolved to make the most of it while it lasted; and from this motive he proceeded to pillage both nobles and people as if they had been enemies rather than his own subjects. Such conduct naturally drove them to seek redress from Malcolm, who during this tyranny had been fully occupied in the defence of Northumberland against the Danish invasions, which had now multiplied against England to an alarming amount. The Prince of Cumberland, on obtaining a breathing interval from his occupations in the Danelagh, gladly responded to the call, and hastened to the defence of his plundered inheritance, which Grim continued to rack without stint. At Monnivaird the two armies approached each other; and as Ascension-day had arrived, which was a usual season of peace over the whole Christian world, Grim resolved on that day to attack his enemies, hoping to find them off their guard and employed in the wonted devotions. But in this he was disappointed: Malcolm was warned and ready to receive him; and in the battle that followed, Grim was deserted by the greater part of his followers, wounded in the head, taken prisoner, and forthwith deprived of his eyes, according to the savage practice then prevalent among both Danes and Saxons. His claims to royalty and power to enforce them being thus extinguished, he died in captivity after a reign of ten years.

The long-delayed sceptre was now eagerly grasped by the conqueror, who succeeded to the kingdom under the title of Malcolm II. (1004). The great national danger as well as chief calamity still continued to be the Danish invasions, which had now nothing less than the conquest of the whole island for their object; and they were repeated at every assailable point whether Scottish or English that promised the easiest entrance to their purposed object. In the reign of Malcolm II. these visitations were renewed in Scotland chiefly from the personal resentment of Sweyn, the son of Harold, King of Denmark. This prince, having been banished from his country, came, after a wild life of unsuccessful war and adventure, into Scotland to obtain assistance against his enemies; and there he embraced Christianity, after having been one of its bitterest persecutors. But his conversion was of the old Norse character, which left ample room for the rooted habits of piracy and bloodshed, and even for a fresh return into heathenism; and he is said to have been baptized more than once into the Christian faith. On receiving aid in the form of a small band of auxiliaries, Sweyn returned to Denmark, and on the murder of his father obtained possession of the Danish throne. After this he was the most terrible of all the northern enemies that England had hitherto encountered, and finally became its conqueror and king. It was in the course of this conquest that Sweyn was encountered by Scottish auxiliaries in the English armies, to whose support they had been sent in accordance with the old agreement that had given Cumberland to Scotland. The merciless conqueror, either ignorant of such a treaty or like a true Dane careless about its sanctions, ordered these troops to return to their own country, and on their refusal he directed his resentment against

DEFEAT OF THE DANES AT LUNCARTY NEAR PERTH (A.D. 973).
HAY WITH HIS TWO SONS ARMED WITH PLOUGH-YOKES TURN THE TIDE OF BATTLE.

the land that had formerly sheltered him, as if it had now abandoned and betrayed him. A Danish army was sent into Scotland, which made a descent upon Moray, and after wasting the whole open country proceeded to besiege the strongholds and fortresses within which the Scots had entrenched themselves. Malcolm hastened to their relief; but the Danes were so numerous that his forces were quickly routed, and himself so severely wounded that he escaped with difficulty from the field. After this unfortunate conflict the castle of Nairn yielded to the conquerors; the other castles of Elgin and Forres imitated the example; and the Danes, having thus obtained a firm footing in Moray, resolved to establish it as a permanent settlement. Accordingly they cut through the peninsula upon which the castle of Nairn stands, thus converting the site into an island that could at all times be reinforced from the sea, and sent their fleet home for their wives and children. They had now won for themselves a commodious harbour and a safe retreat, from which they might carry their devastations over those wealthy inland districts that as yet had remained untouched.

In the meantime Malcolm, alarmed at the establishment of such a dangerous colony within his kingdom, made every preparation to dislodge it; and having collected an army more numerous and better appointed than that which had lost the day at Nairn, he advanced against the invaders, who had now penetrated into Mar. An encounter took place at Mortlach, A.D. 1010. At the commencement the Scots had the worst of it, for they lost three of their principal mormaors, and were driven back to their entrenchments in the rear. But from their skilful enemies they seemed to have already learned the art of defensive warfare; for, instead of betaking themselves to flight after this serious repulse, they strengthened their position with a rampart, ditch, and palisades, leaving only a narrow opening by which they could be assailed. The battle was here renewed and the tide of fortune reversed, for the Danes, who rashly attacked the Scots in their entrenchments, were routed in turn, and so effectually that they fled in great disorder. Malcolm wisely withheld his raw levies from pursuit, and the fugitives were allowed to reach Moray in safety.

When tidings of this defeat came to Sweyn in England he saw too well the value of the occupation won in Scotland to relinquish it, and he accordingly sent a strong reinforcement by sea under the command of Camus to assist his countrymen in Moray. These invaders first attempted a landing in the Frith of Forth; but, on being repulsed, they directed their course to the Redhead in Angus, where they disembarked and pitched their camp at the village of St. Bride. Here they were soon encountered by a strong Scottish force, and defeated with considerable loss; upon which Camus drew off the remains of his army and endeavoured to effect a junction with the Danes in Moray. But he had scarcely proceeded two miles in his retreat through an unknown country and without guides when he was again encountered by the Scots, who obstinately followed his track and brought him to bay; and in this second battle he fell with all his followers. The fate of this Danish army, and the places of those encounters in which it was successively defeated, were plentifully commemorated by names and monuments. The village which rose on the site of this last encounter is still called Camuston; and its obelisk, Camuston Cross, is supposed to have been the cairn of the northern chieftain. At the beginning of the seventeenth century the ploughshare laid open a sepulchre inclosed with four stones beside this monument, in which a gigantic human skeleton was laid, having the skull cleft as with the stroke of a battle-axe; and from the Danish structure of the tomb and its connection with the obelisk, the skeleton, with some degree of justice, was supposed to be that of the unfortunate Camus.

It was probably as part of the same momentous invasion, which had for its object the relief of the Danes of Moray, that another detachment of these formidable rovers was cut to pieces in the neighbourhood of Slains Castle, Aberdeenshire, after they had suffered a signal defeat near the town of Brechin. Those who escaped from the slaughter fled to their ships under shelter of night, and, after being tossed about for several days by contrary winds upon the coast of Buchan, were obliged to land to the number of five hundred for the purpose of obtaining provisions. But scarcely had they set foot upon the shore when they were assailed by Mernun, the mormaor of the district, and driven to a steep hill; and here they made so skilful and determined a rally as kept the pursuers in check notwithstanding their overwhelming numbers. At last the Danes were overpowered and died fighting to a man, well knowing that it was useless to crave for that quarter which they had never been wont to bestow.

These disasters, heavy though they were, could not daunt the conquerors of Normandy and England, more especially under such a leader as Sweyn; and the royal Dane, who either at this time or soon after was proclaimed "full King of England" in consequence of the flight of its despairing sovereign, Ethelred, to Normandy, sent a fresh army into Scotland, at the head of which was his son, afterwards renowned in history under the title of Canute the Great. At the coming of such an antagonist Scotland had the utmost need of all her caution as well as all her valour. The Danes landed in Buchan; and Malcolm, who perhaps was speedily made aware that they were under a better commander than those luckless chieftains who had preceded him, stood cautiously on the defensive. He therefore contented himself with a war of skirmishes and cutting off the foragers of the Danish camp. But the hunger which this occasioned to the enemy was also extended to his own troops, and both armies were impatient for battle. The conflict between two such warriors as the Danish prince and the Scottish king was conducted with equal skill and valour; and after a long struggle, in which great loss was sustained on either side, the weary combatants parted on equal terms. But the advantages of such a doubtful fight remained with the Scots, who had their resources at hand and could be easily reinforced, so that when on the following morning they drew up for a fresh encounter they found the enemy willing to treat for peace. An agreement accordingly was concluded upon the terms that the Danes should evacuate Moray and Brechin; that the Scots and Danes should thenceforth live in mutual peace, neither of them assisting the enemies of the other; and that the battlefield should be set apart and consecrated to the burial of the dead. As a permanent record of this treaty, the memorial-stone called Sweyn's Pillar is supposed to have been erected at Forres. Thus a Danish conquest of Scotland, which seemed as inevitable as that which about the same time befell England, was happily prevented. It is true, indeed, that these events, which our old Scottish historians have related with so much complacency, have been questioned or rejected by the scrupulous historical inquirers of the present day; but they have not attempted to explain, in return, how so many ancient monuments were erected in these localities, or what deeds and heroes they were designed to commemorate.

This compact with Sweyn must have occurred before the year 1014, in which the Danish King of England died. Having thus got rid of the most formidable of his enemies by a treaty which the Dane, who now had higher objects of ambition, was little inclined to interrupt, Malcolm II. had full leisure to prosecute those wars which assailed him from less important antagonists. Accordingly we find him, A.D. 1018, invading Northumberland, with whose earl, Uchtred, he was in hostile collision; and in a desperate battle which ensued between them at Carham, near Werk or Wark, the Northumbrian magnate appears to have been the conqueror. But he did not live to enjoy the fruits of his success, having been assassinated on his way to the court of Canute, who had lately succeeded, by the death of his father Sweyn, to the throne of England; and the earldom of Northumberland devolved upon Eadulf, the brother of Uchtred, between whom and Malcolm the war was continued. Eadulf, however, was less fortunate than his brother, and he consented to a lasting peace by ceding Lothian in perpetuity to the Scots. In this brief and unsatisfactory manner the acquisition of a territory of such vital importance to Scotland is announced by an old English chronicler.[1] Another intimation equally indistinct brings Canute the Great once more into Scotland—unless, indeed, the Canute who formerly invaded it was not the son but the brother of Sweyn, as Boece has declared. Whether the conquest of the kingdom of Scotland or personal resentment at its sovereign was the motive of this portentous arrival of Canute, which is said to have occurred A.D. 1031, is involved in the same obscurity. It is certain, however, that neither the conquest nor the humiliation of Scotland was the result. All that Canute obtained, and all perhaps that he sought, was a more punctual observance of the terms on which Cumberland had been ceded to the Scottish crown, and which Malcolm, during the course of these Border wars, may have been remiss in discharging; and having obtained this, the great king returned, apparently satisfied, to England. Cumberland and Lothian still remained in the secure possession of Scotland.

Such were the chief actions of Malcolm II., as far as they can be ascertained through the glimmer and gloom of so remote a period. It was a reign remarkable for its energy, and the important acquisitions which it secured for Scotland both of territory and political influence; but unfortunately it has been more deeply obscured by antiquarian cavil and debate than any previous portion of our history. And yet all this uncertainty was but the token that the dawn was approaching, and that the light, which had now so faintly commenced, would soon brighten and predominate. The last days of the reign of Malcolm II. are involved in a double portion of this struggling and shifting uncertainty. He is said to have made a division of all the lands of Scotland into baronies at the Mote-hill of Perth, and to have bestowed them upon his nobles according to their services; but we nowhere find evidence of such unlimited power being

---

[1] Simeon of Durham.

possessed by any Scottish sovereign. To him also a code of laws has been attributed that could only have been the growth of a later period. The manner of his death has also been diversified by contending popular traditions which Buchanan has severally specified. According to one of these he was assassinated by the relations of a noble virgin whom he had violated in his old age. According to another he was killed in an ambush that had been laid for him by some adherents of the former kings Grim and Constantine. A third account, more popular than the rest, because more atrocious and picturesque, represents him as perishing by a conspiracy of his nobles. He had resumed, we are gravely told, the rich grants which he had bestowed upon them with such rash liberality at the Mote-hill of Perth, and so pillaged them by extortions that they would endure his growing avarice no longer. Accordingly, having corrupted some of his domestics, they murdered him by night in his bed-chamber at Glammis in Augus. It is added that the criminals, in endeavouring to escape, were so bewildered in their flight by a heavy fall of snow, by which the landmarks had become invisible, that they got at unawares upon the frozen surface of a loch, and that the ice suddenly giving way they were all ingulfed and drowned. It was not till the thaw had dissolved this treacherous shroud of the traitors that their bodies were found, which were forthwith hanged upon gibbets on the highway. Amidst such an exorbitant variety of deaths it is more reasonable to believe that (as stated in the *Register of St. Andrews*) this illustrious sovereign died the death of nature and of old age, after an active and eventful reign of thirty years (1034).

CHAPTER II.

FROM ACCESSION OF DUNCAN TO ACCESSION OF EDGAR (1034-1097).

Reign of Duncan—His connection with England—Fictitious events of his reign—Account of Macbeth—Duncan assassinated—Macbeth becomes king—His useful reign—His defeat and death—Malcolm III. surnamed Canmore succeeds—State of the kingdom at his accession—Circumstances in his favour—Macduff rewarded—Malcolm's connection with Tostig, Earl of Northumberland—Arrival of Edgar Atheling in Scotland—Marriage of Malcolm to the Princess Margaret—He invades England—William the Conqueror invades Scotland—Character of Queen Margaret—Her piety and charities—Her attempts to civilize the Scots—Her debate with the Culdees—Wars between Malcolm Canmore and William Rufus—Nature of the Scottish homage to the English kings—Malcolm invades England—He is slain at Alnwick—His character—Death of his queen—Donald Bane succeeds to the throne—His endeavours to restore the Celtic ascendency—He is displaced by Duncan, son of Malcolm Canmore—Donald Bane recovers the throne by Duncan's assassination—Donald Bane's unwise reign—He is again deposed—Edgar succeeds as king.

When Malcolm II. died he had neither a brother to succeed him according to the Celtic usage, nor yet a son who might immediately occupy the throne according to the innovation of Kenneth Macalpin. But, by his daughter Bethoc, who had married Crinan, abbot of Dunkeld, at a time when priestly marriages were neither unusual nor unlawful, he had a grandson, Duncan, who had been installed Prince of Cumberland as heir-apparent to the kingdom. On the death of Malcolm, therefore, the sceptre came into the hand of Duncan as a regular and undisputed inheritance.

Of Duncan's history while he ruled the principality of Cumberland nothing can be ascertained. The position, however, which he thus held while Dane and Saxon were at fierce war with each other for the possession of England gives probability to the report that he adhered to the English side of the controversy, as he was bound to do by the tenure of his possession, although, from the troubled state of the country, he was unable to repair to the King of England and tender his allegiance in person. When Canute the Great succeeded to the English crown he became the feudal superior of Duncan in England; and as such he required the Prince of Cumberland, now King of Scotland, to invade Northumbria in support of the new Anglo-Danish government. Duncan had no alternative but to obey; and A.D. 1035, the last year of Canute's reign, he invaded Northumberland, and laid siege to the castle of Durham, from which he was driven, if we may believe the old English historian,[1] with heavy loss and signal defeat.

---

[1] Simeon of Durham.

After the death of Canute the Danish dynasty was so firmly established for a season in England that Duncan, as King of Scotland, had no further disturbance from that quarter of the island, and the rest of his short reign appears to have been passed in tranquillity. But such an unwonted lull was irksome to our early historians, and they have filled up the unwelcome blank with armies, actors, and achievements which they seem to have conjured up at will. It was indeed a season of weird sisters and incantations, and its very memory was contagious after centuries had elapsed. According to these legends there was war with Macdowal and his islesmen, war with galloglasses and kernes from Ireland, and war with the Danes, while in every change the master-spirit of the storm was Macbeth, who quelled the elements when they were at the wildest. In the last and most dangerous of these commotions Sweyn, King of Norway, had invaded Scotland, and all but made himself master of the kingdom. In this strait the Scots opened a negotiation in which they flattered the enemy with fallacious hopes; and, to crown their professions of good-will, they sent a bountiful store of provisions, with plenty of wine and ale, into the half-starved Norwegian camp, over which the freebooters revelled with their wonted largeness of appetite and habitual love of good cheer. But the liquors had been treacherously drugged with the narcotic nightshade;[1] and at midnight there was a silence as deep over the whole Norwegian army as over the camp of Sennacherib. Thousands had revelled and slept their last; they drank and died. It was then that the Scottish troops under Macbeth and Banquo came down upon the invaders; and those who woke only fought with a blind resistance, and were struck down like deer crowded within the tinchel. As for Sweyn, who was dead drunk, his more prudent attendants, who were only half drunk, contrived to lay him across a baggage-horse and carry him to the shore, where their shipping had been anchored; but here they found their numbers so few that they could scarcely man the single vessel in which they escaped with their king. As if enough had not been already done to secure so discreditable a victory, Boece and Buchanan then raise a storm upon the unlucky fleet, by which the ships were dashed against each other until they were all wrecked upon that dangerous bank afterwards called the Drumlaw Sands.

But leaving these romantic fictions, and even the prophecies that welcomed the victors upon "the blasted heath"—events which were copied from the Scottish into the English histories, and invested by Shakspere with a power that makes historical reality shrink before it like a mendacious culprit—we gladly turn to those few intelligible incidents upon which this gorgeous but airy superstructure has been based. And here we find that Macbeth, although so deeply branded by the poet as a usurper that no skill can remove the stigma of that terrible branding iron, can yet be spoken of with some extenuation. According to all Celtic reckoning he had injuries to avenge as well as pretensions to maintain, that might make him look upon Duncan as an enemy and supplanter. His wife Gruoch was the granddaughter of Kenneth IV., who lost life and crown in his contest with Malcolm II. Her brother had been murdered by order of the same Malcolm, who feared his pretensions to the crown. Her first husband Gilcomgain, Mormaor of Moray, had been burned within his castle, with fifty of his adherents, while she herself was obliged to fly with her infant son Lulach. Thus, in marrying the lady Gruoch, Macbeth also espoused the injuries she had received from the reigning dynasty, as well as whatever pretensions her family may have enjoyed through their descent from Kenneth IV. But if it be true that he was himself connected also with royalty, and that his mother was Donda or Doaca, a daughter of Malcolm II., he may have thought, and not extravagantly, that his own claims to the crown were at least as strong as those of his cousin Duncan, also the grandson of the same king by a female descent. Upon the strength of the Tanist law, and amidst its perplexing complications, we find royal successions effected among the kings of Scotland apparently upon no better guarantee.

In this way we can perceive that Macbeth needed no weird women to incite him in his attempt to become king. In the seclusion of his bed-chamber were woman's complaints of wrong and suffering; within his own bosom there were the whispers of ambition; and these were enough to embody themselves into the welcome, "All hail, king that shall be." The means to realize this promise were not likely to be of scrupulous selection, and the revolt of another cousin of Duncan furnished the opportunity. This was Thorfin, Mormaor or Earl of

---

[1] "Sueno and his army, rejosing of this fouth of vittallis, begun to wauneht on thair maner, and to have experience quha micht ingorge thair wambe with maist voracite, quhil at last the vennoum of thir beryis was skalit throw all partis of thair bodyis; throw quhilk, thay war resolvit in ane deidly sleip."—Thus far Boece, who did not seem to think that these Danes or Norwegians, so inured to the practice of fraud themselves, might also be suspicious of a retaliation in kind, and would not swill so liberally without having first tested the soundness of the liquors. But this difficulty occurred to Buchanan, and therefore he is careful to tell us that the bearers themselves partook liberally of the liquids, and that after this example the enemy drank without suspicion.

Caithness, who refused to pay the tribute which he owed to the Scottish crown, and against whom Duncan marched to reduce him to obedience. But the king's progress northward was arrested near Elgin, and he was slain at a place called Bothgowanan, or the "smith's dwelling," by assassins in the employ of Macbeth.[1] Thus perished "the pure-breathed Duncan" as he is called by the Celtic bard, the "gracious Duncan" as he is termed by the poet of all time, after a short reign of six years.

The sovereign left two sons, Malcolm and Donald Bane, of whom the eldest had been designated his successor by the usual investiture of the title of Prince of Cumberland; but the young princes were still in early boyhood, and their safety rather than their royal succession was the chief subject of consideration. Accordingly Malcolm, on the death of his father, fled to Cumberland, and Donald Bane to the Hebrides, while Macbeth marched unopposed to the throne, and was crowned at Scone upon the marble chair of destiny in the year 1037. If he must still be accounted a usurper of royalty he was a most beneficent one, and the old chronicles are filled with descriptions of the peace and prosperity that abounded in Scotland during the greater part of his reign. With this, indeed, the people were so well satisfied that they made no movement in behalf of the family of Duncan, so that the aid by which they were restored was derived from aliens and enemies. Macbeth was also devout according to the fashion of the times; and either to signalize his piety or soothe his remorse he made a pilgrimage to Rome, at that time the resource of regal and princely offenders, and of which Canute the Great had lately taken full benefit as well as several of the Anglo-Saxon sovereigns of England. Even in a political point of view, therefore, this devout journey of Macbeth may have been expedient as a full proclamation to Europe of his unquestioned and unquestionable sovereignty.[2]

But a prosperous and tranquil reign of seventeen years only diversified by a commonplace journey to Rome and back again—this was not enough for our historians of the middle ages; and having adopted Macbeth as a romantic personage, they gathered round him the events that were fittest for such a character, as it was at that time understood. Thus, though his mother was a lady of rank and lineage, his father was no other than a demon who had seduced her by his blandishments, and who at his birth predicted for this wondrous babe all the equivocal advantages which Shakspere has only transferred to the cavern of Hecate. His seat was to be secure until Birnam Wood came to the hill of Dunsinane, and his body to be impervious to every weapon wielded by the hand of any one born of woman. Having thus laid the groundwork of the plot, it was easy to expand the few particulars of his after reign into voluminous form, and season them with a due amount of the supernatural--which they have done accordingly. Our task, and it is no easy one, is to reduce all this amplification to its primitive and scanty elements.

By the death of Duncan, irrespective of its cause, Macbeth, in consequence of his being nearest in relationship to the deceased king, succeeded by old established usage to the kingdom; while Malcolm, the eldest son of Duncan, being still a minor, could advance no claim to the throne until the reign of Macbeth was ended. But Malcolm, Prince of Cumberland, was little likely to respect a law which of late had been so rudely thrust aside; and Siward, Earl of Northumberland, whose sister was mother of Malcolm, could not be supposed to sympathize with an order of succession so much at variance with the rest of Europe, and by which his own nephew was unthroned and an exile. Malcolm, therefore, when he had grown towards manhood at the Northumbrian court, found in Siward a willing as well as powerful ally to assert his claims to the crown of Scotland, and nothing was wanting but the favourable moment of onset. That, too, we are told, was afforded by the opportune arrival of Macduff at the court of Northumberland, whose wrongs, and the inducements with which he endeavoured to rouse the apparently reluctant Malcolm, as detailed in the wondrous drama, are to be found at great length in the pages of Boece. Siward the Strong, the hero of Northumbrian romance, who split a rock of granite asunder with a blow

---

[1] The tragic circumstances which Shakspere has so dramatically introduced in the assassination of Duncan were adopted from Boece's account of the assassination of King Duff by Donevald, lord of the castle of Forres. There every point is specified even to the intoxication of the poor grooms, and the manner in which they were made to appear as the guilty actors of the deed.—See Boece's *Chronicles of Scotland*, translated by Bellenden, vol. ii. p. 208. Edin. 1821.

[2] Hoveden and Simeon of Durham inform us that A.D. 1050, "*Rex Scotiæ, Machetad, Romæ argentum spargendo distribuit.*" This it has been alleged means nothing more than that Macbeth *sent* money to Rome— perhaps as an expiation or a bribe. But the statement rather implies that the king was there in person. Of his bounty in this pilgrimage, also, we have the following attestation from Wyntoun:—

"Quhen Pape was Leo the Nynt in Rome,
As pilgryme to the court he come;
And in his almis he sen silver
Till al pur folk, that had myster (*i.e.* need).
In al tyme orsit he to wyrk
Profetabilly for haly kyrk."

of his battle-axe, and who thought that for a warrior to die otherwise than on his legs and in full panoply was to die the death of a cow, advanced with a powerful army of his own retainers into Scotland to vindicate the claims of his nephew. This invasion occurred in 1054; but the nobles and people, instead of flying from Macbeth, seem to have rallied round him, and fought bravely in his cause. A battle ensued in the neighbourhood of Dunsinane Hill; and although Macbeth was defeated, the war was not yet ended. It was there that Siward lost his eldest son Osberne, and refrained from lamentation when he was told that all the young warrior's wounds were in front. The earl was soon recalled to England, and thus the conduct of the war was left to Malcolm, who found in Macbeth an able and dangerous antagonist. After his defeat at Dunsinane the latter retired to the fastnesses of the north, and contrived to protract the war nearly two years longer, until he was brought to bay and slain in a desperate conflict at Lumphanan in Aberdeenshire. Tradition relates, that here also a son of Macbeth died fighting by his father's side; and the same authority attributes the death-stroke of the brave usurper to the hand of the injured Macduff.

On the fall of Macbeth the Scots, instead of repairing to the standard of the victorious Malcolm, continued their resistance, and proclaimed Lulach, the stepson of Macbeth, king. It was not wonderful that such should have been the case, when we remember that this contest for the royal succession was not a civil war but a foreign invasion, and that Malcolm's cause was supported by the Anglo-Danes of Northumberland, the deadliest enemies of the Scots. As for Lulach, who was the great-grandson of Kenneth IV., his claims to the throne would be unintelligible without a full understanding of the complexities of a Celtic pedigree; yet, tried by the Tanist rule, they appear to have been considered more valid than those of Malcolm himself. But Lulach, whose name signifies a "Fool," was no match for his energetic rival, backed by the Danish battle-axes of his Northumbrian auxiliaries; and after a short reign of continual struggle that lasted only a few months his career was terminated by defeat and death in a conflict with Malcolm at Essie in Strathbogie. The date of this battle is given as the 3d of April, 1057; and Malcolm, now without a rival, ascended the throne of Scotland.

This most distinguished of our early Scottish sovereigns, with whose reign the history of the country is reckoned properly to commence, on account of the darkness and uncertainty of its previous annals, is better known under his Celtic appellation of Malcolm Canmore (*caen mohr*, signifying a large head) than his title of Malcolm III. And seldom indeed has large intellect, which the appellation probably signified, or stout heart and warlike arm, which he undoubtedly possessed, been more required for the king of a barbarous age and a disunited discordant people. Looking at the subjects over whom he was called to rule, he was indeed at his accession a "king of shreds and patches." For independently of that congeries of tribes composed of Scots and Picts who constituted the earlier population of Scotland, there were the Britons of Cumbria and Strathclyde, the Danes from Ireland and the Baltic, the Anglo-Saxons of Lothian, and the "wild Scots of Galloway"—men differing in lineage, in speech, in character, and modes of life; differing in the terms of their admission into the country; and differing in the terms of submission which they owed to its royal authority, and even the positive hostility with which they were ready to oppose it; and these, if possible, had to be united into one nation and reduced to a common rule. No ordinary conjunction of favourable circumstances was needed for a king so situated. But these circumstances also in an eminent degree were combined in favour of Malcolm Canmore. By descent he was Saxon as well as Celtic, and therefore a representative of the two great races who now comprised the chief population of Scotland. His training among the Northumbrians had familiarized him to a higher style of civilization than he could have learned in his own country, as well as taught him those "sweet uses of adversity" which princes in exile have such ample means of acquiring. Judging from the probable period of his birth and the terms of his expatriation, he must have been at least thirty years old at the time of his accession, and therefore not a mere pupil in the arts of government. He came to the throne a successful conqueror, after having triumphed over an able and powerful rival; and this, irrespective of any question of right, will always be attractive with a rude and warlike people. Most opportunely also it happened for Malcolm III. and his ill-assorted people, that whereas a contest with England, so much more powerful than themselves, and with which they were now in such close and emulous contact, might have crushed them at the very outset of their political existence, this latter power had too many troubles and grievances of its own to interfere with the progress of Scotland. The dissensions between Edward the Confessor and the Godwin family, the disputed succession of Harold, and finally the Norman conquest of England, disunited and weakened that rival power against which, if united, even Malcolm Canmore could scarcely have made head. Thus the new Scottish king, able, vigorous, well-trained, and having on his side the prestige of a successful warrior, succeeded to the crown under circumstances and at a period when his great qualities could be best exercised for the consolidation of his people and extension of his kingdom.

One of Malcolm's first duties was to reward that Scottish adherent by whom he had been so ably assisted in recovering his patrimonial rights. This was Macduff, the Mormaor of Fife, who had first repaired to Malcolm in England and afterwards joined him with his vassals in Scotland; but instead of accepting a profitable return in grants of crown lands or pensions, Macduff contented himself with honourable distinctions which were freely accorded by the new sovereign. These were that he and his successors, the lords of Fife, should have the right of placing the King of Scotland on the throne at their coronation; that they should lead the van of the Scottish armies whenever the royal banner was displayed; and that he or any of his kin committing unpremeditated slaughter should have a peculiar right of sanctuary and remission of punishment by the payment of a fine.[1]

During four years after the accession of Malcolm a strict peace was maintained with England—a measure which gratitude as well as policy must have dictated to the Scottish king. He had also conceived such a strong friendship for Tostig, the brother of Harold, who had become earl or governor of Northumberland about the time of his own succession to the throne of Scotland, that they were commonly called the sworn brothers.[2] But in 1061 this brotherhood had come to an end, and Malcolm invaded Northumberland, wasted the country, and "violated the peace of St. Cuthbert"[3]—a sacred compact which seems to have been made between the two chiefs over the relics of the saint in the island of Lindisfarne. With which of the parties the demerit of breaking this sacred alliance rested we are not informed; but the profligate and imperious character of Tostig, for which he was finally banished by the Northumbrians, makes it probable that in this case the earl and not the king was the offender.

Rashly prosecuted as this quarrel seems to have been on the part of Malcolm, by an invasion that might have involved his kingdom in a dangerous war, his renewal of friendship with the unprincipled Tostig was more culpable and impolitic still. This earl, burning with resentment against the Northumbrians who had cast him off, and against his own brother Harold, now King of England, who refused to uphold his cause against the just resentment of the men of Northumberland, resolved to take vengeance upon all alike by becoming a traitor and an enemy to his native country; and with this view he went successively to the courts of Flanders, Normandy, Denmark, and Norway, to stir them up to an invasion of England and the deposition of its king. Having obtained a few ships he attempted a descent upon England in the fashion of the northern sea-kings, but was driven from every point at which he attempted a landing; and at length, compelled by extremity and the hopelessness of his enterprise, he came with only twelve small vessels to Scotland. Malcolm received the unnatural rebel with welcome, or at least permitted him to anchor unmolested and remain a whole summer in the country. From Scotland Tostig repaired to Norway, whose king, Hardrada, he persuaded to invade England at the time when William of Normandy was making preparations for its entire conquest. Hardrada and his ally in the course of their expedition touched at the Orkneys, where they were largely reinforced by the Norwegian pirates of these islands; but by this time it appears that the alliance between Malcolm and Earl Tostig had terminated, as the Scottish king did not embrace the tempting opportunity of joining such a formidable invasion. And it was fortunate for himself and his people that he thus abstained; for on their landing in England the Norwegian king and Northumbrian earl were totally defeated at the battle of Stamford Bridge, and slain, with nearly all their followers.

Events now went onward, the inevitable result of which was to bring England and Scotland into close contact and even hostile collision. Only three days after the battle of Stamford Bridge, William of Normandy landed in England, and the battle of Hastings was fought, by which his way was opened to the English throne. During the progress of this Norman conquest the English sought for a leader among their own native princes; but in their sad extremity their choice was limited to Edgar Atheling, son of Edmund the Outlaw, and grandson of Edmund Ironside. Few, indeed, were the men who could have been found less fitted for the sacred office of a national champion and liberator; for besides his indifference to freedom, he was a contented follower in the train of the Norman despot, and his

---

[1] Called Macduff's Law by Fordun, in whose time it was still extant. *Fordun*, lib. v. cap. 9. See also Hailes' *Annals of Scotland*, vol. i. p. 4. Edin. 1797.
[2] Simeon of Durham. [3] Idem.

early life, which had been spent in exile in Hungary, had not only denationalized his feelings, but blunted him to the sense of what was due to his own royal ancestry. But his name at least was something, and it was eagerly secured by Marlswine, Cospatric, and other Northumbrian nobles, who were disgusted with the tyranny of the Conqueror; and when they found their cause hopeless they fled for protection to Malcolm Canmore, carrying with them Edgar Atheling, his mother Agatha, and his two sisters, Margaret and Christina. This, though the most important, was not the first influx of English exiles whom the Conquest had driven into Scotland; for even already several Anglo-Danish and Anglo-Saxon nobles had found a home from Malcolm, and had encouraged their suffering countrymen in England by reports of his liberality. Malcolm received the illustrious fugitives of the line of Alfred with welcome, lodged them in his castle of Dunfermline, and finding Margaret young and beautiful, he soon took her to wife. The precise date of this important union is uncertain, but it appears to have been about A.D. 1067 or 1068. By this marriage the English nobles might hope to find in the Scottish king an assured protector as well as a willing avenger. Malcolm on his part may have hoped, from the example afforded by the history of Kenneth Macalpin, that this marriage might finally blend the royal lines of England and Scotland into one, and entail upon his race the sovereignty of the whole island.

The union of the Scottish king with the English princess was the signal of fresh insurrections against the Norman conqueror; and, instigated by the exiles at the Scottish court, the Northumbrians rose against the garrisons of their oppressors and put them to the sword. In the year 1069 a fleet of Danes, who still remembered their old alliance with the Danelagh, ascended the Humber to act in concert with their kinsmen of Northumberland. It was a formidable but heterogeneous armament, like that with which William himself had effected the conquest of England; for it consisted of 240 ships, manned not only by Danes and Holsteiners, but by Frisians, Saxons, Poles, and the roving adventurers of every country whose trade was war, and whose only pay was plunder. The inhabitants of Northumberland and Yorkshire joined them; and to their united encampment repaired from Scotland Edgar Atheling, Marlswine, Cospatric, Waltheof, the son of Siward, and cousin of Malcolm Canmore, and many other English nobles, all elate in the foreign aid that had arrived, and hopeful of liberty and revenge. Their first attack was upon the city of York, which they took by storm, and inflicted such slaughter upon its Norman garrison as had not been paralleled since the battle of Hastings. But after such a signal commencement nothing more was attempted; and this singular inactivity has been attributed to the non-appearance of Malcolm Canmore, who was to have acted in concert with the Danes and Northumbrians. For this failure his memory has been severely blamed; but it may have originated either in his ignorance of the arrival of the Danes or his inability to collect a sufficient military force when the season for action had arrived. At all events, the opportunity for the recovery of England was utterly lost. In the meantime William broke up this coalition with his wonted activity and success. He first bought off the Danish commander, who withdrew his fleet and army, and won over Cospatric by the promise of the earldom of Northumberland, while Edgar and the rest of his adherents, dismayed at these instances of treachery, abandoned the Northumbrians to the vengeance of the Conqueror and fled once more to Scotland.

At length Malcolm was in readiness to act when the fit time for action had passed away. In 1070 he entered England by the western border through Cumberland, laid waste the district of Teesdale, and, dispersing a small army that opposed his progress at Hunderskelde, near the Derwent, he advanced into Cleveland, apparently hoping still to find his allies upon the east coast. But learning of their dispersion, he proceeded to turn the war to his own account by acting as a hostile invader. He accordingly proceeded through the eastern parts of the bishopric of Durham, marking his progress with fire and sword, in which neither church nor sanctuary was spared; and on learning that the traitor Cospatric was wasting his own district of Cumberland in the service of the Norman he increased the severity of his measures by at first ordering no quarter to be given to either age or sex. These merciless orders were as mercilessly executed; they were too much in accordance with the usages of war, both Saxon and Norman, to excite much surprise, and he afterwards signalized his clemency by ordering that the young men and maidens should only be carried away into bondage instead of being put to death. So great was the number of prisoners on this occasion, that for many years after an English bondman or bondwoman was to be found, as we are assured by Simeon of Durham, not only in every village but even every hovel of Scotland. But here the miseries of devoted Northumberland did not terminate. To chastise its revolt William the Conqueror visited it with a more formidable army than that of Malcolm, and wasted it with such havoc that the visit of the Scots was light in comparison. A terrible famine was the natural consequence, which inflicted still greater evil than the sword. The defeated English fled across the border into Scotland, which was now regarded as the asylum of the oppressed Englishman and discontented Norman; the hunger-worn peasantry who had still the means of flight, imitated the example; and many who had lost their all were fain to sell themselves, their wives, and their children as slaves at the hour of their extremity, and when no other aid remained.

After William had taken full vengeance upon the Northumbrians his next thought was of reprisals upon Scotland; and A.D. 1072 he invaded it by land, while a fleet followed to co-operate by sea. What were his military operations during this campaign we are not informed; but as it was the most formidable invasion which the country had as yet sustained, we are warranted by this silence in concluding that Malcolm gave place to the storm which he could not resist, and allowed the Norman chivalry to waste their valour upon the barren heaths and mountains of his frontier.[1] Supported, however, by his fleet, William was able to maintain his ground so long that Malcolm at last consented to a treaty, which, we are told, was made at Abernethy.[2] Thither the King of Scotland came to the Norman sovereign, and there gave hostages, and did homage to William—but for the lands he held in England, as Fordun is careful to inform us,[3] upon the authority of Vincentius. Malcolm, however, was the losing party by the expedition, as it was probably about this time that William took Cumberland into his own possession, and bestowed it as a military fief upon Renouf (or Ranulf) Meschines, who thereby became the first earl of Cumberland. In this way a debatable ground was created for the future wars between England and Scotland. William also removed Cospatric from the government of Northumberland, under a suspicion that he had encouraged the late rebellion in that quarter. This noble, on being thus bereaved of the price of his treachery, fled once more to Scotland, and was received into favour by Malcolm whom he had betrayed, and who admitted him once more into his confidence. This trust, and the lands with which Cospatric was richly endowed in Scotland, rivetted his wavering fidelity at last, and he became the ancestor of the earls of March, that powerful family who, from the possession of Dunbar, were said to have the keys of Scotland at their belt. On his return to England William also ordered the castle of Durham to be fortified as a barrier against future Scottish inroads. As for Edgar Atheling, the ostensible cause of the war, and of whom such hopes had been formed that he had obtained the title of "England's darling," his utter imbecility was such a complete defence that the Conqueror made no attempt to dislodge him from the hospitable shelter of the Scottish court. Edgar, however, probably weary of its rude simplicity, returned to England in the following year, and made his peace with William, into whose hands he surrendered all his claims and rights, for which he obtained in return a daily allowance of a pound of silver. In this way the descendant of Alfred, and heir of his toils and victories, sold his birthright for a mess of pottage, and stooped to the crumbs that fell from the rich man's table!

From this picture it is pleasing to turn to the noble character of his sister Margaret, the wife of Malcolm Canmore, who was so fortunate in that rude age as to find a faithful biographer in her chaplain Turgot. To her, indeed, he was what Asser had been to Alfred; and from his narrative, written in Latin, we have a full account of the private life of Margaret and her husband. In the proceedings of Malcolm himself we perceive that, although wise, clement, and magnanimous, he was still a barbarian; but, from her sage counsels and gentle conduct, his lion-like ferocity was tamed, and he even learned from her example, as the monk informs us, to pass the night frequently in prayer, and to supplicate with groans and tears. "I confess," he adds, "that I have often marvelled at the wonderful mercy of God, when I beheld a king so devout, and such signs of deep penitence in a layman." Notwithstanding his education in England, Malcolm was unable to read; but he loved her prayer-books and favourite volumes, often turned them over and kissed them, and caused them to be adorned with gold and pre-

---

[1] "Here King William led ship-force and land-force to Scotland, and that land on the sea-half with ships beleaguered, and his land-force at the ford (Gewaede) led in, *and he there nought found that to him the better was.*" This passage from the *Saxon Chronicle* has been supposed by some writers to intimate a complete conquest of the country; but such a conquest without one battle at least is too unreasonable for ordinary belief. It is more natural to suppose that when William found nothing "that to him the better was," the phrase means that the expedition was a most unprofitable one—that it supplied neither plunder nor provisions.

[2] From the impolitic character of the route which must have led William into such gratuitous danger, it is supposed that the English chroniclers have mistaken the name of the place, and that it was at Berwick rather than Abernethy that the treaty was made on this occasion, while Chalmers supposes that the Abernithi in question was the mouth of the Nith in Dumfriesshire.

[3] Anno millesimo septuagesimo secundo, Willelmus Bastard Scotiam intravit, cui occurrens rex Malcolmus, in loco qui dicitur Abirnethy, homo suus devenit *pro terris in Anglia*.

VOL. I.

cious stones. Some of her works of charity, while they evince her ardent benevolence, also indicate the monastic instruction by which they had been trained and directed. For every day she washed the feet of six of the poorest people, and dried and kissed them. She maintained nine orphans, and upon her knees she fed them out of her own hands. She had a custom to treat three hundred poor persons in a hall of her palace, when, on the doors being shut, she and her husband served the guests on either side of the table, and supplied them with food. These deeds, which in modern times might savour of fanaticism or ostentation, were at such a period considered only the natural expressions of a devout affectionate spirit, and as such were practised without a sense of degradation. Other charities of Margaret, however, were of a more queenly and useful character. All superfluity in her ornaments, dress, and expenses of the table were curtailed, that the produce might be given to the poor. She even sent privately among the towns and provinces to discover those who were in extreme want, and especially such as had formerly been in a better rank of life, and to hear of them was to send them relief. When she understood, also, that any of the English were detained as prisoners of war in Scotland, she paid their ransom and sent them home. "As the queen of the bees," says one of her eulogists, "has but very short wings, so she strays not far from the hive, our princess except for necessity and divertisement, which she was obliged to take for her health, went seldom abroad. And if she chanced at any time to go out about the affairs of the kingdom or her devotions, a troop of widows and orphans circled her on all sides as their common mother: she heard them with incomparable sweetness, and permitted none to go away empty-handed."[1]

In her domestic life, Margaret, as a mother and a queen, was a pattern for every age and country. She carefully educated her children, drew up precepts in writing for their moral conduct, and ordered their preceptors to chastise them as often as they merited punishment. Even in her dying moments they were her chief concern, and she bequeathed the charge of their spiritual instruction to her confessor in language which few mothers could read unmoved.[2] In her household she entertained many ladies about her person whose leisure hours were chiefly employed in needlework, and such was the strict decorum she maintained that " in her presence nothing unseemly was ever done or uttered." As an English princess also Margaret must have felt the rude contrast of the Scottish court and its barbarous chieftainry, and seen that to civilize her husband's subjects it was necessary to commence the reformation at the fountain-head. It was easy, therefore, to persuade Malcolm, whose sentiments accorded with her own, to appear in public with the commanding insignia of royalty, to enlarge and improve his retinue, and give frequent banquets to his nobles, where they would have an opportunity of learning the superior festive refinements of those distinguished Norman and Saxon refugees who had sought the asylum of the palace of Dunfermline. At these banquets also she caused the king to be served at table in gold and silver plate—"at least," says the historian, putting a check on his enthusiasm, "the dishes and vessels were gilt or silvered over." And as one of the first as well as most important steps in the civilization of a community originates in the desire of better clothing and more becoming ornaments, Queen Margaret not only dressed gracefully and richly, but facilitated the means of imitation to her court and people by encouraging the foreign merchants to adventure into Scotland with their tempting ware. They came, accordingly, with such rich commodities as the Scots had never seen before, so that when they attired themselves in these strange importations, they seemed, says the chronicler, to "have become new men."

From the devout character of the queen, modelled as it was upon the rule of Rome, which could tolerate no observances but its own, Margaret, at her first entrance into Scotland, must have been startled at the nakedness of the Culdee form of worship, so unlike the gorgeous ritual to which she had been accustomed. But still more grievous offences, in her eyes, belonged to it, the chief of which was the period of the celebration of Easter, in which the Culdees, as we have already seen, followed the computation of the Eastern rather than the Western Church. This to Margaret must have appeared a spiritual rebellion and downright heresy, more especially as the violent controversy which it had stirred up in England was still of notable remembrance. To suppress,

---

[1] *The Idea of a Perfect Princess in the Life of St. Margaret, Queen of Scotland*, &c. Paris, 1661.

[2] After a discourse on her spiritual state she said to Turgot: "Farewell; my life draws to a close, but you may survive me long. To you I commit the charge of my children; teach them above all things to love and fear God; and whenever you see any of them attain to the height of earthly grandeur, oh! then, in an especial manner be to them as a father and a guide. Admonish, and if need be, reprove them, lest they be swelled with the pride of momentary glory, through avarice offend God, or by reason of the prosperity of this world become careless of eternal life. This, in the presence of HIM who is now our only witness, I beseech you to promise and to perform."—Translated in Hailes's *Annals*, vol. i. p. 47.

therefore, what she honestly considered a soul-destroying error, but to suppress it by the gentle weapons of argument and persuasion, was her chief aim. And indeed she was better fitted than most women of the age for so difficult a task; for independently of the unlimited power which her husband seems to have allowed her in the management of the Scottish church, and the ascendency of her own amiable character, she was both learned and eloquent, being able to read the Scriptures in the Vulgate as well as a priest, and illustrate them with fluency and power. "Often," says Turgot, "have I with admiration heard her discourse on subtle questions of theology in presence of the most learned men of the kingdom." A public controversy upon the Easter question was therefore inevitable, and the Scottish clergy were invited into the lists to debate the subject with the queen. There was a difficulty indeed in the case which might have checked an ordinary controversy at the outset or adjourned it to an indefinite period; for while Margaret was ignorant of the Gaelic language, the priests could speak no other. But the king, who could speak both Saxon and Gaelic, acted as interpreter between the parties, and thus the difficulty was surmounted. "Three days," continues Turgot, "did she employ the sword of the Spirit in combating their errors; she seemed another St. Helena, out of the Scriptures convincing the Jews." Against such a disputant, aided by such an interpreter, the issue could scarcely be doubtful; and the monk informs us that the Scottish priests, overcome by the arguments of reason and truth, abandoned their erroneous usage and observed Lent according to the Catholic institution. In recording the history of this strange debate we cannot help thinking of a similar convocation held at Hampton Court by a royal descendant of Malcolm and Margaret, more than five centuries afterwards, when the question was not about Easter, but clerical gowns, tippets, and episcopal ordination; and how differently royal courtesy and discretion were manifested on that occasion by James VI., the Solomon of his age! On account of their zeal for religion and the panegyrics they have received from the clergy it might be supposed that Malcolm and his queen must have signalized their piety, according to the universal fashion of the period, by rich gifts and endowments to the church; but except in certain moderate donations to the Benedictines of Dunfermline and the Culdees of Fife no trace of this kind of liberality can be discovered in their history. The king may have found the royal demesnes not more than sufficient for the endowment of those exiles whose families were to become the nobles of Scotland; and as for Margaret, the honour of saintship which she obtained from her church was won by the purity of her character, not purchased with broad lands and rich offerings.

Reluctantly abandoning such an alluring oasis of green pastures and still waters, we pass from the life of this mother of her people to those political events in which her husband and the nation were involved. Seven years of tranquillity had passed in Scotland since the invasion of William in 1072, and from the foregoing account we can judge how the interval was employed upon the internal affairs of the kingdom. But in 1079, while the Conqueror was warring in Normandy against his unnatural son Robert, Malcolm embraced the opportunity of once more invading England. Of the causes of this inroad we are not informed, but perhaps the resumption of Cumberland to the English crown was the chief. The history of this expedition, which was carried into Northumberland as far as the Tyne, is briefly dismissed by an old historian, who tells us that Malcolm slew many, captured more, and returned with much plunder.[1] William, who had ended his war in Normandy and returned to England, sent his son Robert, to whom he had been reconciled, into Scotland on the following year to revenge the insult. But Robert, although as brave a soldier as his father, had neither his activity nor his prudence, and after an inglorious campaign, in which he is supposed to have advanced as far as the place where Falkirk now stands without finding an enemy to encounter, he returned to England without a battle and without honour. All, indeed, that he seems to have effected was to erect in his retreat a fortress near the Tyne, to repress the invasions of the Scots, which was afterwards called Newcastle.

After this another interval occurred, in which Scottish history is a blank. By the death of William the Conqueror, A.D. 1087, Malcolm was freed from a most dangerous antagonist; but he gained another more quarrelsome still in William surnamed Rufus, the second son of the Conqueror, who succeeded to the throne of England. At first, however, matters went on smoothly, for the new king released a son of Malcolm, who appears to have been held as a hostage in England, and conferred upon him the honour of knighthood. But Rufus still kept possession of Cumberland, and, in addition to this old injury, he is supposed to have withheld certain other lands in England to which Malcolm Canmore had a claim. A fit season for retribution arrived on the absence of Rufus in Normandy,

---

[1] Florence.

and in May, A.D. 1091, Malcolm led an army into England; but when he had penetrated as far as Chester-le-Street between Newcastle and Durham, he learned that an English army was mustered to oppose him, upon which he prudently retreated homeward. Three months after this inroad Rufus arrived in England, with his brother Robert, Duke of Normandy, and prepared to invade Scotland, as his father had done, both by land and sea. Although his ships were blown off the coast and dispersed by a storm he still pressed forward, losing many of his horses by hunger and cold in his march. Malcolm advanced to meet him as far as "Lothian in England," says the *Saxon Chronicle*—but as Lothian already belonged to Scotland, some other place within the English territory of a similar name (perhaps Lothere, now Lowther) must have been the halting-place of Malcolm. No conflict, however, occurred, as Robert of Normandy, who was in the English camp, and Edgar Atheling, who had for a short time been in Scotland, mediated successfully between the contending sovereigns. The result was an agreement by which Malcolm rendered to Rufus the usual homage of the Scottish kings; while the latter restored twelve manors in England which Malcolm had held under the Conqueror, and agreed to pay him annually twelve marks of gold. They parted in mutual peace, which, however, was not to be lasting, for A.D. 1092 William Rufus erected a castle at Carlisle to serve as an additional barrier against Scottish incursions, but which Malcolm regarded as an infringement upon his rights in the district of Cumberland. His remonstrances appear to have been backed by the Norman nobles of England, who were too busily employed in securing their new possessions to covet an unprofitable war with Scotland. The two kings accordingly met at Gloucester to adjust the quarrel by negotiation. Here, however, the imperious character of Rufus broke out, for he required Malcolm at this place, and in presence of the English barons, to render the usual homage; but this the Scottish king refused to do except upon the common frontier, and in presence of the nobility of both kingdoms, according to the fashion which had been hitherto observed. This makes it evident that the homage in question, which afterwards produced such deadly wars, and finally so much literary controversy, was merely for territories held in England, and not for the kingdom of Scotland itself, as in the latter case the Scottish nobles would only have been rere-vassals to the English king, and therefore disqualified to sit in court with the chief lords of his crown. It would have been in vain, therefore, for Malcolm Canmore to have pleaded former usage as the ground of his refusal, had not such meetings, where the nobility of both kingdoms assembled on equal terms, been a fact too well known to be denied. Upon this refusal Rufus was advised by his counsellors to detain the Scottish king as a prisoner; but this he refused, although, it may be, from no high principle of magnanimity. Only the year previous he had gained possession of a large portion of Normandy, and been promised the whole dukedom should he outlive his brother Robert; but such a flagrant violation of all feudal law as the detention of the Scottish king might have reduced his own hope of succession by the same law on the Continent to an absolute nullity. He dismissed Malcolm unharmed, but in a scornful supercilious manner, and the latter, thus insulted, hurried to Scotland and prepared for immediate war.

These preparations appear to have been conducted with angry haste, and were therefore ill fitted to encounter the united weight of England. The meeting at Gloucester occurred on the 24th of August (1093), and little more than two months afterwards Malcolm at the head of a tumultuary army burst into Northumberland, which he wasted as on the former occasion with fire and sword. After having ravaged the open country, he proceeded to lay siege to the castle of Alnwick. Here, however, his career was ended, for, on the 13th of November, he was surprised and slain by Robert de Mowbray, Earl of Northumberland. With him also fell Edward, his eldest son, who would have succeeded to the throne. Such was the end of Malcolm Canmore, after a long and glorious reign, of which the particulars handed down are so scanty that they are chiefly to be surmised from their important results. Like William the Conqueror, his contemporary, his reign forms the great historical epoch and starting-point of the country over which he ruled; and to him those important institutions have been referred whose origin cannot otherwise be ascertained. Succeeding to the rule of an unsettled kingdom and a barbarous and divided people, it speaks highly for his abilities both as a statesman and soldier that he was able to hold his course so successfully against such opponents as the Conqueror and William Rufus. It is in this character that he looms before us in the obscurity of remote ages, and the brief as well as sometimes contradictory statements of the English chronicles from which our knowledge of him is chiefly derived.

During this unfortunate campaign Queen Margaret, worn by the fastings and austerities which her church encouraged, was lying upon her death-bed in the castle of Edinburgh. She had received for the last time the communion, and was employing the few moments that remained to her upon earth in devout supplications for acceptance with Him into whose presence she was about to enter, when a messenger of sorrow glided into the apartment: it was her son Edgar, who had escaped from the carnage at Alnwick, and only arrived in time to see his mother die. Recalled to earthly affections by his appearance, Margaret eagerly exclaimed, "How fares it with the king, and my Edward?" —and the mournful silence of the youth was the only answer. "I know all," she rejoined—"I know all: by the holy cross, by your filial affection, I adjure you, tell me the truth!" He informed her that both husband and son were among the slain. She raised her eyes to heaven, and faintly exclaimed, " Praise and blessing be to thee, Almighty God, that thou hast been pleased to make me endure so bitter anguish in the hour of my departure, thereby, as I trust, to purify me in some measure from the corruption of my sins. And thou, Lord Jesus Christ, who, through the will of the Father, hast enlivened the world by thy death, oh, deliver me!" With these words she expired.

It will at once be seen that a history of Malcolm Canmore would be incomplete if taken apart from that of Margaret. In his government, indeed, she seems throughout to have been his better genius, and to her whatever civilization his subjects acquired was mainly owing. Her wisdom and goodness were also conspicuous in the carefulness with which she avoided all open interference in the government of the kingdom, so that his renown should be undiminished and his authority unimpaired. In all those departments of internal administration in which a queen may be allowed to co-operate with her lord and husband, we seem to recognize the spirit of Alfred, her illustrious ancestor—the same earnest self-sacrificing devotedness to the instruction and civilization of her people, but softened into feminine gentleness, and confined within its proper sphere. With such worth, and diffusing such blessings, it is not wonderful that her name was adopted as a household one for the homes of Scotland, as well as enrolled in the hagiology of a grateful priesthood.

The death of Malcolm Canmore gave every promise of being followed by a troubled succession to the throne. Of his six sons, the eldest had fallen with him in battle; the second, Ethelred, had disqualified himself for a crown by assuming the clerical tonsure; and the other four princes were still minors. Donald Bane was indeed still alive, and in the Hebrides, to which he had escaped on the assassination of his father by Macbeth; but the Tanist law, which of late had sustained so many rude shocks, was not likely to be in favourable acceptance with the Norman chiefs and Anglo-Saxon population, who were already so influential in the affairs of the kingdom. But Donald Bane, although now an old man, was resolved to try the experiment; and, supported by the Norse chieftains of the Hebrides, he set sail with a formidable armament and landed upon the mainland of Scotland. His claims were warmly supported by the Celtic part of the population, who hated the Saxons, and were jealous of foreign innovation; and regarding Donald as the champion and representative of their race they quickly bore him forward to the elevation he coveted. The new king, who appears to have been a genuine savage, soon requited this favour by the expulsion of the obnoxious foreigners; and among those who fled were the four sons of Canmore, who were safely conveyed into England by Edgar Atheling from the fury of their tyrant uncle. Fortunately this backward career of Donald was speedily arrested. The late king, besides his children by Margaret, had an elder illegitimate son, Duncan, whom he had left as a hostage in the hands of the English in the treaty of 1072, who had received knighthood from the hand of Rufus, and been trained under him in military service. At a period when crowns and countships were the prizes of every military adventurer, Duncan sought and quickly obtained permission from the English king to try his fortune in Scotland; and after having sworn fealty to Rufus he commenced the adventure with a miscellaneous army of Normans and English, men who, having failed to carve out estates with their swords in the south, were willing to content themselves with the less profitable acres of the northern kingdom. Donald Bane was expelled by the invaders after he had worn the crown for a short year, and Duncan reigned in his stead.

At this point of our national history the usual darkness gathers doubly around it. It has been alleged, for instance, in justification of Duncan, that he was the legitimate offspring of Malcolm Canmore by a first marriage, and that his occupation therefore of the throne was according to the rule of primogeniture established among every people but the Celts. In this way they explain the aid which Rufus gave to the expedition, and his acquiescence in its result—as if the son of him who was wont to sign himself "Gulielmus Bastardus" would have been a stickler for legitimate succession! It was by such a sovereign also as Duncan, who was his sworn vassal, that the English king could best hope to lay a secure hold upon

Scotland. Others, who are convinced of Duncan's illegitimacy, declare that he did not usurp the crown at all, but merely acted as regent for his lawfully born brothers until they should be of age. But whether he ruled as king or regent it mattered little, for his rule was brought in a few months to a violent termination. Edmund, a son of Canmore, incensed at the usurpation of his step-brother, entered into a league with Donald Bane for the removal of Duncan and the partition of the kingdom between themselves; and in consequence of this compact Duncan was assassinated by Malpedir, Earl of Mearns, one of the conspirators. According to William of Malmesbury a full measure of poetical justice was meted out to the unnatural Edmund, for in a few years after, when order was restored in Scotland, he was condemned to perpetual imprisonment; and in the death-bed anguish of his remorse he ordered his chains to be buried with him as the token of his repentance. If this story be true, it makes for the full legitimacy and lawful royal succession of the unfortunate Duncan.

The way being cleared for his re-entrance into Scotland Donald Bane returned from his shelter in the Hebrides, and A.D. 1095 became once more a king. But neither increasing age nor his late dethronement appear to have added to his wisdom, and on resuming the royal seat he also resumed his baffled plans of restoring the old Celtic ascendency by the suppression and banishment of strangers. These men, however, although as yet the smaller number, were not to be expelled so easily, and they could calculate upon the sympathies of England, from which country they had so recently emigrated. It was no difficult matter, therefore, for Edgar Atheling to obtain permission of Rufus to assemble English forces and make an attempt in Scotland for the restitution of his sister's children. The expedition was crowned with success by the defeat of Donald Bane, who was taken in battle, deprived of his eyes, and thrown into prison, where he soon after died. Edgar, the eldest surviving son of Malcolm Canmore next to Ethelred the priest, succeeded by the deposition of his uncle to the throne of Scotland (A.D. 1097).

CHAPTER III.

HISTORY OF SOCIETY DURING THE PERIOD 843-1097.

Districts into which Celtic Scotland was divided—Additions made to the territory and population of Scotland—Immigration of the Cruithne from Ireland into Galloway—Acquisition of Lothian, Strathclyde, Cumbria, and the Islands—Norwegian population in Scotland—Their character, weapons, shipping, and forts—Their manufactures—Account of the Scoto-Celtic population—Their laws—Their form of coronation—Their military habits, weapons, and war-cries—Their want of traffic and coinage—Their scanty literature.

By the conquest or acquisition of Kenneth Macalpin, Caledonia had now become Scotland, and the two rival races by which it was peopled were fused into one, of which, as was to be expected, the Scoto-Irish had the complete predominance. This fusion, too, was the more easy, as both the Picts and Scots were children of the same great Celtic family, so that there were less demand upon the vanquished either for change or sacrifice.

When the country of many tribes and contending interests had thus become an entire kingdom, it is interesting to mark the portions of which Scotland proper was now composed and to ascertain its historical limits. These have been divided into ten districts, of which division the following is a summary:—

1. FIFE, comprehending the country between the Forth and the Tay below the Ochil Hills.

2. STRATHEARN, comprising Menteith and Breadalbane, which included the country between the Forth and the Ochil Hills on the south and the Tay on the north.

3. ATHOLE, including Stormont, comprehending the central Highlands, and lying between the Tay and Badenoch.

4. ANGUS, which consisted of the country lying between the Tay and the Isla on the south to the river North Esk upon the north.

5. MERNE or Mernes, composing the district from the North Esk to the river Dee.

6. ABERDEEN, including Banff, lying between the river Dee and the Spey.

7. MORAY, extending from the Spey to the Farrar and Beauly, and westward to the boundaries of Northern Argyle.

8. ARGYLE, the ancient kingdom of the Scots, stretching along the continent of Scotland from

the Clyde into the heart of Ross, and comprising the numerous islands in the neighbourhood.
9. Ross, composed of Ross and Cromarty.
10. SUTHERLAND and CAITHNESS.[1]

Such was Celtic Scotland during the present period, subject to one system of law, whatever that might be, and governed by one sovereign. But still the Celtic principle of division into tribes and the patriarchial form of rule prevailed, so that each district was governed by its own mormaor, who if he was strong enough might tyrannize over his neighbour chiefs, or even rebel against the king, should the supreme authority be opposed to his own interests.

The Scoto-Irish population which thus predominated were not entirely composed of the descendants of those who came into the country with Fergus and his brothers. There was a later Irish immigration and conquest in Scotland, to which it now becomes necessary to advert. When the Saxon invasion of England was crowned with success in the south, the spirit of adventure, or the inability to secure a better portion, impelled several of the invaders northward, where large and still unoccupied territories awaited the first comer. On this account the large peninsula formed by the Solway, the Irish Sea, and the Clyde was overrun by the Northumbrian Saxons, so that the district was soon included in the kingdom of Northumberland, although the scanty native population was still more numerous than the Saxon. But at the end of the eighth century the Northumbrian dynasty was extinguished; and the extensive district being so far removed from the parent seat of government, and still so scantily inhabited, lay invitingly open to fresh bands of homeless adventurers. At this crisis the Cruithne of Ulster, overpowered by the invasions of the Danish sea-kings, crossed the narrow sea, as their countrymen the Dalriads had done four centuries earlier, obtained a footing near the Rhinns of Galloway; and being soon after followed during the ninth and tenth centuries by bands of their countrymen, as well as joined by their kinsmen the Scots of Cantire, they took possession of the whole of that extensive district which subsequently obtained the name of Galloway.

One of the most important as well as one of the latest acquisitions of the growing kingdom of Scotland was Lothian, which at the accession of Kenneth Macalpin was still a part of England, although it had often been a debatable ground and battlefield of the Saxons and the Picts. It still continued to belong to England till the eleventh century, when Malcolm II. obtained it by the peaceful concession of Eadwulf, Earl of Northumberland, in 1020. This was a valuable acquisition, as the Lothian (or Loudian) of those days comprised not only what are now called the Lothians, but the Merse, and that part of Roxburghshire which lies on the north of the Tweed.

Among the additions made to Scotland during this period must be mentioned the British kingdom of Strathclyde. This little Welsh territory, which was obliged to maintain its independence successively against the Saxons, the Picts, the Danes, and the Scots, at last was exhausted by its own efforts and fell an easy prey to its overwhelming neighbours, so that it was conquered and annexed to the Scottish crown by Kenneth III. in the tenth century.

Another British kingdom which was not so easily to be won by Scotland, or so permanently retained, was that of Cumbria. After it had long and gallantly resisted both its Saxon and Danish invaders it was at length conquered by the former, and bestowed upon Malcolm I. by Edmund the English king as the price of alliance and aid. On being thus obtained it formed a principality, and furnished a title to the heir of the Scottish throne, who was invested in its government by the sovereign under the title of Prince of Cumberland. But in 1072 this comfortable occupation of so large a principality was interrupted by William the Conqueror, who made a grant of it to Ranulf Meschines, one of his favourite chiefs, who in turn subdivided it into fiefs for the military retainers who followed his banner. The portion of Cumbria, however, which lay nearest Scotland was still retained by the latter, and its claims to the whole were kept in reserve as a ground of future controversy.

In this way was Scotland, a land which nature herself had divided into numerous independent districts by chains of mountains and broad rapid rivers, as well as by the segregation of its families into separate clans, at length rounded into an entire kingdom, with a single people in full predominance. But most important it was for its future safety and prosperity that here its limits should not terminate; for its seas were studded with islands which, as long as they remained independent of its authority, would inclose the kingdom as with a hostile network. A passing glance at these is necessary for a full understanding of the condition of Scotland at this early period.

What was the history of the Orkney and Shetland Islands before the ninth century—if, indeed, they had a history to tell—has never been recorded. They had no tin, like the Cassiterides, to allure the merchant, nor rich acres

---

[1] Chalmers' *Caledonia.*

to invite the conqueror; and we hear of them for the first time in Scottish records as the asylums of rebels and runaways. These were Norwegians, who had fled from Harold Harfagre, their king, in consequence of his naval victory by which he reunited the provinces of Norway into an entire government. Having accomplished this, A.D. 875, he turned his attention to the refugees, whose neighbourhood was still sufficiently dangerous; and he easily reduced these islands to his authority and placed them under the sway of Jarl Sigurd, who ruled them as his deputy. A line of jarls succeeded; but the submission of these Orcadian reguli, who lived by piracy and plunder, to the crown of Norway under which they held rule, could have been little more than nominal. Toward the close of the tenth century the islanders were converted to Christianity by the Culdees, but with little abatement of their spirit of piratical enterprise, for they still continued to harass the eastern coasts of Scotland, and managed to establish a permanent footing in Sutherland, Ross, and Moray. In the course of these conquests also their chiefs, fortunately for Scotland, were often at war among themselves, and in this way the Hebrides were reduced into tributaries to the Lord of the Orkneys and Shetlands. At length, in 1090, Norway was strong enough to bring back these sea-kings to their old allegiance; and Magnus Barefoot, the Norwegian sovereign, visited these islands with long-delayed chastisement, and compelled the Orkneys, Shetlands, Hebrides, and the Isle of Man to recognize themselves as vassal states of his kingdom.

In this way a rival kingdom was established in the Scottish seas and upon the coast which might, under favouring circumstances, have obtained the final ascendency and changed the character of the people as well as the current of their history. But formidable though this Scandinavian power certainly was, there were obvious difficulties which rendered such a consummation all but impossible. These are to be chiefly found in the narrowness of its extent, the poverty of its soil, and the want of union and cohesion among its widely scattered and discordant members, so that their final subjugation to the united power of Scotland, however tedious might be the process, was an inevitable necessity. This accordingly happened, as we shall find, in the course of events, and the infusion of so large a Scandinavian element into the Celtic and Saxon population of Scotland not only added greatly to its strength and resources, but to the high qualities of its national character. Even glancing through a long course of succeeding centuries, we can find that the naval flag of Britain, through which our island at last obtained such a universal dominion, was mainly unfurled and borne onward by the descendants of the Danelagh population of England, and those of the Norwegian islands and districts of Scotland.

It is unfortunate, however, that we know so little of the habits, manners, and mode of life which prevailed among the early settlers of these islands. As it was the custom of the earliest British historians to call all the Norse invaders Danes indifferently, whether they came from Denmark, Norway, Sweden, or even Iceland, the same mistake has been committed in our old Scottish chronicles, where the invaders are called by the general name of Danes instead of the distinctive title of Norwegians. We may therefore safely conclude that these conquerors and colonists of the Orkney, Shetland, and Hebridian islands were similar to their brethren, who about the same period attempted the conquest of England. That in religion they were worshippers of Odin, and in occupation pirates, we assuredly know; and that they did not fall short of that fearless and ruthless character which such a creed inspired and such pursuits cherished, we are fully warranted to conclude. The followers of Halfdane and Guthrun in the days of Alfred are described as unsparing destroyers of churches and murderers of priests; as insatiable plunderers and extortioners; as perfidious trucebreakers whom no oaths could bind; as immeasurable gluttons and drunkards, when the means were within their reach; and as guests, who, after devouring the substance of a house, were wont at their departure to murder the inmates who had waited on them, and set fire to the dwelling that had sheltered them—and the facts which the English historians relate confirm the truth of so revolting a picture. Such, then, were probably those roving freebooters of Norway who inhabited the Scottish islands during the ninth and tenth centuries. But happily their means of mischief were limited by stormy seas and barren rocks; and when they made their descents on the mainland they found a country almost as poor as their own, where hard blows were at least as plentiful as booty. Their invasions, therefore, upon Scotland were neither so formidable nor so sanguinary as those of the Danes in England. The same English histories attest the nautical intrepidity and skill of these rovers; their superiority in castrametation, and the unflinching valour with which they battled against every odds; and in these qualities we may conclude that the Orcadians and Hebridians were not inferior to their congeners. Of the defensive armour of these Norse warriors the helmet and shield were the chief, if not the only portion at this period; the shirt or habergeon of steel chain-work and armour of plate being later inventions. Of offensive weapons, besides the usual missiles of slings, darts, and arrows, and the sword and spear for close fight, the Danes and Norwegians were distinguished by the large double-edged battle-axe and heavy iron mace, which last weapon was adopted from the mighty hammer of their god Thor (the northern Hercules) with which he performed his wonderful achievements. Of the piratical vessels, these dragons of the sea, which so often issued from the rocky bays of the northern and western islands in quest of their prey, we can form a distinct idea from the numerous descriptions to be found in the old runes and northern histories. They were long, narrow, and low, and thus equally adapted for swift sailing and stealthy movements; and they were usually adorned with a figure-head at the prow like the vessels of earliest antiquity. Besides the usual complement of spears, arrows, and darts, each vessel was furnished with a quantity of heavy stones to sink an adversary; and along the sides was a breastwork of shields planted in a row by which the rowers were defended from missiles discharged from a distance, and which they could buckle on when it came to close combat. The missiles of distant fight were discharged from the prow and stern, which were built high for the purpose. In encountering the galley often tilted with its beak against the sides of the opposing vessel; and when they closed the battle was chiefly maintained on the prows. Often two ships were lashed together by mutual agreement, and the fight was maintained until one of the crews was overpowered. In these particulars we recognize the elements of a British naval fight in the nineteenth century.

From a people thus prepared both from choice and necessity for universal aggression unusual precautions in their means of defence were but too necessary, and were therefore not neglected. Accordingly, in the Orkney and Shetland islands, and the Hebrides, in Caithness and Sutherland, and in some parts of the west coasts of Ross and Inverness, Norwegian stone buildings, the tokens of a very early age, still exist, called *burgs* in the Norse language, and *duns* in the Celtic, both names signifying a place of strength. These are often supposed, but erroneously, to have been erected by the Picts, and are sometimes called the Picts' houses or castles, although they are only to be found in those districts which anciently formed the Norwegian part of Scotland. These burgs are constructed of stones without any kind of cement, but well fitted into each other; and they generally stand along the sea-coast, two or three, or even more sometimes being in sight of each other. In form they are circular, or slightly elliptical; and in height they vary from ten to forty feet, having from one to four stories of apartments according to their altitude. They generally had two walls, one within the other, with an open space between from four to five feet wide; and to make an unfriendly visit as difficult as possible, the entrances are both low and small, being generally not more that three feet in height, and two feet and a half in width. Each of these burgs was thus not only a fortress in the hour of danger, but might serve as a signal-station and a lighthouse. In the Shetland Islands and the Hebrides the ruins of some of these towers are on islets in the small lochs, in which case the only approach to them was by a concealed causeway under the surface of the water.[1]

In these indications we trace nothing higher than the restless, adventurous spirit of these early inhabitants of the Scottish islands and the insecure tenure by which property and life were held. But even during this period the energy of the Norwegian character was beginning to manifest itself in other enterprises than those of piracy and plunder; and the cultivation of useful arts and manufactures in which these islanders began to be distinguished, indicated a more settled state of society and the commencement of civilization and refinement. This was especially the case in the Hebrides (called the Sudereyar or Southern Islands by the people of Norway), and the cloths which they manufactured were famous, we are told, in the northern parts of Europe. A proof of this is given by a quotation from a northern poet, who, in describing the splendid dress of a hero, is careful to tell us that it was spun by the Sudereyans.[2] Such was the Scoto-Teutonic branch, which, along with the Saxons and Normaus, was so soon to impose a new people upon the Celtic kingdoms of Scotland.

While the great mass of the population in the meantime consisted of a Pictish, Dalriad, and Cruithne race, it is unfortunate for us that we know so little of the government and legislation, and still less of the manners and customs of the Scottish people before the great transition was effected. On the union of the Scots and Picts into one nation it is probable that a similar union was also formed of the laws of the two peoples. But in this case the Brehon system of legislation which belonged to the Scoto-Irish would assume, as the code of the conquering people, a decided ascendency over the old Pictish, whatever that may have

---

[1] Pennant's *Tour.* Gordon's *Itinerary.* Martin's *Western Islands, Statistical Account of Scotland.*
[2] Macpherson's *Annals of Commerce*, vol. i. p. 200.

been; and especially in the matter of Tanistry, which regulated the succession to regal and chieftain authority. That such was the fact we know from the struggles which took place for the Scottish throne after the death of Malcolm Canmore, when not the son but the brother of the deceased sovereign obtained the suffrages of the people, while his rival had to be imposed upon the royal seat by the Saxon and Norman foreigners. But of the express laws themselves which were in full force during this period of Scottish history we still remain ignorant, and the Macalpin code, to which the inquirer is referred, may be suspected to have originated at a later period. These Celtic laws and Celtic usages continued to predominate during the reigns of Malcolm Canmore and his immediate successors; and it was not till after a hard struggle that this primitive and patriarchal system gave place to the feudal, which was now the general law of Europe. By this the chief of the tribe, to whom all owed unlimited obedience, was changed into the landed proprietor, whose tenants paid him rent in military service; instead of a mormaor he became a thane, an earl, or a sheriff; and his little kingdom, in which he had been wont to rule with absolute sway, became an insignificant portion of the empire, to whose great head he owed the same feudal duty which he exacted from his own tenants and dependants. But how this duty was paid, and how keenly these deposed magnates looked back upon the old days when they had neither check nor superior, may be read in the continual rebellions of the Scottish nobility against their kings until feudalism itself had utterly passed away.

In the coronation of kings, the use of an inaugural stone seems to have been a distinguishing characteristic of the Scoto-Irish race. Hence the many travels and mystic importance of that slab of black marble which now reposes so peacefully in the cathedral of Westminster. It was declared to have been the original stone which Jacob in his flight first used as a pillow and then set up as a memorial. It was brought by Gathelus to Spain, and afterwards by his descendants from Spain to Ireland, where it was set up on the Hill of Tara as the future coronation-seat of the sovereigns of Ireland. After having been used for this august purpose for many ages it was then brought from Ireland to Cantire, and was finally transferred to Scone when the son of Alpin succeeded to the rule of the whole kingdom. The unquestionable antiquity of its history, the many coronations it had witnessed, and, above all, the prophetic promise that accompanied it, and which was supposed to have been verified in all its past wanderings, made it be regarded with such religious veneration that, long after the Celtic dominion had passed away, no Scottish sovereign would have been recognized as a lawful king unless he had received his power by being seated upon this throne of promise and miracle. But this was not all; for the ancient usages of a Celtic coronation formed also the chief part of the ceremonial. What these were we learn from our oldest historical records. When the boy-sovereign, Alexander III., was crowned at Scone, the feudal part of the rite was soon performed by administering to him the usual oaths, first in Latin, and afterwards in Norman-French. This being ended, the Celtic portion of the great national rite commenced. The boy was led to the sacred stone, which was placed before the cross in the eastern division of the chapel; the crown was placed upon his head and the sceptre in his hand; and the nobility, kneeling before him in token of homage, spread their robes beneath his feet. An ancient bard or seannachie with long white hair and clothed in a scarlet mantle then advanced, and, bowing before the throne, rehearsed in Gaelic the names of Alexander's royal ancestors down to the days of Gathelus. But even such a fearful crash of uncouth, unintelligible words may have been gratifying to Saxon ears, because it boded "awful rule and right supremacy." The use of such stones appears to have been common in the inauguration of the chiefs both in Scotland and Ireland. One of the most important of these was at Islay. It was a "large stone seven feet square, in which there was a deep impression that was made to receive the feet of Mac Donald, when he was crowned King of the Isles, and took the coronation oath: whereupon his father's sword was put into his hands, and he was anointed by the Bishop of Argyle and seven priests in the presence of the heads of the tribes."[1]

Of the war-habits of the Scots of this period we have very scanty information. Their chief weapons were a very long and slender spear and the heavy claymore, while besides the small round target covered with leather they

---

[1] Martin's *Western Islands*, p. 241. Spenser (author of the *Faery Queen*) gives the following account of the installation of a chief among the Irish: "They use to place him that shall be their captain upon a stone always reserved to that purpose, and placed commonly upon a hill. In some of which I have seen formed and engraven a foot, which they say was the measure of their first captain's foot; whereon he, standing, receives an oath to preserve all their ancient former customs inviolate, and to deliver up the succession peaceably to his Tanist; and then hath a wand delivered to him by some whose proper office that is; after which, descending from the stone, he turneth himself round thrice forwards and thrice backwards."

seem to have little if any defensive armour. In the wars, therefore, which were waged by Malcolm Canmore and his successors their regular military operations seem chiefly to have depended upon the well-armed and well-disciplined Norman and Saxon soldiery, who now constituted so large a portion of a Scottish army. The use of war-cries, so essential to all armies in the ruder stages of warfare, was especially needed among the Scots, not only to distinguish their tumultuary ranks from those of the enemy, but one clan from another. Hence, as we learn accidentally from Hoveden, the battle-word of the men of Galloway was "Albanich!" which they shouted on advancing to the charge. In later times we find that the cries of separate clans were generally taken from the place of military muster, and reminded them of the district and the homes for which they were fighting, and this may have been the case at an early period. Thus the cry of the Macfarlanes was "Loch Sloy," a small lake in Arrochar parish, Dumbartonshire; that of the Macphersons, "Craig Ubhe," or the black rock; that of the Buchanans, "Clare Inch," the name of a small island in Loch Lomond where their chief resided, &c. Of heraldic cognizances, whether general or particular, the Scots had none; and indeed for men who were so ignorant of pictorial imitation, and so unaccustomed to disguise their persons with a covering of defensive armour, these distinctions were unnecessary, even if their wearers could have carved or painted them. It was only when the Scots became a Teutonic rather than a Celtic nation that these innovations were introduced, in conformity with general European usage. On this account the legend of the national blazoury of Scotland having been devised by Charlemagne, and imparted to King Achaius, may be dismissed without scruple.

In some respects that indicate an advance in national civilization Scotland was considerably behind the other nations of Europe. One of the earliest tokens of a civilized people is the use of coinage, and specimens of money are generally the most abundant as well as the most enduring of a nation's antiquities; but not one trace of an old Scoto-Celtic coin can be discovered in the abundant antiquarian treasury of Scotland. Some have thought that there must have been a national coinage notwithstanding, and the proof they adduce is the historic fact of Macbeth's ample charities during his pilgrimage to Rome. But could he not bestow good largesses of Scottish gold and silver unless it had been coined? Or might he not have furnished himself with the necessary supplies in foreign money by giving sufficient value in exchange?

In the absence of these convenient symbols the traffic of the Scots must have been carried on with the cumbrous realities, and their chief cash must have been in the form of sheep and oxen. This implies the absence of foreign commerce; and accordingly the Scots were so unaccustomed to trade with other countries, that no mention is made of it till the days of Malcolm Canmore. Then, too, it was of the simplest and most primitive kind—a traffic in dress and ornaments by a half-naked people who had not skill enough to make these articles for themselves. At this point, however, a certain mercantile spirit seems to have been awoke among the people, of which we shall afterwards have occasion to trace the progress and results.

In such a period and amidst the wild strife of so many races, Pictish and Celtic, Anglian and Scandinavian, all striving for the possession of the country, an inquiry into the condition of its literature seems all but superfluous. Of ecclesiastical writers, besides Columba, whom we have formerly mentioned as an author, we have Cuminius or Cummin, Abbot of Iona in the middle of the seventh century, who wrote a life of the patron saint of the island; and Adamnan, also abbot during the close of that century, who wrote a *Life of Columba*, and an *Account of the Holy Places in Judæa*. Had the learning of the country been capable of higher efforts the opportunity was lost by the destruction of the college of Iona during the terrible ravages of the northern sea-kings. After this Scottish authorship was silent until the thirteenth century, when it gave tokens of its awakening from repose. As the Celtic character, however, is especially poetical, and as poetry does not depend for its aliment upon books and scholarship, a bardic literature at least might have been expected in the absence of other intellectual indications. But with the exception of the very doubtful Ossianic specimens, no Scottish poetry, whether Celtic, Cumbrian, or Pictish, has survived to distinguish this period of mental barrenness. When deeds of valour or turbulence are achieved poets are naturally produced to record them, and in this way even in Scotland every downright blow may have produced its appropriate rhyme. But beyond the hearth of the chieftain or the circle of a warlike festival these lays seem never to have travelled, and they died with the deeds they recorded or the voices that gave them utterance. Had a poet worthy of the name been produced we surely would have heard of him at least in the pages of Nennius, Geoffrey of Monmouth, and Giraldus Cambrensis.

Such is our scanty knowledge of Scotland during the brief period of Scoto-Irish ascendency and while its Celtic population constituted the bulk of its society. This ascendency is considered to have terminated with Donald Bane, at which period the Teutonic races began to vindicate their superiority and become the dominant power; and when the Celts, gradually driven before the resistless inundation, were finally borne back to the petty kingdom of Ardgael from which they had originally issued. Their disappearance from the foreground, like their entrance, was of a slow and silent and undistinguished character—not a sudden conquest or overthrow, but a gradual yielding before the growth of a foreign and rival power. At a future period they come forward as the Highlanders, and some account of their character and modes of life as such will necessarily occur in a later portion of our history.

PERIOD III.

FROM THE ACCESSION OF EDGAR TO THE DEATH OF ALEXANDER III. (A.D. 1097 TO A.D. 1286).

CHAPTER I.

REIGNS OF EDGAR, ALEXANDER I., DAVID I.—1097-1153.

Accession of Edgar—His tranquil reign—Marriage of his sister to Henry I. of England—His death—Edgar succeeded by Alexander I.—Alexander's contests with the English hierarchy—His efforts to secure the independence of the Scottish church—Appointment of Turgot to the primacy of St. Andrews—Appointment of Eadmer—Alexander's spirited and successful resistance—His donations to the church—His death and character—Alexander I. succeeded by David I.—Ecclesiastical contests renewed—David supports the claim of Matilda to the English throne—He invades England—Battle of the Standard—Defeat of the Scots—David's exertions in the cause of Matilda—The adventurer Wimund—His strange career and defeat—Agreement between David and Henry Plantagenet—Death of David's son Henry—David's liberality to the church—His public administration—His private pursuits—His death and character.

On the deposition of Donald Bane, Edgar, the fourth son of Malcolm Canmore, succeeded to the crown of Scotland, A.D. 1097. As it was by English arms that he had been placed upon the throne, a feeling of gratitude, as well as the consciousness of his own helplessness, may have bound him to that close alliance which he seems to have maintained without interruption with so fierce and imperious a sovereign as William Rufus. In this, perhaps, consisted his chief safety as the king of so unsettled a realm and so many different and contending races, for in character he appears to have been mild, easy, and unenterprising, so that the highest praise bestowed upon him by the old historians is, that in all things he resembled Edward the Confessor. Happily for him, no public event seems to have occurred during his reign to disturb his tranquillity or test his fitness for rule; and a Norwegian invasion that threatened to burst upon the kingdom was exhausted upon its remote boundaries, the Orkneys and Hebrides. This was in consequence of a design of Magnus, King of Norway, to reduce his subjects of these islands to full submission, and afterwards to invade the coasts of England and Ireland. He is said, indeed, in the course of his expedition to have landed in Galloway after he had quelled the rebellious islesmen; but as no conflict is recorded on this occasion, his visit, if he arrived at all, may have only been a partial or temporary landing. Be that as it may, Scotland was soon freed from all apprehension of this terrible pirate-king, as in the year following (A.D. 1103) Magnus carried his devastations to the north of Ireland, where he perished.

The friendly terms which Edgar had maintained with England during the reign of William Rufus, were strengthened by the bond of marriage on the accession of Henry. This was the union of his sister Matilda to Henry I., surnamed Beauclerk, shortly after his accession to the throne of England. This princess, who in early youth had been obliged to escape to England in consequence of the usurpation of Donald Bane, had found shelter with her aunt Christina, the second sister of Edgar Atheling, who was either abbess of Wilton, or of Rumsey in Hampshire. Not only the number of contentious competitors for her hand, but the wild license of the Norman conquerors, obliged her to confine herself within the innermost seclusions of the convent, until reasons of state policy compelled her to become a queen. This arose from the desire of Henry to strengthen his questionable claim to the English crown by an alliance with the royal house of Alfred. He saw, that by such a marriage he should have the whole English nation in his favour, and be thus enabled to maintain himself against the superior right of his elder brother Robert, while the oppressed Anglo-Saxons exulted in the hope that their bondage would be lightened by one of their race becoming a partner in the throne. Thus urged both by king and people, Matilda consented to become the wife of Henry; but here another difficulty occurred: it was the general belief that she had taken the vows of a nun, and consequently, as the bride of heaven, could never become the mate of an earthly husband. But this difficulty was also surmounted. Her aunt, to save her, she said, "from the lust of the Normans, who attacked all females," was accustomed to throw a piece of black stuff over her head; "and when I refused," she added, "to cover myself with it, she treated me very roughly. In her presence I wore that covering; but as soon as she was out of sight, I threw it on the ground and trampled it under my feet in childish anger." This explanation was received with triumph, and there were witnesses in plenty to confirm her statement. It thus appeared that she had worn the veil only occasionally, and as a disguise or mask; and the obstacle being thus removed, she became Queen of England. Her beauty, her love of learning, and charity to the poor, were worthy of the daughter of Margaret of Scotland; and while her marriage reconciled the English to a Norman reign, she continued to the last to be a faithful, affectionate wife to a faithless and hard-hearted husband.

Another marriage in the family of Edgar was that of his sister Mary, A.D. 1102, to Eustace, Count of Boulogne. With this event the history of Edgar may be said to terminate, although his reign continued a few years longer. He died at Edinburgh on the 8th of January, 1106-7, leaving behind him the character of an amiable man and feeble undistinguished sovereign.

As Edgar, like the monastic Edward the Confessor whom he so closely resembled, had no children to succeed him, the throne was immediately filled by Alexander I., his younger brother. The late king appears to have made a partition of the kingdom, by which, while Alexander succeeded to the sovereignty of the country on the north of the Friths, David, their youngest brother, obtained all the districts on the south of the Friths except Lothian as an independent principality. Such an unadvised bequest might, as in other royal instances of a divided government, have been a fruitful source of brotherly contention and civil war by which the nation at large would have been the sufferer, had it not been that Henry of England approved of the partition, which secured his dominion from the chance of a united Scottish invasion, while David himself was secured in his large possessions, in which the Scottish share of Cumberland was included, by the favour of the powerful English barons who advocated his claims. This, indeed, they did so effectually that Alexander, notwithstanding his high spirit, acquiesced in the arrangement. Still further also to secure the alliance of the Scottish king, Henry bestowed upon him his natural daughter Sibylla in marriage. It was a period when illegitimate descent was neither an indelible disgrace, nor yet an insuperable bar to a royal succession, and none were more interested in countenancing this general feeling than the family of William the Conqueror.

The chief contention by which the reign of Alexander I. was signalized was of a religious not a secular character, in which his own rights as a sovereign and the ecclesiastical independence of the kingdom were seriously involved. Hitherto the poverty of the Scottish church, and the unobtrusive lives of the clergy, had secured them from the ambitious designs both of Rome and England, and the pre-eminence which the Archbishop of York had claimed over all the northern sees had as yet been little more than a dead letter. Matters, however, had now altered. The Scottish bishoprics, from late royal endowments, had risen into such importance as made their patronage worth having, and nothing but a fit opportunity was wanting for the English primates to establish their claim. And this opportunity occurred when, in consequence of a vacancy in the bishopric of St. Andrews, Turgot, the monk of Durham, and affectionate chaplain and biographer of Queen Margaret, was selected by Alexander, with the approbation of both clergy and people, to fill the important office of Primate of Scotland. It was now the time for the Archbishop of York to claim the right of consecrating Turgot to the appointment; but it unfortunately happened that the archbishop himself although elected was not consecrated, and therefore could not bestow consecration upon another. In this strait a rumour was carried to Canterbury that a compromise had been devised by the English prelates of the Border by which the Primate of York was to give his presence at the ceremony, while the Bishop of Durham, as his vicar, was to invest Turgot with the necessary episcopal sanction. Of this arrangement Anselm, Archbishop of Canterbury, indignantly disapproved, and commanded his brother of York to come himself to Canterbury and be consecrated, instead of attempting to bestow consecration upon another. After a long and complicated controversy, during which the see of St. Andrews lay vacant, an expedient was devised by the kings of England and Scotland by which the debate was for the present quieted. It was that the Archbishop of York should consecrate Turgot, and that this act should be received "saving the authority of either church," which was to lie over as a subject for future adjustment. In this unwonted fashion Turgot in 1109 became Bishop of St. Andrews. But the good old man was far otherwise than happy in his northern primacy; and while he probably sought to complete those innovations by which the Scottish church might be reduced to a complete conformity with that of England, he had no longer the persuasive influence of Queen Margaret nor the authority of Malcolm Canmore to second his efforts. Be that as it may, he found himself involved in so many trying difficulties that he thought at one time of repairing to Rome for counsel and direction. After six years of trial and vexation he asked permission to revisit the monastery of Durham, in which he had been a monk before he became a prelate; and in that seclusion, which he ought never to have quitted, he soon after died.

With the death of Turgot the late controversy was opened afresh about the question of his successor; and as if to replace it in its former condition, and make the same ground be traversed anew, the present Archbishop of York was precisely in the condition of his predecessor, having not yet received consecration. In this case Alexander endeavoured to escape the control of both the English primates by setting them at variance about the new bishop-elect, who was Eadmer, the English monk of Canterbury, and ecclesiastical historian; but the Archbishops of Canterbury and York had more urgent matters to settle than those of St. Andrews, and did not fall into the snare which the Scottish king had devised for them. Alexander, on his part, was in no hurry to fill up the see, which remained vacant for five years. At length, in 1120, Alexander sent a special messenger to the Archbishop of Canterbury, requesting that Eadmer should be "set at liberty" for the purpose of being invested with the Scottish primacy; and with this the archbishop complied, declaring by letter to the king that he set the monk "wholly at liberty, and advising that Eadmer should be sent back to him with all speed to receive consecration at his hands. On his arrival in Scotland Eadmer, although elected by the clergy and people, and with the full approval of Alexander, did not receive the pastoral staff and ring from the king, nor yet perform homage as a Scottish prelate: he felt as if he were not yet a bishop until he had received the sanction of those high ecclesiastical rulers whose authority he deemed paramount to that of king, clergy, and people. Accordingly, the day after his election, an explanation took place between the king and the bishop, and a rupture was the consequence. Alexander expressed his dislike to Eadmer that he should accept consecration from the Archbishop of York; upon which Eadmer assured him he had no such purpose, but intended to receive it from the Archbishop of Canterbury, the metropolitan, by grace of the pontiff, over the whole island of Britain. This was an abrupt overturn of the king's calculations. By selecting a monk of Canterbury he had secured one who would not be likely to yield to the supremacy of York; and by stipulating that Eadmer should be sent to him *entirely free*, he hoped that this would dispense with any further necessity of episcopal sanction from Canterbury. It was a wholly independent man that he sought for the primacy of Scotland, and not a suffragan of that of England. Abruptly and indignantly he broke off the conference, and commanded the priest who during the vacancy had acted as interim bishop to resume his functions.

After a month of this estrangement had passed, the bishop and king were reconciled by a curious compromise. Eadmer was to accept the ring from the hand of the king, but to take the pastoral staff himself from the altar on which it was to be laid, thus "receiving it from the Lord" instead of an earthly sovereign. In this way he was to be a bishop, partly by grace divine and partly by secular permission. But the Church of Rome understood no such compositions, and therefore they were certain to come to nothing. Thurstan, Archbishop of York, who at present was with Henry I. in Normandy, quickly heard of this movement in Scotland by which his claims of superiority were set at nought, and, at his solicitation, Henry wrote to the Primate of Canterbury, forbidding him to consecrate Eadmer, and to Alexander himself, arrogantly requiring him to prevent such consecration. The Scottish king and Scottish prelate were thus equally in a dilemma. The former was unwilling to provoke a war with England, while the latter, still unconsecrated, felt as if he were not yet wholly a bishop, and could not become so until he had repaired to the fountain-head. This resolution of a journey to Canterbury he imparted to Alexander, who heard it with indignation. "I received you," he said, "altogether free from Canterbury, and while I live I will not permit the Bishop of St. Andrews to be subjected to that see." The reply of Eadmer was equally resolute. "For your whole kingdom," he said, "I would not renounce the dignity of a monk of Canterbury." "Then I have gained nothing," cried the king, "in seeking a bishop out of Canterbury." He thus saw that he had only doubled the difficulty which he had sought to obviate.

The situation of Eadmer was now a trying

one. The proud independent spirit of both king and people was awake; and while he felt the anomalous nature of his position and was anxious to have it settled by what he reckoned the only competent authority, he knew that his motions were watched as well as his purpose prohibited. He craved permission to visit Canterbury to take counsel of the archbishop as to what he should do, "and receive his pontifical blessing for the glory of God and advancement of the Scottish kingdom;" but Alexander, who suspected that this blessing meant nothing less than episcopal consecration, reiterated his former refusal and his declarations of the complete independence of the Scottish church. Being thus debarred from taking counsel at Canterbury, Eadmer sought advice from certain eminent ecclesiastics, both English and Scotch, and among the rest he propounded his difficulties to one Nicolas, supposed to have been a prior of Worcester, and a skilful casuist in matters of ecclesiastical law. The reply of Nicolas affords an amusing picture of the condition of Scotland as well as that of its primate. To Eadmer's complaints of the barbarity of the Scots, and the difficulty of exercising ecclesiastical discipline among them, his counsellor advised him to keep open table and give plentiful dinners. Nothing, he alleged, could better promote sound doctrine and establish ecclesiastical discipline among such a barbarous people, as was shown even in the example of brute animals, that forsook their own kind to follow those men who fed and caressed them. As for the claims of the Archbishop of York and the difficulties that might arise from that quarter, Nicolas regarded them with scorn. Scotland, he observed, had often furnished bishops to York, while York had never furnished a bishop to Scotland till the time of Turgot. The Bishop of St. Andrews, he further asserted, being chief bishop of Scotland, was virtually an archbishop; and that therefore the Archbishop of York could not claim the right to consecrate him, unless he pretended not merely to be a metropolitan but also the primate of another kingdom. As for the contending claims of York and Canterbury and those of Alexander and Henry in this question, he advised Eadmer to get rid of them all by applying for consecration directly from the pope, with permission of the Scottish king. Having thus cut the knot with equal boldness and dexterity, the able casuist ended his letter with the following singular request: "I moreover earnestly beg that you will send me as many white pearls as you can get. Let them be the largest you can find, and I beseech you to send me at least four of this description. If you cannot otherwise obtain them ask them at least as a gift from the king, who of all men is the richest in this kind of treasure." He had not only tendered his counsel as a jurisconsult, but offered to repair to Rome and conduct the cause of Scottish ecclesiastical independence in person. It thus appears that his demand for Scottish pearls was neither unreasonable nor unjust.

These advices were too bold for Eadmer to follow, and he listened to those counsellors who advised him to resign his office and leave the kingdom. He could not indeed be suffered to depart without such a resignation. He therefore returned to the king the episcopal ring which he was now persuaded he should never have accepted from a layman, and laid the pastoral staff on the altar from which he had taken it up; and declaring that he yielded to force, and would not reclaim his bishopric under the reign of Alexander except by the advice of the pope, his own consent, and the King of England, he returned to his cell at Canterbury. Here, however, solitude and the counsels of his friends produced a revolution in his purposes, and he was now persuaded that his canonical election being even a stronger tie to the episcopal office than that of consecration, he could not abandon his bishopric without transgressing the laws of the church. He was now as willing to resume his functions as he had been to relinquish them; and in writing to the King of Scots to that effect he actually offered to relinquish those claims of the superiority of the see of Canterbury for which he had formerly contended with the zeal of a martyr. "I mean not," he wrote, "in any particular to derogate from the freedom and independence of the kingdom of Scotland. Should you continue in your former sentiments I will desist from my opposition; for with respect to the King of England, the Archbishop of Canterbury, and the sacerdotal blessing, I had notions which, as I have since learned, were erroneous. These shall in no way withdraw me from the service of God and your favour, but in them I shall act according to your will if you only permit me to enjoy the other rights which belong to the bishops of St. Andrews." But though this application was backed by an imperious missive from Canterbury, requiring Alexander to recall Eadmer as the canonically-elected Bishop of St. Andrews, and declaring that the see could have no other prelate as long as Eadmer lived, the Scottish king remained obdurate. Thus the bishopric continued vacant till the beginning of 1123-24, when Alexander procured the appointment for Robert, an English monk, and prior of Scone, who was elected to the office. Upon this occasion the Archbishop of York interfered, declaring that St.

Andrews belonged to his see; but the Scots had now fully learned their spiritual independence, and his claims were decisively rejected.

This keen and important controversy, which was continued for fifteen years, was the only war in which Alexander I. was engaged, with the exception of a revolt among his own subjects, which he quelled with equal promptitude and severity. It arose in Moray, A.D. 1120, when Angus, mormaor of the district and grandson of Lulach, the stepson of Macbeth, revived the pretensions of his family to the crown of Scotland. It was so effectually suppressed that no further disturbance arose from that quarter; and it is supposed that from his proceedings on this occasion Alexander obtained the title of "The Fierce," under which he is distinguished in Scottish history.

The rest of the proceedings of this reign of eighteen years, as they are but incidentally announced, may be briefly summed up. Of Alexander's personal valour we are told the following instance. A band of robbers who intended to plunder the palace and perhaps murder the king had been admitted into it by his faithless steward; but, awakened by their coming, Alexander leaped out of bed and defended himself so gallantly that he slew six of the ruffians, along with their treacherous guide, before assistance arrived. He was a liberal benefactor to the church, and his large grant of lands to the church of St. Andrews is still distinguished by the name of the "Boar-Chase." He brought a society of Canons Regular from England and established them as a monastery at Scone. He increased the revenues of the monastery at Dunfermline which had been founded by his parents. The personal piety of Alexander was also attested by a romantic incident. While crossing the Frith of Forth so violent a tempest arose that he and all his company only escaped drowning by being shipwrecked upon the little blank island of Inchcolm in the mouth of the frith. Here, however, they would have perished with hunger during their three days' sojourn before the tempest abated, had there not been a pious hermit on the island, who received them into his cell and supplied them from his own scanty resources. The king, who ascribed his deliverance to the prayers of Columba, the patron saint of Inchcolm, erected upon it the monastery of St. Colm, which was also supplied with Canons Regular.

In the year 1122 died his queen Sibylla, the natural daughter of Henry I., whose death her husband had little cause to deplore, if the testimony of the English historian is to be received,[1] who tells us that she had nothing lovable either in comeliness of person or modesty of behaviour. His own death occurred on the 27th of April, 1124. Another English historian,[2] in describing his character, says in qualified terms that he was not ignorant of letters (meaning thereby, perhaps, that he could read and subscribe his name); that he was humble and courteous to the clergy; zealous in providing them with books and vestments, and in collecting relics and establishing churches. The same authority is careful to make him worthy of the title of Fierce by telling us that he was terrible beyond measure to his subjects, proud, and always attempting things beyond his power; but it is probable that Alexander's gallant and successful resistance to the encroachments of the English hierarchy may have rankled in the mind of the writer. This great attempt to vindicate the independence of Scotland, and in which he persevered so many years, was crowned with the success it merited; and as for his severity, it was perhaps nothing more than the unsettled state of society, thrown loose by the lax government of Edgar, may have demanded from a Scottish king.

As Alexander I. died without legitimate offspring he was succeeded by his brother David, the youngest son of Malcolm Canmore. We have already mentioned the ample sway in which the bequest of Edgar had established him. To these territories David had added the earldom of Northampton by his marriage with Matilda, his cousin, daughter of Waltheof of Northumberland, and widow of Simon de St. Liz, Earl of Northampton, who made him the father of a son, Henry, nine years before he ascended the Scottish throne. As his residence also had been chiefly at the court of Henry I. with his sister Queen Matilda, he had enjoyed such intellectual opportunities for the improvement of his people as his own country could not have afforded.[3] Thus, with advantages which no Scottish sovereign had previously enjoyed, and at the age of fully ripened manhood, the new king entered upon a difficult charge that fully required all his talents and experience.

The first event by which the abilities of David as a sovereign were tested, arose from the still open controversy about ecclesiastical supremacy. Although Robert, Prior of Scone, during the previous reign had been nominated to the bishopric of St. Andrews, he had not as yet been consecrated, and the pretensions of the see of York to the spiritual supremacy of Scotland were at issue upon his consecration. To bring

---

[1] W. Malmsbury.   [2] Aldred.   [3] W. Malmsbury.

this difficulty to a close Cardinal John de Crema, the legate of Pope Honorius II., convoked a council to be held at Roxburgh, to which, by a bull of the pontiff, King David was requested to send the Scottish bishops when their presence should be summoned. Here the prelates of the two kingdoms were to examine into the merits of the question, while Honorius prudently reserved the final decision to himself. But his arbitration was uncalled for, as the council came to no conclusion, and, A.D. 1128, Robert was consecrated by Thurstan, Archbishop of York, without any profession or promise of submission, the archbishop meanwhile declaring that he thus consecrated him "for the love of God and of King David—saving always the claim of the see of York, and the right of the see of St. Andrews."[1] In this way a metropolitan was once more obtained for Scotland without any concession of the national independence.

In the meantime the connection of David with England menaced him with a controversy from that quarter of a very different description. Henry I., having no legitimate family except his daughter Matilda, widow of Henry V., Emperor of Germany, and now married to Geoffrey, Count of Anjou, was ambitious that she should succeed him in the throne of England; and as he knew how monstrous a *she*-king appeared in the eyes of that warlike age, as well as how averse his proud Norman nobility would be to "hold their fiefs under the distaff," he resolved to secure her succession by all the sanctions which the most solemn oaths could impose. He had himself repeatedly violated every obligation of the kind; but with a delusion common to oath-breakers, he imagined that all other persons would be more scrupulous than himself, and would respect the sanctions which he was known to hold in scorn. Accordingly in the year 1126, on Christmas-day, and at Windsor Castle, an assembly met at his summons composed of the bishops, abbots, barons, and chief holders of the crown, who assented to the succession of Matilda after the death of her father, and swore to maintain it to the uttermost, the first who took the oath in his quality of an English earl being David, King of Scotland, the uncle of Matilda. On the 1st of December, 1135, King Henry died, and on the 26th of the same month, not Matilda, but Stephen, Count of Boulogne, was proclaimed sovereign of England. He was the late king's nephew but by the female line, being the son of Adela, the daughter of the Conqueror; but his renown as a warrior, his popular qualities, his wealth, and even his sex compensated for the deficiency of his descent, so that his claim was more attractive to the people than that of Matilda, and the greater part of the high church dignitaries and barons who had lately sworn to maintain the succession of the empress at once adopted his cause. This usurpation called the Scottish king into the field, and though he was related to both parties, in consequence of Stephen being the husband of his niece Maud, it is probable that his sacred engagement to Henry turned the scale, and persuaded him to the dangerous step of a war with England. He accordingly led an army across the Border, took possession of the whole country to the north of Durham, and compelled the northern barons to swear allegiance to Matilda and give hostages for their fidelity. When Stephen heard of this inroad he confidently exclaimed, "What the King of Scotland has obtained by stealth, I will recover by manhood." But there was no need of his moving northward, as David soon found himself confronted by such a powerful combination of the adherents of Stephen that his further progress was effectually checked. A peace, however, was as necessary for the King of England as for himself, and a treaty speedily followed, in which David, although reduced to inactivity at Newcastle, and surrounded by the forces of those northern barons who had broken their oaths to Matilda, was able to extricate himself without loss or dishonour. While refusing to do homage to Stephen for his English possessions, by which he would have recognized the usurper's right to the throne of England, he restored all the lands and castles of which he had taken possession during his inroad. On the other hand, Stephen agreed to bestow upon young Henry, the son of David, the earldom of Huntingdon and the towns of Carlisle and Doncaster, and to take into consideration the prince's claims to the earldom of Northumberland in right of his mother as daughter and heiress of Waltheof. Although David refused to do homage to Stephen for the lands he already possessed in England, he permitted his son to perform this act of vassalage for the new territories conferred upon himself. In this way a new perplexity was added to the question of the suzerainty of the kings of England over those of Scotland, and a fresh claim of exaction for that terrible hour of national reckoning whose coming every act was now tending to accelerate.

In the present state of affairs a treaty like that of Newcastle could only be a brief and uncertain truce. A year had elapsed, and the claims of Prince Henry to Northumberland

---

[1] *Anglia Sacra*, ii. 237. Simeon of Durham. Wilkins's *Concilia*.

which were to be considered did not seem likely to be soon concluded. It was to enforce these claims that David in 1136 resolved to invade Northumberland, but was persuaded by Thurstan, Archbishop of York, to desist from hostilities until Stephen's return, who at that time was in Normandy. At his return the English king gave a flat refusal to the demands of David, upon which the latter commenced the invasion of Northumberland in earnest. The castle of Werk was besieged, but held out so successfully that the Scots, who were unable to take it, vented their rage upon the surrounding country, which they wasted with relentless barbarity. This mood, however, we are carefully informed, did not extend to the Scottish leaders, who doubtless still retained their old affection for the land from which they had emigrated and the kindred by whom it was occupied, and of their diligence to stay these excesses the English historians have given several examples. On one of these occasions, when the abbey of Hexham was stormed and plundered by the Scots, David himself restored to the monks his own share in the partition of the spoil. At length Stephen, having found a short interval in his wars with the adherents of Matilda, flew northward to oppose the Scots, and found them encamped in the neighbourhood of Roxburgh. Avoiding an encounter with an army of which, it is alleged, the leaders were in correspondence with some of his own treacherous nobles, he crossed the Tweed in another direction and carried on the war upon the Scottish Border until want of provisions compelled him to retreat.

These indecisive incursions and reprisals were but preludes to more important events. The principal champion in England of the cause of Matilda was Robert, Earl of Gloucester and illegitimate son of Henry I., who having concerted with David a fresh Scottish invasion by promising to support it with all the nobles of his party and Matilda at their head, had gone abroad to the residence of his half-sister for the purpose of bringing her to England. At the appointed time, and fully expecting their co-operation, David renewed his Northumbrian invasion and advanced to the neighbourhood of Durham. His troops on this occasion were so various in race and so diversified in appearance, but withal so much at one in their deeds of ferocity and plunder, that the monkish Latin of the old English historians sinks under them when they attempt to describe these swarms of "Scottish ants"—these legions of a "barbarous and impure nation."[1] It was such a miscellaneous array as had marched under the banner of Malcolm Canmore, but with sundry strange additions which were of later arrival into Scotland. The first specimen of the insubordination which must prevail among such a host was afforded by the wild Scots of Galloway, who being checked in one of their excesses near Durham, broke out into revolt and threatened to murder the king and his attendants. They were only arrested in their desperate attempt by a cry that the English were upon them; and this alarm, probably raised on purpose, was enough to occasion a temporary retreat of the whole army. Soon after they defeated a body of the English at Clitheroe, took the castle of Norham, and advanced to the neighbourhood of Northallerton. And still Stephen was so closely employed in quelling the seditious barons of the south of England that he could send no aid to the counties of York and Northumberland except a body of cavalry under the command of Bernard de Baliol. But the advance of David was also impeded by the delay of the Earl of Gloucester, who had not yet landed in England; while the invaded counties, recovering from their panic, resolved to rely on their own resources. In this bold resolution they were confirmed by the stout-hearted Thurstan, Archbishop of York, who though worn out with years and infirmity, was the soul of the confederacy. To give this defence of their liberties and homes the character of a holy war the people of the parishes of his diocese were marched out in religious procession by their priests at his command, bearing crosses, holy relics, and consecrated banners, and commanded to take arms in defence of Christ's church against the barbarians, while paradise was promised to those who fell and freedom to those who survived. In like manner Thurstan assembled the barons at York, with whom he fasted three days, and bestowed upon them his pastoral blessing, with the banner of St. Peter brought out for the purpose from the cathedral of York, and his episcopal crozier, which was to be their symbol of command and leading-staff of battle. All being thus animated with the highest of motives, the conduct of the force that was speedily assembled was wisely placed under Walter l'Espec, a veteran warrior of high reputation and experience.

On approaching the Scottish encampment l'Espec resolved to try the effect of negotiation

---

[1] Matthew Paris. *Gesta Stephani*. The enumeration comprises Normans, Germans, Northumbrians, Strathclyde Britons, the men of Teviotdale and Lothian, the Gallowegians, the Islesmen, and the clans of Lorn. The Babel of languages—French, Teutonic, Danish, Celtic, with the different dialects of each that must have been used among them—was sufficiently ludicative of a final dispersion even though no enemy had interposed.

before putting all to the hazard of the sword. He therefore sent as his ambassadors two English nobles whose family names were afterwards to form so essential a part of the history of Scotland; these were Robert de Bruce and Bernard de Baliol. Bruce, who was now an old man, had been the affectionate friend as well as devoted vassal of David, the upholder of his rights while Prince of Cumberland, and afterwards his faithful friend and counsellor when the prince became King of Scotland. The barons offered as a condition of peace to procure from Stephen a grant of the earldom of Northumberland to Henry, David's son, but this proposal was rejected with disdain. That county was already overrun, and David may have considered it as his own, and his honour and good faith as an English baron were pledged to those oaths of fealty which the rest of the nobility had broken. Finding that they could not prevail, these nobles renounced their homage to David for the lands they held in Scotland and returned to Catton Moor, near Northallerton, where the English were encamped. After a few movements in either army, and when a hostile collision was hourly expected, Bruce again repaired to the Scottish king and made a last effort to move him. He described the savage character and atrocities of a Scottish invasion, and entreated David in the name of religion and humanity to turn his thoughts to peace. He suggested the resolute character of those whom he was about to attack, and warned him of the danger of driving them to despair; and bursting into tears at the picture which the suggestion called up, the brave old warrior thus continued: "To see my dearest master, my patron and benefactor, my friend and my companion in arms, with whom I spent the season of youth and festivity, and in whose service I am grown old—to see him thus exposed to the dangers of battle or to the dishonour of flight, it wrings my heart." David also wept, but still continued his refusal, upon which Bruce once more renounced his homage to the Scottish king, and rejoined those ranks that had the chief claim to his services.

In the meantime all was confidence and alacrity in the English camp. The episcopal blessing and absolution had animated the soldiers, and banished every fear of danger or discomfiture; and to confirm the sacred character of their warfare, a high four-wheeled chariot was placed in the midst of the encampment, and rising from it was a tall ship's mast on which streamed the banners of St. Peter of York, St. John of Beverley, and St. Wilfrid of Ripon, while at the top was a little casket containing a consecrated host. It was the same sort of *carroccio* which had been introduced about a century earlier in the wars of Lombardy; and while its towering form, conspicuous over the whole field of battle, served as the most effectual rallying-point for an imperfectly disciplined array, its consecrated emblems were certain to rouse every feeling of religious zeal as well as chivalrous determined courage in the hearts of its brave defenders. But very different from this unanimity was the spirit that prevailed among their invaders. David had resolved to commence the attack with the choicest part of his army, which consisted of Norman men-at-arms and archers; but these strangers, who had lately been subjects of the King of England, were regarded with malignant jealousy by the men of Galloway, who had signalized themselves in the inroad, and now claimed the honour of commencing the onset. "Whence comes the mighty confidence of these Normans?" cried Malise, Earl of Strathearn, indignantly; "I myself wear no armour, yet they who do shall not advance farther than I this day!" The lie was given in his throat by Alan de Piercie of the proud house of Northumberland. "Earl," he exclaimed, "you boast of what you dare not perform!" The Norman and Celtic rivalry seemed ready to contest the quarrel in the very presence of the common enemy who would have laughed at their mutual destruction, when David prudently allayed the strife by conceding to the Gallowegians the honour of leading the van. The second rank was composed of the Norman cavalry and archers under the command of Prince Henry, aided by the military experience of Fitzjohn, lately an Anglo-Norman baron and commander of the castle of Bamborough, who had shifted his allegiance from England to Scotland with the easy fealty of the period. The third rank was composed of the men of Lothian, the volunteers of Teviotdale, and the men of the Isles; while the reserve under the king's own command consisted of the Celtic Scots, the inhabitants of Moray, and a body-guard of Normans and Englishmen. In this array, and with weapons as various as the races to which they belonged, from the small round target of the naked Celt to the complete panoply of the Norman knight, the Scottish army, amounting to twenty-five thousand men, advanced to battle. The English, warned of their approach, rallied as one man around the car from which the titular Bishop of Orkney, whom Thurstan had appointed as his deputy, dispensed absolution, and exhorted the army to fight bravely. "Illustrious chiefs of England," he said, addressing the knights and nobles; "by blood and race Normans, before whom bold France trembles, to whom fierce England has submitted, under whom Apulia has been restored to her station, and whose names are famous at Antioch and Jerusalem—here are the Scots, who have done homage to you, undertaking to drive you from your possessions." "I swear," exclaimed Walter l'Espec, the commander, "that on this day I will overcome the Scots or perish." "So swear we all," cried the assembled barons in reply.

The battle was commenced by the wild Scots of Galloway. Shouting their war-cry, "Albanich! Albanich!" they threw themselves headlong upon the main body of English infantry, whose front ranks they pierced with the impetuosity of their onset. But their naked bodies were defenceless against the shafts with which they were plied by the English archers, and the long slender spears that formed their chief offensive weapons were unavailing against the armour of the Norman men-at-arms, who checked their onward career and encountered them hand to hand. After a desperate but hopeless struggle in which their leaders Ulgric and Davenal were killed, the men of Galloway were borne backward and thrown into disorder. It was now the time for Prince Henry at the head of the second line to act, and this he did with so impetuous a charge that the English phalanx was "rent asunder like a cobweb;" and, pursuing his advantage too eagerly, he fell upon the troops in the rear, thus separating himself from the main battle, where his presence was most needed. The Gallowegians rallied; the third line advanced to support them; but still the English yeomanry and Norman knights and men-at-arms continued an obstinate resistance through a two-hours' fight, and as often as they were driven back they gathered into an impenetrable phalanx around the carriage with its holy ensigns. While the battle was thus maintained on even terms a stratagem turned the fortune of the day in behalf of England; this was occasioned by an English soldier cutting off the head of one of the slain, placing it on the top of a pike, and crying, as he held it triumphantly aloft, "Behold the head of the King of Scotland!" The shallow device succeeded: the Gallowegians gave way, the third line fled without striking a blow, and David himself, after a hopeless effort to rally the fugitives, was forced off the field by the affectionate zeal of his own nobles. With difficulty he reached Carlisle with the remains of his army, now almost reduced to half their number, as the inhabitants of the country, exasperated at the excesses of this invasion, rose everywhere upon the fugitives in their retreat. For several days David remained anxious about the fate of his gallant son, who had not appeared since the conflict; but the young prince, when he saw that all was lost, had saved himself by ordering his followers to throw away their banners and pretend to join in the pursuit, by which means they all at length reached Carlisle in safety.

Such was the conflict of Northallerton (Aug. 2, 1138), commonly called the Battle of the Standard. It was the first great trial of arms between the two rival nations; the commencement of a series of encounters that was to go onward for centuries with scarcely an intermission; and as such the early historians of England have been both ample and minute in describing it.[1] At this great opening of the drama, also, we can distinctly trace the character of the contending parties, and in some measure anticipate the aspect of coming events. In the movements of the Scots especially we see the dissensions and rivalries by which their future operations were so often impeded and their successes negatived—the uncalculating rashness that so frequently hurried them onward to discomfiture, as well as the obstinate valour that finally secured their national liberties when every other hope had departed.

Defeated though he was, David was yet able to act on the offensive; and after having stilled the dissensions of his rallied forces, where each clan or tribe threw the blame on its rival, and having bound all parties by a solemn oath never to desert him in battle, he led them from Carlisle to the siege of Werk, the castle of the victorious Walter l'Espec. The formidable attitude which he was still able to maintain, as well as the helpless condition of the Northumbrian and Yorkshire barons, is attested by the fact that David reduced the castle by famine and razed it to the ground, after which he returned uninterrupted to Scotland. A peace soon followed, chiefly through the mediation of Maud, the wife of Stephen and niece of the King of Scotland, in which David may be said to have secured the advantages of a decisive victory. The point of contest, which was the earldom of Northumberland, was conceded to Prince Henry, the barons of the earldom to hold their lands of Henry saving their allegiance to the English king; and although the fortresses of Newcastle and Bamborough were retained by Stephen, an equivalent of lands in the south of England was granted to David in their stead. In return for these concessions Scotland was to remain neutral in the contest of Stephen with Matilda, and five hostages, the sons of the principal Scottish nobles, were given to Stephen to ratify this promise. This treaty was signed by Prince

---

[1] Matthew Paris. Aldred *de Bello Standardi* in Twisden's *Decem Scriptores.* Richard and John of Hexham. Henry of Huntingdon. Aldred, who lived at the court of David, is abundant in particulars of this national contest.

Henry at Nottingham, after which he accompanied Stephen to the siege of the castle of Ludlow, where he was unhorsed in an encounter, but gallantly rescued by the English king.[1] After the siege he drew this alliance with England still closer by marrying Ada, daughter of the Earl of Warrene and Surrey, a lady related to some of the noblest families both of England and France. On returning homeward after this marriage Henry and his bride would have been taken prisoners by an ambush laid for them by Ranulph, Earl of Chester, had it not been for the kind interposition of Stephen, who frustrated the design. Ranulph had claims either real or imaginary to the lordship of the castle of Carlisle and its surrounding territory, which, however, had been given up to Prince Henry by the treaty of 1135-36, and in this way, so accordant with the spirit of the age when the possession of the fair lands of England were in question, the earl endeavoured to recover what he alleged to be his own. Baulked in his purpose, he went over to the party of Matilda, and became one of Stephen's bitterest enemies.

The course of events in England soon interrupted the friendly relations which had been established between the two kingdoms. Near the end of September (1139) the long-delayed arrival of Matilda took place, who was accompanied only by her half-brother, the Earl of Gloucester, and a train of about a hundred and forty knights. But ridiculous though such a force was for the invasion of a kingdom, the discontent of the English nobles, whose exorbitant demands the king was unable to fulfil, quickly swelled this train into an army, by which Stephen was defeated at Lincoln, deposed, and thrown into prison. Matilda was now full sovereign of England, as her ambitious father had wished; but her arrogant behaviour and harsh proceedings soon justified the English nobles in their dislike of a *she*-king, and made them plot for the restoration of their brave, open-hearted, magnanimous Stephen. Scarcely, therefore, had her coronation robes been prepared when she was driven from London. Soon after her arrival in England David, still mindful of his oaths and relationship, had repaired to the court of Matilda, and endeavoured to correct her unwise proceedings by his wisdom and experience, but in vain: she received his admonitions with scorn, and continued to reject them even after she was driven from the capital. David accompanied her in her flight, was besieged with her in the castle of Winchester, and escaped with her from the exhausted fortress when the assailants were keeping the festival of the Holy Rood, a season when military operations were wont to be suspended. So full of danger and difficulty was their flight from Winchester, and so closely were they pursued, that death or captivity would have been their portion but for the devotedness of a band of gallant knights, who gave battle to their pursuers at Stourbridge, and continued their resistance until they were all cut down or taken prisoners, that the royal fugitives might have time to escape. Matilda reached the castle of Devizes, and was able to continue the war. As for David, his chief endeavour was to reach Scotland in safety through a hostile population, and this he effected after several hair's-breadth escapes. In one of these, being surrounded by the enemy, he was only saved by the dexterity, presence of mind, and courage of a soldier in the army of Stephen, who happened to be no other than David Oliphant, a Scot, and godson of the king.

On returning to Scotland David wisely abandoned all further interference in English affairs, and devoted himself wholly to the welfare of his subjects. This provident design, however, was not without interruption. An English monk named Wimund, after a rambling life of penury and shifts, had settled in the Isle of Man, where his tall comely figure, eloquence, learning, and ingratiating manners won so greatly upon the barbarous Manxmen that they chose him for their bishop. This, however, was not the sort of elevation that could satisfy so restless and ambitious a spirit as Wimund, and he pretended to be the son of Angus, Earl or Regulus of Moray, who had rebelled against David, A.D. 1130, and been defeated and slain at Strickathro. His assertions were maintained with such plausibility that he soon found himself at the head of a fleet and army, while Somerled, Lord of Argyle, bestowed upon him his daughter in marriage. Thus supported, he made war upon the Scottish coasts in the style of a sea-king, while his skill and valour made him such a formidable antagonist that the whole country was alarmed by his piratical visits. His aim in all probability was not merely to be Earl of Moray, but also the head and rallying-point of a Celtic confederacy against the Norman and Anglo-Saxon ascendancy in Scotland. After various successes this Perkin Warbeck of a rude age attempted to levy contributions upon the lands of a certain Scottish prelate, who boldly replied in answer to the demand, "I will never

---

[1] Henry of Huntingdon and Matthew Paris, who are the authorities for this incident, say that the prince was caught by an iron hook, which drew him from his horse and almost made him prisoner. According to the latter historian the hook, which was let down from the wall, had almost hoisted the prince into the fortress, when he was recovered by the gallantry of Stephen. Such cramp-irons have been of use in the rude periods of most countries both in the capture and defence of strongholds.

set the example of one bishop paying tribute to another;" and to make good his words, he advanced at the head of a small force against this belligerent Bishop of Man. He commenced the onset by throwing his light battle-axe at the head of Wimund, and with such good aim that it felled the marauder to the ground; and in the battle that followed, the pirates were so completely defeated that only a few escaped to their ships with their wounded leader. But the career of Wimund was not yet ended. He contrived to gather new partisans, and make himself so formidable that the king was obliged to purchase his forbearance by a full pardon and the grant of a certain portion of territory. In this new situation, however, Wimund could not be at rest; his tyrannical conduct was odious to his vassals, and after a short time they rose against him, deprived him of his eyes, emasculated him, and delivered him into the hands of David, by whom he was subjected to a long imprisonment in the castle of Roxburgh. He was finally pardoned, and thereafter retired to the monastery of Biland in Yorkshire, where he spent the rest of his days not in penitence and mortification, but comfort and jollity, while he amused his brother monks with tales of his strange adventures. "Had my enemies," he was wont to say, "but left me as much light as could be received by the eye of a sparrow, they would have little cause to boast of the injuries they have done me."[1]

While these troubles occasioned by Wimund were occupying the full attention of David, Stephen continued to maintain an uncertain sway in England; for Matilda was still alive, and her son, Henry Plantagenet, who would inherit her claims, was already indicating, although still a boy, those remarkable talents which afterwards made him the greatest sovereign of his age. In the year 1149, when he had now reached the age of sixteen, young Plantagenet crossed the seas from Normandy to the Scottish court to receive knighthood at the hands of his uncle David, and the important ceremony was performed at the ancient city of Carlisle with great pomp and rejoicing. At this meeting also a compact was made by which Henry swore that on becoming King of England he would restore Newcastle to David and give up the whole territory between the Tweed and the Tyne to him and his heirs for ever. Ralph, Earl of Chester, at the same time renounced in favour of Scotland his ancient pretensions to Carlisle, and was to be requited with the earldom of Lancaster, while an infant granddaughter of the Scottish king was to be given in marriage to the son of Ralph when she became of age. The result of this compact was that the Scottish king, the English prince, and the earl were to muster their forces and invade England at an appointed time, for the purpose of dethroning Stephen. But when the season had arrived and David and Henry commenced their inroad, the Earl of Chester broke his engagement, while the approach of Stephen compelled them to retreat into Scotland.

In the year 1152 a mournful event occurred not only to David as a father but the kingdom at large. This was the death of his only son Henry, who expired on the 12th of June. His gallantry and talents for war had been exhibited in the Battle of the Standard; and his other qualities obtained for him the high commendation that in manners he was still more gentle than his father, while in everything else he resembled him.[2] Besides the loss to the whole nation of a future sovereign of such promise, the bereavement was embittered by the thought of the interregnum which it would occasion in so unsettled a country and at such a dangerous period. By his princess, Ada, Henry had three sons—Malcolm, William, and David, of whom the two first were successively kings of Scotland—and three daughters. After the death of Prince Henry, David fixed the succession to the crown by sending his grandson, Malcolm, in royal progress through the kingdom, and causing him to be proclaimed heir to the throne at all the principal towns. He also invested his second grandson, William, with the territories he held in Northumberland, exacting the usual homage of the barons of that territory to the young prince, and taking hostages for their fidelity.

As the long reign of David was chiefly of a peaceful character its history is to be sought in his internal administration and his proceedings as a legislator and judge. And here the particulars have been so fully given by his friend and panegyrist Aldred, that our knowledge of David I. both in his public and private capacity is more intimate than that we have obtained of any of his predecessors. His character as a religious sovereign is the chief aspect under which he has been presented to our notice. Like the illustrious King of Israel whose honoured name he bore, he had shed much blood; and although a single campaign had summed up the principal amount of his military achievements, he reflected with keen remorse upon the wild havoc and massacre with which it had been accompanied. Under these feelings he had

---

[1] W. Newb.; Matt. Paris; Fordun. The last historian gives to Wimund the Celtic name of Malcolm MacHeth.

[2] Aldred.

resolved to expiate his guilt in the manner that was at that time a universal enthusiasm, by abandoning his crown, assuming the red cross of a crusader, and warring in Palestine for the recovery of the Holy Sepulchre. But the urgent necessities of his unsettled kingdom detained him in Scotland, and his penitence was therefore expressed in the other alternative of that stirring and struggling age of superstition—the building of churches and endowment of religious houses.[1] In this way he founded the bishopric of Ross, and probably those of Brechin and Dunblane, while he enriched the revenues of those that had been already established. He transferred the bishopric of Murtlach to the city of Aberdeen and added largely to its endowments. He erected Dunkeld into an episcopal see by converting its old monastery of Culdees into a cathedral. But it was of the abbeys of Scotland that he was especially the nursing father, and the list of those which he founded would be too long to give in full. It is enough, however, to specify as examples the monastic establishments of Holyrood, Melrose, Jedburgh, Kelso, and Dryburgh. This zeal for the establishment of religion on the surest basis, according to the reckoning of the period, David appears to have commenced with his reign, but to have increased with double ardour and liberality towards its close. Little could he calculate either upon the industry of those monks that could convert the myriads of barren acres which he alienated from the royal revenues into rich gardens and fertile corn-fields and pastures; or the reaction which all this luxurious abundance would produce upon their pampered and idle successors. "David I. was ane soir sanct for the crown," said James I. demurely, nearly three centuries afterwards, when the saintship of his predecessor was quoted and its proofs instanced in the richest portions of the soil of Scotland invested in the church, and from which he could therefore derive no revenue. To this taunt David might have answered in a sepulchral voice and amidst the midnight solitudes of Holyrood, that he had acted according to the best wisdom of the age, and erred with Charlemagne and Alfred.

In his political administration this wise and good king was more fortunate, and with more permanent results. This was effected by his anxious endeavours to enlarge his kingdom and secure it with a strong frontier, as well as by his encouragement to those immigrations of superior races by which its power and resources were augmented and its civilization rapidly advanced. In dispensing justice as chief magistrate of the realm, the description which Aldred has given carries us back in imagination to the simple peasant-kings of ancient Greece, or even to the more early patriarchs of the East. David, he tells us, sat at the gate of his palace on certain appointed days to hear cases of complaint and decide controversies; and on these occasions he was careful to give satisfaction by explaining the causes of his decision. He was also fond of hunting; "but I have seen him," says Aldred, "quit his horse and dismiss his hunting equipage when any even of the meanest of his subjects implored an audience." How different this from William the Conqueror and his son Rufus, who laid waste whole counties that they might have a hunting forest, and visited with capital punishment all who molested the deer! At sunrise he commenced the duties of the day and dismissed his attendants at sunset, when he employed himself in meditation and devotion. A gentle trait of character that distinguished him from contemporary sovereigns was his attachment to the humanizing studies of horticulture, and his leisure hours were frequently employed in cultivating his garden and trying experiments in the budding and ingrafting of trees—"that he might provoke his rude subjects by his example to do the same." Few sovereigns also possessed such powers of affectionate, condescending, intelligent intercourse, so that all departed from his presence wiser and happier from the interview.[2] Such, indeed, were David's excellences that Buchanan while contemplating them seems utterly to have forgot his own stern republicanism. "As he equalled the most excellent of the former kings in his warlike achievements"—thus writes the eloquent historian—"and excelled them in his cultivation of the arts of peace, at last, as if he had ceased to contend with others for pre-eminence in virtue, he endeavoured to rival himself; and in this he so succeeded, that the utmost ingenuity of the most learned, who should attempt to delineate the portrait of a good king, would not be able to conceive one so excellent as David during his whole life evinced himself." The close was in keeping with the whole tenor of his life. After having de-

---

[1] In the MSS. Cupr. et Perth quoted in Fordun we are also told that he built at great expense and richly endowed certain hospices for the reception of the sick and the poor, and lazar-houses for lepers—"which like all other such things," the writer adds with a groan, "are now converted by secular abuse into a den of thieves."

[2] "Denique si contingeret ut sacerdos vel miles, vel monachus, dives vel pauper, civis vel peregrinus, negotiator vel rusticus, cum eo sermonem haberet, ita cum singulis, de suis negotiis et officiis, convenienter et humiliter disserebat, ut singulus quisque sua cum tantum curare putaret; et sic omnes jucundos et ædificatos dimitteret."—Fordun, lib. v. cap. 49.

voted his latter days so entirely in preparation for a higher crown and happier existence that the veneration of his subjects was if possible increased, he was found dead in his bed, but with so tranquil a countenance that he seemed as if he still lived, and with his hands closed upon his breast, showing that he had passed away in the midst of prayer. This was on the morning of the 24th of May, 1153, when he had reigned twenty-nine years and a few days.

CHAPTER II.

REIGNS OF MALCOLM IV. AND WILLIAM THE LION (1153-1214).

Minority of Malcolm IV.—Revolt and invasion of Somerled—Interview between Malcolm and Henry II.—Malcolm's rash concessions—He follows Henry to France—Rebellions in Scotland—Death of Malcolm IV., termed the Maiden—His character—William the Lion succeeds to the throne—Alliance between Scotland and France—William joins the rebellion of Henry's sons against their father—He invades England—Taken prisoner at Alnwick—Hard terms of his liberation—The Scottish church escapes the national vassalage—Its resistance to the claims of the English primates—Disturbances in Galloway—William's controversy with the Pope on the appointment of a bishop to St. Andrews—Its termination in favour of William—Marriage of William—Insurrection of Donald—Independence of the Scottish church proclaimed by the Pope—Richard, King of England, absolves Scotland from its vassalage—Terms of the release—The Earl of Huntingdon joins the Crusade—His adventures—William's quarrels and negotiations with John, King of England—Death of William the Lion—His character.

Scotland was now for the first time to be visited with a calamity which was often repeated: she was to have a boy for her sovereign. It was the natural consequence of the law of royal succession which had superseded that of Tanistry, and which, with all its benefits, was necessarily accompanied with an evil that in days of old Heaven had denounced as a curse upon the nations that merited a grievous national punishment.

We have already mentioned that on the death of Prince Henry his eldest son Malcolm had been proclaimed successor to the crown during the life of his grandfather David. The Saxon rule of direct occupation was now so firmly established that the youth ascended the throne without opposition, although only twelve years old, and was the fourth of the name who had filled it.

The first of the inevitable evils of such a minority arose from Somerled, Lord of Argyle and the Hebrides, a chief of almost regal power, and whose subjection to the Scottish crown, if at all acknowledged, was little more than nominal. It appears that no sooner had he heard of the death of David than he resolved to make a descent upon the mainland for the purposes of piracy and plunder; and to give a colour of justice to his invasion, he pretended to be in arms for the rights of his grandchildren, the sons of the adventurer Winnund, to whom he had given his daughter in marriage. The landing of Somerled occurred in November 5, 1153; and although we are unacquainted with the mischiefs it occasioned, these must have been of no small account, as the peace which soon after followed gave a date to several of the Scottish charters of the period under the title of the "Concord of the King and Somerled." Donald, the son of Winnund, was taken prisoner, and confined in the castle of Roxburgh; but Somerled, who renewed his destructive invasions, was not pacified until some time afterwards. It was not till a considerably later period of Scottish history that these dangerous and powerful Lords of the Isles were reduced to the condition of subjects.

But the chief danger to Malcolm IV. and his government arose from the ambition of Henry II., who succeeded to the crown of England by the death of Stephen in A.D. 1154. On his accession he not only forgot the oaths he had sworn to David that he would give up the whole country between the Tyne and the Tweed to Scotland; but he also demanded the restitution of those territories in England that were already held by the Scottish sovereign. A meeting took place upon the subject between the two kings at Chester; but Malcolm, still a minor, was no match in negotiation for the astute Henry, who had already commenced that career of aggrandizement by which he became the most powerful sovereign of the age. Malcolm, therefore, was easily persuaded not only to do homage to the King of England, "saving all his dignities," but to cede to England his possessions in the northern counties, contenting himself with the very unequal requital of the earldom of Huntingdon. Treachery appears to have been practised upon him on this occasion, and his counsellors are alleged to have been corrupted with English gold.[1] Henry had also a hold upon Malcolm that originated in the chivalrous usages of the age. Before a king could be crowned it was deemed necessary that he should receive the honour of knighthood, and the young Scottish sovereign was eager to obtain it from the royal hand of his English senior. For this empty but highly valued honour Malcolm, with the rashness and inexperience of youth, was not only ready to humble himself before his rival and yield to his demands, but even to become the soldier of Henry, and embark with him in those foreign wars with which he had no national connection. He accordingly repaired with the English army to France, where he had for fellow-soldiers Raymond, King of Arragon, a Welsh prince, and the renowned Thomas à Becket, not yet either saint or archbishop, but a gallant warrior full of knightly enterprise; and to reward the compliance of the young Scottish king, Henry there conferred upon him the coveted distinction. But in thus gaining knighthood Malcolm had almost lost his throne. The Scottish nobles, indignant at the concessions of their king, and feeling their country reduced to vassalage by his service under the English banner, sent to him a deputation while he was in France, with the significant declaration that they would not accept Henry for their ruler. This message hastened the return of Malcolm, but it was only to encounter the full brunt of their indignation; for, on holding a parliament at Perth, the Earl of Strathearn and five other nobles attempted to seize the person of the king. He escaped to a tower, which they unsuccessfully assailed, and at last the wild revolt was stilled by the interposition of the clergy.

About the same period that this rebellion was suppressed another broke out in those extensive districts at that time comprised under the name of Galloway. Its wild inhabitants, the most untamed of the Celtic population, had hitherto lived under their own laws and chieftains; and although they partially acknowledged submission to the Scottish crown, they regarded the progress of the Saxon population with jealousy and rage. In 1160 these feelings broke out into open warfare, encouraged, it is probable, by the dissensions that prevailed between the king and his nobility. But this outbreak of a common enemy must have tended to reconcile these dissensions, and the nobles so lately in arms against their sovereign found ample occupation among the swamps and forests of the revolted province. Malcolm invaded Galloway, but in two encounters was defeated. A third attempt was more successful, and was crowned with so signal a defeat of the Gallowegians, that Fergus their chief submitted, gave his son Uchtred as a hostage to the king, and retired from the world to the Abbey of Holyrood, where he assumed the habit of a canon-regular, and died the following year.

A similar rebellion, and from the same rivalry of dissimilar and hostile races, quickly followed in Morayshire, whose Celtic inhabitants had never been reconciled to the Saxon innovations and the race of Malcolm Canmore. But they, too, were conquered and reduced to submission by the vigour of Malcolm. The character given of them by Fordun is, that they could neither be allured by gifts, bound by treaties, nor influenced by oaths; but this picture, which would apply to the Danes of the age of Ragnar Lodbrog or of Guthrun, is so peculiarly *un*-Celtic that we may suspect the historian of gross mistake or downright exaggeration.

The only other important movement which occurred during the reign of Malcolm IV. arose from an invasion of Somerled, the Lord of the Isles, who had resumed his hostile attempts upon Scotland, and (A.D. 1164) entered the Clyde with a formidable armament which he landed at Renfrew. His forces, which on this occasion were very numerous, were not drawn from Argyle and the Hebrides alone, but from Ireland and other quarters: it seems, indeed, to have been a great struggle upon the oft-renewed question of supremacy between Celt and Saxon. He was completely defeated, however, on his landing by a small array of the inhabitants of the district, and both he and his son Gillecolane were left among the dead.[2]

The death of Malcolm followed on the 28th of December, 1165, at Jedburgh, while he was yet only twenty-four years old. He was called Malcolm the Maiden; and it is said that he obtained this title, so honoured in those days when monkish celibacy was of recent imposition in Scotland, by observing through life the strict continence of Edward the Confessor. But he scarcely can be claimed for the convent, as it is certain that he had at least one natural child, a son, who died during his young father's lifetime. Following out the same idea of monastic continence, they endow him with the other attributes of a perfect monk, and describe him as mild, gentle, inoffensive, and almost wholly devoted to religious contemplation. And yet when we study his character in his actions we

---

[1] Fordun, lib. viii. c. 3.   [2] *Chron. Melros.* p. 109.

find him a rash but gallant warrior, bold and active in his movements, successful in his attempts, and ripening into the full promise of a skilful leader and wise politician. It is probable, therefore, that his title "the Maiden," upon which so much has been attempted to be established, may have originated in nothing more than a delicate complexion or comely countenance, at a period when such surnames were common as personal cognomens.

On the death of Malcolm IV. his younger brother William was crowned on the 24th of December, 1165. His first endeavour as King of Scotland was to recover Northumberland, which had been bestowed upon him by his grandfather David I.; and to effect this object he repaired to France, as his brother had done, and became a soldier under the banner of Henry II. of England. But Henry of most kings was the least disposed to relinquish any territorial acquisition which he had once secured, and William in return for his military services obtained nothing but empty promises. All that Henry would definitely assent to was a continuation of the truce with Scotland, which his unsuccessful wars in Brittany as well as against the Welsh made necessary for his own interests. At length his eyes being opened to the true meaning of these delays, William returned to Scotland and adopted a step which his view of the state of affairs on the Continent may have suggested as a hopeful expedient; this was to establish an alliance with France, the confirmed enemy of England, and whose interests would be most effectually served upon the Scottish Border by the impediments that could be thrown in the way of the English invasions upon the Continent. Ambassadors were accordingly sent for that purpose from Scotland to the French court, and that alliance between the two kingdoms was for the first time commenced which continued for centuries, and was productive of such important consequences, especially to the poorer and weaker kingdom. Never did the selfish and calculating Henry II. more effectually overreach himself than in the case of those short-sighted measures by which he compelled Scotland, already almost an English kingdom, to renounce its island brotherhood with the south and have recourse to aliens and strangers.

In the meantime William still continued on terms of peace with Henry, and in 1170 he repaired to England with his brother David, Earl of Huntingdon, and held Easter with the King of England and his nobles in the stately halls of Windsor. Here also David received knighthood from Henry; and on the eldest son of the latter being crowned as King of England, thus rashly anticipating his succession, the Scottish king and prince paid the usual homage to the junior potentate for their English territories, at the requirement of the rash and overfond father. But in spite of these compliances William could not obtain the restitution of Northumberland, and he retired indignantly to Scotland, where he waited the opportunity of revenge.

And that opportunity soon came in a form that might have satisfied the most revengeful. As if to punish his lust of power and the crimes by which it was gratified, Henry was unable to rule his own family, and the domestic rebellions that embittered all the triumphs of William the Conqueror were repeated, and with aggravations, by the race of the Plantagenets. Like William also, Henry II. had armed his sons, Henry, Geoffrey, Richard, and John, with the effectual means of rebellion by investing them with such appanages as made them independent sovereigns. The first to commence this unholy warfare was Henry, the junior king, who was impatient to be king indeed, and who demanded that either England or Normandy should be entirely resigned to his independent rule; while in this extravagant demand he was backed not only by the King of France and a large party of the nobility of England, but by his own mother and brothers. Encouraged by such examples, it is not to be wondered at that William of Scotland should have joined the unnatural coalition; and he may have soothed his conscience with the hope that in such a strife he could best secure the independence of his kingdom and recover the territories of which it had been defrauded. The stripling-king welcomed this valuable ally by conferring upon him a full grant of Northumberland, and upon his brother David the earldom of Cambridge. Upon this William, in 1173, invaded England and besieged the castles of Werk and Carlisle, but was able to reduce neither of them, while the excesses of his army only wasted the country which he sought to make part of his kingdom, and drove its inhabitants into the ranks of his enemies. A counter invasion followed, in which Richard de Lacy, the Justiciary of England, crossed the Tweed and inflicted similar havoc upon the Scottish districts, but without signalizing his inroad by an engagement. A truce succeeded these indecisive movements, by which De Lacy was enabled to defend his sovereign's cause in the south; and this he did so effectually that he defeated the Earl of Leicester, one of the principal adherents of the junior-king, and took him prisoner. On being deprived of their leader, the troops of Leicester invited David, Earl of Huntingdon, to take the command of them, and put him in possession of the castle of Leicester; while King William, his brother, made a furious irruption into Northumberland, which he afflicted with wilder havoc than before.

The cause of the King of England now seemed well-nigh hopeless. His eldest son Henry, aided by the King of France, was assailing the frontiers of Normandy; Geoffrey, his second son, was in arms against him in Brittany; and Richard, the third of this unnatural brood, was at the head of a rebellion of the men of Aquitaine and Poitou, and warring as fiercely against his own father as he did in after years against the unbelieving Saracens. While Henry II. was thus beset on every side and obliged to confront each assailant in turn, a messenger from England arrived with tidings of the Scottish invasion and a meditated descent from Flanders upon the English coast. He instantly left his camp in Poitou and hurried homeward, where his presence was most needed; but had scarcely landed at Southampton, sick, fevered, and broken-hearted with the filial ingratitude of his sons and disloyalty of his nobles, when he commenced his famous penitential pilgrimage to the tomb of Thomas à Becket at Canterbury. His late soldier, chancellor, and archbishop was now worshipped as a saint; and Henry, who was not superior to the superstitions of the age, was not only doubly accessible to such feelings in his present condition, but conscious that his own resentment and angry words had armed the assassins of Becket. He spent a whole night in prayer and weeping at the tomb; he submitted his naked back to the scourges of the monks of Canterbury; and on receiving absolution he hastened to London for the purpose of making head against his Scottish and English enemies. But no sooner had he reached his palace than a burning fever, the fruit of his late astounding mortifications and penance, stretched him helplessly upon a sick bed when his enemies were strongest and his presence and activity most required.

During these events William was driving onward through Northumberland without mercy or check, and after he had taken several towns and castles he laid siege to Alnwick. In the meantime his brave but miscellaneous army made forays upon the country in every direction, where they slew and plundered without discrimination. At length a small band of Yorkshire barons resolved to make a bold effort for their neighbours of Northumberland, and although they could muster not more than four hundred horsemen they set out upon their perilous adventure under the command of Ranulph de Glanville, the sheriff of York. They began their march at daybreak from Newcastle on the 11th of July, and loaded as they were with complete armour they contrived to effect a march of twenty-four miles in less than five hours. On their route so thick a fog arose that the barons drew bridle and proposed to return; but on Bernard de Baliol, one of their number, reproaching them for faintheartedness, and vowing that rather than turn back he would go forward alone, they continued their journey. The fog that had concealed their approach suddenly dispersed when they came near Alnwick, and they saw before them the invested castle, and soon afterwards an open plain, upon which the King of Scotland and about sixty or seventy horsemen were careering in military sport and exercise, apprehending no hostile interruption. William, on seeing the approach of the English, at first mistook them for a detachment of his own army; but no sooner did he recognize their banners than, instead of falling back upon the Scottish leaguer, he couched his lance, and exclaiming, "Now shall it be seen who are good knights!" he rode in full tilt against the enemy, followed by his whole retinue. His chivalrous madness fared as it merited: he was unhorsed at the first shock, and made prisoner, with nearly all his men, while several of his nobles who were at no great distance hurried to the scene, but only in time to share his captivity instead of effecting his rescue. The English barons quickly retreated with their prize, whom they secured that evening within the walls of Newcastle, and on the following day removed for greater safety to the castle of Richmond. As for the Scottish army of Normans, Saxons, Scots, Gallowegians, and Flemings, who were scattered in marauding parties over the country, acting with little concert, and each plundering on its own account, they were so dispirited by the loss of their king that they hurried back to Scotland without striking a parting blow. They were soon followed by David, Earl of Huntingdon, who abandoned the castles which he had fortified against King Henry in Leicestershire, and marched homeward to superintend the distracted affairs of his own country.

When this brilliant enterprise of the Yorkshire barons was achieved at Alnwick, Henry was still languishing upon his sickbed. But at midnight the royal household was awoke by the sudden arrival of a page, who brought important missives for the king, and demanded immediate access; and on being brought to the bedside of Henry he announced himself as the servant of Ranulph de Glanville, and the messenger of good tidings. "Is Ranulph de Glanville in good health?" inquired the king affectionately; "He is well," replied the youth, "and holds your enemy, the King of Scotland, in hands at the castle of Richmond in Yorkshire." The astonished king bade him repeat what he had said, which the page did, and produced the letter of his master; and when Henry had perused it he leaped out of bed and gave thanks to heaven with tears of joy and gratitude. The joyful shock had flung sickness aside, and he summoned together his friends and counsellors, that they might share in his happiness. This reverse of good fortune, so singular in itself, was exalted by the worshippers of Becket into a miracle; and they alleged that the Scottish king had been taken prisoner on the day and at the very hour that Henry had submitted his back to the stripes of the ecclesiastics at Canterbury.[1] Unfortunately for this calculation, the penance had been done on a Thursday and the capture made on Saturday. On the day after the intelligence had reached him Henry was in his war-saddle; and so utterly were the rebellious barons dismayed by the defeat of their allies the Scots, that castle after castle was yielded to the active sovereign, and all chance of a civil war so effectually suppressed that within three weeks Henry at the head of a numerous army was ready to cross the seas and make reprisals upon his foreign enemies in Normandy.

Very different in the meantime was the condition of the captive king of Scotland. He had assisted in hounding on a parricide brood to war against their own father; and he had entered into their hostile measures by a campaign in England, by which the father was to be dethroned or even murdered; but just at the moment when all seemed to promise a successful termination, he had fallen into the hands of a justly-indignant enemy through his own boy-like rashness in a petty skirmish. It was a severe lesson of retribution and rebuke on which he had full time to meditate in the solitude of his prison. But the largest portion of his humiliation was yet to come. Henry's flagellation at the tomb of Becket seems to have taught him neither Christian charity nor kingly magnanimity, and therefore eighteen days after the capture at Alnwick, William of Scotland was brought before him, not as a royal prisoner but as an apprehended felon, with his legs tied under his horse's belly, while the English nobles and their sovereign looked proudly on. He was then sent to Falaise in Normandy, and committed to close custody. Henry having subdued his rebellious sons on the Continent by a successful campaign, was occupied at the end of the year in prescribing conditions of peace, and settling the ransom of his prisoners; and while he liberated the greater part of them on very easy terms, the heaviest price was exacted from the captive of Falaise. Henry required that William should become his liegeman not merely for the territories he held in England, but for the crown and kingdom of Scotland; that he should surrender to him the castles of Roxburgh, Berwick, Jedburgh, Edinburgh, and Stirling; and that he should give his brother David and his principal barons as hostages for his faithful observance of the treaty. To these extortionate terms William submitted; the national assent was given by the Scottish barons and clergy on the 8th of December, 1174, in Valogne, and afterwards at Falaise; and thus Scotland ceased for the present to be an independent nation, and for the first time recognized the feudal superiority of England. It might have been expected that in such a case the submission of the Scottish church to that of England, so often a ground of contention between the two countries, would have been exacted also, by which the vassalage would have been complete; but the clause which was drawn up by the Scottish clergy to this effect, while it seemed to grant everything, in reality conceded nothing. It stated that the Scottish church in time to come would yield such submission as it "ought of right, and was wont to pay" in the days of Henry's predecessors—that it would give that right to the English church "which in justice it ought to have." Even in the most trivial act of everyday chaffering we know what such phrases mean, and for how much they are valued. The Archbishop of York upon the strength of this condition could demand nothing more of Scotland than it had been hitherto wont to pay, and that was simply—nothing.

A choice opportunity soon occurred of bringing these ambiguous expressions to the test: this was A.D. 1176, when Cardinal Huguccio, the papal legate, assembled a council of the English church at Northampton. On this occasion not only Henry II. was present, but also William of Scotland, and six of his principal bishops. Henry ordered these prelates "to yield that obedience to the English church which they ought to yield, and were wont to yield, in the days of his predecessors;" but the bishops, who had no doubt prepared their answer to such a demand, howsoever proposed, replied boldly, that they had never yielded subjection to the English church, neither ought they. This was an appeal to history, upon which the whole merit of the question rested. Roger, Archbishop of York, here asserted, and endeavoured to prove, that the Bishops of Glasgow and Galloway had been formerly subject to his see; but to this Jocelyn, Bishop of Glasgow, replied that by the

---

[1] W. Newbur.

special grace of Rome, whose spiritual daughter Glasgow was, that diocese had been exempted from the jurisdiction of all other bishops and archbishops. This was supposed to have been obtained by a bull granted by Pope Alexander III. only twelve years previously. If, therefore, his see had been subject to the archbishops of York before that period, he added that such a claim was of force no longer. Here the pride of the Archbishop of Canterbury, who bore no good-will to his spiritual brother of York, was effectually kindled: he contradicted the assertion of the latter, and declared that the subjection of the Scottish church was not to the see of York, but to that of Canterbury. This contention of the rival primates was a happy interruption for the Scottish bishops, who must have felt some misgiving for their cause before such a tribunal, and Henry, without repeating his demand, allowed them to depart.[1] Already Scotland was politically his own; but as a spiritual vassal it could only belong to the church, whose growing power he was earnestly labouring to curtail. The late case of Becket had likewise taught him how formidable a sceptre the crozier of Canterbury might become when wielded by a vigorous hand, and probably warned him how dangerous it might become if it was extended not only over England, but Scotland also.

The captivity of William, brief as it was, had shown the still insecure state of the Scottish monarchy, from the strifes and divisions of the many races which it sought to coerce and the rival sovereignties it comprised. This was especially the case with the wild Scots of Galloway who had attended William in his luckless inroad upon Northumberland, and who, like the rest of the army, had made a hasty retreat to their own home as soon as he was taken prisoner. Emboldened by the absence of the king they set up for independence in their own desperate fashion by expelling his officers, razing his castles, and slaying or driving out all strangers settled among them, whether Scotch or English, whether Norman or Flemish; and having thus rid themselves of their masters, they quarrelled among themselves. At this time two brothers, Uchtred and Gilbert, possessed the large district of Galloway between them; but impatient of a divided rule, Gilbert, in 1174, assassinated his brother. To punish him the king marched into Galloway as soon as he had regained his liberty, but effected nothing against him beyond mulcting him in the fine of homicide. Having thus bought a pardon, Gilbert, in 1176, attended Henry II. at York, to whom he did homage, and whose protection he obtained, as is alleged,

by the bribe of a thousand merks. Thus assured of powerful countenance and support, the favoured fratricide commenced war against William in 1184, but, fortunately for Scotland, died in the following year.

The place of Gilbert, as lord of Galloway, was now assumed by a very different personage; this was the gallant Roland, the son of the murdered Uchtred, who, on the death of his unnatural uncle, advanced his claim to the succession of his fathers; and this he made good, not only by defeating the forces of the late usurper, but by clearing the whole of Galloway from the hordes of rebels that infested it. These brave deeds, which were beneficial to Scotland and grateful to the king, were odious to Henry II., whose hold upon Scotland was chiefly to be maintained by its dissensions; and A.D. 1186 he mustered a formidable army at Carlisle for the invasion of Galloway and the removal of its gallant chief. But Roland, undismayed by such an enemy, prepared himself for a war of independence, and so effectually fortified the passes of his rugged dominions that it would have been dangerous to assail him. In this case Henry, who had tried a similar campaign in Wales, A.D. 1165, and been baffled by the natives and the elements, consented that Roland's claims against those of Duncan, the son of Gilbert, should be adjusted by a peaceful and legal compromise. This was done to the satisfaction of all parties, so that while Roland was put in possession of the greater part of the district, Duncan was invested by William with the barony of Carrick, at that time a portion of Galloway.

While these disturbances were still pending William was once more involved in an ecclesiastical controversy. His opponent in this case was neither Archbishop of York nor King of England, but one of more formidable character, even the sovereign pontiff himself. The question at issue was the right of electing bishops, which was now once more to be contested in Scotland, and in consequence, as before, of a vacancy in the see of St. Andrews. This event having occurred A.D. 1178, the chapter assembled, and upon their own authority elected to the bishopric John Scot, one of its arch-deacons —a man distinguished above his brethren in that rude age by his literary attainments. But the king had destined this high office for Hugh, his own chaplain; and on learning the proceedings of the chapter, which seem to have been so cunning or precipitate as to have taken him by surprise, he indignantly exclaimed, "By the arm of St. James, while I live John Scot shall never be Bishop of St. Andrews!" To make good his declaration he seized the revenues of St.

---

[1] Hoveden.

W. H. MARGETSON.

JOCELYN, BISHOP OF GLASGOW, IN THE PRESENCE OF HENRY II.

AND THE PAPAL LEGATE, REPUDIATES THE JURISDICTION OF THE ARCHBISHOP OF YORK, AT COUNCIL OF ENGLISH CHURCH CONVENED AT NORTHAMPTON (A.D. 1176).

Vol. i. p. 117.

Andrews and commanded the bishops to consecrate the man of his election; and although Scot appealed to Rome, Hugh was consecrated and put in possession of his benefice. The pontiff, Alexander III., reversed this election in A.D. 1180, and caused Scot to be consecrated by the Scottish prelates; but as soon as this was done the king sent Scot into banishment, proclaimed Hugh the rightful Bishop of St. Andrews, and put him in possession of its temporalities.

In this way William the Lion, one of the most limited sovereigns of Europe, and sovereign of one of its poorest territories, braved an authority at which kings and emperors trembled. The example of his conqueror Henry II., who had tried the same conflict and been miserably foiled, seems only to have nerved him for the feat. As Bishop Hugh, under shelter of the king, asserted his election to be lawful, Alexius, the papal legate, who had hitherto managed this vexatious controversy on the part of the pontiff, laid the diocese of St. Andrews under an interdict, hoping he had thereby shut the mouth and tied up the hands of the rebellious Hugh from the exercise of his clerical functions. Even this, however, was of no avail, so that the pope himself was obliged to descend into the arena; and he sent a mandate to the Scottish clergy, commanding them within eight days to instal John Scot as their bishop and yield him clerical obedience. "Should the king will otherwise," he added, "or be inclined so to will by the counsel of the wicked, you ought to yield your obedience to God and to the holy Roman Church rather than to men." By another mandate they were also to excommunicate Hugh, the pretended bishop, for his contumacy, and yield due obedience to their lawful prelate John; and should the latter be still rejected by William, the pontiff empowered the Archbishop of York and the Bishop of Durham to excommunicate the king and lay Scotland under an interdict. It is said that at this terrible threat even John Scot himself was willing to end the controversy by renouncing his pretensions; but the pope had gone too far to permit the controversy to be thus adjusted, and he commanded the fainthearted prelate, by the solemn obligation of his "clerical obedience," to stand firm and hold out to the last.

As the menaced excommunication and interdict was the last of Rome's dreaded weapons, and therefore not to be hastily produced or idly hazarded, attempts were yet to be made before it should finally descend and strike. Accordingly Hugh, Bishop of Durham, who had been invested with legatine powers, with John Scot in his company, who had been banished to England, visited William for the purpose of persuading him to relent. Their arguments were in vain. Scot then proceeded to excommunicate, as disturbers of the church, some of the king's chief counsellors; but even by this foretaste of what awaited himself William remained unmoved. On hearing of this strange case of obduracy the pope wrote an angry letter to the Scottish king, commanding him within twenty days to admit Scot to his charge, threatening not only excommunication in case of refusal, but also to throw the Scottish church into subjection to that of England. But William was still as resolute as at the first that John Scot should never be Bishop of St. Andrews; he offered, indeed, to appoint him chancellor and give him some other vacant bishopric, but further than this he would not concede. The legatine authorities of York and Durham then proceeded to pass sentence of suspension upon all those priests who refused obedience to Scot, and William retaliated by banishing those who yielded it. And now the long-gathering thunderstorm exploded, for the sentence of excommunication was at last pronounced upon William, and of interdict upon the kingdom, by the prelates of York and Durham, in name and by authority of the pontiff. By this dread sentence the churches should have been closed upon the living and the very churchyards upon the dead; the nation should have been shunned as a leper or persecuted as an outlaw by every community of Europe, until it grovelled in the dust and craved in abject terms for pity and forgiveness. But this, or even the more terrible alternative of utter extinction among the nations, was averted by what might be deemed a vulgar accident. Pope Alexander III. died; and as it was not uncommon for a pontiff at his accession to taste the sweets of power or ingratiate his new sovereignty by reversing the sentences of his predecessor, Lucius III., who succeeded Alexander III. in 1182, abrogated those which had been inflicted on Scotland and its king. It was even declared in the bull to that effect that William, through Joceline, Bishop of Glasgow, and his ambassadors, "had presented many and sufficient reasons for retracting the judgments pronounced by authority of Alexander III."

Thus was Scotland freed from that strangling nightmare of the nations, whose inflictions, during the long night of the dark ages, were so dreaded and often so fatal. The controversy, indeed, was not yet fully ended, for the question of Scot's reposition or exclusion had to be settled anew even though the excommunication of William had been reversed and the interdict recalled. This, however, was very speedily terminated by the mediation of the Bishop of Dol and the Abbot of Rievaux, who were sent into Scotland by the new pope. William offered to bestow upon Scot the bishopric of Dunkeld, the dignity of chancellor, and the emoluments of the archdeaconry of St. Andrews, with an annual pension of forty merks, while Scot was to destroy all the instruments which he had received from the late pontiff. Should it be absolutely required, the king also offered to remove Hugh from St. Andrews to Glasgow, but not for the sake of John, from whom in that case he would withhold his personal favour. John consented; and although he refused to destroy the papal instruments in question, he pledged himself to renounce all their benefits, if such should be the pleasure of the king. His greatest obstacle to a full reconciliation was the fact of his rival's remaining in possession of the see of St. Andrews, to which he declared he could never give his consent; but even this difficulty was surmounted by an ingenious compromise—a compromise resembling that of two angry schoolboys rather than the reconciliation of two great rival ecclesiastics, with the interests of a church and a nation at stake. Both bishops having resigned their pretensions to the see of St. Andrews, the pope nominated Hugh, the man of the king's own choice, to the bishopric; while John Scot was appointed to that of Dunkeld, according to the king's own consent. Not only did William thus maintain his independence in a trial where defeat seemed inevitable, but also secure the favour of the pope, who at the ensuing festival of Lent sent him the golden rose in token of his especial grace and also his pontifical blessing.

In the year 1186 William married Ermengarde, whose grandmother was an illegitimate daughter of Henry I. This union, recommended by Henry II., appears to have been entered into by the Scottish king with some reluctance. The dowry settled upon his new queen was the castle of Edinburgh, which Henry restored to William, the service of forty knights, and an annual revenue of a hundred pounds.

In the following year the country was once more disturbed by a Celtic insurrection, headed by Donald or MacWilliam, who was or pretended to be the son of that William whose father, Duncan (the illegitimate son of Malcolm Canmore), had ascended the Scottish throne, A.D. 1094, and held it only for a few months. The pretensions of Donald were no doubt founded upon the legitimacy of his grandfather, and his own right to wear the crown of Scotland in preference to the present sovereign. He was soon able upon the strength of these pretensions to take possession of the district of Ross, and lay waste that of Moray, so that the king in person was obliged to advance against him at the head of a numerous army. A part of the royal force under the leading of the gallant Roland, Lord of Galloway, encountered the pretender by accident upon a heath in the neighbourhood of Inverness, and in the skirmish Donald or MacWilliam was slain, upon which his army dispersed.

In 1188 an event occurred that must have been gratifying to the heart of William, as it secured the ecclesiastical independence of his kingdom, which was now constantly menaced by the claims of the English hierarchy. This was in consequence of a bull of Clement III., in which he declared the Church of Scotland to be the daughter of Rome by special grace, and subject to her alone, not mediately, but directly. Only the pope, or his legate *a latere*, was to have authority to pronounce against Scotland the sentences of excommunication and interdict: none was to hold the office of legate there, except a Scottish subject, or a member of the Sacred College deputed by the apostolic see; and no appeal concerning Scottish benefices was to be made out of Scotland, except to the court of Rome. In this way the claims of the primates of Canterbury and York were laid to rest by an authority which they could not question or gainsay.

A recognition so important, by which the national church was proclaimed free and independent, was but the happy prelude of that political liberation which succeeded. Soon after the restoration of the castle of Edinburgh to the crown of Scotland Henry II. offered to give back the castles of Roxburgh and Berwick also, if William would consent to pay the tenths of his kingdom towards the expenses of the crusade. It was not that the King of England cared for the recovery of the Holy Sepulchre, or the expulsion of the Saracens from Palestine, but to him the crusading mania, now the great European epidemic, was a most profitable pretext, under which he extorted money both from priest and layman, both from Jew and Christian.[1] It was not wonderful, therefore, that he should offer to sell these castles, which were too expensive for him to keep, or that he should calculate upon the Scottish national feeling when he rated them at so high a price. But the exorbitance of the royal bargain-maker in this case overshot itself; for in a meeting of the Scottish parliament where the offer was presented, the barons and clergy answered that they would not agree to these terms, though both kings should have sworn to levy them.

Soon after this Henry II. died, and was suc-

---

[1] From the Jews alone, who were assessed at the rate of a fourth of their property, but condemned to redeem themselves at a still heavier amount, Henry II. is said to have wrung the then enormous sum of £60,000.

ceeded by his eldest surviving son, Richard, better known by the title of Cœur de Lion. As the new King of England was heart and soul a crusader, he proceeded to gather money with still greater eagerness than his father; but in his case it was with the honest purpose of expending it freely in the undertaking. A few months after his accession he invited the Scottish king to his court at Canterbury; and in the intercourse which was thus renewed between Richard the Lion-hearted and William the Lion, it was impossible for the former to forget how greatly the latter had suffered as the ally of himself and his brothers. This feeling, combined with his pecuniary necessities, may have suggested to him not only the renunciation of the superiority over Scotland, but the generous and easy terms upon which it was relinquished. Accordingly, for ten thousand merks Scotland was absolved from her degrading allegiance to England, and declared completely free and independent. The separate conditions of this momentous national instrument, dated December 5th, 1189, were the following:—

The castles of Roxburgh and Berwick were given up to William and his heirs for ever as their own proper inheritance.—All obligations extorted from William by new instruments, in consequence of his captivity, were remitted, upon condition that he should fully perform to the King of England whatever Malcolm, the brother of William, had performed to Richard's predecessors.—The boundaries of the two kingdoms were to be re-established as they had stood at the period of William's captivity. Richard on his part became bound to put William in full possession of all his feofs in the earldom of Huntingdon and elsewhere—and to deliver up such of the evidences of the homage done to Henry II. by the barons and clergy of Scotland as were in his possession; declaring also, that all evidences of that homage, whether delivered up or not, should be held as cancelled.

Such were the terms on which Richard I. absolved a whole kingdom from vassalage. His act has been condemned as one of those deeds of thoughtless prodigality or chivalrous quixotism of which his whole history was so largely composed. But even setting aside the common calls of gratitude, which demanded the redress of grievances that had been incurred in his own behalf, there is sufficient evidence that this deed of generosity was an act of political wisdom. Not only was Scotland too poor to be taxed, but too turbulent to be coerced, and it was impossible but that, amidst the political changes of England, she would reassert her liberty by far other modes than a peaceful money composition. Richard, too, be it remembered, was about to depart to Palestine on a long and doubtful expedition, by which the military resources as well as the wealth of the kingdom would be exhausted; and in such a case it was wise to convert a dangerous enemy like Scotland into a grateful affectionate ally. This was shown by the amity that was now established between the two nations, and which continued to prevail after the two contracting sovereigns had descended to their tombs. These considerations might have justified the Lion-hearted had he even rated the quittance of Scotland no higher than a pepper-corn. As for the ten thousand merks of ransom, at which English historians have expressed such contemptuous derision, it was no such frivolous matter to the Scots, with whom silver was scarce, and gold a downright rarity; and our writers have been puzzled to conjecture how it was raised and paid by a people whose scanty commerce was limited to the sale of wool, hides, and skins. It is certain that it could not be raised at once, or paid otherwise than by instalments. Even the two thousand merks which William is said to have contributed for the liberation of Richard from the Austrian prison was perhaps nothing more than a portion of his own ransom.[1]

With the splendid army of Richard I. which left England A.D. 1190, and of which so few were fated to return, was David, the brother of William, and now Earl of Huntingdon in reality as well as name by the late renunciation of Richard. As an English earl he was bound to follow the banner of the King of England, and before his departure he allied himself still more closely to the country by his marriage with Maud, the daughter of Ranulph, Earl of Chester. The adventures of this prince while a soldier in Palestine are unknown, and therefore have left a free field for the romancist; but in history he is chiefly distinguished by the disastrous events of his return from the crusade, in which he was as sorely tried as Richard Cœur de Lion himself. The vessel in which he embarked was shipwrecked on the coast of Egypt; and on reaching land he was conveyed by the natives to Alexandria, where, his rank being unknown, he was sold as a slave to certain Venetian merchants, who brought him to Constantinople and afterwards to Venice. At this last city he was recognized and ransomed by some English traders, with whom he travelled to Flanders; but on embarking a second time for Scotland he was again assailed by such a tempest that in his extremity he vowed to the Virgin that if he reached home in safety he would erect a church to her honour. After

---

[1] Lord Hailes, vol. i. pp. 146 149.

being driven about on the coasts of Norway and Shetland his vessel, stripped both of helm and tackle, entered the Tay and reached Dundee. After landing he fulfilled his vow by erecting the Abbey of Lindores for the order of Benedictines.[1]

The succeeding events of the reign of William, although it was still extended over a course of years, afford little scope for notice, partly from their unimportant nature, but still more from the obscurity with which they are surrounded. Its chief troubles arose from revolts in Caithness which were easily suppressed, and by misunderstandings with the unreasonable John, the successor of Cœur de Lion, which could not be so easily terminated. On the accession of John to the throne of England William did homage to him in the usual form for the land held by him in England, but followed this act by a demand for the restitution of the three English counties that had formerly belonged to Scotland —a demand which John vaguely promised to take into consideration. The latter, however, gave unequivocal proofs of an encroaching spirit against his neighbour by attempting to erect a castle at Tweedmouth for the purpose of overawing Berwick; but as fast as it was built the castle was demolished by the orders of William. After this angry altercation had continued a few years matters seemed, in 1209, to be ripened for actual warfare, and the two kings were on the eve of meeting, each at the head of an army. But when John had arrived at Norham and William at Berwick the barons of both kingdoms interposed, and the quarrel was ended by payment on the part of William of a sum of money for the demolition of the castle of Tweedmouth, and a promise on the part of John that it should never be rebuilt. He also delivered to the guardianship of John his two daughters, Margaret and Isabella, that they might be provided with suitable husbands in England. It has been added that the paction on this occasion was that Henry and Richard, the sons of John, should marry the two Scottish princesses. Throughout the whole treaty William appears as the weaker party, and this especially when we find that, to purchase the good-will of the King of England and fulfil certain agreements not specified, he consented to pay the large sum of fifteen thousand merks. As the price of a demolished castle it was certainly by far too much; but if it was to be understood as a dowry for the princesses on their marriage with the sons of John, it becomes more intelligible. Such a pacification gave little satisfaction to William's subjects, whom it must have considerably impoverished; but he was no longer the bold adventurous knight-errant of former years, but a cautious old man surrounded by difficulties, and having none but an infant son to succeed him. The peace into which he had entered he therefore steadfastly maintained to the close of his life, notwithstanding the temptations arising from the troubled state of John's affairs with not only his barons but the church arrayed against him. In the last year of his reign he allowed his young son Alexander, Prince of Scotland, now in his seventeenth year, to receive knighthood from John, although lying under the excommunication of the church; and this circumstance, which might have deterred other sovereigns, was perhaps an additional recommendation in the eyes of William, who had himself braved the danger and shown how it might be overcome. His death occurred after a long illness at Stirling on the 4th of December, 1214, in the seventy-second year of his age and forty-ninth of his reign.

The character of this king may be distinctly traced in the actions that signalized his government. In his youth his unreflecting unscrupulous disposition was manifested not only in public life by the encouragement he gave to the English princes in warring against their own father, but in private by his licentiousness, so that an illegitimate family of two sons and four daughters were the fruits of his seductions, to which several young maidens of rank had fallen victims. Then followed his military operations, which were conducted without wisdom, and which ended, as they deserved, in discomfiture and disgrace. It was a bitter lesson, but he laid it to heart; and this is evident from his subsequent proceedings, which seem to have been a continual and systematic effort to repair the wrongs he had committed and the suffering he had entailed. He thus was enabled not only to compose the internal troubles of his kingdom but to restore it to the independence from which it had fallen. In the duties of legislation, also, which were so much in request for a people like the Scots, he was eminently distinguished, and his labours in this department are attested by his statutes in thirty-nine chapters which are included in the collection of the ancient laws of Scotland.

This king is usually distinguished in our old histories by the title of William the Lion; and he was so called, Boece informs us, "for his singular justice." But how such a resemblance could be established he has not ventured to suggest. The title most probably arose from his being the first of our Scottish kings who assumed an armorial cognizance, which was a lion rampant, and this is the figure that appears on his seal.

---

[1] Boece, lib. xiii. c. 7

CHAPTER III.

REIGN OF ALEXANDER II. (1214-1249).

Succession of Alexander II.—Insurrection of Donald MacWilliam—Alexander invades England—Scotland invaded by John, King of England—Merciless character of the invasion—Alexander again invades England—Pacification between Alexander and Henry III.—Rebellions in Caithness and Moray—Rebellion in Galloway—Its suppression—Pacific interviews between Alexander and Henry III.—Terms of their agreement—The papal legate proposes to visit Scotland—He is deterred by Alexander—Feud between the families of Athole and Bisset—Its cause—Bisset's unpatriotic conduct—Henry III. invades Scotland—The invasion amicably terminated—Disturbances in Galloway—Rebellion in Argyle—Alexander's expedition to suppress it—He dies on the way—His character.

Alexander, the son of William the Lion, and second of the name, was crowned at Scone on the 5th of December, 1214. Although as yet only in his seventeenth year he had already a foretaste of the cares of royalty, in a Celtic insurrection headed by Donald MacWilliam, son of that rebel of the same name who claimed to be grandson of King Duncan, the son of Malcolm Canmore, and was slain in battle, A.D. 1187. The present MacWilliam, aided by an Irish chieftain, invaded the district of Moray, the scene of his father's inroads; but his forces were defeated, and himself slain by MacIntagurt, Earl of Ross. The insurgent's gory head was presented to the young king in token of the victory.

During the important events which were now taking place in England it was impossible that Scotland would be allowed to remain neutral. The great civil conflict between John and his barons had commenced in which the important principles embodied in Magna Charta were contested and won. The support of Scotland and its king in such a controversy was of high importance, and the price offered for it by the barons of England was such as a patriotic Scottish sovereign of the day could not well refuse: it was the surrender of Carlisle and the investiture of Northumberland. Allured by this prospect of regaining the northern counties of England, Alexander II. joined the barons against John, and at the commencement of the first winter of his reign made an inroad into Northumberland, and laid siege to the castle of Norham. During the forty days of this leaguer, in which he was unsuccessful, the English barons gave him a formal investment of Northumberland by the hands of Eustace de Vesci. But in this payment it soon appeared that they were too hasty, for Norham successfully stood out, the desperate cause of John obtained new strength through the countenance and protection of the pope, whom he propitiated by becoming his vassal, and the English tyrant at the head of an army composed of the military scum and refuse of Europe—Brabançons, Poitevins, Gascons, Flemings, and men of countries more obscure—was able to overrun a large portion of England, and reduce the barons to the last extremity. It was now his turn to take vengeance on the Scots; and after having wasted the northern counties with such excesses of avaricious cruelty on the part of his followers that it was alleged a portion of them were Jews, he entered Scotland with such an array as even Scotland itself had never as yet matched either in strange materials or sanguinary proceedings. The very names in which his principal captains rejoiced, such as Lattim the Merciless, Walter Birch the Murderer, Godeschal the Ironhearted, Mauleon the Bloody, and Falco without Bowels, were sufficient to attest their characters as soldiers and the nature of their military operations. After burning the towns of Haddington and Dunbar, John continued his destructive inroad, swearing that he would rouse the little red fox out of his den, for so he called Alexander from the colour of his hair. The little red fox, however, was too cunning to oppose the first view-halloo of such a huntsman, and he allowed him to exhaust himself in a useless chase upon bleak heaths and barren mountains. Thus finding no enemy in the field, and starved by the desolation which his own wild fury had created, John was obliged to make a hasty retreat, setting fire to the priory of Coldingham and the town of Berwick on his way, as if to announce his return into England. To show himself a leader worthy of such troops, and to encourage their excesses, his own hand commenced the burning of the town by applying a firebrand to the house that had been honoured with his residence.[1]

In the meantime the young King of Scotland had encamped between the Pentland Hills and the Esk, intending there to give battle to the

---

[1] Matthew Paris. *Chron. Melros.*

invader; but the hasty retreat of John and its direction along the sea-coast disappointed his calculations. The retreat of the English forces and the desire of revenge were enough to incite Alexander to invade England in return, and penetrating through the western marches, he advanced through Northumberland as far as Richmond. But the wild followers of his banner, and especially the men of Galloway, committed such havoc that the king was glad to detach them from their prey by the signal of retreat. Nor did these merciless marauders escape the visible judgment of Heaven, if we are to put faith in monkish history, for, after burning the monastery of Holmcultram in Cumberland, a thousand Gallowegians in their retreat were drowned in the river Eden.[1] On reaching home Alexander dismissed from his army the unmanageable freebooters of Galloway, and resuming his incursion into England he took possession of the town of Carlisle. In the meantime Louis, the Dauphin of France, whom the enemies of John had invited to their aid with the offer of the crown of England, landed at Dover, and on his being recognized as king, Alexander marched forward to join the armed coalition against John, and do homage to the dauphin as the sovereign of England for the territories he held in that country. As Bernard Castle, the family seat of Hugh de Baliol, a principal adherent of John, lay in his route, Alexander laid siege to it; but while he rode round the walls, attended by some of the nobles of the district, a bolt from a cross-bow killed Eustace de Vesci, the same baron who had invested him with livery and sasine in the county of Northumberland, and who had married Alexander's sister.[2] By the same authority we are informed that the Scottish king did homage to Louis at Dover. In the compact which was made against John, the dauphin had sworn that he would not agree to terms of peace without his allies; but, by the unexpected death of the tyrant on the 17th of October (1216), this agreement was set aside in consequence of Louis making a peace on his own account, and retiring to France, and the English nobles swearing allegiance to Henry III., the successor of John. In this way the Scottish king was left to shift for himself as he best could. This sudden abandonment of the enterprise was chiefly occasioned by the abject humiliation of John, who had bequeathed England to the rule and protection of Rome, in consequence of which Gualo, the papal legate, pronounced sentence of excommunication against all who were opposed to the dominion of the church. This terrible sentence also extended to Alexander II., to his army, and the whole kingdom of Scotland; but so far from the Scottish king regarding it as the dauphin and the English barons had done, it was not proclaimed in Scotland till a whole twelvemonth afterwards. But however indifferent he might be to a papal excommunication, Alexander found that he could not make war unsupported against the whole power of England, and was compelled to retreat. At the close of the following year the king and nation were absolved from that papal sentence which they seemed to value so lightly, and peace was restored between England and Scotland by Alexander performing homage to Henry III. for the earldom of Huntingdon and all his other English possessions. In 1221 a still closer amity was established between the two kingdoms by the marriage of Alexander to Joan, the sister of the English king.

After this the cares of the Scottish king were chiefly occupied with the internal concerns of the country, which the late unprofitable invasion of England had not tended to propitiate. The first outbreak was an insurrection in Argyle, the inhabitants of which, the original lords of the country, could not tamely witness those changes by which they were reduced to insignificance. The king marched against them, reduced them to submission, and compelled them to give hostages for their future obedience. The flight of their principal ringleaders enabled him to supply the country with new chieftains of the Teutonic race, who were endowed with the lands of the defaulters, and who introduced a higher civilization among the wild tribes committed to their rule.[3]

Another revolt but of a different character occurred about the same time (A.D. 1222) in Caithness. Adam, the bishop of that see, was odious to the people by his rigorous exaction of tithes, and at last they rose in rebellion and besieged his episcopal dwelling. The bishop, hemmed in by a furious multitude and unable to resist, sent to the military lord of the district, the Earl of Orkney and Caithness, praying him to come to his assistance; but the earl, who was supposed to have a fellow-feeling with the revolters, coolly answered, "Let the bishop come to me and I will protect him." In the meantime the dwelling was fired and the unfortunate prelate burned alive. Alexander received the tidings of this atrocity while he was on a journey to England; but instantly abandoning his purposed route, he repaired to the place of insurrection, subdued the rioters, and inflicted upon them a punishment even more terrible than their crime. He caused four hun-

---

[1] *Chron. Melros.*   [2] *Matt. Paris.*   [3] Fordun, lib. ix. c. 34.

dred of them to be put to death, and not content with this, it is added that he emasculated their children in order that none of such an accursed brood should be continued to trouble the country in after years.[1] This odious form of justice does not constitute a solitary instance in the pages of our early chronicles. Nor did the earl wholly escape, for he was deprived of his estate, although he was afterwards suffered to redeem it. Justice, however, was not yet satisfied, and the full measure was meted out to him by his own servants, who murdered him in his house and afterwards set it on fire. Bishop Adam was reckoned a sort of martyr by his brethren because he had perished for the rights of the church; and it is not unlikely that this popular canonization, as well as the spirit of rebellion or love of plunder, may have animated his avengers.

Almost six years after this insurrection in Caithness another broke out in the turbulent district of Moray, headed by a chieftain named Gillespie, an inhabitant of Ross. After burning several primitive castles of timber in Moray he fired the town of Inverness, wasted the crownlands in the neighbourhood, and compelled every one on pain of death to join his party. The king went against him, but was unsuccessful. In the following year the Earl of Buchan conducted an expedition against Gillespie, and with better fortune, for he tracked the formidable marauder, surprised him in his lurking-place, and having beheaded him as well as his two sons, sent their heads to the king.[2]

The scene of insubordination and turbulence once more shifted to Galloway. Allan, the lord of that district and son of Roland, died in A.D. 1234, leaving three daughters by different marriages and an illegitimate son. Of these ladies Helen was married to Roger de Quinci, Earl of Winchester; Devorgoil, to John de Baliol, Lord of Bernard Castle; and Christian, to William des Forts, son of the Earl of Albemarle. As they were the joint-heiresses of their father's powerful principality, the men of Galloway were dismayed at the prospect of having their political consequence humbled by the partition of their country into three lordships, with English barons for their chiefs; and they besought the king to set aside the succession of Allan's daughters and assume the inheritance for himself. But justice and policy equally forbade this daring step; the Saxon laws of succession were as yet too recent to be safely violated, and the English nobles were too powerful to be provoked. Alexander, therefore, dismissed the appeal of the Gallowegians and confirmed the disposition made by their deceased lord. They next requested that Thomas, the illegitimate son of Allan, might be appointed their chief; but the king, who must have felt the necessity of dividing them, refused to sanction the appointment. The Bastard of Galloway, who had such a fair field opened for his ambition, was not thus to be rejected, and a combination to support his claims was formed consisting of the King of Man, several Irish chiefs, and the discontented lords of Galloway, who swore by a solemn covenant of blood-drinking to instal him into his father's rule. Thomas, thus supported, commenced open war, and not only secured Galloway but carried his daring inroads into the heart of Scotland, in company with Gilrodh, a powerful chief from Ireland, who was the principal supporter of his cause. At the head of a numerous army Alexander marched against the insurgents, and in advancing into Galloway he found the obstacles presented by that rugged country augmented by those of famine, for the chiefs had wasted their own lands and destroyed their houses, that the invaders might find neither shelter nor sustenance. But the king persevered, brought the rebels to an open battle, and defeated them with such loss that several thousands were slain in fight, while those who were taken prisoners were put to the sword without mercy. As for the chiefs of the insurrection, their lands were confiscated and bestowed upon stranger occupants, while the three Anglo-Norman barons were placed in full possession of the allotments that belonged to their wives. In this way Galloway was reduced from a separate principality into a congeries of baronies and an integral part of Scotland. In the following year, indeed, Thomas and Gilrodh endeavoured to renew the war; and landing on the coast of Galloway with a strong body of Irish auxiliaries, they burned their vessels as soon as they had stepped on shore, like men who had come to conquer or die. But subsequent events made this menace a mere bravado. The men of Galloway were so effectually subdued by their late defeat that they offered little or no aid to the invaders, and the Bastard and his Irish ally surrendered themselves without resistance to the Earl of March. Thus forsaken by their chiefs, the unfortunate Irish kernes endeavoured to open their way homeward by the river Clyde, and for that purpose had reached Glasgow, when they were set upon by the men of that city, overpowered, and all of them beheaded except two, who were reserved to be hanged and quartered at Edinburgh.[3]

Although there still continued to be a smoul-

---

[1] Fordun, lib. ix. c. 37.   [2] Fordun; Buchanan.   [3] Wynton; Matt. Paris; Chron. Melros.

dering of indignation between the courts of Scotland and England, no open flame broke forth, and the occasional interviews between the Scottish king and Henry III. lasted during the whole of Alexander's reign. The chief subject of contention between them was the land in England which pertained to the Scottish crown—a question in which the royal as well as national honour of the two parties was at stake, and which they were at all times ready to contest, if need should be, by the final assize of battle. Among other claims of Alexander II. was one for the possession of the county of Northumberland, which King John had assigned as the marriage portion of his daughter Joan, but which her brother Henry persisted in withholding. Upon this ground an interview occurred in 1236 between the two kings at York, and afterwards at Newcastle; but the whole terminated for the time in the gift of an English manor to the Scottish queen, and the promise of a revenue to her husband from land in some part of England that would not serve as a door and inlet to invasions from Scotland.

On the following year a still more important meeting occurred between the two kings at York, which Henry convened for the purpose of a final and peaceful adjudication. On this occasion the demands of the Scottish king enable us more perfectly to understand the points of controversy that were at issue. He claimed the counties of Northumberland, Cumberland, and Westmoreland, by right of inheritance—thus laying open all the territorial demands which Scotland had ever at any time established in England either by conquest or cession. He required the repayment of 15,000 merks which his father, William the Lion, had given to King John of England on condition that his sons Henry and Richard should espouse Margaret and Isabella (William's daughters), but which engagement had never been implemented. He also alluded to an engagement by which Henry had pledged himself to marry Marjory, another daughter of William the Lion. These large demands were evidently made that the instalment offered in return should bear some adequate proportion. And in this spirit they were met and settled by the united wisdoms of England and Scotland. Henry offered, and Alexander consented to accept, in lieu of all demands territorial and pecuniary, six manors in the counties of Northumberland and Cumberland yielding an annual rental of £200, and to render homage for these in the usual form—all the Scottish nobles present binding themselves by oath to maintain the terms of the agreement.[1]

At this meeting of Christian pacification Cardinal Otto, the papal legate in England, was an effectual assistant. Mindful of the interests of his church, he took the opportunity of the happy termination of the treaty to intimate to Alexander his wish to visit Scotland, and to examine into its ecclesiastical affairs, as he had done into those of England. But this proposal was wormwood to the Scottish king. His predecessors had striven hard and successfully for the ecclesiastical independence of the kingdom; as yet it had been free from the imperious visitations of papal legates; and in 1225 the Scottish bishops had been gratified with the pope's permission to hold a council of their own, which they not only did for the time, but still continued to do without troubling themselves with a fresh application to the pontiff. Alexander's reply on this occasion was equally bold and politic. "I do not remember," he said, "ever to have seen a legate in my territories, nor that it has been necessary for one to be summoned there, thanks to God; and there is not now any need of one, for all goes on well; neither was any legate allowed ingress into that kingdom during the time of my father, or any of my ancestors, and I will not allow it as long as I am able. However, since report pronounces you to be a man of sanctity, I warn you, if you should happen to enter my territories, to proceed cautiously, lest anything untoward happen to you. For ungovernable, wild men dwell there, who thirst after human blood, and whom I myself cannot tame, and if they were to attack you I should be unable to restrain them: it is but lately, as you have perhaps heard, that they wanted to attack me and drive me from my kingdom."[2] On hearing this the cardinal, who does not appear to have been allured with such a prospect of the crown of martyrdom, wisely remained in England. He sent, however, an Italian, a kinsman of his own, to the Scottish court; and Alexander, that he might not seem discourteous at such a mark of confidence, bestowed upon the foreigner a portion of land and the honour of knighthood. In this way the independence of the Scottish church was still maintained inviolate.

During the same year (1237) Joan, the daughter of King John of England, and Queen of Alexander II., died in her native country of a painful and lingering complaint, for which she had vainly sought a cure at the shrine of St. Thomas à Becket. As she had left her husband no offspring, Alexander in 1239 espoused Mary, the daughter of Ingelram de Couci, a powerful

---

[1] Chron. Melros.; Matt. Paris.

[2] Matthew Paris, vol. i. p. 76. Translation of Rev. J. A. Giles, D.C.L.

count of Picardy, by whom, two years after, he had a son who succeeded him in the Scottish throne.

About this time an event occurred sufficiently characteristic of the rude state of society and mode of administering justice in Scotland during the thirteenth century. At a tournament upon the English borders Patrick, Earl of Athole, a young nobleman distinguished for his knightly accomplishments, unhorsed his antagonist, Walter Bisset. This mischance, which should have been received in all love and courtesy, was supposed to have rankled in the mind of the discomfited knight, and engendered purposes of deadly revenge. Shortly after, while Earl Patrick was lodging at a large barn-like building (probably a hostelry of the period) at Haddington, the door was blocked up with trunks of trees at midnight, the pile was set on fire, and the earl and his attendants perished in the flames. Bisset was immediately suspected of the deed, and the kindred of Athol, now landed in a death-feud, were prepared to pursue the supposed murderer to the last extremity. In the meantime no means were left untried by Bisset to prove his innocence. He procured a sentence of excommunication to be pronounced with its most imposing accompaniments[1] not only in his own chapel, but in all the churches of Scotland against the actors and abettors of the deed; he asserted that he had been fifty miles distant when it was perpetrated; and he offered to clear himself by the ordeal of combat against any who should charge him with the crime. The young and beautiful queen, also, Mary de Couci, only lately a mother, was so assured of Bisset's innocence, that she offered to make oath that he could never have attempted such a crime. But all these expurgations were of no avail against men resolved to condemn him; and when a trial by jury was offered he rejected it on account of the popular prejudice, which gave him no chance of a deliberate hearing. He had thrown himself upon the protection of the king; but against such a feud even royalty was helpless in Scotland; and when Alexander offered to strip Bisset of all his possessions and banish him from Scotland, the Athole faction consented, in the hope of being able to waylay the exile at his departure. This design, however, becoming known to the king, he concealed Bisset for three months before dismissing him; and when the fugitive at last was able to steal forth one dark night undetected it was with a solemn vow that he would make a pilgrimage to the Holy Land, there to pray for the dead Athole's soul and his own, and never to return.

If such was really the devout, self-denying purpose of the fugitive at his egress from concealment, it seems to have been left behind when he had fairly distanced his pursuers; for, instead of repairing to Palestine, he went no farther than London, and there he endeavoured to revenge his own personal quarrel by stirring up a war against his native country. To effect this traitorous purpose he appealed to Henry III., and complained of the injustice he had sustained. Although he had, as he said, proved his innocence, and offered to justify himself by combat, he had been driven from Scotland a banished and disinherited man, and all because his sovereign was unable to do him justice. He further represented that this sentence of his king was illegal and unconstitutional as well as unjust, for that Alexander as the liege vassal of the King of England could not thus deprive and banish a Scottish nobleman convicted of no crime without the sovereign of England's consent. After this disloyal and unpatriotic argument, he adduced a statement which, even if actually true, was a mean breach of confidence on the part of Bisset towards Alexander, who had concealed and sheltered him, and with whose more private doings he must thus have become acquainted:—he declared that the Scottish king harboured Geoffrey Marsh, a fugitive from Ireland, and traitor to Henry, whose son, William, had lately been tried for treason, and hanged at London as his father's accomplice.

These unworthy arguments and insinuations were suited to such a mind as that of Henry III., who had much of the weakness and meanness of his father John. Alexander's alliance with France also by his marriage with Mary de Couci had further irritated him, as he was now prosecuting a war with that country which brought him nothing but loss and disgrace. This French war, and quarrels with his parliament about grants of subsidies and the ratification of Magna Charta, prevented an immediate invasion into Scotland; but in 1244, when Henry found himself at leisure, he prepared for the undertaking in earnest. On this occasion the inducements given by Bisset were strengthened by a report which was rumoured of Alexander, to the effect that he had sent a message to England, declaring that he did not hold the least particle of his kingdom from Henry; that he ought not to do so; and that he would not. The King of England hindered John de Couci, the brother of the Scottish queen, from coming to Alexander's assistance by stirring up a war against him in Picardy; and he secured the co-operation of the

---

[1] "Idem Willelmus Bisset in capella sua omnes factores et fautores hujus incendii, et per omnes ecclesias Scotiæ, accensis et extinctis candelis, excommunicare fecit." Fordun, lib. ix. c. 59.

Count of Flanders, who arrived in England with a strong body of knights and men-at-arms to co-operate in the invasion of Scotland. Henry also enlisted twenty-two Irish chiefs to serve under his banner. When all were in readiness he assembled his army at Newcastle; and, in proclaiming the causes of the war, he not only announced Alexander's alliance with France, and the protection he afforded to Geoffrey Marsh, but also that Walter Comyn, Earl of Menteith, had given matter of offence to England by erecting two castles, the one in Galloway and the other in Lothian. On the other hand, the King of Scotland had not been idle, and the army which he mustered gives a formidable picture not only of the population but the military resources of Scotland at so early a period. It consisted of 100,000 infantry and 1000 horsemen. This was but a small amount of cavalry compared with what the King of England brought into the field;[1] but the Scottish horsemen were knights, and although they were not mounted upon the large fleet war-horses that were usually imported from Spain and Italy, their bodies were well protected by armour of steel or linen. The whole army was also in hearty trim for fight, for the soldiers had shrived themselves, and were encouraged by their preachers to fight to the death in defence of the liberty of Scotland. This imposing army prevented the necessity of a battle; Henry, an unlucky warrior, was in no mood to risk his doubtful fortunes in such a trial; and the King of Scotland, in consequence of his amiable qualities, was almost as much beloved by the English as by his own people. Under such circumstances a peace was speedily concluded between the contending parties at Newcastle. By this treaty the Scots engaged to enter into no alliance with the enemies of England as long as the English did them no harm; and, satisfied with this promise of neutrality, Henry led his splendid army from Newcastle to make a campaign against the Welsh, and to beg or extort money for its maintenance.[2] Little did Scotland know, amidst the joy of such a riddance, how all this would be reversed by a little child of Henry as yet only five years old, and whose boyish attention was thus roused into life by the din and pomp of a Scottish invasion.[3]

After three years of peace the tranquillity of Scotland was disturbed by internal dissension. The Scots of Galloway had not yet been reconciled to the manner in which their country was parcelled out among the husbands of their chief's daughters; and of these new lords the most obnoxious seems to have been Roger de Quinci, Earl of Winchester, whom his Scottish vassals hated as an oppressive taskmaster. His feudal exactions, even if conducted with strict Norman justice, would have been enough to outrage their Celtic ideas of patriarchal right and rule; but in the case of De Quinci they seem to have been imposed with more than the usual rigour. A rebellion of his people followed in 1247; they besieged him in his castle and reduced him to such extremity that he only escaped by a desperate sally, in which he cut his way through the besiegers and fled to the king, whose aid he invoked to replace him. Alexander soon suppressed the rebellion, and Roger was reinstated in his chieftainship. At his death he also, like Allan, his father-in-law, left three daughters, among whom his Scottish possessions were divided; and in this way Galloway, lately such a dangerous sovereignty, with laws and a government of its own, was with each generation becoming more innocuous.

The last disturbance with which the reign of Alexander II. was troubled arose from Angus, Lord of Argyle. This potent chief had been wont to do homage to the King of Norway for certain islands of the Hebrides of which he held possession; and on Alexander requiring that this homage should be transferred to himself, Angus refused to comply. He doubtless felt himself more independent in a foreign vassalage that would have been little more than nominal, than in one which would have placed him under constant watchfulness and control. In consequence of his refusal Alexander set out in person to reduce him to submission; but on his way he was attacked by fever, of which he died in the little island of Kerrera, near the coast of Argyle, in the fifty-first year of his age and thirty-fifth of his reign. His decease occurred on the 8th of July, 1249. By his own desire his body was conveyed to Scotland and buried in the Abbey of Melrose. His actions and his whole life show that the eulogiums bestowed upon him so profusely by Fordun were not unmerited, and that he was one of the best as well as ablest of Scottish kings. He signalized his piety by founding eight monasteries in Scotland; and his prudence by filling them with Dominicans or Black Friars, in preference to the more expensive monastic orders which David I. had patronized. It was not often thus that the kings of his day reconciled their donations to the church with their own royal rights and the welfare of their subjects.

---

[1] These according to Matthew Paris amounted to about 5000 well-armed knights.
[2] Matthew Paris; Fordun; Fœdera.
[3] Edward I. was born on June 18th, 1239; this treaty at Newcastle was ratified on the 4th of August, 1244.

CHAPTER IV.

REIGN OF ALEXANDER III. (1249-1286).

Alexander III. succeeds to the crown—Difficulties about his coronation—His marriage to the daughter of Henry III.—Case of Alan Durward—Interference of Henry III. in Scottish affairs—Complaints of Alexander's queen—Henry's visit to Scotland—Contentions between the Comyn and the English factions—Trial and banishment of the Countess of Menteith—Alexander III. and his queen visit England—Haco, King of Norway, prepares to invade Scotland—Arrival of the Norwegian fleet—Its operations—Its losses by shipwreck—Battle of Largs—Haco retires to Norway—Death of Haco—Alexander reduces the Western Islands to submission—Unites with his clergy for the independence of the Scottish church—Their successful resistance to the pope—Romantic marriage of Robert Bruce to the Countess of Carrick—Edward I. succeeds to the crown of England—Alexander visits him—Ragimont's Roll—Homage rendered by Alexander to Edward I.—Extinction of Alexander's family—He marries anew—Startling pageant at his marriage—His sudden death—His character.

By the death of Alexander II. the crown of Scotland was once more exposed to the perils of a minority, as his only son, Alexander III., was but eight years old. An attempt was made to delay the period of his coronation by representing that the day appointed was an unlucky one, and that the young prince ought to receive knighthood before he was called to the throne. These objections appear to have arisen from Alan Durward, the great justiciary of Scotland, who being also at the head of the Scottish chivalry, had hoped that the honour of conferring knighthood upon the sovereign should fall upon himself. These objections were overruled by Walter Comyn, Earl of Menteith, who represented the danger of delay, and suggested that the Bishop of St. Andrews might perform both ceremonies, as had been done in England by Lanfranc, Archbishop of Canterbury, in the case of William Rufus. Menteith's arguments prevailed, and Alexander III. was invested by the prelate both with the belt of knighthood and the crown of royalty on the 13th of July, 1249. It was well that on this occasion the proposed delay had been set aside, for Henry III., hoping to succeed in what had now become his favourite object, had applied to Pope Innocent IV. for a prohibition of the young sovereign's coronation without his permission, Alexander, as he alleged, being his liegeman. He also requested Innocent to grant him a tenth of the ecclesiastical revenues of Scotland, under the pretext of using it in a new crusade for the recovery of the Holy Sepulchre. The pontiff was not to be deceived with these professions which the English king had so often used for raising money, and he rejected both applications—the first, because it would be an insult to a sovereign prince; and the second, because it was without a precedent.

In the second year of Alexander's reign a scarcely less dangerous event for his independence occurred; this was his marriage with Margaret, the daughter of Henry, to whom he had been betrothed in infancy. The union was celebrated at York on the 26th of December, 1251, when the bridegroom was only ten years old and the bride still younger; and the extravagant pomp and display of the marriage feast would have been truly ludicrous had it not been the type of an alliance between two great rival kingdoms. Such was the immense concourse which assembled in York that the ceremony had to be performed in secret and at an earlier hour than that announced. Of illustrious attendants alone there were more than a thousand knights and nobles, English, Scotch, and French, glittering in silken robes; while to the marriage feast itself more than sixty pasture-fed oxen were contributed by the Archbishop of York—which formed the first and principal course at table. The archbishop, indeed, as prince of the county, was the chief landlord and entertainer of this aristocratic multitude; and by banquets, accommodations to the guests, and presents of gold and silver, "he sowed on a barren shore four thousand marks which he never afterwards reaped."[1] Henry, indeed, attempted to make a harvest out of the prelate's liberality by endeavouring to entrap the inexperienced boy into concessions unfavourable to the liberties of his kingdom; and accordingly, when Alexander had done homage for the territories he held in England, his father-in-law demanded homage to be done for Scotland also, according, as he alleged, to the practice of his predecessors. But Alexander, who had probably been prepared by his counsellors for such an event, answered boldly and briefly. He had come, he said, upon a peaceful purpose, and in full reliance upon the honour of the English king, and not to

---

[1] Matthew Paris.

answer such a difficult question, especially as he had not consulted upon it with his nobles or given it due deliberation. This reply silenced the King of England; and after the usual tournaments, pageants, and merry-makings, Alexander returned to his kingdom as free as he had left it.

It was during these York festivities also that the King of England, as if desirous to increase the difficulties of Scottish affairs, pretended to have discovered a plot by which, if real, the succession of his daughter's children would have been placed in imminent jeopardy. Alan Durward, that is Doorward, or in Latin Ostiarius, the Justiciary of Scotland, and a nobleman of great influence and ambition, had married a natural daughter of Alexander II., whom he had persuaded Robert, Abbot of Dunfermline and chancellor of the kingdom, to legitimatize according to the form of law. The King of England now accused Durward of having sent messengers and presents to the pope to obtain the legitimation of his daughters also by the king's sister, so that, in the event of the young sovereign's death, they should be lawful heirs to the crown. These charges by another account were brought forward not by Henry himself, but by the Earls of Menteith and Mar, who seem to have been at feud with the Ostiarius; but if they were the accusers, it is probable, from the reward they reaped, that they acted under the English king's direction. Certain persons who were accused as partakers in this conspiracy fled from York; Roger, the Scottish chancellor, resigned his office, and took shelter as a monk in the cloisters of Newbattle; while Alan Durward some time after became a soldier of Henry, and followed him in his wars to France. As for Menteith and Mar they were appointed, through the influence of Henry, to the guardianship of their young king.[1]

Besides the train of English knights which Henry III. sent to escort his daughter into Scotland, he had promised to Alexander that he would send him prudent and faithful counsellors to advise with the Scottish nobles on all matters connected with him and his queen. This promise he fulfilled by sending Geoffrey de Langley, his keeper of forests, who, under the guise of counsellor, was to perform the office of spy at the Scottish court and promoter of his master's designs against its independence. But his odious function, and the arrogance with which he discharged it, soon made him be expelled from the kingdom. Still harping upon an expedition to the Holy Land, Henry in 1254 obtained a grant from Pope Innocent IV. not of a tenth, but a twentieth of the ecclesiastical revenues of Scotland for three years, which were afterwards extended to four. It is unnecessary to add that none of this money found its way to Palestine. On the same year he sent into Scotland Simon de Montfort, Earl of Leicester. With what particular mission this most politic of England's barons was intrusted by his sovereign does not appear; but its nature may be surmised from the increase of dissensions that followed among the Scottish nobility. At the head of one faction were the Comyns, of whom Robert de Ros and John de Baliol were ostensibly, but not in fact, the regents of the distracted kingdom; while among their opponents who were supported by the King of England, were Robert de Brus or Bruce, and Alexander steward of Scotland. In this portentous antagonism we recognize the commencement of that rivalry and those contending claims, which were afterwards so pregnant with calamities to the nation at large.

Among the several pretexts of the English faction in Scotland were the pretended sufferings of the young queen; and these complaints afforded Henry an opportunity of sending his chief secretary Maunsell and the Earl of Gloucester into Scotland ostensibly to inquire into her grievances and redress them, but in reality to strengthen that coalition of the nobles who were opposed to the Comyns. To second their efforts he approached with an army towards the Border, and from Newcastle on the 25th of August (1255) he issued a proclamation couched in the most gentle terms, professing that his journey was one of love and courtesy towards his dear son Alexander, and that he would do nothing prejudicial to his rights and the liberties of Scotland. In the meantime Gloucester and Maunsell, on approaching Edinburgh, dismissed their train, and pretending to be humble knights of the household of Robert de Ros, they obtained admittance into the castle, where the king and queen resided. There they were soon joined by their armed followers, and by the Earls of Carrick, Strathern, and Dunbar; and, having both the castle and the royal couple in their possession they proceeded to inquire into the queen's alleged grievances. But these for the most part were either frivolous or unfounded. She complained that she was immured in this sad and solitary castle, where she could neither breathe a wholesome air nor enjoy the sight of green fields. She was not allowed to travel through the kingdom as a queen ought to do, or to have special attendants, or even her young damosels to wait upon her as ladies of the chamber. She also complained of her conventual life, as being secluded from the marital

---

[1] Fordun, lib. x. c. 5; *Chron. Melros*, 219.

society of Alexander, who was now almost fourteen years old. By all this it was made to appear that the Comyns had plotted not only to engross the present rule of the kingdom, but peradventure the future royal succession also, on account of the nearness of their relationship to the throne. The last of the young queen's grievances was immediately redressed, and the removal of the rest in due time was promised. But the treacherous capture of the castle of Edinburgh had roused the indignation of the Comyns; the nobles of their party flew to arms, and surrounded the fortress; but, on learning the safety of the royal pair, or rather finding that they were at one with the English faction, they retired, Robert de Ros, as the chief person inculpated, offering on certain conditions ensuring his own personal safety, to appear before the royal tribunal and answer every charge brought against him. But as it did not suit Henry and the English party to give him a hearing, Ros and John Baliol were deprived of the regency, and at the instance of Henry, who had come as far as Kelso for the purpose, a new government was appointed that included the whole of the clergy and nobility who were favourable to the views of England. This new rule was to continue, with Henry as "principal counsellor," till Alexander had reached the age of twenty-one. Having thus settled the administration of Scottish affairs according to his own selfish purposes, the English king returned home, taking care to indemnify himself on the way for the expenses of the expedition. Not contented, therefore, with confiscating the estates of de Ros which he held in England, and selling a pardon to John de Baliol, he visited the abbeys and priories of his homeward route through the English counties, commending himself to the prayers of the abbots, and extorting from them their money. In this way, after devoutly worshipping in the cathedral of Durham at the tomb of St. Cuthbert, he rose from his knees to break open the rich treasury which had been considered inviolate, and to carry from it by force all the gold and silver he could find under the name of a loan. Such was the king by whom the Scottish counsels were now to be directed.[1]

The departure of Henry was the signal for the Comyns to rally from their depression; and the first victory they obtained over their opponents was the restoration of Gamelin, one of their clerical adherents, to the bishopric of St. Andrews, from which he had been displaced by the opposite faction. Independently of the three earls and thirty-two knights who comprised their powerful family, and the numerous barons who adopted their cause as a patriotic quarrel, the Comyns had the pope in their favour, who excommunicated the new counsellors, and were supported by Mary de Couci, widow of Alexander II., and her husband John of Acre, who happened at that time to visit Scotland. Thus armed with political and spiritual arguments, and having at their call the lance of the man-at-arms and the censures of the priest, they increased in boldness; and being desirous of recovering possession of their young monarch, they attacked Kinross, where he was sojourning, at midnight, surprised him in his bed, and carried him off with his young queen to Stirling. Possessed of the person of royalty, they were now more than a match for their Scottish rivals; and, to strengthen themselves against an invasion from England, they entered into a league with the Welsh, at that time struggling for their independence. Feeling that they could now dictate their own terms at the sword-point, they mustered their armed retainers, and with the king in their company marched against their opponents; but the adherents of the cause of Henry, not finding themselves strong enough to meet their rivals in the field, fled to England. Here they opened negotiations, in the course of which they endeavoured to recover their influence by seizing the young king's person; but Alexander was too well guarded by the Comyns to fall into the snares that were laid for him. By the treaty which was at last concluded between the parties, Henry III. lost the greater part of those advantages for which he had been so insidiously toiling. The counsellors of his former election were, with a few exceptions, displaced, and in their room a new regency was appointed, of which the principal personages were Mary de Couci, and her husband John of Acre, Gamelin, Bishop of St. Andrews, the three earls of the house of Comyn, and Alan Durward, who had shifted sides, and been alternately the ablest ally and most dangerous antagonist of the patriotic party. Such were the principal changes of this singular drama, as far as they can be distinguished in so remote a distance and among such rude actors. In the movements of Henry we recognize a craft upon which his son Edward I. greatly refined, and to which he brought such boldness, military skill, and political wisdom as Henry never possessed.

These events in Scotland were succeeded by a domestic tragedy with which the public history of the period was closely connected. The hero of the Comyn faction, by whose sagacity and courage its proceedings had been so prosperously conducted, was Walter, Earl of Menteith —the same powerful noble who had advocated the immediate coronation of Alexander III. in

---

[1] Matthew Paris.

opposition to the suspicious delays proposed by Alan Durward. Walter, who might now be considered as the head of the new regency, most suddenly and mysteriously died; but while it was asserted in England that he had been killed by a fall from his horse, in Scotland it was declared that he had been carried off by poison administered by his countess. This lady, who seems to have possessed the lands of Menteith in her own right, soon after shocked the feelings of the Scottish nobility by marrying John Russel, a certain obscure Englishman who was alleged to have been her paramour, and to make way for whom she was now openly accused of having removed her late husband. In consequence of this charge she and her partner were thrown into prison, and Walter Stewart, a brother of the Steward of Scotland, who had married the younger sister of the countess, now laid claim in right of his wife to the lands and earldom of Menteith which had been forfeited by the crime. The parliament sustained his appeal, and the elder countess, branded with the double crime of poisoning her husband and contracting a clandestine marriage with a foreigner, was stripped of her possessions and banished.

In these prompt proceedings the Scottish parliament had probably acted according to the established law. But here the matter was not to rest. Four years afterwards (A.D. 1262) Pope Urban IV. adopted it as a matrimonial question, and therefore lying under the cognizance of the church; and he sent to York his deputy Pontius, with full power to inquire into the wrongs complained of by the banished and bereaved countess. Walter Stewart, now Earl of Menteith, most of the nobility of Scotland, and the principal priests and prelates of the kingdom were accordingly summoned by Pontius to appear at York and give their testimony in the case before this ecclesiastical tribunal. But this citation awoke the old spirit of independence, and Alexander, standing upon his royal rights, refused the legate as a judge, and referred himself and his subjects to the direct judgment of the pope. In this way the tribunal erected at York was unable to pronounce a decision. Again, however, this vexatious controversy was revived in 1273, and under different circumstances, for it was in behalf of William Comyn, who had married the daughter of the elder Countess of Menteith, and who now claimed to succeed to her inheritance. He was backed in his application by his father John, the head of the family, who probably thought his power sufficient to shake the firmness of Alexander and obtain his permission for a new trial to be held at York; but the king still refused his consent, and this second attempt was also abortive; he would not allow a court to be held for the trial of Scottish subjects beyond the limits of his own kingdom. At length, in 1285, the controversy, which was now mainly reduced to one of civil inheritance, was brought before the parliament at Scone as its proper place, and with a more decisive result. Walter Stewart was allowed to retain the title of the earldom and half of the lands of Menteith, while the other half was erected into a barony and bestowed upon William Comyn.

While such were the legal results occasioned by the suspicious death of Walter Comyn, Earl of Menteith, the event was of great importance to Henry. The greatest opponent of his schemes against Scottish independence was thus removed, and Alexander bereaved of his wisest counsellor. Eager to profit by such an unexpected chance, the King of England invited his son-in-law and daughter to visit him in London, and there treat with him of important matters connected with the welfare of both kingdoms. But the nature of the message and the character of Henry roused the jealousy of the Scottish nobles; they suspected the tenor of these important matters which were thus withheld from the council, and were indignant at this continual interference of the English king in the affairs of an independent kingdom. A mission of certain of their number to London was the result, and their consent to the royal visit was only obtained under certain concessions to which Henry solemnly pledged himself. These were that neither the King of Scotland nor his attendants should be required to treat of state affairs during his visit; that if the queen became pregnant in England Henry would not detain her, nor her child, if it should be born there; that the queen should undergo her expected confinement at her father's court; and that in the event of Alexander's death Henry would surrender the infant to the thirteen Scottish prelates and nobles who now composed the regency, or to any three of their number. With these guarantees Alexander with a noble train repaired to England, while his queen, who would soon become a mother, followed him by easy stages. But more important affairs than those of court ceremony and chivalrous pageants were connected with the Scottish king's visit, although of these there was great profusion; he wished to be invested in his rights over Huntingdon, the grant of which had been renewed to him by Henry on a visit he made to London in 1256, and to obtain payment of the queen's marriage portion, which Henry had hitherto been too poor to discharge.[1] During this visit

---

[1] It was not till A.D. 1263 (nearly three years afterwards

the period of the queen's delivery drew nigh, and she was prevailed upon to await the event at the English court; while her husband, satisfied with Henry's guarantees on this head, returned to Scotland. In February, 1261, was born his daughter Margaret at Windsor, who twenty years afterwards was married to Eric, King of Norway.

While the Scots were thus resisting the encroachments of England, their independence was threatened from a different quarter. The Norse chieftains, who had established numerous small sovereignties of their own over the Western Islands, had ever been dangerous neighbours to Scotland; but the superior power of the latter had at length prevailed, and several of the island chiefs who had hitherto maintained their allegiance to the parent country of Norway were glad to transfer it to the Scottish crown. But those who still resisted were too formidable to be overlooked; the possessions which in some instances they had established upon the Scottish coasts made their piratical visits dangerous to the peace of the country; and Alexander II., as we have already seen, had died in the expedition which had for its object the reduction of these northern reguli to peaceful and obedient Scottish liegemen. This purpose was resumed by Alexander III., and the Hebrides were invaded by the Earl of Ross aided by several island chieftains. It was, therefore, a wild war of one set of barbarians against another, in which every passion was let loose and all the atrocities of the old Norse campaigns resumed; but the heaviest visitation seems to have fallen upon the invaded of these islands, whose churches were wantonly destroyed, and whose children were impaled alive in savage sport upon the pikes of the ruthless invaders.

Loud complaints of these atrocities were carried to the court of Norway, and Haco its king resolved to exact a terrible retribution. He therefore made preparations not only to protect his faithful vassals of the Hebrides but to invade Scotland itself, and his muster of troops and shipping at the port of Bergen was upon the most formidable scale. But this danger which threatened Scotland in the first instance might, if the expedition should succeed, be extended to England also; and the invasion of Hardrada could not be forgot, through which the English army had been so seriously weakened before the battle of Hastings. This was enough to make Henry III. interpose his good offices, independently of his wish that no one should intermeddle with Scotland but himself, and A.D. 1262 he sent messengers to Haco to persuade him to desist from his purpose. The Norwegian monarch assured Henry in reply that he had no purpose to invade Scotland, and hastened his preparations.

All being in readiness the Norwegian fleet, commanded by Haco in person, set sail on the 7th of July, and directed its course to the Scottish coasts. If we may believe the Norse accounts to such storm from the north had gathered against the shores of Albion since the piratical days of Harold and Cnute, when whole kingdoms were plundered or won by a single onset. The armament consisted of more than a hundred tall ships, the decks of which were crowded with soldiers arrayed in shining armour, while from the top-masts fluttered the banners of their jarls and captains. The ship of Haco, towering over the rest, was furnished with twenty-seven banks of oars. The protection or plunder of the islands was the first object of the armament, and after visiting Shetland it anchored for some time in a bay of the Orkneys, from which parties were sent out to ravage the coast of Caithness, lately in allegiance to Norway, but now reduced to a Scottish province. The fleet then crossed the Pentland Firth, and directed its course by the Lewes and the Isle of Skye, gathering in its progress reinforcements from the King of Man and other tributary chieftains of the isles, until it amounted to an hundred and fifty ships. But grievous was the condition of those little potentates who had abandoned their fealty to Norway as a country too remote either to trouble or protect them. Their rejected sovereign was now at their doors, and his legions made terrible havoc upon the lands of those who still halted in their allegiance between him and King Alexander. After carrying dismay or compelling submission over the islands of the Hebrides and the neighbouring coasts, while their presence was little known, or but vaguely understood in the heart of the kingdom, the whole fleet of 150 ships entered the Firth of Clyde, presenting such a spectacle to its shores as they had never yet witnessed.

In this manner the Scottish government was taken in a great measure at unawares, and only warned of the danger by the actual presence of the enemy. To treat with assailants whom at present they were too weak to resist was the sole expedient of Alexander and his counsellors, and a deputation of Barefooted Friars was sent to Haco, to learn upon what terms he would agree to peace. Haco claimed as its price not only the whole Hebrides, but also the islands of Bute, Arran, and the Cumbraes in the Firth

---

that Henry contrived to pay five hundred marks of this dowry, by which his treasury was fairly emptied. For payment of the rest he was obliged to crave a delay, with the promise that he would be more punctual than he had been hitherto.—Lord Hailes, vol. i.

of Clyde, while Alexander, who was willing to yield possession of the islands of the Hebrides to Norway, refused to cede those of the Clyde, which would have established a formidable enemy within a two-days' march of his capital. Thus the negotiation was protracted, and nothing granted, although Haco, impatient of delay, at last proposed in chivalrous phrase the final arbitration of kings and conquerors, and invited Alexander to meet him at the head of his army, and try the question by a decisive battle between Scotland and Norway. But the wisdom of this dilatoriness on the part of the Scots was soon apparent. Their forces were mustering in every quarter; the provisions of the invaders were exhausted; and the mild autumnal breezes, which had been so propitious to the Norwegian sails, were now beginning to be exchanged for those winter storms against which no fleet could keep together, and which were especially dangerous among rocks and treacherous sands that would baffle the pilotage of strangers. The Norwegians had been lulled into security until the elements themselves, as well as Scottish valour, should strike for Scotland.

Finding a peaceful settlement hopeless, Haco at last resorted to those measures which he should have adopted at the beginning. He had already expended the best season for action in the recovery of petty islands and the chastisement of revolted chieftains, instead of striking at Scotland itself when his coming would have been unexpected; and he now sent at the last hour a fleet of forty sail up the Clyde under the command of Magnus, King of Man, accompanied by four Hebridian chiefs and two Norwegian captains. They sailed into Loch Long, and on reaching the head of the loch they dragged several galleys across the narrow isthmus separating it from Loch Lomond and launched them upon the peaceful waters of the latter lake. The beautiful islands with which that lake is begemmed, and upon which the eyes of travellers from every land were centuries afterwards to gaze with such delight, were then, it seems, studded with cottages, and at this season of danger were probably more populous than was wont, from the crowds that may have fled to them as places of safety. But soon the houses were ashes, and the islands themselves the homes of desolation and death, as well as the shores in the neighbourhood, which the rovers wasted with fire and sword. Allan, one of the chiefs of the expedition, then made a dash across the country into Stirlingshire, where he slew many of the inhabitants, and returned with welcome supplies in the form of many hundreds of cattle. But now the winter storms commenced, and announced to the Norwegians the fate that was in store for them; for ten of their ships were wrecked in Loch Long, and Ivar Howm, one of their captains, died either of fatigue or grief. Soon after a second storm burst upon the main body of the fleet that was anchored between the Cumbraes on Monday, the 1st of October, and such was its violence, that at midnight the stout ship of Haco was all but thrown on shore in spite of the eight anchors that were successively thrown out to keep her fast to her moorings. Five ships that were not so well found as the royal galley were flung upon the coast and reduced to wrecks, and the rovers that manned them were attacked by the Scots on the shore, and would have been overcome but for the boats' crews which Haco sent to bring them off. When the morning dawned upon the scattered armament of dismasted ships, and the hulks lying on shore, the Norwegians, accustomed as they were to the wars of the ocean, thought that such a storm could only have been raised by the supernatural agency of magic; and in this belief the king caused his boat to be put out and rowed to the Cumbraes, where he caused a solemn mass to be performed, in the hope that it would counteract the powers of darkness and bridle the fury of the elements.

After this act of devotion, and when the morning had fully broke, Haco went ashore upon the mainland with about eight or nine hundred men to prepare for the disembarking of his whole forces; and while he occupied the strand with this detachment, an additional band of two hundred men was stationed further onward upon the height. The Scottish army now appeared in full march for the encounter, and presented a very formidable aspect; for, besides their numerous infantry, chiefly armed with bows and spears, they had fifteen hundred horsemen, who were knights or barons armed completely in mail, and many of them mounted upon Spanish horses that, like their riders, were protected with steel armour. The first brunt of their onset fell upon the Norwegians stationed on the height above where the town of Largs now stands; but this body fell back toward the shore, seeing the hopelessness of resistance, and fearing to be surrounded. In the meantime Haco, who was at the head of the main detachment, had resolved to abide the unequal encounter in person until reinforcements should arrive from the shipping; but in this generous purpose he was opposed by the equal devotedness of his officers, who feared for his safety, and compelled him to return to the fleet that he might hasten the landing of their comrades.

And now commenced what has been called the Battle of Largs, which was rather a series of skirmishes along the shore than a single regular engagement. It commenced also with great advantage to the Scots, for the Norwegians upon the height who had retired at their approach soon changed their retreat into a flight, and communicated their panic to the main body; and while some were preparing for the encounter, others were hurrying to the boats in headlong confusion, or to the transport that lay near the shore. While thus overloaded boats were sinking, and the shouts of commanders recalling the fugitives only added to the wild uproar, the Scots, who are described as having outnumbered their enemies by ten to one, began the battle with a shower of stones and darts, and then pressed onward to closer encounter. One incident of this fight will show the spirit in which it was conducted. A gallant Scottish knight called Sir Piers de Curry, distinguished by a helmet and armour inlaid with gold, and adorned with gay sparkling stones, was also conspicuous by his daring courage, for he repeatedly galloped alone up to the front of the Norsemen and defied them to the encounter. At length Andrew Nickolson, one of the Norse commanders, accepted the challenge, and dealt Sir Piers such a blow with his sword that it shore through his leg-armour, lopped his thigh from his body, and left a dint in the saddle where the edge of the weapon was arrested. A furious struggle now commenced over the body, the Norwegians struggling to spoil it of the rich armour which they coveted; and at this point their resistance was the keenest and the greatest slaughter committed. It was in vain, however, that the more anxious of the invaders looked seaward for the arrival of fresh troops and their king: during the fight a third storm had arisen, and with such violence that no troops could be landed, except a few volunteers who boldly threw themselves into boats without permission, and fought their way through the war of the tempest to the shore to aid their countrymen. This slight reinforcement revived the courage of the Norsemen: they made a desperate rally against their assailants, whom they drove back to the heights above the shore, and thus gained time to secure a retreat for the whole detachment in their boats, that pulled for the Cumbraes, and reached their tempest-beaten fleet in safety.

But even when the wrath of man had done its worst the storm still continued to war against the armament, and ship after ship was stranded upon the lee shore of Ayrshire, broken upon the rocks, or shattered in collision with other vessels running adrift; so that besides the slain who had fallen in battle the shore was covered with the corpses of the drowned and heaps of drifted tackle and broken timbers. Haco then craved a short truce to bury the dead, which was done upon the shore and in the Cumbraes, where mounds and memorial-stones were erected to their memory. After setting fire to those stranded vessels that could not be removed, he directed his course to Arran and cast anchor in Lamlash Bay. Here he was met by a deputation he had sent to the Danish party in Ireland called the Ostmen, who had formerly applied to him when he first arrived at the Hebrides, offering to become his vassals if he would abandon the Scottish expedition and come to their aid against the English. These messengers returned with such promises of help from the Ostmen, and flattering hopes of conquest and booty in Ireland, that the Norwegian king was willing to attempt the trial rather than return home without honour; but in this he was opposed by his captains, whose marauding ardour had been cooled by their late disasters. He therefore sailed back to the Hebrides; but his shattered fleet was so unlike the resistless armament which had formerly exacted their homage that the Hebridian chieftains stood aloof, or even attacked and cut off his followers when they landed. On the 29th of October the fleet anchored in Orkney after more storm and shipwreck and still greater diminutions from desertion, as many of the vessels had parted company and straggled back to Norway without leave or notice. At Orkney permission was issued that all might return home; but as for the king, he was too sick of heart and exhausted in body to return with them. His expedition that had ended so differently from the triumphs of his predecessors, the disgrace that had closed the wings of his raven banner which had lately soared so proudly, and the trials and anxieties he had sustained, had settled into a mortal disease; and in his chamber in Orkney this, the last of those dreaded Scandinavian pirate kings whose visits had been so ominous to Britain, was stretched upon an inglorious death-bed like a sick woman or a monk. His death was a strange mixture of the old Runic warrior and the half-taught Norse Christian of the thirteenth century. He joined in pious conversation with the attendant priests, and in the prayers and services that were to prepare him for his final departure; and when these were over he consoled his last moments with the chronicles of the kings of Norway, which he caused to be read to him that their tales of rapine and adventure might soothe him into sleep. He received extreme unction in the midst of this solace, and on the 15th of December he expired.

Such was the event usually called the Battle of Largs, which forms an important date in the history of Scotland. The accounts of it, however, are so contradictory, and have been so extravagantly magnified, that, in spite of the Norwegian graves on the spot and the tokens that have been exhumed from them, it has often been questioned whether any battle or encounter did actually take place. But upon this head the Norse accounts of the expedition are too full and minute, and the acknowledgment of its failure too full and express, to tolerate such scepticism. These accounts probably lessen the number of the Norwegian combatants and the magnitude of their defeat; but still they show that Norway sustained a heavy national loss, while Scotland obtained a signal deliverance. All that they can do is to magnify the valour of the "shielded warriors," the "throwers of the whizzing spear," and tell how gallantly they resisted before they were driven to their ships. From the contradictory accounts it has also been considered doubtful whether the Scottish king was present at the engagement. But Alexander was now twenty-two years old, and can therefore scarcely be supposed to be absent when the military strength of his kingdom was mustered for such an encounter. The common account, which seems also the most probable, is that the Scottish army consisted of three divisions; that one of these, composed of the men of Perth, Angus, the Mearns, and the north, was commanded by the king; the second, of the men of Athole, Argyle, Lennox, and Galloway, by Alexander, the High Steward of Scotland; and the third, comprising the troops of Lothian, Fife, Stirling, Berwick, and the Merse, by Patrick, Earl of Dunbar.

As if to fill up the measure of his triumph, Alexander, on the same day that tidings reached him of the death of his formidable enemy Haco, was also advertised of the birth of a son, his expected successor in the throne. This event occurred at Jedburgh on the 21st of January, 1264. Anxious to secure the fruits of his success, the king collected troops for the purpose of invading the island of Man and reducing it to its former submission; but this movement was anticipated by Magnus, the king of that island, who repaired to Alexander at Dumfries and renewed his homage, engaging, as the token of his submission, to furnish to his liegelord of Scotland the services of five galleys with twenty-four oars, and as many with twelve. The Western Islands that had revolted from their allegiance to the Scottish crown during the late invasion were next to be chastised; and this was done by the Earl of Mar, who repaired thither with an army and discharged his commission with the military severity of the period by executing the principal leaders of the revolt and wasting their territories. These islands, with the exception of Orkney and Shetland, were now to form a part of the Scottish government; such of the inhabitants as would not consent to live under its laws were allowed to emigrate; while Alexander bound himself on his own part and that of his successors to pay 4000 marks, and a yearly sum of 100 marks ever after, to the Norwegian government as a quit-rent for the possession of these islands. To this important agreement between the two kingdoms the pope was made arbiter, with full power, on the failure of either, to exact a penalty of 10,000 marks from the offender.

While this negotiation with the court of Norway was under discussion, by which the integrity of the Scottish kingdom was advancing to completion, that of England was rent by a civil war raised by the commons under the Earl of Leicester against the privileges and despotism of the nobles. Although Scotland as a nation abstained from interfering, this neutrality could scarcely be expected from those of her Norman magnates who had large possessions in England, and whose feudal rights and interests were therefore so much at stake. Accordingly John Comyn, John Baliol, and Robert Bruce, at the head of a large party of their Scottish military retainers, marched into England as auxiliaries of Henry III. and took part in his changeful fortunes, until they were relieved by his son, afterwards Edward I., in the victory over Leicester at Evesham. During the battle of Lewes which preceded it Bruce and Comyn were taken prisoners, and the greater part of their Scottish followers slain.

The rest of the reign of Alexander III. was happily exempted from further war, but his tranquillity was disturbed and the independence of the kingdom threatened from a more formidable quarter than Norway. Cardinal Ottobon de Fieschi, the papal legate in England, in order to defray the expenses of his visitation to the British islands, thought fit to extend the impost over Scotland, which he had never visited, of six marks from each cathedral and four from each parish church. This exaction the king, with the advice of the clergy, refused to sanction; and on his appealing against it to Rome, they contributed 2000 marks to defray the expenses of the appeal. This fortunate union, however, between the king and the priesthood in behalf of their national rights was almost destroyed by a serious misunderstanding. A knight named Sir John Dunmore having been excommunicated for certain offences against the prior and convent of St. Andrews, was shielded by the king, who required Gamelin, the Bishop of St. Andrews, to rescind the sentence. This the bishop could not do without satisfaction being rendered by the culprit; and on being further urged he not only confirmed the sentence, but excommunicated all who should adopt the cause of Dunmore, with the exception of the royal family. Incensed at this, the king gave way to the legate and allowed him to levy a part of the demanded contributions. It was well, in the midst of this unhappy variance between king and prelate, in which the great question at issue was about to be sacrificed, that the party interposed who could do it with the best effect. Sir John Dunmore, the original cause of quarrel, submitted to ecclesiastical discipline, confessed his guilt, and was absolved. The king and his clergy were once more united, and the fruits of their union were soon apparent. The legate had resolved to visit Scotland, but to his demand for admission they sent him a flat refusal. Offended with his resistance and resolved to punish them, Ottobon then sent a summons to all the Scottish bishops requiring them to attend him in England at whatever place he should think fit; he also sent in like manner to the clergy ordering them to send two of their number, heads of monasteries, as their representatives. But this requisition, instead of being obeyed either in letter or spirit, was answered in a different fashion; for the bishops sent only two of their number, and the clergy as many—not, however, to tender the submission of the rest, but to watch over the proceedings of the council; and when several canons affecting Scotland were enacted at this meeting they interposed and refused to recognize them.[1] They were there as the representatives of a national independent church, and they furnished such an example of ecclesiastical intrepidity as was rare among the priesthood of Europe. Such moral courage, silent and unostentatious though it was, ought to occupy a high place in the history of Scottish heroism.

To punish this dangerous example of disobedience was now the aim of the pontiff, and to effect it he resolved that the chastisement should fall upon the lean purses of the Scottish clergy as well as their national pride. He therefore required them to pay a tenth of their benefices to assist in the Crusade, and to pay it to Henry III. of England, who in concert with the King of France had resolved to make a fresh effort to recover Palestine from the infidels. But this demand also Alexander and the clergy rejected, declaring that Scotland itself would furnish a proper complement of armed men for the expedition. On this occasion, indeed, the Crusade in question was no longer an empty pretext, for Ottobon had preached its necessity with such effect that Edward, the son of Henry, and 150 English barons and knights had assumed the red cross and were preparing to join the expedition of Louis IX. of France, afterwards called Saint Louis. True to the promise that Scotland would furnish its own contingent of crusading soldiers, David Earl of Athole, Adam Earl of Carrick, and several other Scottish nobles embarked with their military followers in 1268 to join the ill-fated expedition from which so few returned. It was the last effort of that religious spirit of Christendom into which its chivalry had been directed. Religious wars were still to continue, but to be waged with different weapons as well as upon questions of higher import.

In the meantime another part of the Scottish dispute of independence had to be adjusted, which referred to the right of England in the collection of the tenths of the Scottish ecclesiastical revenues. Of this authorization of the legate Henry III. was not likely to be neglectful, and he had proceeded immediately to put it into active use. His claims were resisted by the Scottish bishops, who once more appealed from the legate to the pope. But something more decisive than this was necessary, and they resolved that the question should be tried at another tribunal than that of the English church or a Roman legate. Accordingly they held a provincial council of their own at Perth, over which presided one of their bishops. It was a daring step, but in justification they adverted to the bull of Honorius IV. granted to the Scottish clergy A.D. 1225, by which, in consequence of their dislike to receive a legate from Rome, they were permitted to hold such a council for the regulation of the affairs of the church. This permission, indeed, could have been only meant to be temporary, but the ambiguous language in which it was expressed might be accepted as a grant for all time coming; and in this way the Scottish prelates were not slow to interpret it. At this meeting of Perth the business was commenced by two canons being enacted, which continued in full force in Scotland until the church itself was overthrown by the Reformation. By the first canon it was decreed that an annual council should be held in the kingdom; and by the second, that each of the bishops should exercise in rotation the office of "Protector of the Statutes." In this way the Scottish priesthood decreed their entire independence both of legatine and English interference.

---

[1] Fordun, lib. x. c. 24. The prelates sent on this occasion were the Bishops of Dunkeld and Dunblane; the representatives of the clergy were the Abbots of Dunfermline and Lindores.

About this period a romantic incident occurred by which the future destinies of Scotland were to be mainly directed. Adam, Earl of Carrick, who in 1268 had repaired to the Crusade, and died in Palestine two years after, left no family except a daughter Marjory, who in her own right became Countess of Carrick. It happened one day when this young lady had gone out to hunt in full feudal state, attended by a throng of armed retainers and fair serving-women, that their path was accidentally crossed by Robert de Bruce, a young Scottish knight, the son of a noble of the same name who was Lord of Annandale in Scotland and Cleveland in England. The knight was distinguished by that personal beauty in which his family was afterwards so pre-eminent, and the lady no sooner saw him than she addressed him with kind salutations, and besought him to join them in the recreations of the chase. The noble stranger demurred, but his refusal only increased her importunity; and laying her own fair hands upon his bridle-reins, "with a certain violence, if it is right to say so,"[1] she conducted him to her castle of Turnberry, and there kept him in gentle captivity for the space of fifteen days or more. The result of this strange wooing may be easily conjectured: the knight's reluctance was speedily overcome, and the pair were wedded, not, however, in open day, and amidst a happy assemblage of their kindred, but by stealth, and in the silent recesses of the towers of Turnberry; for the countess was a ward of the crown, and as such, had committed treason by marrying without the sanction of her liege sovereign. The union could not long be concealed from the king, and he proceeded to punish the chief delinquent by the seizure of her castle and estates; but these were afterwards restored to her upon the payment of a heavy fine, and the fortunate stranger in right of his wife became Earl of Carrick, and one of the most powerful of the Scottish nobles. From this union of romance one of the most romantic of the heroes of history was born on the 11th of July, 1274. This was Robert Bruce, the restorer of the Scottish monarchy and liberator of Scotland, whose origin, although so singular, was to be even outdone by his subsequent career.

The course of events in England was now going onward in that direction which foreboded a most undesirable connection with the safety of Scotland. We have already seen the tortuous and underhand measures which Henry III. pursued in order to establish his claims of superiority over the latter country. These, as well as the troubles which his insincere administration produced in England, were brought to a close on the 16th of November, 1272, when he died after a reign of fifty-six years. But a more terrible enemy to Scotland was to succeed in Edward I., his son, the heir of his ambitious hopes and purposes as well as of his crown and sceptre. Edward, indeed, was at a distance, being in France, on his return from the Crusades, and apparently in no hurry to occupy the throne that awaited him in England; but he knew that England was quiet, and might be left for a time to itself, while he scanned with severe scrutiny the affairs of the kingdom of France, in which he was afterwards to be an important actor. His whole career, indeed, had been a stern but most effectual apprenticeship for the varied course of war and politics of which his after life was to be composed. At the battle of Lewes, when only twenty-two years old, his first military blunder was also his last; and so much did he profit by the warning, that at the battle of Evesham, which occurred only fifteen months after, he succeeded by his skilful arrangements in defeating the Earl of Leicester, justly accounted one of the best warriors of the age. His next military service was as a soldier of the cross; and in this character, while he endeared himself to the religious enthusiasm of Europe, he showed himself by his wonderful deeds in this Syrian campaign to be almost the equal of Richard Cœur de Lion in personal prowess, and his superior in skilful generalship. With a character and renown thus fitted to acquire ascendency in a warlike age and over men who valued strength and courage as the best attributes of humanity, he possessed a natural sagacity that penetrated events with a glance, and a hardness of feeling that never allowed him to be diverted from his purpose by the pleadings of pity or sympathy. Such was the king who after more than four years' absence landed in England, and was crowned on the 19th of August, 1274. The English, proud of his warlike renown, received him with an ecstasy of triumph. They had been long weary of the inglorious reign of his father, and they hoped that under their new sovereign the losses which England had sustained under Henry III. would be repaired, and its defeats exchanged for victories and conquests.

As yet, however, all wore the appearance of calm between England and Scotland, and Alexander, with his queen Margaret, the sister of Edward, and a splendid retinue, repaired to London to the coronation, the Scottish king being first careful to stipulate that this friendly visit should be prejudicial in nothing to the independence of his kingdom. The two kings who thus met as equals and as brothers were of

---

[1] Fordun, l. x. c. 29.

ALFRED HEARSE.

THE COUNTESS OF CARRICK AND ROBERT DE BRUCE.

THE COUNTESS CAPTURES DE BRUCE AND CARRIES HIM OFF TO TURNBERRY CASTLE, WHERE THEY WERE
AFTERWARDS WEDDED. THEIR SON ROBERT BRUCE WAS THE VICTOR OF BANNOCKBURN.

almost the same age, Alexander having commenced and Edward just completed his thirty-fourth year. If the bill of fare which Edward sent before him from France as the rule for the coronation feast had been properly obeyed, which doubtless was the case, the Scots must have been astonished at the profusion of the banquet; for it consisted of 380 head of cattle, 430 sheep, 450 pigs, 18 wild boars, 278 flitches of bacon, and 19,660 capons and fowls,[1] not to speak of pasties, "soteltes (subtleties)," cakes, jellies, and fruits, with which it must have been accompanied, or the floods of wine, ale, and hippocras which such mountains of good cheer demanded. Half a year afterwards Margaret, Queen of Scotland, died, by which a connecting tie between the two sovereigns was dissolved.

Although the recovery of the Holy Land was now a hopeless enterprise, the proclamation of a crusade was too profitable a pretext for taxation to be abandoned by the Roman see. Accordingly, among the other imposts of this kind, was the tax of a tenth of all ecclesiastical benefices in Scotland. This rate was also to be levied, not according to former rating, but the real and present value, and for this the clergy were obliged to return truly and upon oath, under the terror of excommunication. To collect this the pope sent Benemund de Vicci, or, as he was vulgarly called, Bagimont, into Scotland in 1275, and the rent-roll of Scottish benefices which was drawn up on this occasion is known under the name of Bagimont's Roll. Finding this tax oppressive, the clergy employed him as their advocate at Rome to obtain an abatement by the restoration of the old rating, but without effect.[2]

Hitherto Edward had found sufficient occupation in the conquest and subjugation of Wales, which he partially accomplished in 1277. Having now found a breathing interval in the temporary submission of the Welsh, he directed his attention to Scotland, not, however, with the design of invading it, but of entrapping its king into such feudal concessions as might at fit opportunity be turned to good account. And nothing could be better suited for the purpose than the form of homage rendered by the Scottish kings for the lands they held in England, as either some vague word or thoughtless ceremonial might be interpreted into submission for the kingdom at large. Accordingly Alexander III. was required to render the wonted homage before the English parliament at the feast of Michaelmas, A.D. 1278, and this he did at Westminster in the form which was usual on such occasions: "I, Alexander, King of Scotland, do acknowledge myself the liegeman of my lord King of England against all deadly." It was a feudal observance that implied no degradation, for in this manner it was performed not only by kings and sovereign princes to their equals, but even in some cases their inferiors; and it was thus that Edward himself was a feudatory and liegeman to the King of France. As if aware, however, of the purposes founded on this visit, and careful to guard himself against the appearance of submission even in the slightest points of the ceremony, Alexander desired that the oath of homage should be received through Robert Bruce, Earl of Carrick; and when this was granted the substitute took the oath for his sovereign in the following words: "I, Robert, Earl of Carrick, according to the authority given to me by my lord the King of Scotland, in presence of the King of England, and other prelates and barons, by which the power of swearing upon the soul of the King of Scotland was conferred upon me, have, in presence of the King of Scotland, and commissioned thereto by his special precept, sworn fealty to Lord Edward, King of England, in these words:—I, Alexander, King of Scotland, shall bear faith to my Lord Edward, King of England, and his heirs, with my life and members, and worldly substance; and I shall faithfully perform the services, used and wont, *for the lands and tenements which I hold of the said king.*" Such was the fealty which Alexander III. rendered, and which Edward I. consented to receive. Even at this late hour, and before the arrogant claimant himself who was so soon to demand the submission of the whole kingdom of Scotland, Alexander conceded nothing beyond what had been usually rendered for the possessions of the Scottish crown in England.[3]

Having thus vindicated the liberties of his kingdom and enjoyed a prosperous reign, Alexander was anxious to provide for a succession in the throne; and in 1281 he married his daughter Margaret to Eric, King of Norway. From the disparity of ages—the bride being twenty-one years old, while the royal bridegroom was only in his fourteenth year—it was evidently a marriage of kingdoms and a union of political interests; but as such it was a desirable measure for Scotland, as it satisfied the rival claims of Norway, and had a tendency to reconcile the Norwegian population of the islands to the Scottish rule. In the year following Alexander, the Prince of Scotland, then a youth in the nineteenth year of his age, married Margaret, the daughter of Guy, Earl of Flanders. But here the fortunes of the Scottish king had reached their culminating point,

---

[1] Rymer. [2] Fordun, l. x. c. 35. [3] Fœdera; Lord Hailes; Tytler's *History of Scotland.*

and all that followed was disappointment and disaster. Soon after the last of these marriages Margaret, the Queen of Norway, died, after having been the mother of an infant daughter known in Scottish history as the Maiden of Norway; and in a few months after her brother Alexander died, leaving no succession. The King of Scotland was now childless, and the only survivor to occupy his throne was an infant, a female, and a foreigner. As it was necessary to guarantee so precarious a succession by all the sanctions that law could furnish, Alexander III., a few days after the death of his son, convoked a parliament, which was held at Scone on the 5th of February, 1283-4. There the prelates and nobles became bound to receive the Maid of Norway as their sovereign, failing any children who might be born to the king, and failing the issue of the Prince of Scotland, deceased.

These hopeful reservations were well advised. The recentness of the young prince's marriage made it uncertain as yet whether his widow might not present an heir to the Scottish crown; and as for the king, he was a widower and still in the prime of life. After a sufficient lapse of time had shown that the first expectation was fruitless, Alexander again married, and his choice was Joleta or Ioland, the young and beautiful daughter of the Count of Dreux. The future queen was brought over in royal state to Scotland, and the marriage, as a joyful national event, was celebrated at Jedburgh with great pomp, the French nobles who attended Ioland seeming to vie with those of Scotland in the processions, pageantries, and masqueradings with which the forest of Jedwood was animated on this happy occasion (April, 1285). But amidst this mirth there came forth a handwriting on the wall. A gay choral march was presented, but there followed in a figure with regard to which the onlookers were in doubts whether it might be human or a phantom, for it was a form in the likeness of Death; and while it seemed to glide, rather than touch the ground as it walked, it suddenly vanished from their view, they knew not how. The laugh that arose was suddenly checked with a shudder; the acting of such a stern reality was too good to be pleasant, and after-events made it be remembered with compunction as a profanity, or awe as a prophecy.[1]

In the same year the unconscious prediction of the masquerading phantom was fearfully realized. Riding at a late hour near Kinghorn, Alexander was advised by his attendants, as the night was dark and the road dangerous, not to continue his journey to Inverkeithing till the morning; but rejecting their counsel, he continued to gallop forward until his horse suddenly stumbled upon a rocky cliff, by which he was thrown from the saddle and killed on the spot. This unexpected close occurred when he had lived forty-five years and reigned thirty-seven (March 16, 1285-86). "Let no one," says Fordun earnestly and affectionately, "be in doubt, from the suddenness of his death, about the entrance of such a king into heaven, for, as it is said, 'He cannot die ill who has lived well.'"

Seldom has a royal demise been so deeply deplored by a whole nation, and this not merely from the immediate loss, but the whole centuries of calamity it occasioned. Alexander III. is described as having been large-boned, of tall and commanding stature, and a pleasant open countenance—the index of his mind—while his affability endeared him to his subjects. He was also devout notwithstanding his ecclesiastical quarrels, and chaste and temperate at a period when royal and princely examples went strongly in an opposite current. The firmness of his administration was attested in the resolute stand which he made for the independence of his kingdom both against Rome and England; and its wisdom in the annexation of the Western Islands to the Scottish crown, and his propitiation of Norway to the measure. He was a strict unwearied dispenser of justice, and in this character he made an annual progress through his kingdom, which he divided into four circuits, visiting each in turn, attended by its sheriff and armed militia. At these tribunals his prompt decisions were grateful to his subjects, who, like all rude communities, were impatient of the delays and refinements of a perfected legislation. Thus the people were happy and the nation was steadily advancing in prosperity, in political consequence, and the arts of civilization. It speaks, indeed, not a little for his reign that the following stanzas, so often quoted in commemoration of its blessings, constitute the earliest effort of the Scottish muse, as far as has yet been discovered:—

> "Quhen Alysandyr, our kyng was dede,
> That Scotland led in luwe and le,
> Away wes sons of ale and brede,
> Of wyne and wax, of gamyn and gle.
> Oure gold wes changyd into lede.—
> Christ, born into virgynyte,
> Succour Scotland, and remede,
> That stad is in perplexyte."

---
[1] Fordun, l. x. c. 40.

CHAPTER V.

HISTORY OF RELIGION (650-1286).

Condition of the Culdee Church—Doctrines of the Culdees—Opposition of their doctrines to those of Rome—Attempt to suppress the Culdees commenced in Northumbria—Council held at Whitby for a trial between the two churches—Debate on the occasion—The Roman Church preferred—Suppression of the Culdee Church in England—Adamnan, Abbot of Iona, converted to the Church of Rome—Mode of his conversion—His ineffectual attempts to gain over his brethren of Iona—Endeavours of King Nectan to establish the Roman Church in Pictland—His treatment of the monks of Iona—Iona ravaged by the Danes—Gradual suppression of the Culdees in Scotland—Modes in which it was effected—Ascendency obtained by the Church of Rome in Scotland—First Scottish bishops—Appointment of Turgot to the bishopric of St. Andrews—Contention between the Archbishops of Canterbury and York for the right of consecrating Turgot—Its adjustment by the kings of England and Scotland—Eadmer appointed Bishop of St. Andrews—The controversy between the archbishops revived—Eadmer retires to Canterbury—His ineffectual intercession to be recalled to St. Andrews—The claims of the Archbishop of York to the homage of the Scottish Church unsuccessful—Liberal endowment of the church by David I.—Its immediate and remote effects—Attempts to establish the supremacy of the English over the Scottish Church in the treaty for the liberation of William the Lion—Terms agreed to by the Scottish clergy—Meeting held at Southampton to receive their submission—The claim of the English Church eluded by the Scots—Speech of Canon Gilbert on the occasion—Fresh troubles in the election of a Bishop of St. Andrews—Mode of John Scot's election—Scot banished by the king—The pope interferes in his behalf—His unsuccessful attempts to obtain the submission of the king and the Scottish Church—The king excommunicated and Scotland laid under an interdict—Unexpected and favourable termination of the controversy—Avaricious and oppressive treatment of the Scottish Church by Cardinal Gualo—Establishment of new monastic orders in the kingdom—Continued resistance of the Scottish Church to the usurpations of Rome.

Although what may be called the Culdee Church, as distinguished from that of Rome, was established in Ireland, Scotland, the kingdom of Northumbria, and various other portions of England, its tenure of the islands of Britain and Hibernia could neither be secure nor lasting. Ireland was fast relapsing into barbarism and national insignificance. Scotland was too remote in position and too uninfluential in political character to have a potential voice in the great family of European nations. As for Northumbria, it was but a fraction of England which the other heptarchic kingdoms were already regarding with the *odium theologicum*—the keen relentless eye of religious jealousy and hatred. On the other hand, Romanism had commenced that unfaltering march which had the Eastern Church for its animating object of rivalry, and universal spiritual dominion for its final accomplishment. That resistless progress which had already extended over the principal kingdoms of Europe was not likely to be bounded by the bleak rocks of Lindisfarne and Iona. The pompous and alluring ritual of Rome, her spiritual assumptions and unscrupulous policy, must in the end prove too much in Britain, as they had done elsewhere, for the primitive apostolic church which St. John had established in the East and Columba transplanted to our shores. Thus the days of Culdeeism were numbered, and she was now awaiting the martyr's doom. An event so important in the earliest stage of Scottish ecclesiastical history as the downfall of the Culdees—an event extending in point of time from the days of Kenneth Macalpin to those of Alexander III.—is worthy of our particular attention.

It would greatly aid us at the outset of the narrative if we could clearly ascertain those particular tenets of the Culdees which so distinguished them from the prevailing corruptions of Christendom and exposed them to its hatred and persecution. But here, unfortunately, our knowledge is so limited that our account must be confined to the following brief particulars, which are chiefly derived from the testimony of their enemies themselves, and therefore the more worthy of credit.

We find, then, that the Culdees rejected the doctrine of the necessity of auricular confession, and consequently that of penance and priestly absolution.

They did not believe in the existence of the real presence in the sacrament, but regarded the eucharist as a solemn act of religious commemoration.

They rejected the worship of saints and angels, and on this account they dedicated their churches to the Holy Trinity alone. It was only when they were supplanted by a new order of monks that a change was introduced in the case of the church of Scone, which was dedicated anew by Alexander I. not only to the Holy Trinity as before, but also "to God himself, and St. Mary, and St. Michael, and St. John, and St. Laurence, and St. Augustine." If this was the commencement of saint-worship in Scotland, of which there appears a strong probability, it does not date earlier than A.D. 1114, when this new form of consecration took place.

The Culdees rejected the doctrine of works of supererogation, hoping for salvation not in the merit of themselves or others, but only in the mercy of God through faith in Jesus Christ.

While refusing to pray to dead men, the Culdees also rejected prayers *for* the dead, believing that when we come before the tribunal of Christ neither Job, nor Daniel, nor Noah can intercede for any one, but that every one must bear his own burden.

They were opposed to all traditions of the church—and in this is to be found the summary of their errors and their guilt according to the views of Rome. "They observed only those things," says Bede, "which they found written in the prophets, evangelists, and apostles, and diligently fulfilled the duties of purity and piety."

In such doctrines as these, and the basis on which they were founded, the western church in Britain met with a stumbling-stone in its progress which must be broken or removed from its path. But even more irritating than these subjects merely doctrinal, and therefore the less dangerous in such a rude age, must have been the external indications that characterized these Culdees, and which the simplest could mark and understand. They were of the primitive apostolic type, and therefore in startling opposition to the innovating spirit which had now set in like a spring-flood. Clerical celibacy, which was regarded as the perfection of sanctity, these Culdees would not understand; and they had their wives and children either dwelling in the monastery or its immediate neighbourhood. Instead of exacting their support from the industry of others and making this a source of indolence, luxury, and wealth, they lived by the labour of their hands, and were more ready to give than to receive. While the external pomp of the Roman ritual was of yearly increase, until the palace at last was eclipsed by the church, and the purple of the emperor outshone by that of the pope, the Culdees were contented to assemble in humble chapels, perform the rites of worship without incense and tapers, and administer baptism without the consecrated chrism. Even in the chief badge of clerical distinction the Culdee differed from the Romish mouk or priest; for while his tonsure consisted of a shaven brow, that of the latter was made by shaving the middle of the head. Thus, not only in doctrine, but in form of ecclesiastical polity and mode of public worship, nay, even in external distinction and costume, the followers of Columba were so opposite to the predominating church that the only question with the latter was regarding the means with which, and the manner in which, they should be suppressed or annihilated. In this case it was well for the Culdees that crusades and inquisitions were the refinements of a later age. As yet persuasion and argument were the chief instruments of conversion, and these were brought into full play.

We have given an account in a former chapter of the conversion of the heathen Northumbrians to Christianity by the united efforts of Oswald their king, and Aidan, the missionary from Iona. Their Christianity, however, being of the Culdee form, stood in silent antagonism to that which Augustine and his monks had established in the rest of England. Here, then, was the vantage-ground for the western church to commence that warfare which had for its object the establishment of a universal conformity. Culdeeism, being the weaker party, could be represented as being not only a heresy but a national dissent or schism. But above all, Oswy, the powerful king of Northumberland, whose conscience was laden with the crimes of regicide and usurpation, and who therefore needed the full assurance of absolution, had already manifested strong leanings towards a church whose penances were soon to be so persuasive with the Anglo-Saxon kings. It was easy, therefore, to induce him to convoke a public meeting at which the claims of the two rival churches should be contested by their respective champions, and the strongest be established as the only faith of Northumbria. It was indeed a simple and summary mode of deciding the choice of a national faith; but this religious levity had already become a characteristic of the Anglo-Saxon people. If a ruler willed, in spite of the Italian preachers, to remain an idolater, his subjects continued to worship Thor and Odin; but if he became a Christian they submitted to baptism without a murmur.

The meeting for so important a debate and decision was held in the convent of Whitby, on the coast of Yorkshire, A.D. 664. On either side was a throng of disputants, the one party being headed by Colman, originally a monk of Iona, and now Bishop of Lindisfarne; the other by the ambitious and enterprising Bishop Wilfrid, who, more than any one, had bestirred himself in Northumbria in behalf of the cause of Rome. The king presided over this great assize, accompanied by his principal courtiers, while Hilda, daughter of King Edwin, and prioress of Whitby, was present with her attendants. But in the debate the simple-minded Colman and his Culdees proved no match for the astucious Wilfrid, whose great natural talents had been matured by foreign education and residence at the papal court. He dexterously shifted the argument from those essentials which might have been tested by argument or Scripture to mere unimportant externals, such as the form of the clerical tonsure and the proper date of Easter; and when Colman appealed to the Bible the other opposed him with the authority of what were termed the Apostolical Canons. Having thus obtained a ground of his own choosing, Wilfrid was both eloquent and persuasive, for he could prove that the observances which he advocated were in universal use, except among the Picts and Britons, whom he named with contempt. When Colman quoted Saint John and Columba as his authorities for the Culdee mode of keeping Easter Wilfrid, in the course of argument, dexterously dropped the name of the apostle and used only that of Columba, as if the Culdees could claim no higher origin for their church than an Irish missionary, while he boldly proclaimed St. Peter and St. Paul to be the founders of the Church of Rome. "And now," he triumphantly added, "after having heard the decrees of the apostolic chair, yea, of the whole church, and these confirmed by sacred missives, if you still persist in rejecting them you are undoubtedly guilty of sin. For although your founders were holy men, are they, a handful occupying a mere nook of a remote island, to be preferred to the universal church of Christ extended over the whole world? And even though this Columba of yours was both holy and endowed with graces, can he be preferred to the most blessed prince of the apostles, to whom our Lord said, 'Thou art Peter, and upon this rock I will build my church, and the gates of hell shall not prevail against it?'"

This part of the argument seemed to startle King Oswy. He turned to Colman, and anxiously asked him if these words were really addressed by our Lord to Peter; who confessed that they were. "And can you adduce," said Oswy, "any such words addressed to your Columba?"—and Colman replied that he could not. "You both, then, agree in this discussion," rejoined the king, "that these were spoken to Peter alone, and that to him the keys of heaven were committed?" Both disputants assented; upon which Oswy thus closed the controversy: "I now tell you, that as Saint Peter is the doorkeeper, I will no longer be opposed to him, but will obey him in every point, lest, when I come to heaven's gates, he should be displeased with me, and refuse to open them." The bystanders shouted their applause at this decision, and the fate of the Northumbrian church was sealed: Colman, with his Scottish brethren and thirty English Culdees, retreated to Iona, while Wilfrid, raised to the dignity of Bishop of Northumberland, found little difficulty in reducing his whole diocese to conformity. With equal or with greater facility the people were withdrawn from Culdeeism wherever it had been established throughout England, and by the same cunning form of management: the controversy, instead of dealing with doctrines, was limited to a question of fashion and expediency—to a few strokes of the razor and a new version of the calendar —to the proper form of the clerical tonsure and the right date of Easter holidays.

England being thus won to Rome, the next conquest was to be that of Scotland. And here, also, the insidious character of that Italian policy which had been so successful with England was strikingly manifested. Adamnan, the ninth in succession from Columba, who as Abbot of Iona must have been regarded by strangers as head of the Culdees and primate of Scotland, was, in spite of his piety, his learning, and position, allured into the western church. For this conversion an interesting incident had prepared the way. A Gaulish ship having been wrecked in a storm upon Iona, the passengers were received to the hospitality of the monastery; and among these was Arculf, a bishop of Gaul, who had visited Jerusalem, travelled through the whole of Palestine, and sojourned at Damascus, Constantinople, Alexandria, and other places of religious pilgrimage. Such a guest was thrice welcome to the lonely sojourners of that bleak little island, and especially to Abbot Adamnan, who eagerly listened to the accounts of his far-travelled guest about the scenes he had visited, and digested them into a volume entitled "Concerning Holy Places." This work, of which Venerable Bede gives a copious abstract, was also highly commended by the renowned monk of Jarrow as very useful to the ignorant, and to all who had no opportunity of visiting these sacred localities.[1] In the course of his public duties Adamnan had occasion to visit the court of Northumbria, and thither he carried his literary production, which he presented to King Aldfrid, by whom it was highly commended, and by whose order it was transcribed for circulation. The Romish priests were not long in discovering both his learning and his weakness, and marking him for their own. He was urged with arguments similar to those which had been used in the controversy of Whitby; and while the discussion was confined to mere ceremonies and the Easter question, he was overwhelmed

---

[1] *Bedæ Hist.* lib. v. c. 15.

with the authority of the church universal as opposed to the obstinacy of a few monks entrenched within an unknown corner of the island. Overcome by their arguments, and perhaps by the flattery of King Aldfrid, the abbot yielded, embraced the cause of the Romish Church, and returned with all the zeal of a fresh convert to lead his brethren into the new path. But the monks of Iona, notwithstanding this defection of their superior, stood firm; and Adamnan, finding that he could not persuade them, left the island, and repaired as a missionary to Ireland, where he was more successful, for he persuaded several of the Culdee establishments in that quarter to shave their heads anew, and adopt the computation of the western calendar, by which they were Romanized to the full. After several years spent in this manner he returned again to Iona; but here his success was no better than before. This resolute constancy of the Scottish Culdees, notwithstanding the example of their father and head, presents an honourable contrast to the weakness of the Saxons of Northumbria.

But authority of a more secular and formidable character was now to be brought against the brotherhood of Iona, and persecution was to follow when persuasion had failed. Nectan III., King of Pictland, having joined the Roman Church, resolved that his subjects should follow his example, and for this purpose he applied for aid to Ceolfrid, Abbot of Girwy, in Northumbria. The kind of assistance he requested was twofold. The one was pastoral letters from the abbot, containing such arguments as might avail for the conversion of his people: the other was for some English architects to build for him a church of stone, which he promised to dedicate to Peter, the prince of the apostles. Both letters and masons were readily sent, and the former proved so available, that in a short time, as we are informed by Bede, the monks of Iona, with the other monasteries subject to them, were, "by the assistance of our Lord," reduced to canonical uniformity with Rome and England. But the previous steadfastness of these Culdees would incline us to suspect that more cogent arguments than those of the Abbot of Girwy must have been used by the royal disputant; and accordingly, in the year assigned for this conversion (A.D. 716) we are told in the *Ulster Annals* that the brethren were expelled by Nectan from Iona, and driven beyond the Grampian Mountains into the country of the southern Picts. In this way we can easily understand the acquiescence of the island of Columba. The voice of dissent was silenced when no one was left to raise it.

The overthrow and death of Nectan III., about A.D. 725, seemed to produce a favourable change for the Culdees; and we are informed that Iona was in peace for sixty years. In spite of the monkish legend of Bede about the miraculous success of Egbert the monk in converting the whole island—and which appears to be nothing more than a legendary episode—we may more rationally account for this peace by supposing that on the death of their persecutor the brethren of Iona returned to their cells, and that Nectan's violence produced nothing more than a temporary expatriation. But more terrible enemies than the Pictish king were now to enter upon the scene. These were the merciless Norsemen, the kings of the sea and pirates of every coast. In 793 their shielded galleys and raven banner were borne through the Western Isles, which were swept and desolated by their ravages. In 801 they burned the monastery of Iona. In 805 they returned and repeated the work of havoc with such severity that not more than sixty-four of the brotherhood were left in the island. Iona was now a helpless frontier exposed to an unsparing enemy, and the repetition of these visits made further residence there neither desirable nor safe. Raising, therefore, the bones of their honoured founder from the grave in which they could no longer rest in peace, the monks of the holy island emigrated to Dunkeld, and in its church, which had recently been built by Kenneth Macalpin, they deposited the remains of Columba and established their future home.

In this way was the capital of the Culdees destroyed. A lonely and mysterious star amidst a sky where all was darkness—a Patmos with its exiled witness amidst the growth of a universal apostasy—this little island of the Hebrides has for ages arrested the gaze alike of the theologian and the scholar, until by distance its history has assumed the character of a myth or a fable rather than a veritable reality. But however bright and delusive the fata morgana may be, this wonderful phantasm has its substantial impersonation in rock and strand, and the attestation of its departed greatness in crumbling walls and tombstones instead of vague surmise or uncertain tradition. And above all, its reality has been evinced in the spirit it implanted upon the national character and the effects it produced on the religious history of the people. But thus the living Iona became a grave, a monument, and a place of pilgrimage. Although not destroyed with its revered metropolis, Culdeeism was rudely shaken and prepared for its final overthrow.

This consummation was now so certain that its accomplishment was nothing more than a question of time. The work itself extended, indeed, over a long course of years; but it was managed with that artful policy which could well afford to wait, and which was never wont to mar its purposes by precipitate haste and rashness. Of the various agencies by which the extinction of Culdeeism was effected we can only afford to give a very brief summary. One of the foremost and most influential of these has been detailed in a preceding chapter; it was the amicable disputation to which the leaders of the Culdees were invited, where they had for their opponents an energetic sovereign and an amiable, talented, popular queen. It was difficult, indeed, to resist the gentle Margaret, armed as she must have been with the strongest and subtlest arguments which the Rome of that day could furnish. Another device was the establishment of the episcopal over the presbyterian form of church polity. Whether the new Anglo-Saxon dynasty established by Malcolm Canmore had taken the alarm at the rapid growth of the feudal power, and sought to counteract the aristocracy of warlike nobles by one of learned priests, we are unable to determine, but it was pursued with as much zeal as if royalty itself had had a personal interest in the measure. It was so steadfastly prosecuted at the outset that four bishoprics were founded by David I. alone, independently of his numerous abbacies and priories. By this device Culdeeism was met, pressed back, and hemmed in on every side until its parishes were absorbed by the surrounding sees, and even the most talented of the brethren in many cases won over with the allurements of monastic and episcopal mitres. And yet, even in spite of these aggressions, the church of Columba might have retained its hold of the popular affections and been cherished as the church of the people, let that of the state be what it might—a political anomaly which Scotchmen can well understand—had not another plan been introduced by which the people themselves were to be allured from their old spiritual pastors and guides. This was the establishment of canons regular in Scotland— an order of recent origin in the Roman Church, but which occupied the same place in advancing its interests that was held at a later day by the Jesuits. And against these new rivals the Culdees had little chance of maintaining their ground. The latter, as we have seen, were handicraftsmen and farmers as well as presbyters; their ritual was simple and unadorned; and, like the rustics whom they taught, they led an everyday domestic life with their wives and children around them. Such a style was only fit for a primitive stage of society which every step in advance must alter or leave behind. But in opposition to this half-laic, half-ecclesiastical character, the canons regular were priests and nothing else, while their spiritual character was emphatically marked by their celibacy, which kept them apart from the world, while it seemed to exalt them above its weaknesses and its cares. Theirs was also a ritual which the land of genius and the fine arts had constructed, and the attractions of which the rude communities of Europe had been everywhere unable to resist. In this way the proscribed Culdees, now a diminished band, with Christendom itself arrayed against them, were fated, during the present period of our narrative, to disappear as a community and a church from the page of history. Still, indeed, its spirit remained and its remembrance was kept alive in a corner of the national heart; but with what healing influences it may have leavened the new and successful church, and in what manner these influences may have been manifested, it would now be in vain to conjecture.

Although a large portion of Scotland had been Christianized by the missionaries of the Western Church, who were careful to establish the ecclesiastical polity of Rome in contradistinction to the Culdeeism of Pictland, and who had therefore their presiding bishops, yet it is worthy of notice that these prelates do not seem to have had their separate and specific dioceses. They merely bore the general title of *Episcopi* or *Episcopi Scotorum;* and thus, though Scotland had its bishops, it had no bishopric, so far as can be learned, until near the close of the ninth century. The honour of the innovation is ascribed to King Grig, who founded the bishopric of St. Andrews, thenceforth to be regarded as the parent see of Scotland; and it was probably for this pious deed that the monkish writers afterwards expanded Grig, the Celtic chief, into Gregory the Great, and made him the conqueror of England and Ireland. Still, however, the country was so obscure that its bishoprics offered few temptations to clerical ambition, whether from Rome or England. For two centuries, therefore, the Scottish church remained unnoticed until its growing wealth and importance made it worth regarding. It was then that Turgot, Prior of Scone and confessor of Queen Margaret, was nominated by Alexander I. to the bishopric of St. Andrews. But from whom was this primate of Scotland to receive episcopal consecration? According to the new canonical rule and usage he could only be made a bishop by one who held a still higher office in the church—by an archbishop, a cardinal, or the pope. In this case Anselm, the Archbishop of Canterbury, claimed the right of investiture, as primate of the whole island of Britain; while Thomas, the Archbishop of York, declared that both St. Andrews and the kingdom of Scotland itself were included within his diocese. But unfortunately for the claim of the latter, although elected to the archbishopric of York, he was not yet consecrated, and therefore unable to invest another with the mitre. The two English prelates were kindled into antagonism, and while each regarded the other with jealous watchfulness, the attention of both was directed with unwonted interest to every clerical movement in Scotland. In this state of things a report reached Anselm that a plan had been devised by which Turgot was to be consecrated by the Bishop of Durham and the Bishop of Orkney, while Thomas was to attend and ratify the act by his presence. Indignant at this stratagem, Anselm interposed his prohibition, declaring that a mere archbishop-elect could not consecrate a bishop either personally or by deputy, and he commanded Thomas to come to Canterbury and be consecrated himself. The conflict between the two English arch-prelates was keenly watched by the Scottish clergy, whose independence was thus at issue; and they declared that neither by right nor by usage could the Archbishop of York lay claim to consecrate a bishop to the see of St. Andrews. To divide such a knot when it could not be untied, the civil sword was necessary; and the two kings of England and Scotland interposed to restore peace and concord between the two archbishops. From such sovereigns as Alexander the Fierce and Henry Beauclerk sharp and short work was to be expected. And yet all they could obtain was but a temporary adjustment. It was to the effect that King Henry should command the Archbishop of York to consecrate Turgot, "saving the authority of either church." The worth of such a saving clause was afterwards to be tried by Beauclerk's grandson, Henry II., in his controversy with Thomas à Becket. In the meantime, as far as Scotland was concerned, the compromise decided nothing beyond the personal claim of Turgot, and left the whole question open for future strife and discussion. As for Turgot himself, who after this decision was consecrated with great pomp at York, Cardinal Ulric being present at the ceremony, the elevation little availed him, for in consequence of misunderstandings with the king he resolved to travel to Rome to seek counsel of the pope. But already worn out with age and sorrow, he was unfit for such a journey, and therefore he went no farther than his own cell at Durham, where he died in peace.[1]

On the retirement of Turgot another bishop would have been nominated for St. Andrews,

but, apprehensive of a fresh controversy from the claims of York and Canterbury, Alexander I. kept the see vacant for several years. At last, when the delay could be no longer continued, the king wrote in 1120 to the Archbishop of Canterbury, blaming himself for having allowed the flock to wander so long without a shepherd, and requesting that Eadmer, a monk of Canterbury, should be "set free" and sent to him, for the purpose of being "enthroned with episcopal dignity" at St. Andrews. This application to Canterbury instead of York was a decided rejection of the claims of supremacy made by the latter, while the king's demand that Eadmer should be *set free* implied that thenceforth the monk should owe no allegiance even to Canterbury itself. Such at least appears to have been the understanding of Alexander, and in this way he attempted to provide for the independence of the Scottish church and the maintenance of concord between the two kingdoms. But neither Eadmer nor his metropolitan had taken these considerations into account; and this was shown as soon as the former had arrived in Scotland. How or by whom was he to be consecrated? This was the anxious question of the king in his first interview with Eadmer, while he expressed his repugnance at any application being made for the purpose to York. Eadmer cordially assented: he was as little disposed to acknowledge the superiority of that see as the king himself; but he added that he meant to apply to Canterbury, as its primate by ancient right held the episcopal supremacy over the whole island of Britain. At this proposal Alexander started and recoiled. Had the Scottish church been freed from York only to be given up to Canterbury? The particulars of the quarrel between the king and the bishop-elect have been elsewhere noticed: it is enough for the present to state, that while Eadmer considered himself to be still the spiritual subject of Canterbury, whether as English monk or Scottish prelate, the king conceived that by being set free every such tie of allegiance was broken—that the priest was sent to him absolved from every restriction. He was willing, indeed, that the Scottish church, like other national churches, should render homage to Rome as the unquestioned fountain-head of spiritual authority; but to subject it either to York or Canterbury was to sacrifice its national independence, and make it a mere suffragan diocese of England. At last, finding that he could neither persuade nor awe the strong-headed sovereign, Eadmer was induced to abandon the struggle by resigning his bishopric and retiring to Canterbury. Even here, however, the controversy could not well termi-

---

[1] Sim. Dunelm; Eadmer.

nate. On his return home he was rebuked by his English superiors and advisers for having so hastily abandoned the contest. It was not thus that they were willing to lose their hold of Scotland, and the desponding priest was urged to make such concessions as might warrant his reposition. On resigning the bishopric he had engaged not to reclaim it during the life of Alexander, unless by the advice of the pope, the convent of Canterbury, and the King of England; but, under the influence of his new light he wrote a humble supplication to the Scottish king, in which he offered to be more submissive for the time to come. "Lest you should think," he said, "that I am in any way desirous to detract from the liberty and dignity of the King of Scots, I wish you to be satisfied on this point. For, with respect to the King of England, the Archbishop of Canterbury, and the sacerdotal benediction, I have now learned, that in what you demanded, and I was unwilling to grant, my opinions were erroneous. Should you therefore still persist in your sentiments you will no longer find me contrary, nor these differences withholding me from the service of God and your affection. Only permit me to enjoy the other privileges belonging to the see of St. Andrews, and I shall act according to your will."[1] This surrender was sufficiently humble and complete; but the time had gone by when it could be effectual, and Alexander was unwilling to tamper with the victory he had already won, or to provoke a fresh contest which was no longer necessary. Perhaps, too, the submissiveness of this application was marred instead of mended by an imperious letter from the Archbishop of Canterbury, demanding the recall of Eadmer as a right, because he had been canonically elected, and declaring that as long as the latter lived no other could be bishop of St. Andrews without the crime of spiritual adultery. But Alexander was deaf to either appeal; and here the controversy as far as Eadmer, its victim and historian, was concerned, was brought to a close. It is worthy of notice as the first assumption of superiority by England over Scotland, and the first display of that Scottish independence which subsequent events were to call into action. As such it was a needful preparation for the weaker country that was so soon to be summoned into the field, and there to decide the question, not by arguments but the sword.

As Alexander had resolved that Eadmer should not return to Scotland, his next choice for the vacant bishopric fell upon Robert, Prior of Scone, who, like his two predecessors, was a native of England. In each choice there was not only a manifest recognition of the superior learning and fitness of the English clergy, but the absence of that national jealousy and suspicion of which as yet both countries seem to have been unconscious. But the new election was not to be undisturbed; and Thurstan, Archbishop of York, afterwards renowned as one of the English heroes in the Battle of the Standard, renewed the claims of ecclesiastical homage that had been made by his predecessors. But now there was less chance than before that they would meet with dutiful attention, and rather than submit, the consecration of Robert was delayed for five years. At last Thurstan was fain to succumb, and the Bishop of St. Andrews was consecrated by the English prelate without doing homage to the see of York. "Be it known to all both now and hereafter"—thus Archbishop Thurstan's instrument attested— "that I have absolutely consecrated without profession or promise of obedience, Robert, Bishop of St. Andrews, for the love of God and King David, saving the claim of the see of York and the right of the see of St. Andrews."[2] But this last exception, if anything more than an unmeaning form, was an absolute confession of defeat, and the independence of the Scottish church upon that of England might now be considered as confirmed.

The reign of David I. is memorable in the history of the Scottish church for the liberality with which he endowed it. His munificence, which was extravagantly applauded in his own day, was as keenly reprobated in later ages; and it happened, singularly enough, that both the censure and the praise were bestowed according to the strictest justice. In conferring such extensive dotations of land upon the church he merely gave away unproductive acres which none had cared to occupy, and he gave them to the only men of the period who had industry and skill enough to turn them to account. He invited communities of monks both from England and France into Scotland, and provided stately homes for their residence; but as these ecclesiastics were the only scholars of the age it was in this way alone that he could provide for the instruction of a barbarous and illiterate people. In thus founding monasteries he was establishing schools and colleges. Moreover, during the earlier part of his reign the warfare commenced under his father Malcolm Canmore with England was rising into a confirmed national feud, and he may have thought that by consecrating such ample territories to the church, especially upon the Border, he placed them under the surest of protections, and gua-

---

[1] Eadmer.   [2] Wharton's *Anglia Sacra*, t. ii. p. 237.

ranteed them from the worst calamities of war. Nor were his hopes in the first instance disappointed. The churchmen proved themselves skilful, industrious agriculturists and tolerant landlords, so that their lands were the best cultivated, and their peasantry the most comfortable in Scotland. In every district their scholarship was of the utmost importance, where, except themselves, there were none who could read and write. In the high church dignitaries also, the bishops and abbots, whose number David so greatly augmented, he created a political power which served as a counterpoise and a check to the overgrown feudal power of the nobility. Thus his wisdom was the highest wisdom of the age, and his expedients were the best which circumstances suggested. But unfortunately, while a reaction, whether soon or late, was inevitable, it was certain to come with those peculiar aggravations which attend upon a church that has become too wealthy and too powerful. The account of this reaction belongs to a later period of our history.

With the exception of a single attempt of the Archbishop of York to impose his supremacy upon Scotland, its church remained untroubled from that quarter during the reign of Malcolm IV. The occasion, indeed, seemed especially opportune, as the archbishop, having been invested with legatine authority by Pope Alexander III., was hopeful that he might be able to extend it over the whole Scottish clergy; but the claim was so decisively rejected that he quietly allowed it to go to sleep. But in the reign of William it was resumed, and under circumstances that promised full compliance. The Scottish king had been taken prisoner, and to obtain his liberation had been compelled to become the liegeman of Henry II. The kingdom being thus deprived of its independence through the vassalage of the sovereign, a similar demand was made upon the liberties of its church, and to this David, his brother, and the Scottish barons had been obliged to yield. Nothing was now wanting but the assent of the Scottish clergy, and a deputation of their highest dignitaries was sent to the place of conference to ratify their part of the treaty. But while they ostensibly assented, they secured their independence by agreeing that the English church should hold the same authority over that of Scotland "which *of right* it ought to have." By these vague terms, by this most flexible of conditions, all and nothing was promised, and the question was left open as before to a controversy of history and tradition. It seems passing strange that the Anglican church should have been satisfied with such specious generalities, more especially as these had been her own favourite weapons during the whole course of this clerical war. But none are so easily deceived as deceivers themselves, especially when their own form of craft is used against them.

It was not long before the worth of these concessions was brought to the test. A meeting was convoked at Norham for the purpose of receiving the recognition of the Scottish clergy to the archbishop's supremacy; but the former, unprepared for open refusal and unwilling to yield, craved a postponement. This was granted. In the following year (1176) Hugo, Cardinal of St. Angelo, being then in England, sent his apparitors to Scotland to summon its clergy before him at Northampton, and accordingly a great number repaired thither at the time appointed. It was a trying occasion, for here the subject of submission was resumed not only by the cardinal, who presided over the meeting, but by Henry II. himself, who was present. The demand thus made upon English ground and by such authority must have staggered the Scottish ecclesiastics; but they soon rallied sufficiently to show what they meant by the late treaty. In accordance with its words the king required that they should yield that obedience to the English church which they ought to yield, and had been wont to yield in the days of his predecessors;—but to this the northern bishops replied that they never had yielded, and ought not to yield, subjection to the Church of England. The Archbishop of York asserted the contrary, and endeavoured by fact and argument to maintain his claim; but this kindled, as on previous occasions, the rivalry of the Canterbury primate, who declared that Scotland was comprised within his own see. This revival of quarrel between the two English hierarchs was fortunate for the Scots, who had only to stand aside; and Henry, who had already experienced enough of Canterbury under Becket, was glad to dismiss the Scottish prelates without repeating his demands, or exacting any token of submission.

Thus far goes the account of an English historian who probably was present at the meeting.[1] But during the course of these incidents there was an important episode upon which our Scottish writers have dwelt with peculiar satisfaction, as it shows the honourable relation in which their ancient church stood to that of England. According to this account, while the Scottish bishops were daunted by the demand of submission and remained silent, not knowing what to answer, Gilbert Murray, a young Scottish clerk, started forward as speaker on the

---

[1] Hoveden.

occasion and arrested the attention of the auditory by the following bold harangue:—

"It is true, English nation, thou mightest have been noble, and more noble than some other nations, if thou hadst not craftily turned the power of thy nobility and the strength of thy fearful might into the presumption of tyranny, and thy knowledge of liberal science into the shifting glosses of sophistry. But thou disposest not thy purposes as if thou wert led with reason; and being puffed up with thy strong armies and trusting in thy great wealth, thou attemptest in thy wretched ambition and lust of domineering to bring under thy subjection thy neighbour provinces and nations, more noble I will not say in multitude or power, but in lineage and antiquity—unto whom, if thou wilt consider ancient records, thou shouldest rather have been humbly obedient; or at least laying aside thy rancour, have reigned together in perpetual love. And now, with all wickedness of pride that thou showest without any reason or law, but in thy ambitious power, thou seekest to oppress thy mother, the Church of Scotland, which from the beginning hath been catholic and free, and which brought thee, when thou wast straying in the wilderness of heathenism, into the safeguard of the true faith and way unto life—even unto Jesus Christ, the author of eternal rest. She did wash thy kings, and princes, and people in the laver of holy baptism; she taught thee the commandments of God and instructed thee in moral duties; she did accept many of thy nobles and others of meaner rank when they were desirous to learn to read, and gladly gave them daily entertainment without price, books also to read, and instruction freely; she did also appoint, ordain, and consecrate thy bishops and priests; by the space of thirty years and above she maintained the primacy and pontifical dignity within thee on the north side of Thames, as Beda witnesseth.

"And now, I pray, what recompense renderest thou unto her that hath bestowed so many benefits on thee? Is it bondage? or such as Judæa rendered unto Christ—evil for good? It seemeth no other thing. Thou unkind vine, how art thou turned into bitterness! We looked for grapes, and thou bringest forth wild grapes; for judgment, and behold iniquity and crying. If thou couldest do as thou wouldest, thou wouldest draw thy mother, the Church of Scotland, whom thou shouldst honour with all reverence, into the basest and most wretched bondage. Fie for shame! What is more base, when thou wilt do no good, to continue in doing wrong? Even the serpents will not do harm to their own, albeit they cast forth to the hurt of others. The vice of ingratitude hath not so much moderation; an ungrateful man doth rack and massacre himself, and he despiseth and mineeth the benefits for which he should be thankful, but multiplieth and enlargeth injuries. It was a true saying of Seneca, I see, 'The more some do owe, they hate the more; a small debt maketh a grievous enemy.' What sayest thou, David? It is true; 'they rendered me evil for good, and hatred for my love.' It is a wretched thing (saith Gregory) to serve a lord who cannot be appeased with whatsoever obeysance.

"Therefore thou, Church of England, doest as becomes thee not. Thou thinkest to carry what thou cravest, and to take what is not granted. Seek what is just, if thou wilt have pleasure in what thou seekest. And to the end I do not weary others with my words, albeit I have no charge to speak for the liberty of the Church of Scotland, and albeit all the clergy of Scotland would think otherwise, yet I dissent from subjecting her, and I do appeal to the apostolical lord unto whom immediately she is subject; and if it were needful for me to die in the cause, here I am ready to lay down my neck unto the sword. Nor do I think it expedient to advise any more with my lords the prelates, nor if they will do otherwise do I consent unto them; for it is more honest to deny quickly what is demanded unjustly than to drive off time by delays, seeing he is the less deceived who is refused betimes."

The effect of this eloquent and unexpected speech was striking; some of the English, both nobles and prelates, commended it highly for its bold patriotic spirit, while others regarded it as an effervescence of the ardent Scottish temperament, and quoted what perhaps at that time was a proverb, "In naso Scoti piper."[1] But the person most affected was Roger, Archbishop of York, whose authority and claims it so violently shook. He uttered a groan, but speedily recollecting himself, he assumed a merry countenance, and laying his hand upon the young man's head, said, "Ex tua pharetra non exiit illa sagitta;"[2] insinuating by this that Gilbert had not spoken of himself, but according to the prompting of others. From the same historical authority we learn that the speech was attended with important consequences. This appeal to the protection of the pope, and acknowledgment in behalf of Scotland of his sole and supreme authority, was so gratifying to the pontiff that he abandoned the interests of the Archbishop of York by sending a bull soon after to King William, granting that

---

[1] There is pepper in the nose of a Scot.
[2] That arrow did not come from your own quiver.

neither in ecclesiastical nor civil affairs the Scottish nation should answer to any foreign judge whatsoever, but only to the pope, or his legate specially constituted.[1]

This successful conclusion of a long struggle for independence was gratifying both to the Scottish king and the national church, and the universal approbation was testified in the rapid rise of the canon Gilbert, who soon after was made Bishop of Caithness, and subsequently chancellor of the kingdom. A few years, however, sufficed to make it doubtful whether they had acted wisely in escaping from the dominion of England by taking shelter under that of Rome. An event followed which showed that the supreme pontiff might prove a more dangerous taskmaster than any English archbishop. We allude to the affair of John Scot in his election to the bishopric of St. Andrews; and although an outline of this controversy has already been given in the civil department of the narrative, we revert to it at greater length on account of its importance in the religious history of Scotland.

The see of St. Andrews having become vacant in 1178 by the death of its bishop, Richard, the chapter assembled and elected John Scot as his successor. This man, if we may believe the old Scottish historian[2] whose account we chiefly follow, was one of those characters whom the Scottish church at this time especially needed; for, independently of his piety and moral worth, he had studied first at Oxford and afterwards at Paris, and was learned in the liberal arts, in science as it then existed, and in theology beyond the general standard of the age. After returning from the foreign schools he visited Scotland, and on arriving at St. Andrews was received, not as a stranger, but as a friend and brother. Here he settled and became archdeacon of the diocese, until, on the vacancy occurring, he was elected by his brethren to be their bishop. But in this hasty election several errors had been committed. Notwithstanding his name, and probably his ancestry, the prelate-elect was an Englishman, being a native of the county of Chester; and thus the recent controversy excited by the national leanings of Turgot and Eadmer might be revived in all its bitterness. But worse than even this was the fact that in electing him they had usurped an important function of the royal prerogative. Hitherto the practice both in Scotland and England had been for the sovereign to nominate and present, and the chapter to accept and confirm the choice by their election. In this way even the Archbishops of Canterbury, and Becket, the greatest of them all, had owed their appointment in the first instance to William the Conqueror and his successors. It happened unfortunately also for the chapter that the king had already destined the bishopric for Hugh, his chaplain. On hearing, therefore, of the election, William indignantly exclaimed, "By the arm of St. James, while I live John Scot shall never be Bishop of St. Andrews!" This favourite oath of the king, which was final and conclusive, was followed by vigorous action; he seized the revenues of the diocese; commanded the chapter to rescind John's appointment, and elect and consecrate Hugh in his stead; and when Scot, after a hopeless resistance, appealed to the authority of Rome, William drove him from Scotland as a traitor, and extended the punishment to all his relations, friends, and supporters, who by the same summary process were banished from the kingdom.

On this expulsion John Scot repaired to Rome, as Becket had done a few years earlier, to plead his cause in person, and was favourably received by Pope Alexander III., who annulled the election of Hugh as illegal. Nothing, indeed, could be more welcome to the Roman conclave than the appeal of the displaced and exiled bishop. To have the sole right of appointing to all the high offices of the church throughout Christendom was now the great aim of Rome, as it would not only be a source of unlimited power and influence but of boundless wealth; and that kings might be reduced to acquiescence the experiment, which a short time afterwards was so successful with John of England, was in the first case to be attempted with the King of Scots. He was to be taught that none had a right to bestow church livings but the earthly father of the church and those who acted under his authority; and if William yielded, the proud Norman potentates of England would more readily follow the example. Acting, therefore, as supreme and divinely-constituted judge, Alexander III. took the case in hand, and after announcing Hugh's deposition he sent Alexius, a sub-dean of Rome, into Scotland as his delegate, with full power to repossess the injured and punish the guilty. A favourable verdict for John Scot was the consequence, and in 1180 he was consecrated to the bishopric. But such a verdict was as yet but a dead letter in Scotland; and while Hugh continued to enjoy the revenues and exercise the functions of a rightly-appointed and

---

[1] This story, which is given differently by Boece, we have taken from Petrie's *History of the Catholic Church* (fol. 1662, p. 373), this accurate and diligent antiquary having transcribed the speech from an old register of Dunkeld no longer extant. An entirely different version of the speech will be found in Spottiswood's *History of the Church of Scotland* (fol. 1667, p. 33). In Fordun (lib. viii. c. 26) the speech is nearly the same as that in the Dunkeld register.

[2] Fordun.

consecrated bishop, Scot, dreading the indignation of the king, found himself once more obliged to quit the kingdom and repair to Rome. The pope then wrote gentle letters to William, demanding the recall and reposition of Scot; but to these the king closed his ears "like the deaf adder, and would not listen to the voice of the charmer." At this exhibition of contumacy the pope assumed a harsher tone, and announced his purpose to lay Scotland itself under an interdict; but Scot threw himself at the feet of the pontiff and implored him to forego his purpose. "Holy father," he cried, "I would rather yield to the decree and resign my episcopal office into your hands than that mass for the deliverance of the souls in purgatory should be omitted for a single day on my account." But such a termination of the strife would ill have suited the papal interests, and the relenting prelate was enjoined upon his clerical obedience to stand firm in his resistance.

All these movements had merely been prelusive, compared with the conflict which now commenced in earnest. To silence Bishop Hugh, when he was unable to eject him, Alexius laid the diocese of St. Andrews under an interdict; but the public rites of religion were still continued as if no sentence had been passed. The Scottish clergy were commanded by the pontiff to install, within eight days after receiving the mandate, their rightful bishop, John Scot, and yield him dutiful obedience, and to excommunicate Hugh, the pretended bishop of St. Andrews; but the obdurate priests paid no heed to the order. The king's chief officers, Richard de Moreville, Constable of Scotland, Richard de Prebenda, the royal secretary, and several of William's counsellors, were excommunicated, as "wicked ones" who stirred up their master to evil; but their master remained as unmollified as ever. The same fearless courage which had animated his desperate charge upon the English chivalry at Alnwick, but guided by better prudence and a nobler motive, carried him onward to confront the ghostly terrors of the conclave, and brave in behalf of the rights of his people those terrors before which kings and emperors were learning to quail. Finding him still unmoved, the avenging sword of Rome, which had struck down his defences in front and on either side, was now raised over his own head; and he was threatened with the terrible doom of excommunication if, after twenty days of grace, he refused to install John Scot in the bishopric. But even at this threat the utmost he would offer was to make Scot his chancellor, and appoint him to any other bishopric that happened to fall vacant. Henry of England, also, his late conqueror and master—ashamed, perhaps, of his own conduct in a similar warfare in which he had been scourged into submission—offered to mediate, and endeavoured to obtain from William conditions more ample and satisfactory; but the Scottish king stood firm to his purpose, and refused any further concession.

Astonished and provoked by a resistance so unwonted, but still unwilling to strike a crowned offender, the next expedient of Rome was to visit the chief clerical delinquents, and by the chastisement of her own children give a warning to kings and princes. The clergy of the diocese of St. Andrews were peremptorily required to obey Scot as their bishop under pain of suspension; and, as if to embitter the command, it was delivered through the Archbishop of York and the Bishop of Durham, who no doubt exulted in the humiliation of their old antagonists, especially as they were authorized to carry the sentence into execution. Under dread of the penalty several of the St. Andrews clergy yielded; but for this opposition to the royal command they were banished by the king from Scotland. The decisive step of inflicting the last punishment was now inevitable, and to this the Archbishop of York, whom the pope had invested with legatine authority for the purpose, addressed himself with hearty alacrity. He excommunicated William, and laid the kingdom under an interdict. By this proceeding the king was proclaimed to have no longer right to reign, or even to enjoy the privileges of an ordinary Christian; his society as an accursed man was to be abjured even by the meanest of his subjects; and whosoever raised against him the assassin's weapon, instead of having committed a crime, would be held to have rendered to God and the church such good services as would cancel all his past sins, and ensure his entrance into paradise. And terribly would the interdict fall upon the kingdom; for the churches would be closed, the images of the saints laid prostrate upon the pavement, the public rites of religion suspended, the dead left unhouseled and unburied in their homes, or upon the highway, and all the social confidence and kindly intercourse of society suspended as by a deadly stroke. The direful consequences involved in such a doom, as well as the danger of provoking reaction, had as yet made Rome very careful in using it, so that it had never been brought forward except at the last extremity, and when all other means had failed. Hence, especially in the present instance, had proceeded that dilatoriness, and those successive monitory punishments by which Rome had endeavoured to succeed before trying the final resource with such a sovereign as William the Lion, and a people so obdurate as the Scots. And how was the death-sentence endured? "By reason of the rumour and dread of the interdict," says the old chronicler,[1] writing in the spirit of a churchman, " the king was troubled, and all Scotland with him." But, in looking at the narrative, we find no signs of this universal tribulation; on the contrary, both king and people, both church and government, appear to have held onward in their tranquil course. And ominous, indeed, it would have been for the papacy, if at this early stage it had been shown by the hardihood of Scotland that its heaviest penalty might be safely defied, that its choicest thunderbolt was only *brutum fulmen*. It was a singular combination of fortunate circumstances that freed it from such a hazard. At the critical moment of execution Pope Alexander III. died; his delegate, the Archbishop of York, also died; and as their sentence could be little more than a dead letter, until it was renewed by the succeeding pontiff, both the Scottish church and its enemies had to wait for further orders. But Lucius III., who succeeded to the chair of St. Peter, after receiving a gracious embassy from William, revoked both the excommunication and the interdict. In his bull on this occasion he even became the apologist of these rebellious outstanders; for he declared, that to reverence excellent kings is an apostolical precept, and that the King of Scots was inexorably opposed to the election and consecration of Bishop John! So notable a concession on the part of infallibility deserved some requital, and William accordingly recalled John Scot from banishment, treated him at his return with high distinction, and humbly received the papal absolution at his hands. We are told that he would even have replaced him in St. Andrews, but for the oath he had sworn to the contrary, in which he had shown himself as wicked as Herod and as rash as Jephtha.[2] But the good bishop was not to lose his reward amidst the happy reconciliation; and at this season of opportune deaths the decease of the Bishop of Dunkeld, which occurred at the time of Scot's recall, gave William a choice opportunity of testifying his good-will to the exile, who was forthwith inducted into the vacancy. And inasmuch as Dunkeld was a poor bishopric compared with the other, Scot was compensated for this difference, as well as for the expenses of his banishment, by being allowed to retain the revenues of his old archdeaconry of St. Andrews along with his new charge. As for Hugh, the intrusive bishop of St. Andrews, he too was in good time received into the grace of the church; for, after he had held office ten years and ten months, he repaired to the Eternal City and was absolved by the pope, but died after starting on his return within six miles of Rome.[3]

Of the history of the Scottish church during the reign of Alexander II. few particulars have been recorded that would interest the present generation. His adherence to the party of the English barons against John, and the aid he afforded them, brought him into hostile collision with the Roman conclave after the tyrant of England had placed his kingdom under the protection of the pope. The consequence was that Cardinal Gualo, the pope's legate in England, laid Scotland under an interdict—a sentence, however, which was so little regarded that it was not published in the country until twelve months afterwards. This indifference was a notable contrast to the effects produced by the same penalty upon England during the reign of John. On the return of peace the removal of the interdict was one of the conditions of the treaty, and it was removed accordingly by the Archbishop of York and the Bishop of Salisbury at the command of Gualo. But the cardinal, who was an avaricious man and had made a plentiful harvest in England, was incensed at his deputies for having let off the Scottish churchmen so easily, instead of exacting from them a heavy ransom which would have flowed into his own coffers. He therefore declared that the general absolution did not comprehend the clergy, whom he summoned to appear before him at Alnwick. Thither accordingly went the high church dignitaries, bishops, abbots, and priors, and were compelled by his threats to compound for individual absolution by the payment of large fines. With the common churchmen of Scotland he adopted a more summary and oppressive method, although it was ostensibly for their accommodation: this was to send a commission of two ecclesiastics for the purpose of absolving them in their own districts instead of requiring them to travel to England for the purpose. But by this device Gualo inclosed the whole of Scotland within his net, for the commission commencing their inquisition at Berwick, extended it over the kingdom, so that no priest, however humble, could escape. Their practice was to assemble the priests and canons of the district at each principal town, and require them to confess truly and upon oath, and answer every question; and when their confessions were taken they were compelled by threats of deprivation not only to pay large sums for absolution, but to crave it barefooted and in the most abject terms at the church-door. This double tyranny was so intolerable that the Scottish clergy sent a deputation of three bishops to

---

[1] *Scotichron.* [2] Ibid. l. vi. c. 38. [3] Hoveden; Benedictus Abbas; *Scotichronicon.*

plead their cause at Rome, and complain of the legate's extortions, upon which Gualo was fined in a round sum. Thus "he escaped," says Spottiswood, by dividing the spoil (which he had made in those parts) betwixt his master and himself." These Scottish bishops, on humbly confessing their offence, were absolved by the pope. On this occasion one of the cardinals present observed with a sneer, "It is the sign of a truly pious disposition to confess a fault where no fault has been committed." In return for this submission the pontiff, Honorius III., confirmed anew those liberties of the Scottish church which had already been conceded by four of his predecessors. Among other causes announced for this concession one was the respect and obedience which Alexander had manifested to the papal see! It would be difficult for any eye short of infallibility to discover any such token on the part of the king throughout the whole proceeding.[1]

The increase of monachism in Scotland was still going onward, to the great indignation of the secular clergy, who found their consequence diminished by the superior pretensions to piety and moral strictness with which these monks ingratiated themselves into the popular favour. It is possible that the papal court encouraged the establishment of these monastic orders in Scotland, where they were so well fitted to advance its interests among a people proud of their independence and jealous of every foreign interference. The Cistertians and Canons Regular, costly though they were, seem now to have been thought too little for the country; and at this time there was a fresh immigration from France, composed of new communities—Dominicans or black friars, Franciscans, Jacobins, and monks of Vallombrosa—brought over by the Bishop of St. Andrews, and established in the country by the liberality of the king, who founded for them no fewer than eight monasteries in the principal towns of Scotland. They came professing poverty and humility, and in this way they speedily became rich. Of the readiness of the Scottish nobles to favour these new-comers and enrich the church a striking example was afforded in the case of Gilbert, Earl of Strathern, who, having divided his inheritance into three parts, gave one to the see of Dunblane, and another to the Abbey of Inchaffray, while he reserved only the third portion for himself and his descendants.[2]

The rest of the history of the Scottish Kirk during this period, filled though it be with incidents, must be dismissed with a few general notices. The growing importance of the office of a Scottish bishop, and especially a Bishop of St. Andrews, was accompanied with the usual amount of clerical ambition and intrigue; and as in these quarrels Rome naturally became the umpire, its influence over the country was augmented by every contested election. The increasing wealth of Scotland under the reign of Alexander III. was also an additional incentive to the popes; and their applications for money, under the pretext of establishing a new Crusade for the deliverance of the Holy Sepulchre, were both frequent and vexatious. But these demands were in most cases met either by procrastination and excuse or by downright refusal. That love of independence inherent in the Scottish Church, by which it had baffled the claims of the Archbishops of York, was now arrayed against the pontiffs themselves; and this especially when the latter attempted, either directly or indirectly, to make Scotland subservient to England. The admission, therefore, of even a papal legate into the kingdom was opposed, and with success, as an intrusion upon the rights and liberties of the Scottish Church, and an attempt to subject it to that of the wealthier and more powerful kingdom. In 1280 a letter of the Bishop of Moray to the meeting convened at Perth shows us of what office-bearers a Scottish ecclesiastical council was at this time composed, being addressed to "the bishops, abbots, priors, deans, archdeacons, and other prelates of the church." These were reckoned sufficient for the purposes of government and legislation without being presided over by a representative of the pope.

---

[1] *Foedera*, i. 227-28, 374; *Scotichron*.

[2] *Scotichron*.; Spottiswood, p. 48.

CHAPTER VI.

HISTORY OF SOCIETY (1097-1286).

Scantiness of our information on the early condition of Scotland—Aids derived on the subject from English historians—Saxon population of Scotland—Arrival of Norman visitors and exiles—Their reception and influence—Establishment of the feudal system in Scotland—Devotedness of the Scots to feudalism—Causes of this devotedness—Effects of the half-Celtic, half-Teutonic descent of the Scots upon the national character—Arrival of the Flemings into Scotland—Effects produced by their arrival—Change in the government from the Saxon predominance—Chief officers under the Scoto-Saxon kings—Administration of justice—Laws and legislation of Scotland at this period—Amount of slavery in the kingdom—The *Mercheta Mulierum*—Commercial condition of Scotland at this period—Progress of merchandise under the Scoto-Saxon kings—Its prosperity in the reign of Alexander III.—Commercial regulations during his reign—Style of royal life—Warlike sports of the nobles—Hunting—Masquerades—State of clerical society in Scotland—Public and domestic architecture—General state of Scottish living—Scottish schools of the period—Eminent Scotchmen—Michael Scot—Thomas Rymer.

Although the events of Scottish history from its commencement to the present period of the narrative are so obscure and unimportant, and require to be so briefly related, this defect does not arise either from poverty of incident or infrequency of change. Its cause is rather to be traced to the deficiency of our early annals, and the masses of vague and contradictory conjectures with which their place has been supplied. The fact that three different peoples had already predominated in Scotland, and that three different forms of speech had successively prevailed as the national language, is a sufficient proof that incidents sufficiently numerous and stirring and revolutions abundantly important had filled up the interval. The early Britons, Caledonians, or Picts had been supplanted by the Scoto-Irish, who were in turn superseded by the Saxons; and these last were now to become the representatives of the Scottish as they had long been of the English people. But where was the Homer to immortalize their deeds, or the Herodotus to chronicle these successive changes? And even had such an Iliad or history existed, would the destructive wrath of the conqueror have allowed it to descend to posterity?

It was fortunate for Scotland that when the enduring portion of her national existence was to commence by the introduction of a Saxon population, England abounded in historians, and that part of their office was to note the incidents by which the two countries had come into such close collision. It was also equally fortunate when this change commenced by which the Scottish population was to be transformed, and its history directed into its final current, that the change was impersonated in a man too distinguished to be overlooked, and that Malcolm Canmore, himself half-Celt and half-Saxon, half-Scottish and half-English, was the living type as well as the chief agent of the transformation. His reign was therefore the favourable starting-point for the chroniclers of England, and it is from them that we learn the successive steps by which Scotland was transformed from a Celtic into a Saxon kingdom. Under this guidance we have already recorded in our narrative the principal periods and modes in which the change of population was effected; and we have seen how original occupation, warlike aggressions, conquests, exile, and emigration maintained a steady influx from the southern into the northern part of the island, as well as the conflict that commenced between the old and the new elements before the latter could acquire a permanent lodgment. The perseverance of the Teutonic race, so conspicuous in their character from the beginning, was too overwhelming for the fierce but irregular resistance of the people whom it displaced; so that even at the accession of Edgar the history of Scotland commences as that essentially of a Saxon kingdom.

While England was thus supplying a new population as well as a new character and destiny for Scotland, the change was not to be effected by the Anglo-Saxon race alone. With them came also Anglo-Normans, their conquerors and masters, in quest of new settlements; and in such a competition it would have been singular if these Normans had not maintained their wonted pre-eminence. As invaders, they were wont to conquer the land they coveted; even as exiles or fugitives, they gradually became its magnates and the founders of its principal families. It was as refugees and exiles or as guests that they chiefly entered Scotland. Disappointed of the rich possessions they had hoped to win in England, discontented with the arrogance of William the Conqueror, or dispossessed of the estates they had already won amidst the cruel wars and court intrigues of the Norman Conquest, they arrived, not in formidable bands, but singly or in small parties, and as homeless men, to try once more in the north that game of ambition which had gone against them in the south. Such able and enterprising adventurers were certain of welcome at the court of Malcolm Canmore and his descendants. Their weight was of the utmost consequence in the struggle for ascendency that was still pending between Celt and Saxon; their skill in arms and renown in war made them doubly welcome to a brave people who only wanted good leaders to head them; while in a land so abundant in uncultivated acres, no great stretch of generosity was needed to reward the services of these gallant wanderers with large estates of heath and mountain. By these royal grants, by fortunate intermarriages, and other means of aggrandizement it was not long before they became the principal aristocracy of the land, so that there was scarcely a noble family in the kingdom that could not trace its origin to some adventurous Norman. Even the boundary of the Lowlands of Scotland was no obstacle to the enterprise or check to the ambition of these daring strangers, who won their way into the Highlands, and became at length the principal chieftains of the fierce and jealous mountaineers. This was the greatest victory of all, when we remember the Celtic prejudice and devotedness to patriarchal descent that had to be overcome before these Norman intruders—men of yesterday and nowhere, according to Highland reckoning—became the Grants, the Gordons, and the Campbells of a Celtic community. And yet in a few generations the descendants of these men were to be found as mountain satraps, wearing no dress but the tartan, speaking no language but Gaelic, and identifying themselves with the politics of Highland feuds and the literature of Highland genealogies. Men who could thus surmount or conquer the law of Tanistry itself, in its own stronghold, were assuredly worthy of their elevation.

To this ready welcome so frankly accorded to the strangers may be traced the easy and silent establishment of the feudal system in Scotland, in contrast to the example of England. Into the latter country the Normans had come as hostile aliens and invaders, whose avowed object was to slay and take possession; and the land which they had won by the sword they were obliged to defend by the sword against a people who had envied them as conquerors and hated them as tyrants and usurpers. Hence it is that so large and important a portion of the history of England is the record of a systematic war against feudalism, and a struggle of the commons with the nobility, until, after centuries of a life-and-death conflict, the latter were obliged to succumb. But the different mode of their entrance into Scotland was followed by different results. Their superiority was recognized by a free and willing people, and their establishment in place and power was a spontaneous reward for gallant and useful services. This principle of gratitude, however, of itself could scarcely have withstood the wear and tear of centuries; and when these reciprocities had ceased to be remembered—when the mutual jealousy between the rulers and the ruled had produced its wonted fruits in the form of oppression on the one hand and resistance on the other—it might have been expected that the Scots, like their brethren of England, would have rebelled against the descendants of the aliens, and ejected them from a supremacy which they were no longer worthy to hold. But against such a reaction a hereditary principle of the national character opposed an effectual barrier. This was the patriarchal or clannish devotedness of the people, which they had derived from their Asiatic ancestry. The whole nation had been Celtic before they became Teutonic; and the Saxon immigrations, instead of being visits, as in England, of conquest and extinction, were only those of interfusion and amalgamation. In this manner Caledonian and Pict, and Dalriad and Cruithne Scot, had been able to unite on equal and amicable terms with the Norwegian, the Dane, and the Belgian, the Saxon and the Norman; and the result of this union was a mingled race, half Celtic, half Teutonic, in which they differed from the English, who were almost wholly Teuton. And to this large proportion of Celtic blood and character which was retained unsubdued, and which blended with the Gothic current, may be traced many of those peculiarities of national character by which the Lowland Scots were distinguished from their Saxon kinsmen of England. It especially inspired them with the tendency to separate into tribes and families—to abide by territorial and consanguineous instead of national and common distinctions—to follow out their feuds against each other when they should have been united for their common welfare—and above all, to rally round their own chief or noble, let whosoever might be sovereign of the kingdom, and to follow him implicitly through good and through evil. This devotedness was nothing more, and nothing else, than the old patriarchal system of the Celts, which still continues to predominate wherever that race is found; and the feudal system which was engrafted upon it made little alteration in its spirit or additional weight in its obligations. It was from these compounded nationalities of two different races, from whom they were equally derived, that the Scots during the feudal ages adhered to their nobles with a pertinacity which neither time nor misfortunes could impair, while the English looked on and wondered. The latter could not comprehend such an Asiatic devotedness in a people speaking the same language as themselves, and were apt to laugh at it as unreasonable, or despise it as abject and slavish. Even modern philosophers and historians also, either overlooking the twofold ancestry of the Scots, or holding it in little account, have been too apt to sympathize with this wonderment or derision. They cannot comprehend why, against all right and reason, Scotland should have persisted in cherishing its feudal predilections, when the other nations of Europe had given them to the winds.

When the influence of original descent upon the formation of national as well as individual character has been more fully investigated and better ascertained, many of those anomalies which are so perplexing in Scottish history may be found of easy solution upon the principle we have already stated. It often seems, indeed, as if we were perusing the record of two different peoples, when we find them at one time so ready to yield to bondage, and at another to fight for freedom to the death—at one time so fickle in their purposes, and at another so pertinacious and unyielding—so irregularly great and noble, and so subject to sudden transitions, that their whole history is a series of startling changes, in which victories and defeats are alternated like the fictions of a romance rather than the orderly developments of usual history. How were the men of one and the same nation so hot, headstrong, and rash, and yet so proverbially cautious and calculating? Was it according as the Celtic or the Saxon element might chance for the time to prevail? And did the two contradictory elements continue to divide the national character upon equal terms, until the heavier and more substantial, aided by political and religious circumstances from without, at length obtained the predominance? These questions, which are offered as suggestive hints rather than solutions, may go far to explain the mystery.

While Scotland, still a Celtic kingdom, was receiving a foreign population, by which its power and resources were to be so greatly augmented, another branch of the great Gothic family arrived to impart a new element of strength which the country still needed. These were the Flemings, who were now to add their commercial skill and enterprise to the agricultural industry of the Saxon and the military qualities of the Norman. Originally called into England during the civil wars of Stephen, they had so increased in strength and numbers as to excite the national jealousy: on this account many of them being expelled on the accession of Henry II., repaired to Scotland in the middle of the twelfth century. Their offers of military service were readily accepted by William the Lion; and, finding them brave and useful auxiliaries in his wars against the English, he granted them settlements, where they congregated into towns and villages, until at length they were to be found in large communities in most of the districts of Scotland. As traders, handicraftsmen, and fishers they introduced into Scotland those manufacturing and commercial arts by which they had not only enriched, but in a great measure created the land of their nativity. As merchants they appear to have been sometimes incorporated into companies, and invested with extraordinary privileges;—as in the instance of the Red-hall of Berwick, which they were allowed to occupy on the tenure of defending it against the English. But they were stout warriors as well as industrious traffickers and manufacturers; and as such they founded several noble families that were afterwards conspicuous in Scottish history. Of these it is enough to mention the Flemings, the Leslies, and the Murrays. But a still more illustrious Scottish race from this Belgic ancestry was that of the Douglases, which, after all its mythic and lofty pretensions to the earliest of origins, can go no higher than "Theobaldus Flammaticus." This Theobald the Fleming about the middle of the twelfth century received a grant of some lands on the Duglas Water, in Lanarkshire, from Arnald, Abbot of Kelso; and William, the son and heir of Theobald, was the first who attached the distinction of de Duglas to his name.

The change of Scotland from a Celtic to an Anglo-Saxon kingdom was necessarily accompanied with corresponding changes in the form of government. The first and most important of these was the recognition of one man as the chief ruler or sovereign of the land instead of a host of independent kinglings; and the northern law of direct royal succession instead of the Tanist rule. This king by established right, instead of temporary election and voluntary concession, could claim the leadership of the national armies, the convocation of parliaments and councils, the enactment of laws, and the administration of public justice. These important offices, however, were not to be exercised by his own sole authority, but with the advice and consent of those who held the highest influence in the realm. And foremost of these were the principal clergy, the spiritual guides of the people. Hence it is that as soon as we read of Scottish parliaments, we always find the bishops, abbots, and priors placed at the head of the list. Next to them were the earls and lords, the chief nobility of the kingdom and custodiers of its civil and military resources. At what precise time the title of earl was introduced into Scotland does not clearly appear; but the change was one in name only, and not in character and substance, for the Celtic mormaors and their descendants under the new appellations still retained their old possessions and privileges.

Independently of a royal council, in which every national movement was discussed, high and influential officers were needed to carry its decisions into action; and accordingly offices were established both in court and state to which these duties were attached. In most cases, also, as in other sovereign courts from the earliest commencement of royalty, these important functionaries were generally chosen from the persons who were nearest the king, and who superintended the menial duties of the palace. From the high families they founded, and the important influence they exercised in the subsequent events of the national history, a brief enumeration of the principal officers of the Anglo-Norman sovereigns of Scotland may here be not out of place. These were—

The Butler, under the various titles of *Pincerna*, *Buttelarius*, and *Minister Poculorum*. Although so essential an appendage to royalty is not mentioned in our Scottish annals previous to the reign of Edgar, some such functionary assuredly must have existed in the early Pictish and Scottish courts. Under the new Saxon and Anglo-Norman dynasty, the office was hereditarily established in the powerful family of de Soulis.

The Doorkeeper or Door-ward (*Ostiarius*). The most distinguished of these doorkeepers was Alan Durward, who was also Chief Justiciary, and so distinguished by talent and ambition as to give uneasiness to Henry III. of England, who procured his displacement.

The Steward (*Seneschalus*). This office, which was first conferred by David I. on Walter Fitzalan, an English knight, was established hereditarily in his family by Malcolm IV. Little could it have been surmised at the time that this office would furnish the patronymic for the future dynasty not only of Scotland but of the island at large; and that descendants of Walter the Steward would rule over territories then undreamt of.

The Constable (*Constabularius*). This office we first hear of in Scotland under the reign of Alexander I. It was held successively by the Morevilles, lords of Galloway, the Earl of Winchester, and the Earl of Buchan, until at the close of this period it fell into the powerful family of the Comyns. Afterwards it was confirmed in the family of De la Hay, where it still remains.

The Marshall (*Mareschalus*). This office existed in Scotland during the reign of David I., and was made hereditary in the family of Keith, by William the Lion, before the close of the twelfth century.

The Chamberlain (*Camerarius*). This office was held by several high nobles successively without being established in any particular family.

The Chancellor (*Cancelarius*). We do not hear in Scotland of a royal chancellor until the reign of Alexander I., although a much earlier antiquity is pleaded for the office.

The Treasurer (*Expensarius*). At first this duty, which in Scotland must have been a sinecure, was discharged by the chamberlain until William the Lion had a purse-bearer of his own. When there was so little to expend, the office did not come fully into notice until a considerably later period.

Such were the titles and offices, originally humble enough, out of which the high civil and military leaders of the nation were established; they rose with the rise of royalty itself and participated in its grandeur and power. It will be seen that both title and office were the same as had been established in the English court under the Anglo-Saxon and Anglo-Norman sovereigns, whose example it was natural for the new dynasty of Scotland to adopt as its model. As in England, also, some of them were of arbitrary and others of hereditary appointment. The Norman nobles of England in their castles followed the example of the sovereign in his palace by appointing similar office-bearers, through whom they ruled their limited domains in the style and with the authority of kings; and the tempting example was not lost upon the Scottish magnates, who, in imitation of their richer brethren of the south, exalted their favoured dependants into constables, stewards, cup-bearers, butlers, and marshalls, and invested them with substantial rule as well as title. In this way even a Scottish peel was a palace upon a humble scale, and the domain that belonged to it a little kingdom ruled by its civil and military officials. This example, too, was adopted even by the spiritual lords, who had a feudal grandeur of living to maintain as well as wars to wage and trespassers to punish. Accordingly, in an old charter of the latter part of the twelfth century containing a grant made by

Richard, Bishop of Saint Andrews, the document is witnessed by his chaplains, steward, cupbearer, chancellor, marshall, and doorkeeper.

During the reigns of the first three Scoto-Saxon kings the administration of public justice seems to have been exercised by the sovereign in person, as is the usual custom of governments and kingdoms in their youthful and primitive form. But these duties soon become too burdensome for one man; and such was the case in Scotland, so that during the reigns of Alexander I. and David I. we find two great justiciaries presiding, the one over the northern and the other over the southern division of the kingdom. During the minority of Alexander III. an additional justiciary was appointed over the troubled districts of Galloway. But besides these three principal dispensers of law, the country, as Saxon rule extended, began to be divided into sheriffdoms, as in England, each having its presiding magistrate or sheriff, who in the earliest instances was appointed by the king; and following the royal example, the great lords and barons had also their sheriffs who administered justice over the districts of their feudal superiors.

An office of this period also which has been magnified into undue importance was that of the thane or *thegn*, which is erroneously supposed to have been of Celtic origin and to have existed in Scotland from the earliest period, while the authority of its honoured holder is supposed to have been next to that of royalty itself. But the name as well as office is evidently Saxon, and can only date in Scotland from the accession of the Scoto-Saxon sovereigns. Instead, also, of being high nobles and royal counsellors, the dispensers of royal decrees and the leaders of armies, these Scottish thanes appear to have been land-stewards or bailiffs over districts and royal manors. Such were their thanages, in which their chief duty was to superintend the agricultural proceedings and collect the rents and imposts. As the church lands and manors continued to multiply similar officials were needed for ecclesiastical property, and on this account abthanes were also appointed by the bishops and abbots. After the present period of our history they disappear from public notice, having probably sunk into mere rent-collectors and land-factors.

Of the laws of Scotland and the mode of their administration during this period of obscurity and turmoil it is still more difficult to treat, and after all that has been written upon the subject we can only dismiss it with a very summary and uncertain notice. It is evident from the mixed state of society where so many rude elements of the future population were brought into closer contact, and from the transition state which they were now undergoing in the process of incorporation, that a struggle must have been going on for the mastery among the laws and rights of the different tribes and races; and that the conflict must have been especially strong between the new Anglo-Saxon and Anglo-Norman institutions, which were now acquiring the ascendency, and the old Celtic laws and usages, that would not relinquish their rule without a keen resistance. Much, therefore, must have depended upon the kind of population, whether Norse, Belgian, Celtic, or Saxon, that happened to predominate in the different districts, and upon the discretion or arbitrary decisions of the judges who were placed over them. No entire code could be thrust upon the nation at once and at swordpoint, as had been done in England, first by the Saxon and afterwards by the Norman conquerors; and even when Scottish legislation had finally subsided into a national code it was a compromise formed by the union of the old laws with the new. In the meantime the adoption of the usage of England by the division of the country into shires, and the establishment of sheriffs, was a gradual work that went on with the advance and increase of the Saxon population in Scotland; and it was not until considerably after the present period that the division of the whole kingdom into sheriffdoms was fully effected. The sovereign still continued to appoint his judges for counties, and the lord his magistrates for baronies, who dispensed justice in that summary form which characterizes every rude age and people. The utter absence of any authenticated code of Scottish legislation during this transition period has given rise to many theories upon the subject; and the *Leges Malcolmi*, the *Regiam Majestatem*, and the *Leges Burgorum* have all had their advocates to prove that each of these constituted the statute-book of Scotland. But these conjectures are so vague as to be unsuited to the purposes of history, and may be safely left to the caprice of the controversialist. We know, however, that the difficulties of the judge must have been but too well simplified in those days, from the condition of the people who depended upon his awards. Over him there was no control but that of his feudal superior. As yet what is called the middle class was too limited to be influential, and the population almost wholly consisted of the two extremes of the ruler and ruled—the master and the slave. On the other hand, however, it is gratifying to find that these laws, whatever they may have been or however derived, which existed from the period of the accession of Edgar to the death of Alexander III., seem to have suited the condition of the people and to have been as cordially cherished as laws are wont to be. This was manifested at the close of the period, when the death of the last-mentioned king threatened the subversion of the old order of things with the introduction of a new dynasty. On this occasion, when the marriage of Margaret of Norway to the English Prince of Wales was proposed, the people regarded their laws as the national palladium, so that the marriage contract stipulated for their entire and unchanged maintenance.

The amount of slavery at this time existing in Scotland appears to have been as great as in any other European nation, and to have originated in similar causes. We know not to what extent, or in what condition, the distinction of the people into bond and free may have existed during the Celtic period; but in the Saxon it must have greatly accumulated from the destructive inroads which the Scots were wont to make into the English counties. On these occasions prisoners, who were converted into slaves, were in as great demand as any other article of booty; and the Scots are described as driving them like flocks of sheep before them, and in such numbers, that every house in Scotland was supplied with an English slave. Besides this supply from the resources of war, the frequent famines of this age of ill-understood and scantily-practised agriculture were so severe, that whole multitudes frequently sold themselves and their children into slavery when death from starvation was the only alternative. But, besides these captives and purchased bondmen, there were the peasantry of the royal and noble manors, who belonged to the land, and were sold or transferred along with it—and in many cases without it. This enslaved peasantry, whether foreign or native, who were considered as part of the landowner's chattels, and distinguished by the title of his "men," or villeyns, are also specified in old charters of transfer under the titles of *nativi, servi, cottarii, captivi, bondi, bondagii, tenandii, husbandii, drengi.* From the time of Malcolm Canmore till the close of the present period we find this change of ownership so frequent, and the cultivators of the soil so invariably treated as part of the live stock, as to give a melancholy picture of the condition of the greater part of the Scottish peasantry. Onward also to the fifteenth century this practice continued, as a right of property in selling or granting land, to hand it over *"cum nativis et eorum sequelis."* Still Scotland was not singular in this degrading practice: it was the law of the period, and it prevailed not only in England but throughout Europe at large.

As if the serfdom, however, of the Scottish peasantry had not already been sufficiently oppressive, many authors have been pleased to add to its aggravations the law called *mercheta mulierum*. According to Boece this law was devised by the profligate King Evenus, who reigned a short time before the commencement of the Christian era; and it granted to every feudal lord the right of a husband to the daughter of any of his vassals on the first night of her espousal. He adds that this practice continued in full force till the reign of Malcolm Canmore, by whom it was commuted into a fine in money. But Scotland was not the only country to which this odium was confined: the same law is stated also to have prevailed in England, France, and several countries of the Continent; and modern writers have in many cases exhausted their learning to prove that such was one of the many feudal rights which were generally recognized during the dark ages, when feudalism was at its height. But after all that has been written upon the subject, it appears to have been nothing more than the mistake of a later period, founded upon a misinterpretation of the old feudal phraseology. Stripped, therefore, of its terrors, this Scottish *mercheta mulierum* dwindles into a landlord's trifling money-tax for the loss of the services of one of his vassals, who, by marriage away from his land and to a stranger, became the property of another. As we have already seen, not only the villeyn, but his children and descendants, were the property of the lord of the soil. If his sons attempted to escape from their master they could be reclaimed and punished; but not so his daughters, when they transferred themselves from his yoke to that of matrimony; and in this case his only recompense was a fine paid by the father of the bride on obtaining his lord's allowance for the marriage. In this way, also, pious prelates and abbots were repaid for the loss of their female vassals, instead of having recourse to the strange composition permitted or enjoined by the law of Evenus. By the same right of fine the landlord was also the protector of female chastity among his dependants, as in the case of seduction he could also impose upon the offenders the same pecuniary compensation.

In turning our attention to the commercial history of Scotland during this period, we find that the traffic with foreign merchants, so wisely commenced by Malcolm Canmore and his queen Margaret, had been actively followed by his successors. This we gather from the fact incidentally mentioned by Wyntoun, that Alexander I. presented to the church of St. Andrews an Arabian horse with its velvet trappings and a suit of Turkish armour. The fact of a Scottish king possessing such unwonted luxuries, seems to indicate the rich foreign produce which was already in request in so remote a market as that of Scotland. From the letter of Nicolas to Eadmer we also hear of the rich pearls found in the Scottish rivers, which this sovereign possessed, and that no doubt served as an article of barter in this foreign traffic. The commerce of the country was extended under the administration of David I., who had profited by the mercantile experience he had acquired by his residence in England. He encouraged the entrance of foreign merchandise into the Scottish harbours, and is described by Ailred as the protector of strangers and merchants, to whose applications he always lent a ready ear. To him is generally attributed the first erection of Scottish burghs, and a code of laws for the manufacturers, dyers, and dressers of woollen cloth. It is certain, however, that a great source of national wealth, the herring fishery of Scotland, was mainly commenced under his reign, when the Firth of Forth was often filled with the fishing-boats, not only of his own subjects, but of those from the English coasts, and even from Belgium. At this early period the following Scottish ports are mentioned as commercial towns: Berwick, Leith, Stirling, Perth, Old and New Aberdeen, and probably Banff. That, however, which was to become the greatest and most important of all our Scottish trading cities and ports, was only as yet indicated by a stately cathedral and a shallow river, the former of which owed its foundation to David, while Earl of Cumberland. Such, with a few straggling hamlets round the church, was Glasgow in the early part of the twelfth century. About sixty years after its consequence was raised by being made a burgh subject to its bishops, to whom was granted the privilege of holding an annual fair.

During the reign of William the Lion the progress of Scottish merchandise and manufactures had so much increased that the burghs alone were able to contribute 6000 marks to the 15,000 which was to form the marriage portion of his two daughters. It is unfortunate, however, that we are still unable to ascertain the particular laws by which the burghs were governed, the different handicrafts that were pursued in them, the proficiency they had attained, and the commercial condition of the kingdom at large at the accession of Alexander III. This period at all events seems to have been the commencement of a new era in the history of Scottish merchandise. During the minority of the young king, as we learn from the *Scotichronicon*, a new coinage had to be introduced into the country in imitation of the example of England, where the clipping of money had lessened the intrinsic value of the standard coinage. But the best proof of progress was the reputation for skill in ship-building which the Scots had already acquired among foreign nations, of which a signal proof was given at this period by the French Count of St. Paul and Blois. When he was to join his sovereign Louis IX. in the Crusade, his ship, which was one of the great vessels of the fleet, was constructed at Inverness. That a quarter reckoned so obscure should at that time have been so renowned, and its carpenters so skilful as to procure such an application from France itself, gives a higher measure of the resources of the country and ability of its workmen than has generally been conceded.

The reign of Alexander III. is reckoned the golden age of Scotland; and it stands out in strong relief on account of the darkness by which it was so suddenly succeeded. Descending to particulars, we find that his mother, the queen-dowager, was entitled to a third of the net royal revenue, and that she derived from it an income of 4000 marks. This information, which we derive from a notice of Matthew Paris, raises the royal revenue of Scotland to 12,000 marks yearly. Although we cannot now fully estimate its real value, we may conjecture that this was a very large sum, when we remember that Henry III. of England, who engaged to pay Alexander 5000 marks as his daughter's portion, in a period of four years was unable to raise the money, and had to crave a year additional. If we are to receive the *Statuta Gildæ* and *Iter Camerarii*, as published by Skene, for authentic documents, we learn much in the details of the Scottish merchandise of this period. In these we find that there was a court of the four burghs, composed of representatives from Berwick, Edinburgh, Roxburgh, and Stirling, and that they judged in all matters pertaining to commerce and the constitutions and customs of the burghs. There was also the chamberlain's court which superintended the trade, the burghs, and the general police of the kingdom. The chamberlain made periodical visits to the towns throughout the land, carrying with him standard weights and measures, by which he tested those that were in use in different places. It was his duty, also, to prevent those who took up goods on the king's behalf from using their office dishonestly by paying less for them than the appointed value, or not paying at all. Belonging to this court, moreover, we are told there were inspectors, who examined cloth, bread, and casks of liquor, to ascertain that they were of due quantity and quality, and to attest them with their seals of office; while other officers, called trovers, had the inspection of wool. By this chamberlain's court, also, the salmon fishery was regulated, and fishing for salmon during the night, or when they were not in season, prohibited.[1]

Of the other particulars of the reign of Alexander III. connected with the commercial prosperity of Scotland the following are stated by Wyntoun and Fordun. His laws for the promotion of agricultural industry were so effectual that the land produced crops of grain in greater abundance than it had done in any former period. His regulations abridged the useless and unwieldy trains of barons and prelates, so that horses were kept for industry and the national defence instead of lordly parade. He promoted the fisheries of the country; and the processes of curing fish were practised by the Scots perhaps even earlier than in Flanders, while this article of traffic was in considerable request both in England and upon the Continent. He strictly enforced the laws of debtor and creditor, by which the movable property of the former was sold by the sheriff to satisfy the just claims of the latter. By the laws of shipwreck, which were probably adopted from England and established during his reign, the property of vessels wrecked on the Scottish coast, instead of being treated as a waif, was preserved for the owners. A market so well regulated and so profitable as that of Scotland had now become was certain to attract the attention of foreign merchants; and among these were a body of Lombards, at this time the wealthiest and most enterprising traffickers in Europe. Their design was to settle in the country, and for this purpose they requested the king to grant them the mount above Queensferry or the small island near Cramond for the establishment of their chief factory. But unfortunately these modest demands, which might have proved so profitable to Scotland, were opposed by some of the most influential of the courtiers, and the plan of Lombard settlements was abandoned. Another instance also shows that the spirit of mercantile adventure had to contend with the prejudices of the age. The loss of Scottish vessels by shipwreck, pirates, and arrest in foreign ports, had so alarmed the king that his subjects for a time were prohibited from exporting goods in their own ships — a heavy discouragement, among other evils, to that naval architecture which, as we have already seen, was already making considerable progress in Scotland. Another restriction upon commerce was a law by which foreign merchants arriving from abroad were limited from disposing of their cargoes to any but burgesses. Still, however, the mercantile spirit, though impeded, could not be arrested by such hindrances; and the old historian, who regarded them as wise precautions, tells us that in consequence of these the kingdom abounded in corn, money, cattle, sheep, and every kind of merchandise.

Having thus noticed the growth of the kingdom at large during the course of nearly two centuries, our interest naturally turns to the individual manners and customs, modes of life, and condition of the various classes of society during such a period of progress and change. But here, unfortunately, the materials are still so scanty and so casual that we are almost wholly left to inference and conjecture. Of public royal life and its simple patriarchal character we have already seen as much as can be learned during the course of the narrative. The Scoto-Saxon descent of the sovereigns had no doubt its influence in assimilating, as far as could be done, the palace life of Scotland to that of England. The allowance granted from the treasury of England to these Scottish kings, when invited to the English court, may, in the absence of other information, be perhaps taken as a general standard of their way of living at home. It was fixed at 100s. per diem during their journey in going and returning, and 30s. per day during their attendance at the English court. While the last-mentioned allowance continued there was added to it a provision supply consisting of twelve loaves of wastel bread, twelve wheaten loaves; twelve quarts of wine, of which four were of superior quality, for the king's own use; two stone of wax or four tapers; 120 candles, of which forty were for the king's use; two pounds of pepper and four pounds of cinnamon. These, with the 30s., seem to have been considered an ample daily allowance for the royal household and table. The inordinate quantity of spice can be easily accounted for by the supposition that the Scots, like the English, used it largely in their cookery, until their dishes were "burning with wildfire," and that they were also partial to the use of hypocras. Besides the ordinary train Alexander III., in his journey to London, had among his attendants a harper, minstrels, and trumpeters, whose expenses during the visit were paid by the English king.

Of the amusements of the Scottish kings and nobles during this period we have almost no account. That tournaments were not unknown among them we learn incidentally, but the greater poverty and rudeness of Scotland must have made these chivalrous pageants less frequent than among the nobility of France and

---

[1] Macpherson's *Annals of Commerce*, vol. i. p. 440.

England. Chivalry itself, also, having been a recent importation into Scotland, and chiefly limited to the Norman strangers, must have had its sports and exercises for the present confined within a very limited range. The same may be surmised of the military amusements of the people at large, on account of the rude weapons they used and the little skill required in wielding them. Indeed, the brief sketch given by Aldred of the equipments of the Scottish army that fought the battle of the Standard exhibits the nature of the warlike practices that must have been used among the different classes, as well as the contrast between the high-spirited and well-trained knight and the half-armed, half-naked Celtic or Saxon military serf. The Norman chivalry under the command of Henry was a small but chosen band, armed in linked mail and mounted upon strong foreign war-horses; and their gallant charge alone had well-nigh won the victory for Scotland. On the other hand, the bulk of that array seem to have had nothing better than their brittle ill-tempered swords, their enormously long and fragile spears, and light small leather-covered targets—the same weapons with which the legions of Agricola had been encountered at the battle of the Grampians. In this dearth, however, of sports and amusements of a wholly military character, which would have ensured better weapons and a more perfect discipline, these bold Scots betook themselves to other sources for enlivening the dulness of a campaign; and we learn from the same authority that jesters as well as male and female dancers accompanied them in their march. These dancers, and jesters or fools, were also in high request among the nobles of England, although we do not find them brought into the field along with their military retainers.

In the absence of more intellectual resources hunting forms a principal amusement of every people; but this sport, which was a passion with the Anglo-Saxons, became a downright frenzy with the Norman conquerors of England. It would have been strange, therefore, if Scotland during its change from a Celtic into a Saxon kingdom had not exhibited this characteristic tendency, and prosecuted for pleasure what had originally been followed as a necessity. Accordingly we find more ample notices of hunting in the old Scottish records than of any other kind of royal or noble amusement. The kings were ardent hunters, and in several shires had forests and hunting-lodges for their exclusive pursuit of this favourite recreation; and from the charters of the period we learn that a tenth of the venison, or skins of animals killed in the chase, was frequently bestowed upon the neighbouring monastery. The nobility also had their hunting-grounds, and in grants of land to their followers often reserved for themselves all right to the beasts of venery, such as stags, wild boars, and wild goats, and the birds of game; leaving no right to the new possessors to lay any snares or gins upon the grounds except for the purpose of catching wolves. With hunting the stirring sport of hawking was also pursued at this period, and from Ranulph, the falconer of William the Lion, was descended the family of the Falconers of Halkerton, hereditary grand falconers of Scotland, ancestors of the earls of Kintore. It is gratifying, however, to add that the inordinate passion for the chase which, as well as the love of war, formed the chief characteristic of the Norman race, was kept in wholesome check in Scotland, so that neither its Saxon sovereigns nor its Norman nobility could lay waste whole counties, as was done by William the Conqueror and his successors in England. This was only the stern right of conquest and the right of the stronger, which, as we have already seen, the royal dynasty and nobility of Scotland were in no condition to claim.

In the less stirring amusements of the period may be classed dancing and those rude masquerades which are common to all nations. Under this last particular the reader cannot yet have forgot the loathly phantasm which presented itself at the marriage festival of Alexander III. While the mirth was at its height this ghost appeared among the dancers, we are told, wearing the form of a corpse whose flesh had departed from the bones, and who seemed to glide along rather than touch the ground. Such mumming and masquerading, though not carried to such a height, was perhaps becoming the usual accompaniment of noble festivals at the close of this period.

Of the condition of clerical society and the manners of the Scottish priesthood our information is, if possible, still more scanty; their refectories and their cells, their studies and recreations, are alike unknown to us. But that the order produced no chroniclers or poets of mark, and even no skilful illuminators of psalters and missals, seems to be gathered from the fact that no trace of their labours in this way has survived or even been announced by tradition. In the absence of other information we may therefore imagine that their studies and cares were chiefly occupied in maintaining their ecclesiastical independence against Rome and England, improving their revenues, and cultivating their gardens and orchards. That they were liberal of their charity we learn from a fact incidentally stated by Fordun, of Waltheof, Abbot of Melrose. In one of those severe famines in the reign of David I., with which the land was often visited, 4000 half-starved wretches took up their abode in the neighbourhood of the abbey, where they were fed by the provident bounty of the superior for three months until the public calamity had abated. That these generous benefactors were not also negligent of their own comforts we may guess from a statement of the same historian. It is to the effect that William de Malvoison, Bishop of St. Andrews, during the earlier part of the thirteenth century, deprived the abbey of Dunfermline of the presentation to two churches because its monks had neglected to supply him with enough of wine for his collation after supper. It is added, indeed, that the good men had not really failed in this token of respect to their spiritual superior, but that his own attendants had consumed the supply. In this belligerent age also, when the prelate was ready to become a warlike captain and the monk a bold man-at-arms, the athletic military exercises that formed the needful training were not likely to be unknown even within the peaceful precincts of the monastery. Having thus weapons within their reach, and skill to use them, the temptation could sometimes induce the high church dignitaries to settle their feuds with the carnal but convincing arguments of feudal barons rather than of peaceful priests and studious logicians. Such a case occurred A.D. 1269, when the Abbot of Melrose made a hostile sally into the district of Stow, assaulted certain houses belonging to the Bishop of St. Andrews, and slaughtered a priest, besides wounding many others. It is gratifying, however, to find that for this unprofessional outbreak the abbot and most of his monks were excommunicated in a provincial council held at Perth.[1] At this time the coldness of the climate of Scotland was so remarkable that the monks of Lindores, before the close of this period, received a papal dispensation not usually required in other countries; it was that they might wear silk caps in processions and public worship, as they were liable to take cold "in terra frigida." This precaution in guarding tonsured heads gives probability to the statement of Boece, that in the first winter of the thirteenth century the cold was so intense that beer was frozen into lumps and sold by the pound!

Although Scottish towns were now rising into historical notice, they as yet gave little promise of the magnitude and importance they were afterwards to attain, being little better than irregular clusters of hovels that were chiefly made of twigs or timber. Houses constructed of such materials were, of course, often subjected to accidents from fire; and accordingly we learn from Fordun that about the year 1244 Roxburgh, Haddington, Lanark, Stirling, Perth, Forfar, Montrose, and Aberdeen were thus destroyed. In a country where wood at that period was so plentiful and the standard of domestic comfort so low, such a loss, which sounds to modern ears like a great national calamity, must have been little heeded and easily repaired. The influx, however, of foreigners accustomed to greater refinement began to introduce houses of stone, and when these were erected they seem to have been remarkable rather for strength and security than for elegance, as is still attested by their ruins. As for the kings, nobles, and bishops of such a rude and unsettled period, they seem to have pitched their residences on a rock, where they could be least subject to surprise or capture. Even upon these, however, the storm was gathering that was soon to lay them low, and the succeeding generation saw most of them in ruins.

It would be well if we could redeem our general ignorance of the Scottish architecture of this early period by referring to the splendid monasteries and sacred buildings, which date their foundation from the twelfth and thirteenth centuries, and especially those which owed their foundation to the piety of David I. But such have been the effects of time, and tempest, and human violence, of ruin and restoration, upon these time-honoured memorials, that even their primitive types can no longer be accurately ascertained. The gorgeous ruins of Melrose, Dryburgh, Kelso, and Jedburgh still arrest the eye of the native, and allure the step of the foreign visitor, while the universal wonder is, that so poor a country could have supplied such expenditure, and so rude an age have manifested such taste. But we are abruptly wakened from this delusion by the records of the building itself, which inform us how often its several portions yielded to decay, how frequently they were visited with demolition, and how often the same profuse but mistaken piety which first erected them, had also to be summoned from century to century to renew or replace them. We are thus compelled to acknowledge that these wondrous fabrics were not the work of a single epoch or generation of workmen, but of ages, and that they extend from the commencement to the close of the history of Scottish ecclesiastical architecture.

The notices of the general mode of Scottish living during this period are so scanty and brief, that they may be hastily dismissed. Agriculture was still so imperfectly practised that famines were frequent—a circumstance which was afterwards to make a war with Eng-

---

[1] *Scotichron.* x. c. 25.

land, and an invasion of its well-stored granaries and larders, no unwelcome enterprise to the Scots. They chiefly used the labours of the ox in cultivating their fields in preference to the horse, while the chief grain which they raised at this time, as well as for ages afterwards, was oats. The insecurity of a country so exposed to strife and change made it necessary for the rural population to congregate in villages for mutual protection, instead of dispersing themselves into separate farms, while the territory annexed to the village, divided into stripes of arable or pasture land, furnished employment and subsistence to the villagers. Of the little intercourse which was thus maintained between the different communities, and the risks of passing from one to another, an idea may be formed from the fact, that in 1253 one mark was the hire paid to a person for conveying the sum of twenty marks from Badenoch to Berwick. The condition of one of these villages at the close of the present period is pretty clearly indicated in the Chartulary of Kelso. We there find that the village of Bolden in Roxburghshire, which belonged to the abbey of Kelso, had twenty-eight husbandmen, thirty-six cottagers, a miller, and four brewers. Each agriculturist held a husband-land from the abbey, for which he paid a rental of 6s. 8d., with certain services and carriages. Of the cottagers each had nearly half an acre of arable land, with the right of common pasture, and for these they paid conjointly 55s. 8d., with certain additional services. There was a mill in the village which was rented for eight marks, and four brewhouses that were let for ten shillings each, the brewers being also obliged to furnish the abbot with a lagen and a half of ale for a penny. (This lagen was a copious measure, though we cannot now ascertain its precise amount.) In these and other ancient charters we find frequent mention of breweries, showing that ale was the principal beverage of the people, and that they drank it in abundance. This was especially the case during the reign of Alexander III., when wine and wax, no longer dainties, were also in plentiful use both for lighting and cheering the festive board.

Concerning the schools of so early and so rude a period, it might at first sight appear almost superfluous to speak. But that regular seminaries for the education of the young existed throughout Scotland there is abundant proof. To hold the superintendence of these schools, either from motives of benevolence or ambition or both, became an important object with the monks, and accordingly they obtained grants for the management of the principal schools throughout the kingdom. In this manner David I. conceded to the monastery of Kelso not only the superintendence of all the churches, but all the schools within the district of Roxburgh; and in the latter part of the twelfth century, the Bishop of St. Andrews confirmed to the monks of Dunfermline the school of Perth and that of Stirling. It was natural that these *magistri scholarum* should become influential both in the civil and ecclesiastical community, and accordingly they frequently appeared by name and title in the chartularies of the period. What may have been the amount of learning possessed by these reverend preceptors to fit them for their office does not clearly appear; but it is evident, that in the present condition of society they were its best scholars, and therefore the best fitted for the office. They taught their pupils to read and write, and they must have taught them Latin, the principal written language of the period. It is probable, also, that they taught them Norman-French, the court language of England as well as France. In the schools of Aberdeen at the middle of the thirteenth century it was required, that among their other branches of instruction the pupils should be taught grammar and logic. We may conclude, however, that as yet these schools were not very numerously attended, and that only the children of the high-born and the rich, or those who were destined for the church, frequented them. But let us beware how we smile at such schools and such teachers when we remember the pupils who at its close were in training. A school-boy, William Wallace, was taking lessons in Latin from his uncle, who was priest and schoolmaster—and was engraving upon his memory the leonine Latin verse which taught him there was nothing like liberty, and exhorted him never to live in bondage. Robert Bruce, also a stripling, was acquiring that scholarship which enabled him to read the romance of *Ferembras*, with which he cheered his followers in their wanderings, and persuaded them that nothing was impossible to the brave. And alas! must we also be reminded that school-boys were learning the art of writing, the only evidence of whose proficiency should remain in the signatures of the Ragman Roll, by which they gave their own freedom and that of their country away?

During this age, however, so unintellectual and undistinguished in other respects, Scotland was so fortunate as to possess both an erudite scholar and a distinguished poet. The first of these was Sir Michael Scot of Balwearie; the second, Thomas Rymer, author of the metrical romance of *Sir Tristram*.

Michael Scot is supposed to have been born

somewhere about the year 1214, although the exact place of his birth and also his parentage are unknown. Of a studious inquiring mind he soon exhausted the few means of learning which his country afforded, and betook himself to the University of Oxford, where he became distinguished for his proficiency in the sciences of astronomy and chemistry as they were then taught, and in the Latin and Arabic languages. He next proceeded to the University of Paris, where he so highly signalized himself by his progress in mathematics as to obtain the name of "Michael the Mathematician," and in divinity, as to be made a doctor in theology. His thirst of knowledge still increasing with every fresh acquirement, he next went to the college of Padua; and here he turned his studies in astronomy to the usual account by making them subservient to astrology, in which he showed himself a devout believer, so that his essays on that science and his predictions spread his renown over Europe, and made him be regarded as one of the greatest soothsayers of the age. Afterwards he was successively a student at Toledo, a royal astrologer to Frederick II. of Germany, and a physician; in every change a restless inquirer after knowledge, and in every place an honoured guest on account of his prophetic character. On his return homeward, after many years spent in study and travel, he passed through England, where he made some stay at the court of Edward I., by whom he was treated with great distinction: he arrived in Scotland shortly after the death of Alexander III., in consequence of which event he was sent, with Sir David Weems, to Norway, for the purpose of bringing the Maid of Norway to her Scottish throne. Thus far extends the credible history of Michael Scot, who died at a good old age, A.D. 1292, and was buried, as is generally supposed, in the abbey of Melrose. That he was one of the most accomplished scholars of that early age, and yet not in advance of its superstitions, is manifest from the list of his various writings. It was not, however, as a scholar, but as a mighty magician, that he was reverenced, perhaps also dreaded, by his countrymen; and while they lost sight of his books, which they were unable to understand or to read, they perpetuated for ages the renown of his enchantments and wonderful deeds of *diablerie.*

The other eminent Scot of this period was one who has been commemorated under the various names of Thomas Rymer or the Rhimer, Thomas Learmont, and Thomas of Erceldoun, the first name probably being in reference to his poetical character, and the last to his residence in the village of Erceldoun or Earlston, near Melrose, while Learmont was, it may be, his patronymic. He appears to have lived during the greater part of the thirteenth century; and his romance of *Sir Tristram* was so well known, that it was quoted by Gottfried of Strasburg, the German minstrel of this period, and Robert de Brunne, the English poetical annalist, also a writer of the thirteenth century. So current also were his rhyming predictions, or at least those attributed to him, that they were referred to by a succession of old Scottish historians—Fordun, Barbour, Winton, and Henry the Minstrel—as the unquestionable utterances of true prophetic inspiration. The romance of *Sir Tristram*, after being long lost, was discovered and published in the beginning of this century under the editorship of Sir Walter Scott. Although very complicated and artificial in structure and obscure in style, this poem is yet a wonderful production for the age, abounding in poetical description expressed in vigorous language.

But it was his poetical prophecies that kept Thomas's name alive. These floated throughout the country, and continued to accumulate with every great national event, until they were collected and published in Latin and English at Edinburgh in 1615. It was not wonderful, indeed, that such credence should have been attached to them, when we find Archbishop Spottiswood, so late as the middle of the seventeenth century, thus expressing his belief in the prophetic inspiration of the poet: "Whence or how he had this knowledge can hardly be affirmed; but sure it is, that he did divine and answer truly of many things to come." Even yet, perhaps, the same amount of belief is still to be found in many of the cottages of Scotland that have never heard of the discovery of the Auchinleck manuscript.

One instance of the prophetic power of Thomas given by Boece was no doubt a cherished tradition in Scotland. On the day before the sudden death of Alexander III. the seer was asked by the Earl of March what sort of weather would be on the morrow; who answered that before noon it should blow the greatest wind that ever was heard before in Scotland. When the morrow came, and noon approached, there was neither wind nor tempest, and the sky was silent and cloudless. The earl then reproached him for his prediction; but all the answer he received was, "Noon is not yet gone." Almost immediately after a hasty messenger of evil tidings arrived at the gate, who reported the death of the king, and the manner in which it happened. "This," said Thomas, "is the wind I foretold, and that shall blow to the great calamity and trouble of all Scotland."

PERIOD IV.

FROM THE DEATH OF ALEXANDER III. TO THE DEATH OF ROBERT BRUCE (A.D. 1286 TO A.D. 1329).

CHAPTER I.

THE INTERREGNUM FROM THE DEATH OF ALEXANDER III. TO THE CROWNING OF BALIOL (1286-1292).

Interregnum—Troubles of Scotland on the death of Alexander III.—Plots of Edward I. to obtain possession of the kingdom—Margaret of Norway affianced to his son—Edward's intrigues with Norway and Scotland to obtain consent to the marriage—Conditions of the marriage ratified by Edward to the Scots—Manifestations of his ambitious designs on Scotland—Death of Margaret at Orkney—Competition for the crown at her death—Edward claims the right of decision as superior lord of Scotland—His claim recognized by the competitors—Meetings held for the decision—The ten pretenders and their claims—The choice limited to John Baliol and Robert Bruce—The claims of Baliol proclaimed superior—He is declared King of Scotland by Edward I. as umpire—Humbling limitations annexed by Edward to Baliol's sovereignty.

NEVER yet had so heavy a calamity befallen Scotland as the sudden death of Alexander III. While the only heir to the throne was an infant and a female, the land was filled with those rivalries and dissensions which the energy of the late sovereign had scarcely sufficed to hold in check; and the English claims of superiority had fallen into the hands of one who more than others was qualified to watch the turn of events, as well as to strike a decisive blow when the moment for action arrived. On recovering from the stunning effects of their bereavement the Scottish parliament assembled at Scone on the 11th of April, 1286, and appointed a regency of six persons as guardians of the realm during the infancy of their sovereign, Margaret of Norway. These were William Fraser, Bishop of St. Andrews; Duncan, Earl of Fife; and Alexander Comyn, Earl of Buchan, for the northern division of Scotland beyond the Firth of Forth; while the country to the south of that boundary was intrusted to Robert Wishart, Bishop of Glasgow; John Comyn, Lord of Badenoch; and James, the High Steward of Scotland.[1]

Even at this meeting of parliament a bitter foretaste was given of the calamities that awaited the kingdom from the rivalry of the Bruce and Baliol factions, who put forward their respective claims not only to the present leadership of affairs, but to the royal succession also in the event of the death of Margaret. Of these ambitious competitors the most active was Robert Bruce, father of the Earl of Carrick, who claimed through his descent from David, Earl of Huntingdon, the brother of William the Lion; and to make his pretensions good in a trial where force could only decide he was backed by the powerful English Earls of Gloucester and Ulster, who were his kinsmen by marriage, as well as by the Scottish Earls of Menteith and Dunbar, the High Steward of Scotland, the family of Donald, Lord of the Isles, and the lords and barons of his own powerful house. Of these formidable magnates a meeting took place at Turnberry Castle on the 20th September (1286) to support the claims of the Bruce, as if the rights of Margaret had been already a nullity; and there they bound themselves in a mutual covenant against all who should oppose them, saving their allegiance to the King of England, and him on whom the crown of Scotland might afterwards devolve by right of descent. As might be expected, the faction of the Comyns took the alarm at this league and banded themselves in opposition, the result of which was a civil war of skirmishes that extended over the greater part of the kingdom during the two years that succeeded the death of the late king. The regency was unable to tranquillize the dissension of two such rival powers; for of the six persons that had originally composed it the Earl of Fife was assassinated in 1288, the Earl of Buchan died

---
[1] Fordun, lib. xi. cap. 1.

about the same time, and the High Steward was wholly in favour of the Bruces. Nor could Norway, although so deeply interested in such a contest, interpose with effect; for Eric its king was as yet but a youth of eighteen, while his daughter was only three years old. All that he could do was to keep the royal infant safe in his own custody instead of intrusting her to such guardianship as that of the Scottish nobles, and to wait the chance of events, or until the storm had exhausted its violence.

But a more powerful umpire than Eric had also been on the watch. Edward I., although employed in France, was not inattentive to the state of affairs in Scotland; and he must have been aware that the existing rivalries would in the end render his mediation necessary. Even the contest of the different parties, by which they were mutually weakening each other, would prepare the way for making Scotland his own by marrying his son Edward to the infant Scottish queen. He therefore continued his French campaign uninterrupted until his interposition in Scottish affairs was formally entreated; and this was done not only by the King of Norway, who was solicitous about his daughter's inheritance, but also by the Scottish estates, who sent to him an embassy to that effect. Having settled his affairs in France, he therefore returned to England and addressed himself to a more substantial acquisition than that of continental conquests. On receiving the Scottish message, we are told, he exclaimed exultingly to his counsellors, "The fit time has come at last to reduce Scotland and its kinglings under my rule."[1]

After this betrayal of his cherished purpose Edward prepared to treat with the Norwegian and Scottish commissioners, and this he did with such a show of moderation that neither of the parties suspected his designs. The place of meeting was Salisbury, and thither he sent as his commissioners the Bishops of Worcester and Durham and the Earls of Pembroke and Warrenne. The first article of the treaty here arranged, which had for its object the establishment of the young queen upon the throne of Scotland, was from the Norwegian deputation, who promised that Margaret, free from all matrimonial engagements, should be conveyed immediately either to England or her own territories. On the part of England it was then promised that if Edward received the young queen thus free, he would on demand deliver her equally free to Scotland, provided that good order should be previously established there, so that she could reside in the kingdom with safety; and provided also that the Scots should give security to the King of England not to bestow her in marriage without his ordinance, will, and advice, and the assent of Eric her father. Interpreted by after events, this promise of Edward was only worth as much or as little as he was pleased to assign to it. At what time would he discover that this "good order" was established in Scotland, more especially if he found it his interest to disturb it? In this way he might constitute himself perpetual guardian of the queen, and keep her for life within the safe precincts of Windsor Castle. The Norwegian and English parties having thus pledged themselves, it was now the turn of the Scots, who delivered on the part of their nation the following promises: 1. That previous to their queen's arrival they would establish good order in Scotland, and that they would grant full security for her coming there with safety and residing there in all freedom; 2. That they would remove any of the guardians or ministers of Scotland whom the King of Norway should reckon unfit for their offices or liable to suspicion, and place persons of the best rank and character in their room, by the determination of the *good men* of Norway and Scotland; and if they differed in their choice, by the arbitration of the commissioners whom Edward might appoint. Of these terms of agreement three copies were made; one, which was in Latin, was sent to the King of Norway, and the others, which were in Norman-French— now the state language of the Scottish as well as the English nobility—were retained for the use of the two nations.

During the negotiation no mention had been made of the projected marriage of the Queen of Scots to the son of the English king. But Edward, who had indirectly secured so many advantages by the treaty, had already made arrangements for the matrimonial union by which these advantages were to be turned to account. His first task was to procure a papal dispensation for the marriage, the parties being within the prohibited degrees, for Prince Edward was cousin-german to the mother of the bride; and accordingly the English king had already obtained the full consent of Pope Nicholas IV. by inducements which the pontiff could not well reject. It was represented that if Margaret married any other husband dissensions might arise between the kingdoms of England and Scotland, and that Edward would thereby be prevented from undertaking the Crusade which he had promised. The dispensation accordingly had arrived from Rome even before the meeting of Salisbury. His next step was to obtain

---

[1] Fordun, l. xi. c. 3.

the consent of the Scots, and although we have no account of the negotiations with Edward to that effect, we know that they were successful. The report of the coming marriage arose in Scotland in the form of a popular rumour; and the favour with which it was regarded was announced in a letter addressed to King Edward from the Scottish estates assembled at Brigham, a village on the Tweed near Roxburgh. "We rejoice," they said, "to hear the general report that your highness has procured a dispensation from the Apostle[1] for the marriage of your son, Prince Edward, with our sovereign lady. We beseech your highness to inform us whether the report be true; if it is, we on our part heartily consent to the alliance, not doubting that you will agree to such reasonable conditions as we shall propose to your parliament." This letter, which was written in the name of the four regents of Scotland, ten bishops, twenty-three abbots, eleven priors, twelve earls, including Robert Bruce Earl of Carrick, and forty-eight barons, including Robert Bruce Lord of Annandale, shows the earnestness of the Scottish clergy and nobility either to obtain peace for their country or to propitiate the favour of such a powerful king as Edward. Not content with this, they at the same time sent an address to the King of Norway announcing their consent to the marriage, and requesting him to send Margaret to Scotland before the feast of All-Saints, according to the treaty of Salisbury. "If you should fail," they added, "in granting our request, we must in this extremity follow the best counsel which God may give us for the state of the kingdom and its inhabitants."[2]

Nothing was now required but the consent of Eric, which, however, was not to be so easily won. To intrust his helpless child, the object of so much political intrigue, to such a guardian as the King of England, or such subjects as these Scottish nobles were likely to prove, was no safe or trivial experiment, and therefore he demurred to the proposal. But Edward was too powerful a king, and too cunning a politician, to be thus arrested in his purpose. Accordingly, in the summer of the following year (1290), he not only repeated his urgent request for the arrival of the princess from Norway, but sent to its court Anthony Beck, Bishop of Durham, a soldier and diplomatist after his own heart, to overcome Eric's reluctance. The prelate went wisely to work, and with golden arguments, which, since the suppression of the piratical trade of the kingdom, were now of double force in Norway. He distributed large sums of money to the chief counsellors, which, under the delicate name of pensions, were to be annually continued until Margaret should have reached the age of fifteen;[3] and as each head had its price as distinctly marked as if it had been ticketed by the merchant, his difficulties were soon got over, and consent to the marriage obtained in a full Norwegian Storthing. So confident, indeed, was Edward in the efficacy of the means, that when the Scots, who were ignorant of his proceedings, became clamorous at the delay, he bound himself in a penalty of 3000 merks, to be paid to the Scottish guardians, that Margaret should either be landed in Britain or delivered to his commissioners in Norway for the purpose before the 1st of November. Fortunately for him this royal obligation, so like a modern wager, did not need to be proclaimed a forfeit, as the princess set sail before the period. All parties being thus reconciled and at one, the only task that remained was to draw up such articles for the marriage as would be compatible with the rights and independence of the two kingdoms of Scotland and England; and for this purpose a great national meeting was convened at Brigham on the 18th of July, 1290. It was attended not only by the guardians, clergy, earls, and barons of Scotland, but the representatives of the Scottish community at large; while, on the part of England, appeared the Bishop of Durham and five other dignitaries. The articles which the English proposed and the Scots accepted are worthy of consideration, not only as illustrative of the extreme jealousy of the latter in preserving their national independence, but as showing more clearly the merits of the war into which they were afterwards compelled to enter. In the event of the marriage it was agreed—

I. That the rights, laws, liberties, and customs of Scotland should remain for ever entire and inviolable throughout the whole realm and its marches—saving always the right of the King of England and of all others, which, before the date of this treaty, belonged to him or any of them in the marches or elsewhere, or which ought to belong to him or any of them in all time coming. This saving clause, so honest in its appearance, was afterwards distorted into strange meaning under Edward's interpretation.

---

[1] This title was usually given to the popes, and what effect it imparted to their dispensations may be easily surmised.

[2] Rymer's *Fœdera*, ii. p. 473.

[3] Forty pounds, divided among the whole, was the sum for which the Norwegian counsellors sold their services on this occasion, and this by their own express demand and rating. Such was the price of a northern court in those days of cheap diplomacy, and such the straightforward mode in which the bargain was struck. This instance will help to illustrate the venality of the Scottish nobles in their subsequent trafficking with Edward I.

It formed the groundwork of those claims which he afterwards brought forward for the sovereignty over Scotland under which the other guarantees for its independence were nothing but idle words.

II. Failing Margaret and Prince Edward or either of them without issue, it was agreed that the kingdom should return to the nearest heirs to whom it ought of right to return wholly, freely, absolutely, and without any subjection; so that thereby nothing should accrue or decrease to the King of England, to his heirs, or to any one else. If Margaret survived her husband she was to be delivered to the Scottish nation free from all matrimonial engagements. In the meantime it was agreed, that immediately upon the marriage she should be secured in such a jointure suitable to her rank as would be satisfactory to herself and her friends.

III. Of the kingdom of Scotland it was agreed that it should remain separate and divided from England, free in itself, and without subjection, according to its right, boundaries, and marches, as heretofore. The chapters of churches possessing right of election were not to be compelled to go out of Scotland for obtaining leave to elect, for presenting persons elected, or for swearing allegiance to the sovereign. No crown vassal was to be compelled to go out of Scotland to perform homage or fealty, or transact for his relief. A similar provision was declared for widows, orphans, and all others peculiarly entitled to the protection of the state. To receive these homages a person was to be appointed in Scotland to act by the authority of the queen and her husband, a reservation being made in those cases where homage ought to be performed in presence of the sovereign. Fealty having been once done, each man was to have sasine of his land immediately by brief from chancery. In thus providing for the individual liberty of the subject it was also granted that no native of Scotland should in any case, whether of covenant made, or crime committed in Scotland, be compelled to answer out of the kingdom contrary to the laws and usage of the country.

The other articles of this treaty, which had reference mainly to the independence of the Scots as a nation, were equally express and conciliatory. The great seal of the kingdom, which had been used since the death of Alexander III., was to continue in use until the new queen had taken the coronation oath, after which a new great seal was to be made with the arms accustomed, and with the name of the sovereign of Scotland, exclusively of any other, and to be delivered into the custody of the chancellor for the time being; and this chancellor was to be a native of Scotland and resident also within the kingdom. The same conditions were also to apply to the chamberlains, clerk of the rolls of chancery, justiciaries, and other officers of the realm. Of the mere inanimate symbols of national independence care was also taken, so that all relics, charters, grants, and other muniments connected with the royal dignity of Scotland, were to be deposited in a safe place within the kingdom, and in sure custody under the seals of the nobility and subject to their inspection, until the queen should arrive and have living issue. During the same interval, also, no incumbrance, alienation, or obligation was to be created in matters respecting the royal dignity of the kingdom; no disparagement by marriage effected upon the heirs of the nobility who were wards of the crown; no parliament to be held beyond the boundaries of Scotland in matters respecting the kingdom, its marches, and its inhabitants; no tallage, aids, levies of men, or extraordinary exactions demanded from it, or imposed upon its inhabitants, unless to promote the common interests of the realm, or in cases where the kings of Scotland had been wont to demand them.[1]

Such was the treaty of Brigham. These conditions, offered by a stronger power to a proud, jealous, sensitive people, were guarded by all the scrupulosity which language could furnish, as well as all the impressive sanctions which the church could impart; and when the English commissioners who offered these terms, as well as their king who ratified them, had sworn by every oath to their observance, and committed themselves to heavy spiritual and ecclesiastical penalties for breach or non-fulfilment, the Scots accepted them in the same good faith in which they believed them to be tendered. Yet scarcely had his signature dried upon the parchment, when Edward adopted a line of conduct which tended to nullify the whole treaty. His first step was to appoint Anthony Beck, Bishop of Durham, who had so ably signalized himself in his negotiations with the court of Norway, Lieutenant of Scotland in the name of Queen Margaret and his son Edward. Decent pretexts were needed to veil such a usurpation; and therefore, while the new governor's commission announced that he was to act in concert with the guardians, and by the advice of the prelates and nobles of the realm, Edward pretended that the obligation of his oath to maintain the laws of Scotland made such an appointment necessary. But the king well knew that even among the four Scottish guardians the bishop would be certain to have the preponderance, as two of

---

[1] *Fœdera*, ii. p. 482, *et sequen*.

their number were already in the English interest. Edward's next step was of a still bolder character: pretending to be alarmed by some rumours of danger impending over Scotland, he demanded that the fortresses of the kingdom should be instantly committed to his custody. The Scots were startled at the summons, and sent through their ambassadors a decisive refusal: they would retain their castles and fortresses in their own keeping until the arrival of their queen and her intended husband, to whom alone they would deliver them. To soften this refusal, however, they took the oath of fidelity to Margaret and Prince Edward as their future joint-sovereigns, engaged to consent to no other marriage for their queen, and offered to remove those keepers of the fortresses whose fidelity was suspected, and appoint others in their room. With these answers, from which the English king must have discovered that he had been too precipitate, he was obliged for the present to be contented.

While these negotiations, so pregnant with national quarrel and danger, were still in agitation, the Maiden of Norway, as Margaret was poetically called, had set sail for Scotland. We are not told with what misgivings this child, as yet only in her eighth year, was committed to the hazards of the ocean, that she might rule over a kingdom more stormy and uncertain still. Upon so frail a tenure the hopes of the Scottish nation were now embarked, and amidst these ominous aggressions of Edward many must have felt that her arrival was the country's only hope of escape from a destructive war, and perhaps from final vassalage. But an untimely death released Margaret from the woes that in later times awaited Mary Stuart. On her passage from Norway she was attacked by a mortal disease, so that she had to be landed at Orkney, and there she died towards the close of September, A.D. 1290.

By the death of the Maiden of Norway the Scottish throne was left not only without an occupant, but without a recognized successor; and the two great competitors for its possession, Robert Bruce Lord of Annandale, and John Baliol Lord of Galloway, had already prepared themselves for the contest. The first to move was Bruce, who, as soon as the mournful tidings arrived, appeared at Perth with a formidable array of his armed retainers; and, being joined by the powerful earls of Mar and Athol, who mustered their forces to support him, his chance of success seemed all but certain, as Baliol was at present resident in England. But the Lord of Galloway had an assured friend to his interests in William Fraser, Bishop of St. Andrews, and one of the regents of the kingdom, whose devotedness to his patron seems to have obscured, or absolutely extinguished, that spirit of patriotic independence for which the Scottish clergy had hitherto been remarkable. He wrote to the King of England, describing the troubled state of the kingdom, and inviting his dangerous interposition. He even advised him to approach the Scottish borders for the prevention of civil war and bloodshed, and for the peaceful appointment of a successor to Margaret, should the tidings of her death, as yet uncertain, be confirmed. He was particularly careful to point out the person whom he judged worthiest of the succession. "Should John de Baliol," he wrote, "present himself before you, my advice is that you treat with him so that, in all events, your honour and interest may be preserved." Again returning at the close of his letter to the subject most at heart, he thus counselled his royal correspondent: "Should the queen die, which Heaven forbid, I entreat that your highness may approach our borders, that the people of Scotland may be comforted, and the effusion of blood prevented; and that the faithful of the land may be enabled to preserve their oath inviolate, and to prefer him to be king who ought of right to inherit, provided always that he is willing to follow your counsel." In this last qualification who could fail to recognize the man of Edward's subsequent choice? The "faithful of the land" were no doubt the adherents of Baliol and supporters of the English interest; but of the oath to which the prelate alludes, the dark records of the period have made no mention.

This advice, which was too shrewdly traitorous to have been merely a random suggestion, as some have charitably supposed, completely coincided with Edward's crafty policy; and it is probable that he would have speedily advanced upon the Scottish border but for the sickness and death of Eleanor, his queen, whom he loved with all the intensity of an iron heart that was proof to every other kind of affection. But the bereavement only made his ambition more pitiless and insatiate, and he returned with renewed ardour to his favourite project, which was the reduction of the whole island into a united British empire. Even before the death of Margaret he had assumed in writing to his confidential supporters the title of Lord Paramount of the kingdom of Scotland; and after that event he had declared in a meeting of his council that he meant to bring Scotland under his rule in the same way that he had subdued Wales. His first step was to establish his claim to the feudal sovereignty of the kingdom; and this could be best done by becoming the umpire of the royal succession, and appointing a king for Scotland who would receive the crown as his gift. The fact has been assumed that, dismayed at the prospect of a civil war, the nation at large chose Edward as the arbitrator, but of any such choice no evidence has been adduced; and in the absence of this we are justified in suspecting that the invitation came from the competitors themselves and their supporters. But even less than this would have sufficed for such a king as Edward, and with such an interest at stake. He ordered the barons of Yorkshire, Westmoreland, Lancashire, Cumberland, and Northumberland to assemble at Norham with all their military retainers on the 3d of June (1291); and the clergy and nobility of Scotland, including John Baliol and Robert Bruce, to meet him at the same place but at an earlier period, being the 10th of May. By giving the Scots this priority of meeting Edward avoided the appearance of an armed intervention, which the divisions among the Scottish nobles and the helplessness of the people rendered unnecessary; and therefore he repaired to it not with an army, but a train of peaceful counsellors and attendants.

The proceedings of this momentous assembly were commenced by an opening speech on the part of Edward, which was delivered by Roger Brabazon, justiciary of England. The latter stated the anxiety of his royal master at the difficulties in which the death of Alexander III. and his daughter had involved the Scottish kingdom, and his good-will to the Scots collectively and individually; "for in their defence," added the speaker, "he himself is interested." He had therefore called the Scots together on this occasion that justice might be done to the competitors for the crown and the peace of the kingdom established; he had also undertaken a long journey that, as Superior and Lord Paramount of the kingdom of Scotland, he might in person do justice to all. "Wherefore," added the speaker, coming down upon his terrible conclusion which he had so cautiously preluded, "our lord the king, for the due accomplishment of this purpose, doth require your hearty recognition of his title of Lord Paramount of the kingdom of Scotland."

The whole assembly was thunderstruck; none, even the most selfish or unpatriotic, had been prepared for such a declaration, and the Scottish nobles gazed at each other in silence. At length a solitary voice ventured to exclaim, "No answer can be given while the throne is vacant." This interruption awoke the ire of the King of England. "By holy Edward, whose crown I wear," he cried, "I will vindicate my just rights or perish in the attempt!" Knowing that his army was mustering, the Scots requested a delay that they might consult among themselves, as well as advertise those who were absent; but Edward replied gruffly, "You were all sufficiently informed by my summons, but I grant you a delay till to-morrow." The morrow came, but only with a request for further delay, which Edward granted for three weeks, well knowing their inability to unite for any common measure, and that at the end of this time his forces would be assembled. Through his intrigues in Scotland ten competitors were already in the field, the representatives of as many contending factions. On the nobles returning home each was more solicitous for his own personal interests or those of his favourite candidate than for the rights of the insulted kingdom and its down-trodden people; and therefore, after the interval had elapsed, all were ready to appear before the foreign tribunal and submit their cause to the decision of the English king.

On the 2d of June this meeting was held, not, however, at Norham, as before, but in an open field called Holywell Haugh, near Upsettlington, and opposite Norham Castle, but within the Scottish boundary. This change of place had been ordered by Edward during the interval with the politic design of giving the meeting a free and national character. Eight competitors presented themselves on the occasion, viz. Robert Bruce, Lord of Annandale; Florence, Count of Holland; John Hastings, Lord of Abergavenny; Patrick Dunbar, Earl of March; William de Ross, William de Vesci, Robert de Pynkeny, and Nicholas de Soulis. The proceedings were resumed at the point where they had broken off at the meeting of Norham; and the speaker on this occasion was Robert Burnel, Bishop of Bath and Wells and Chancellor of England. He stated that the English kings were Lords Paramount of Scotland because they had either enjoyed or claimed that right from the earliest ages; and that King Edward, although he was open to inquiry and conviction, and had required the Scots to produce their counter-evidence against his claims, had remained unanswered. As they had produced nothing in reply the king was therefore resolved to act as Lord Paramount, and decide the succession to the Scottish crown. Then turning to Robert Bruce, the bishop asked him, "Do you acknowledge Edward as Lord Paramount of Scotland, and are you willing to act and receive judgment from him in that character?" "Definitively, distinctly, publicly, and openly," as the instrument declares, Bruce announced his assent. The same question was put to the other competitors successively, and they all gave the same reply. Sir Thomas Randolph then stated that John Baliol, Lord of Galloway, who was not present, had mistaken the day of meeting; and he requested that this nobleman should be admitted on the following day, that he might give his answer in person. The delay was granted, and on the 3d of June Baliol appeared, and after some coy demur assented like the rest. Having thus inclosed the competitors within his net, the chancellor-bishop declared in his master's name that although Edward at present asserted his right of superiority for the purpose of pronouncing judgment in the competition, he did not purpose to relinquish his right of property in the kingdom of Scotland, but would reserve his claim to that right in whatever time and manner he judged most convenient. In this way he declared Scotland to be a male fief, so that as all the competitors claimed by the female line, the person elected could only reign by his sufferance and might be deposed at his pleasure. Edward himself then harangued the assembly. After reviewing its proceedings and confirming the declarations that had been made by his chancellor, he talked of his affection for the Scottish nation and the toils he had undergone and would still be ready to undergo to bring its affairs to a happy issue. He promised also that he would give a prompt and impartial judgment in the pending competition, and secure for the kingdom the administration of its laws and customs, the redress of abuses, and the establishment of national tranquillity. Then, invoking the divine aid, and expressing his hope that the whole affair would be conducted to the glory of God, he ended by once more expressing his determination to keep his claim to the property of Scotland as its feudal superior entire and complete.

The Scottish competitors were now as compliant as Edward himself could have desired; they were ready with their homage to this formidable superior who claimed it as his right and had power to enforce it. Baliol was the first to succumb by acknowledging Edward as his lord and craving his judgment; and he was followed by John Comyn, Lord of Badenoch, one of the Scottish regents, who made the same recognition and presented his claims as a competitor. The ten candidates subscribed an instrument acknowledging the right of Edward to decide in the competition, and submitting themselves to his award; and on the following day (June 4th) they agreed to give Edward entire possession of Scotland and its places of strength, because, as they declared, "judgment cannot be without execution, nor execution without possessing the subject to be awarded." This possession, however, was only to continue for two months, and with full security of restitution, while the revenues of the kingdom were to remain untouched except the allowance for the expenses of government. It was also unanimously agreed by the whole assembly that Baliol and Comyn, for themselves and their adherents, should nominate forty commissioners, and Bruce in like manner as many, to which Edward should add twenty-four, or more or fewer, to consider the claims of the competitors and make their report to the king. On the 11th of June the Scottish regents solemnly resigned the kingdom into Edward's hands, and the keepers of the castles in like manner surrendered their trust. Amidst this universal national degradation only one bright example of manly independence was afforded; this was by Gilbert de Umfraville, Earl of Angus, who held the castles of Dundee and Forfar. On being required to deliver up his charge he refused, declaring that he had received the keeping of these castles from the National Estates, and would not surrender them to England unless Edward and all the competitors joined to exonerate him from blame. A letter of indemnity was accordingly drawn up by the regents and competitors which Edward was willing to receive; and it was only then that the gallant patriot consented to resign his trust into English hands. Thus far unopposed and successful, Edward proceeded to act as the lawful and recognized King of Scotland. He restored to the regents the custody of the kingdom which they had so abjectly surrendered; but to keep them in the right way he gave them Allan, Bishop of Caithness, an Englishman, for their chancellor, and Walter Agmondesham, another Englishman, for his colleague. He also added to the regency a fifth member in Brian Fitzallan, an English baron. He was likewise careful to state that, although this meeting had been held by his consent in Scotland, the example should not debar him from pronouncing judgment in England whenever a similar case should happen. He also ordered that no Scottish breves should be excepted against or rejected by the King's Bench in London, "because," said the declaration, "the two kingdoms are now joined on account of the superiority over Scotland which the King of England enjoys." Thus early did he consider the union of the two kingdoms as complete and indissoluble, with himself for their sole king and master. These proceedings were completed by the 13th of July; and as nothing remained except to try the claims of the candidates and pronounce his award, Edward appointed the 2d of August for that purpose, with the town of Berwick as the place of meeting. During the short interval he was eager to improve his advantages by receiving the homage of the people, who were universally required to swear allegiance; and for this purpose he made a tour through the principal cities of Scotland, and exacted the oaths of fealty, not only from the earls and barons, but also from the burgesses and commons. Even into those parts of the country which he did not visit he sent commissioners to demand the oaths of the people, and compel them, if need should be, by imprisonment, to acknowledge themselves vassals of the King of England. He also surveyed with a critical eye the strength and military resources of the kingdom, so that in the event of any popular reaction he might know at once the danger and the remedy.

On the 2d of August the great assize was assembled at Berwick, and on the 3d the candidates presented their claims before the 104 commissioners selected by the Bruce and Baliol parties, and by the King of England, who were assembled in the church of the Dominicans. The competitors had now increased to thirteen, chiefly through the intrigues of Edward, who by this increase had sought to magnify the importance of his arbitration, and deepen the submission of the applicants. A short glance at the names of these claimants and the ground of their expectations is necessary for a more perfect understanding of this dark and disastrous portion of Scottish history. Of these there were—

1. Florence, Count of Holland, who competed as great-grandson of Ada, sister of William the Lion.

2. Robert de Pynkeny, great-grandson of Marjory, another sister of William the Lion.

3. Patrick Dunbar, Earl of March, who claimed as grandson of Ada, illegitimate daughter of William the Lion.

4. William de Ross, who claimed as great-grandson of Isabella, illegitimate daughter of William the Lion.

5. William de Vesey, grandson of Marjory, another illegitimate daughter of William.

6. Patrick Galythly, whose father Henry, he asserted, was the lawfully begotten son of William the Lion. But this claim, which would have settled the competition at once, could not be proved, and therefore he was classed among the other illegitimate scions of royalty.

7. Nicholas de Soulis, who claimed as the descendant of Marjory, illegitimate daughter of Alexander II. As has already been mentioned in the course of this history, Alan Durward, the husband of Marjory, endeavoured, but unlawfully, to procure her legitimization, in the hope that his posterity might succeed to the crown.

8. Roger de Mandeville. This was a new claimant, a descendant of Aurica, whom he endeavoured to prove a lawfully begotten daughter of William the Lion; but his tale for this purpose was too romantic even for that age of romance, although he appealed to the legends of Scotland, England, and Ireland in testimony of the fact.

9. John Comyn, Lord of Badenoch, and one of the regents of Scotland, known in our history as the "Black Comyn," to distinguish him from the younger John, who was called the "Red." He claimed as the fifth in descent from Donald Bane, brother of Malcolm Canmore. But his claim, even allowing the correctness of the pedigree which he produced on the occasion, could only be established upon the fact of his ancestor having been the lawful king of Scotland and all the successors of Canmore usurpers.

10. Eric, King of Norway. He also was a new candidate in the competition, and he claimed as heir to his infant daughter Margaret. But this claim, however, good in a question of personal property, was not enough to win a kingdom; and of this it is evident he was aware by the lateness of his application and the readiness with which he renounced it. His competition, indeed, seems to have been only put forward to strengthen certain money demands which he made upon the kingdom of Scotland, and that were still more extravagant than his claim to the crown itself. He required that the revenues of the country which had been due during his daughter's lifetime should be given over to himself as her administrator, and that the nation should pay him £100,000 sterling (!) for not receiving their queen—who had died before she reached them. At length, however, he contented himself with 200 merks per annum, which he demanded as the debt still owing to him in the portion of his wife Margaret, daughter of Alexander III., which had been imperfectly paid; and this being allowed, he vanished from Scottish history.

Of these ten claimants the pretensions were weak and inadmissible, being founded upon remote, uncertain, or illegitimate descent; but they served for the moment to embroil the controversy and heighten its interest. But of the other three candidates no such declaration could be made, as they were the descendants and representatives of David, Earl of Huntingdon, brother of William the Lion, and whose progeny had therefore an indisputable claim on the extinction of the family of William. It unfortunately happened, however, that these candidates were three in number; and not only were their claims so nicely balanced that it was difficult to adjust them, but backed with such power and influence as would have filled the whole kingdom with commotion and civil war.

These were John Baliol, Robert Bruce, and John Hastings.

It was not, however, at this stage of the proceedings that Edward meant to decide. A delay would tame the expectants into full subservience, and vindicate his own claim as Lord Paramount of Scotland, and therefore he adjourned the final trial to the 2d of June in the following year. Before that time arrived the unfortunate ten, who seem to have been led into the arena either by fallacious promises or against their own choice, had become conscious of the weakness of their claims, and had withdrawn them, thus leaving an open field for Baliol, Bruce, and Hastings.

Into the particulars of this long and important but tedious trial, which was adjourned to the 15th of October, and afterwards to the 17th of November, we do not propose to enter. It was sufficiently characterized by the mean subserviency of the eighty Scottish commissioners, who in questions touching the laws of their own country about succession, pleaded their ignorance, and bowed before the superior knowledge of the judges from England. In this confession, indeed, they scarcely erred, when it was made before the tribunal of the English Justinian. David of Huntingdon, whose son John died without issue, had also left three daughters, of whom the eldest, Margaret, was married to Alan of Galloway; Isabella, the second, to Robert Bruce; and Ada, the third, to Henry Hastings. Now Bruce was the son of the second daughter, and Baliol the grandson of the first, by his mother, the daughter of Margaret. Between these two claimants, therefore, the controversy chiefly lay, and the question at issue was, whether the claim of Baliol as the representative of the senior branch, was not vitiated by the intervention of a female representative. After learned and long and keen discussion the whole was summed up in the following query of the King of England to the judges: "By the laws and usages of both kingdoms does the issue of the eldest sister, though more remote in one degree, exclude the issue of the second sister, though nearer in one degree; or ought the nearer in one degree, issuing from the second sister to exclude the more remote in one degree issuing from the eldest sister?" To this the commissioners and the whole parliament unanimously answered, that "by the laws and usages of both kingdoms in every heritable succession, the more remote in one degree, lineally descended from the eldest sister, was preferable to the nearer in degree issuing from the second sister."

As the deliberations at this stage were auspicious to the claim of Baliol, Bruce and Hastings took the alarm, more especially as Edward had declared that Bruce should take nothing in the competition with Baliol. At an earlier period it had been asked, whether Scotland, as a kingdom to be inherited, was entire and inseparable, or might be divided into portions; and to this the Lord of Annandale, trusting in the fancied superiority of his descent over that of his rival, and hoping to obtain all, had replied that Scotland was indivisible. But now, when he saw that this chance had escaped, he resolved to secure at least a part. Forgetting, therefore, his former concession, he now insisted that Scotland was a divisible inheritance; that as such, he was entitled to one-third of the kingdom; and that in return for this he was willing to acknowledge the right of Baliol to the title of king and the royal dignity on account of his descent from the eldest sister. The same claim in his own behalf was made by John Hastings on account of his descent from the youngest sister. In this way these three ambitious competitors would have parted the kingdom to its ruin for the paltry distinction of ruling as a feudal prince over a stripe of barren territory. But this division did not suit Edward, who had resolved to secure for himself even more than the lion's share. He therefore put the two following questions to the commissioners and parliament: Is the kingdom of Scotland divisible? If it is not divisible, are its revenues divisible? They answered in one voice that the kingdom was indivisible, and that its revenues, if once in the hand of the sovereign, were indivisible also. Edward therefore decreed that neither John Hastings nor Robert Bruce should take anything in the competition, as Scotland was indivisible like other kingdoms.

The closing scene of this terrible trial, in which a kingdom and its people, like a few paltry acres and the cattle that grazed upon it, were to be transferred by the chicanery of law and the imperious sentence of a selfish interested judge to a new possessor, who demanded them as his right, was made on the 17th of November, 1292. Throughout the trial the show of justice had been retained with the utmost scrupulosity, for it was but too much needed to veil an enormity of fraud that could not endure the light. The final and conclusive sentence, although it announced a decision which had probably been adopted eighteen months earlier, when the court was first opened, must have been heard with mingled feelings of awe and disappointment and deep misgivings for the future. "As it is admitted," said the royal judge, "that the kingdom of Scotland is indivisible, and as the King of England must judge of the rights of his subjects according to the laws and usages of the kingdoms over which he reigns; and as by the laws and usages of England and Scotland in the succession to indivisible heritage, the more remote in degree of the first line of descent is preferable to the nearer in degree of the second;—therefore it is decreed that John Baliol shall have sasine of the kingdom of Scotland."

In this way did John Baliol become sovereign of the country—but a servant-sovereign, with an imperious master over him. And of this fact he was not for a moment allowed to remain in doubt, for the same breath that announced his kingship, also proclaimed his vassalage. When the decree was ended Edward was careful to repeat the declaration he had formerly uttered, that this decision should not in any way impair his own claim to the property of Scotland. He then read Baliol a lecture upon his royal duties, charging him to act justly towards his people, and threatening to interpose as Lord Paramount in case of neglect. It was a painful foretaste of the uneasiness which a crown inflicts upon the head that wears it, and a humbling preparative for the indignities that were sure to follow. Two days after Edward ordered the five Scottish regents to resign the government of the kingdom into Baliol's hands, and he surrendered the castles that had been intrusted to his keeping; but as if to convert this act into an indignity, by showing that he needed no such guarantee for their submission, he, in presence of the new king and Scottish nobles, broke the great seal of the kingdom which had been used since the death of Alexander III., and sent the fragments to be laid up in his royal treasury in England, "in testimony to future ages of his right of superiority over Scotland." On the following day Baliol swore fealty to Edward at Norham, and ten days after (on the 30th of November, 1292) he was crowned at Scone. Even in the ceremonial of his coronation the ominous shadow of the King of England seemed to be present, to cloud its otherwise diminished lustre; for he was placed upon the royal and prophetic chair not by the Earl of Fife, to whom the office hereditarily pertained, but by John de St. John, whom Edward appointed for the purpose, the young Macduff being at present a minor. After Baliol was crowned his first obligation was to repeat as king the submission which he had rendered as a baron, and accordingly, on the 26th of December, he did homage to Edward at Newcastle in his royal capacity, and for the kingdom of Scotland.

CHAPTER II.

REIGN OF JOHN BALIOL (1292-1296).

Reign of John Baliol—Commencement of its troubles—Appeals to English tribunals against the decisions of Scottish courts—Edward I. justifies this usurpation—Baliol cited to appear in England against an appeal of one of his subjects—He is obliged to comply—He refuses submission to the award of the English parliament—Despotic conduct of Edward towards the King of Scotland—The Scots form an alliance with France against England—War commences between Scotland and England—Unsuccessful invasion of England by the Scots—Edward invades Scotland—He takes Berwick by storm—Baliol renounces his allegiance to Edward—Defeat of the Scots at Dunbar—Bruce's hopes of succession to the Scottish crown destroyed by Edward—Baliol's humble submission and deposition—The Scots compelled to receive Edward as their sovereign—His arrangements for the government of Scotland—Commencement of Scottish resistance to his rule.

At the mature age of forty-three John Baliol ascended his precarious throne. Scarcely had he been seated when the troubles of his position commenced by appeals of the discontented from the decisions of the Scottish tribunals to the superior authority of England. Security, indeed, had been promised against such license by an article in the treaty of Brigham, in which it was declared that no Scottish subject should be compelled to answer in any suit, whether civil or criminal, beyond the bounds of the kingdom. Regardless of this Roger Bartholomew, a citizen of Berwick, whose case had been tried and decided by the regents during the interregnum, appealed from their verdict to the decision of the King of England. Baliol opposed this transference as a violation of the treaty, of which he reminded Edward; but to the Scottish king's protest, the latter replied that he had scrupulously observed his promise, but that the hearing of complaints against the ministers of his own appointing belonged to himself, and was not to be interfered with by his subjects. He then summoned Baliol, and the Scottish prelates and nobles who attended him into his privy chamber, and there declared to them in express terms the manner in which he purposed to exercise his sovereignty over Scotland. He had been induced, he said, to make these promises during the interregnum; but now that the Scots had a king, these promises were binding no longer. He therefore considered himself at liberty to judge in every cause that was regularly brought before him from Scotland: he would hear them in England, and decide upon them as Lord Paramount; and should it be necessary in such cases he would summon the King of Scotland himself to appear in his presence. To show, also, that these were no hasty and idle threats, Edward reduced them into a formal instrument, in which he renounced as Lord Paramount every engagement and promise contained in the treaty of Brigham. This interview, so humbling to Baliol, occurred at Newcastle on the 31st of December, 1292, only five days after he had done homage to Edward for his kingdoms; and although there was such manifest perjury in this summary renunciation, he was obliged to hear and submit in silence. After this final confirmation of his authority, and when resistance was no longer to be feared, Edward restored to the chamberlain of Scotland the national documents, records, and accounts that had been forwarded from Edinburgh to Roxburgh, and granted possession to Baliol of the Isle of Man in like manner as it had been held by Alexander III., reserving, however, his own rights as feudal superior and the rights of all others.

The threat held out of summoning Baliol before an English tribunal, as often as an appeal on the part of his subjects should make his personal appearance necessary, was not an empty menace; and a case of this kind occurred only a few weeks after the bitter interview at Newcastle. The causes were the following:—Duncan, Earl of Fife, having died in 1288, had left a son, a minor, under the guardianship of the Bishop of St. Andrews. But the lands of Reres and Crey, which pertained to the earldom, had been seized by Macduff, grand-uncle of the minor, under the allegation that these had been bequeathed to him as his patrimonial inheritance. Such, however, did not appear manifest to William, Bishop of St. Andrews, who dispossessed Macduff in favour of his ward, whom he considered the rightful heir of the lands in question. As this occurred during the interregnum, Edward, to whom Macduff appealed, had referred him to the regents, who, after trial of the cause, sustained his claim and replaced him in possession. Here, however, a question involving the rightful occupation of so much property was not allowed to rest; and at the first parliament held under the new reign, which met at Scone on the 10th of February, Macduff was required to answer for taking possession of lands which, being the property of a minor, were under royal custody. Macduff might have preferred to rest his case upon the argument of rightful and confirmed inheritance, which, however, he failed to make out to the satisfaction of his judges, and by them he was committed to prison as guilty of trespass. After his imprisonment, which was a brief one, had ended, he petitioned Baliol for a renewal of the trial; but on this being refused, he appealed to Edward as superior judge.

So choice an opportunity of giving a practical lesson on obedience to the King of Scots was not likely to be neglected by Edward, and he summoned Baliol to appear before him on the 25th of March to answer the complaint of Macduff in person. But Baliol did not obey. He was again summoned to make his appearance by the 14th of October; and still further to aggravate the demand, or subdue him into utter submission, Edward in the interval caused his parliament to pass several orders by which the King of Scots might at pleasure be made to appear personally in England at whatever appeal of any of his subjects. "No excuse of absence," said one of these regulations, "shall be ever received either from the appellant or the King of Scots, respondent." Baliol was now obliged to comply, and he appeared before the English parliament that was held after Michaelmas, his own subject, Macduff, being also present as his accuser. On being asked for his defence, Baliol replied boldly and briefly, "I am King of Scotland; to the complaint of Macduff, or to any other matters regarding my kingdom, I dare not give answer without the advice of my people." "What means this refusal?" cried Edward; "you are my liegeman, you have done homage to me, you are present in consequence of my summons." "In matters that pertain to my kingdom I dare not and I cannot answer in this place without the advice of my people," replied Baliol. These were bold answers—the courage of despair. Feeling that he had been more urgent than prudent, Edward artfully proposed that Baliol should desire an adjournment for the purpose of taking counsel with the nation; but Baliol, aware that every future demand upon his personal appearance would be sanctioned by such a precedent if he yielded in the present case, replied firmly that he would neither ask a longer day nor consent to an adjournment. In consequence of his refusal the English parliament resolved that this case was still before their king; that Baliol should be held to have offered no defence; and that his answers were derogatory to the authority of his liege lord and a manifest contempt of the court. They further decreed that Macduff should have damages, to be assessed by this court, from the King of Scots, for his imprisonment; and that the inquiry should be held anew as to whether he had been lawfully dispossessed of his property. As every one also ought to be punished in that which emboldens him to offend, they resolved that the three principal castles of Scotland, with their towns, should be taken into the custody of the King of England until the King of Scots had made satisfaction for his contempt and disobedience. But before these hard conclusions could be officially announced Baliol interposed. "My lord," he said, addressing Edward, "I am your liegeman for the kingdom of Scotland; and as that of which you have lately treated concerns my people no less than myself, I therefore entreat you to delay judgment until I have consulted my people, lest I be surprised through want of counsel. They who are now with me neither will nor dare advise me in the absence of the rest of my kingdom. After having advised with them I will report the result in your first parliament held after Easter, and perform what I ought to do." With this request it suited Edward to comply, for the resolutions of the parliament were too violent, and the occupation of the three Scottish castles could not be accomplished without the commencement of open war. It was therefore resolved that the final judgment should be delayed until the day after the feast of the Trinity in the following year.

This delay was of importance to Baliol and his kingdom, for such at this time were the relations of England with the Continent that at any day or hour Edward might be summoned to a French invasion, and compelled to stake his life upon the hazard. And one of these contingencies speedily arrived. At or near the port of Bayonne some English and Norman sailors had assembled to fill their water-casks; a quarrel arose about the right of priority, and in the scuffle that ensued one of the Norman sailors was killed. This led to wholesale reprisals, and finally to a great naval war in which the fleets of Normandy, France, and Genoa were combined against that of England, aided by the ships of Gascony, Ireland, and Holland. To punish Edward, who was his vassal for the dukedom of Aquitaine, Philip le Bel, the French sovereign, summoned the King of England to answer personally in Paris for these outrages; and on Edward failing to appear as Duke of Aquitaine before his French peers, the dukedom was declared forfeited to the crown of France. In this manner Edward was made to feel that the feudal law was two-edged, and he stood in the same relation to Philip that Baliol stood to himself. But here the resemblance ended, for he was neither so weak in character nor resources as to sit down under the insult; while his parliament, which assembled at London in May, 1294, entered heartily into the quarrel and agreed to assist him in the war. At this meeting also Baliol appeared, and gave evidence of his compliant spirit by yielding up the whole revenues for three years of his rich estates in England, to support the campaign against France. It is probable from this wonderful liberality that the Scottish king already contemplated rebellion against his oppressive taskmaster; and that what he thus surrendered so readily was scarcely his own to give, on account of the confiscation that was sure to follow of all his English possessions. Whatever may have been the suspicions of Edward to that effect he did not allow them to appear, but still continued to treat Baliol as a willing and subservient vassal. Having therefore laid an embargo on all ships within his English dominions, he required the same to be laid upon the Scottish ports, and to continue until further orders; he demanded reinforcements of Scottish troops for his expedition into Gascony; and he sent to the chief nobility of Scotland, requiring and commanding them, by their faith and homage as his vassals, to send their armed retainers to his banner. On receiving this message the Scottish parliament assembled at Scone—not, however, for the purpose of compliance, but to organize a decisive and open resistance. Their measures on this occasion were characterized by boldness and sagacity. Their first proceeding was to persuade their passive king to dismiss all those Englishmen who, either as visitors or as functionaries, resided at the Scottish court, and to do this under the pretext of economizing the public expenditure. Having thus rid themselves of troublesome spies, by whom their whole proceedings would be watched and reported, they appointed a committee for the regulation of national affairs, consisting of four bishops, four earls, and four barons, without whose advice and consent no public measure was to be transacted. Alarmed also at the facile character of Baliol, the English historians add that a watchful eye was kept upon all his motions, so that he was held in a sort of honourable captivity. But the most important as well as the most unfortunate of all these preparations for resistance was an alliance with France, the confirmed enemy of England, which was concluded at Paris on the 23d of October, 1295. By this treaty the King of Scots engaged to assist Philip le Bel in his wars, with all his power and at his own charges, and especially in the event of an invasion of France by the King of England. On the other hand Philip engaged, if Scotland was invaded by Edward, to assist the Scots either by making a diversion or sending supplies of men and money. It was further stipulated that neither sovereign was to conclude a peace with England separate from the other. To confirm these engagements Baliol's son and heir was to espouse the eldest daughter of the Count of Anjou, brother of Philip le Bel, while Baliol agreed not to contract a second marriage without the advice of the French king.

Although the English spies were removed from the Scottish court, and the negotiation with France was conducted by stealth, the aspect of Scottish affairs was sufficient to excite the suspicions of Edward. But Baliol, or probably the new regency acting in his name, endeavoured before the treaty was signed to quiet his doubts by offering to surrender into his keeping the castles of Berwick, Roxburgh, and Jedburgh during the continuance of the war between France and England, Edward engaging on his part to restore them when a peace should be concluded. When the time arrived that was judged fit for action, the Scots threw off the mask by invading England, according to the terms of their agreement with the French king. They entered Cumberland on the 26th of March, to the number, it is asserted by English historians, of 40,000 foot and 500 horse; but the proceedings of this mighty host soon showed the enervating effects of the long peace that had hitherto subsisted between the two countries. After the usual preliminaries of waste and havoc, they attacked Carlisle, which they succeeded in setting on fire; but while the townsmen were employed in quenching the flames, their wives flew to the walls, repelled the assailants, and forced them to retreat into Scotland. Even without giving full credence to this English story, it is evident that the expedition was unwise and contemptible. A few days after they renewed hostilities by an inroad into Northumberland, but their late campaign of forty-eight hours had taught them neither discipline nor valour, for after burning a nunnery and a monastery, they attacked the castle of Harbottle, from which they were beaten off with ease.

By these invasions Edward had obtained the opportunity he desired, and for which he had so diligently intrigued; he had now a pretext for accomplishing the utter subjugation of Scotland by force, while, in consequence of the divided state of the country, such a conquest promised to be an easy achievement. At the head of 30,000 foot and 4000 mounted men-at-arms, who had been trained in his continental wars, he advanced upon the eastern borders, being joined in his march by Anthony Beck, the warlike Bishop of Durham, with 1000 foot and 500 horse. The first operation was the siege of Berwick, which the Scots instead of surrendering to Edward, had strongly garrisoned and placed under the command of Sir William Douglas. This city, already distinguished by its commercial enterprise and wealth, so as to be called by the English themselves a second Alexandria, was not only a tempting prize, but had given offence by plundering several English vessels that had unsuspectingly entered the harbour at the commencement of the revolt. Ill fitted though the town was for resistance, being defended only by a dike, its inhabitants rejected Edward's summons to surrender, upon which he assailed it both by land and sea. The naval portion of this combined attack was unsuccessful; the townsmen and the garrison fell upon the ships, burned three of them, and drove the rest in a crippled condition out to sea. But Edward, who had carefully surveyed the ground, conducted the land attack with equal valour and skill, drove back the Scottish garrison, and, mounted upon his horse Bayard, was the first who leaped the dike. Berwick was entered and the work of massacre and plunder commenced, which was conducted with all the rancour of a newly kindled national hatred; neither age nor sex, neither church nor monastery, was spared. In this indiscriminate carnage the loss of life has been variously estimated, but it is probable that not less than 10,000 or 12,000 perished, while for two days the streets ran with blood. Amidst these horrors the fate of a body of Flemish merchants who resided in the town is worthy of especial notice. Their factory was a building called the Red-hall, which they occupied upon the tenure of defending it at all times against the English king. True not only to the spirit, but the very letter of their feudal engagements, these merchant-heroes, although only thirty in number, defended the Red-hall till night against the whole English army; and on the building being set on fire they still kept their post, and perished to a man in the flames. Alas for the fidelity of Scottish knights and nobles compared with these strangers and traffickers! Sir William Douglas, commander of the castle, and his garrison of 200 men, seeing the hopelessness of resistance, capitulated on the same day, and were allowed to march out with the honours of war, after making oath that they would never bear arms against England. From this terrible blow, which it sustained on the 30th of March (1296), Berwick never fully recovered.

After these events the war could no longer

be considered as the mere outbreak of a discontented party; the victorious enemy was in the midst of the country, and must be met by a united and national resistance. The measures of Baliol, therefore, or at least those which were adopted by the Scottish council in his name, were marked with boldness and decision, although they were too late to be availing. Decrees were issued that all English ecclesiastics who held benefices in Scotland should be expelled, and that all attached to the cause of England, or who remained neutral, should be visited with the penalties of treason. This last enactment was especially levelled against the party of Bruce, who hoped that the revolt of Baliol would elevate their own chief to the forfeited sovereignty. By the advice of his parliament, also, Baliol sent to the King of England a solemn and formal renunciation of his allegiance, with a statement of the causes on which this renunciation was founded. These were, that he, the King of Scotland, had been wantonly and upon frivolous causes summoned to the English court; that his estates in England had been seized; that his goods and the goods of his subjects had been spoliated; and that natives of Scotland had been forcibly carried off, and were still detained in England. He also declared that when he had remonstrated against these injuries, Edward, instead of redressing them, had only added to their amount, and was now wasting his kingdom with fire and sword. "Wherefore," the missive concluded, "I renounce the fealty and homage that have been extorted from me, and in defence of my kingdom bid defiance to Edward, King of England." When the messengers, who were Henry, Abbot of Arbroath, and three of his monks, arrived at the camp of Edward, they found him employed in constructing new fortifications to secure his tenure of the town of Berwick. The nature of the message, which he had provoked and doubtless expected, only filled him with contempt; and having hastily read it to the end, he exclaimed, "The senseless traitor! But since he will not come to us, we will go to him."

The invasion of Scotland, and the severities with which it was accompanied, provoked retaliation, and a counter invasion was made into England under the Earls of Menteith, Ross, and Athole. But wild though its devastation was over the districts of Redesdale and Tynedale, in which towns and villages were plundered and reduced to ashes, it was only a desperate foray to provoke and justify the vengeance of the conqueror. Edward advanced upon Dunbar, the gate of the Scottish kingdom on the side of England, of which he lately possessed the key; for a small garrison attached to his cause held the castle, while Patrick, Earl of Dunbar, was serving in his ranks. But the Countess of Dunbar, whose heart was wholly with her country, admitted the Scottish party within the walls, who ejected the adherents of Edward, and took possession of the town and castle in the name of Baliol. To recover this important place Edward sent Warrenne, Earl of Surrey, with 10,000 infantry and 1000 horse; and on being summoned to surrender, the Scottish garrison agreed to yield if not relieved within three days. The utmost efforts were made by the Scots to bring assistance within the limited period, and with such effect that 40,000 foot and 1500 horse were mustered upon the heights near Spot for the relief of Dunbar. The besieged exulted at the prospect, and cried to the enemy from the ramparts, "Now, you long-tailed English dogs, we will kill you all, and chop your tails off." Warrenne, resolving to attack this numerous enemy upon its own vantage ground, put his forces in motion; but the Scots, imagining that they detected signs of confusion in the march of the English ranks through a valley which they had to pass, and that they intended a retreat, came down from their heights in tumultuous array, as if to exterminate a flying enemy. But when too late they found their career arrested by a wall of brown bills and levelled spears, and a destructive shower of arrows. The battle that followed was brief; the Scots endeavoured to restore their broken ranks, but in vain; and after a confused fight they fled, with a loss of 10,000 in the battle and pursuit. Among the slain Sir Patrick de Graham, a Scottish baron, is particularly mentioned by an English historian,[1] as one of the wisest and noblest of his country, who, disdaining to ask for quarter, fought to the last with a valour that extorted the praise of his enemies. Among the prisoners were the Earls of Ross, Menteith, and Athole, with four barons and seventy knights, of whom the greater part were loaded by Edward with chains, and committed to close confinement in the castles of England and Wales. Attempts have been made to soften the shame of this defeat by attributing treachery to the leaders of the Scottish army; but its want of discipline and rash headlong confidence were of themselves sufficient to ensure its discomfiture. This terrible opening of the great drama of the Scottish and English wars was fated to have its ending at the same place and under similar circumstances, more than three centuries afterwards, when a Scottish army, advantageously posted at or very near these heights, rushed down upon Cromwell and his iron men,

---

[1] Hemingford.

in the fear that they would escape into England, and were chastised with an equally shameful defeat.

After this event, when the cause of Baliol was at the lowest ebb, the opportunity of the Bruces seemed to have arrived, in which their claims would be reconsidered and favourably accorded. To lull them into this delusion Edward had tampered with their patriotism and held out prospects, by which they were deterred from joining the cause of their countrymen; while, on the other hand, Baliol and his council had aggravated this neutrality into positive opposition by bestowing the rich lordship of Annandale, belonging to the son of the competitor, upon John Comyn, Earl of Buchan. This insult as well as injury drove the Lord of Annandale into the arms of Edward, his old fellow-crusader, who received him with a show of affectionate sympathy, and promised him the throne of Scotland, which his rival was now unworthy to hold; and allured with this prospect, Robert Bruce had not only repeated his oaths of homage to Edward, but had prevailed upon the Earls of March and Angus to do the like. He now reminded Edward of his promises, which the latter treated with contempt. "Have I no other business," he exclaimed, "than to conquer kingdoms for you?" Silenced and stung to the quick the disappointed noble retired. He saw that the coveted crown would never be his.

Edward now commenced avowedly and openly to conquer Scotland for himself; and as the kingdom was prostrated by the defeat at Dunbar his progress was rapid and triumphant. The castles of Roxburgh, Dumbarton, Edinburgh, and Stirling were surrendered to him almost as soon as they were summoned, while the Scottish nobility abjured the alliance with France, and tendered him their oaths of fealty. They saw that in the present case resistance could only be a dying struggle, as the English army had been reinforced by 15,000 men from Wales, and 30,000 from Ireland under the Earl of Ulster. Thus everywhere successful, and experiencing no check to his progress, Edward kept the feast of the nativity of John the Baptist at Perth, where the services of a religious festival were blended with the pageantries of a military triumph. It was in the midst of this revelry of feasting, mutual congratulation, and creation of new knights, that a mournful spectacle was seen, which only served to complete the pleasure of this joyous occasion. It was the utter humiliation of John Baliol, King of Scotland. He sent messengers to implore the mercy of the conqueror, and was ordered in reply to repair to the castle of Brechin, and there await the pleasure of his liege lord. Thither accordingly he went a few days after, to undergo such conditions as only a merciless enemy could impose. In the presence of the Bishop of Durham and the English barons he was divested of his royal robes, stripped of his crown and sceptre, and standing with a white rod in his hand, like a criminal before the assembly, he was compelled to make a confession of his manifold offences and acknowledge the justice of his punishment. He averred that, misled by evil counsellors, he had grievously offended against Edward his king. He acknowledged the errors of his government, and above all, the crime of which he had been guilty in forming an alliance with France, and making war upon England. He finally recognized the justice of Edward in visiting this rebellion with the severities of invasion. In this humbling pageant the King of England, as in many other instances, allowed his pride and his love of vengeance to overcome his policy. It was most unwise thus to displume a sovereign before his own hard-ruled and high-spirited rebellious barons; and this very spectacle, which they could not fail to treasure up in their memories, they afterwards re-enacted with fearful additions upon his own son, Edward II. Three days after this Baliol made a voluntary resignation of his crown, kingdom, and people into the hands of Edward, and gave up his eldest son Edward as a hostage for his future obedience, when he had been nominally a sovereign three years, seven months, and two days. After this cession both father and son were sent by sea to the Tower of London, where they were kept in captivity three years. The name of John became thenceforth one of evil signification in the royal family of Scotland, and was therefore carefully avoided, while the decisive epithet of *Toom-tabard*[1] was applied to Baliol himself, as if he had been nothing more than a herald's empty coat. The nickname was too well merited, not only by the showy promise of his reign compared with the unsubstantial reality, but by the mere pageant office which he was selected to fulfil, and the carelessness with which he was thrown aside when the play was ended. Such a king was best suited to the purposes of Edward upon Scotland.

Having thus displaced the nominal sovereign of the kingdom, and being armed with all the rights of conquest as well as his fabulous claims of feudal superiority, the English king now resolved to complete the work of subjugation and rule Scotland, without giving it any longer even a pretext of independence to cover the shame of its submission. He therefore proceeded

---

[1] *Toom* in Scotch is empty; it is the Icel. *tóm*, Dan. *tom*, empty.

northward in his military progress, receiving as he advanced the submission of both priests and nobles, and their abjuration of the French league, from which they had derived so little benefit, notwithstanding the high promises and professions of France. In this way he proceeded as far as Elgin in Morayshire without meeting the least resistance. Thus finding the whole country apparently subdued and submissive, he retraced his steps for the purpose of holding a parliament at Berwick; and, in passing the Abbey of Scone, he despoiled it of its famous prophetic stone on which the kings of Scotland were crowned, and sent it to Westminster Abbey as a proof and memorial of the full cession and conquest of Scotland.[1] Having thus treated the great palladium of its national independence, it was not to be supposed that he would be more lenient with its less venerated symbols; and accordingly the memory of Edward I., notwithstanding the attempts that have been made to clear it, will still continue, and perhaps justly, to be aspersed with the crime of mutilating or destroying the charters and historical documents in the Abbey of Scone that exposed the fallacy of his pretensions to the feudal sovereignty over Scotland. On arriving at Berwick he held a parliament on the 28th of August (1296), and there the priests, nobles, and gentry of Scotland, hitherto so divided among themselves and so unfitted for a united effort when the moment of trial had arrived, were unanimous in their submission to the conqueror. Their subscriptions to the oaths of homage to the King of England as their liege lord, and their abandonment of the French alliance, covered thirty-five skins of parchment, and under the name of Ragman Rolls are still preserved among the archives of London. Among these names we might probably have found that of Robert Bruce, the competitor; but, more fortunate than his successful rival, Baliol, he had died in the preceding year. The name, however, of his son, Robert Bruce, Earl of Carrick, whose appeal Edward had so contemptuously rejected after the battle of Dunbar, is to be found in that roll, and so would also that of Robert Bruce, the future liberator and king have been, but that he was still a minor, although already acting by commission under the King of England in tranquillizing the districts of Carrick and Annandale.

The other measures adopted by Edward for the government of the subjugated country, now that this was accomplished, were both wise and clement. He ordered the lands of the clergy that had been confiscated at the commencement of the war to be restored to them. The widows of those Scottish barons whose husbands had died before the French alliance were put in possession of their jointure lands on their promise of fealty to him as sovereign of the kingdom. He even appointed decent pensions for the wives of several who had risen in arms against him, and were now his prisoners. With the exception of the government of the more dangerous districts, and the custody of castles and places of strength, most of those persons who had held office under Baliol were continued in their charges. The Scottish prelates were also conciliated by his granting to them the privilege of bequeathing their effects by will, "in the same manner as that privilege was enjoyed by the archbishops and bishops in England." For the future government of the country Edward appointed John Warrenne, Earl of Surrey, and victor at Dunbar, to the office of Guardian of Scotland, Hugh de Cressingham to be Treasurer, and William Ormesby, Justiciary, while the four principal strengths of the kingdom, which were the castles of Edinburgh, Berwick, Roxburgh, and Jedburgh, were placed under the keeping of trustworthy English commanders, with well-appointed English garrisons.

Satisfied with these arrangements Edward returned to England; and, suspecting no further trouble from Scotland, he turned his attention to France and the recovery of his continental possessions. But the expense of the late Scottish invasion had impoverished his exchequer, and when he demanded fresh supplies for the prosecution of the French war his application was met by his parliament with discontented murmurs, and by his chief barons with a flat refusal. In the midst of these embarrassments, while the clergy were withholding from him their money and the nobles their military attendance, and when the general discontent seemed ripening into open revolt, alarming tidings reached him from Scotland that more than doubled his perplexity. The people, whom he had not taken into account when he received the submission of their nobles, had risen of their own accord against their English governors— were plundering the lands of his adherents, attacking the castles he had garrisoned, and defeating his veteran soldiers in several bloody encounters. These, indeed, which at first were but riots, and as such might have been quickly extinguished, were daily growing into a great national rebellion which armies and years might be insufficient to suppress; for a master-spirit was at their head. Sir William Wallace had already entered upon his divine mission—the mission of setting his country free.

---

[1] Et hoc in signum regni conquesti et resignati.—Walsingham.

CHAPTER III.

RESISTANCE TO EDWARD I. UNDER WILLIAM WALLACE (1296-1298).

Sir William Wallace—Commencement of his patriotic career—He kills the sheriff of Lanark—Successful exploits of Wallace—He is joined by several of the nobles—Their envy of Wallace and secession from his standard—Wallace defeats the English at Stirling—He recovers the castles and expels the English from Scotland—Wallace invades England—Summons Newcastle to surrender—Protects the monks of Hexham—He is appointed Guardian of Scotland—His strict and able government—Difficulties of Edward I.—He invades Scotland—Plan of defence adopted by Wallace—Military operations of Edward in Scotland—Battle of Falkirk and defeat of Wallace.

Sir William Wallace, who now appears upon the scene, was the second son of Sir Malcolm Wallace of Ellerslie, near Paisley. At what period the family had settled in that part of Scotland is unknown, and it appears also to have lived unnoticed until the exploits of the national champion gave it an imperishable name in history. As Sir Malcolm, his father, belonged to the lower order of barons who owed nothing to England, and whom Edward had overlooked after the ready submission of their superiors, Sir William belonged to that class of the Scottish population which was most alive to sentiments of national liberty and best fitted to maintain it. The boyhood and youth of Sir William Wallace were chiefly passed with his uncle, a wealthy priest at Dunipace, in Stirlingshire, by whom he was imbued with a greater portion of learning than was commonly imparted to the rude young squires of the period;[1] and his education, thus auspiciously commenced, was afterwards improved and matured in the schools of Dundee. Thus early prepared by mental training for command and leadership during a period of anarchy and oppression, he also possessed in an eminent degree those personal qualifications without which mere intellectual superiority would have remained unrecognized. His stature, which was almost gigantic, at once announced and claimed pre-eminence over the common herd; his strength was commensurate with his stature, so that his personal prowess, which kindled the emulation and inspired the confidence of his followers, was a banner around which despair itself could rally; while his powers of hardy endurance in every change rose superior to the dangers, fatigues, and privations of that arduous self-denying career to which his whole life was devoted. Thus has the rude poetry of Henry the Minstrel described the Scottish Achilles of the thirteenth century; and the deeds of Wallace, as they are recorded by the veritable historian, completely authenticate the description of the poet. And it is thus, and thus only, that he still passes before the enthusiastic fancy of his countrymen as a glorious living reality, while nothing but the names of his contemporaries have survived.

Circumstanced as Scotland was at this period, any accidental spark was enough to kindle such a spirit as that of Wallace into a flame; and a street brawl in the town of Lanark was the commencement of his patriotic course. He was walking peacefully along when certain English soldiers of the garrison, who had marked him for some time with no friendly eye, accosted him with insulting language and made a pull at his sword as if he had no right to wear one. After a short and sharp dialogue Wallace drew, and so bravely bestirred himself that more than one assailant bit the dust. He would soon have been overpowered in that unequal conflict but for the affection of his mistress,[2] who, as he retreated fighting, threw open her door and gave him shelter, and afterwards, on their forcing their way into the apartment, secured his escape by a private passage, and delayed the pursuers until he had safely reached the neighbouring greenwood. This outbreak alarmed Hislop,[3] the English sheriff; and as the culprit was beyond his reach, he revenged the injury upon the affectionate woman by putting her to death. So unmanly and cold-blooded a murder was followed by swift retribution. Wallace in

---

[1] We are told that a Latin lesson which the young hero learned from his uncle, and never afterwards forgot, was the following leonine verses, which he often delighted to repeat:—
"Dico tibi verum, Libertas optima rerum,
Nunquam servili sub nexu vivito, fili."

Of these lines Monipennie has given the following translation:—
"My sonne (I say) Freedom is best,
Then never yield to thrall's arrest."

[2] The old tradition, which is worthy of credit, makes her the wife of Wallace, and states that her maiden name was Bradfute.

[3] Also called Heselrig by the old historians.

WALLACE, ATTACKED BY LORD PERCY'S FOLLOWERS
WHILE FISHING IN IRVINE WATER, DEFENDS HIMSELF WITH HIS NET POLE, AS TOLD BY
HENRY THE MINSTREL (circa A.D. 1274)

the greenwood was soon at the head of thirty men who, like himself, burned with indignation at the oppressors, and were ready at every hazard to turn upon them. At midnight he led his band into the town to assail the murderer in his place of strength; he burst open the door of the lodging in which the sheriff slept; and on that functionary starting up in bed and asking who was there, he received the terrible answer, "It is I, William Wallace, come to requite thee for the deed of yesterday!" Seizing Hislop by the throat, he dragged him down the stairs and slew him in the open street, where his soldiers might have heard his outcries, and, if they so pleased, have attempted a rescue.

This daring deed, which made Wallace a fugitive and an outlaw, and compelled him to find his home among forests and mountain-caves, also made him an open avowed patriot, the leader of a gallant troop, and finally the general of a victorious army. At first his exploits were confined to petty skirmishes and a shifting guerrilla warfare; but in these his military sagacity, personal valour, and unfailing success were so distinguished that public attention was aroused, and those who hitherto despaired for their country were now encouraged to hope. Not only many a patriotic spirit also, but many a desperado proscribed by the laws of both countries, and whose only safety could be found among the armed ranks of insurrection, repaired to this flying camp; and in a short time Wallace was at the head of a strange miscellaneous assemblage whose deeds as well as motives could not always sustain a rigid inquest. But his power of harmonizing and directing the movements of such discordant materials, of pervading them with one generous heroic purpose, and inspiring them with such confidence against an enemy from whom they had lately fled in abject terror, speak strongly of his fitness for command, and this especially when his years are taken into account. For he was still little more than a stripling when gray-haired outlaws and distinguished veterans elected him to the difficult and dangerous office of leader. Circumstances favourable to the insurrection were also to be found in the character of the English rulers and the nature of their government. Warrenne, whose military talents at least appear to have been of a high order, had been obliged on account of ill health to retire to the north of England when his presence was most needed. Hugh de Cressingham, the treasurer, although a priest, was more attached to military than ecclesiastical studies, and in consequence of this unholy apostasy from his sacred calling was a presumptuous, blundering, and ignorant soldier, and a selfish tyrannical clergyman, whose rochet the people hated and despised more than they feared his corselet. As for Ormesby, the justiciary, whose especial charge was to exact the oath of fealty to the King of England from the lesser barons and commons, and punish the recusants, he discharged his odious duty with such despotic severity as made the people at large fully conscious of their bondage and impatient for deliverance.

In the meantime Wallace, whose successful exploits rang far and wide, and whose following was daily augmented, at length received a powerful accession in Sir William Douglas, who joined him with a large array of military retainers. Sir William had commanded the garrison of Berwick when it was besieged by the English, and on the surrender of the town had been allowed to depart on swearing fealty to Edward. As Surrey and Cressingham had repaired to England to attend the parliament, leaving the whole charge of affairs in the hands of Ormesby, Wallace and Douglas resolved to attack the justiciary while thus unsupported by his more able associates. Accordingly they marched to Scone, where he was holding a justice-court, with such celerity that his military followers were surprised and routed, and himself all but taken prisoner. Animated by this victory and enriched with its spoils, the insurgents no longer confined themselves to guerrilla operations, but made war in open fashion, at first by dispossessing the English in the open country, and afterwards by laying siege to the castles.[1] In this manner, while Wallace swept the country to the west and advanced into Lennox, Douglas took the castles of Sanquhar and Disdeir. Their cause, indeed, was now so promising that some of the most powerful of the Scottish nobility ventured to join it, the chief of whom were the Steward of Scotland and his brother; Alexander de Lindesay, Sir Richard Lundin, and the best and truest of them all, Sir Andrew Moray of Bothwell. To these were added the politic head and wise counsels of Robert Wishart, Bishop of Glasgow. A still more important adherent soon followed; this was Robert Bruce, grandson of the competitor and future King of Scotland, whose proceedings as yet had been marked by little else than youthful thoughtlessness and irresolution. For this, however, not only his tender years might have formed some apology, and the vacillating selfish examples afforded by his father and grandfather, but also his English descent which he shared in common with most of the nobility of Scotland. But his power and

---

[1] Hemingford.

influence were of immense consequence; for in right of his mother, the Countess of Carrick, and by the concession of his father, who was Lord of Annandale, his possessions extended from the Frith of Clyde to the Solway. Aware of the uncertain tenure of his allegiance and the dangerous example that would be given by his secession, the English guardians of Scotland resolved to assure themselves of his fidelity; and for this purpose they summoned him to attend at Carlisle on a certain day, there to consult with them for the interests of the king, provided he still recognized their king as his sovereign.[1] The young Bruce complied with the mandate enforced by such a test of obedience, and he swore fealty to Edward and truth and vigilance to the utmost in his service, upon a consecrated host and upon the holy sword of St. Thomas à Becket. Eager to prove his sincerity, he then invaded the estate of Sir William Douglas, which he wasted with fire and sword, and carried off his wife and children prisoners. But repentance quickly followed; he was impatient to recant his apostasy; and having assembled the men of Annandale, he tried to lead them over to the ranks of the insurgents, declaring that the oath of homage had been extorted from him through fear and by violence; that although he had uttered it with his lips, he had not taken it in his heart; and that now he repented of it, and, as he hoped, would soon be absolved from it. But the men of Annan were the vassals of his father, who was now with Edward in England; and on their refusal to compromise the safety of their lord, young Bruce collected his own feudal retainers and went over to the party of Wallace.[2]

These events had followed so rapidly and had matured so quickly into a national revolt that Edward could not believe the tidings when they reached him; and he despatched Anthony Beck, his favourite bishop, northward to learn the real state of matters, or if he could, to extinguish the rebellion. But the warlike prelate, on crossing the Scottish border, found the insurrection so formidable that his report astonished and irritated Edward, who was ready to embark for Flanders, after having overcome the opposition of his own subjects, and extorted their consent to a continental war. To stay the expedition was impossible; and he thought that this outbreak of the Scots might be easily suppressed, as their principal nobles were in his custody, either as feudal attendants or prisoners; he therefore ordered Warrenne to muster the whole military force north of the Trent, suppress the revolt in Scotland at once, and inflict due chastisement upon its leaders. He also sent the two Comyns, John Earl of Buchan, and John Lord of Badenoch, into the north, to recall the people to their allegiance. Surrey, whose remissness in England during the progress of late events even the plea of sickness can scarcely explain, now bestirred himself in earnest; and having mustered his forces at York, he sent 40,000 foot and 300 mounted men-at-arms into Scotland under the command of Henry Percy, his nephew. The invaders entered Annandale on the 10th of August (1297), and encamped at Lochmaben in full security. But their motions had been watched, and at midnight they were attacked by such a furious onset of the Scots that they only escaped the fatal effects of a surprise by setting fire to the wooden houses, and fighting by the light of the flames. In this way they were able to form their ranks and drive back the enemy, after which they marched to Ayr to receive the Gallowegians into the king's peace. So strong, however, was the spirit of revolt in that quarter that only a few knights tendered the required submission.

While the progress of the invaders was so unsatisfactory, tidings came to Percy that the Scottish army was within four miles of his quarters and ready to give him battle, upon which he advanced to the neighbourhood of Irvine, where he found them drawn up on the border of a small loch. Their numbers were nearly equal to his own, and with them was Wallace, who was worth whole armies; but he was no longer the leader whom all were ready to obey and proud to follow. The late acquisitions of the high-born and noble who had flocked to his standard, instead of strengthening, had only weakened the cause of national liberty; for, while each contended for pre-eminence over his fellows, all were united in refusing to have for their leader a man who, however brave and fortunate, was but the son of a private knight, and a mere man of the people. It was upon the banks of that little lake near Irvine that the evil first distinctly manifested itself, which was for ages to prove the bane and the political curse of Scotland. With an enemy in front of them, all was feud, faction, and quarrel, so that they were unfit either to give battle or to retreat; and on seeing the hopeless state of matters, Sir Richard Lundin, one of the bravest and most experienced of their warriors, went over to the enemy, exclaiming, that he would no longer fight by the side of those who were divided and at variance among themselves.[3] His departure was an evil prestige to the cause

---

[1] "Tractaturus cum eis de negotiis regis, si tamen in fide ipsius regis perseverando maneret."—Hemingford.
[2] Hemingford.

[3] Hemingford.

of Scottish liberty, for hitherto he had refused allegiance to the King of England, and now only submitted in utter despair. His example was as the beginning of the letting out of water, for Bruce, the Steward of Scotland, and his brother; Alexander de Lindesay, Sir William Douglas, and the Bishop of Glasgow immediately opened a negotiation with the enemy, went over to them with all their followers, and subscribed themselves once more the vassals of England. Of all the men of rank who had lately joined the young champion of Scotland none remained with him but Sir Andrew Moray of Bothwell. Unable to give battle after these desertions, and scorning every proposal to surrender, Wallace drew off with his own well-tried veterans, and resumed that flying warfare which the professed aid of the barons had only interrupted. Nor was his cause so hopeless as it appeared. He had already won for himself a nobility of his own in the hearts of the common people which no titles could impart; and even the affections and wishes of the military vassals of the nobles were with him, though their presence and services were on the adverse side.[1]

In the meantime the condition of the apostate nobles, who had maintained their pride of place at such a ransom, was far from enviable. In their instrument of treaty with Lord Percy they had confessed their treasonable offences, such as "burning, slaying, and committing divers robberies" in Galloway and Scotland; and on their supplication had been once more received to Edward's mercy; but the first brunt of danger being over, they found themselves suspected persons, and treated as mere prisoners at large. Such was especially the case with Robert Bruce, whose submission and oaths, after those he had taken at Carlisle had been so readily violated, were now of such little account, that, in addition to these, his infant daughter, Marjory, was required of him as a hostage for his sincerity. Even yet, also, they endeavoured to make a stand upon the ground of patriotism, by withholding the pledges of their future submission until certain reservations they had made in the treaty for the rights of their country should be complied with; but by the act of making these very reservations they had completely deprived themselves of the power of enforcing them. Their shallow compromise, as is usually the case in a question of national and vital interest, had lost them the confidence of the party they forsook, without winning that of their new allies, and this the unfortunate Bishop of Glasgow was soon fated to experience. He had negotiated the treaty of surrender; and upon the demur of his associates, he had repaired to Roxburgh, and given himself up unconditionally as a prisoner; but Edward treated him harshly, under the pretext that he was still a traitor in his heart, and that he had only repaired to Roxburgh to betray its castle to the Scots. On the other hand, Wallace, incensed at the bishop's treachery, attacked his house, plundered it of its stores, arms, and horses, and carried off his sons, who lived with him under the decent name of nephews.[2]

It is not impossible that this surrender of the insurgent Scottish nobles acted as favourably for the cause of their forsaken country as their stoutest resistance could have done. In the latter case Edward, foregoing his intended campaign to Flanders, would have brought his whole military force to bear upon the more important acquisition of Scotland, and thus the new-born patriotism of the people would have been overwhelmed and crushed at the outset. But now that the nobles had forsaken it, it could be nothing more than a mob-riot of contemptible undisciplined villains, whom the onset of a few knights would suffice to scatter to the wind. Thus Edward must have calculated; and according to the feudal reckoning of the period, his conclusion was sound. Even in Wallace, too, a mere Robin Hood of outlaws, who had neither years, nor rank, nor military name according to the reports that must have reached him, he could never expect to find a greater king of the people, and more formidable military antagonist than his old opponent, the Earl of Leicester. Edward, therefore, without pausing for a moment in preparations for his war in Flanders, where leaders of high name were to be encountered and knightly deeds achieved, made hasty arrangements at his departure for the extinction of these Scottish disturbances. He liberated the more doubtful of the Scottish barons who had been taken prisoners at Dunbar, and restored their forfeited lands, on condition of their serving with him in Flanders, and leaving their eldest sons in England as hostages. Others of the nobles, in whom he had more confidence, he allowed to return to their country, on promising to assist his officers in suppressing the rebellion. He also detached as many of the troops as he could spare from the continental expedition to join the northern army which was to act against the Scots. But to crown all these prudential measures by a great political blunder,

---

[1] Such is the confession of Hemingford even when he is speaking most bitterly of "ille latro Willelmus Wallays." His words are: "Tota etiam familia magnatum adhærebat ei, et licet ipsi magnates cum rege nostro essent corpore, cor tamen eorum longe erat ab eo."

[2] "Filios etiam episcopi, nepotum nomine nuncupatos, secum adduxit."—Hemingford.

he deprived Warrenne of the office of Governor of Scotland on account of the dilatoriness of his proceedings in suppressing the rebellion, while he continued him in the principal command of that army upon which the fresh conquest and subjugation of Scotland was mainly to depend.

It is unfortunate that we have no certain account of the exploits of Wallace for a few months after this treaty of Irvine, and when he was thrown upon his original resources; but that they were sufficiently brilliant as well as successful is evident from the fact that he had taken the castles of Forfar, Brechin, and Montrose, and expelled the English from most of the places they had garrisoned northward of the Forth. He was now besieging the castle of Dundee, when he heard that the English army was advancing upon Stirling; upon which, charging the citizens of Dundee upon pain of death to continue the blockade of the castle, he drew off his forces, and by a rapid march advanced upon Stirling, with the ground of which he was well acquainted, to secure a fit position for his army. The place he selected for giving battle was admirably chosen, being a rising ground on the Forth above the Abbey of Cambuskenneth, and with full command of the passage of the river; and having secured these advantages before the arrival of the English, Wallace, at the head of 40,000 foot and 180 horse, awaited the issue of what was probably his first pitched battle upon a large scale. The English soon appeared, and in greater force than the Scots, independently of their superior equipments; for they numbered in their ranks 50,000 foot and 1000 well-armed horse. They might have advanced indeed in still greater array, as Lord Henry Percy had hastened from Carlisle towards Stirling to join them with 8000 foot and 300 horse, but for the parsimony and vanity of Cressingham, who ordered these troops to be disbanded on the plea that their maintenance would be an additional expense, and that their aid was not needed. This was not the only evil omen under which the English approached the place of conflict. The Earl of Lennox, with the Steward of Scotland and other Scottish lords who had seceded from Wallace and were now in the enemy's camp, requested Surrey to halt for a short space while they should negotiate with their countrymen, to prevent useless resistance and bloodshed. This was granted; but they soon found their mission hopeless, upon which they promised at their return to the English quarters that they would come back to the camp on the following day with a reinforcement of sixty horsemen. On their departure at evening with their armed train they met on their way a foraging party of English soldiers; an affray commenced between the two bands, and in the skirmish the Earl of Lennox drove his sword through an English soldier's throat. The whole English camp was in commotion as soon as the tidings reached them; the soldiers ran to their arms, declaring that the Scottish barons had betrayed them and formed a compact with their insurgent countrymen; and in proof of this they pointed to their bleeding companion, whom they carried before Warrenne. "Contain yourselves for this night," said the earl, "and if to-morrow they do not fulfil their promises we shall exact the greater vengeance." To pacify their impatience he also issued orders that all should be in readiness to cross the Bridge of Stirling on the following day.[1]

Early on the next morning a body of more than 5000 English infantry and a great number of Welsh crossed the bridge; but on finding themselves unsupported by the rest of the army, they returned to their camp, where the Earl of Surrey, their commander, was still asleep. An hour afterwards he rose; but, instead of proceeding to action, he conferred the honour of knighthood upon several young chivalrous aspirants, some of whom were not destined to live till sunset. He then ordered the bridge to be passed, but speedily revoked the order, because the Scottish barons, with their promised reinforcement of sixty horse, had not arrived; and when they came at last it was without their followers, and only to announce that their efforts to treat with the Scottish army had been in vain — that they could withdraw from their ranks neither horse nor horseman.[2] On looking across the river and marking the encampment of the Scots, Surrey appears for the first time to have discovered the strength of their position and the danger of attacking it, so that he had recourse to negotiation; and he sent two preaching friars of Cambuskenneth to propose terms of peaceable surrender. "Return to your employers," cried Wallace to the messengers, "and tell them that we are here not to treat about safety, but prepared for battle, and to set our country free. Let them then come hither when they please, and they shall find us ready to meet them beard to beard."[3] This answer raised the resentment of the English army to fury. "Let us march upon them," they cried; "they defy us!" and a headlong onset would have instantly been ordered had not Sir Richard Lundin interposed. "My lords," said that prudent warrior to the English leaders, "if we

---
[1] Hemingford.
[2] "Dicentes, se non posse ab eis eripere nec equos nec arma."—Hemingford.
[3] "Nos paratos invenient etiam in barbas eorum."—Hemingford.

cross the bridge we are dead men. See ye not that we cannot enter upon it except two by two, while the enemy commands our flank and can be upon us when they please in full force. But there is a ford not far off, where we can cross sixty abreast. Give me then 500 horse and a small body of foot, with which I will attack them in the rear and throw them into confusion, while you, lord earl, and the rest can meanwhile cross the bridge in full security." To this wise advice, which might have saved the English army, Cressingham the treasurer interposed a haughty negative. "Lord earl, it is not right," he impatiently exclaimed, "to spend further time, or waste the king's money to no purpose: let us attack the enemy at once, and do our devoir as we are bound to do."

In an evil hour Surrey consented. He had already been superseded for remissness, and his prudent delay on the present occasion might be liable to a similar charge. He therefore gave the word to cross that narrow bridge whose danger Lundin had not exaggerated. And the fact is marvellous to tell, as well as the fearful result, exclaims the old historian,[1] how so many and such prudent men crowded upon a bridge where scarcely two could ride together, and when they knew that the enemy were in readiness to receive them! The van was led by Sir Marmaduke Twenge, a brave knight and skilful leader, and joined with him in command was the presumptuous Cressingham. When about half of the English army had defiled along the narrow passage, in which they occupied several hours, Wallace, who had kept his ranks in quiet until a sufficient number were within his reach, wheeled round a body of spearmen, who took possession of the foot of the bridge and barred all further communication between the two portions of the severed army. Twenge, ignorant of this movement, by which support or retreat were equally prevented, and impatient for battle, rushed up the heights to assail the Scots; but this impetuous movement threw his ranks into disorder; they were assailed, broken, and thrown down the hill; and when driven back to the bridge, they discovered when too late that their only hope of safety was in possession of the Scots. Seeing the infantry dispersed and cut down, and his heavily-armed horsemen plunging into the river in the vain attempt to reach the opposite side, Sir Marmaduke Twenge was advised by his attendants to follow their example; but he indignantly replied, "It never shall be said of me that I consented to be drowned. Follow me, and I will open your way to the bridge!" Exerting his utmost prowess, he struck down his enemies to right and left, cleared for himself a passage through the press, and reached the opposite side, carrying his nephew with him, whom he had rescued when thrown down and wounded, and followed by his armour-bearer. But Cressingham was not equally fortunate, being slain at the commencement of the encounter. It would be difficult to tell whether he was most hated by his own countrymen whom his arrogance had offended, or by the Scots whom his tyranny had oppressed. The contumelies which the latter inflicted on his body have been magnified into the absurd story that his skin was converted into saddles or horse-girths. Even the modified report that Wallace made of it a sword-belt is scarcely worthy of admission, when we remember how useless such a belt would have been to sustain the weight of a two-handed sword.

In the meantime Surrey from the opposite bank saw half of his fine army destroyed at a blow without power to interpose. He even seems to have forgot the ford in the neighbourhood mentioned by Lundin through which he might have sent a rescue, or perhaps have renewed the battle and done all that a brave man might and ought. He appears, indeed, to have been utterly stunned and deprived of all power of judging. To add to his perplexity, the Earl of Lennox, the steward, and other Scottish barons, who had been watching the tide of events, were now able to find the promised troops which at morning had not been forthcoming; and with a band of their armed followers they fell upon the scattered Englishmen and gathered abundance of spoil. Seeing that all was lost, and apprehending that the Scots would cross the river, the earl ordered the bridge to be destroyed and charged Twenge to occupy Stirling Castle, with the promise that in ten days he would return to his relief. His only purpose, however, seems to have been to escape out of Scotland, and to effect this he spurred with such unknightly haste to Berwick that when he alighted at the monastery of the Minorites his steed, on being stabled, was too exhausted to eat. Such was the crowning close of the victory of Stirling, fought on the 11th of September, 1297. Of the English at least 25,000 must have fallen, as the Scots took few prisoners; and the plunder was so abundant that many wagons were filled with it. Independently, however, of its moral effect in elevating the hopes and confirming the resistance of the Scots, this victory was attended with immediate political consequences of the utmost importance. Dundee immediately surrendered. The castles of Edinburgh and Roxburgh were dismantled, and Berwick was aban-

---

[1] Hemingford.

doned by its English garrison. Over the whole land not a single stronghold was retained for Edward, and Scotland was completely free. All this, too, had been achieved in a few months by a young chieftain of outlaws and fugitives, who had not only the ablest king and best soldiers of Europe, but also the nobility of his own country, arrayed against him. His success also at Stirling was accompanied with the gratifying thought that it had been effected with little loss to his own army, if we except the death of the brave and patriotic Sir Andrew Moray of Bothwell, who was mortally wounded in the engagement.

After this victory a severe famine succeeded in Scotland, in consequence of the neglect of tillage during the period of strife and insecurity. As the maintenance of his army was of the utmost consequence Wallace, instead of disbanding his troops, resolved to quarter them upon the resources of the north of England, and thus weaken the enemy, while he spared the destitution of his own countrymen. The movement was to be made upon a great national scale instead of being a common inroad; and on this occasion Wallace associated with himself in command the young Sir Andrew Moray of Bothwell, the son of him who had fallen in the battle of Stirling. The great difficulty of Wallace on this occasion arose from the principle of feudal obedience; the vassals of those nobles who were with Edward, or in the interest of England, refused to repair to his standard; and he was obliged to have recourse to such severe modes of impressment as the state of the times and the necessity justified. He accordingly ordered every county, barony, town, and village to send him a certain proportion of their fighting men between the ages of sixteen and sixty; and to enforce compliance he caused gibbets to be erected in each barony and county town on which those who disobeyed were to be hanged. To show that this was no idle threat, several burgesses of Aberdeen who refused to repair to the muster were in this manner executed. By these stringent measures a larger Scottish army was raised than had ever yet invaded England; and on entering Northumberland the inhabitants fled with their wives, children, goods, and cattle, and took refuge in Newcastle and the inland provinces. After halting for a while, and thinking that the enemy had retired, the fugitives ventured to return to their homes; but the Scots, who had only waited for the opportunity, made a rapid avance from their headquarters in the forest of Rothebury, swept the counties of Cumberland and Northumberland, and made booty of all that had been brought back. In this manner the invading bands issued from their lair in the forest, moving wherever they pleased, and finding none to oppose them. "During this time," says the English historian of the period,[1] "the praise of God ceased in all the churches and monasteries of the whole province from Newcastle-upon-Tyne even to Carlisle, for all the monks, the canons regular, and other priests, the servants of the Lord, with all the people, had fled from the face of the Scots; and thus the Scots continued to lay waste with burning and plundering from the festival of St. Luke (18th of October) even to the festival of St. Martin (11th of November), and there were none to oppose them except certain of our men in garrison at Alnwick and other fortified places, who sometimes sallied out and killed a few stragglers." Thus strangely had the tide of victory and desolation rolled backward from Scotland into England. And merciless, indeed, must that invasion have been in which neither monk nor priest could be assured of his safety!

For eight days after the festival of Saint Martin the Scottish array continued to advance, destroying all in their progress till they came to the city of Carlisle, which was strongly fortified. They summoned it to surrender by a priest, who delivered his message in the following terms: "My master, William the Conqueror, charges you that, having due regard to your lives, you surrender to him your town and castle without resistance or bloodshed, for which he will give you immunity in life, limb, and cattle; but if you refuse he will forthwith assail you and put you to the sword." "Who is this conqueror?" "He is William, whom you call Wallace," replied the envoy. They refused to surrender a trust which they had received from their king, and defied the leader of the Scots to do his worst. "Tell him," they added, "if he wishes to win the town, to come and attack it in the fashion of a right conqueror, when, if he is able, he may win city and castle and all." After this answer of defiance and contempt they bent their ballistas and other warlike engines to welcome the expected assailants. Instead of spending time in an unprofitable siege for which his army was not provided, Wallace turned his course to the forest of Inglewood and laid waste the country from Allerdale in Cumberland to Derwentwater and Cockermouth. He then resolved to invade the county of Durham, which was so slightly guarded at this time that it could only muster about 3000 foot and 100 horse; but according to the old English historians Saint Cuthbert himself was at hand to defend his own sacred patrimony, and raised such a tempest

---

[1] Hemingford.

of hail, snow, and frost that many of the Scots perished from cold and hunger. Independently, indeed, of the guardian saint of Durham, winter had set in, and with such unwonted severity that it was time for the Scots, who had effected their purposes, to commence their retreat. On their return to Hexham they found at the monastery three canons, who after the first hostile visit of the invaders had ventured to come back to their cloisters and were repairing the ruined oratory. Brandishing their long lances, the foremost of the Scots rushed into this violated sanctuary, exclaiming, "Show us the treasury of your church or you shall instantly die!" "Alas!" replied one of the old men, trembling, "it is not long since you and your people carried off all we had; you best know where you have laid it up; since that time we have only gathered the few things which you see before you." At this moment Wallace entered; and sternly checking the rude soldiers, he requested one of the canons to celebrate mass. This was done; but before the host was elevated, Wallace, who was completely armed, retired that he might wash his hands and lay aside his helmet and weapons before receiving the sacred emblems. His momentary departure was the signal for fresh violence; his wild followers snatched the chalice from the altar, spoiled it of its ornaments, and even stole the missal with which the service had been commenced. At his return Wallace, shocked at the profanation, ordered the plunderers to be searched out and executed; "but they were not found," adds Hemingford, "for the search that was made was a dissembled one." "Abide with me," he then said to the trembling monks, "and do not leave my side, for there only you can be safe; my people are evil-doers whom I can neither justify nor punish." They were indeed evil-doers when they had plundered a monastery dedicated to Saint Andrew, the patron of Scotland, and chartered by David, the best of its kings! Still further to ensure the safety of the brotherhood, Wallace, in the name of Sir Andrew Moray and himself as joint-leaders of the Scottish army, granted a charter of protection to the monastery, by which all its members and property were admitted under the peace of the King of Scotland, and all persons prohibited from doing them injury. Having thus wasted the northern districts during more than three weeks without opposition, Wallace led back his army into Scotland.

The English attempted a reprisal by an invasion of Scotland in turn, and for this purpose Lord Robert Clifford, having collected 20,000 infantry and 100 horse, advanced into Annandale. But nothing was achieved by such formidable numbers which might not have been effected by a mere band of Border freebooters, in consequence of the blunder of Lord Clifford, who on crossing the Solway made proclamation that every soldier should plunder for himself and retain what booty he might find. Through this rash license the whole army was broken into loose bands of marauders and scattered over the country, intent on nothing but spoil, while none kept together except the small troop of 100 horsemen. The paltry result of this expedition was that they burned ten hamlets, killed 308 inhabitants of Annandale, and carried off a few captives. These exploits were so much to the taste of Lord Clifford that soon after he repeated his inroad, and with similar success, for he plundered and burned the town of Annan and the church of Gysborne, and carried off a few captives. But the only effect of these injuries was to irritate Robert Bruce, the Lord of Annandale, and drive him once more from the cause of England into the ranks of the patriots.

The victories of Sir William Wallace, his successful expedition into England, and the prospect of a long and arduous struggle to secure the national liberty which he had so bravely recovered, all pointed him out as the only man fitted for the supreme command until order could be effectually restored; and such appears to have been the general popularity as well as strength of this conviction that the jealous nobles were compelled to acquiesce or be silent. As far, therefore, as can be discovered or surmised in such a doubtful matter as the tenure on which Wallace held that office of regency upon which he acted after his return from England, he appears to have been invested with it in the earlier part of the year 1298, and at a national assembly held at the Forest Kirk in Selkirkshire. Several of the principal nobility attended, among whom are mentioned the Earl of Lennox and Sir William Douglas; and there he was solemnly invested in office with the title of "Governor of Scotland, in name of King John and by the consent of the Scottish nation."[1] Let the secret murmurings of the envious be what they might, it appears to have been a national election as well as a most urgent national necessity; and he assumed office under the name of that only sovereign whom the kingdom as yet recognized, and as whose lieutenant he had already levied armies and granted letters of protection. On becoming guardian of the realm by legal election Wallace was resolved that the stern duties of his invidious office should be properly exercised both in the

---

[1] Anderson's *Diplomata Scotiæ*, No. 44; Fordun; Crawford's *History of the Douglases*, quoted by Sir R. Sibbald.

suppression of offenders and the military defence of the kingdom. One of his first acts was to exercise his vice-regal authority by appointing Alexander Skrymgeour or Skirmishur, the Royal Standard-bearer of Scotland, to the important office of Constable of Dundee. He laboured to check the wild license of his soldiers, and improve them by military discipline. To place the whole kingdom in a defensible condition and have troops in readiness for any sudden call, he divided it into military districts, in which every serviceable man between the age of sixteen and sixty was enrolled, and obliged to attend the summons whether for war or muster. And as this trenched sorely upon the feudal usurpations of the nobility, whose military vassals could thus be called out for national service instead of being kept in reserve for the personal quarrels of their masters, Wallace controlled these nobles and compelled their acquiescence by the fears of imprisonment.[1] It was no wonder that the indignation of these proud magnates was augmented under such restrictions, and that their general sentiment was, "We will not have this man to reign over us."

During these disasters to the arms of England Edward was in Flanders. But the tidings of this Scottish revolution, upon which he could not previously calculate, arrested him in the midst of his continental operations, and he sent letters to the lords of the English regency commanding them to muster their military retainers and march with all speed into Scotland under his lieutenant, Warrenne, Earl of Surrey. The nobles met accordingly, but it was to murmur and remonstrate, not to obey; and they agreed to withhold their military service until Edward had ratified the Great Charter and the Charter of the Forests, and prohibited the levying of taxes without the consent of the people expressed through the national parliament. Edward was obliged to comply; and satisfied with these concessions, the chief nobles, with the Earl Marshal and the High Constable of England at their head, mustered their vassals in great force at York upon the day appointed, which was the 14th of January (1298). The king had also written to the Scottish nobility, commanding them on their allegiance, and on pain of being treated as enemies and rebels, to attend this muster at York with all their military retainers; but their dread of Wallace was superior to their fear of Edward, and they failed to appear. Still the assembled English force was sufficient to overwhelm resistance without their aid, for it numbered 100,000 foot and 2000 heavily-armed cavalry; and, in obedience to the king's order they crossed the Border under the command of the Earl of Surrey, relieved Roxburgh, which was besieged by the Scots, and took possession of the town of Berwick. At Roxburgh they were joined by Edward in person, who had hurried from Flanders to the scene of action after having made a truce with the French king. He was now impatient for conquest and revenge, and having been strongly reinforced with cavalry he gave orders to set forward; but to his astonishment this vast array refused to move. He had signified his assent in Flanders to the demands of his nobles; but this they reckoned not enough; and, warned by past experience of the insecurity of their rights without the most solemn sanctions, they refused to march unless he ratified in person and upon the spot the promises which he had transmitted from abroad. Nor were their suspicions unreasonable, for Edward, instead of direct compliance, gave them nothing but promises which he had no intention to keep. Accordingly he declared that upon his return, if he was victorious over the Scots, he would grant their demands in full; and in the meantime Anthony Beck, Bishop of Durham, and the Earls of Surrey, Lincoln, and Norfolk, who were the royal sureties, solemnly swore upon the soul of the king that at his return he would fulfil his promise. This satisfied them, and they commenced their march. We thus perceive that Edward himself was hampered by the same causes that impeded the movements of Wallace; but in the resistance of the English nobility we see a more generous and patriotic motive than that which animated their contemporaries of Scotland. It is interesting, moreover, to mark how the sword of Wallace, while protecting the liberties of Scotland, was unintentionally advancing those of England also. Edward I. was almost as dangerous an enemy to his own kingdom as to that which he sought to conquer.

After these delays Edward marched into Scotland by the eastern borders; and, to make sure of supplies for his numerous host, he directed his fleet to sail from Berwick to the Firth of Forth, and attend upon the movements of the army. In the meantime Wallace had made every preparation which his limited means would allow for the defence for the country. But at a crisis when the utmost of simultaneous effort was needed, and when all would have been little enough to repel such an invasion, the Scottish nobles still continued to prefer their own personal interests, or the estates they held in England, to the welfare of a land of which they scarcely yet were natives; and although they had refused to repair to the English ren-

---

[1] Fordun, lib. xi. c. 28.

dezvous, they also failed to attend the Scottish muster: their fear of Wallace was exchanged for an equal dread of Edward, who was now at hand, and they seem to have waited the turn of events to make terms with the winning side. In this way even Robert Bruce, the future hero and king, although now on the side of Scotland on account of the invasion of his lands by Lord Clifford, instead of repairing to the national banner, took his post in the castle of Ayr, ostensibly to protect the western districts against the invaders. The only men of rank who appear to have responded to the summons were John Comyn of Badenoch, the younger; Sir John Stewart of Bonkill, brother of the Stewart of Scotland; Macduff, the grand uncle of the Earl of Fife; and Sir John Graham of Abercorn. The utmost that Wallace could effect was a defensive war, and for this his preparations were a model of military skill, and served for ages afterwards as the best defence of the country. Instead of risking a hopeless encounter with such an overwhelming enemy, his plan was to retreat slowly before their advance, wasting the districts as he retired, and garrisoning the places of strength, so that the English, even though they should march into the heart of the kingdom, would be compelled to a ruinous retreat from the impossibility of finding subsistence. It was then that his light-armed troops would be able to act with full effect by hanging upon the rear of the invaders, assailing them at every point of advantage, and wasting them in detail. In this way, as was shown by the events of later periods, without a pitched battle, the half of that resistless army might have melted away before it reached its home in England.

Edward continued his march into Scotland through Berwickshire until he came to Temple-liston (now called Kirkliston), near Edinburgh, without seeing the Scottish army or meeting with any resistance. Here he halted, expecting the tardy arrival of his ships, for his army was now distressed from want of provisions, which had been carefully removed by the Scots as he advanced, and he even began to make preparations for a retreat. It was necessary for this purpose to secure the strong castle of Dirleton and two other strongholds, the garrisons of which were already assailing the rear of his army and cutting off his foraging parties, and he sent the Bishop of Durham to reduce them. But the warlike prelate after a siege of several days, in which he was gallantly resisted by the garrisons, being unable from want of battering engines to make any impression upon the walls, despatched Sir John Marmaduke to the king for further advice. "Return to Anthony Beck,"

said Edward, "and tell him that though it is right to be scrupulous as a bishop, there is no need of his pious scruples in deeds of this description. But you," he added, complimenting the messenger, "are a man right pitiless, whom I have often been obliged to check for over-much cruelty, and triumphing over fallen enemies. Now, however, return, and be as merciless as you please, for, instead of rebuking, I will laud you for doing so. But beware how you appear before me again without having razed these three castles." Having given the messenger this hopeful charge, the king blessed him and sent him back to the bishop,[1] who by this time was enabled to execute the royal commission through the arrival of three ships laden with provisions. The garrison of Dirleton yielded upon terms of security to life and limb, and the other two castles were abandoned to the English after being set on fire by their defenders.

In the meantime the situation of Edward was critical. A month had already been wasted, but nothing achieved. A single victory, of which his ample means ensured him, would suffice to crush the rebels; but of the place where they were encamped he could learn no tidings. The country was laid waste before and around him, and while his mighty host was already half conquered by famine he looked wistfully seaward for his fleet, in vain, for it had been detained by contrary winds. At length a few ships arrived with a scanty store of food, a large share of which was dealt out to the Welsh troops, who had suffered most severely from hunger, and to it the king bountifully added a supply of wine; but this drink, acting upon the empty stomachs and fiery brains of the ill-used and enslaved Cambro-Britons, drove them into downright madness, under which they made a furious night attack upon the English quarters, and murdered eighteen priests and wounded many others. Enraged at this, the English horsemen charged the drunken rabble-rout, and put them to flight after cutting down eighty of their number. On the morning Edward was told that the Welsh, who were 40,000 strong, were in full mutiny, and had resolved to go over to the Scots. "What matters it," cried the proud, stout-hearted king, "though my enemies should join with my enemies, since both are foes alike? Let them depart when they please, for I hope, with the help of God, to chastise both the one and the other in a single day." On learning this the Welsh abode in the encampment, but apart from the English, upon whom, it was believed, they meant to fall as

---
[1] "Dataque benedictione, dismisit eum."—Hemingford.

soon as the Scottish army had advanced. So critical was now the situation of Edward that in a few days more he must have commenced a ruinous retreat, but for the treachery of Patrick, Earl of Dunbar, and the Earl of Angus. These Scottish nobles at the earliest dawn of the 21st of July repaired privately to the Bishop of Durham's quarter, and not daring personally to appear before Edward, as they had ostensibly joined the patriotic party, they sent a young page to inform him that Wallace and his army were encamped not far off in the Forest of Falkirk, and that they meant to surprise him by a night attack, or at least to harass him in retreat. "Praise be to God, who till now has freed me from every difficulty!" cried the king, rejoiced at the tidings: "they shall not need to follow me, since I shall set out forthwith to meet them." He instantly gave orders that all should arm, without announcing whither they were to march, and was himself the first to buckle on his armour and mount his war-steed. He also commanded the sutlers and traffickers of the camp to pack up their wares and follow the march. At three o'clock the army left Kirkliston, wondering at this new movement and ignorant of its course; and on reaching Linlithgow they there halted for the night, each soldier lying down upon the ground in his armour with his shield for a pillow, and every horseman having his horse still equipped beside him. At midnight a cry of treason arose; for the royal destrier, which had been intrusted to the careless keeping of a boy, had trod upon the king as he slept and severely bruised him: his soldiers started to their weapons, thinking that the enemy was upon them, and all was confusion until the cause of the alarm was known. As it was near morning the march was resumed, and after having passed through Linlithgow near sunrise they saw the glitter of lances upon the distant hills, which fell back at their approach, for it was only an advanced guard of the Scottish army; but on taking possession of the heights the English saw the army itself making prompt arrangements for battle. Through the treachery of the earls their place of encampment had been betrayed, and the English had stolen upon them by a silent and unexpected march. Wallace saw that his plan was defeated, that even retreat was impossible, and he calmly prepared for battle as the only alternative.

The English army to the number of 100,000 men, of whom more than 15,000 were cavalry, were now arrayed against 30,000 Scots. As these were almost wholly infantry, and inferior in their equipments to the enemy, Wallace availed himself to the utmost of every advantage which their mode of warfare and the nature of the ground could afford. He divided his troops into four bodies, called schiltrons, of which the front line kneeled and presented their long spears obliquely, while the lances of those behind rose, tier over tier, as they stood in such close array that they resembled a stone rampart. In this way only they could hope to resist the overwhelming charges of the English cavalry. Between the intervals of these schiltrons the Scottish archers were posted; and behind them in the rear were drawn up their horse, which amounted only to 1000, and could therefore merely act as a protection to the infantry. These, indeed, according to the military reckoning of the times, were the élite of the Scottish army, for they were of chivalrous rank and equipments; but besides their small number as compared to the enemy, they could not be trusted, as they were the allies and retainers of those nobles who had joined the army on compulsion, and would be ready to desert it, or turn against it. Having finished his arrangements, Wallace made to his troops that brief address of which so many versions have been handed down that the true one cannot be discovered. He either bade them merrily to dance their best, as they were now in the ring—or to flinch if they dared, seeing the enemy was now in front of them.

Having heard mass, Edward proposed that the tents should be pitched and the soldiers refreshed before commencing the onset; but from this he was dissuaded by his chief officers, as the Scots were at hand, while only a rivulet parted the two armies. "What shall we do then?" he asked. "Let us ride against them, in the name of the Lord," they cried, "since ours is the field and ours the victory!" "Be it so then," he replied, "in the name of the Father, and of the Son, and of the Holy Ghost."[1] The English van, under the command of the earl-marshal and the Earls of Hereford and Lincoln, marched to the encounter in a direct line; but their extended array was interrupted by a moss or peat-bog in front of the Scottish army, along the side of which they were obliged to defile to the west. The second line, over whose numerous array thirty-six banners floated, next advanced under the command of the warlike Bishop of Durham; and on discovering the obstacle of the bog, began to make a cautious circuit eastward. This was too much for the third line, already impatient for action; and Ralph Basset of Drayton, one of its leaders, shouted to the prelate as he paused at the quag-

---

[1] This mixture of religious and warlike phraseology, which was characteristic of the period, is carefully preserved by Hemingford.

mire, "Hold to your mass, bishop, instead of teaching us our duty in front of an enemy." "Set on, then, in your own fashion," cried the bishop; "we are all soldiers to-day, and must do our utmost." They drove through the bog and assailed the foremost schiltron; while the first line, that had surmounted the difficulty, also entered into action. It was a torrent of man, and horse, and heavy mail, and axe and sword, such as had never before swept down upon a Scottish phalanx to test its firmness to the uttermost. And nobly did the schiltrons endure it. The 1000 Scottish horse that were drawn up in the rear fled without striking a blow; the gallant archers of Selkirk, placed in the intervals between the schiltrous, rallied round their leader, Sir John Stewart of Bonkill, when he was thrown to the ground, and perished in his defence; while the tall, handsome, athletic forms of these brave men, who had fallen each in the place where he fought, called forth, when the battle had ended, the admiration of their enemies. But the Scottish masses, though thus uncovered and inclosed, continued the desperate conflict, and presented to the fierce mail-clad riders of England an unyielding rampart of spears through which they could not penetrate. The skill of Wallace had drawn them up, and the soul of Wallace animated their resistance. Enraged at the length and obstinacy of the conflict Edward brought up his reserves and assailed the serried ranks of the Scots by a mode of attack which they had no means of requiting; his archers and slingers discharged their missiles among them, and under these destructive volleys large gaps were opened through which the English cavalry dashed with loosened rein. After this resistance was at an end or hopeless, and all that Wallace could effect was to secure a retreat to the neighbouring wood, having left half of his army dead on the field. This loss has been extravagantly magnified by English chroniclers, some making it amount to 50,000 or even 60,000 men; but it is certain that scarcely less than 15,000 must have perished. What was almost of equal account was that the three best and most steadfast of the Scottish patriots of rank and influence, who abode by the cause of their country when their compeers had deserted it, were numbered with the slain at Falkirk. These were Sir John Stewart of Bonkill; Macduff, the grand uncle of the Earl of Fife, who brought the retainers of his nephew into the field; and Sir John Graham, whom tradition has affectionately commemorated as the "fidus Achates" of Wallace, and next to him the bravest champion and truest heart in Scotland. Who they were who fled from the field as soon as the first onset was given cannot now be ascertained, and therefore to their memory must still be conceded the full benefit of oblivion. The English chronicles, that represent so plentiful a slaughter of the Scots in this engagement, make amends by their clemency to the other side, of whom they tell us few fell, and only one man of note; this was Sir Bryan de Jaye, the Master of the Scottish Templars, who was slain in the pursuit while he too eagerly pressed upon the fugitives. This memorable battle of Falkirk, so fatal in its consequences to Scotland, was fought on the 22d of July, 1298.

CHAPTER IV.

WAR OF INDEPENDENCE, FROM THE BATTLE OF FALKIRK TO THE EXECUTION OF WALLACE (1298-1305).

Progress of Edward I. in Scotland after the battle of Falkirk—Is obliged to make a speedy retreat—His injudicious disposal of Scottish estates—Baliol's conduct in prison during the war—He is dismissed by Edward to France—Wallace resigns his guardianship of Scotland—His surmised movements after his resignation—The Scots elect new guardians—Edward unsuccessfully invades Scotland—He repeats the invasion—Strange claim of the pope over Scotland—He orders Edward to acknowledge it—Controversy between Edward and the pope about their respective rights to Scotland—Answers of Edward and the English parliament—Edward again invades Scotland, and retreats without battle—The pope and the French king abandon the interests of Scotland—Treachery of the French king to his Scottish allies—The English invade Scotland—They sustain three defeats in one day at Roslin—Edward enters Scotland—He captures the castle of Brechin—He defeats the Scots at Stirling—Wallace refuses to surrender himself to Edward—He is outlawed and proscribed—Edward besieges the castle of Stirling—Its surrender—Wallace betrayed to the English—His trial and execution.

After his victory of Falkirk the progress of Edward I. in Scotland was that of a conqueror whose arms nothing could resist. Wallace with the remains of his army had retreated from Falkirk to Stirling, where he endeavoured to rally and renew the war; but, unable to maintain the town against the English, who followed closely on his track, he on the fourth day burned both town and castle and continued his retreat. Edward entered Stirling, now a heap of ashes except the Dominican convent, which had escaped; and here he took up his residence to recover from the effects of the severe bruise which he had received on the night before the battle of Falkirk. During his short stay at this place he caused the castle to be repaired and garrisoned, and sent a strong body of troops across the Forth to ravage the districts of Clackmannan, Menteith, and Fife, which they did with great severity. The latter county seems to have been the especial mark of their vengeance on account of the aid which had been given by Macduff and his vassals to Wallace at Falkirk; and accordingly military execution was inflicted upon the inhabitants in its fullest extent with fire and sword. St. Andrews, which the English found deserted, was given to the flames, and the richest of the Scottish districts was quickly reduced to a wilderness. Unable to subsist in the county they had thus wasted, the English then advanced to Perth, but found that the Scots had anticipated their arrival by setting fire to the town; and thus, in a more hungry condition than they had set out, they hastily returned to Stirling.

Edward, having now recovered from his ailments, was impatient for the arrival of his fleet with provisions from Berwick, and in the hope of meeting it he proceeded from Stirling to Abercorn; but the winds were still contrary and not a ship appeared. Disappointed and impatient, he marched to Glasgow, and afterwards proceeded towards Ayr, the castle of which was in the custody of Robert Bruce, whom he was desirous to call to a strict reckoning for his late equivocal movements; but Bruce, who liked neither the subject nor the catechist, eschewed the meeting by setting fire to the castle and escaping into the wilds of Galloway. The king followed, being still eager for an interview with his refractory pupil, which in all likelihood would have changed the whole current of Scottish history; but the famine which Wallace had prepared for the enemy so effectually saved the Bruce that Edward was obliged to make a hasty return through Annandale after wreaking his resentment by the capture of Bruce's castle of Lochmaben. In all these marches Edward, wherever he turned, seemed still to be confronted with the presence of the Scottish guardian, from the impossibility of subsisting his troops, so that in spite of his victory he was obliged to retreat from a country that lay prostrate at his feet. It was now, indeed, that the wisdom of Wallace's plan was apparent, and which would have been successful but for the treachery that compelled him to abide the late encounter. All that Edward obtained by his victory was an unmolested retreat to Carlisle through the western borders, thus leaving Scotland almost wholly in the same state as he found it.

On reaching Carlisle and putting his famine-worn troops into cantonment, the King of England was speedily beset by a Scottish difficulty of his own creation. He there called a parliament; and although at the present period only a small portion of Scotland could be called his own, he proceeded to reward his friends and punish his enemies by assigning the estates of several of the Scottish lords to his own followers. By this rash deed the former were turned irrevocably into patriots and good Scotsmen, while the latter were little gratified by a grant of possessions which were neither his to give nor theirs to enjoy. These, however, the historian is careful to inform us were only given "in hope." The same writer gives a particular instance of Edward's princely liberality in such kind of donations. One of those unscrupulous military adventurers with which the age abounded, called Thomas Bisset, had come from Ireland to the island of Arran, to the aid, as was commonly reported, of the Scots, and under that character appears to have taken possession; but no sooner did he hear of the defeat of the Scots at Falkirk than he applied to Edward, declaring that he had come to assist the English, and had conquered Arran in their name; and his request was that the island should be granted in possession to him and his heirs after him. Edward had readily acceded to this request at Lochmaben, and Bisset the adventurer was confirmed in this fair lordship. But in this instance, as in those that afterwards were repeated at Carlisle, the king had violated a solemn compact made with the earl-marshal and the Earl of Hereford that he would confer no new grants without their advice and consent. This was not the first ground of quarrel between Edward and these powerful nobles; and the latter, indignant at the fresh breach of promise, returned home with all their followers under the pretext that their men and horses were worn out and needed repose.

Amidst these disasters and changes in Scotland, by which the country had been alternately enslaved and liberated, our thoughts naturally revert to that phantom king Baliol in whose name the struggle for liberty had been maintained, but who the while had been a prisoner in the Tower of London. After a year's captivity a gleam of hope, the promise of deliverance, lighted his cell, from the intervention of the King of France, who, in the truce which he made with Edward I., endeavoured to have the Scots included in the treaty. He therefore proposed that John Baliol as his ally should be set free; that all the other Scottish prisoners in England should be sent home on the delivery of hostages, and that all the inhabitants of Scotland of whatever degree and holding should share in the benefits of the truce. But Edward was in no temper to forego his hold on Scotland, or allow the Scots to escape unpunished; and as he was already raising an army for their final subjugation he sent an evasive answer to Philip craving time for deliberation, instead of a direct refusal, and continued his military preparations. That period of leisure came after his victory of Falkirk, and his answer was what might have been expected. The alliance, he said, between Scotland and France had been deliberately and freely renounced by the former, which country could therefore claim nothing from it. To this it was objected by the French king that this renunciation had been obtained through force and fear; but Edward, who had now the rights of a victor, stood firmly upon his refusal. In the meantime Baliol himself had shown that he was unworthy of liberty by the contemptible shifts he had used to obtain it. He declared that he renounced all intercourse with the Scots; that he had found them a false and treasonable people; and that he had good cause to suspect they intended to poison him. These professions, however, seem to have availed him as little as the interposition of his royal ally of France, for he still remained inclosed in the Tower. At length Pope Boniface VIII., at the instance of Philip, applied in behalf of the discrowned captive, and his appeal was successful; but even then Edward consented with murmuring and reluctance. "I will send Baliol to the pope," he spitefully exclaimed, "as a perjured man and a seducer of the people." The King of Scots was accordingly marched for deportation to Whitsand, near Calais; and before he was suffered to embark his baggage and mails were rummaged, that he might carry no contraband matter forth from England. In this search a considerable sum of money was found, which was allowed to pass free as his own private property; but the great seal of Scotland, which was laid up with his treasure, was seized and retained, as was also a golden crown, which Edward hung up in the shrine of St. Thomas of Canterbury. Thus thoroughly denuded, Baliol was suffered to depart in peace to France, where he took up his abode at Bailleul, the original seat of his family before it became English,

Scotch, or royal, and there he spent the rest of his obscure life. As for his English estates these Edward, in a sudden fit of generosity and in consequence of the pope's application, had resolved to remit to the impoverished exile; but on further thoughts he retained them all in his own possession, and some years afterwards bestowed them upon John Count of Bretagne, his own nephew.[1]

But a greater and better man than Baliol disappeared about the same time from public life, and became an exile and a wanderer. This was Sir William Wallace, whose career had hitherto been so romantic and so wonderful. In little more than the brief space of a year the stripling hero, without birth, without rank, without political influence, had won his way from obscurity to imperishable renown, and from the condition of a hunted outlaw among the mountains to that of the ruler of the land and the commander of its armies—had raised the hearts of the people from the depths of despair to the height of heroic daring—had swept away, as with an irresistible storm, the net-work of garrisons with which the whole land was inclosed—and without instructors to train, or past experience to enlighten him, had displayed a military skill that outgeneralled the best leaders of the age, as well as a political sagacity which, if left to itself, might have established the liberty he had won, and antedated the period when his country was to become great and happy as well as free. Of no other land is the history of its national hero so unpromising at its commencement, and yet so glorious; so brief in point of time, and yet so lasting in its effects. A biography of which such is the summary, can easily resign those romantic particulars with which it has been filled to the cavils of the coldhearted or queries of the doubtful, and yet find in it enough of the great and the wonderful. But where was Wallace now, after that one defeat which the guile and treachery of his false supporters had made inevitable? After the battle of Falkirk he was as ready as ever to continue the war; and from the precautions he had previously adopted he well knew that Edward, in spite of his victory, would be compelled to make a hasty retreat. But the envy of the nobles was as intense as ever, and after that disastrous conflict it could make itself be more effectually heard. Instead, therefore, of being able to levy a fresh muster, the Guardian of Scotland was threatened with impeachment; and foremost among his accusers were the Comyns and the Bruces, the two most powerful families in Scotland. It was evident that at

[1] Rymer's *Fœdera*; Walsingham; Prynne's *Edward I*.

every step his leadership would be thwarted; that the war for liberty would degenerate into a wasteful civil conflict of feuds and factions; and aware of this, Wallace resigned his office and retired into private life.¹ Here Scottish history generally loses sight of him till the period of his execution seven years afterwards. But it is impossible to imagine that during this period he remained in Scotland unnoticed by friend or enemy, or that he utterly abandoned those patriotic labours for which at last he laid down his life. The general tradition, therefore, as embodied in our oldest histories, is that he repaired to France, whose alliance had already cost Scotland so dear; and that at the French court he endeavoured to obtain by negotiation that aid for his country which he was no longer permitted to give by action in the field.² It is the simplest mode of accounting for the entire disappearance of Wallace from the scene; and yet it has become the fashion to discard it, from the contemptuous indifference with which these early authorities have been treated by modern investigation. Recent discoveries, however, have established the fact, and vindicated the truthfulness of our early cherished traditions; and from these we may assume as historical facts the following particulars in the Scottish champion's eventful career.

After the defeat of Falkirk and his own abdication of office Sir William Wallace saw that there was no hope of national deliverance in the selfish and divided nobility. He therefore resolved to apply to Philip le Bel, who not only owed a debt of gratitude to Scotland, but had a long account of injuries to settle with Edward and the English nation. He accordingly embarked for France with a few brave companions, who, like himself, preferred exile to a home in which they could be no longer free. Even his voyage was not without adventures; and while one of our oldest authorities mentions in general terms that he cleared the sea of pirates, and was celebrated in the French songs and ballads of the day,³ another embodies in heroic rhyme his capture of the terrible Red Rover, who at the close of the thirteenth century was an imitator of the vikingr of the eleventh.⁴ Such an encounter upon the high seas was perfectly consistent with the condition of the period; and on arriving at the French court this exploit of Wallace, by which he had rid their coasts of a destructive enemy to their merchandise, would enhance the welcome which his recent renown and deeds against the English had already ensured. But this flattering prospect was quickly overcast. Philip was one of those politicians who never allow the claims either of private gratitude or abstract justice to interfere with their plans for the public good; and the change of events had now made it evident that an alliance with the powerful Edward would be more profitable to France than a chivalrous defence of Scotland and its fugitive hero. The Flemings, aided by Edward, were in revolt against Philip just as the Scots were against the King of England; and the proposal between these two selfish potentates was, that each should leave the enslaved country to the tender mercies of the other, so that while Edward withdrew his help from Flanders, the French king was to give no aid to Scotland. Philip entered so cordially into this compact that he threw Wallace into prison, and sent a letter to Edward advertising him of the fact, and offering to surrender the Scottish hero to his keeping. Edward gladly accepted the offer, and the fate of Wallace was apparently sealed. But either a touch of compunction, or what is more likely, a change in his prospects of advantage, withheld the hands of Philip, so that, instead of surrendering Wallace he released him from prison, and furnished him with credentials to his agents residing in Rome.⁵ To Rome accordingly Wallace may be supposed to have repaired, in the devout hope that his just appeal in behalf of Scotland would obtain a more favourable hearing from the reverend father of Christendom than from the selfish potentates of France and England. It was his last resource, and he would not leave it untried. It was the refuge of the destitute when secular arms had failed, and its mandates had more than once arrested the progress of a conqueror. Even the quick natural sagacity of the young Scot may have taught him that Rome could scarcely desire the aggrandizement of such a restive vassal as Edward I., and might be inclined to check him with Scotland as a counterpoise. Thither, therefore, it is likely that he went, not as a public functionary or accredited agent, but as a private suppliant, or even as a fugitive from prison, and instructed in no case to show the passport of the French king in behalf of "our beloved William le Waloys of Scotland, knight," except in urgent extremity. And yet this document at last found its way to the possession of Edward I. himself, who must have read it with no very friendly feelings towards his royal brother Philip. It would be curious to learn the progress of Wallace as a negotiator among Italian priests and cardinals, and how

---

¹ Wyntoun; Fordun.
² Cupar and Perth MS. quoted in Goodall's *Fordun*, lib. xi. cap. 34, 35. Henry the Minstrel.
³ MSS. Cup. et Per. in Fordun. ⁴ Henry the Minstrel.

⁵ Document found in the Record Office of the Tower of London, and published in the *Wallace Papers*, Maitland Club Series, No. xvii. p. 163.

WAR OF INDEPENDENCE.

much the half-forgotten Latin which his uncle had taught him may have stood him in good stead. It may be that his representations mainly influenced that interference in behalf of Scotland which Boniface VIII. attempted, and which might have been available with any other king than Edward I. of England. But, finding after months or years of hope deferred that his labours were in vain, the heart-broken patriot turned his back upon the grandeur of the "Eternal City," and the bright skies and fair scenery of Italy, that he might become once more a hunted fugitive among his own native hills, and die for the land which he could no longer save.

We now return to the regular course of public events in Scotland. On the abdication of the guardianship by Sir William Wallace a new regency was chosen, which consisted of William Lamberton Bishop of St. Andrews, Robert Bruce Earl of Carrick, and John Comyn the younger of Badenoch. These held their office as Guardians of Scotland in the name of Baliol; but how Bruce consented to forego his royal pretensions by acting under such authority is one of those inconsistencies in the early life of that hero which we are unable to explain. As yet, thanks to the efforts of Wallace, Scotland was free, and the new guardians were ready to continue the war. Enraged at this unexpected decision, Edward, although greatly weakened by the departure of the Earls of Norfolk and Hereford, resolved to return and effect the entire subjugation of Scotland. He would, indeed, have repeated his campaigns at once had not the season been too far advanced; but during the following spring and summer he hastened his preparations for a conquest that should be final and complete. Even his disputes with his barons, who now felt their importance and stood boldly out for their rights, could not make him alter his purpose. Being a widower, one of his politic projects was to detach France from the interests of Scotland by a marriage with the sister of the French king; and having effected this in September (1299) he appointed his troops to muster at York, made a pilgrimage to the shrine of St. Alban, and ordered prayers to be offered up in all the churches of his kingdom for the success of his enterprise. In the meantime the Scottish guardians had already commenced operations by besieging the castle of Stirling, which the English garrison was too small to maintain for any length of time; and Edward, aware of this, and grudging to lose this token of his hold upon Scotland, was anxious to relieve it. The Guardians of Scotland, who had assembled their army at Torwood, alarmed at these formidable preparations, endeavoured to avert the storm by negotiation; and adverting to the truce which had lately been formed between the Kings of England and France, they offered to suspend their military operations if Edward would follow the example. But the latter was too resolute and had gone too far to pause midway, and without vouchsafing to reply to the application he hastened to York to open his parliament and commence the new northern campaign.

The military muster that had repaired to that city was so numerous and so well appointed as to give every promise of success; the greater barons were in attendance with their numerous retainers, and the populous county had supplied its full contingents of militia; there was every promise of a greater victory than that of Falkirk, more especially when the great Scottish leader was no longer to oppose them. To prevent every kind of unnecessary delay and keep his troops in hand for instant action, Edward issued strict proclamations that during the war there should be no tournaments, no weapon-shows, no wandering from headquarters upon adventure except by his orders; and though it was now the beginning of November, with the full promise of a severe northern winter, he marched to Berwick-on-Tweed. But here the march suddenly paused and the campaign was ended, for the barons refused to proceed. Notwithstanding his many promises Edward had eluded the due fulfilment of their privileges, as secured by the Great Charter and the forest laws; and now that they were in arms and at the head of their own vassals, their season for resentment and remonstrance had arrived. Without adducing, however, the real causes of their discontent, they alleged the severe winter, the impassable nature of the northern roads, and the difficulty of obtaining provisions as the dissuasives from further operations; and having done this, they marched to their own homes and left the royal banner in its solitude. In spite of this desertion Edward marched forward at the head of the small force that still abode with him; but on learning the strong position of the Scottish army at Torwood he saw the hopelessness of the enterprise and prudently desisted, after ordering the garrison of Stirling to capitulate and surrender the castle to the Scots.

In the following year (1300) and during the summer Edward once more invaded Scotland by the western marches, but with almost as little effect as on the previous occasion, for the Scots, taught by fatal experience, prudently confined themselves to that defensive system of warfare for which the nature of the country was so well adapted. They therefore skilfully selected their ground where they could not safely be attacked, and shunned a general action, so that Edward menaced an enemy whom he could not reach. In addition to the uselessness of his powerful cavalry, that could not act among the bogs, rocks, and mountains by which the Scots were intrenched, his Welsh auxiliaries, who were accustomed to such a mode of warfare, refused, as they had done at Falkirk, to give their hearty co-operation, and thus the enemy remained unassailed.[1] All that Edward could accomplish, therefore, during this profitless campaign, which lasted five months, was to lay waste Annandale and receive the submission of the inhabitants of Galloway. As winter was at hand he was now in a mood to listen to overtures which at the commencement of the invasion he had scornfully rejected, and pretending to accede to the earnest wishes of the French king in their behalf, he granted to the Scots a truce which was to last till Whitsunday in the following year. He also set Wishart, Bishop of Glasgow, who had long been his prisoner, at liberty after receiving anew his oaths of allegiance. After these concessions Edward left his headquarters of Dumfries in the beginning of November and returned to England.

Such peaceful proceedings were so little in accordance with the character of the English king that this unwonted cessation must be traced to other causes than Edward's courtesy towards the King of France, or even the growing difficulties of the invasion. So fixed, indeed, was his resolution to conquer Scotland and annex it to the English crown, that he felt as if without it neither life could give him pleasure nor death itself repose. But a new claimant for Scotland had unexpectedly entered into the field, whom he must encounter and if possible overcome before he proceeded on his course, and this rival was no other than the pope! At the commencement of this year the Scottish rulers had sent a commission to Rome to represent the unjust and oppressive conduct of Edward towards Scotland and to crave the interposition of the pontiff. Boniface VIII. did, indeed, interpose, but it was according to the tactics of the Roman conclave; he had discovered that Scotland belonged to Rome, and therefore could never become the property of England. He accordingly sent a bull to England which Winchelsea, Archbishop of Canterbury, was required to present to the king without delay; and as Edward was at present in the wilds of Galloway the English primate had to undertake the dangerous journey in person. An account which he afterwards wrote to the pontiff of this most perilous pilgrimage across the sands of Solway and to Caerlaverock, the roaring floods he had passed through, and the bands of Scottish robbers thirsting for English blood whom he had escaped, would form a valuable episode for a volume of English hagiology.[2] After three days of struggle the weary messenger reached his sovereign's camp and presented the bull, which being written in Latin he was also obliged to translate. In this singular manifesto Edward was informed that his claims to the superiority of Scotland were naught, because that ancient kingdom had belonged, and did still belong, to the see of Rome. An investigation was also made into his (Edward's) feudal rights over Scotland, and a historical refutation of them given, which must have been gall and wormwood to the royal listener. The pope then established his own claims and rights by those arguments which simple laymen and ultramontanes found difficult to refute, and often too hard to understand; and Edward was finally required, as a token of his submission, to set free the Scottish ecclesiastics whom he had imprisoned, and to withdraw all his officers from Scotland whom he had appointed to govern the kingdom under him. He was also required, if he had any pretensions to all or any part of Scotland, to send his proctors to Rome within six months, when the pope would himself hear and determine the case according to the rules of equity; and in order that Edward might be assured of full justice being done Boniface added, "I take the cause under my own particular cognizance."[3] He thus made himself the judge of a trial in which he was also the plaintiff! When this astounding manifesto was ended the archbishop rounded the papal mandate by a ghostly and unctuous exhortation; he advised the king to yield dutiful submission; and reminded him how Jerusalem would not fail to protect her citizens, and Mount Zion to cherish those who put their trust in the Lord.

It would be impossible to describe the astonishment and rage of Edward at the arrogance of the pope and the hardihood of his own archbishop; it was the more mortifying as the charge was delivered in the presence of his assembled nobles and warriors; and starting up, he ex-

---

[1] After describing the behaviour of the Welsh at Falkirk, who stood upon a hill until the battle was over, the French Metrical Chronicle, translated into English by Robert de Brunne, thus characterizes these allies in general:—

"Was neuer withouten gile Walsh man no Breton.
For thei were ouer in wone, men so of tham told,
Whilk was best banere, with that side forto hold.
Saint Bede sais it for lore, and I say it in ryme,
Walsh man salle neuer more luf Inglis man no tyme."

[2] The letter is contained in full in Prynne's *Edward I.*, book v. chap. 4, p. 882.

[3] Rymer's *Fœdera*, vol. i. part 2, p. 907; *et* Prynne's *Ed. I.*, p. 879.

claimed in a voice of thunder, "By God's blood! I will not be silent for the sake of Zion, nor rest in peace on account of Jerusalem, while there is breath in my nostrils, but will show to the whole world, which knows my right, that I am also able to defend it."[1] Some days after, when his ire had cooled, it was blown into fresh fury by the Scots, who, trusting in the papal protection, requested him to suspend his proceedings until their rulers had consulted with the King of France. "What man of you," he cried, "who has done me homage as his liege lord of Scotland can think me so gullible or so weak as to abandon my right which I hold over you? Beware how you appear before me again with such a message! If you do, I swear by the Lord that I will lay waste all Scotland from sea to sea."[2] But when second thoughts prevailed Edward was well aware that these new claims of the pope were not to be averted by angry threats and assertions, and he prepared for the encounter with those aids and weapons that gave him the only chance of success. On returning home, therefore, he disbanded his army and commenced an active muster of casuists and documents. He ordered a full parliament to assemble at Lincoln upon the ensuing term of St. Hilary, of which the special summons to peers, prelates, and commons bore that they were called to defend the rights of his crown against this new claim of the papacy. He issued special writs to several deans, archdeacons, and other learned scholars, enjoining and commanding them without fail to repair to Lincoln, to advise with the lawyers and others of his council concerning his right to the realm of Scotland. He ordered the Chancellor and University of Oxford to send four or five of their most discreet and expert scholars in the written law to confer with him and his counsellors upon the great question at issue, while the University of Cambridge was required to send two or three similar scholars for the same purpose. He also issued writs to several abbots, priors, deans, and chapters, to search diligently amongst all the chronicles, archives, and private documents of their institutions, that they might find whatever could touch in any way upon the said kingdom of Scotland. And never, perhaps, was there such an antiquarian exploration in England either before or since; for the fate of a kingdom was at stake, and Scotland was to be fought and won by a campaign of old parchments!

The period at length arrived; the parliament was held at Lincoln—and very strange to the nostrils of knight and baron must have been the dust of this new battle-field. The result, however, was, that they proved to their own entire satisfaction the feudal superiority of England over Scotland, and this conclusion, with the grounds on which it rested, Edward transmitted in a long letter to the pope. We could scarcely believe that he kept his countenance while he indited it, did we not know how earnest he was for the possession of Scotland, and how implicitly under such a feeling the heart can admit the veriest shadows as full and substantial proofs. He went back to the days of Eli and Samuel, the judges of Israel, when a certain brave and illustrious Trojan called Brutus arrived in Britain, and having slain the giants by which it was inhabited, took possession of the whole island, and afterwards parted it among his three sons, reserving for the eldest, whose portion was England, the supreme and kingly dignity. Thus the kings of England by conquest, by express appointment, and by hereditary right had been overlords of Scotland from the earliest possible periods. He then summed up the long array of his shadowy predecessors, in which King Arthur, in whom he devoutly believed, was not forgot, and showed how in every case the Scots had recognized them as feudal superiors. As all this right, however, was heathenish at the best, it would have little availed against the orthodox argument of the pope, who claimed Scotland for the holy see, because it had been miraculously converted to Christianity by the relics of St. Andrew, carried thither by St. Regulus. These wonder-working relics, as we learn from Fordun, consisted of a joint of St. Andrew's arm, three fingers of his right hand, one tooth, and one knee-pan. But this miracle Edward matched with another that triumphantly established his cause. He told of Athelstane, King of England, who by his sovereign right made Constantine king over Scotland, accompanying the act with the sage remark, that to make a king was still more glorious than to be one. The Scots afterwards rebelled; but Athelstane overcame them through the help of St. John of Beverley. "And having devoutly given thanks to God (thus Edward wrote), he prayed that forthwith through the same blessed agency some visible signs should be given, by which the living of that day and of ages to come should know that the Scots were rightfully the subjects of England. And seeing certain rocks in the place, which was near Dunbar, he drew his sword from the sheath, and struck the flint; and, through the power of God acting upon the sword-stroke, the rock was so cleft that the opening was an ell in length." This Edward declared to be an incontrovertible fact, because

---

[1] Walsingham, p. 78; Prynne, *Edward I.*, p. 878.
[2] Prynne, *Ed. I.*, p. 878.

the cleft in the rock was still to be seen, and the legend of the miracle continued to be recited every week in the church of Beverley to the praise and glory of St. John. Having thus set aside the relics of St. Andrew, and established his own claim to Scotland by right divine and miracle, Edward continued the narrative to his own period; and while he stated the homage which Baliol and the kingdom had rendered to his superiority, he was careful to enumerate with severe aggravations the many atrocities which the Scots had committed in their late rebellion against him.[1]

While the King of England thus answered for himself, the parliament had prepared a reply for themselves; and though it was very brief compared with that of their sovereign, it was equally decisive. It was a fact, they said, notorious to all, that from the earliest times the temporalities of Scotland had never belonged, and did not now belong by any kind of right, to the holy see. On the contrary from the earliest times Scotland had been a fief of England, and of the predecessors of their present king. In temporalities, also, the kings of England were not amenable to the see of Rome. They had therefore all and each resolved that they would not allow their sovereign's independence to be questioned; that he should send no advocates or envoys to plead his rights; and that they cannot and would not permit him to yield to such demands, even though he were willing so to do. This spirited reply had 104 seals of the nobles, knights, and chief commoners attached to it.[2]

Having thus silenced his ecclesiastical rival in a war of words, Edward hastened his military preparations to invade Scotland anew, and put the question of its actual possession beyond the power of cavil. As before, the invasion was to be conducted both by land and sea, so that while his barons were ordered to muster at Berwick, a fleet of seventy ships was commanded to be in readiness at its port. Again, also, he was mindful of his religious duties; and before he joined his army he made a pilgrimage to the shrine of St. Thomas à Becket and other holy places to obtain the blessing of the saints upon his enterprise. He then crossed the Borders accompanied by his young son, the Prince of Wales, to whose command he intrusted a division of his army, and advanced as far as Linlithgow. But his great preparations were signalized by no adequate achievement; for the Scots, as wary as before, avoided a pitched battle and confined themselves to skirmishes with straggling parties of the English, while his cavalry lost many of their horses from cold and want of forage. Instead of returning to England, he resolved to winter at Linlithgow, where he built a castle; but before the season for resuming hostilities had arrived he was prevailed upon to grant the Scots a second truce through the mediation of the French king, which was to last from January (1302) to St. Andrew's Day. Into this treaty, however, he would allow no recognition of Baliol as King of Scotland, or the alliance of that country with France, which the negotiation had attempted to establish, as such an acknowledgment would have been fatal to his designs against Scottish independence. The useless campaigns being thus ended, Edward withdrew his army into England.

Although the storm that thus threatened to burst upon Scotland had been averted, it was only for a brief season; and symptoms now gave promise that it would return in greater violence, and with more deadly effect. The allies of the oppressed country were about to desert it and leave it to its fate. The foremost of these was Pope Boniface, who had lately been so anxious to rescue it from the gripe of England, but only to secure it for himself. The answer of the English parliament had distinctly shown him, that while grasping a shadow he might lose the substance—that by advocating the cause of remote and barren Scotland, he might inevitably offend, and perhaps wholly alienate England, the most profitable portion of the whole inheritance of St. Peter—and true to the policy of his government, he made haste to undo his error and adopt the winning side. An opportunity also presented itself in the case of Wishart, Bishop of Glasgow, who, after being dismissed from prison by Edward, was now active in Scotland against the English interests. To him Boniface wrote a reproving letter, in which the political apostasy of the pontiff is rendered doubly disgusting by the religious strain in which it is embodied. "With astonishment I have heard," he thus wrote, "that you, as a stone of stumbling and rock of offence, have been the chief instigator and promoter of the fatal disputes at issue between the Scottish nation and Edward, King of England, *my dearly beloved son in Christ*, to the displeasure of the divine majesty, the peril of your own honour and salvation, and the unspeakable injury of the kingdom of Scotland. If such is the case, you have made yourself odious to God and man. You ought to repent, and strive by earnest endeavours in procuring peace to obtain forgiveness." The pope also addressed a bull in a

---

[1] Mat. Westminster; Knyghton; Walsingham; Prynne, *Ed. I.* p. 887.
[2] Rymer, vol. II. p. 875; Prynne, *Ed. I.* p. 802.

similar style and to the same effect to the Scottish bishops, which he closed with these ominous words: "Listen to my advices, and study to promote the national peace, lest I should be compelled, in addition to all I have said, to apply another remedy." It was now the turn of Philip of France to follow this backward apostolic march, which he did with a readiness that trod upon the papal heel. He had suffered a severe defeat from the Flemings; and that he might work his will upon them, he was ready to make peace with Edward, their ally, and leave the Scots to their fate. In the treaties, therefore, of truce and peace that were negotiated between the two kings, neither Scotland nor Flanders was allowed to participate. Even this act of treachery, also, could not be perpetrated on the part of Philip towards the Scots without flavouring it with certain iniquitous refinements. He was a very epicure in political craft and cruelty, as his oppressions of the Flemings and destruction of the order of the Templars fully showed; and on the present occasion he was resolved that the unsuspicious Scots should be the victims of his morbid predilection. At his court as negotiators for their country were the Earl of Buchan, Lord Soulis, James the Steward of Scotland, and Ingelram de Umfraville; and as these were among the bravest and most influential of the Scottish nobility, he resolved to deprive their country of their services until the season of action had expired. While he therefore continued to treat with Edward until a lasting peace was ratified, he pretended to these commissioners that although he had made no stipulation for Scotland, he intended to make its independence the subject of a separate treaty; and he besought them to remain in Paris until this good object could be accomplished. They stayed accordingly and listened to his promises until it was too late to return.

While these negotiations were in progress the truce between Scotland and England had expired; the war was resumed, and the Scots not only succeeded in expelling the enemy from the country, but threatened an invasion of England. Edward, alarmed at this, ordered twenty-six of his chief northern barons to repair immediately with all the force they could muster to the assistance of John de Segrave, his governor in Scotland, intending soon to follow them with his whole army; and he sent down Ralph de Manton, commonly called, from his office, Ralph the Cofferer, with supplies of money for their expedition. Segrave, thus reinforced, commenced aggressive operations at the head of 20,000 soldiers, most of whom were cavalry, separated into three divisions that the work of havoc might be more widely extended; they marched from Berwick towards Edinburgh, and encamped near Roslin, each division by itself, and without any communication with the rest. The Scots, however, although they had retired before their advance, had neither been idle nor faint-hearted; they had watched for the opportunity which the careless encampment at Roslin now presented; and to the number of 8000 horse, under the command of Sir John Comyn, one of the guardians of Scotland, and Sir Simon Fraser, they marched from Biggar to Roslin to surprise the enemy by a night attack. So secure were the English that they had kept no watch, and the only notice they received was from a boy, who rushed into the camp of the first division, commanded by Segrave himself, and cried that the Scots were at hand. There was no time for preparation to receive them, and after a confused resistance they were completely routed, Segrave himself, who was wounded, being taken, with his brother and son, as well as sixteen knights and thirty squires. The victors had scarcely breathed when they were obliged to prepare afresh for battle, for the second division under Ralph the Cofferer was advancing with furious haste to retrieve the defeat of their companions. In this strait the Scots had recourse to the remedy afterwards adopted by Henry V. at Azincourt, and which seems to have been no uncommon military usage of the day — they slew their prisoners, whom they could no longer retain or liberate with safety to themselves, and commenced a fresh encounter. The English at this time also were better prepared, and the Scots had a still harder struggle to maintain than before; but the latter were again victorious, and the Cofferer with many of his best soldiers was taken. Two such victories were toil and glory enough for a single morning; and the conquerors, who had also made a weary night march, were longing for repose when signals for new action were given; the third division, greatly reinforced by the fugitives and commanded by Robert de Neville, a baron of high renown in the wars against the Welsh, were seen advancing in order of battle, and apparently strong enough to trample down the exhausted Scots with a single onset. Maddened at the interruption, as well as the prospect of having the victory snatched from them at the last moment, the Scots were again reduced to the cruel necessity of slaying their captives; and on this occasion a deed so revolting to brave soldiers seems to have been committed with resentful severity. Such was especially shown in the fate of Ralph the Cofferer, who though a priest was clad in the full panoply of knighthood, and who now begged hard for his life with the promise of a princely ransom. "Where is thine albe or thy hood, sir priest?" cried Fraser, his captor, in savage derision; "this laced hauberk of thine, I wot, is no holy garb. Oft hast thou harmed us and robbed us of our wages, and now it is our turn to have quittance." With these words he first lopped off the hands of the soldier-ecclesiastic and afterwards struck his head from his shoulders. In this battle also the English were so completely defeated that the remains of the army fled to England, leaving Neville among the slain.[1] The renown of this three-fold victory, which rang far and wide, was grateful to the ears of the French, notwithstanding their cessation of hostilities with England; and the Scottish envoys at the court of Philip thus alluded to it in their letter to the Scottish guardians:—"You would greatly rejoice if you knew what reputation you have acquired all over the world by your late conflict with the English."[2] In reading of this wonderful achievement at Roslin we are apt to ask, "Was not Wallace there?" So ready, indeed, were the English to connect his dreaded name with such a defeat that by some[3] he is asserted to have commanded the Scots on this occasion. That he had already returned to Scotland is certain from the proscriptions afterwards issued, in which his name frequently appears. But it is equally certain that he neither could have been offered, nor ought to have accepted, the chief command where a duly-appointed Scottish governor was in the field. It was not likely, however, that he would be lurking in his cave or idly nourishing his resentment when the country was invaded and resistance prepared; and therefore it is not improbable that he was at Roslin as an unknown knight or private volunteer, and that his war-cry heard amidst the din of onset may have struck terror into the English, and made them think that their dreaded enemy was once more in the ascendant.

The destruction of so gallant an army and the infliction of such a lasting disgrace were enough to madden the chivalrous as well as resentful spirit of Edward; and with terrible oaths he swore that he would either reduce the Scots to obedience, or make their land so desolate that the beasts of the field alone should inhabit it. He was now also in a condition to make good his threats, from the cessation of his wars on the Continent, which left the whole military resources of the kingdom at his disposal. Accordingly towards the end of May, 1303, he entered Scotland with such an army as made resistance hopeless. It was parted into two divisions, one commanded by his son the Prince of Wales, and the other by himself, that the eastern and western Scottish borders might be invaded at the same time, and the threatened desolation of the country more effectually consummated. And the proceedings of both these divisions, as they advanced by their respective routes towards Edinburgh, seemed to show a competition in cruelty between father and son, that made it difficult to tell which of them had the pre-eminence. Behind them was a waste of desolated fields, of plundered cities, and burning villages and huts, while before them was the unresisting submission of those whom the unsparing havoc had quelled into abjectness, or whose age, sex, or profession unfitted them for action. All that could be done by the Scots was only in the form of a guerrilla warfare; and accordingly, at the head of small bands that still dared to remain in arms, Comyn and Fraser, the heroes of Roslin, and Wallace himself, who now reappears on the field in the humble form of an insurgent captain, hovered round the skirts of these overwhelming phalanxes, and could only retard the progress which they were unable to encounter or prevent. From Edinburgh Edward continued his destructive march, in which he visited or passed the towns of Linlithgow, Perth, Dundee, and Aberdeen, meeting no resistance of moment in his progress except from the castle of Brechin, which was garrisoned by Sir Thomas Maule. This gallant knight, at the approach of Edward, refused to surrender; and so confident was he in the strength of the walls, that in scorn of his assailants he wiped off from his face with a towel the dust which was raised by their battering-engines. So strong, indeed, were the ramparts that no impression was made on them, and the siege, which lasted twenty days, threatened to be tedious or unsuccessful when the brave-hearted Maule was struck down by a mortal blow from one of the missiles. "May we not surrender now?" cried his dispirited soldiers as they hung over their expiring leader. "What, cowards!" he exclaimed indignantly, "yield up the castle?—no, never!" and with these words he expired.[4] But the life and soul of resistance had passed away with his last breath, and the garrison opened their gates to the enemy. After the surrender of the castle of Brechin Edward proceeded to Dunfermline, where he resolved to pass the winter. The chief ornament of this old capital of Malcolm Canmore was the Benedictine monastery—a building of such extent,

---

[1] Tyrrel; Langtoft; Wynton; Fordun; Hemingford; Trivet. [2] Rymer.
[3] Walsingham, and the *Chronicle of Abingdon*.

[4] M. Westminster.

as we are told by an English historian, that three sovereigns with all their retinues might have found accommodation within its walls.[1] It had also occasionally been used as a place of meeting for the Scottish parliament. Being on these accounts a fair mark for destruction, the English army set it on fire; and the same historian whom we have already mentioned endeavours to justify the deed. "They beheld," he says, " that this temple of the Lord was no longer a church but a den of thieves, and as it were a sty in the eyes of the English nation," and therefore they destroyed it; but he is careful to tell us that the church itself and a few cells, "good enough for the residence of monks," were exempted from the general destruction.

As Stirling Castle, garrisoned by Sir William Oliphant, was the only fortress of consequence in possession of the Scots, they made a last effort to preserve it; and for this purpose Comyn the governor, having assembled an army, posted himself upon the same ground which Wallace had occupied when he so signally defeated the army of Surrey. But the ground little availed where the spirit of Wallace was absent. Edward, rejoicing that his enemies were now arrayed before him on one field, instead of being everywhere and invisible, advanced to end all by a single battle. In his eagerness also he intended to reach them by the same bridge which had given passage to Cressingham; but even this trap, which might have allured him to a similar destruction, had been foolishly destroyed by the Scots, and thus he was obliged to cross the river by a ford—the same ford, in all likelihood, which Lundin had recommended to the impetuous Cressingham. Edward thus crossed the river with little difficulty, and on charging with all his cavalry the Scots were quickly routed and dispersed.[2]

The last army of Scotland was thus thrown away, and nothing remained but submission. Bruce had already surrendered, and Comyn, with the other insurgent nobles, followed the example, after obtaining the most favourable terms which the conqueror was willing to concede. These stipulations were for their lives, liberties, and estates, reserving to Edward the right of inflicting upon their rebellion whatever pecuniary fine he pleased. Certain persons, however, were excepted from this amnesty as being worthy of heavier punishment; and these were Wishart, Bishop of Glasgow, the Steward, Sir John Soulis, David de Graham, Alexander de Lyndesay, Simon Fraser, Thomas Bois—and William Wallace. Wishart, the Steward, and Soulis were sentenced to exile for two years, and not to pass to the north of the Trent; Graham and Lyndesay were banished from Scotland for six months, and Fraser and Bois for three years, with prohibition to enter France, or any of Edward's territories. As for Wallace, the greatest defaulter of the whole, no conditions of mercy were held out to him: he was advertised, that if he surrendered himself it must be unconditionally to the clemency of the King of England; and of what that clemency consisted the past experience of Scotland had learned but too well. Soon afterwards Edward held an English parliament at St. Andrews to receive to his mercy such of those barons as consented to the stipulated terms; and all came forward and submitted, with the exception of Fraser and Wallace, who were immediately proclaimed outlaws. Weary at last of such a life of suspense, and hopeless of the national spirit, even Fraser at length succumbed to his sentence of banishment, and Wallace stood alone. He indeed made a show of surrender also, but it was in full consistency with his heroic character. Scorning the idea of yielding unconditionally, he proposed terms through his friends to the King of England, which were those of a soldier, a free man, and an independent chieftain, who had borne rule and might bear it again, rather than a hunted outlaw in the forest of Dunfermline. Edward was "full grim" when he received this tender; and sending Wallace with curses to the foul fiend as an arch-traitor, and all who sustained and abetted him, he set a price of 300 marks upon his head. Confirmed by this answer, Wallace confined himself to his hiding-places, subsisting as before on the plunder of his enemies.[3]

The castle of Stirling still held out, on which account Sir William Oliphant, its commander, and the garrison had been included in the sentence of outlawry proclaimed against Fraser and Wallace. Edward now laid siege to this last stronghold of Scottish liberty; but on being summoned to surrender, Oliphant, in the true spirit of chivalry, replied that the fortress had been committed to his keeping by his feudal superior Sir John Soulis, without whose express permission he could not yield it up: he offered, however, immediately to repair to France, where Soulis was in exile, and return with his answer whatever it might be. But Edward, who cared little for knightly fidelity when it was arrayed

---

[3] "Whan thei brouht that tething Edward was fulle grim,
And bitauht him the fende, als his traytoure in lond,
And ever-ilkon his frende that him austeynd or fond.
Three hundreth marke he hette unto his warisoun,
That with him so motte, or bring his hede to toun.
Now flies William Waleis, of pres nouht he spedis,
In mores and mareis with robberie him fedis."
—Langtoft, vol. II. p. 324.

[1] M. Westminster.   [2] Trivet.

against himself, received the proposal with insult: "I am not to wait for the orders of Soulis; defend you the castle as you best can." The castle in those days was reckoned all but impregnable, and to storm it every engine was brought forward which military science had devised. Thirteen of these played against the walls, and discharged huge stones, leaden balls, and javelins; but they were answered by machines from the ramparts fully as terrible, that made destructive gaps in the ranks of the besiegers, and were seconded by daring and successful sallies of the garrison. The difficulties of the siege and the gallant deeds of arms with which it was accompanied roused the spirit of Edward, now an old man, into all the military ardour of his youth, so that he was eager to throw himself into the foremost press of conflict. On one of these occasions his daring had almost cost him dear; for, while riding too near the walls, a dart aimed at him from a balista struck him on the breast, and but for his well-tempered cuirass would have pierced him to the heart. He was, however, unhurt; and, plucking out the weapon, he shook it aloft, and cried that he would hang the caitiff who had shot it. At another time a huge stone boomed so close to him, that with the noise and wind his horse backed and fell, so that his soldiers thought he had been slain. The siege had lasted a month, when, finding that the shot of his engines was of little avail against walls so strong and high, Edward sent to York, Lincoln, and London, ordering all their most effective war machines to be forwarded to his camp; and he constructed two new ones that discharged leaden balls of 300 pounds weight with such force as to command the lofty battlements; he also caused arrows to be shot into the tower round the heads of which balls of cotton were wrapped that were kindled with Greek fire to consume the buildings. The perseverance of the stern old monarch, who was determined not to leave the castle untaken, prevailed; and after the siege had lasted three months the small band of brave defenders, reduced to the last extremity, were forced to capitulate. Nothing less than their unconditional surrender would satisfy the pride of Edward; and they were obliged to appear before him with their heads and feet bare, with ropes round their necks, and their bodies stripped to their drawers and shirts, and in this condition to crave for mercy upon their knees. In this way he ungenerously endeavoured to degrade 140 brave soldiers—for this was their scanty number—who had kept his whole army at bay for three months, and who had only yielded when their last meal was consumed and their last defence thrown down. After this the whole were consigned to prisons in England.

Every castle in Scotland had now surrendered, and the conquest was more complete than ever. But Sir William Wallace still survived; and as long as he lived the conquest of his country could never be sure and certain, no, not for a single day. Of this Edward was well assured; and he employed every means, not only of open pursuit but secret craft and treachery, either to destroy the national champion or entrap him within his toils. There were Scotchmen also base enough to co-operate in his designs; and of these recreants Sir John Menteith is doomed to the imperishable infamy of having been the successful traitor, notwithstanding all the historical cavil and denial that has attempted to clear his memory. Whether the promised reward was his sole motive, or whether he was instigated by some personal or family feud, it is impossible now to discover, and perhaps does not greatly matter—for it was a deed of such damning iniquity as to defy extenuation. Menteith employed a servant of Wallace, called Jack Short,[1] to watch and betray his master; and so successfully did this emissary play his part, that the hero was apprehended in his bed in Glasgow, at the house of a certain Ralph Raa or Ray.[2] On being secured the captive was brought to London, and led to a place of confinement "with great numbers of men and women wondering upon him."[3] On the day after his arrival, so expeditious were his judges, he was brought on horseback to Westminster for trial, and attended by the mayor, sheriffs, and aldermen of London, with a strong guard of horse and foot. In derision, also, a crown of laurel was placed on his head, when he was arraigned in Westminster Hall, because, according to the report of his enemies, he had said that he ought to wear a crown in that hall. His impeachment, which was made by Sir Peter Mallorie, the royal justice, contained a long array of deeds in behalf of his country, but each a deed of treason, because committed against Edward. After the conquest of Scotland and the submission of Baliol and the nobles, this William Wallace, it was declared, had traitorously levied war against his liege sovereign of England; he had gathered to himself an immense host of felons, with whom he assailed the king's officers and servants; he had slain William Heselreg,[4] governor of Lanark; he had driven out the king's garrisons

---

[1] *Chronicle of Robert de Brunne.*
[2] Arundel MSS. in *Illustrations of Scottish History* of the Maitland Publications. Wyntoun.
[3] Stow.
[4] This person is named Hislop, Haselrig, and Heselreg indifferently by the old English historians.

from the towns, cities, and castles of Scotland, and by his own authority had convoked parliaments to form an alliance with France for its aid against the King of England. With his accomplices he had also invaded the counties of Northumberland, Cumberland, and Westmoreland; and in addition to the atrocities committed against the laity of these counties, slaying old and young, man, woman, and child, he had slaughtered monks and holy men, burned churches, and destroyed their sacred relics. Moreover, when King Edward with his army had again entered Scotland, and granted it a lasting peace, the aforesaid William Wallace had persisted in his felonious and seditious practices, refusing to submit to the king's peace, and for this he had been outlawed according to the statutes and customs both of England and Scotland.[1] Wallace indignantly denied that he was a traitor. He had never sworn fealty to Edward, and his resistance was nothing more than which the English had offered to Louis the Dauphin in defence of Edward's own father and of the rights of England, when they were invaded by a foreign master. As for the hostility he had waged, and the damage he had inflicted upon the English, these were deeds too notorious to be denied, as well as too consistent with the usages of war to be excused, and therefore he offered no defence. The sentence of the judge was inflicted upon him with all its horrible details (23d August, 1305). In chains he was dragged through the streets at the tails of horses to the Elms in Smithfield, the common place of execution; he was hanged for a short space, and then cut down; and while still living his bowels were taken out and burned before his face. No parting speech, no dying words of Wallace, have been recorded: they may have been unheeded or suppressed; but one little incident connected with his execution, although delivered by an authority whom it is the fashion of our day utterly to discard,[2] is too natural, as well as too affecting to be rejected, while it forms a welcome relief to the horrors of the scaffold. From childhood a cherished book of Wallace was a psalter, which he always carried with him wherever he went; but it had been taken from him with his weapons when he was apprehended. At his request Lord Clifford caused it to be brought to him; and on receiving it the Scottish hero, whose hands were bound, had it held before his eyes by a priest, and he continued to look upon it to the last. His head was struck off, and consigned to its place on London Bridge; his four quarters were sent to Newcastle, Berwick, Stirling, and Perth, to be set up and exhibited as a scorn, a gazing-stock, and a warning. Thus equally was he parted between England, which he had so sorely chastised, and Scotland which he had raised into rebellion. But without him, where would have been the civic privileges of these fair cities, or even the liberty of England and Scotland themselves, in which they have learned so cordially to participate? Even the boasted Magna Charta, which the Plantagenets would have torn into shreds, found its truest and ablest champion and preserver in Wallace, the hero of Scotland.

---

[1] These offences were all and each to be visited with a correspondent punishment, which was thus expressed in his sentence: "Consideratum est quod prædictus Willelmus pro manifesta seditione . . . detrahatur a palatio Westmonasterii usque Turrim Londoñ, et a Turri usque Allegate, et sic per medium civitatis usque Elmes; et pro robbertis et homicidiis et feloniis, quas in regno Angliæ et terra Scotiæ fecit, ibidem suspendatur et postea devaletur. Et quia utlegatus fuit, nec postea ad pacem domini regis restitutus, decolletur et decapitetur. Et postea pro inmensa vilitate, quam Deo et sacrosanctæ ecclesiæ fecit comburendo ecclesias, vasa et feretra, in quibus corpus Christi et corpora sanctorum et reliquiæ eorundem collocabantur, cor, epar, et pulmo et omnia interiora ipsius Willelmi, a quibus tam perversæ cogitationes processerunt, in igneni mittantur et comburentur. Et etiam quia non solum ipsi domino regi, sed toti plebi Angliæ et Scotiæ, prædictus seditionem, deprædationes, incendia, et homicidia et felonias fecerat, corpus illius Willelmi in quatuor quarteria scindatur et dividatur, et caput sic abscissum assedatur super pontem Londoñ, in conspectu tam per terram quam per aquam transeuntium, et unum quarterium in gibetto apud Novum Castrum super Tynam, aliud quarterium apud Berwyk, tertium quarterium apud Stryvelyn, et quartum quarterium apud Villam Sancti Johannis, in metum et castigationem omnium præteriuntium et ea conspicientium," &c.—Wallace Papers of Maitland Club, pp. 102-3. The same causes are specified with equal minuteness in De Brunne's *Chronicle*.

[2] Henry the Minstrel.

CHAPTER V.

WAR OF INDEPENDENCE CONTINUED—ROBERT BRUCE (1305-1307).

New government established by Edward I. for Scotland—Robert Bruce—Review of Bruce's previous career—His early inconsistencies—He proposes to liberate Scotland—His singular compact with Comyn—Assassination of Comyn—Coronation of Bruce at Scone—Difficulties of his situation—Edward's preparations to suppress this new insurrection—Defeat of Bruce at Methven Wood—His subsequent wanderings and dangers—He is attacked and defeated by the Lord of Lorn—Bruce's gallantry in the retreat—His passage across Loch Lomond—He takes refuge in Rachrin—Edward's merciless execution of his Scottish prisoners—Capture of the castle of Kildrummy—Execution of Nigel Bruce.

Edward I. having thus freed himself by the execution of Sir William Wallace from the only obstacle he apprehended, found no difficulty in making those arrangements by which Scotland was to be governed as a dependency of England. Nothing, indeed, appeared more easy than such a task; for the fortresses were in his possession, the nobility had sworn allegiance to his rule, and the people at large were not only without courage but without a leader. He commanded the Scottish nation to elect ten commissioners to represent them in the English parliament, this representation to consist of two bishops, two abbots, two earls, two barons, and two persons for the commons; and on their repairing to London they were joined by twenty English commissioners, with whose aid a new constitution and laws were to be framed for the kingdom of Scotland. They set to work in compliance with his decree, and took care that their enactments should be in accordance with his wishes. The new government thus formulated was more lenient than could have been expected. The country was to be governed by the king's lieutenant, and under him the chief offices were to be held indifferently by Englishmen and Scots; the districts were to be superintended by sheriffs who should act for the king's profit and the maintenance of order; and while the old laws, under the name of the "custom of the Scots and Brets," were abrogated, the new Saxon code, that had been growing upon the old since the time of David I., was still further assimilated to that of England. In these changes, although the defaulters in the late revolt were not allowed to escape, their punishment was more lenient than could have been expected, consisting of a fine varying from one to five years of rental, according to the length or obstinacy of their resistance. But let the new government be as mild as it might, it was still the token of national degradation and subjection; and its leniency only indicated the confidence of the victor, and his determination that the conquest should be sure and lasting.

Little, however, did it matter how wise or just or gentle it might be when, before the ink had dried, the parchment was torn into shreds and thrown to the winds. Another Wallace was in the field. Scottish resistance had been resumed. The kingdom, instead of being peacefully ruled, must be conquered anew.

The hero of this formidable revolt was Robert Bruce, Earl of Carrick, and grandson of the competitor whose conduct during the preceding years had been so changeable and perplexing. As he has hitherto flitted only for a few moments and at irregular intervals before our notice, a more collected account of his antecedent career will be necessary for the better understanding of his future proceedings, and this especially as he impersonates the most important epoch of Scottish history.

The circumstances that occasioned the romantic union of the Lord of Annandale to the Countess of Carrick have been already related.[1] Their son Robert, the future champion and King of Scotland, was born on the 11th of July, 1274. At the period, therefore, of the execution of Wallace, which occurred on the 23d of August, 1305, Bruce had ended his thirty-first year. The competition for the crown of Scotland, in which he had such a deep personal interest, must have kindled within his young heart an ambition which, though occasionally suppressed by after events, could never be extinguished; and to this ruling principle of his youth, waging a constant war with those patriotic feelings which seem to have been of slower and later growth, may be mainly attributed that early fickleness of conduct which concealed the native strength and nobleness of his character. It may have also proved his best safeguard against the watchfulness of Edward, who could little suspect that a young man of so many changes would prove such a formidable and successful rival. In this spirit young Robert, who with his father was in the service of Ed-

---
[1] See above, p. 138.

ward, could be little expected to dissent from the proceedings of the English king in 1295-96, which had for their object the deposition of Baliol, more especially as the Earl of Carrick had been allured with the hope that he would be placed upon the throne of his rival. Both father and son had also been irritated by John Baliol, who during his short and unsuccessful revolt had deprived Bruce of the earldom of Carrick and bestowed it upon his own kinsman, John Comyn, Earl of Buchan.

After these events, and when the war of national independence succeeded, Robert Bruce was in a situation of considerable difficulty. With the insurgents were patriotism, victory, and the tempting allurements of military renown and adventure; but Wallace, as guardian of Scotland, acted in the name of John Baliol, and every success he achieved was a step towards the reposition of the fallen king. It was not wonderful that Bruce should demur in behalf of a cause he hated and a rival who had sought to bereave him of his patrimony, and persuade himself that Scotland was not to be benefited by such agencies in behalf of such a sovereign. But as the revolt of Wallace went onward and became more formidable this neutrality of the Bruce became suspicious to the English powers whom he most sought to propitiate; and a summons from the Bishop of Carlisle to meet him and the barons to whom the charge of that district had been committed, and consult with them on the troubled state of Scottish affairs, could not be refused. To Carlisle he accordingly went, followed by his vassals of Galloway. This was not enough, however, and he was obliged to swear upon the host and the sword of Thomas à Becket that he would be a true liegeman to Edward, and the active enemy of all his enemies, whether Scots or others. After this guarantee so doubly sanctioned Bruce returned home; and to prove the sincerity of his allegiance to the King of England he ravaged the lands of Sir William Douglas, who was serving under the banner of Wallace, and carried off as prisoners that nobleman's wife and children. If this rash deed was done in sincerity it was quickly repented of, or if it was adopted to blind the English the mask was speedily thrown aside; for he joined the secret councils of the Scottish patriots, and mustering his father's vassals of Annandale, he endeavoured to enlist them on the same side by appealing to their national feelings, and declaring that the oaths he had sworn at Carlisle had been wrung from him by force and fear. But these men of Annandale had a lord whom they preferred to their country; and as he was now serving under Edward they would not compromise his safety let the jeopardy of Scotland be what it might. They therefore stole away in the night from their young master, whom they must have regarded as a rash or undutiful son, and left him to prosecute the adventure alone. Bruce then joined the insurgents along with those other Scottish nobles whose accession was such a doubtful aid to Wallace and national liberty; but his new-born ardour was so short-lived that at the capitulation of Irvine he accepted the terms of peace, became once more the liegeman of England, and gave his daughter Marjory, the mother of the future dynasty of Scotland, as the hostage of his faith. In this way he deprived himself of a share which he might otherwise have enjoyed in the glorious victory of Stirling, and escaped the punishment with which, in all likelihood, such a participation would have been visited.

After this narrow escape Bruce returned to his cautious neutrality and shut himself up in the castle of Ayr, apparently indifferent to the claims of either party, although his father and uncle were in the service of England. But if he thus exempted himself from the dangers of the defeat at Falkirk, he found it still more difficult to escape the wrath of the victorious Edward, in whose eyes such neutrality was nothing but passive hostility, and who marched westward after the battle to chastise his lukewarm vassal. But Bruce fled at his approach, and his castle of Lochmaben was seized by Edward as the foretaste of a worse punishment. It is possible, however, that the services of his father pleaded in his behalf, for in the sharp sentences of Edward that visited the other Scottish nobles Robert Bruce, the younger, was wholly exempted from either fine or imprisonment.

The fluctuations of the unsteady young hero, numerous though they had been, had not yet terminated. In Scotland, indeed, at this time political oscillation had become a national epidemic; it was at least a vertigo or St. Vitus's dance which had visited the nobility; and upon Bruce, unhappily, a double portion of the malady seems to have fallen. After the resignation of the guardianship by Wallace a regency was chosen for the restoration of the national independence; and among these new rulers who attempted such a perilous experiment was the young Earl of Carrick. What was still more surprising was that he took office with John Comyn, the younger of Badenoch, the enemy of his house and the rival of his royal claims. But on this occasion Bruce was obliged to take a decided part, for he felt that the suspicious eye of Edward was upon him; and in such a strait it was much that he should adopt the cause of his fallen country, instead of seeking to remove Edward's suspicions by following an opposite course. This, however, produced the chastisement that might have been expected; for during his invasion of Scotland, A.D. 1300, the King of England wasted the lands of Bruce and took his castle of Lochmaben. Quelled by this demonstration, or foreseeing the hopelessness of the national resistance, the young Earl of Carrick returned once more to the predominant side and left his brother guardians to shift for themselves, so that he had no share in the victory of Roslin, the renown of which fell to his rival, John Comyn. In this way, when the Scottish reverses succeeded, Bruce had secured the confidence and favour of Edward, while Comyn was punished by a heavy fine. He was now also the head of his powerful house, his father having died in 1304, and he had succeeded to its great estates in England and Scotland without diminution. In all these changes we cannot help detecting a mind that was very slow in learning the principle either of decision or patriotism. How much would his heroic reputation have been enhanced if his early history had corresponded with that of his more matured years!—if, like Wallace, he had started at the first summons of his country and thrown every selfish calculation aside! But he was as yet, by the circumstances of descent and hereditary feeling, only half a Scot; and independently of his princely possessions, which would have been staked on the chances of a desperate game, he had, it may be, the prospect of a crown in reversion, which a single step might have exchanged into the scaffold of Smithfield. All this may explain and palliate, although it cannot excuse, the manifold shiftings of Robert Bruce between two countries and two contending interests whose claims upon him seemed to be almost equal, and amidst whose alternate rise and fall the most experienced wisdom found it often hard to choose.

But events had ripened, and the time had arrived when not only his choice must be decisively made, but firmly and consistently adhered to. He had now reached an age when ambition is likely to be fully matured, and the powers of thought and action developed for its full exercise; and if he would obtain the crown to which his secret aspirations had been directed, he must now show himself able to win and worthy to wear it. To effect this, but without revealing his ultimate intent, he had formed those bonds of alliance with several nobles and barons which were common to the Norman aristocracy both of England and Scotland, in which they engaged to support each other in every feud, let the enemy or the cause be what it might; and he had adopted for his principal supporter and counsellor the politic and patriotic William de Lamberton, Bishop of St. Andrews. But the most singular union of this kind into which Bruce entered was with John Comyn, his rival, who, as the son of John Baliol's sister Marjory, had inherited since the abdication of his uncle all the royal claims of the Baliol family, which, after the utmost consideration, had been proclaimed stronger than those of the rival house. This portentous alliance between the two claimants for such a prize occurred, as we are told, while they were riding from Stirling and mutually lamenting the misgovernment of the country through the oppressive rule of Edward. It was then that Comyn, after acknowledging the superior right of his companion to the crown, made the following proposal: "Make yourself king, in which I shall aid you, and give me your estate in return; or if you do not choose the offer, take my estate, and aid me in becoming king." It was a startling proposal according to modern reckoning; but taking into account the spirit of the times and the risk of the enterprise it was, if made in good faith, a fair and reasonable offer. Bruce chose the more heroic alternative. "Since you will have it so," he said, "I will blithely take upon me the royal state, for I wot that I have the right, and right often makes the feeble strong." That night at the close of their journey the indenture was written out and subscribed between them, by which Bruce was to become King of Scotland, and John Comyn, the younger of Badenoch, commonly called the Red Comyn, the wealthiest and most powerful of its nobles.[1]

It was not long, however, before the Lord of Badenoch repented of his bargain; and eager to secure his own safety, as well as to involve his dangerous rival, he revealed to Edward the secret machinations of Bruce with which he had been made privy during the late interview, and even sent the indenture which had been drawn up and subscribed between them. Edward's eyes were opened at last, and the wiles of Bruce could no longer avail him: his death was resolved by a king whose ambition never relented, and in a few hours Bruce, who was in attendance upon the court in London, would have found himself in prison or before a tribunal. But in the midst of his unsuspecting security he was advertised of the treachery of Comyn and the purposes of Edward. Here the story becomes so dark, and the events so numerous and contradictory, that selection is at a loss; and amidst the many romantic incidents with which the detection of Bruce and his fortunate escape into

---

[1] Barbour's *Bruce*, book i. p. 18; Jamieson's edition.

Scotland are crowded, the historian can do little else than rejoin the hero at the last stage of his flight.[1] He had successfully achieved his escape from London, and baffled or outstripped pursuit; and on the seventh day[2] he arrived at his castle of Lochmaben. The English judges were about to hold a justiciary court at Dumfries; and as both Comyn and Bruce were freeholders in the district their duties required them to give attendance on the occasion. A dangerous meeting between the rivals was therefore a natural event; and there Bruce, the circumstances of whose departure from London were still unknown, invited Comyn to a private interview in the convent of the Minorites. From the sacredness of the place it may be reasonably inferred that he contemplated using no sharper weapons than angry words. The rivals met: Bruce accused the other of treachery, and a hot altercation followed, in which Comyn used the insulting expression, "You lie!" At these words, though the pair had then reached the foot of the altar, Bruce was so blinded with rage that he plucked out his dagger, struck it into the body of the insulter, and instantly, as if overwhelmed with the atrocity of the deed, he rushed from the building, and called eagerly for his horse. His friends, Kirkpatrick and Lindsay, on seeing his agitation, asked what was the matter, to whom he replied, "I doubt I have slain Comyn!" "Do you only doubt it?" cried the truculent Kirkpatrick; "I mak sikkar!" and with these words he rushed into the sanctuary, and killed the wounded man who was lying bleeding on the steps of the altar. To this account of a deed in itself so awfully criminal, other circumstances have been added that deepen its atrocity. We are told, for instance, that both Lindsay and Kirkpatrick entered the church; that they asked the wounded man if he thought he should recover; and that when he told them his hurt was not beyond cure if a skilful leech could be found, they made his death sure by fresh wounds. This was not all; for with him was also slain Sir Robert Comyn while hurrying to the rescue of his uncle. Barbour has also added that several others fell on this occasion, as if the single deed of assassination had drawn onlookers to the spot, and swelled into a deadly feudal skirmish. Whatever the truth regarding the concomitant circumstances, we know for certain that Comyn fell by the hand of Bruce after a hot and hasty debate, and that Kirkpatrick gloried in having finished the deed, adopting a gory hand and dagger as his military cognizance, and his own memorable exclamation for a motto.

The terrible deed, which Bruce had committed without premeditation and in a moment of frenzy, was fraught with such a fearful accumulation of consequences, that his stout heart must have sunk within him at the reflections which followed. He had murdered a man not only in a sanctuary, but at the very altar; he had slain him under breach of trust, and in a meeting for conference and discussion. By that one act he would not only be an accursed and excommunicated man, but accounted a false and perfidious knight and soldier. He had murdered the head of the most powerful family in Scotland, and involved himself in a death-feud with its numerous dependencies; and he had thereby involved himself in deadly quarrel with Edward, whose vengeance was certain to follow. As a Christian, a noble, a knight; as a subject, whether under English or Scottish law, he was now a manifest criminal, whom every class might hunt to execution, and his only chance of escape from a scaffold was the shelter of that throne with the allurements of which he had coyed so long and so inconsistently. Willingly or perforce he must now be a king, and he hesitated no longer. His first step, therefore, was a proclamation of defiance to England. Assembling his followers, he took possession of the castle of Dumfries; and as the English justiciaries who held their court in the great hall felt that their lives were in danger, and barricaded the door, the building was set on fire, and on their surrender they were dismissed unharmed, and sent to England. His next step was to hasten to his castle of Lochmaben, and summon his few adherents to repair to him for his coronation at Scone, and the maintenance of his cause against Edward. That castle was more than sufficient to receive and entertain the few supporters who assembled at his summons; but their names, which are dear to Scottish patriotism, ought not to be omitted. Of the clergy there were William de Lamberton, Bishop of St. Andrews, Robert Wishart, Bishop of Glasgow, David, Bishop of Moray, and the

---

[1] The account of Barbour seems most worthy of credence, who makes the revelation of Bruce's danger to have come from Edward himself, who showed him the indenture, and questioned him sharply about its authenticity. Bruce, pretending that he would satisfy the king by good proof on the morrow that the whole was a forgery, was allowed to retire to his lodging, that he might prepare his evidences; but long before the promised hour of appearance he had mounted his horse, and rode none could tell whither. Of the marvellous incidents with which the tale is garnished, such as the warning of twelve pence and a pair of spurs sent by the Earl of Montgomery (or of Gloucester), the Cacus expedient of inverted horse-shoes with which Bruce endeavoured to give a false track to his pursuers, and his slaying and despoiling Comyn's servant of his master's letters on the Border—these are not noticed by Barbour, who, if they had been true, or even talked of in his day, would scarcely have neglected such choice poetical embellishments.

[2] The fifth day according to Barbour.

Abbot of Scone. Of the higher nobility there were only two, the Earls of Athole and Lennox. Of the barons there were Edward, Nigel, Thomas, and Alexander, the brothers of Bruce; Thomas Randolph, his nephew; Christopher Seton, his brother-in-law; Gilbert de la Haye of Errol, and his brother Hugh de la Haye, David Barclay of Cairns, Alexander Fraser of Oliver Castle, Walter de Sommerville of Linton and Carnwath, David of Inchmartin, Robert Boyd, and Robert Fleming. As this little band set out on their apparently hopeless adventure they were met on their way and joined by a gallant young knight whose aid was of itself worth armies: this was Sir James Douglas, the son of that Lord William Douglas who had joined the banner of Wallace, and afterwards suffered grievous injury at the hands of Edward, who had given his estate to Lord Clifford. Barbour, who describes the circumstances under which this gallant youth sets forth to join the desperate cause, exclaims in a burst of poetical and affectionate fervour, "Dear God, who art king of heaven, save him and shield him from his enemies!" The band rode through Glasgow, where it was increased by a few adherents, and they all proceeded to Scone, where Bruce was crowned on Friday the 27th of March (1306), but with maimed rites and obscured ceremonial; for crown and sceptre had been carried away by Edward, and above all, the sacred stone which would have imparted promise and blessing to the new dynasty. The Bishop of Glasgow furnished such robes as would look most kingly from his own wardrobe; a golden circlet, probably borrowed from the head of a saint, supplied the place of a crown; and Bruce was placed upon the throne—or what was adopted to represent it—not by the Earl of Fife, to whom that duty hereditarily pertained, but who now was in the service of Edward, but by a fair lady, Isabella, Countess of Buchan, and sister of the Earl of Fife, who claimed the family right, and was eager to perform a ceremony which her brother on this occasion would have repudiated. She also brought good aid to the new king by presenting to him her husband's war-horses. For all this she was afterwards punished not only by English historians, who unjustly traduced her good name as a chaste woman and a wife, but by the King of England himself, who subjected her to the penalties of treason.

In this manner, without an army save the few friends who accompanied him, and without a fortress except the castle of Kildrummy in Aberdeenshire, Robert Bruce became King of Scotland. Nothing, indeed, but the imperious force of necessity could have induced him to adventure such a perilous step at so unpromising a period. The King of England whom he thus so daringly defied was, although now an old man, still fresh and vigorous for action, and as politic and relentless in following out his purposes as he had been at the ripest period of manhood, while the armies which he could collect would make resistance a desperate trial even though the whole of Scotland should be combined for the effort. On the other hand the Scottish nobles were either cowed into submission, and therefore deaf to the summons of Bruce, or friendly to the Comyn faction and therefore ready to oppose him. Even at the best, half the nation would be disposed to ask whether Bruce could be lawfully and legitimately king; but under the present most unfavourable circumstances he had scarcely a supporter beyond the members of his own family. And what career could be more inauspicious than one commenced with sacrilege and murder? On the other side, however, there were contingencies which Bruce had doubtless taken into account. The example of Wallace had already shown what a love of national freedom was cherished in the hearts of the common people, and of what sacrifice and exertion they were capable in its behalf. The nobility of Scotland, too, who had held aloof from the late champion on account of his inferior rank and birth, could not thus demur when the new candidate was one of the highest of their own order, who would be careful of its interests as well as his own. In this way, let him be but successful in his first attempts, though they should be but adventurous skirmishes, and a reaction both of noble and peasant might take place in his favour. By such calculations it is not unlikely that Bruce nerved himself for the coming struggle, and that over the gloom the example of Wallace rose like a guiding star to enlighten his cheerless path and lead him on to victory. All in the first instance depended upon his own efforts, whether of daring or endurance, and these he resolved should not be wanting. Besides all this the terrible Edward, whose talents and resources were most to be dreaded, had now reached the age of sixty-five; he must die in a few years, and perhaps might die in a few months; and the Prince of Wales, who would succeed, had already evinced a very different character from that of his illustrious father. These, indeed, were nothing more than chances; but what young aspiring mind in the situation of Bruce would not clutch at such chances with the firm resolve of converting them into realities? For one imminent danger, indeed, which perhaps weighed heaviest of all, Bruce had made good preparation. The curse of the church, which already had struck down kings and emperors in the very height of their power, was about to be launched at his head. But Scotland was still far from Rome and cared little for the thunder of the Vatican; while the chiefs of the Scottish clergy were upon his side, and would effectually interpose in a warfare which they were best fitted to encounter.

It would be difficult to describe the rage and astonishment of Edward when tidings of these events were carried to England. Little more than five months had elapsed since Wallace had died upon the scaffold, and in him it was thought that the light of Scotland had been quenched and its hope annihilated. But another Wallace had appeared, and yet again must Scotland be subdued. Crippled with disease or the lassitude of old age, so as to be unable to mount his horse or to travel but in a chariot, Edward, during the season of Lent, was peacefully reposing at Winchester when the tale reached him, first of the murder of Comyn, and afterwards of the coronation of Bruce. Roused as by the defiance of a war-trumpet, the worn-out veteran king once more started into action and made his preparations for a new war and conquest with all the promptitude of his earlier years. To provide against the chance of an invasion from Scotland he ordered the garrisons of Berwick and Carlisle to be strengthened, and he appointed Aymer de Valence, Earl of Pembroke, to be guardian of Scotland, with full power to levy all the military resources of York and Northumberland for the suppression of this new rebellion. Nor was he neglectful of those spiritual weapons which the case so temptingly offered; and, after sending to Clement V. an account of the murder of Comyn in the sanctuary of Dumfries, he applied for a sentence of excommunication against the impious homicide, which was forthwith transmitted from Rome, while the Archbishop of York and the Bishop of Carlisle were authorized to proclaim it. And that no means might be omitted for the punishment of Bruce and his adherents, Edward also arrayed against them all those formidable resources which chivalry could so effectually furnish. He proclaimed a solemn festival, to be held at Westminster on the feast of Pentecost, for the purpose of investing his son Edward of Caernarvon and other young noble aspirants with the order of knighthood; and so splendid an assemblage repaired on the occasion that the palace was too small to hold them, so that they had to repair to the orchard of the New Temple, the trees of which were cut down for the occasion. Three hundred youths of illustrious families, with the Prince of Wales at their head, were knighted with all that magnificence of military and religious ceremonial which the stately institution of chivalry could use with such imposing effect; and at the feast given on the occasion two swans inclosed in a golden net-work, the knightly emblems of constancy and truth, were brought in with a fanfare of trumpets, psalteries, and shawms, and reverently placed upon the table. The venerable sovereign then rose, and stretching forth his hands, made a solemn vow "to the God of heaven and to the swans" that he would inflict severe vengeance upon Bruce for his outrage against God and the church, and upon the Scots for their treachery; and that after this he would never more unsheathe his sword against a Christian foe, but hasten to Palestine to wage war against the Saracens and die in the Holy Land. After this strange oath, so accordant with the religious spirit of the age, the Prince of Wales solemnly swore that he would not remain two nights in the same place until he reached Scotland.[1]

Edward having thus imparted his hatred to the rising generation, and raised a storm against his enemies which would not expire at his death, made preparations on an ample scale for a war of extermination. To defray its expenses the merchants agreed to contribute a tenth, and the clergy and laity a thirtieth, while the armed muster was appointed to meet at Carlisle fifteen days after midsummer. Thither Edward came by slow and easy stages; but he was too feeble and exhausted to accompany his army into Scotland, and he therefore sent thither the Earl of Pembroke as commander of the expedition, while the Prince of Wales and his young chivalrous companions followed in the rear. Whatever might have been the personal courage of the prince on this occasion, or the benefits of his presence to such an enterprise, it is certain that clemency was not one of them, and his conduct gave the Scots a sharp warning of the treatment they might expect should he become their king. Such, indeed, was his merciless ferocity in wasting the country and sparing neither age nor sex, that his father himself, incensed as he was at the whole Scottish nation, was obliged, it is said, to interpose.

While this formidable army had been mustering against Scotland its new king had not been idle, but of his particular movements for three months after his coronation we have no distinct account. This, however, can be easily accounted for by the smallness of his party and the hostility of the Comyns, who had the greater part of the kingdom at their disposal. We can easily imagine that, amidst such danger and opposition, the movements of Bruce were numerous and rapid, and more like the shiftings of a fugitive outlaw than a candidate for a throne; and that

---

[1] M. Westminster.

his appeals to the patriotism both of nobles and people were urgent and incessant. At length he laid siege to Perth, where the Earl of Pembroke had established his headquarters with a strong garrison. As the town was well fortified with strong towers and high ramparts the limited means of Bruce did not permit a regular siege; and he therefore endeavoured to tempt his enemy into the field, there to try the right of possession by a pitched battle. Kindled by this challenge, and being stronger by 1500 men than the assailants, Pembroke would at once have issued from the walls but for the sage counsel of Sir Ingelram de Umfraville, who represented to him the valour of the enemy and their leader, and advised that they should be assailed by a night attack when it was least expected. This advice prevailed, and Pembroke sent in answer to the defiance of Bruce that he would march out of Perth and meet him in battle on the morrow. Trusting more than a leader should have done to the fantastic obligations of chivalry, Bruce drew off his troops to the neighbouring wood of Methven, where they encamped in full security, while a third part of their number dispersed themselves in quest of forage. But at night, while the soldiers were cooking their supper, they were roused by the cry that the enemy was upon them. Bruce himself had so little expected this onset that he was unarmed; but he hastily girded on his mail, mounted his war-steed, and ordered his banner to be displayed. The fight that followed was but a tumult and confusion on the part of the Scots, although their king by almost incredible efforts of prowess endeavoured to check the assailants and repair his error. Thrice was he unhorsed amidst the press of opposing multitudes and as often remounted; and on one occasion his bridle-rein was seized by Sir Philip Mowbray, who shouted, "Help, help! I have got the new-made king!" when a blow from Sir Christopher Seton struck Mowbray to the ground. Seeing all resistance hopeless, Bruce counselled retreat, advising his followers to disperse in small parties to baffle pursuit, and be ready to assemble when the danger was over; and with five hundred of his men who kept together in a body he extricated himself from the perilous wood of Methven. But in this fatal night engagement, besides those who had fallen, several of his best friends and supporters were taken prisoners, the chief of whom were Sir Thomas Randolph, his nephew, at that time a young bachelor of arms or esquire; Sir Alexander Fraser, Sir David Barclay, Sir David Inchmartin, Sir Hugh de la Haye, and Hugh, the chaplain of Bruce. On Pembroke advising his master of the victory Edward commanded him to execute instantly all his prisoners—an order which the earl did not carry into effect; and in consequence of this delay, while only a few knights were afterwards hanged and quartered, some were ransomed, and others liberated on promising to be the liegemen of the King of England. Among these last was Sir Thomas Randolph, who was not yet confirmed in his principles or superior to the shifting character which distinguished that mutable period.

After this disheartening defeat Bruce retreated for shelter to the wilds and mountains of Athole; and among the band that accompanied him were Sir Edward Bruce his brother, the Earl of Athole, Sir James Douglas, Sir Gilbert de la Haye, Sir Nigel Campbell, and Sir William de Barondoun. Nothing could be more wretched and hopeless than the condition of this band of wanderers cooped up in a barren country where they could find little subsistence, and yet afraid to venture into the plains where their followers might be tempted to desert them. In a short time their apparel was worn out and rent; they had no shoes but such as they made of the untanned hides of the beasts they killed in hunting; and even this sorry subsistence was so scanty and precarious that they were obliged by hunger to descend into the low country of Aberdeenshire at the risk of falling into the hands of their enemies. At Aberdeen Bruce was joined by his queen, and by the wives and daughters of the principal wanderers, who were anxious to share or alleviate the privations of their husbands and fathers, and who had come to them escorted by Sir Nigel Bruce, the king's brother. Bruce rejoiced at their coming, although it only increased his difficulties, for he learned that the English had heard of their resort, and meant to fall upon them by surprise. This report hastily broke up their encampment, and the band of patriots with their affectionate partners retreated from the town to the bleak shelter of the wilderness. As their wants were increased they were obliged to be doubly assiduous in hunting and fishing, and in these desperate shifts none was so useful as Sir James Douglas. This young knight, who had been educated among the refinements of the French court, was as gentle, courteous, and debonnair as he was valiant; and therefore, while he comforted the king with his wit and scholarly conversation, he was constant in his attention to the sufferings of the ladies, and no one was so dexterous as he in making gins and nets to snare the wary game, or so successful in hunting and fishing. He was indeed a "very perfect knight" of a rude age and ruder country.

In the course of their wanderings the party arrived at the head of the Tay; and here their dangers were increased, for they were now in the country of Breadalbane, which was ruled by Alexander, Lord of Argyle and Lorn, who had married the aunt of the murdered Comyn, and was therefore at deadly feud with Bruce and all his family. On hearing that his hated enemy was so nigh, this mountain satrap collected a thousand of his hardy and devoted followers, and rushed down to take the royal party by surprise. Bruce was fortunately aware of his coming; but the superior numbers of the enemy, and the warfare of the mountainous passes for which his heavy-armed soldiers were unfitted, made the conflict every way unequal. They bore themselves indeed bravely and made a stout resistance; but their armour of plate and mail was an insecure defence against the heavy Lochaber axes of the Highlanders, while their footing among rock and morass deprived them of the full use of their horses and weapons and their wonted modes of warfare. Sir James Douglas and Sir Gilbert de la Haye were wounded; the floundering steeds of the men-at-arms were struck down; and seeing the hopelessness of resistance on such dangerous ground, Bruce gave orders to retreat, taking his place meanwhile in the rear to hold the pursuers in check, which he effected to the terror and admiration of his enemies. One of his deeds on this occasion extorted their applause, and put an end to the pursuit. Three devoted vassals of the Lord of Lorn had resolved to destroy this enemy of their chief, and followed him for the purpose, until they overtook him at a part of the pass where there was a loch on one side and a precipitous bank on the other, with a path so narrow between as scarcely to give him room to wheel his war-steed. At this place of advantage they all sprang upon him at the same instant, and one of them seized the king's bridle; but Bruce with a blow of his sword lopped off the captor's arm by the shoulder. The second seized the king's foot to drag him from the saddle; but Bruce jammed the fellow's hand between the mailed foot and iron stirrup, so that he held him as in a trap, and drew him after him by rising in his seat and giving his horse the spur. The third Highlander with a tiger-like spring leaped upon the horse behind, hoping to pinion the arms of Bruce, or stab him in the back; but, exerting his great strength to the utmost, Bruce turned in the saddle, dragged the man forward upon his horse's neck, and despatched him with a single blow, after which he made an end of the prostrate enemy whom he still held fast by the stirrup. This threefold task, as it required great promptitude, seems to have been scarcely the work of as many seconds. One of Lorn's barons called MacNaughton, on seeing the gallant efforts of Bruce to protect his followers, and especially the last deed we have mentioned, was loud in his praises. "In what a little time," he cried, "he has felled three of our strongest to the earth, so that none dare follow him: he is the bravest champion I ever beheld." "You seem to be delighted," said Lorn angrily, "at the slaughter he makes among our followers." "Not so," replied the other, "but we ought to praise a gallant deed whether done by friend or enemy." On perceiving that his enemies had cleared the dangerous pass, Lorn discontinued the pursuit. The place where this fatal skirmish happened is still called Dalry, or the king's field, in commemoration of the event.

As winter was now approaching the hardships of the wanderers were increased, and their scanty resources of hunting and fishing began to fail. It was therefore judged expedient that the ladies should no longer accompany them; and after a tender parting they were sent under a strong escort commanded by Nigel Bruce to the castle of Kildrummy, and provided with all the horses of the company to carry them on their way. Bruce and his attendants, who were now reduced to 200 men, continued their pilgrimage on foot, oppressed with hunger, winter storms, and cold, but resolving to force their passage to Cantire, and afterwards proceed to Ireland, where the Earl of Ulster might provide them with shelter for the winter. With this design they prosecuted their route through Perthshire, but on reaching the banks of Loch Lomond they were brought to a sudden pause, for they had no means of crossing the loch, while to travel round it would only lead them into the hostile territory of the Lord of Argyle and Lorn. When pursuit in the meantime was every moment to be apprehended the fortunate Douglas found a boat sunk in the water; and although it was a crazy leaky skiff that could only hold three persons, it carried over a part of the band by frequent trips, the others crossing by swimming. A night and a day, however, were spent in this weary transit, and to cheer his drooping followers during the delay, Bruce, who appears to have read much during his years of leisure, recounted to them the romance of *Ferembras* and other tales of chivalry, in which the weak triumphed, and the many were overcome by the few.[1] Having crossed the lake the hunger-worn party explored the neighbouring woods in search of food, although the enemy was on their track. On hearing the noise of their coming the Earl of Lennox, who was among the neighbour-

---

[1] Barbour informs us that he *read* the romance of *Ferembras*. In this case Bruce must have carried about with him in his wanderings a story-book just as Wallace carried his psalter.

ing hills, came down with his attendants to learn the meaning of this arrival. He had been a firm supporter of the cause of Bruce, whom he had not seen since the battle of Methven, and whom he already believed to be dead; but on meeting thus unexpectedly with his royal friend and master the two embraced each other with tears of joyful congratulation. He was himself indeed a homeless wanderer like the king; but he had not been reduced to such straits, and he was able to supply the whole company with a plentiful meal. As no time was to be lost they continued their route to Cantire by sea, in vessels furnished by Sir Nigel Campbell, where they were hospitably received by Angus of Isla, the Lord of Cantire, in his castle of Dunaverty. It was indeed in a happy hour that they thus set sail, for the pursuit was so close upon them that the Earl of Lennox, the last who embarked, would have been overtaken by the English, had he not escaped by hard rowing and throwing everything overboard that could be spared.

After residing three days at the castle of Dunaverty, and receiving the homage of Angus of Isla, Bruce, who knew that even this extreme point of Scotland could furnish him with neither defence nor shelter, prepared for his temporary departure from the country. The bleak and obscure little island of Rachrin (or Rathlin) on the northern coast of Ireland was his place of choice, and thither he sailed with 300 followers in the small flotilla which the care of Sir Nigel Campbell had provided. Their landing upon the island dismayed the simple inhabitants as much as if it had been one of the old Norwegian invasions of which they may have preserved a traditionary remembrance; and when they saw their strand glittering with the arrival of mail-clad men, they collected their cattle in haste and fled to a place of strength in the interior. Their fears were quickly removed by the courteous words and explanations of the strangers, so that they received them with hospitality; and in this inclement and obscure hiding-place, concealed alike from friend and enemy, Bruce resolved to abide until a dawn of hope from Scotland should invite his return.

This escape of an enemy whose claims so formidably interfered with his own prospects highly aggravated the rage of the King of England, and his persecutions of the rebellious Scots, merciless though they had hitherto been, were now prosecuted with double severity. Too old and feeble to enter in person upon the scene, although he had got as near it as Lanercost, he issued his stern orders to Pembroke, the English Guardian of Scotland, who acted accordingly. He made proclamation that all Scottish people should search for and pursue every person who had been in arms against the English government, and had not surrendered to it; that all who had committed other crimes should be apprehended dead or alive; and that all who were negligent in this search should be punished with the forfeiture of their castles and dwellings, and be imprisoned during pleasure. The guardian was also empowered to punish at his discretion all who harboured the offenders above specified. While these decrees were sufficiently comprehensive a special measure of severity was reserved for all who might in any way countenance the crime of the murder of Comyn; and on this head it was proclaimed that all who had been present at the deed, or who abetted it, or who voluntarily and knowingly harboured any of the actors or abettors, should be drawn and hanged; and that all those already taken in arms, or who might afterwards be so taken, and all who harboured such persons, should be hanged or beheaded. The chief of those who had been in arms, and had surrendered themselves to mercy, were to be imprisoned during the King of England's pleasure. As for the common people, those who had been compelled to rise in arms at the command of their feudal superiors, but contrary to their own inclination, the guardian was commissioned to fine and ransom them as he judged fit.[1]

The proceedings of Edward in the condemnation of high and noble prisoners who had fallen or who soon after fell into his hands, evinced his resolution that these enactments should be anything but a dead letter; and the fate of his victims, although painful to tell, is yet necessary to be recorded for a more complete understanding of the times and the Scottish history of the period. We select in the first instance, as the least revolting, the punishment of those ecclesiastics who had sanctioned the cause of the excommunicated Bruce by their presence as well as aided it with their resources. Of these Lamberton, Bishop of St. Andrews, and the Abbot of Scone, who were taken in the full harness of knighthood by the Earl of Pembroke, were sent in fetters to Edward; and soon after Robert Wishart, Bishop of Glasgow, who had taken refuge in the castle of Cupar, was captured in the same unpriestly garb and sent in chains upon the same journey. They were accused of manifold acts of treason; but the whole amounted to the fact that before the battle of Methven they had supplied Bruce with money and the aid of armed retainers, and were still earnest in his cause. Edward would assuredly have sent them to the same gallows on which

---

[1] Rymer, *Fœd.*; Ryley; Tyrrel's *History of England.*

men of equally high estate were immolated had he not feared the perilous consequences of a new Thomas à Becket warfare, with all Christendom arrayed against him; and therefore stopping short of this, he inflicted as much as he dared, so that their places should know them no more. He accordingly applied to the pope, to whom the right alone pertained, requesting not only that the two bishops should be deposed, but that Walter Comyn, brother to the Earl of Buchan, might be appointed to the primacy of St. Andrews, and Jeffrey de Mowbray to the bishopric of Glasgow. But with this dictation in church government from a layman, even although he was a powerful sovereign, the pontiff did not think fit to comply, more especially when no particular benefit to Rome was to accrue from it. Edward, thus disappointed in his revenge against the patriotic churchmen, escheated their temporalities and condemned them to an imprisonment which he resolved should be perpetual.

Other victims more worthy of commiseration were those unfortunate ladies who had accompanied the wanderings of Bruce until his scanty resources could sustain them no longer. Of those who had been sent to the shelter of Kildrummy, his queen, Elizabeth, not judging the castle strong enough to protect her, had resolved to betake herself to that sanctuary where even felons and murderers were safe under the powerful guardianship of the church. With her young step-daughter Marjory, whose very childhood had been doomed to share in the sufferings of her country, the anxious queen set out for the sanctuary of St. Duthac, at Tain in Ross-shire, accompanied by an armed escort from the garrison of Kildrummy. But the Earl of Ross, under a craven dread of Edward, violated the sanctuary, took the ladies and their escort prisoners, and sent them to the English king, who threw the ladies into prison, where they endured eight years of captivity, and executed the knights and squires who had accompanied them as traitors. Mary and Christina, the sisters of Bruce, who afterwards fell into his hands, were also imprisoned, the former in a cage built for the purpose in one of the outer turrets of the castle of Berwick, and the latter in a convent. Nor did that heroic lady escape who had so boldly repaired to Scone that she might fulfil, as a Macduff, the sacred obligations of a Scottish coronation by placing the king upon the royal seat. Isabella, Countess of Buchan, was made prisoner at Tain, and her place of confinement was also a cage constructed in one of the turrets of Berwick Castle similar to that which contained the Lady Mary Bruce. These strange places of bondage were latticed and cross-barred with wood and secured with iron, so that while they were strong enough to prevent escape or rescue, they were so open that the noble captives, in spite of their rank and sex, were exposed to the ribald gaze of all who passed by. In this place of shameful captivity the countess was immured during four long years.[1]

While such were Edward's modes of dealing with priests and ladies, no mercy was to be expected for those gallant knights and nobles who were not so fortunate as to perish in the battle-field. Of these one of the bravest and best-beloved of the Scottish nation was Sir Christopher de Seton, brother-in-law of Robert Bruce, whom he was also accused of having abetted in the murder of Comyn.[2] After having fought for his royal brother until the cause seemed hopeless he took shelter, it is said, in his castle of Loch Doon; but he was betrayed into the hands of the English by a false Scot, a "disciple of Judas" named MacNab, according to Barbour, who, kindling into rage at the deed and forgetting his priestly character, exclaims, "For this may he be condemned to hell!" Seton was hurried to Dumfries, and after a short trial was hanged as a traitor and an assistant in the death of Comyn. So dear was he to his brother-in-law that when better times succeeded Bruce erected a little chapel on the spot where he had been executed, and caused masses to be said there for his soul. As if to show that even a participation in his own royal blood could be no protection to those who partook in the Scottish rebellion, Edward selected for another of his victims John de Strathbogie, Earl of Athole, his own cousin, being the son of Matilda of Doune, the aunt of the King of England.[3] Athole, however, who remembered more his Scottish birth and nobility than his relationship to the English tyrant, had attended Bruce at his coronation, fought for him at Methven, and afterwards, on attempting to escape by sea, was apprehended by the enemy. Strong intercession was made on his behalf by certain English nobles on account of his royal descent; but Edward, swearing that this should procure him nothing more than a loftier gibbet, caused him to be hanged on a gallows fifty feet high. When only half-dead he was then cut down; his entrails were taken out and burned before his face, and his head, on being struck off, was sent to join that of Wallace on London Bridge. Edward, who at that time was suffering heavily from disease, is said to have experienced great relief from his pain when he heard of the capture of Athole.

---

[1] Ford. Anglia, II. 1014.   [2] Matt. West. p. 456.
[3] Matilda of Doune was daughter of Richard, the illegitimate son of King John.

A more formidable enemy than even the Earl of Athole also gratified, by his execution, the remorseless rage of Edward. This was the gallant veteran Sir Simon Fraser of Oliver Castle, a soldier renowned in the wars of the Continent, and afterwards in the threefold victory at Roslin, where he commanded the Scottish army in conjunction with Sir John Comyn. Only less persevering than Wallace, to whom he was reckoned but second in military skill and prowess, he had yielded at last when the other persisted to the death; and he had been received to mercy on such hard terms as showed the obstinacy of his resistance and the dread he had inspired by his deeds. But on the rising of Bruce he was again in the field, and when it failed he betook himself to that outlaw and fugitive mode of life which was now the only refuge of Scottish patriotism. Every effort was made to apprehend him, but such were his boldness and ingenuity that the Scottish prisoners who had fallen into Edward's hands had said confidently that Fraser could not be taken. But he was at last overpowered and compelled to surrender after an unsuccessful stand at Kirkencliff, near Stirling; and on being sent to London he was brought into the city loaded with chains, and with his legs tied under the horse's belly, while in mockery his head was crowned with a wreath of periwinkle. His trial and sentence were also similar to those of Wallace, and fulfilled with the same horrid circumstances, even to the exposure of his head, which was also set up beside that of the champion of Scotland upon London Bridge. His body, indeed, was not dismembered, to be sent to the principal towns in Scotland; but it was hung in chains, and strictly guarded that no one might give it burial.

These were but a few of the Scottish victims of Edward, the gleanings of those fields over which the harvest of battle had passed, and that were as carefully collected as if the soil had been doomed never more to produce the fair fruits of heroic patriotism and national independence. And still, as the capture of more and yet more prisoners was reported, their fate was collectively sealed by the king from his sick-bed in the brief sentence, "Hang and draw!" which he exclaimed with his utmost strength and grinning with rage.[1] And thus the axe, the cord, and fire were kept in constant exercise. And fearful must have been the misgivings and anticipations of those Scottish persons of noble and knightly rank, to the number of twenty-seven, who were confined in English prisons, any of whom an additional twinge of Edward's grievous malady might have sent to the scaffold.

From these painful episodes we return to the regular course of events. And here the eye naturally reverts to the castle of Kildrummy, the only stronghold which Bruce possessed in Scotland, and to the handful of gallant defenders who, under his young brother, Sir Nigel, had resolved to hold it out against the whole force of England. Under such circumstances it was not unadvisedly that Queen Elizabeth, fearing the event, had withdrawn from it with her step-daughter Marjory, although the close of her flight was so unfortunate. Resolved to win this last hope of the Scottish rebels, Edward commanded the Earls of Lancaster and Hereford to besiege it in due form, and destroy all that held it without ransom, or take them prisoners without conditions. Barbour also adds the not unlikely circumstance, that with these earls he sent his son Edward, Prince of Wales. He must have felt, indeed, that his own end could not be far distant, and he was anxious to bequeath his ambitious purposes towards Scotland as a sacred legacy to him who should succeed him in the throne, and to train him in the warfare by which the conquest was to be secured. The castle thus assailed maintained a gallant resistance, and as it was strong and well provisioned there was every prospect of a long-continued siege. But there was a traitor named Osborne among the garrison, who set fire to the granary by throwing among the grain a piece of red-hot iron, and their corn being thus destroyed, the defenders were obliged to yield. The prisoners were sent to Berwick, where the chief of them were tried, and as a matter of course executed. The fate of Nigel Bruce, the young, and brave, and courteous, who excelled in that personal beauty by which his family were distinguished, and whose bright but brief career was terminated on the scaffold, where he was hanged and quartered, excited not only the deep sorrow of all Scottish hearts, but even the commiseration of his enemies.[2]

Thus was the measure of Bruce's punishment by the close of this year (1306) apparently filled up. In addition to these sufferings with which he had been visited through the merciless executions inflicted upon his friends and kindred, and the alienation of all his estates both Scottish and English, which Edward bestowed upon English nobles, he was solemnly excommunicated by the church, and the sentence pronounced in February (1306-7) at Carlisle by Cardinal St. Sabinus,[3] with all those imposing accompaniments which made it more fearful in

---

[1] Barbour, book iii. 1. 550.   [2] Matt. Westminst.; Barbour.   [3] Hemingford.

the eyes of men than the worst doom of any earthly tribunal. Hopeless, indeed, must his case have been accounted, when, if he still existed, he was now an utterly bereaved and doubly branded criminal, with heaven and earth equally closed upon his recovery.

CHAPTER VI.

WAR OF INDEPENDENCE CONTINUED—ROBERT BRUCE (1307-1312).

Sir James Douglas crosses from Rachrin to Arran—Defeats an English escort—Bruce lands in Arran—He passes over to Carrick—The false beacon—Bruce defeats a party of English soldiers at Turnberry—Douglas surprises his own castle of Douglasdale—The "Douglas Larder"—Bruce kills three conspirators—Defeat and execution of Bruce's brothers—Bruce pursued by the men of Galloway—His single-handed defence of a ford—Douglas defeats the garrison who held his castle—Bruce defeated by the Earl of Pembroke and Lord Lorn—His escape from the pursuit—He kills three assassins—He defeats the English at Glentruel—Douglas defeats the English at Makyrnock—Bruce's victory over the Earl of Pembroke at Loudon Hill—He defeats the Earl of Gloucester—Edward I. makes a dying attempt to invade Scotland—His death at Burgh-upon-Sands—Imbecile proceedings of Edward II. in Scotland—Bruce's victory at Old Meldrum—Successes of the Scots—Victories of Edward Bruce in Galloway—Douglas again captures his paternal castle—Takes Sir Thomas Randolph prisoner—Randolph reconciled to his uncle—Bruce's victory over the Lord of Lorn—Recognitions of his royal authority—Edward II. ineffectually invades Scotland—Invasion of England by Bruce—His capture of Perth—Growing helplessness of Edward II.—Bruce a third time invades England.

In the meantime the fortunes of Scotland were inclosed within the little island of Rachrin. So obscure was this place, and so remote from intercourse with the world, that it seemed expressly fitted to ensure the full safety of the fugitives; and the belief was prevalent over England and Scotland, both with friend and foe, that Bruce must be assuredly dead—that nothing but the grave itself could be the cause of such silence. But this concealment, in spite of its advantages, became intolerable to those swelling adventurous spirits, that longed to be free and employed once more in a world of enterprise and danger. Accordingly, after the dreary winter had passed and spring commenced, this feverish yearning for action was expressed by Sir James Douglas, who thought it foul shame that they should be a useless burden upon the poor islanders, when castles were to be surprised, and Englishmen put to the sword.[1] Having obtained the king's permission, he crossed with Sir Robert Boyd to the island of Arran to attempt the surprise of the castle of Brodick, with the defences of which they were well acquainted. As the building was strongly garrisoned with English soldiers under the command of Sir John Hastings, Douglas, who had landed by night, placed his small party in ambush, and waited till three boats arrived near the place commanded by the under warden, and laden with provisions, arms, and clothing for the garrison. Douglas and his followers instantly attacked the escort, slew forty of the soldiers, and captured their whole cargo. He then intrenched himself in a secure part of the island to wait the arrival of the king, while the enemy, unaware of the small number of their assailants, kept within the protection of their walls.

On the tenth day Bruce himself landed in Arran with all his company conveyed in thirty-three vessels which had been supplied by Christina of the Isles. In stepping upon the cliff-crowned shore of that romantic island of rock and promontory his first anxiety was to find the hiding-place of his advanced party under the gallant Douglas, and three blasts upon his horn that reached the dell in which they were living in free outlaw fashion proclaimed his approach, and brought them speedily to his side. As his own fair coast of Carrick loomed distinctly in the distance, where he hoped to find faithful retainers, he resolved to commence his operations there, and begin with an attack upon his castle of Turnberry, now strongly garrisoned by English soldiers under Sir Henry Percy. It was necessary, however, to ascertain the strength of the enemy and the dispositions of the people for a rising; and for this purpose he sent his trusty servant Cuthbert to the opposite coast, with orders, if he found matters favourable for a landing, to kindle a fire upon a certain eminence near Turnberry Castle as the signal. The king in the meantime traversed the beach with

---

[1] Barbour.

his eye fixed upon the appointed spot of warning, and at the time he had specified a bonfire gleamed upon the hill-top, and sent its cloudy pillar high into the air. The mission of Cuthbert, therefore, had been successful: Scotland might yet be redeemed. There was an instant hurrying to the beach and launching of skiffs upon the water. When Bruce was about to step on board, the poor woman who had been his hostess during his short stay in Arran brought to him her two sons, and assuring him in her character of prophetess that he would triumph over all his enemies, she besought him to enlist her sons in his dangers, and reward them when he became king. He embarked and would have landed in Carrick in full daylight; but fortunately for his cause on this occasion the wind was against him, so that night set in, and the weary rowers were obliged to direct their course by the beacon-light that still continued to blaze. But on landing near the point of Turnberry, they found Cuthbert awaiting them with sorrowful tidings. The garrison in the castle was fully 300 strong: two parties of the enemy were quartered in the town; and the hearts of the people of Carrick were so utterly quelled, that there was no hope of their assistance. "Traitor!" cried the king in a rage, "why, then, did you kindle the fire?" "Alas, sir!" replied the man, "the fire was not made by me; but, observing it and fearing it might deceive you, I hurried hither to warn you of your danger." In this strait a consultation was held; but the impetuous Edward Bruce, declaring that no peril on land should drive him back to the sea, and that he would follow the adventure whether for good or evil, quickly swayed the rest and overcame Robert's hesitation, who resolved to attack the parties in the town in the midst of their careless security. This was done; and the night assault was so successful that 200 of the enemy were put to the sword, while the garrison in the castle, who heard the din of conflict, were too much alarmed to sally out to the rescue. The conquerors were richly rewarded with the spoil, among which were Percy's household plate and war-horses.[1] Three days did the king remain in the neighbourhood of the castle while the English confined themselves within its walls; and during this period a lady of high rank, a kinswoman of his own, but whose name has not been mentioned, came to Bruce with supplies of money and refreshments, and a reinforcement of forty men. Seldom, indeed, was even a hero of romance so heroically and bountifully aided by woman's generous devotedness as this fugitive and persecuted king: in his sufferings they were ever ready to suffer with him, and in want to relieve him, even though their kinsmen should stand aloof or be opposed to him. Alas, that a spirit so pure and noble should also have been so undiscriminating as finally to settle upon the head of his unworthy descendant, the "Young Chevalier!"

In the meantime the English soldiers in Turnberry Castle, as well as the still greater party in that of Ayr, confined themselves within their strongholds; a mysterious dread of their opponents, from the uncertainty of their numbers and resources, prevented them from entering the field—in which case Bruce and his party might have been overpowered or dispersed. At length, on learning that a reinforcement of a thousand soldiers from Northumberland, under Sir Roger St. John, were marching to the relief of Turnberry Castle, Bruce retired before the arrival of this superior force and took refuge among the mountainous parts of the district. His cause was still in imminent hazard, as none of the inhabitants of Carrick had joined his banner; and it was only from the lady who had lately left him that he learned the calamities that had befallen his friends during his absence in Rachrin. He thus found that his castle of Kildrummy was in the hands of the enemy; that his beloved brother Nigel and his brave associates had been butchered by a judicial sentence; and that Athole, Seton, and other noble friends had died on the scaffold. The king vowed a severe retribution, and only waited for the opportunity.

While he was thus shifting among the mountains as he best could, his adventurous follower, Sir James Douglas, resolved to attempt the recovery of his native castle of Douglas, which Edward had bestowed upon Lord Clifford, who now occupied it with a strong English garrison. Having obtained Bruce's permission, Sir James set off upon his hardy enterprise attended only by two yeomen—"a simple staff," says Barbour, "to take a land or a castle withal." But he knew the devotedness of his faithful vassals, and that he should find them ready in the hour of need. He was received in the house of his trusty tenant named Dickson; and in disguise he was enabled to travel over Douglasdale, visit his people, and lay plans for the coming onslaught. Palm Sunday, which was at hand, was the day appointed, and the place the kirk of St. Bride, at which the country people as well as the soldiers of the garrison would meet as on common ground with palm branches in their hands in honour of the festival. Sir James and an armed party, but with their weapons concealed, entered the church unsuspected among the worshippers, and in the midst of the service

---

[1] Hemingford; Barbour.

suddenly threw off their disguises, shouted the dreaded war-cry, "A Douglas! a Douglas!" and fell upon the English soldiers. A furious conflict ensued, for the enemy, though so unexpectedly assailed, made a brave resistance; but at length the whole, to the number of thirty, were killed or taken prisoners. He then proceeded to the defenceless castle, which he plundered of all that was worth carrying away, after which he made a pile of the malt, corn, and provisions, staved the casks of wine and other liquors amidst the heap, crowned the loathsome mass with the bodies of the prisoners, whose heads were struck off without mercy, and set the whole, with the castle itself, on fire. He knew that he could not garrison the home of his fathers, and he was resolved that it should give no shelter to the enemy. But the savageness of the deed, although it was commemorated as a choice pleasantry under the title of the "Douglas Larder," and although it has been extenuated by the declaration that only ten prisoners thus suffered, will ever remain a foul blot upon the otherwise stainless reputation of the "good Lord James."

During the absence of this gallant partisan the difficulties of the Scottish king continued to multiply. De Valence, Earl of Pembroke, on hearing of his landing in Carrick, sent a strong force to Ayr under Sir Ingram Bell, who, being unable to reach the royal fugitive, resolved to entrap him, as had been done in the case of Wallace and other patriots. He therefore tampered with an inhabitant of Carrick who often had communications with Bruce; and this traitor, with his two sons, engaged either to assassinate the king or give him into the hands of the English. Bruce continued to trust them until he received a private hint which put him on his guard. These men, knowing his place of daily retirement, planted themselves in ambush, and on his appearance approached as if for friendly intercourse; but suspecting their purpose, he sternly warned them back. They still endeavoured to win upon his guard; and as they were powerful and well-armed men, while Bruce had no weapon but his sword and no attendant but a boy, every step of their advance made his peril more imminent. Finding they were resolute to reach him, he snatched the bow from his page and sent a well-directed arrow into the eye of the old man, which penetrated to his brain. The two sons instantly rushed upon Bruce, the one armed with sword and axe and the other with sword and spear; but in the encounter he cleft the spearsman's head asunder, and sent that of the other brother flying from his shoulders. "May our Lord be praised!" ejaculated the wondering boy, "who has given you such might as to quell three enemies in so short a space!" "They would have been worthy men, all three of them," said the compassionate hero, "had they not been full of treason, which has undone them." The warning which saved him on this as well as other similar occasions he is supposed to have received from affectionate women, who were captivated by his personal appearance as well as his high rank and adventurous career.[1]

The king continued to hold his flying camp in Carrick with not more than 200 followers, but in hourly expectation of the arrival of his brothers, Thomas and Alexander, from Ireland, to which he had sent them for reinforcements. They were so successful that they collected 700 Irish soldiers, with whom they crossed over to Loch Ryan in Galloway. But here their career terminated. Macdowall, one of the chiefs of Galloway, but in the interests of England, had prepared for their arrival; and on their troops attempting to land he attacked and completely defeated them, and took both Thomas and Alexander Bruce prisoners after they had been severely wounded in the engagement. Regardless of their wounds and sufferings, they were carried at once to England and presented to Edward at Carlisle, who instantly ordered them to execution and caused their heads to be set upon the gates of the castle and town.[2]

Calamities once more had deepened around the career of the heroic Bruce, and of the brave band of brothers who had gathered by his side and fought in his cause none remained but Edward. He was now so stinted in provisions that he seldom had around him more than sixty followers at one time; while the Gallowegians, flushed with their late success, gathered closer upon his track and endeavoured to hunt him down with bloodhounds. At one time when his band was thus reduced, the rest being scattered abroad in quest of provisions, the men of Galloway to the number of 200, and directed by the keen quest of the bloodhounds they had brought with them, threaded the woods and morasses and advanced nigh his encampment. Warned of their coming by his sentinels, Bruce hastily withdrew his troops across a mountain-river that had only a single ford and posted them in a bog about two bow-shots off. Hav-

---

[1] "I wate nocht quha the warnyng maid;
Bot on all tym sic hap he had,
That quhen men schup thaim to betraiss,
He gat witting tharoff all wayis;
And mony tyme as I herd say,
Throu wemen, ...
That wald tell all that thai mycht her,
And swa mycht happyn that it fell ther."
— Barbour, b. v. l. 537.

[2] M. Westminster Langtoft; Hemingford.

ing thus led them to a secure position, he left them under the command of Sir Gilbert de la Haye, and returned to the ford to watch the motions of the enemy, attended only by two men. It was now night; he could hear distinctly the baying of a hound and the voices of the pursuers that cheered it on; but anxious to learn their purposes fully, and finding that they designed to cross the river, he sent his two attendants to give the alarm to his party, resolving in the meantime to make good the ford single-handed until they arrived. The place was favourable to such a daring purpose, for the banks were steep and rugged; the gorge at which he took his stand was so narrow that he could not be easily surrounded, while the ford in front of him could scarcely give passage to more than one at a time. A long file of the enemy entered the water, but as fast as they came within reach of his spear five of them successively were lifeless corpses floating down the river. The boldest paused; this startling interruption was most unexpected; but the light of the moon, that revealed the fate of their companions, also glittered upon the king's mail and showed that they had only a single enemy to deal with. Enraged and ashamed, they redoubled their efforts to win the landing and overwhelm their opponent; but the mighty arm and good weapon of Bruce soon raised such a rampart of fallen men and horses in front of him as to make the difficulties of the assailants more perilous. "Ah, dear God!" exclaims Barbour in a transport of admiration, "whoever had been by and seen how hardily he addressed himself against them all, I wot well that they would have called him the best that lived in his day!" On the hasty arrival of the king's party the Gallowegians fled, while Bruce was found by his friends unwounded, but hot with his exertions, sitting on the ground and wiping his brow, having taken off his helmet for the purpose, while the bodies of fourteen dead enemies attested his successful prowess. At the spectacle his men declared that henceforth they would fear nothing, since their chief had been so brave and mighty and had adventured upon such an enterprise in their behalf.[1]

The shifting drama of chivalrous events now suddenly transports us to Douglasdale, where its gallant lord, after the surprise of his castle, had betaken himself with his companions to the greenwood. But the castle had been rebuilt in greater strength than ever, and intrusted to the keeping of one Thirlwall, whom Sir James Douglas was resolved, if possible, to eject. He therefore laid an ambush of his men at a place called Sandilands, near the castle, and at an early hour of the morning sent a small party to allure the garrison into the fields by driving off some cattle that were feeding in their neighbourhood. The bait took; for, indignant that the Scots should dare to plunder so near him, Thirlwall rushed out in such haste that he did not take time to put on his helmet, and was followed by a large part of the garrison. The spoilers fled, but it was only to allure the pursuers into the ambush upon which they most unexpectedly stumbled, and by whom they were assailed, struck down, and routed before they could recover from their confusion. The survivors fled to the castle, followed pell-mell by the Scots, who would also have entered with the fliers, but for the precaution of those within the castle, who hastily barred the gates and manned the ramparts. As it was, however, the presence of Douglas in the district and his successful exploits had roused the drooping spirits of the Scottish patriots, and made the keeping of his castle a task of dread and danger to his enemies. Having learned in the course of his nimble movements that Aymer de Valence, Earl of Pembroke, was collecting a great force both of English and Scots to assail Bruce and crush the insurrection, Sir James gathered all the followers he could, and joined his master at Cumnock in Ayrshire.

The difficulties of Bruce were not yet ended. The Earl of Pembroke advanced into Carrick with a formidable array, and was reinforced by John of Lorn at the head of 800 Highlanders. Bruce, who was ignorant of this addition, resolved to give battle to Pembroke, although he had not more than 400 men. He accordingly became the assailant; but while he was engaged in front with both English and Scots, among the latter of whom was his own nephew Randolph, now in the service of England, the men of Lorn, to whom this mountain warfare was familiar and who had been concealed in ambush till the decisive moment, fell upon his rear. This unexpected shock turned the tide of battle against him, and his small array would have been overpowered and cut to pieces, but for the rule which he had already provided for any such emergency. It was, that his troops should hastily disperse in parties and by different directions, so as to disconcert the pursuers, and afterwards rally at a certain given point when the danger was over. His soldiers accordingly retired in three bands; but Lorn, who had a Highland blood-feud against the king, stuck close to the party which Bruce commanded, and was assisted effectually in the pursuit not only by his nimble keen-eyed followers but by a bloodhound once belonging to Bruce himself, which

---

[1] Barbour, b. iv. l. 970.

they had brought with them to track its old master. Perilous, therefore, was the chase, and closely followed, while five of the fleetest Highlanders, who had been selected for the service, overtook Bruce, who was in the rear of his party. He turned round upon the assailants and struck four of them down in quick succession, while the fifth was despatched by his henchman, who was also his foster-brother. The pair, now left alone with the chase in full cry, and the hound at its head, were fain to plunge into a thick wood through which, fortunately for them, ran a brook; for, by wading a bowshot down the stream before they crossed it, the hound lost the scent, and could track them no farther. According to another tradition the troublesome animal was arrested by an arrow shot by one of Bruce's followers from behind a thicket. It is said, also, that in this battle Sir Thomas Randolph captured his uncle's banner, and for this exploit was held in great favour by the English king. Having thus thrown off the pursuers, Bruce and his companion in danger were proceeding to the appointed place of rendezvous, when they were met by three suspicious-looking men well armed, one of them carrying a sheep, who pretended they were in search of the king, and desirous to join him. Although he did not reveal himself, they suspected that he was the Bruce, and invited him to a lone deserted hut on their way, where they dressed part of the sheep for his entertainment. After dinner he lay down to rest, his follower keeping guard over him. It was now the time for the ruffians, who intended to betray the king to the English: they advanced upon the faithful sentinel, whom they slew; but before he fell he was able to waken his master, who was upon his feet in an instant. The combat that followed was brief, for such was the gigantic strength of Bruce, the goodness of his armour, and his skill in using his weapons, that the three traitors were soon laid lifeless on the floor.

On arriving at the rendezvous Bruce found not only his own party who had preceded him, but also his brother Edward and Sir James Douglas, with a reinforcement of 150 men. Resolved to act once more on the offensive, and trusting in the security of his enemies, who supposed him to be at a distance and in full flight, he surprised 200 English, an advanced party of Pembroke's army, who were carelessly cantoned about a mile or two apart from the main body, and put them to the sword. Weary of such a kind of warfare, or hoping to entrap such a wakeful enemy, Pembroke then withdrew himself to Carlisle, taking care, however, to appoint spies who should advertise him of all Bruce's movements. Soon after, hearing that the latter was deer-hunting with all his company in Glentruel, the earl rode in haste from Carlisle with a large body of cavalry, and arrived in secrecy by night within a mile of the Scottish encampment. But his purpose was discovered from one of his own spies, who was arrested by the Scots; and Bruce at the head of 300 men was so well prepared for the encounter that the assailants, to the number of 1500, who had dismounted and advanced on foot in full security, were themselves surprised at a thick part of the wood and fairly put to the rout. Indignant at their defeat the English leaders quarrelled among themselves, and Pembroke was forced to return to Carlisle. Bruce having thus obtained a free interval, employed it so effectually that he soon reduced the three districts of Carrick, Kyle, and Cunningham to obedience, and dispossessed the English of the strengths they held in Ayrshire. About the same time, or soon after, Pembroke, having detached 1000 men under the command of Sir Philip Mowbray to advance from Bothwell into Kyle and Cunningham for the purpose of arresting the progress of Bruce, was met at Makyrnock by an ambush laid by Sir James Douglas, consisting of only forty men. They were planted, however, on a narrow way between two morasses where cavalry could not act, and through which the enemy had to defile; and here the English were attacked at a point where their ranks only encumbered them, and with such suddenness and vigour that they fled back in disorder to Bothwell, leaving sixty of their companions dead on the field. As for Mowbray himself, he had advanced so far into the pass that retreat was impossible, and he only escaped by spurring his horse through the Scots, and riding at full speed by Kilmarnock, Kilwinning, Ardrossan, and Largs, to the English garrison at Inverkip.

It was by such skirmishes, insignificant as they may appear, that the affairs of Bruce were retrieved when their state seemed utterly desperate. He was now a matchless knight of whose personal deeds his followers were justly proud, a skilful and successful leader whom they could confidently follow, and each man felt as if a threefold might were in his own right arm under such guidance and example. This inspiration, the best and surest promise of success, was soon after manifested at London Hill, where Bannockburn itself was singularly prefaced both in its movements and results.

The late encounters, in which his troops were so utterly defeated by a few, seem to have roused to full height the indignation of the Earl of Pembroke: he must have felt not only that his military reputation was disgraced, but his authority as Guardian of Scotland put in imminent peril. Such reflections, too, could scarcely be mitigated by the thought that the actor of these deeds was one whom at the outset he had baffled, defeated, and driven into exile and obscurity. Resolving, therefore, to retrieve his character as publicly as it had been lowered and sunk, he sent a herald to Bruce, now at Galston, and in the full career of his success, informing him that on the 10th of May he purposed to come to Loudon Hill, and inviting him, if he dared, to meet him then and there. This chivalrous invitation Bruce courteously accepted, and doubtless it was with the resolution that no such mistake should occur as that which had happened at Methven. He carefully surveyed the place of meeting, which was in the neighbourhood of Galston, and made ample preparations for the reception of Aymer de Valence. His small force, almost entirely of infantry, and amounting only to 600, he drew up upon a road that led through a piece of dry level ground bounded on either side by extensive and deep morasses; and, to prevent it from being outflanked on either wing by the overwhelming cavalry that were certain to be brought against him, he drew deep trenches on either side so as to allow his army to be assailed only in front, and by not more than about 500 men. Three several sets of these trenches were also drawn on either side, that his troops might have as many rallying points in succession before they could be overpowered. Within this narrow range, protected alike in flank and rear, this little army of spearmen was drawn up; and to the eye that judged according to the military standard of the period, it must have appeared miserably inadequate to encounter the storm that was to burst upon it. But Bruce, who had tried the materials of which that little compact mass was composed, knew that it was a rock around which the whirlwinds might rage in vain, and against which the billows might dash only to be broken and baffled.

Very different was the appearance of the English army which advanced impatient for the onset. It consisted of 3000 well-armed cavalry, and the splendour of their appointments, as described by the poetical historian, was such as to give war its most attractive aspect. Their polished helmets, he tells us, glittered in the sun; the light of their spears, pennons, and shields flashed over the whole field; their banners of various colours waved aloft, while the coat-armour and hauberks of the knights imparted to the wearers the dazzling appearance of angels.[1] Pembroke had arranged them in two lines, and he ordered the first to advance to the charge. With heads lowered and lances couched, the living torrent of man, horse, and steel came on at full speed; it seemed impossible that any opposing force could check such a career; but they were met by the close unflinching array of Scottish spears and brought to a pause—they were sent reeling backward, and in a short time 100 steeds were flying masterless over the field or floundering in the morasses. Giving them no time to recover, Bruce advanced upon them with his main body, and charged with such vigour that the front and rear ranks of the English were soon mixed together, and incapable of a fresh onset; the panic among them became universal; and the hasty flight which followed was that of men who had been thrown in one instant from the height of presumptuous confidence to the deepest despair. It was, indeed, not only a glorious victory to the Scots, but easily won; for, after the first terrible repulse, the enemy seem to have offered little resistance, and been more eager to escape to Bothwell than to rally for a fresh onset. That men, habitually so brave in an open field, should have been so easily turned to a shameful flight, can only be attributed to that new and perplexing mode of warfare which was thenceforth to be the chief characteristic of Scottish campaigns. After a long period of forgetfulness the old lessons of warfare were revived, and the proud chivalry of the middle ages were to be taught that the might of a nation lies among its people at large, and the strength of an army in its steady compact infantry.

Only three days after this signal victory at Loudon Hill Bruce gained another over Ralph Monthermer, Earl of Gloucester, whom he defeated with great slaughter and chased into the castle of Ayr, to which he immediately laid siege. To this, perhaps, he was the more inclined, as not only Gloucester, but also his chief antagonist, the Earl of Pembroke, had taken shelter within the castle.

While the cause of Bruce was thus reviving and the liberties of Scotland were once more in controversy, the condition of Edward of England was daily becoming more pitiable. He had only been withheld from the field by a painful and wasting sickness which had long confined him to his couch at Carlisle, where his feverish irritation at the successive tidings of Scottish revolts and skirmishes could only be soothed by fresh executions of his prisoners. Weary of dictating military operations in which he could not share, and at last provoked beyond endurance by the defeats of his great captains, Pembroke and Gloucester, the king issued an order for his military vassals to repair to him at Car-

---

[1] Barbour.

lisle three weeks after the feast of John the Baptist. This was to be the last and most decisive of all his Scottish campaigns, and also the most terrible and merciless, while the energy of his purpose so invigorated his feeble frame that he believed his recovery from sickness to have already and fully commenced. Under this flattering hope, and to dispel the reports of his death which even already were in circulation, he offered up the horse-litter which he had used in journeying, in the cathedral of Carlisle, and once more mounted his war-steed. But it was a useless effort, for in four days he could only advance six miles, when he reached the little village of Burgh-upon-Sands on the 6th of July (1307). Nothing more of the world now remained for him but a single day of life; and its hours as they passed must have been filled not only with bitter regrets, but ominous fears and surmisings. For Scotland was still unconquered, while the character of his son and successor was such that instead of winning another kingdom he was more likely to lose his own. As such a ruler as Edward was not likely to pass away from the earth without prophetic warning, at least in popular report, a story of this kind which was afterwards current among the Scots has been devoutly rehearsed by Barbour. According to this legend, when Edward at the last stage of his journey and life alighted or was lifted to the ground, he asked the name of the village; and on being told that it was Burgh-upon-Sands, he exclaimed, "Ah me! my hope is now fordone; for I weened that I should never have tasted the pain of death until through my prowess I had won the burgh of Jerusalem, and that there I should die. Here, then, my journey is ended."[1] Breathing with difficulty and speaking in a very low voice,[2] he uttered the testament of a dying man; and it was in full accordance with his character and the whole purpose of his life. His heart was to be conveyed to the Holy Land, and 100 knights were to be maintained there for a whole year in honour of the cross and in defence of the Holy Sepulchre. As for his body, it was to be carried into Scotland with the expedition, and not consigned to a tomb until the country was completely subdued. Froissart has thus detailed this singular part of the dying king's charge: "When he perceived that he could not recover, he called to him his eldest son, who was afterwards king, and made him swear, in presence of all his barons, by the saints, that as soon as he should be dead he would have his body boiled in a large cauldron until the flesh should be separated from the bones; that he should have the flesh buried and the bones preserved; and that every time the Scots should rebel against him he should summon his people and carry with him the bones of his father; for he believed most firmly that, as long as his bones should be carried against the Scots, they would never be victorious."[3]

Edward of Carnarvon, who succeeded to the English throne as Edward II., was not the prudent king and able warrior who was needed to carry out his father's dying request; and he was more anxious for the society of his worthless minion, Gaveston, who had been banished from the kingdom, than for the recovery of Scotland to the English crown. Had he but possessed a tithe of his father's energetic spirit, he would instantly have crossed the border, and with the powerful army at his disposal and the Scottish lords who would have joined his banner he might have succeeded even yet in crushing the insurrection, and dispersing the handful of its supporters. But his proceedings at Carlisle were such as Bruce himself, or Edward's worst enemy, could have wished. He recalled Gaveston from exile. He loitered three weeks at Carlisle for the arrival of more troops, although every hour of delay was equal to a defeat. And as if to show even already his indifference about the conquest of Scotland, he caused his father's body to be committed to the royal tomb at Westminster. After these useless preliminaries he marched to Dumfries, where he received the homage of certain Scottish nobles who were in the English interests, and executed a grant of the earldom of Cornwall and other princely possessions which had belonged to his cousin Edmund in favour of the infamous Gaveston, by whom he was speedily joined in Scotland. Then rousing himself to a semblance of action, he held onward in his course as far as Cumnock, on the borders of Ayrshire; but there, instead of commencing the dangerous chase after Bruce, whose lair he had approached, he suddenly wheeled about and hastily returned to England.

Very different were the proceedings of his active antagonist. As soon as the new king of England had retired Bruce made an irruption into Galloway, and, mindful of their inveterate hostility to the cause of national independence and the defeat and execution of his brothers, he wasted the territories of the Gallowegians with

---

[1] This will remind the readers of English history or Shakspere of Henry IV., who expected to die in Jerusalem, and found that the neighbouring chamber in which he was to breathe his last was called by that name.

[2] "He wes sa stad, that he na mocht
Hys aynd bot with gret paynys draw;
Na spek bot giff it war weill law."
—Barbour, book iii. l. 426.

[3] Froissart (Johnes' translation), chap. xxv. p. 70.

fire and sword. The Earl of Richmond, whom Edward II. had appointed Guardian of Scotland, after reinstating Pembroke in the office and almost immediately afterwards deposing him, now advanced for the protection of Galloway; but Bruce, whose interest it was for the present to avoid committing all to a single hazard, retired before the greatly superior force brought against him, and went into the north of Scotland. On reaching that part of the Grampian range called the Mounth, Bruce, who was accompanied by his brother Edward, the Earl of Lennox, Sir Gilbert de la Haye, and Sir Robert Boyd, was here joined by Alexander and Simon Fraser (probably sons of the brave old Sir Simon) with their military retainers; and it appears that several successful operations followed this accession of strength. At length Bruce was advertised that Comyn, Earl of Buchan, aided by Sir John Mowbray, and his nephew, Sir David de Brechin, were collecting their forces to attack him. For him the season was most unwelcome, for in consequence of his toils and privations he was at present so enfeebled that he had to be carried about in a horse-litter. While his troops were intrenched at Old Meldrum, and standing on the defensive waiting for his recovery, the enemy made a furious attack on his outposts under de Brechin, and put his soldiers in that quarter to flight. Bruce was so stung by this military insult that rage inspired him with temporary vigour; he caused himself to be set on horseback and supported by a man on either side, and in this condition he led his soldiers against the enemy, whom he routed and pursued to the borders of Buchan. This rough remedy of warlike exertion acting upon an iron frame, and the exhilaration of success that followed, appear to have wrought a speedy cure, and he was able to follow up his victory by an invasion of Comyn's territory, which he wasted with all the severity of feudal and hereditary hatred. Fifty years afterwards, says Barbour, men still continued to bewail the "hership (that is harrying or ravaging) of Buchan."

It was not merely where Bruce acted in person that the cause of Scottish liberty now began to triumph. Other hearts caught the inspiration of his own, and received his successes as signals for correspondent efforts. Such was the case in Aberdeen, where the citizens rose against their oppressors, stormed the castle, and put its English garrison to the sword. Afterwards, when the English had collected in that quarter to recover the town, the citizens manfully sallied out upon them and put them to flight. Soon after a person, evidently of station beneath that of knighthood, whom Barbour calls Philip the Forester of Platane,[1] gathered a few hardy men like himself, with whom he surprised the castle of Forfar by escalade, and afterwards destroyed the fortifications by orders from the king. Another event that must have gladdened the affectionate heart of Bruce was the return of Sir David de Brechin, who about this time seceded from the cause of England and joined his uncle with all his followers.

Independently of these indications of popular feeling, the hazardous warfare which Bruce had waged was such an effectual military school that his chief captains were able to conduct adventurous enterprises with his own skill and success. Such was the case with his brother Edward, who to the character of a fiery soldier and reckless knight-errant had now added that of an able leader. On being commissioned by his brother to carry an invasion into Galloway, where their enemies, both Scotch and English, were in great strength, Edward advanced to the water of Cree, where they were assembled to the number of 1200 men under the command of Sir Ingelram de Umfraville, a Scottish baron on the side of England, Sir John de St. John, and Donegal, a powerful Gallovidian chieftain. Of these leaders Barbour tells us Sir Ingelram had acquired such renown that he was wont to have a red bonnet carried before him on the point of a spear, in token that he was the best of all knightly champions. Although the enemy were superior in numbers Edward Bruce attacked them with such vigour that, after losing 200 men, they were fain to betake themselves to flight. This success enabled Edward Bruce to tame the wild Scots of Galloway and reduce them to the rule of his brother. Indignant at his late defeat, Sir John de St. John returned from England to Galloway with 1500 horsemen, and hoped to surprise the victor by a forced march; but Edward Bruce, who was aware of his coming, prepared for him such a reception as was beyond even the daring calculations of chivalry; with but a handful of his soldiers he resolved to attack this multitude and scatter them by a daring onset. Having, therefore, strongly intrenched his infantry, he sallied out with only 50 horsemen, gained the rear of the enemy, and turned upon them under favour of a thick fog. But just before the moment of onset the fog suddenly dispersed, surprise was impossible, and it was too late to retreat with safety. Edward therefore bore down upon the English before they recovered from their surprise at his coming, and his first charge was so impetuous that their front ranks reeled and were thrown

---

[1] Platane forest was in Forfarshire, in the Kirriemuir district.

into disorder; a second attack followed as desperate as the first; and at a third assault the enemy, confounded at his daring and borne down by his fiery valour, fled in confusion and at full gallop. Barbour, who is minute in describing this gallant passage of arms, informs us that he received the particulars from Sir Allan Cathcart, one of the actors in the adventure.[1]

We now gladly turn our narrative to another pupil of King Robert—to Sir James Douglas, that attractive model of knighthood, in whom skill in battle and prowess unmatched in combat were so amiably blended with gentleness, courtesy, and every knightly accomplishment. While Edward Bruce was successfully warring in Galloway, Sir James had been commissioned to attempt the reduction of Douglasdale, and the forests of Selkirk and Jedburgh. His first aim was his own castle of Douglas, which the enemy was especially careful to garrison on account of the strength of its position, and which on that account he was magnanimously bent upon destroying, so that not one stone should be left upon another to shelter them. Having approached it undiscovered and placed an ambush near to the gate, he sent fourteen of his men, disguised as peasants, with their arms concealed, and having sacks filled with grass across their horses, who passed in sight of the castle as if they were on their way to the fair at Lanark. As the garrison was sorely pinched from want of provisions, Sir John de Webeton, their commander, no sooner espied this welcome convoy than he sallied out with most of his soldiers in pursuit, and was drawn by the pretended rustics beyond the place where the ambush was planted. Having thus made sure of the enemy, they suddenly wheeled about, threw off their disguises, and gave the signal to their companions, who started from their concealment, and the English, thus attacked in front and rear, were cut down to a man. After this, the survivors of the garrison capitulated, and the castle was razed to the ground. Among the spoil was found a box belonging to Webeton in which was a letter from an English lady, his mistress, engaging to marry him if he could make good for a whole year this perilous castle of Douglas against every assailant. It was one of those heroic freaks of chivalry so often introduced to alleviate the dulness of serious warfare, in which a knight would undertake an exploit that was astounding from its difficulty or extravagance, and peril both life and reputation upon the issue. In this way the unfortunate Webeton had undoubtedly pledged himself, and might perhaps have made his promise good had he been pitted against a less daring and skilful enemy.

While Sir James Douglas was thus employed, he happened in the course of his forest adventures to approach a house on the water of Lyne, and as it was night he advanced with his wonted caution to discover by what inmates it was tenanted. "The devil"—such was the exclamation that first greeted his ears; and as profane swearing was in those days a privilege confined to martialists, he concluded that soldiers must be within, whom therefore it behoved him to know whether as friends or enemies. He soon found that they were no other than Alexander Stewart of Bonkill, Thomas Randolph, the nephew of Bruce, and Sir Adam Gordon, men of the highest military renown, and also his countrymen, but who had joined the side of the English, and were now combined for the enterprise of taking him or driving him out of the forest. They were themselves captured after a short conflict, with the exception of Gordon, and brought to the king. "Nephew," said Bruce to Randolph, "you have for some time renounced your allegiance, but you must now be reconciled to me." "You chastise me," replied Sir Thomas angrily, "when you better deserve chastisement yourself; for since you warred against England you should have justified your claims by fair fighting, instead of such covert stratagems and cunning." "That fair fighting," said Bruce calmly, "may be hereafter, and peradventure ere long; but since you speak so rudely, it is fit that your proud words should be chastised, until you learn what is right and yield to its authority." Randolph was ordered to close confinement, and there the lesson recommended to his attention was so carefully conned that he was soon at liberty and in full concord with his royal uncle. Stewart of Bonkill also forsook the cause of England and joined that of the patriots.

The promised time for open and aggressive warfare had now arrived, and Bruce resolved to commence it with an attack upon his inveterate enemy the Lord of Lorn. The mountain chief was not slow to meet the invader, and having placed 2000 men in a narrow defile which only one horseman could enter at a time, he embarked on Loch Etive the rest of his forces in a fleet of light lymphads, and hovered within sight of the pass. It was a skilful arrangement in mountainous warfare; for the pass where the land troops lay in ambuscade runs along the bottom of Ben Cruachan, a high and rugged

---

[1] "A knycht that then wes in his [Bruce's] rowt,
Worthi and wycht, stalwart and stout,
Curtaiss, and fayr, and off gud fame,
Schyr Alane off Catkert by name,
Tauld me this taile, as I sall tell."

mountain between Loch Awe and Loch Etive, and consists of ground where the light-footed natives could act with every advantage; and while Bruce was entangled in this difficult pass the troops at sea could be speedily debarked to take him in the rear. But Bruce appears to have had secret intelligence of these arrangements, and he had learned by fatal trial the nature of this kind of warfare. While he marched forward as if he intended to enter the pass and fall into the snare, he sent his light-armed troops and archers under Sir James Douglas to make a circuit, climb the mountain behind the pass, and come down unexpectedly upon the Highlanders in the rear while he was occupying their attention in front. This important movement Douglas executed with his wonted skill and activity, and while the mountaineers were occupied with the king, whose soldiers were lightly armed for the occasion, and who boldly met the enemy half-way, Sir James and his party suddenly appeared, and, after pouring down a shower of arrows, advanced to close conflict. The men of Lorn, thus unexpectedly taken in their own subtle fashion, and assailed at once both in front and rear, were broken, struck down, and scattered with fearful slaughter, while the Lord of Lorn, who saw from his galleys the havoc and discomfiture of his clansmen, was unable to come to their rescue. Bruce followed up this success by wasting the district of Lorn and capturing the strong castle of Dunstaffnage, which he garrisoned to bridle the insurrections of the natives.

As if these remarkable exertions of Bruce had not of themselves been sufficient for the recovery of Scotland, they were fully aided and accelerated by the infatuation and the blunders of Edward II. He was still so besotted by his attachment to the infamous Gaveston as to be averse to all military exertion; while he disgusted the warlike barons by the honours and possessions which he still continued to heap upon him. And the only instances in which he occupied himself with Scottish affairs served merely to complicate his difficulties; for in less than a year he had appointed six guardians successively to the charge of that distracted kingdom. Thus the office soon became little more than nominal, and each entrant, before he could well examine his position or his duties, was obliged to give place to a successor. Edward was moreover so unadvised as to set William de Lamberton, Bishop of St. Andrews, free, and permit him to return to Scotland. This able and politic man, while war was at the hottest, in which he could not personally take a part, seemed to think himself justified in the full use of the resources of craft and cunning since carnal weapons were denied him, and had trimmed and shifted, promised and recanted, according to the changes of the tide, but always with a heart devoted to the interests of his country. He had been a prisoner in England since the defeat of the Scots in Methven, but had easily succeeded in duping the weak Edward, to whom he solemnly swore fidelity, and engaged to publish in Scotland the papal excommunication that had been issued against Bruce and his adherents. It is perhaps unnecessary to add of such a man that he eluded his engagements and pursued an opposite course as soon as he found himself within the shelter of his see. At this time, also, it suited the interests of the King of France to interpose in behalf of Scotland, and he sent his envoy, Oliver de Roches, to negotiate with Bruce and Lamberton about a truce between their country and England. The French envoy, joined by agents of the pope and the King of England, met for this purpose in Scotland; and the result of their agreement with the Scottish king was a truce which was to continue between the two countries until the ensuing feast of All Saints.[1] Such a treaty, and so conducted, was a significant recognition of Bruce's royal authority on the part of those who still accounted him an excommunicated man and a traitor. Another incident equally indicative of the leaning of France towards the cause of Bruce occurred shortly afterwards. The Sieur de Varennes, Philip's ambassador at the English court, sent a letter to Bruce openly addressed to him merely as Earl of Carrick, while secret missives accompanied it in which he was recognized as King of Scots. These double-dealing despatches, which were intercepted before they reached their destination, excited the indignation of Edward, but he could do nothing more than murmur his resentment.[2] He even commissioned the guardian for the time being to *purchase* a truce from the Scots, if such a mode of bargaining should be found necessary.[3] A strange reverse and humiliation! But all this arose from his crazy partiality for Gaveston. A warlike muster which would have brought his barons together would only have united them against him, and before the march for a northern campaign had commenced they would have demanded the favourite's head.

Gratifying although these growing acknowledgments of his sovereignty must have been to the heart of Bruce, another instance followed of greatly higher account, as it showed that a similar

[1] Rymer's *Fœdera*. [2] Idem.
[3] Hemingford, vol. i. p. 246.

recognition had now taken root in the affections of his own divided subjects. On the 24th of February, 1310, an assembly of the estates of Scotland was held at Dundee to designate by special law the rightful holder of the royal authority. Here it was solemnly determined and declared that Robert, Lord of Annandale, the competitor, ought by the laws and customs of Scotland in former times to have been preferred in the competition for the crown to Baliol—that they, therefore, recognize Robert Bruce now reigning as their just and lawful sovereign; that they engage to defend his right, and the liberties and independence of Scotland, against all opponents of every rank, power, or dignity; and that they declare all contraveners of the same to be guilty of treason against the king, and to be held as traitors against the nation.[1] At the same time the representatives of the Scottish church—the bishops, abbots, priors, and procurators—issued a pastoral declaration to all the faithful of the land, announcing "That the Scottish nation, seeing the kingdom betrayed and enslaved, had assumed Robert Bruce for their king, and that the clergy had willingly done homage to him in that character."[2] Although Lamberton as primate did not appear in the front of this clerical movement, his secret influence was undoubtedly its mainspring; and while he still continued to keep well with the Absalom of England, he may have thought that he could thus more effectually counteract the designs of the royal epicure and his Ahithophels.

The truce, which had been little respected on either side, was abruptly and prematurely terminated. Such could scarcely have been otherwise as long as Scottish estates were held by English proprietors, and Scottish castles garrisoned by English soldiers. On the resumption of hostilities Bruce was so strong, that, instead of resting on a defensive war, he was eager to become the assailant, and had made preparations for besieging Perth, at that time the most powerful town in Scotland, but which was held by a strong English garrison under the command of Sir John Fitz-Marmaduke. Alarmed at these demonstrations, Edward resolved in earnest upon a Scottish invasion, and sent out his orders over England and Ireland for the great crown vassals to assemble their retainers for the purpose. But so low had his credit fallen, that many of his principal nobles, although they sent their military contingents, refused to give their personal attendance. Still the Earls of Gloucester and Warrenne, the Lords Henry Percy and James Clifford, and many others of high rank and military reputation, followed his banner, while the army in strength and numbers seemed sufficient for the full reconquest of Scotland. Of this, indeed, Bruce was so well aware that he resolved to let it roll onward unconfronted, and content himself with hovering on its outskirts. Fortunately, also, the wonted irresolution of the English king so far prevailed, that although he persevered in the invasion, it was too late to make it effectual, for it was not commenced till near the end of September, when the approaching winter would be certain to waste it with starvation, or drive it back to England. The whole of his march and the proceedings that accompanied were characterized by the same irresolution and imbecility. Instead of keeping coastward for his fleet to co-operate, he drove right inland as if with his eyes shut, and proceeded from Roxburgh to the Forest of Selkirk, from Selkirk to Biggar, and from Biggar to Renfrew, without finding an enemy to encounter, or even much mischief to accomplish. At length, on the failure of forage and provisions, he commenced his retreat by Linlithgow, and through the Lothians and the eastern part of Lammermoor, until he arrived at his starting-point at Berwick, which he reached about the 10th of November, having thus spent somewhat more than two months in useless marching and countermarching. During this time Bruce had neither stood idle nor aloof, but had kept up a continual war of skirmishes by which convoys were cut off, and provisions intercepted, and in one of these he killed 300 English and Welsh. Vain of his expedition because his enemy had not met him in the field, Edward wrote an account of it to the pope, and boasted that he had made Bruce and his traitorous accomplices fly to their earth-holes like foxes. But for eight months he lingered at Berwick within the security of its walls, not daring to venture into England on account of the unpopularity into which he had fallen. So little, indeed, did his subjects sympathize with him, that during the campaign many of them had supplied the Scots with provisions, horses, and arms. Anxious to cover the disgrace of his useless inroad, or more probably to give his favourite an opportunity of recommending himself by warlike achievements, he sent Gaveston at the close of this year (1310) from Berwick into Scotland at the head of a strong detachment. But Gaveston, although he penetrated into the country as far as the Forth, which he appears to have crossed, was as unsuccessful as his master, having been unable to force the Scots to an engagement.

---

[1] Instrument in the General Register House, Edinburgh, quoted in Kerr's *Life of Bruce*, vol. I. p. 370.
[2] Anderson, *Indep. Ap.* No. 1.

After this unsatisfactory retreat of the English it was time for Bruce to make reprisals by an invasion of England, to which his enlarged resources could now afford the opportunity; and he accordingly crossed the Solway, and for eight days ravaged the districts of Gillsland and Tynedale, from which his soldiers returned with abundance of booty. If they exercised the law of retaliation in this inroad to the full of its requirements, nothing less at such a period and under such circumstances could be expected: for years they had been the helpless victims of a cruel oppression, and the first moment of deliverance had but now arrived. Fordun indeed regards their doings as nothing worse than a righteous retribution.[1] Different, indeed, was the view of Edward, who endeavoured to enlist the church in his quarrel; and in writing to the pope of the late invasion he was careful to describe the atrocities which the Scots had committed in a portion of the patrimony of St. Peter. "Robert and his accomplices," he thus complained, "having invaded our realm of England, perpetrated the most horrible ravages, depredations, burnings, and murders in the border counties of our kingdom, but more especially in the bishopric of Durham; not sparing the innocent youth or the female sex, and paying no respect, alas! even to the immunities of ecclesiastical liberty."[2] Against such complaints it was fortunate that Bruce had the Scottish clergy on his side, and that they cared more for their sovereign than for the pontiff. Leaving, therefore, the pope and the King of England to condole with each other, Bruce in September repeated his invasion through Redesdale and Tynedale, in which also the bishopric of Durham, the see of the merciless Anthony Beck, was not spared.

As the recovery of Perth was an important object, Bruce, after his return from England, resumed the siege, which he was now able to do without fear of interruption. The town, however, was so strong in towers and ramparts, and so well garrisoned under William Olifant, an anglicized Scot, that its capture promised to be a work of difficulty, more especially as the King of England had promised to relieve it. Thus emboldened the garrison held out for six weeks, and might have protracted the siege till the arrival of assistance, but for the prudence and daring of the King of Scots. Having carefully surveyed the defences of the town, and matured his plans, he pretended to raise the siege, and marched to a considerable distance, where he remained for eight days. He then quickly and silently returned by night well furnished with scaling ladders of due height; at the head of his troops he entered the ditch or moat that surrounded the wall, with a scaling ladder on his shoulders, the water reaching to his throat, and steadying his steps with his spear, being the first person who crossed, and the second who mounted the wall. Thus the ditch was passed, and the ramparts were won in darkness, and so fierce and unexpected was the attack which followed, that the garrison threw down their arms and surrendered. An incident of chivalrous and generous daring enlivened the history of this important capture. A knight of France who happened to be among the captors had seen with surprise the devotedness of Bruce in placing himself in the front of danger to show the way to his followers; and no longer able to contain himself, the gallant stranger exclaimed, "Good heavens! what shall we say of our French lords that fare so luxuriously, and will only eat, drink, and dance, when such a worthy knight will throw himself into such peril to win a wretched hamlet?" He immediately plunged into the water, crossed the moat, and was one of the first who mounted the wall. Only the Scots among the garrison were put to the sword as traitors; the English soldiers were dismissed unharmed, and the fortifications of Perth were dismantled.

The infatuation of Edward still continued, and during these humbling reverses he was more anxious to retain the wretched Gaveston, whom his nobility were bent to drive from the kingdom, than to recover Scotland to his rule. Such was mainly the history of England at this period—and such the result of the conquests of Edward I.! All had degenerated into a pitiful brawl between the besotted king and his indignant barons, during which the nation could only stand still and look on; and all that the son of the dreaded Edward Longshanks could at this time achieve against Scotland was in the form of empty threats and menaces, or equally empty negotiation. We therefore find him at this time (1311-12) writing to the despairing English castellans of the few strongholds that remained in Scotland untaken, exhorting them to hold out—writing to John of Lorn exhorting him to try once more the fortune of his arms against the Bruce—and writing to the pontiff beseeching him to direct his spiritual artillery against the rebellious Scots, and to hold in fast durance at Rome, Wishart, Bishop of Glasgow, instead of allowing him to return home, where he would be certain by his cunning counsels to strengthen the insurgents. Edward even descended to such humiliation as to negotiate for a fresh truce; but this the King of Scots decidedly refused: he had tried his strength;

---

[1] *Scotichronicon*, lib. xii. c. 18. [2] *Fœd. Angl.* iii. 283.

he was aware of his advantages; and now was the time beyond all others to work for the deliverance of Scotland.

A third invasion of England was the result of Bruce's decision. This he undertook at the close of 1312, and his advance across the border was in greater force than on the previous occasions, and with still greater havoc. Having burned the towns of Hexham and Corbridge, he made a rapid march upon the rich town of Durham, surprised it by a night attack, and reduced a great part of the city to ashes, while the people of the bishopric were so dismayed that they offered to purchase a truce at the price of £2000. But humbling though the offer was, they were not let off so easily, for the Scots stipulated that so often as they were pleased to invade England, they should have a free passage through the county of Durham. Even these terms also appeared so desirable that the counties of Northumberland, Cumberland, and Westmoreland paid £2000 each for the privilege of being included in the same treaty. Bruce having established his headquarters within reach of the town of Hartlepool, once a part of his own English property, resolved to indemnify himself for the loss of fair, market, and harbour dues that had now passed into other hands; and for this purpose Sir James Douglas was sent forward as collector of the alienated revenues. This active chief discharged his commission so ably, that he sacked the town, and returned with many of its inhabitants prisoners. The return, however, of this expedition to Scotland was not quite so prosperous, and the Scots appear to have presumed too much upon their own strength and the dispirited plight of their enemies. Thus Bruce attempted the strong city of Carlisle; but in the assault his troops were beaten back, and Sir James Douglas with several others wounded. Undeterred by this failure Douglas also attempted to surprise Berwick by a night attack; but at the critical moment when his soldiers were mounting the walls the barking of a dog alarmed the garrison, and the assailants were beaten off. Notwithstanding these partial reverses the invasion was a prosperous one, for the Scots had not only secured a rich booty, but given fresh life to their cause, while the hearts of their lately victorious enemies were proportionally depressed and dispirited. During this year also (1312) the castles of Bute, Dumfries, Dalswinton, and several fortalices which the English held in Scotland, surrendered to Bruce, which he caused immediately to be razed to the ground. In this way he wisely increased the difficulty of a reconquest of Scotland by giving no place of shelter to the invaders. It is possible, also, that warned from the example of England during the reign of Stephen, he saw what dangerous possessions these might prove in the hands of the proud nobility of Scotland; and how easily, under such protection, they might establish themselves into petty tyrants when the national enemy was suppressed and the land delivered from their presence.

CHAPTER VII.

THE WAR OF INDEPENDENCE CONTINUED: BATTLE OF BANNOCKBURN (1312-1314).

A war of sieges—Capture of Roxburgh Castle by Douglas—Of Edinburgh Castle by Randolph—Of Linlithgow Castle by William Binning—Growing strength of Bruce's cause—He reduces the Isle of Man—Stirling Castle ineffectually besieged by Edward Bruce—His rash agreement for its surrender—A whole year's muster of England and Scotland for a decisive conflict—Their respective resources—Bruce's army—His arrangements for battle—His encampment at Bannockburn—Advance of the English army—Skirmish of Randolph with a body of English cavalry—Bruce's combat with De Boune—Bruce's address to his army before the battle—Morning of battle—Preliminaries of the conflict—BATTLE OF BANNOCKBURN—Total defeat and dispersion of the English—Flight of Edward II. from the field—His narrow escape—Immense spoil won by the Scots—Generous conduct of Bruce after his victory—Capture of Baston the poet—His poetical ransom—Important consequences of the victory of Bannockburn—Death of John Baliol.

The tide of warfare having now turned in favour of Scotland, the chief efforts of Bruce and his compatriots were directed to the ejection of the English by the capture of those more important castles in the kingdom which they still continued to occupy. Of these the castle of Roxburgh held a conspicuous place, as it was one of the keys of the Scottish border, and while the English had it in their keeping Scotland could always be invaded with advantage. It was, therefore, a tempting prize between the two contending nations, around which the warfare was speedily collected; and Douglas, who according to his wont was lurking in the forest of Jedburgh, resolved to signalize himself by its capture. His plan was laid with that sagacity which ensured such success to his many romantic adventures both in siege and battle. For escalade he employed a certain Simon of the Lead-house, "a crafty man and a curious," to make him rope ladders of a peculiar construction, with iron steps and cranks; and the time he selected for the attempt upon the castle was the night of Shrove Tuesday, when he knew well that the garrison would be employed in feasting and revelry as a preparative for the fasting and penance of Lent, which would commence next day. With only sixty soldiers, whose armour was covered with black frocks, and sheltered by the darkness of midnight, the hardy band approached the castle undetected. On arriving at the bank on which it is situated they began to ascend cautiously on all-fours; and while thus employed they could overhear a conversation between two sentinels, by which they knew that their motions had not been wholly undiscovered. Naming a neighbouring farmer whose cattle were used to graze upon the plain, the one sentry exclaimed, "Surely he is making good cheer to-night when he thus leaves his oxen shut out." "Yes," cried the other, "of a surety he will make merry to-night though the Douglas should drive them away." Cheered by the discovery that they were mistaken for oxen, and passed over without further notice, the assailants reached the walls, fixed their ladders, and silently ascended. The first who stepped on the wall was Simon of the Lead-house; but the soldier on guard who was stationed there, instead of raising the alarm, rushed forward to throw him headlong from the ramparts, in which case he would have borne down his companions who were following after. But in this critical moment, when a single step in advance of the Englishman would have defeated the whole enterprise, Simon met the assailant, laid him dead with a stroke of his dagger, and threw the body over the wall. Almost immediately after another Englishman advanced to the spot, but Simon quickly silenced him and sent him after his companion. The wall being thus won and no alarm sounded, the Scots rushed forward to the keep, where all was a mirthful revel of dancing and singing, and made their presence known by the terrible war-cry, "A Douglas, a Douglas!" and a furious unexpected onset. Little resistance followed; the revellers were driven across the hall, and all could have been easily struck down but that Douglas gave them quarter. In the meantime the commander of the garrison, Sir Gillemin de Fiennes, a knight of Burgundy, made good his retreat with a few followers to a tower which he endeavoured to defend, but he was mortally wounded and compelled to surrender. The gallant Simon of the Lead-house, who had so greatly contributed to the success of the enterprise, was commissioned to carry the tidings to Bruce, by whom he was royally rewarded. Roxburgh Castle, by the Scottish king's orders, was forthwith demolished by his brother Edward, who also reduced the rest of Teviotdale, except Jedburgh, which was garrisoned by the English, to full submission.[1]

It was now that Thomas Randolph of Strathdon, the pardoned nephew of Bruce, by whom he had been raised to the earldom of Moray, was ready to show the reality of his repentance as well as the sincerity of his devotedness to the cause of national liberty. At this time also that noble rivalry seems to have commenced between him and his captor, Sir James Douglas, which had for its great object the complete liberation of their country. He therefore resolved to distinguish himself by the capture of the castle of Edinburgh, which the English had held for twenty years, and which, from its commanding site and the imperfect resources of the military science of the period, could only be reduced by famine or taken by a sudden and desperate onset. Randolph commenced the siege in form, which threatened to be tedious if not abortive, for the garrison were not only numerous but abundantly supplied with provisions. Suspecting also the fidelity of their commander, Sir Piers de Luband, a knight of Gascony and a relation of Gaveston, they deposed him from office and placed one of their own number in his room. These precautions and their obstinate resistance had protracted the siege for six weeks, during which the Scots made no progress; and Randolph saw that his only chance of success lay in winning the castle by surprise. His inquiries as to whether there was no private access to the walls more easy than the others were answered by William Frank, an English soldier now in his service. When a young man he had been a soldier in the castle, from which, having a love intrigue with a woman dwelling in the town, he was wont to descend at night by a ladder of ropes and return before his absence could be detected. He still remembered distinctly the winding track among the precipices along which he had descended and returned in safety, and he offered to conduct a party by the same way and be foremost in the adventure. Randolph, having weighed his statement, resolved to make the attempt. He selected thirty bold and agile men for the purpose, whom he accompanied in person; under

---

[1] Fordun, lib. xii. c. 19; Barbour, lib. vii.

the cover of a dark night they glided to the foot of the rock, and, preceded by Frank, their guide, they began to ascend the slippery perpendicular steep, availing themselves of every cleft and projection, and aware that a single false step might precipitate the whole party to the bottom. Midway up the rock was a narrow ledge or shelf where they halted to rest themselves, and there they could hear the officers going their round upon the walls to ascertain that the sentinels were at their posts. At this moment, also, a still more startling incident alarmed them; one of the watchmen on the ramparts directly above their heads, either seeing something move or in mere thoughtless play, threw a stone down the rock and exclaimed, "Away! I see you well!" They heard the words and the missile that whizzed over their heads; but hoping, from the silence which followed, that they had been unnoticed, they resumed their perilous ascent and reached at last the bottom of the wall, where it was only twelve feet high. Here they fixed their rope-ladder by its iron hook to the top of the wall and mounted in breathless silence, William Frank being the first, Sir Andrew Gray the second, and Randolph himself the third who ascended. When only a few had reached the parapet they heard a whispering and a movement of weapons among the guards; it was followed by a rush of armed men upon them, and the alarm-cry of "Treason! treason!" but the Scots quickly cleared the walls of their defenders and made onward for the keep, where the whole garrison had rallied. The darkness of the night, the strange and sudden onset, and their ignorance of the force of their assailants, quelled the wonted valour of the English, while the Scots rushed on with those advantages on their side which, in such a night surprise, can make a small band equal to a whole legion. The confused resistance of the panic-struck garrison was soon over; the governor, who made a desperate rally, was slain; some leaped over the walls and were dashed to pieces; but the rest, still greatly more numerous than their assailants, threw down their arms and received quarter. "Never in any land," exclaims Barbour, "have I heard of a castle which was taken so hardily!" Taking into account the difficulties of the feat and the admirable skill and daring with which they were surmounted, it forms, indeed, an episode in this war of gallant and romantic incidents that can scarcely be paralleled, and in no case surpassed. After the surrender Sir Piers Luband, the deposed governor, was released from the prison to which the garrison had committed him, and easily persuaded to become a liegeman of the King of Scotland; while the castle itself, in conformity with Bruce's wise policy, was razed to the ground.[1]

These splendid feats of heroic daring and devotedness were no longer confined to knights and high-born nobles, for the spirit of the land was now fully awake, and even the peasantry were producing brave champions and skilful leaders. This was especially manifested in the capture of the castle of Linlithgow, a feat which was achieved by a common hind. This castle, which is described by Barbour as being large and strong, and "well stuffed with Englishmen," was also formidable as a rallying point to the enemy and a place of communication between the garrisons of Stirling and Edinburgh. Aware of its great importance to the English, as well as annoyed by the oppressions of its garrison, William Binning, "a stout carle and a stoure," who was in the practice of supplying hay to the fort, and who well knew its defences, resolved to attempt its surprisal. He communicated this purpose to his companions and found them hearty to second him. He placed a party of them in ambush near to the gate, concealed eight of them well armed within his wagon, covering them with hay, and accompanied by a servant ostensibly to drive the oxen, Binning walked with his wonted air of carelessness at the side of his wain. The portcullis was raised, the vehicle entered; but, instead of passing through the gateway, the driver, by cutting the harness of the oxen, left it standing and thus prevented the portcullis from descending, while Binning raised his concerted warning of "Call all! call all!" At that signal the eight men leaped from the wagon and secured the gate; the ambush rushed from their concealment, and entered the castle; and the astounded garrison made but a short resistance, and were glad to escape to Edinburgh and Stirling. The king worthily rewarded the gallant peasant, and ordered the castle to be demolished.

These substantial successes, by which the English hold upon Scotland was so greatly enfeebled, began to manifest their effects in winning fresh adherents to the cause of Bruce. He was now a king in reality as well as in title and pretension, and several who had hitherto held aloof from him, or joined his enemies, began to suspect that his was the winning side. Of those new convertites to his cause was David, Earl of Athole, who had long been of the party of England, and had lately been rewarded by King Edward with a grant of English lands, but who now subscribed to their forfeiture by acknowledging Bruce as his sovereign. Alarmed at the capture of the castles of Edinburgh and Rox-

---

[1] Barbour, lib. vii.

burgh, Edward was apprehensive that Berwick might share the same fate, and he therefore caused the Countess of Buchan, who had been there ignominiously imprisoned during seven long years, to be transferred from her cage to a more inland place of duresse. About the same time also (A.D. 1313), and while negotiations were going on for a truce between England and Scotland through the mediation of the King of France, Bruce invaded Cumberland, where he inflicted considerable damage. A more important enterprise, however, to which this invasion was but a prelude, was an expedition for the recovery of the Isle of Man to the Scottish crown, which Bruce conducted in person. In this he was successful, for he overthrew the governor, and reduced the whole island to subjection. This governor, who in the Manx Chronicle is called Dingaway Dowill, was probably that same Duncan Macdowall, formerly a lord of Galloway, who had surprised Thomas and Alexander Bruce at Loch Ryan, and delivered them bound and bleeding into the hands of their remorseless enemies. If such was the case, the defeat of Macdowall in the island to which he had fled as a place of shelter, after his expulsion from Galloway, was but a righteous retribution.

During this period of successful sieges Edward Bruce had been pursuing an adventurous career which was to lead to a most important termination. He had reduced the whole of Galloway and Nithsdale, expelling the English and razing their strongholds according to his brother's orders; he had also destroyed the castle of Rutherglen, near Glasgow, and captured that of Dundee. Continuing his course of success he next laid siege to the castle of Stirling, now the only fortress of consequence which the English possessed in Scotland; and as the military honour of each nation was at issue in this last relic of the campaigns of Edward I., the attack and defence were maintained with equal pertinacity. But Edward Bruce, although as daring a knight in the open field as ever couched a lance, was no tactician in sieges; and the height of the walls, as well as the bravery of the garrison, checked his impetuous career, and obliged him to exchange his favourite plan of straightforward attack into a dull tedious blockade. Weary of this process, which had lasted from spring till midsummer, he at length entered into an agreement with Sir Philip Mowbray, the governor, that the operations of siege or blockade should be suspended for a year, and that by the ensuing midsummer the castle should be surrendered, if not previously relieved by the English.

Nothing could be more perilous to the cause of the Scottish king than this rash compact of his brother. It compelled him to abandon that desultory warfare for which Scotland was so admirably fitted, and in which he had hitherto been so successful, and to risk all in a battle in the open field, where every chance would be against him. The utmost of England was thus challenged and defied to raise the siege, and its whole might would be collected for the effort. A whole year was allowed for the attempt, and during the interval England had full time to collect her immense resources not only at home, but from the Continent. Hitherto, also, the ill-feeling between the English nobles and their king had proved one of the best sources of Bruce's growing strength and ascendency; but such a national cause, in which the chivalrous honour of both parties was at stake, would be certain to compose their dissensions and unite them into one great resistless army for the invasion and final overthrow of Scotland. And to meet all this Bruce had as yet but a divided nobility and the half of a kingdom, for a strife in which the whole might prove too little. These obvious circumstances he stated to his brother Edward, and added thoughtfully, "God may dispose the issue to our advantage, but the peril to win or lose all at once is fearful." "Let the King of England come and all his following," cried Edward boldly; "we shall fight them all were they still more numerous." At these words, so full of that daring courage which formed so great an element of Robert Bruce's character, "he prized his brother greatly in his heart," and gave full consent to the arrangement.

The twelve months that followed were of too important a character to be wasted in skirmishes and deeds of knightly prowess; the two nations were "hushed in grim repose" that looked like peace, but which was more terrible than a usual course of war, because it was the gathering of the storm; the long breathing for the death-struggle by which the contest should be ended. The preparations made by England were worthy of her national spirit, independently of the feeble character of her king. The great lords and barons who were holders of the crown to the number of ninety-three mustered their military retainers; and while nearly the whole repaired in person to the place of meeting, the few who still preferred their resentment against their king to their hatred of Scotland or the welfare of their own country, were careful to send their vassals. From the English Pale in Ireland came the retainers of the crown of England under the Earl of Ulster, and with them were joined twenty-six Irish chiefs and their followers who owed allegiance to the conquerors. The counties of Wales also sent their numerous and hardy

ALFRED PEARSE.

LINLITHGOW CASTLE CAPTURED FROM THE ENGLISH.

BINNING BLOCKS THE PORTCULLIS AND TAKES THE GATE. (A.D. 1313.)

contingents, which, with those of the free counties of England alone, composed an army of 27,000. Scottish aid also was not neglected against Scotland, and while those northern chiefs who held grants of land from the English king were ordered to repair to the banner of the Earl of Pembroke, their governor, John of Argyle, the old antagonist of Bruce, was appointed to co-operate with the invading army by sea, with the title of high-admiral of the western fleet of England. And besides these, the mercenary soldiers of the Continent who owed allegiance as yet to England, or whose trade was war, were not omitted; and accordingly we are told that reinforcements were drawn to England from Hainault, Gascony, and Aquitaine; from Poictou, Provence, and Brittany; from Holland, Germany, and Bohemia. Such was the mustering for an army the numbers of which have often been a subject of controversy, for while some have extravagantly magnified them into more than 200,000 soldiers, others have sought to reduce them to less than half the amount. It is evident, however, from the great resources of England, from the length of time spent in collecting them, and from the writs and orders issued on the occasion, that they exceeded rather than fell short of 100,000 soldiers, independently of an immense array of servants, artisans, sutlers, and camp followers, who swelled the bulk and formidable appearance, while they encumbered the operations of the army. Every nerve had been tasked for the occasion, so that not only all the clergy as well as the nobles, but all the widows and other women who in any way held of the crown, were summoned to furnish their allotment of men, horses, and arms. Something more was to be effected than the relief of the castle of Stirling; this was to be but a prelude to the conquest of the whole Scottish kingdom. In descending to the details of this immense host, and the portions into which it was divided, Barbour is as reasonable as when he estimates its numbers at "100,000 men and more."[1] He tells us that there were 40,000 cavalry well armed; and of these 3000 were completely armed both man and horse in plate and mail, who composed the front rank. The archers were 50,000. The whole army, he also tells us, was arrayed in ten divisions, each comprising at least 10,000 men. As to march such a numerous army into Scotland, without providing for its sustenance independently of the country, would have been to march it into the jaws of famine and starvation, not only an ample land commissariat was attached to it, but a numerous fleet was provided, both for the purpose of invading Scotland by sea and supplying the troops with provisions.

While such were the vast preparations of England during a year of peaceful interval, those of Bruce were correspondent to his high character both for valour and wisdom. His orders to arm and muster in the Torwood, near Stirling, went forth in every direction; but it was evident from the small numbers that had hitherto followed his banner, and the scanty resources with which he had been obliged to conduct his military operations, that these orders would be but partially obeyed. Many could disobey them with impunity; not a few must have been daunted by the formidable power of the enemy; and the chief of the nobility still kept aloof from his cause, or were ready to act against him. No force, therefore, so far as concerned mere numbers, could be expected to meet that would bear a comparison with the English host. Accordingly scarcely more than 30,000 men were finally assembled at the place of rendezvous, with about 20,000 undisciplined and unarmed camp followers, who could take no part in the engagement. This array was brought together from various quarters chiefly by the exertions of Edward Bruce, Sir James Douglas, Randolph Earl of Moray, and Walter the Steward of Scotland. Beyond this meagre list we look in vain for the names of the highest of the Scottish nobles. But the gallant soldiers whom they brought were men who had set their lives upon a cast which they were ready to throw without wincing, and most of them had been trained to every emergency of unequal conflict in the wars of Bruce and Wallace. The good king Robert received them graciously, and his courteous language and kind demeanour made them doubly ready to die for such a sovereign. With so great a disparity of numbers he resolved to abide the encounter, after availing himself of every resource which the nature of the ground and the character of his troops could afford him.

On the assembling of this army Bruce held a council of war and explained to his chief officers his plan of operation. From the condition of their array they must fight the battle lightly armed and on foot, instead of trusting to their cavalry, which was so inferior to that of England. Such a mode of warfare might appear utterly hopeless, environed and borne down as they could be by the mail-clad and mounted squadrons of the English, by which alone their whole force was outnumbered; but the wars of Wallace and his own victory at London Hill, as well as the example of the Flemish burghers at Courtray, who on foot had met and routed the best chivalry of France, had demonstrated the efficacy of a compact body of infantry

---

[1] *The Bruce*, lib. viii. 1. 105.

in resisting the charges of cavalry. In this way, therefore, his troops must abide the encounter and do their utmost to win the victory. For such a kind of resistance, as well as for closing up every passage by which relief could be sent to the castle, the New Park, near Stirling, was the fittest place. There, he showed them, they would have every advantage, because on such a ground the enemy's cavalry, from the trees and morasses by which the park was skirted, would be deprived of their chief power of action. His representations were cordially received by men so well fitted to estimate them, and to the New Park accordingly the whole army was moved, where every troop was arranged according to his orders and under his own experienced eye.

These arrangements were worthy of the great issue and formed a masterpiece of strategic wisdom. The ground thus chosen was on the declivity along the east side of the marshes of Halbert and Milton. The right of his army was protected by a marshy ground intersected by numerous sykes; the left by the rivulet of Bannock and the deep ravine through which it flows. In this way his wings were sheltered from those terrible attacks of cavalry which were chiefly to be dreaded in the coming fight. But still further to increase the difficulties of the ground, Bruce caused pits to be dug on the level ground between his right wing and the morass, three feet in depth, over which the turf was replaced and covered with brushwood, so that they were concealed from the eye and might serve as traps for the horsemen. These "pots," as Barbour calls them, were so numerous "that they might be likened to a wax comb that bees make." It has been added that at the bottom of these pits sharp pointed stakes were placed upright to transfix all who fell into them, and that iron caltrops or crows'-feet were planted in the intervals to lame those who had escaped the pits. By these precautions the Scots could only be assailed in front and by equal numbers, while the rest of the English army were more likely to prove an encumbrance than a help to those who were engaged in combat. Having thus got a fair field for action where every brave soldier could bring his efforts into full play, Bruce resolved that even the refuse of his army—the stragglers and followers of the camp—should be turned to good account. These, which numbered nearly 20,000, along with certain bodies of undisciplined Highlanders who had joined his ranks, were sent with the baggage to a valley in the neighbourhood by which the Gillies' Hill is divided; and from this concealment they could sally out and join the chase if the day went in favour of Scot-

land, or be a covering party if the army was compelled to retreat. His whole front array was divided into three battles or battalions, of which the command of the right was given to Edward Bruce, of the left to Sir James Douglas and Walter the Steward of Scotland, and of the centre to Randolph, Earl of Moray. Behind these was the reserve, commanded by Bruce in person, consisting of his own military vassals of Carrick, the men of Argyle, Cantire, and the Isles, and Lord Angus of Islay, with his followers of Islay and Bute. Immediately behind the van, commanded by Randolph, Bruce himself took his station, where he could oversee all that passed and give aid where it was most required.

This movement of the Scottish army from the Torwood to the field of Bannockburn and these skilful preparations were not made until Saturday, the 22d of June, when the English had reached Edinburgh. By thus delaying the execution of his carefully-conceived plan, Bruce effectually prevented the enemy from devising means to counteract it, and led them on in their blind confidence until it was too late to pause. On that day the place of every troop was assigned as it arrived, and at night, when all was dark and silent, the pits were dug and the stakes planted. On the following morning mass was performed throughout the army, and many of the soldiers made their shrift, as men ready to conquer or destined to die, and anxious to be prepared for either. As it was also the vigil of St. John, they devoutly obeyed its stern requirement by eating no dinner and fasting on bread and water. After mass and confession Bruce went to examine the pits and satisfy himself that his directions had been rightly fulfilled. He then caused proclamation to be made through the army that all who were not ready to win bravely or die with honour had still permission to depart, as he wished to keep none with him except those who would stand by him to the last and take whatever God would send them. But a loud thunder-peal of 30,000 voices assured him that none would flinch—that all would strive and endure to the last.

The English army was as great a contrast to the Scotch in its prudence and precaution as in its numbers and its military equipments. Divided into ten battalions, each of which consisted of about 10,000 men, they overspread the land as they entered; while the carriages which accompanied their march were so numerous that, had they been extended in a single line, we are told, they would have been sixty miles in length. Never had so large an army marched from England; and, confident in their strength, their language had been, "I will pursue, I will overtake, I will divide the spoil;" for not only the conquest of the land but the partitioning of its estates, and the share that was to fall to each, had been settled long before their enemies were in sight. In this spirit they had advanced to Edinburgh in such haste that both horses and men were wearied and half-famished. On their approach towards Stirling Bruce sent Sir James Douglas and Sir Robert Keith, hereditary marshal of Scotland, to reconnoitre; and they returned with intelligence of the vast numbers of the invaders, the blaze of their burnished armour that lighted up the whole line of march, and the steadiness and rapidity of their approach; but as this report was calculated to daunt his soldiers, he advised them to give out that the enemy, though numerous, were without order and discipline.

When the English had advanced within two miles of the Scottish army they detached a party for the relief of the castle. These consisted of 800 gallant and completely armed horsemen, the choice of their cavalry, under the command of four lords, the chief of whom was Sir Robert Clifford. Avoiding the New Park, and making a circuit by the low grounds to the east and north of the church of St. Ninians, they thus eluded the observation of the Earl of Moray, who had received a special charge to watch the approaches to the castle and prevent the English from reinforcing it. But the quick military eye of Bruce detected the movement, and hastening to his nephew he cried sharply, "The enemy has passed your guard; heedless man! a rose has dropped from your chaplet!" Stung by this rebuke and aware of the magnitude of his error, Randolph hurried off with 500 spearmen to throw himself between the English and the castle. The enemy, thus finding an obstacle in their way, and scorning it as only composed of infantry, advanced upon the Scots in full career, expecting to ride them down in an instant; but throwing themselves into a square according to the orders of Randolph, and presenting a front on all sides with their spears rising tier above tier, the Scots awaited the onset. The shock was terrible; but the little phalanx remained unbroken while many of the English were thrown to the ground, and one of their bravest knights, Sir William Daynecourt, who was foremost in the charge, was slain. Enraged at being thus foiled, the English closed round the ring of spearmen and followed with charge upon charge like the waves of a tempest; but, in spite of their panoply, their mighty war-horses, and their numbers, the little forest of spears was unbroken, while the Scots, who were unencumbered with defensive armour, made wild work upon the unwieldy dismounted cavaliers with their short knives, daggers, and battle-axes. But still to the Scottish army that looked on in the distance the fate of their companions appeared imminent, surrounded by such overwhelming masses of cavalry and almost hid by the dust of conflict; and Sir James Douglas, no longer able to endure the sight of his rival's danger, hurried to the king exclaiming, "Ah, sir! the Earl of Moray is in peril, and if not aided will be slain; with your leave I will hasten to his rescue, for he has great need." "You shall not go a step," replied Bruce; "if he wins let him take the benefit, but whether he wins or loses I may not break my arrangements on his account." But Douglas was not to be thus repelled; "Certes! I cannot endure," he said, "to see him overborne by his enemies when I can bring him help; and therefore, with your leave, will aid him or die with him." "Then, go," replied the king reluctantly, "but let your return be speedy." The words were scarcely uttered when Douglas had hurried off to the rescue; "and I trow," exclaims Barbour, "that he shall help him so well that all his enemies shall feel it!" But on approaching the place of conflict he saw that the English ranks wavered, reeled, and would speedily be put to flight. He instantly ordered his band to halt, and said, "Our friends yonder fight so bravely that they will soon be victorious; let us not, then, lessen their glory by taking a share of the encounter." The event was as he had foreseen; the English were charged by Randolph in turn and driven back in confusion to their own army, while in this desperate struggle, in which they inflicted a heavy loss upon their assailants, the victors lost only one man.

This was not the only deed of chivalrous emprise by which the great national fight of Bannockburn was prefaced. While the English army continued to advance towards the Scots King Edward suddenly called a halt that he might consult with his officers upon the expediency of commencing battle immediately, or deferring it till the following day. But so unwieldy a mass, when once put in motion, could not be so easily arrested, and the front rank, consisting of cavalry armed from head to foot, that had not heard the king's order, continued to advance until they came near the Scottish vanguard, while its commander, Randolph, was absent. Bruce was riding in front of it, armed at all points, with a battle-axe in his hand, marshalling the ranks for the expected conflict, when Sir Henry Bohun or De Boune, an English knight of the opposite army, hoped to end the conflict at once by the death of the Scottish king, whom he recognized by the golden coronet which he wore upon his helmet. He accordingly laid his lance in the rest, spurred his strong war-steed, and came onward in sudden and full career. Bruce, who had no offensive weapon but his short axe, which served as a truncheon, and who was mounted only on a light palfrey, might have shunned the unequal encounter without disgrace; but, aware of the discouraging effects of such a retreat, and confident in his strength and skill in combat, in which no knight of England or Scotland was his equal, he turned and rode forward to meet his antagonist. At the moment when the shock would have rolled himself and palfrey in the dust he dexterously avoided the collision; and, rising in his stirrups at the same instant, he dealt such a blow upon the head of De Boune with the full swing of his battle-axe that head and helmet were shattered with the stroke, and the handle of the axe itself split in two. The English front recoiled at the spectacle and fell back in confusion, while Bruce's friends gathered round him and affectionately blamed him for meeting at such disadvantage a knight so well armed and horsed as his opponent. The king felt the justice of their remonstrance; and to turn it aside he held up his weapon and said with a look of comic regret, "I have broken my good battle-axe!"

Nothing could be better calculated to encourage the Scots than the skirmish and the combat: they were omens of success which even scepticism would scarcely reject; and while the soldiers were proud of the matchless prowess of their king, they saw that his skilful plan of warfare could countervail their scanty equipments as well as inferior numbers, and lead them to victory and triumph. Bruce availed himself of the opportunity to animate their spirit and confirm their hopes, and his speech to the army on the occasion, recorded at full by Barbour, who must have received it from those who listened to it and treasured it in their hearts, is a masterpiece of military and patriotic eloquence. "We ought," he thus began, "to love and extol Almighty God who sends us so fair a beginning. It is a great discomforting to our foes, that in this wise, and so quickly, they have been twice signally checked." The discomfiture of their choicest soldiers, he added, and the hasty retreat of their van, would so dismay their hearts and quell their courage, that their bodies and personal strength would be of little worth. A good ending would assuredly follow from such a beginning. Were they then still ready for the fight? The choice should be theirs, not his; he would fight or abstain according to their pleasure; let them then express freely their will. Here he was interrupted by their loud cheerful voices: "Good king, give battle as soon as you may, and think not that we shall fail you; for neither danger nor death will we shun till we have made our country free!" "Since you will have it so," he joyfully answered, "let every man be in his place, and all in readiness to-morrow morning at sunrise, as soon as mass has been performed." He besought them in nowise to break their array; to stand as one man; to receive the enemy on their spears, and set heart and will and strength to the struggle. He reminded them that they had three advantages on their side. They had the right, and the right was the cause of God. The enemy in their overweening confidence to possess the land had brought with them their wealth; "and this," he said, "they have brought to our hand, and in such abundance that the poorest of you shall be both rich and powerful." And finally he reminded his soldiers that they were fighting for their own lives and those of their wives and children, and for their freedom, and for their country, while their enemies were arrayed only in the cause of injustice, cruelty, and oppression, and if successful, would have no mercy. Let them then meet the onset so stoutly that the hindmost ranks of the English shall tremble at the shock. If they conquered, as he was assured that they should, he besought them to waste no time upon the spoil, or in taking prisoners, until the field was wholly their own. With regard to those who should fall in battle, he pledged his royal promise, that their heirs, however young, should immediately inherit their lands free from wardship, relief, or the customary feudal exactions. Having delivered this address to the army at large through their officers he dismissed them with the admonition to rest for the night under arms, that they might be in full readiness for fight on the ensuing morning.

The English, although they had advanced so rapidly, showed none of their wonted eagerness for the fight: they were weary with their march, and dispirited by the events of the day, which had convinced them that their victory would neither be so easy nor so certain as they had expected. In more than five hundred places over the field they gathered in groups to discuss and blame the proceedings of their leaders, and to prove that matters which at present were evil enough would soon be greatly worse. To silence this "routing," as Barbour terms it, heralds were sent by the English lords through the host to assure them their discomforts would be speedily amended, and exhorting them to fight bravely on the following day. King Edward, after having deliberated with his council and concluded to defer the battle, drew off his troops to the right and rear of the position they originally occupied, and encamped them in the Carse, where the ground was low and abounding in pools of water; but these, the English bridged over by demolishing houses and using the materials for the purpose. They then addressed themselves to supper; and the festive cries that were soon heard far and wide, showed how they were indemnifying themselves for past toils and preparing for future exertions. While they were thus revelling to the full one Alexander Seton, a Scot in the service of England, stole away from their encampment, and showed to Bruce how easily he might defeat the English if he became the assailant, and gave battle on the morning at an earlier hour. But Bruce had chosen his position too carefully, and had too much at stake, to alter his arrangements.[1]

At an early hour of the morning of Monday the 24th of June the Scots rose fully equipped for battle, and all took their places at once, and without confusion owing to the skilful precautions of their king. Their comparatively small numbers, their being on foot, even the compactness of their array showed most unfavourably, as contrasted with the wide-spread and almost countless enemy; while their half-naked bodies, only defended by helm and target, bore but a poor comparison with the myriads of mail-clad men and barbed horses of England, and gave little promise of security against the deadly showers of arrows that would soon fall as thick as a hailstorm. But it was in their offensive weapons that they were to put their trust—the long Scottish spear that could hold the iron-clad rider at bay, the axe that could hew his armour asunder in close fight, and the short knife that could despatch him when he was dismounted and thrown to the earth. As soon as they were astir, and before they advanced to their allotted places, the soldiers breakfasted, and afterwards had mass performed by Maurice, the Abbot of Inchaffray, who stood on an eminence in front of the line that he might be visible to the whole host. As soon as the army was arrayed Bruce, who was observant of every point of chivalry, proceeded to invest the most deserving with the honour of knighthood; and accordingly, with displayed banners and proclamation of heralds and trumpets, he conferred that distinction on Sir James Douglas, Walter the young Steward of Scotland, and several other noble aspirants.

The English army was now in motion, and its front had advanced within a bowshot of the Scots. Owing to the narrowness of the ground which the forecast of Bruce had selected, the other nine divisions, instead of arranging themselves to support the van, were obliged to follow at some distance, and with small intervals between each. The King of England, who in person acted as general of this cooped-up and unwieldy mass, was attended by 500 chosen cavalry as his body-guards; and at his bridle-rein on either side were stationed Sir Aymer de Valence, Earl of Pembroke, and Sir Giles de Argentine, a gallant knight of Rhodes, who next to Bruce was accounted the bravest and best combatant of the age. When King Edward drew near, and observed the admirable manner in which the Scots were drawn up, and the confident steady front they maintained, he was astonished at their presumption. "What! will you Scotchmen fight us?" he cried to Sir Ingram Umfraville, a Scot in his service. "Yea, and sickerly," replied Sir Ingram, who knew well his countrymen and their king: he advised, therefore, that a retreat should be feigned, in which case the Scots would abandon their ground and pursue in such disorder, in spite of their leaders, that they would easily be overwhelmed and crushed; but fortunately for Scotland, Edward was too confident in his strength to have recourse to stratagem. A few moments after the whole Scottish army knelt as one man, sending up their orisons to Heaven for aid in the approaching fight, while Abbot Maurice, barefooted, and holding aloft a crucifix in his hand, walked along the front of their line. "See," cried Edward, "they kneel! they ask mercy!" "They ask mercy indeed," replied Sir Ingram, "but not from you: it is to God that they appeal, and upon that field they will conquer or die." "Then, be it so!" cried the king angrily, and ordered the trumpets to sound the charge.

That signal was the warning and first note of a thunderstorm under which the ground rocked and trembled—for on came the English van with lances couched, and at the full career of their war-steeds: the whole mass threw itself upon the right wing of the Scots commanded by Edward Bruce, which was opposed to it, while the shock of such a terrible meeting was felt over the whole field. But a wall of spear-points met the charge, and the sharp-edged axe made deadly work upon the hundreds who were swept from their saddles in the onset. This onset of the van left an open space that was immediately occupied by the main body of the English, who, moving obliquely to the right, advanced upon the Scottish centre commanded by Randolph, Earl of Moray. But the earl met the attack midway, although the English were at least ten to one, and when his troops entered the unequal conflict they seemed to disappear among their enemies "as if they were plunged into the sea."[2]

---

[1] Leland, *Collec.* ii. p. 547.   [2] Barbour.

The Scottish left wing commanded by Douglas and the Steward now advanced into conflict, and thus there were three battles extending over the whole field, while nothing was heard but groans, and the ringing of blows that struck fire from the steel armour on which they lighted, instead of the shouts and cries of an ordinary battlefield. Fearful, indeed, must have been the silence of that earnestness when two such nations were so engaged—a silence more appalling than that of death itself.[1] The English cavalry, in whom the hope of victory chiefly rested, indignant at the resistance of mere churls that fought on foot, threw themselves incessantly on the masses of spearmen, but only to deepen their own disasters; for the Scottish phalanxes stood firm against every onset, while men and horses at every charge were impaled and gored upon the thickset palisade of lances that confronted them, let them assail where they might. And where was the dreaded archery of England in such an hour of need? They had decided the fight of Falkirk, and they were numerous enough to decide that of Bannockburn. Nor were they idle on this occasion; for at the commencement of the fight they plied their arrows with deadly effect, especially upon the right wing of the Scots. But Bruce had anticipated this danger, and prepared for it. He ordered 500 light-armed cavalry, the whole of his force of this description, and which he had kept in reserve for the purpose under Sir Robert Keith, marshal of Scotland, to make a compass so as to avoid a conflict with the English horse, and charge the left flank of the archers. This order was bravely and skilfully executed, and levelling their lances, the whole mounted array charged through and through the groups of bowmen who had no weapons for close fight, and who were trampled down in that sudden onset or driven back in confusion upon the main body. The ground being thus cleared, the Scottish archers advanced; and although inferior in skill to those of England, they shot with such effect as greatly to impede the charges of the English cavalry. In the meantime Keith pursued his advantage so successfully that the splendid archery of England was cut down, chased off the field, or driven in panic-struck heaps to the far distant rear of their own army, from which it was impossible to recall them.

In this manner the battle was gallantly contested, and with equal, if not superior advantage on the side of Scotland; for the enemy's bowmen were scattered, while the greater part of their unwieldy host, from the narrowness of the Scottish front and the defences on either flank, were unable to enter into action. Bruce, whose eye and attention were everywhere, beheld with satisfaction the unbroken condition of his ranks, the unabated vigour of their continued resistance, and the dispersion of the English bowmen, and he cheered his officers with encouraging assurances that they would soon be victorious. He then brought up his fourth line, which he had kept as a reserve, into the forefront of the battle, by which the fight was kindled into fresh vigour: his whole army now presented an entire front which the fierce onsets of the English, now becoming less confident and more faint, were unable to break asunder; and the Scottish archers, who carried axes as well as bows, took an effectual part in hand-to-hand combat after they had emptied their quivers. The four Scottish battalions were thus arrayed side by side, each under the other's observance and all under the eye of their heroic king, and the efforts both of soldiers and leaders were strung to the height of chivalrous emulation and patriotic zeal. At last the scales that had so long remained in even balance began to turn: there was an evident yielding among the English ranks, the general symptom in a fight of such closeness and continuance that the flagging party were on the point of yielding; and the Scots, cheered by the prospect, raised the cry, "On them! on them!—they fail!" and charged them with double vigour. Even yet, however, the English might retreat in order and with little loss of honour—they might rally on more open ground where the Scots would not dare to follow them—they might renew the fight on the following day with better experience, and forces still sufficient to overwhelm and crush their adversaries! But of all these chances they were utterly deprived by an unexpected event that was to turn their yielding into flight and their defeat into rout and hopeless confusion.

Mention has already been made of the rabble of camp-followers which Bruce had dismissed into shelter behind the Gillies' Hill. It has been thought, from the circumstance of several brave but undisciplined Highland clans having been mixed with them, that they were intended to play a more important part than that of mere onlookers — that, in fact, they were designed by Bruce to enter upon the scene in the

---

[1] A lang quhill thus fechtand thai war,
That men no noyis mycht her thar;
Men hard noucht bot granys and dintis,
That flew fyr, as men slayis on flintis.
Thai faucht ilk ane sa egerly,
That thai maid nothir noyis na cry.
—Barbour, book ix. l. 214.

It is interesting to mark at what an early period the "terrible silence" which characterizes a British charge in modern warfare had been adopted. Was Bannockburn the place of its commencement? At all events it is here that history notices its first appearance and earnest appalling character.

warlike fashion they did, and at the critical moment when their appearance would be most effectual. And that their purpose was of no timid or pacific character was evident from their preparations to descend into the field; for they elected officers, mounted some on the baggage-ponies, arranged themselves in troops of horse and foot, and marched with sheets hoisted upon tent-poles and spears, which looked in the distance like pennons and gonfalons. Thus extemporized into a warlike array, the motley groups descended from the Gillies' Hill and directed their imposing march towards the battle-field. The English, already slackening in their efforts, were confounded at this apparition, which they mistook for a fresh Scottish army advancing to the relief of their countrymen, and began to give way in earnest; the disorder increased into a panic; and Bruce at that instant raising his war-cry, made such a terrible charge upon the wavering ranks that their flight and fate were sealed. Their whole array was now a confused mass of broken ranks and despairing fugitives; the rear was crowded up or trampled down by the van; while those who hopelessly rallied to renew the battle or die with honour were borne along by their flying countrymen, or struck down by the close onset of the Scots in full pursuit. Never had England witnessed, either among her own armies or among those of her enemies, whether far or near, so terrible and so complete a discomfiture. Nearly 30,000 were slain in the battle or in the pursuit. Many fell into the pits, which had been escaped during the whole course of the engagement, and were impaled or captured. Many were drowned in the Forth after they had escaped the first danger of the pursuit. So completely was the Bannock choked with dead bodies of the English that the pursuing Scots passed over it dry-footed. Of Englishmen of rank, besides the Earl of Gloucester, Sir Robert Clifford, an experienced leader, Sir Edmund Mauley, the seneschal of England, and others of almost equal note, 200 knights and 700 esquires were numbered among the slain. So many fled for protection to the castle that they were clustered upon the rock "like bees," until they were dislodged and captured by the Scots. A large body of Welsh, under the command of Sir Maurice de Berkeley, who had thrown off their upper clothing before they entered into battle, and had afterwards escaped the pursuit, were slain or captured by the peasantry before they could reach the English Border. Even when the victory was assured and his army in full chase Bruce prudently kept his reserve in hand, to prevent the scattered enemy from using the castle as a rallying point. His glorious victory was the more gratifying as it had been obtained with little loss, only two persons of knightly rank being slain; these were Sir Walter Ross and Sir William Vipont.

Of the conduct of Edward II. during the conflict we have no account; and from this silence both of English and Scottish historians it has been surmised that he cautiously kept aloof from the danger, and was little more than a passive spectator. At length, when the last shock was given by which his ranks were broken and turned to flight, the Earl of Pembroke, who attended at his bridle, led the king from the field. With Edward, also, retreated the gallant Sir Giles de Argentine, but not far; for when he had seen his royal master free from immediate danger he turned, saying, "I never yet fled; and here, therefore, I will abide and die with honour, rather than escape with disgrace." Putting his lance in rest and shouting the cry of, "An Argentine!" he charged the foremost rank of Scottish pursuers under the command of Edward Bruce, and fell covered with wounds.

In the meantime the King of England, attended by the 500 chosen horsemen that composed his body-guard, continued his ignominious flight. Distracted, apparently, by his fears, he directed his first course to Stirling Castle, into which he sought to be received; but on Sir Philip Mowbray, the governor, representing to him that an immediate siege was certain, against which he could not hold out, and that England would raise no second army to relieve the castle, Edward turned his bridle and rode off in the direction of Linlithgow with all his attendants. It was well for him that the horse he rode, the princely present of the Bishop of Durham, was of matchless speed, for a terrible pursuer was already on his track; this was Sir James Douglas, who, on seeing the flight of the king, resolved to seal the victory by his capture or death. But he could muster no more for the chase than sixty horsemen. As he passed the Torwood in full pursuit he met Sir Lawrence Abernethy, with twenty-four mounted retainers, on his way to join the English; but on hearing of their defeat Sir Lawrence immediately threw away his allegiance and joined the Douglas in the chase. Still they were not strong enough to give battle, although they overtook the royal escort a little beyond Linlithgow; all that they could do was to hang upon the rear of the fugitives, and cut down every straggler that fell behind. Edward, thus closely pressed, was not allowed a single moment to draw bridle; and as he spurred his horse he vowed a vow to the Virgin that if she would aid him in this strait he would erect a splendid building to her glory, and as a home for her poor Carmelites.[1] At length he reached Dunbar, full sixty miles from the field of battle, and was received into the castle by Patrick, Earl of March, its governor, after which he embarked in a small boat and went by sea to Bamborough. As for Douglas, he halted the pursuit at Tranent, the weary horses of his party being unable to carry them farther.

The victors, now in full possession of the field, were at leisure to collect and divide the spoil, which, according to the generous promise of Bruce, was parted among the army at large. It was enough to raise the country at a single step from hunger to abundance, and from poverty to wealth; for besides the numerous flocks and herds and the vast store of provisions which the English had brought along with them for their permanent support after a complete conquest, there were vessels of gold and silver, and rich apparel and costly ornaments; there was armour in heaps, and good steeds in thousands; and there were the money-chests which had been brought for the payment of the soldiers. There was, besides, for future consideration, the ransom of the prisoners of rank, who numbered twenty-two barons and bannerets and sixty knights. The whole amount of wealth that thus passed into the hands of the Scots is estimated by an old English writer[2] at £200,000 of the money of that period, an equivalent to £3,000,000 of the present day. Besides this treasure there was among the spoil a large amount of warlike engines for the defence and attack of castles and walled cities, that were carefully laid aside for the protection of the land which they had been brought to subdue. An honourable trophy of their victory was also found by the Scots; this was the privy seal of England; but Bruce, instead of retaining it, as he might have done after the example of Edward I., who carried off that of Scotland as a token of his conquest, restored it to the English king, only stipulating that it should not again be put to use.[3] Indeed, the whole conduct of Bruce after the battle was so full of generous magnanimity towards the enemy, notwithstanding the provocations he had received, that fatal beyond all others though their defeat had been, the English were as much subdued by his clemency as his valour. He buried the illustrious fallen with all the honours of their rank, and treated the prisoners with courtesy and kindness, admitting them to easy terms of ransom. Mindful, also, of his friends who were still in English captivity, he exchanged John de Segrave, who was taken at Bannockburn, for five Scottish barons; and soon afterwards he liberated the Earl of Hereford, who surrendered with the castle of Bothwell, in exchange for his queen, his sister Christina, his daughter Marjory, Wishart, Bishop of Glasgow, and the young Earl of Mar. One little incident in his proceedings after the victory it would be unpardonable to omit. At night he had caused the funeral obsequies of the Earl of Gloucester to be celebrated in a neighbouring church; and at an early hour of the morning he walked over the battle-field, where a living English warrior suddenly rose from behind some bushes where he had sheltered himself for the night after the rout and dispersion of his followers. This was Sir Marmaduke Twenge — perhaps the same stalwart knight who seventeen years previous had led the advanced party of English in conjunction with Cressingham at the battle of Stirling, and who afterwards so gallantly cut his way through the Scots and crossed the Forth in safety. His purpose in the present case was surrender, not resistance, and upon his knee he yielded himself prisoner to the king. Bruce received him with the welcome of a friend, entertained him kindly for several days, and then dismissed him not only without ransom but enriched with gifts. The luckless fate of another prisoner seems to have excited the somewhat irreverent mirth of the conquerors. This was Baston, a Carmelite friar and famous poet of his day, whom King Edward had brought with him as his laureate to celebrate his victories and conquests in Scotland. But the unfortunate bard fell into the hands of his enemies; and having probably, like his tribe, neither silver nor gold with which to redeem his captivity, he was required, as the price of his deliverance, to change his theme and compose a poem on the victory of the Scots at Bannockburn. This palinode he accordingly produced; and it has been preserved by Fordun, in whose eyes it found such favour that he declares it ought not to be hid under a bushel but set upon a candlestick.[4] Although one of the strangest jingles of Latin rhyme which that monastic age, fruitful in such puerile and artificial productions, has bequeathed to us, it is still not without such touches of pathetic feeling and genuine poetry as suffice to redeem it from absolute contempt.

On the day after the battle Sir Philip Mowbray surrendered the castle of Stirling according to the terms of agreement. He also abandoned the service of England for that of Bruce, to whom he afterwards adhered with unshaken fidelity.

---

[1] This vow he afterwards fulfilled by erecting a monastery for the Carmelites at Oxford.
[2] *Monk of Malmesbury*, p. 152.   [3] Trivet; *Fœd. Ang.*
[4] *Scotichron.* lib. xii. cap. 22.

Such was the great fight of Bannockburn, and the immediate advantages it produced in wealth, trophies, and military reputation. But the moral as well as lasting benefits who can estimate? So utterly had it daunted the courage and quelled the pride of the enemy, that "100 English would not hesitate to fly from two or three Scottish soldiers.[1] It so strongly established the liberty of the country, that although afterwards it was often rudely shaken, it could never be destroyed. Even when afterwards Scotland was at the lowest point of depression, a vigorous reaction was sure to follow; and when the national spirit thus sprang up into new life and exertion it was the remembrance of Bannockburn and the name of Robert Bruce that formed the stimulant and the watchword of this awakening. Nor has its influence yet perished, or even waxed faint; for "Bannockburn" is still a household word among Scotland's children. And not perhaps until the field itself has passed away amidst the universal dissolution of nature will its deeds be forgot, or its influences unfelt. The name of Marathon is immortal, although its people have disappeared; and its tale has inspired the heroism of nations long before whose beginning Greece herself had expired. And thus it may be with Bannockburn when Scotland is no more.

During the same year in which this great national deliverance was achieved a humbled and heart-broken old man who was strangely connected with the event expired. This was John Baliol, formerly king of the liberated country, but now a despised exile. In his castle of Bailleul in France he could scarcely be indifferent to tidings of Scotland; and the rising, the sufferings, and exploits of Bruce may have often formed the theme of the pilgrim who asked bread at his gate, or the wandering troubadour who harped in his hall. It would be hard to guess the mingled feelings of patriotic pride and family envy with which he may have listened to each successive report; or whether the irritated feelings of a deposed king or the disinterested satisfaction of a true-hearted Scot was most prevalent. And how did he welcome the crowning victory by which the country was set free, remembering, as he must have done, that his own abject surrender had sold it into bondage, and invested his rival with the glorious office of its liberator? Even through old age, and dotage, and the advancing infirmities of his last sickness, these thoughts must have haunted him, and disquieted his lonely and perhaps unpitied departure. Peace be to his memory, which we are unable to honour! He died towards the close of the year.

CHAPTER VIII.

REIGN OF ROBERT BRUCE—FROM BANNOCKBURN TO THE END OF THE IRISH EXPEDITION (1314–1318).

Happy effects of the victory of Bannockburn—Bruce's cares as a legislator—England invaded—A famine—Edward II. attempts to enlist it against Scotland—Bruce settles the succession to the Scottish throne—The crown of Ireland offered to Edward Bruce—He accepts the offer—His exploits and victories in Ireland—Robert Bruce invades the Western Isles—His curious voyage across the isthmus of Tarbet—The islands reduced to submission—Robert Bruce invades England—He crosses to Ireland to aid his brother—Defeats the Earl of Ulster—March of the Bruces through Ireland—Generous conduct of Robert Bruce to a poor woman—Scotland invaded in his absence—Gallant defence of the country by Sir James Douglas—He defeats the English at Linthaughlee—His victories over Sir Edmund de Cailou and Sir Robert Neville—The English routed at Donibristle by the Bishop of Dunkeld—Return of Robert Bruce from Ireland—Edward II. has recourse to the aid of the church—Devices of the pope to compel the Scots to a truce with England—Failure of the negotiation—The cardinals plundered and stripped—Their fruitless attempts to establish the truce by a messenger—His account of his mission—Bruce surprises the town and castle of Berwick—He invades England—Misfortunes of Edward Bruce in Ireland—His defeat and death near Dundalk—Retreat of the Scots from Ireland.

After the glorious victory of Bannockburn the whole aspect of the land was suddenly changed: the storm was hushed, the clouds and shadows were dispersed, and the sunshine had returned. Where there had been poverty there was wealth and abundance, and the possession of these was sweetened by the thought of the toil with which they had been purchased, and the freedom with which they might be enjoyed. "There was universal mirth, and solace, and

---

[1] Walsingham, p. 106.

blitheness," says Barbour, "for every man was blithe and jolly." But the watchful prudence of Bruce would not permit him for a moment to repose upon his triumphs. Liberty had still to be secured and order restored, without which his victory would have been no better than a successful tournament. One of his first cares as a legislator was to settle the tenure of lands, which had constantly fluctuated by the usurpations of war and conquest since 1286, and to make them available for the supply of that royal revenue which was necessary for the maintenance of his government. With the advice of his council he accordingly issued a proclamation that all who had claims to land in Scotland should produce their titles within twelve months and render the usual homage for it, otherwise the estates should be forfeited to the crown. By this simple rule the dispossessed families could be replaced, and those Scots who still remained in England recalled to their allegiance. The estates held by royal charter could be placed upon a permanent footing, and their debts to the crown as the price of infeftment or livery could be regularly and impartially exacted.[1]

Having issued this order the next care of Bruce was to maintain by war the advantages he had already won, and this, too, before the enemy had recovered from their panic. His first military operation, therefore, was an invasion of England, by a force which he sent under the conduct of Sir James Douglas and Edward Bruce, whom he had made Earl of Carrick on account of his own rise to the throne. The Scottish army crossed the eastern marches, wasted Northumberland, and laid the bishopric under heavy contributions. After having penetrated as far as Richmond in Yorkshire without being opposed, so complete was the depression of the English, the invaders turned their course westward, burned Appleby and several other towns, and marched back to Scotland laden with plunder. During this inroad we are told that many of the Northumbrians joined the Scots against their own countrymen and aided them in their devastations.[2]

In this reverse of affairs between the two kingdoms the proceedings of Edward II. were indicative of nothing but loss and humiliation. There was no longer word of a fresh invasion of Scotland: the utmost he now aimed at was the defence of his own border and the security of England against the victorious Scots; and for this purpose he appointed the Earl of Pembroke warden over the country between Berwick and the Trent, to repress their incursions.

The king also issued proclamations of levies in troops and shipping for the protection of the English border both by land and sea. But these orders were soon rendered ineffectual by a fresh Scottish invasion that was as little resisted as the former, and which swept over Redesdale and Tynedale, wasting every town, village, and hamlet in its course, and compelling the inhabitants to ransom their lives at a heavy price. The Scots then directed their march into Cumberland, from which they exacted large sums, while many of its inhabitants swore allegiance to the King of Scotland, and made common cause with the Scots against their own country. These were doubtless the broken clans of the Border, the scum and refuse of both countries, who now began to constitute a people by themselves indifferent alike to the welfare of England and Scotland, and only faithful to their own separate interests. Finding that little aid was to be received from their king, who was at variance with his own nobles and parliament, the barons of the northern counties assembled at York, entered into a mutual league for the defence of their own districts against the Scots, and elected four of their number to command the forces raised for the occasion. But even this wise precaution was frustrated by circumstances which they could not control: the royal exchequer, from which they should have been supported, was empty, or its resources otherwise employed, and the troops which the barons had raised, but were unable to pay, indemnified themselves by plundering their employers and assisting the invading enemy.

During the course of this successful career Bruce hoped that the opportunity had at last arrived of securing an honourable and lasting peace, which was necessary for the welfare of both countries alike. He signified this desire by letter to Edward II., who granted a passport to four Scottish commissioners for their coming to England, and negotiating with the members of his council. But the English were not yet ready to recognize the claims of Scottish independence, and the treaty was abruptly terminated. The winter of 1314 having thus passed, the commencement of the following year saw England afflicted with a severe famine which had been aggravated by the late Scottish inroads, and which the enactments of the English parliament to lower the price of provisions could neither remove nor alleviate. As might be expected, the same calamity extended to Scotland, and Edward II., unable for the present to raise an army against the Scots on account of the lowness of his exchequer and the discontent of his barons, resolved to enlist the general calamity upon his side, and encounter

---

[1] Barbour, L ix. [2] *Chron. Lanercost;* Walsingham.

the enemy with their own favourite weapon. He therefore issued strict prohibitions against every supply of provisions to Scotland by the merchants of England, Ireland, and Wales. As the Scots at this time also were chiefly dependent upon the continental markets he sent missives to Holland, Flanders, Brabant, and Lunenburgh, requesting them to stop the importation of grain and cattle into Scotland. But at so low an ebb was his influence in these small states, and so greatly had the reputation of the rival kingdom been increased by the victories of Bruce, that Edward's entreaties, which in the days of his father would have been received as authoritative commands, were disobeyed and set at nought, even though he sent small squadrons of ships to cruise round the island, and intercept all foreign supplies to the Scots. The Scots, also, in the spring retaliated this new form of English aggression by invading Northumberland, upon which they renewed all their former severities: they ravaged the bishopric of Durham, plundered the seaport of Hartlepool, compelling the inhabitants everywhere to pay heavy ransom, and penetrated to the gates of York. And still, amidst the miseries of his subjects on the Border, the King of England was obliged to sit inert and helpless in his capital. He could raise no supplies from his parliament even for a defensive war; and though Gaveston was dead, the barons, who had put him to death, were too apprehensive of the vengeance of Edward to intrust him with the command of an army.

After this invasion the wise foresight of Bruce made preparations for the settlement of the crown of Scotland, by which the evils of a disputed succession, whence the country had already suffered so much, might for the time to come be avoided. The season also was favourable for the purpose; for not only were his own royal claims now in general acceptance on account of the deliverance which he had achieved for the land, but those of the rival house were considered as forfeited by the calamities it had entailed, and also by the voluntary abdication of its head and representative. John Baliol had also lately died in France, while his son Edward was an unnoticed resident in England and a pensionary of its king. The Scottish parliament was accordingly assembled at Ayr on Sunday the 26th of April (1315), and in a full meeting of clergy, lords, and commons the important subject was unanimously settled. It was decreed, with full consent of the king and his daughter Marjory, that should Robert Bruce die without heirs male of his own body, in that case his brother Edward, as a man of tried valour and experience, and therefore best fitted to rule and defend the kingdom, should succeed to the throne. With the consent of the king and of his brother Edward, it was provided, failing Edward and heirs male of his body, that Marjory, and failing her the nearest heir male descended from King Robert, should succeed to the crown—under condition, however, that Marjory should marry with consent of her father, or, in the event of his death, with the consent of the majority of the estates of Scotland. Should both the king and his brother die during the minority of an heir male, Thomas Randolph, Earl of Moray, was to be guardian of the heir and kingdom until the heir was of age; and should Marjory die in widowhood, leaving an heir under age, or should there be no male heir, Randolph was to be appointed guardian of the kingdom until the estates should determine upon the rightful succession to the crown.[1] In these enactments it will be distinctly seen how the Scots had laid the warning of the past to heart; and how anxious they were that there should be no parallel between the history of Marjory Bruce and that of Margaret of Norway. Soon afterwards Marjory was married to Walter, the hereditary steward of Scotland, a most important national event, as it was the source of the Stewart dynasty.

It was now that after a lapse of centuries Scotland was once more to enter into a close connection with Ireland. The Anglo-Norman conquest of that island in the reign of Henry II. had been succeeded by those severities and oppressions with which conquerors, when few in numbers, endeavoured to enforce the submission of the conquered; while the Irish, a Celtic people, and therefore tenaciously wedded to their peculiar institutions, hated the English not only as tyrants but as innovators. There was no congeniality of race, character, or language between the two peoples that might have softened the asperities of conquest and resolved them into a single nation; on the contrary, every year only added to the list of Irish injuries, and made the separation more complete and inveterate. In such a state it is not surprising that the present condition of Scotland should inspire them with the hope of liberty and revenge. They had watched the course of events; and while they triumphed in the calamities that had fallen on their oppressors, they no doubt hoped that with Scottish aid they might make Ireland as free as Scotland. The result was an application to Robert Bruce from the chieftains of Ulster entreating his assistance, and offering to make his brother Edward their king. It has often been matter of sur-

---

[1] *Scotichron.* l. xii. c. 24.

prise that Bruce assented to their appeal. The recovery of Scotland was but of yesterday, and could only be maintained by the same course that had won it. The strength of England was still unbroken, and might soon rally under a better leader than its present inefficient ruler; while the resources of Scotland at the best were so inferior that their uttermost would be needed for the trial. It was certain also that this alluring prospect of Irish conquests and settlements would attract those gallant spirits who were most needful as well as most effective for home defence. These considerations were doubtless taken into account and allowed their full weight. But how to dispose of his brother was also Robert's difficulty. Edward Bruce, "that stouter was than a libbard," we are told, was too restless to remain in peace, and thought that Scotland was too little for his brother and himself.[1] The only chance, therefore, of maintaining the undivided rule of Scotland, perhaps of transmitting it in peace, was to assist this restless, ambitious, and popular knight-errant in winning a kingdom of his own. Besides this politic consideration there was the promise of an easy conquest, by which the power and fame of Scotland might be increased and the resources of England weakened and divided; and Robert Bruce was a bold ambitious soldier as well as a prudent king and sagacious politician. His consent to the expedition was given, and towards the close of May (1315) Edward Bruce embarked an army of 6000 Scots in 300 small vessels at Ayr to win his new kingdom. Among the many brave captains who accompanied him, and whose absence it might be thought Scotland could least spare at such a crisis, were Randolph, Earl of Moray, Sir Philip Mowbray, his late antagonist in the defence of Stirling Castle, Sir John Soulis, Sir Allan Stewart, and Sir John Campbell, the nephew of the Scottish king. On landing, Edward Bruce with characteristic boldness sent back to Scotland the shipping in which his troops had been exported, thus showing his resolution to win or die by renouncing the means of retreat.

The narrative of this expedition is in the highest degree romantic, abounding with daring deeds and surprising victories; but this, indeed, might have been expected from such an army and leader, as well as the state of the country and the object at stake. On landing, the Scots commenced their daring march into the interior in two bodies or battles, the van being commanded by the Earl of Moray and the rear by Edward Bruce. They were soon confronted by an army of nearly 20,000 English settlers and Irish natives; but this ill-assorted and undisciplined array was attacked and quickly put to the rout with little loss to the invaders. After this success Edward Bruce took possession of the town of Carrickfergus, and here he was joined by ten or twelve of the Irish reguli or chiefs, who swore allegiance to him as King of Ireland. The next exploit of the Scots was to storm a strong pass occupied by 4000 archers and spearmen, who were stationed there to block up the communication between Carrickfergus and the interior. This the Scots achieved with the same boldness and success that had distinguished them in the mountain warfare of their own country; and by this victory they procured great store of cattle for the subsistence of their army, of which they stood greatly in need. They then advanced into the country, burning and slaying in their progress, but confining their merciless inflictions to the English settlers and their Irish adherents. To repel the invaders Richard de Burgh, Earl of Ulster, mustered his military vassals and the English of the province, and, assisted by those Irish chieftains who had not joined the enemy, he advanced to give them battle. He was so far connected with the Scots as to be brother-in-law to their king, who had married his sister; but his interests as well as his allegiance were wholly on the opposite side. As he advanced against the Scots he exceeded them in the havoc with which he visited the territories of those who had joined them. Edward Bruce, although greatly outnumbered, marched forward and encountered the Anglo-Irish near Dundalk. A long contested battle followed in which the earl's forces were defeated; and on flying for shelter to Dundalk, the victors followed at their heels and forced an entrance into the town, which they pillaged after slaying or ejecting the fugitives. Edward Bruce then continued his march southward with the Anglo-Irish hovering upon his flanks, and after a series of unimportant skirmishes reached a great forest called Kilrose, where the enemy had collected an army which, according to Barbour, amounted to 50,000, while the Scots, even though reinforced by their Irish auxiliaries, were only a fifth of that number. But dismounting and charging on foot, which was now the favourite mode of Scottish warfare, they utterly routed the enemy, who were chiefly on horseback, and drove them into the recesses of the forest, whither they prudently forebore to pursue them.

After this specimen of the opening of the

---

[1] Barbour, lib. x. This view of the character of Edward Bruce in connection with the Scoto-Irish war is also repeated by Fordun:—"Causa hujus guerræ hæc est; iste Eadwardus erat homo alti cordis, non valens cohabitare cum fratre suo rege Scotiæ, tanquam regnum istud non foret ulrique sufficiens."—*Scotichron.* l. xii. c. 37.

Scottish campaign in Ireland, a campaign which continued to be filled with other marvellous successes, although their precise nature has baffled historical research, we return to the affairs of Scotland. These, during the years 1315 and 1316, were signalized by unwonted tranquillity, the English being too closely occupied with the distracted condition of their own affairs to attempt a Scottish invasion. Bruce therefore availed himself of the interval to collect and reconstruct the fragments of his still divided kingdom; and for this purpose it was necessary to recover full possession of the Western Isles, without which he could have no effectual protection for the Scottish coasts or a fleet to resist the English at sea. But the greater part of these islands were under the dominion of his deadly enemy John of Lorn, who since his defeat at Ben Cruachan and expulsion from the mainland, had fled thither, and there he ruled with the authority of an old Norse sea-king and under the protection of Edward II., who had dignified him with the title of Admiral of the Western Fleet of England. For this naval invasion Robert Bruce used the fleet of small vessels which his brother had sent home; and to conceal the purpose of the expedition he collected them at East Tarbet, as if he meant to direct his course to Ireland. Across the narrow isthmus between the lochs of East and West Tarbet the distance from sea to sea is little more than a mile; and as doubling the Mull of Kantire is often a dangerous enterprise for such small craft as he possessed, he boldly resolved to transport his whole fleet across by land and launch it into the opposite sea. He may have been also induced to this singular attempt from a prophecy in which the western islanders trusted; it was that they would never be subdued until a fleet had crossed the isthmus of Tarbet to invade them. Two rows of trees by his orders were properly smoothed and laid lengthways and parallel across this low-lying neck of land; large rollers of trees cut into convenient lengths were likewise added to the slides where they were most needed; and along this singular railway the ships were dragged by the troops and mariners and launched into West Tarbet Loch. It is said also that to facilitate the movements of the vessels in this voyage by dry land every sail was hoisted, as the wind was favourable for the purpose. Dismayed by this unexpected approach, and recognizing it as the fulfilment of the augury, the superstitious islesmen offered no resistance, but everywhere submitted. John of Lorn, who was taken prisoner, was confined in the castle of Dumbarton, and afterwards in that of Lochleven, where he died. To confirm his authority, and perhaps to improve the opportunity of relaxation from his oppressive trials, the king spent a considerable time in these islands enjoying the pleasures of the chase; and it is probable that at this period he invested his young son-in-law, Walter the Steward, with the lordship of the Western Isles—a title that was perpetuated in the family of the future dynasty. A more important event for the house of Stuart, which also occurred about this time, was the birth of Robert, the son of the steward and grandson of the king, who ascended the throne of Scotland as Robert II. fifty-five years afterwards. But this birth of an heir to royalty and promise of a regular succession was clouded by the death of Marjory, which occurred a few hours afterwards.

In the meantime the war between Scotland and England continued, and the fact that no regular battle signalized it is a full proof of the growing ascendency of Scotland and the depressed condition of her formidable rival. The Scots, now the assailants at every point, carried their invasions into Wales, and with such effect that Edward II., instead of calling the Welsh levies into the field, was obliged to leave them for the defence of their own territories. About midsummer Bruce also conducted in person an expedition into England, and advanced as far as Richmond unopposed, which town was only spared from the flames by a heavy ransom from the inhabitants. Bruce then penetrated into the West Riding, and after devastating the country for sixty miles round he brought back the army to Scotland enriched with spoil.

The attention of Robert Bruce was now turned towards Ireland, into which country the war had mainly been directed. Edward Bruce had taken the castle of Carrickfergus after a long siege; he had soon after been crowned King of Ireland; and England was using every effort to recover her dominion of the island. The safety of his brother and the brave army under his command, the hope of wasting the enemy's resources, and the desire of giving Scotland a breathing time of recovery may have influenced the Scottish king, as immediate advantages worth securing; and, intrusting the defence of the kingdom to Sir James Douglas and Walter the Steward, he embarked about the end of the year (1316) at Loch Ryan, and landed at Carrickfergus. At the head of an army of 20,000 men, half of whom appear to have been Irish auxiliaries, the two royal brothers made a military progress through the island, Edward leading the van, and King Robert and the Earl of Moray the rear. Their line of march lay through an extensive forest; and here the Earl of Ulster awaited them at the head of 40,000 horse and foot, intending to let the van of the Scots pass unopposed through the defile, and afterwards to attack and crush the rear with the weight of his onset. The rashness of Edward Bruce aided this well-devised plan of the earl, for he hastily marched through the wood without previous exploration, and continued his route in confidence that the rear would safely follow. But as soon as Robert had entered the pass, the appearance of small parties of archers that hovered on the outskirts of his division gave tokens that their army was at hand; and perceiving this he gave prompt command that his troops should march in close order of battle, and that no man under any pretence whatever should quit the ranks. So urgent was the need of this precaution, and so rigidly was it enforced, that when Sir Colin Campbell, the king's nephew, rode off at full speed to attack two archers who had shot at him, Robert chastised the lordly trespasser with a heavy blow of his truncheon. "Breaking of orders," he cried, "might cause our utter ruin: ween you that yon ribbalds durst assail us, were not their army at hand?" His calculation was justified, for a short advance brought them in front of the whole Anglo-Irish army. But the Scottish rear from the late precaution was in trim for instant action; they charged the enemy though eight times their number, and after a keen contest defeated them with great slaughter. As soon as tidings of this victory reached the ears of Edward Bruce he bitterly lamented that he had obtained no share in it. "It was owing to your own folly," replied his elder brother reprovingly: "no man who commands the vaward should pass wholly out of sight of the rear."

The march of the Scots was continued, but with greater circumspection, and meeting no enemy they arrived at Dublin, which they attempted to capture; but the citizens adopted such effectual means of defence that the Bruces turned aside and directed their course through Kildare, until they reached the town of Limerick. If they had hoped that their appearance would be the signal for the Irish to rise against their oppressors they were disappointed: the English conquest of the country had been too complete and of too old a date to be thus shaken off; and this long march across the island from Carrickfergus to Limerick, if we except the glory of the enterprise and the spirit with which it animated the Scots, produced no result. They retraced their steps to Kildare, the English still not venturing to give them battle. On their homeward return an incident occurred which has endeared the memory of Robert Bruce more highly to many an affectionate heart than all his splendid victories. He was one day aroused by outcries of female lamentation; and on asking the cause he was told that they were uttered by a washerwoman or laundry-woman following the army, who had fallen in travail, and was bewailing the necessity that would leave her behind to the English, or the wild kernes their auxiliaries. To stop the march of an army for such a humble and every-day incident, and that, too, while the enemy were following and might soon close upon them, had seldom, if ever, entered into the possibilities of military calculation. But good King Robert's lion heart was as keenly alive to gentlest emotions as to deeds of daring and the charms of military glory. "Certes," he said, "it were pity that she should be left at such a point; and I trow there is no man who will not have compassion upon a woman so bested." He immediately caused his army to halt, and a tent to be raised for her comfortable reception; ordered the women of the army to attend upon her, and gave careful directions about her safe conveyance in the march after her delivery. Such is the tale as Barbour relates it; and he truthfully and affectionately adds, "This was a great act of courtesy that such and so great a king should make his army delay in this manner for only a poor washerwoman."

The absence of Robert Bruce in Ireland was welcomed by the English as a choice opportunity for invading Scotland; and to this Edward II. was the more inclined from a temporary reconciliation which had taken place between him and his offended barons. He accordingly ordered his army to assemble for the purpose at Newcastle about the end of September, 1317; but this command, instead of meeting with obedience, only woke anew the hostility of the English lords, and they failed to appear with their vassals at the time appointed. Instead of a united expedition the enterprise therefore broke down into a series of smaller inroads, which were successively encountered and gallantly defeated by Sir James Douglas, the temporary guardian of Scotland. This renowned knight, whose especial charge was the defence of the middle borders, and whose favourite haunt was Jedburgh Forest, was selected as a fit antagonist by the Earl of Arundel, who commanded the opposite marches. Knowing that Douglas had built for himself a spacious mansion at Linthaughlee, near Jedburgh, and meant to celebrate its completion by a banquet to his captains and military vassals, the earl deemed this a choice opportunity to surprise his antagonist when off his guard. He accordingly mustered a strong force of 10,000 men well armed, and also provided with axes; for he meant not only to disperse the Scots, but to clear the forest of trees, so that it should no longer be a shelter to the enemy. But Douglas, who was constantly wakeful and had his spies abroad, was soon aware of the design of these unbidden visitors to disturb his revel, and made preparations for a correspondent welcome. He collected a band of fifty men-at-arms and fifty archers, with whom he planted himself in ambush at the narrowest part of the approach, his men-at-arms on one side and the archers on the other, with an interval of only twenty yards of clear ground between them; taking care also to secure his archers from an attack of cavalry by interlacing the branches of trees behind which they were posted into a close, strong-set hedge. The Earl of Arundel advanced with his powerful array, little weening of the entertainment awaiting him; his troops were silently marched into the opening of the wood, where it afforded a wide entrance that narrowed as it went inward; but on nearing the place of ambush, and when their ranks were crowded together from want of room, the signal to the Scottish archers was given, and volleys of arrows were discharged from their safe concealment with deadly effect. Confounded at this unexpected greeting, the English ranks recoiled on each other and were wedged into an unwieldy mass, when Douglas unexpectedly burst upon them from the opposite side with his fifty horsemen in full charge. This completed their confusion; they could neither effectually resist nor escape; and after sustaining terrible loss they were finally driven back through the pass and into the open country, where Douglas with his small band knew it would be unwise to follow them. In this battle, also, as was his wont, he combined the office of a brave combatant with that of a skilful leader; and singling out Sir Thomas de Richemont, a gallant knight of Brittany who fought in the ranks of Arundel, he closed with him and slew him with his dagger. Over his helmet the Briton wore a furred hat, a material at that time rare in Scotland, and this rich ornament the Douglas was careful to secure as a trophy.

Thus the forest was cleared and the enemy routed by a daring and successful surprise. But the work of the victors was not yet quite ended. During the march of the English, and probably before they entered the wood, they had detached 300 men under the command of a bellicose churchman named Ellis to make a circuit and attack the stronghold of the Scots in another direction, so as to multiply the chances of success. The ecclesiastic found his way to the mansion of Linthaughlee and its savoury larders, where all was in readiness for the promised feast; and thinking, no doubt, that their owner was already dead or in full flight, he yielded to the tempting opportunity, and sat down with his companions to eat, drink, and be merry. But the Scots soon returned both hungry and weary, and were therefore in the worst of moods to find their places occupied; their swords flew from their sheaths; and the battle that followed, which was very brief, proved a fatal reckoning to most of the guests, who were stretched lifeless on the floor. The remnant that escaped reached the main body, already driven out to the plain; and when they had told their tale Arundel felt no inclination to return to the forest and tempt a fresh encounter. Instead of this he hastily retreated across the Border.

After the departure of the Earl of Arundel another antagonist to Sir James Douglas soon entered the field; this was Sir Edmund de Cailou, a knight of Gascony, and countryman of the late favourite Gaveston, to whom Edward II. had intrusted the important government of Berwick. Resolved to signalize himself by a deed of arms against the Scots, and enrich himself with their plunder, Sir Edmund advanced into the lower part of Teviotdale and the Merse, spreading his devastations in every direction. Sir Alam Gordon, now a reconciled Scot, brought tidings of the inroad to Douglas, who resolved to meet the invader and recover the spoil. He gathered his followers for the purpose; but on approaching the enemy, who were on their way back to Berwick, he found that their numbers far exceeded his own, and were much greater than had been reported. While he hesitated on this account to attack them de Cailou sent his plunder to Berwick, and advanced to the encounter. It was an unequal conflict in an open field, as the English were two to one, while their commander was an able and gallant leader. At length Douglas, on finding his men hard pressed, resolved to decide the contest by the death of de Cailou, and was successful, for the Gascon fell beneath his sword; his followers took to flight, and the plunder they were carrying off was recovered.

The personal prowess of Douglas was now so famed that an encounter with him on superior or even equal terms was one of the highest marks of knightly ambition. This was the case with Sir Robert Neville, at that time residing in Berwick, who, on hearing the terrible tales of the might of Sir James which were brought to Berwick by the fugitives, declared that he would meet this dreaded knight in combat if he dared to display his banner before the walls of Berwick. Douglas was not a man to overlook such challenges; he was soon within sight of the town; and, to rouse his adversary and bring him forth, he caused his troops to waste the adjacent country and set fire to the villages.

Sir Robert rushed out, hoping to surprise the Scots while thus dispersed; but Douglas quickly recalled them and advanced in order of battle. When the fight was at the hottest the promised combat between the two leaders commenced; but the Englishman proved the weaker and fell lifeless to the earth. The rout of his followers was complete; several of high rank were made prisoners; and Douglas, after wasting and plundering the country at pleasure, returned unopposed to the forest. A usual practice with him after such forays, which he observed on the present occasion, was to divide the spoil among his soldiers, reserving none to himself. It was not wonderful, therefore, that they were so ready to follow him, or that they bestowed on him the title of "The Good Lord James."

By these successes of the gallant Scottish guardian during the absence of the king in Ireland the army which Edward II. had collected at Newcastle was destroyed in detail and the safety of the country ensured. Another attempt at invasion which the English made by sea was equally unsuccessful. A strong body of troops embarked on the Humber, sailed up the Firth of Forth, and landed at Donibristle, with the intent of laying waste the peninsula of Fife. To oppose their landing 500 horse were hastily collected by the sheriff of the county; but, on seeing the superior force of the invaders, the horsemen drew bridle and were soon in full flight. At the sight of this disgraceful spectacle William Sinclair, Bishop of Dunkeld, met and arrested the fugitives with indignant taunts: "Ha! my good knights, whither away?—the king should hack off your gilt spurs from your heels for taking such care of the country in his absence!" Throwing off his priestly raiment and seizing a spear he cried, "Let every one who loves his king and country follow me!" and with these words he turned the tide of flight and charged the English, who were little prepared for such a sudden change. The desperate onset of this strong-limbed, stout-hearted, soldier-looking prelate, ably seconded by the riders of Fife, drove the English back in disorder to their shipping; 500 of them were slain in the conflict and chase, and many were drowned from the sinking of several vessels into which they too eagerly crowded. This deed, among the other achievements of the war, was so welcome to the king at his return from Ireland that he honoured Sinclair with the title of "My own Bishop."[1]

The return of Bruce was so welcome to his people that the whole land rejoiced at his arrival; and on his way from the coast of Galloway, where he landed, he was feasted by the nobles and followed by crowds. There was, indeed, good cause for such a popular ovation, for the whole country was now recovered from the yoke of England with the exception of the town and castle of Berwick; while the Scottish nobles were obedient to his authority, such as refused having been previously sent into banishment. In this state of affairs, which he was unable to subvert by arms, Edward II. had recourse to the church. But it was not now the repossession of Scotland which he aimed at; his utmost wish seems to have been nothing more than to be protected from the aggressions of the Scots. He found in Pope John XXII. a ready ally, who about the beginning of 1317 issued a bull from Avignon, his place of residence, commanding a truce to be established between the two contending countries on pain of excommunication. But it was evident to what side this partial arbitrator inclined by the title which he gave to the Scottish sovereign, whom he only recognized as "his beloved son, the noble Lord Robert Bruce, carrying himself as King of Scotland." The pontiff also sent two cardinals into England to enforce the establishment of the truce, and empowered them to inflict the highest ecclesiastical punishments upon Bruce and all his adherents in the event of their refusal, which was expected to follow. Another formidable weapon with which they were privately intrusted in the event of his opposition, and upon which in this case they were to act, was a papal sentence by which Robert Bruce and his brother Edward were declared excommunicated persons. By another bull the Minorite Friars were denounced for preaching rebellion in Ireland and stirring up the natives to join the Scottish invasion. Thus armed at all points with the weapons of the church they arrived in England, and commenced the campaign by obtaining letters of safe-conduct for themselves and their nuncios to open their communication with the King of Scots. But Bruce in the stern school of experience had learned a wisdom which was more than a match for the craft of the cardinals, and his war with the church was not the least important in the record of his battles and victories.

The particulars of this new invasion of Scotland, which were detailed at length by the cardinals themselves to their ecclesiastical superior, are well worth noting.[2] Halting at Durham, where a new bishop was about to be consecrated, they sent the Bishop of Corbeil and Master Aumery, their nuncios, across the Border, of whom, when the conference with the

---

[1] Barbour; Scotichron.

[2] Fœd. Angl. p. 661, et sequent. Their missive was dated 7th September, 1317, from Durham.

Scottish king was ended, the one was to return speedily with the tidings, while the other was to follow at his leisure. They were courteously received by Robert Bruce; and in answer to their proposals he expressed his acquiescence in their wish for a good, firm, and perpetual peace; but as he was only addressed as Governor of Scotland he stated that he could not admit them to a definitive interview upon the subject while so addressed without the permission of his barons in full council. Upon the same plea he refused to receive and open the papal letters addressed to Lord Robert Bruce; "for," said he, "there are other barons in Scotland of the name of Robert Bruce who have a share in the government of the country." Thus the papal epistles were returned, like the "mis-sent" billets of a modern post-office. The nonplussed messengers then attempted to rally by an excuse for the omission of his royal title; it was not customary, they said, for his holy mother the church to prejudge a question which was still in controversy; but to this apology his reply was bold and distinct: "Since my father the pope and my mother the church are unwilling to prejudice either party by giving me the title of king, they ought not to prejudice me during the controversy by withholding it; for I not only have possession of the kingdom and receive the title of king from its people, but am addressed under that title by other princes. But my spiritual parents assume an evident partiality among their sons. Had you presumed to offer letters so addressed to other kings, you might perhaps have been otherwise answered." All this, the messengers declared, was delivered in an affable manner and with a pleasant countenance, "evincing all due reverence for your holiness and the church;" but they must have felt the bitterness that lurked under his words and the shame of their defeat. And this, too, at their own weapons and by a barbarian king! They then besought him to cease from hostilities with England for the present at least; but were told that this could not be done without the advice and assent of his barons, more especially as the English were daily committing hostilities upon various parts of Scotland.

Thus terminated this singular interview between the King of Scots and the ambassadors of the pope; and although the proposals of peace were to be taken into consideration at a remote day when a full Scottish parliament could be assembled, the nuncios were convinced that nothing could be accomplished until Bruce's royal title was acknowledged by the Roman conclave. They therefore returned to England; but even yet the vexations of their mission had not ended. The English Border at this time swarmed with unemployed or disbanded soldiers; and in the troubled state of the country they were becoming formidable outlaws, ready to side with whatever cause was strongest, and attack wherever plunder was most plentiful. It is supposed that Bruce was in communication with these desperate allies, and had incited them to a deed in full keeping with their character; this was nothing less than an onslaught upon those churchmen, who, under the peaceful character of arbitrators, were seeking to enslave the kingdom to England and drive him from the throne. The deed was perpetrated a few miles from Darlington, where the cardinals and their returning messengers seem to have met in council upon the affairs of the church. On this occasion a formidable band of these English freebooters, under Gilbert Middleton and Walter Selby, their leaders, rushed from the wood in which they were ambushed, and not only made the nuncios prisoners but also the two cardinals, the new Bishop of Durham who accompanied them, and Henry de Beaumont, his brother. The churchmen were plundered, stripped, and dismissed, with the exception of the two Beaumonts, whom the chief outlaw kept as prisoners in his castle until their liberty was purchased by a heavy ransom. Such were the chief particulars of an event very confusedly related, and of which neither the distinct date nor the object is specified. If it was a mere marauding exploit it is sufficiently intelligible according to Border usages, but if its purpose was to capture the papal missives it certainly failed.

Having thus been baffled in their first attempt the cardinals resolved to make full use of those extraordinary powers with which they were invested. As yet they had only talked of truce and pretended to act as impartial peacemakers; but now they resolved to proceed to the extremities of interdict and excommunication, which they had kept in secret as a last resource. A pretext was necessary for their use, but this they could easily create: it was merely to proclaim the two years' truce in Scotland as authorized by the pope, well knowing that Bruce would indignantly refuse it, and thus commit himself to their censures. To find a martyr to carry their proclamation into Scotland was their only difficulty, but this they easily procured in Adam Newton, father-guardian of the Minorite Friars of the monastery of Berwick, who set off on his perilous mission furnished with letters from the cardinals to the principal clergy of Scotland, charging them upon their vow of spiritual obedience to enforce the requisitions of the pope. But Adam's own account of his proceedings on this occasion is too important to be omitted.

In his letter to the cardinals he thus writes from Berwick on his return:—

"In the first place, after passing through England I arrived, with God's assistance, at the town of Berwick, and then set out safe and sound with all my letters for Scotland, yet not without great danger and difficulty. And on the Friday before the feast of St. Thomas the Apostle I set out in the morning from Berwick, and arrived at a certain town called Old Cambus, distant about twelve miles from Berwick, nigh to which town the Lord Robert Bruce was encamped with his accomplices, and labouring night and day in the construction of various machines for the siege and destruction of Berwick. And what I feared at first, afterwards befell me. But that I might proceed with caution, I left the bulls and all the letters, with your process, in safe custody at Berwick, until I should have a safe-conduct from the aforesaid Lord Robert, which I received from Lord Alexander de Seton his seneschal, and Master John de Montforth his clerk.

"And having returned from Berwick with the bulls and other letters to the said town of Old Cambus, they refused to let me have personal treaty with the above-mentioned Robert, but ordered me to give them the letters that they might themselves present them to him, and ascertain whether they were for him or against him. And before them, and a great crowd there assembled, I proclaimed publicly and expressly the truce that had been ordained and established by our high pontiff between England and Scotland; which proclamation they scouted. And because he was not addressed as King of Scotland in the bulls he returned them and the other letters with contempt, declaring that he would receive neither the bulls nor your processes, unless he was addressed as King of Scotland, and until he had taken the town of Berwick. And on having seen and heard all this I was greatly troubled in heart as to how I should escape from the hands of my enemies, difficulties being on every side, not only for the preservation of my letters, but mine own mortal life. And I entreated and adjured them in the name of the Lord, that in charity and compassion, and from their reverence to the Holy See, they would give me a safe-conduct to Berwick, which they refused; neither would they grant me one to pass further into Scotland to transact affairs with certain prelates of the country, as you gave me in charge, but dismissed me bereft on all hands, and ordered me to be gone from Scotland as soon and as fast as I could.

"And in the morning, being disturbed, I hurried away from them, and journeyed back towards Berwick. But in my journey I was encountered by four armed ruffians, who spoiled me of all my letters and of my raiment even to the skin. It is also rumoured that the said Lord Robert and his accomplices, who instigated this outrage, have the letters in their possession. What ought now to be done against these contumacious rebels and despisers of apostolic authority, your wisdoms can better decree than I am able to surmise; but I declare to you before God, that I am even yet ready, as I have hitherto been, to labour unremittingly in your affairs."[1]

In this strange episode of the unfortunate Adam Newton we have a papal controversy curiously carried on and as oddly terminated. On the one side is John XXII. devoted to the cause of the richer and stronger kingdom, and the members of his conclave, many of whom were the purchased pensionaries of Edward II.; on the other is a bold, rough warrior-king, contending for national independence, and surrounded by a court of iron-clad barons, few of whom were able to read the letters which they were so eager to clutch and destroy; while the place of interview and negotiation was a forest ringing with the din of falling trees that were to be converted into battering-rams and turrets. According to the mood in which it is received it is a hostile meeting of mind and matter; a warlike interchange of defiance between the corporeal and the spiritual; a confronting of the boldest and bravest against those terrors before which the bravest were wont to succumb. But still, in the conduct of Bruce we recognize the predominance of a commanding intellect that held onward in its path of duty in spite of the sophistries that might have perplexed, or the terrors that might have daunted it, and gallantly persevering in a species of warfare beneath which kings and emperors had fallen. Even the *ultima ratio* of each was in keeping with his character; and when the thunderbolt of excommunication was finally drawn forth it was extinguished; and by what?—a pail of water. Four Border thieves, or soldiers who needed little disguise to pass as such, are let loose when every other form of argument has failed, who quash the whole proceeding by a simple act of highway robbery. It was probably not without reason that a rumour was prevalent of the bulls and letters having found their way into Bruce's own keeping.

The devoted and brave-hearted friar, as we have seen, found the King of Scotland employed in preparations for the reduction of the last English possession in Scotland. Its defence

---

[1] *Fœdera Ang.* vol. ii. p. 351; Edward II. An. Dom. 1317.

was as important to England as its recovery could be to the Scots, as it was a gate between both kingdoms, and therefore available for the purposes of invasion to whatever power might possess it. Of this the English were well aware, and had fortified it so strongly that the limited resources of Bruce for a lengthened siege might have proved unavailing. It happened, however, that Roger Horsely, the governor of Berwick, having maltreated an English burgess named Simon Spalding, the latter resolved to have ample revenge by betraying the town to the Scots. He accordingly sent intimation to an influential officer in the Scottish army, to whom he was related by marriage, that on a particular night he would be upon guard at a certain part of the walls, where they were low and might be easily scaled; and that if the Scots advanced upon this quarter he would admit them into the town. The officer carried this important intimation to Bruce himself, who said, "You did well in discovering this first to me; for had you told it either to Randolph or Douglas you would have offended the one from whom you kept it back; but I will make use of both, and they shall aid you in the enterprise." He ordered him to repair with his band to Dunse Park, about fourteen miles from Berwick, and there hold himself in readiness for the appointed evening; and thither also he afterwards sent Douglas and Randolph at the head of a strong party. This rendezvous at so distant a point was doubtless for the purpose of misleading the English garrison in Berwick, who could scarcely imagine that this muster was for any other purpose than an inroad into England. Marching rapidly and secretly from Dunse Park, the assailing party reached the walls near the Cow Port, and with the aid of Spalding fixed their scaling-ladders and mounted without opposition. They rushed into the streets, and the garrison that ran hither and thither in small parties were either cut to pieces or driven into the castle. It was fortunate, however, that in this night surprise Randolph and Douglas kept a strong party of their men together, for their comrades had flown upon the spoil, while the English in the castle, who still outnumbered the Scots, made a sally in the hope of recovering the town. But they were driven back to their stronghold by the two chiefs at the head of the reserve. The town being thus taken, Bruce advanced with the rest of his army and laid siege to the castle in form, which surrendered five days after. Thus fell the last as well as the most important of the English possessions in Scotland, and the conquests of Edward I., on the 3d of April, 1318, and the land was now completely free. As its capture by the King of England also had been an unsparing massacre, its recovery by Bruce was signalized by his wonted magnanimity and clemency, for he gave quarter to all who sought it. Berwick had continued to be used by the English as an important mercantile emporium, so that the victors were enriched with its plunder; and Bruce, being well aware both of the military and political importance of the place, instead of demolishing its defences, as he had done with other recovered strongholds, resolved to retain it in all its integrity as a barrier of the kingdom. He therefore intrusted the government of the town and castle to his son-in-law, Walter the Steward, and stored it with every engine of defence which the military science of the age could devise.

This important capture was almost immediately followed in the same month by a Scottish inroad into Northumberland, in which Bruce reduced the castles of Werk and Harbottle by siege, and took by surprise the castle of Mitford. On this occasion he laid the country under contributions of victual instead of money; and the provision thus collected was stored up in Berwick against the chances of a future siege. On the following month the invasion was repeated in greater force and over a wider range, for the Scottish army penetrated into Yorkshire, plundered and burned the towns of Northallerton, Burroughbridge, Scarborough, and Skipton in Craven, and obliged the inhabitants of Ripon to free themselves from a like calamity by the ransom of 1000 marks, equal to about £10,000 of modern money. This visitation was so destructive that those places which had endured it were in the following year exempted by the King of England from a general taxation. The Scottish army, after wasting the country at pleasure, returned home without opposition, laden with booty, and with so many prisoners that they are described by the English historian as "driving them like sheep before them."[*]

While the Scottish war against England was thus prosperously conducted at home, the campaign in Ireland was hastening to a melancholy termination. After the departure of the Scottish king, Edward Bruce continued his adventurous career; but although his course had hitherto been so victorious he had been unable to establish his rule anywhere but in Ulster, and even there it was of a precarious character. At length Lord John de Berningham, the English commander, mustered a numerous army to drive these intruders from the soil, and on the 5th of October, 1318, advanced to Fagher, near Dundalk. His army is swelled by Barbour to

---

[*] *Chron. Lanercost*, iii. 272; *Fœd. Angl.*

more than 40,000 strong; but if we rate it at half the amount it was still sufficient to exterminate the handful to whom it was opposed, for the army of Edward Bruce amounted to little more than 2000 Scots. It is added, indeed, that this force was supported by 20,000 of his Irish subjects or auxiliaries, but they were an undisciplined mob on whom no reliance could be placed; they even refused to take a share in the coming conflict, alleging that it was not their mode of warfare to contend in pitched battles, but to maintain it by flying retreats, ambuscades, and skirmishes. As the enemy were so numerous, and as the Scottish king was expected to return speedily with reinforcements, the captains of Edward Bruce counselled a retreat; but his many successes made him over-confident, and he scorned a suggestion which his own brave brother would have adopted without scruple. His only precaution was one often adopted in ancient warfare, of arraying one of his bravest officers in his own arms and armorial cognizances while he fought himself in the harness of a common knight. In the battle the Scots were speedily overwhelmed by the enemy's numerous cavalry; Edward Bruce himself was slain at the first charge by John Manpas, an English champion, who fell dead upon the body of his brave antagonist; and nearly the whole of the Scottish captains shared the fate of their leader. In this manner, after eighteen victories, was the meteoric course of the new King of Ireland extinguished, and the hopes of a Scottish ascendency in that country brought to an abrupt close. But subsequent events showed that this unfortunate expedition had effected all the benefit which it was fitted to produce, by causing a temporary diversion of the English arms from Scotland, and animating the Scots with fresh courage by its victories; while its prosecution would have uselessly drained their kingdom of its brave adventurers whose services were soon to be so needful at home, and added the necessity of defending Ireland to their own numerous difficulties in the maintenance of national independence.

After this victory of the English at Fagher the field of battle was searched and the body of Edward Bruce found; but the conduct of the victors on this occasion was different from that of his brother after the victory at Bannockburn, for they quartered the body and exposed the mangled remains in four different places in Ireland, while the head was sent to England as an acceptable present to Edward II. De Berningham was richly guerdoned with the earldom of Lowth and other special distinctions. The handful of Scots who survived the defeat were rallied by John Thomson, the leader of the men of Carrick; and having extricated them from the throng he effected a dangerous retreat to Carrickfergus, where they embarked for Scotland.[1]

CHAPTER IX.

REIGN OF ROBERT BRUCE CONTINUED (1318-1326).

New arrangement in the succession to the Scottish throne—Military enactments for the defence of the kingdom—Regulations for the arms and conduct of soldiers—Machinations of King Edward against the Scots—He invades Scotland—Berwick besieged by the English—Engines used in its defence—Berwick attacked by land and sea—Engines used in the attack—Gallant defence of the town—The Scots, under Randolph and Douglas, invade England—Their victory at Mytton—The siege of Berwick raised—A short truce between England and Scotland—Remonstrance and justification sent by the Scottish parliament to the pope—Conspiracy against Bruce—Its authors tried and punished by the "Black Parliament"—Conspiracy of the English nobles against Edward—Its suppression—His vainglorious confidence—England twice invaded by the Scots—Edward enters Scotland with an immense army—He is driven back by famine—Bruce follows the invaders into England—He defeats Edward at Biland—Bruce's conduct to the prisoners—Plot of the Earl of Carlisle against Edward—The earl is executed—Another truce established between Scotland and England—Bruce seeks a reconciliation with the pope—He sends Randolph for this purpose—Randolph's dexterous and successful diplomacy—Birth of Bruce's son, afterwards David II.—Death of Walter the Steward.

The death of Marjory Bruce as well as that of her uncle Edward had rendered new regulations for the royal succession necessary, and a parliament was accordingly held for the purpose at Scone in the beginning of December, 1318. Here, after engaging to maintain the royal rights of Robert Bruce, their king, against all who should oppose them, it was decreed by the

[1] Barbour, xii.; *Irish Annals.*

prelates, earls, barons, and others of the community, that should he die without an heir male, Robert, the son of Marjory, should succeed him in the throne; and that if the said Robert, or any heir male of Robert Bruce, should be a minor at the period of succession, Thomas Randolph, Earl of Moray and Lord of Man, should be tutor and curator of the young heir and guardian of the kingdom; or failing him, Sir James Douglas, until Robert Stuart should be capable of governing. As doubts also had risen in times past about the rule by which the succession to the kingdom of Scotland should be judged and determined, it was likewise decreed that this rule ought not to have been regulated, nor should be in future, according to the practice observed in inferior fiefs and inheritances, as such had not been the custom in regard to the succession of the kingdom; "but that the male nearest to the king at his death, descending in the direct line, or failing such male, the nearest female in the same direct line; or failing the whole direct line, the nearest male in the collateral line; respect being always had to the right of blood by which the deceased king reigned; and which heir so designed shall succeed to the kingdom without any let, hinderance, or contradiction whatsoever."[1] On this assignment of the offices of tutor, curator, and guardian, the Earl of Moray and Sir James Douglas laid their hands upon the holy gospel and relics of the saints and solemnly swore to perform the duties of these offices according to the best of their ability. In like manner this decree of guardianship and law of royal succession was sworn to by all the members, both lay and clerical, of parliament, who also affixed their seals.

Besides this readjustment of the important question of royal succession, other useful regulations were decreed, which had for their object the safety and welfare of the kingdom. As might be expected from the condition of Scotland at the time, they were chiefly of a military character. Every layman possessed of land who had £10 worth of movable property[2] was ordered to provide himself with a hacqueton, a basnet, and gloves of plate, with a sword and spear; he who had not a hacqueton and basnet was to have, instead, a habergeon, a good iron jack, and an iron knapiskay, with gloves of plate; and all this under forfeiture of his goods or movable property, half to the king and half to his feudal superior. Every man having the value of a cow was to be provided with a bow and a sheaf of twenty-four arrows or a spear.

The lords and sheriffs were enjoined to enforce this law, and hold a wapinschaw for the purpose. In repairing to the royal army every man was to subsist upon the road at his own charges; if he came from a place near the rendezvous he was to bring his own carriage and provisions, and if his place of residence was too remote for such a purpose he was to furnish himself with a sufficient sum of money. Such persons were to be adequately supplied with necessaries on payment; and if these were refused them, they were authorized to take what was needed, but always at the sight of the bailies or magistrates of the district or the nearest neighbours. Having thus facilitated their journey to headquarters, every security was taken against that military license in which armed men in every country are so prone to indulge during a march; and whoever committed murder, robbery, or theft while coming to the army, remaining in it, or departing from it, was to be punished by the justiciary according to the crime and the law; while the bailie or judge of the district where the offender dwelt was to compel his appearance before the justiciary of the place where the offence was committed. In another law of peculiar stringency, by which the military resources of the kingdom were to be husbanded for self-defence, it was decreed that to supply the English with bows or arrows, or with any kind of weapons or armour, or with horses, or with any kind of aid or assistance whatever, was a capital offence and to be punished accordingly. It was, moreover, decreed that no ecclesiastics should remit money to Rome for the purchase of papal bulls—although without the sanction of these bulls, according to the reckoning of the church, no ecclesiastical dignity could be confirmed. In the same statute also it was enacted that all absentees in England who possessed lands in Scotland should draw no money out of the kingdom. The other laws that were passed at this parliament of Scone were directed against the civil offences of theft-boot and leasing-making, which during this disturbed period must have been of frequent occurrence.[3]

In the meantime Edward II. had been doing his utmost to move heaven and earth against Scotland and its king. Not satisfied that Robert Bruce had already been excommunicated, he caused the two cardinals who were still in England to pronounce the sentence anew; and when the Scots appealed to the papal court at Avignon against the sentence he procured their appeal to be disallowed and set aside. He endeavoured to enlist the pontiff's aid in promoting treason among the Scots by offering to

---

[1] *Scotichron.* l. xiii. c. 13.
[2] Equal to about £160 in modern money.

[3] *Regiam Majest.* chap. v. stat. Robert I.

those who were excommunicated a full absolution if they would desert their king and turn to the cause of England.¹ In the same spirit Edward endeavoured to prevent all commercial intercourse of Flanders, Brabant, and the Netherlands with the Scottish ports, by representing to these continental states that the Scots were an excommunicated people, and therefore unworthy to have dealings with Christian men.² And having now effected a reconciliation with the Lancastrian party, he resolved to try once more the chances of war and signalize its commencement by the recovery of Berwick. He accordingly summoned his military vassals of England and Wales to assemble at Newcastle-upon-Tyne on the 24th of July, 1319, and appointed a powerful fleet to block up the mouth of the Tweed in order to prevent all supplies from being sent into Berwick, while he besieged it by land. All things being in readiness, and the prayers of the church having been secured for the success of the enterprise, the march commenced about the beginning of September: and so confident was Edward on this occasion of a complete conquest of Scotland, that, like a munificent patron, he had already parcelled out several of its best church livings among his adherents.³ With these preliminaries he commenced the siege both by land and sea; and as his army was numerous, while the best and bravest of the English nobles were present in person, there was every prospect that Berwick would be speedily taken. Having secured his camp by lines of circumvallations consisting of strong ramparts and deep ditches, to prevent the Scots from relieving the town by land, and closed up the river with his shipping, Edward resolved to effect the capture by storm, and fixed St. Mary's Eve (7th September) for the period of assault.

The condition of Berwick thus isolated from all aid, and so formidably beleaguered, might well make the friends of Scottish liberty anxious for the result. Since its first capture by Edward I. in 1296 its defences had been considerably increased, so that the wall which surrounded it was about fifteen feet high; but this height was reckoned no formidable obstacle in ancient escalade; and those parts of the wall that were to be attempted were confronted by high mounds of earth that had been raised by the besiegers. The success of resistance had mainly to depend upon the gallant hearts within, the nature and amount of their resources, and their skill in using them. And here we find that Walter the Steward, the commander of Berwick, though young and unexperienced, was possessed of that high courage that made him worthy to be the father of an illustrious race of kings; five hundred knights and gentlemen, who were officers of the garrison, were his own kinsmen; and his zeal and activity in preparing the defences had won the confidence of the soldiers. Of the warlike engines, originally taken by Bruce himself from the English at Bannockburn, and which were now to be used against them, there was no lack: these consisted of arblasts or large cross-bows; of balistæ that discharged iron darts; and of springalds and cranes, that threw heavy masses of stone or metal. All these, in fact, were of the same nature as the sieging artillery of ancient Rome long before she became full mistress of the world—the resources of a people newly emerged from barbarism, and beginning to apply their first lessons in science to the arts of destruction or the necessities of defence. It was fortunate for the Scots within the town of Berwick that they had for their chief engineer a foreigner, who possessed the skill for directing these machines of which they were still deficient: this was John Crab, a Fleming, one of a nation accustomed to contend with the ocean itself when its waves were at the fiercest, and therefore, from sheer necessity, the most skilful of all people in withstanding the onsets of living ranks, and making good the defence of mound and rampart.⁴

Early on the morning of the day called St. Mary's Eve the English advanced to the assault in separate divisions, each provided with scaling-ladders to mount the walls, and pickaxes to undermine them; with scaffolds and coverings for shelter, and slings and arrows for annoyance; and each division having its separate portion of the wall as its place of onset. Against this multiplied attack the Steward divided his garrison into troops that were stationed over the assailed points of the wall, while at the head of a chosen band he kept moving over the whole circuit, cheering the soldiers, and bringing aid where it was most needed. The trumpets sounded and the assault commenced; scaling-ladders were planted and thrown down; and while the stones and arrows of the assailants swept the top of the wall, the defenders could also be reached by the spear-points of those below. The desperate onset was met by a resistance as stubborn, and the struggle was continued with equal fortune till noon, when the danger of the Scots was deepened by the approach of the English ships, that sailed up the river with the rise of the tide. One of these ships that

---

¹ *Fœder. Ang.* iii. 764. ² Ibid. iii. 759.
³ Ibid. iii. 785–6.

⁴ Barbour, l. xvii.

had been prepared for the purpose, was drawn up close to the town; and from its rigging, to which a drawbridge was attached, the soldiers of the armament were to descend upon the wall. The device was well planned, but it proved abortive; for the luckless vessel struck upon a bank, and when the tide had left it the townsmen set it on fire. Disheartened by this failure and their loss of men, the assailants by land sounded the retreat, and withdrew from the well-defended wall. But it was only for a new assault both by land and sea of a still more formidable character; and to prepare for this five days of peaceful interval occurred, during which nothing was heard among the besiegers and besieged but the din of the axe, the hammer, and the saw, the one party constructing means of annoyance, and the other of resistance.

As it was found that Berwick could not easily be stormed, the English now resolved to attempt its capture by undermining the walls; and a formidable machine had been framed, roofed with strong timbers covered with hides, under which a large band of armed soldiers and miners could safely approach the ramparts. This engine, from its shape, was called a *sow*. Still further, also, to ensure its efficiency, several movable scaffolds were constructed of greater height than the walls, from which drawbridges could be let down upon the parapets, and their defenders encountered hand to hand by the soldiers who manned the scaffolds. An equally formidable sea-attack was to be made at the same time; and to make it more successful than the former one, several ships were prepared as the other had been: the boat of each vessel being filled with armed men, was to be drawn half-mast high, until it was upon a level with the top of the wall; while the round tops of the masts were to be filled with archers, whose discharges would clear the way for the assault of their comrades from the boats below. These were terrible means of attack; but Crab had not been idle, and to match the sow he had built a *crane*, so called also from its shape, having a long neck bent backward, like that of a crane or stork. It appears to have been mainly a Roman catapult that moved on wheels, and discharged huge stones with great force and accuracy. Besides this engine, Crab had caused strong chains and hooks to be made for catching and holding fast the sow and its attendant scaffolds when they reached the walls; and large store of faggots made of dry branches intermixed with flax and tow soaked with pitch and sulphur and rolled into bundles as large as casks, to set fire to the English engines as soon as they were grappled and secured. He had also caused several new springalds to be constructed, that shot large heavy arrows winged with copper. In the last assault an English engineer had been taken prisoner, and he was now unwillingly compelled to become the assistant of Crab in defending Berwick against his own countrymen.[1]

All being in readiness, the English commenced a fresh onset on the 13th of September. They filled up the ditch, as in the former attack, with fascines, and advanced to the walls, which they attempted to win by escalade; but the most forward of the assailants were beaten off, or crushed by large stones which the defenders discharged from their engines. Baffled in this storming attempt, the English had then recourse to undermining; and about noon the formidable sow, in which they confidently trusted, was set in action, and moved towards the walls with a numerous mining party sheltered under its strong and ample covering. At its dreaded advance the Scots made every preparation to meet it; and not relying wholly upon their own skill, they had recourse to that of the English engineer whom they had lately captured. He was taken from prison to the wall, where the crane was planted, and ordered to do his utmost to destroy the sow, on pain of instant death. With trembling hands he wound up the machine, took aim, and touched the spring; but the huge stone which it discharged went beyond the mark. He once more bent and discharged the crane; but in this case the stone fell short. Furious at these failures, more especially as the sow was triumphantly advancing, and had nearly reached the wall where it would have been safe from such attacks, the Scots renewed their threats, and the engineer prepared for a third and final trial. He wound up the engine to its utmost force and took a steady deadly aim; the huge stone flew upward, while nothing was heard but its boom as it ascended, watched by the breathless onlookers, and in coming down it fell so direct and true upon the back of the advancing sow that a tremendous crash proclaimed the demolition of its roof, and the uselessness of its protection. A roar of triumph burst from the Scots, followed by peals of laughter, when they saw the miners and armed men scampering on all sides from under the ruin, and "The English sow has farrowed her pigs!" was their derisive cry. The hooks and chains were thrown out to make it fast, and the burning faggots soon reduced it to ashes. While thus it fared with the land attack, that by sea was not more fortunate. Aided by the tide the English ships advanced to the town

---

[1] Barbour, xvii.

with their boats and drawbridges in readiness, but against these assailants the Scots directed a second crane which they had prepared and kept in readiness. This they plied with such effect that a stone hit the foremost vessel and swept off a number of her crew, while the other ships, dismayed at this reception, were fain to sheer off. In spite of these mischances the English continued to press onward to the walls, which they thought to win by main force, though their science had failed; while the Scots continued their defence so stubbornly, that out of the hundred chosen men who attended the Steward in his rounds to the different places of attack, only one was at last left unwounded. Even the women and boys of the town were not idle; for during the whole conflict they gathered up the stones and arrows in the streets, which had been shot by the English, and carried them as supplies to their own men upon the walls. Barbour adds, that none of these were slain, and he attributes their safety to the miraculous working of Providence. Towards evening the English made a last attempt upon the Marygate, broke through the barrier that defended it, and after demolishing the drawbridge attempted to burn down the gate. On the alarm being carried to the Steward he gathered a reserve of soldiers that were still in the castle, and ordering the gate to be thrown open he made such a sudden and vigorous sally upon the assailants that they were beaten back with great loss. This was the last attempt of a desperate struggle that had continued from morning till evening, and having utterly failed at every point the English forces reluctantly retired.

During this period Bruce had not been unmindful of the brave garrison of Berwick and his gallant son-in-law; but finding the English army too numerous and strongly intrenched to risk a battle for the relief of the town, he resolved to draw them off to the defence of their own country by an invasion of England. This expedition he intrusted to the Earl of Moray and Sir James Douglas, who, at the head of 15,000 men, crossed the Border and advanced into Yorkshire. As the Queen of England was at this time residing in the city of York while her husband was employed before Berwick, a part of the plan of the Scottish leaders was to capture her by surprise, in which case her husband might have been compelled to more reasonable terms of peace than he had hitherto been willing to accord. It would have been well for him if they had succeeded—better still if they had kept her in perpetual duresse; but this "she-wolf of France" had probably been made aware of their design, for she hastily retired inland to a place of greater security. Thus disappointed of their prey, Randolph and Douglas held onward in a course of wild devastation, in which Ripon, Wetherby, and Mytton were successively visited and plundered. To check this havoc the Archbishop of York collected 20,000 men of all professions, few of whom were soldiers, and with these he marched towards Mytton near the river Swale, where the Scots were encamped. But his miscellaneous and undisciplined host was ill fitted to encounter their veteran opponents; for even at the approach of the Scots they wavered, and at the first charge they were broken and scattered. 4000 English were slain in this inglorious encounter, many were drowned in the Swale; and among the dead were 300 priests, who had covered their shaven crowns with steel helmets. This circumstance made the battle be termed in savage pleasantry by the Scots the "Chapter of Mytton."[1]

This inroad, as had been expected by the Scottish king, broke up the leaguer of Berwick. As soon as tidings of the archbishop's defeat reached the English camp, Edward II. held a council of war, at which many of the barons whose estates were in the north of England and near the seat of war expressed their purpose to depart for the defence of their own homes; and in this they were encouraged by the Earl of Lancaster, who soon after retired in disgust with all his forces, which constituted a third part of the army. Edward, thus deserted, saw that the prosecution of the siege was hopeless; but, eager to signalize his retreat, he marched southwards in the hope of encountering the Scots on their return. But Douglas and Randolph, having effected their purpose as well as secured much booty and many prisoners, eluded the meeting, and returned unmolested to Scotland. In this expedition, besides their victory on the Swale they had inflicted terrible loss on the enemy: eighty-four towns and villages were burned and plundered, and before it could recover, the West Riding of Yorkshire had to be exempted from the usual taxations. This gallant defence of a place so important to the Scots as Berwick was doubly gratifying to Bruce, as it had been effected by his son-in-law. As the walls of the town were so low that in future wars they would be constantly exposed to the risk of escalade, he gave orders that they should be raised ten feet higher all round.[2]

The time now appeared propitious for the establishment of an honourable peace to which the heart of the Scottish king was so earnestly

---

[1] Walsingham, 112; Barbour; Fordun.
[2] Walsingham; Barbour; J. de Trokelowe.

inclined, and to that effect he sent commissioners to Newcastle to negotiate with those appointed on the part of England. Nothing more, however, than a two years' truce could be settled, which was to commence at Christmas, 1319, and during its continuance all intercourse between the two nations was strictly prohibited.[1] It was no doubt found that such intercourse after the recent injuries on either side would inevitably lead to quarrel and conflict, and mar all hopes of a lasting peace, to which the truce was intended only as a preparative. Edward II. had now lowered his tone; for, in announcing to the pope the conditions of the truce, he no longer termed the Scots *rebels* but enemies.[2] The next attempt of Bruce was to reconcile himself to the church, a step that was necessary on account of the hostility of the pontiff, which still continued unmitigated: in fact, by the orders of the pope the sentence of excommunication was to be repeated every Sunday and festival-day against the King of Scotland and all his adherents by the Archbishop of York and the Bishops of London and Carlisle. To effect this reconciliation the Scottish parliament was assembled at Arbroath; and the defence which they drew up of their proceedings in the war with England was characterized by that manly uncompromising independence which had now become a striking characteristic of the Scots. To vindicate their rights as a free and independent nation they went back to the earliest days of the Scots—to their emigration from Egypt to Spain, and from Spain to Ireland and Scotland—an origin as good, and as devoutly believed in by the few readers of the age, as that which derived the English nation from Brute and his redoubtable Trojans. They mentioned the hundred and thirteen kings, from the accession of Fergus I., who had reigned over Scotland; its final conversion to Christianity by St. Andrew, the brother of St. Peter; and the privileges which the Scots had enjoyed from their spiritual father, the pope, as the flock of the brother of St. Peter. Thus they had continued from the earliest periods until Edward I., the father of the present King of England, under the disguise of a friend and ally, had invaded them with fraud and violence, and had cruelly oppressed them and bereaved them of their freedom, until their present valiant king, Robert Bruce, under the help of God, had arisen like a second Joshua or Judas Maccabæus to deliver them from bondage. His also was the right of descent as well as of their own choice, and to him they would adhere as their king in the defence of their rights and liberties. But bound though they thus were to him, should he desert their cause, or endeavour to reduce them to the dominion of England, they added that even him, too, they would drive from the throne, elect another king, and not submit to England as long as a hundred of them remained alive. Finally, assuming a still bolder strain, in consequence of the pope's partiality for England, they declared, that if he persevered in thus favouring the designs of their enemies they would "hold him guilty in the sight of the Almighty of the loss of lives, perdition of souls, and all the other miserable consequences that might ensue from the continuance of this war between the two nations." This singular cartel of admonition and defiance was dated the 6th of April, 1320, and was subscribed by eight earls and thirty-one barons in the name of the whole Scottish community. On being sent to Rome it was speedily seen by the pontiff that such a national manifesto was not to be idly thrown aside. He therefore became an equal mediator between the two kingdoms, but with little effect, for Edward would not yet succumb to the Scottish demand of independence, while a civil insurrection in England inspired Bruce with the hope that a more favourable opportunity for an honourable peace would yet occur, which the course of events was likely to accelerate. This English insurrection was headed by the Earl of Lancaster, with whom he was in close communication.[3]

But while the King of Scots was thus weakening the power of Edward II. by stirring up his own nobles against him, the latter was retaliating in kind by a conspiracy among certain Scottish barons which had the dethronement and death of Bruce for its object. At the head of this dark plot, which came and passed like a horrid dream, and the particulars of which are briefly and confusedly narrated, was William de Soulis, the seneschal of Scotland, and grandson of Nicholas de Soulis, the competitor for the crown, but whose claims had been set aside as derived from an illegitimate source. It is supposed that Lord William still continued to nourish those dreams of ambition which his royal descent would have fully warranted but for the cross-bar that marred it, and that in the King of England he found a ready encourager and supporter. But in Sir David de Brechin, the nephew of Bruce, Lord Soulis obtained a still more effectual accomplice; and if De Brechin was not absolutely participant in the design of destroying his uncle, he was at least guilty of concealing the conspiracy and allowing it to go on unchecked. In the same foul design several

---

[1] *Fœd. Ang.* iii. [2] *Fœd. Ang.* [3] Fordun; *Fœd. Ang.*; Anderson's *Diplomata Scotiæ*.

others were also implicated, among whom were five knights and three esquires, whose names have been handed down to us in the brief notice of their trial. This dangerous plot was at last betrayed by the Countess of Strathern, who was privy to it, and the conspirators, with their formidable train of 360 squires, were suddenly arrested at Berwick, and arraigned before the parliament held at Scone in the beginning of August, 1320. The particulars of the trial having been destroyed, we only know the result. Lord de Soulis and the Countess of Strathern were convicted upon their own confession and sentenced to imprisonment for life; Sir Gilbert de Malherbe and Sir John Logie, knights, and Richard Brown, an esquire, were executed as traitors. But the fate of Sir David de Brechin, who also suffered capital punishment, occasioned much lamentation among the people, for he was young and brave, and had fought against the infidels; but while the popular voices condemned the severity of his uncle, and lamented their young favourite as the martyr of an unjust sentence, they were little aware how fully his doom had been merited. Although he had been pardoned for fighting in the ranks of England he had connived at the conspiracy by which his king and uncle was to be murdered, and the established dynasty subverted in favour of a pretender. This meeting at Scone was long after remembered in Scotland under the name of the "Black Parliament."[1]

The fate of these Scottish conspirators, whom Edward was so ready to support, was but a prelude to that which awaited those English nobles who were enlisted in the behalf of Bruce. Disgusted with the inglorious reign of their sovereign, and his shameful attachment to unworthy favourites, the Earls of Lancaster and Hertford and their associates longed for deliverance, even though it should come from Scotland; and with this view had entered into a treaty with Bruce, by which their rising in open rebellion was to be seconded by a Scottish invasion. In the event of their success they agreed to use their best efforts to procure a peace for the Scots upon their own terms, and establish the family of Bruce upon the Scottish throne. But Edward was made aware of this negotiation, and roused into unwonted activity he took the field, and pressed the party of Lancaster so vigorously that they were defeated before their allies could come to their aid. The earl fled northward with his broken forces, hoping to shelter himself in Scotland and renew the war, but was met and defeated near Bossaugh-bridge by Sir Andrew Hartela, warden of Carlisle, and Sir Simon Ward, sheriff of Yorkshire. Thus the conspiracy was shattered at a stroke: the Earl of Hertford fell in the conflict, and Lancaster, who surrendered himself, was forthwith tried and beheaded.

This single instance of success so highly elated the weak mind of the English king that he thought the conquest of Scotland would be an easy and certain achievement. He accordingly wrote a vainglorious letter to the pope, requesting him to give himself no further trouble about peace or truce between the two kingdoms, as he was resolved to subdue the Scots by force of arms; all that he now desired was that the pontiff should repeat his spiritual sentences against these obdurate rebels, so that their resistance should be without excuse.[2] He then issued orders to the holders of the crown for a military muster; but as the late Earl of Lancaster had been not only a favourite among the nobles, but also the idol of the people, who after his death regarded him as a saint, the royal commands were met by no correspondent alacrity. But it was very different with the Scots, to whom an English invasion had now become a safe and profitable adventure; and under the command of Randolph they broke through the western marches, extended their havoc over Cumberland and Westmoreland into Lancashire, and returned laden with spoil. A second expedition, conducted by Bruce himself, speedily followed, in which Lancashire was so effectually desolated that all the growing crops and everything that could not be carried off were laid waste and destroyed. For twenty-four days this destructive visit continued, during which the Scots appear to have met with no resistance, and on their return to Scotland they encamped five days in the neighbourhood of Carlisle, thus defying the English to battle, a challenge which, however, was not answered. They continued their homeward march unchecked, and with a long train of wagons laden with church plate, ornaments of gold and silver, and other valuables, and followed by droves of sheep and herds of oxen which they had collected at pleasure.[3]

While these events were transacted four months had elapsed since the summons of Edward II. to his military vassals without an English army appearing in the field. But such intolerable insults were to be endured no longer; and when the king repeated his order the people armed with such alacrity that he was soon at the head of 100,000 men. He was resolved with this overwhelming force to bring the issue to a decisive battle—a second Bannockburn, in which the blunders of the first should be fully repaired and its result gloriously reversed. But

---

[1] Fordun, l. xiii. c. 1; Barbour, xix.

[2] Fœd. Ang. iii. 944.   [3] Knyghton, 2542; Fordun, xiii. 4.

on the other hand Bruce had no such motives to abide the trial as formerly, for Scotland was already free and his own authority recognized over the whole kingdom, so that he could fight or abstain as best suited his own convenience. Wisely resolving, therefore, not to hazard what he had already won, and against such dangerous odds, he adopted the plan of a defensive warfare by starving the English in their advance, and harassing them in their compelled retreat. It was the system of Wallace—the true defence of Scotland. All the cattle of the Merse, Teviotdale, and the Lothians were accordingly removed, as likewise all the provisions and every article of value, so that when the English army advanced from Newcastle into Scotland they found no enemy to encounter but famine, which they wisely dreaded more than they did the Scots. So thorough, indeed, had been the clearance that the English found nothing but a lame bull at Tranent, in East Lothian, which the Scots had been unable to drive away. "Is this all ye have brought?" said Earl Warenne to his hungry followers when they returned from foraging with this trophy of their success; "I never saw beef cost so much." When the English reached Edinburgh their provisions were exhausted, and here they halted three days expecting the arrival of their fleet with supplies; but their ships had been detained by contrary winds, and after several soldiers had died of hunger the army was compelled to retrace its steps. They plundered the abbey of Holyrood at their departure, and afterwards the abbeys of Melrose and Dryburgh in their retreat, venting their rage by slaying the prior of Melrose and a few old monks who were too frail to take to flight, and carrying off a pyx from the altar after they had contemptuously thrown away the host.[1] To this narrow compass were the exploits of such an army reduced by the wise precautions of their opponent! On reaching their own border, which they entered like fugitives, the starved soldiers dispersed themselves in quest of food, and ate so voraciously that nearly half the army, according to one English historian, but 16,000 men according to the more probable account of another, died of repletion.[2]

With this disgraceful campaign the misfortunes of Edward were not to terminate; for scarcely had he issued his commands for the defence of the Borders when Bruce had crossed them and laid siege to the castle of Norham. Learning that the English king had collected the remains of his army and was securely reposing in the abbey of Biland, near Malton, in Yorkshire, Bruce raised the siege and hastily advanced to Biland, hoping to surprise and capture his enemy; but this chance was lost owing, it is supposed, to a warning which Edward had previously received. The plan of surprisal was exchanged for one of open battle, although in this case every advantage was on the side of the English, for they were not only still very numerous, but occupied a strong position on the ridge of a hill that was so rocky and steep as to be assailable only by one narrow pass. This pass the gallant Douglas undertook to force; and his generous rival, the Earl of Moray, on hearing this, offered himself as a volunteer in the enterprise, and with four squires ranked himself under the Douglas banner. The pass was assailed by the noble pair and their followers, but defended with equal gallantry by Sir Thomas Ughtred and Sir Ralph Cobham. The struggle of the Scots to win the pass was desperate; but the steep ascent and the showers of missiles that encountered them at every step inflicted heavy loss upon the party, and increased their chance of failure. It was then that Bruce had recourse to that mountain warfare which he had practised so successfully upon the Lord of Lorn when he defeated him among his fastnesses; and selecting the men of Argyle and the Isles, to whom such difficulties were of little account, he ordered them to climb the steep ridge at a distance from the battle and fall upon the English flank. This skilful plan was effectually executed, and the enemy, thus unexpectedly assailed, were driven from their defences with great slaughter, while Douglas and Randolph quickly reached the summit. As for Edward, on finding himself so suddenly defeated he fled to Bridlington, after losing his great seal, as he had done at Bannockburn, in the tumult, and leaving all his baggage and treasure to the Scots, his flight in the meantime being accelerated by the Steward of Scotland, who pursued him at the head of 500 horse. Among the prisoners who fell into the hands of the Scots by this victory were John de Bretagne, Earl of Richmond, and Henry de Sully, grand butler of the King of France. Richmond had been in the habit of speaking despitefully and slanderously of Bruce, and now that he was a captive his season of chastisement had arrived; for the Scottish king, after rebuking him sharply for his offences, imposed upon him such a heavy ransom that some years appear to have elapsed before it could be raised. The treatment of Sully and his companions was very different. "I know," said Bruce, "that you fought to prove yourselves valiant knights in a strange land, and not from hatred to me;" and with

---

[1] *Scotichron.* l. xiii. c. 4.   [2] Walsingham; Knyghton.

that he dismissed them not only free of ransom but enriched with presents. After their success the Scottish army extended their ravages through Yorkshire and almost to the banks of the Humber, imposing heavy contributions upon the towns and monasteries that were spared from destruction. They returned to Scotland, as was now usual after such expeditions, with a great number of prisoners, and enriched with cattle and other spoil.[1]

The discontent of the English nobles with their king still continued, for Edward persisted in bestowing upon the worthless De Spencer the same inordinate attachment and extravagant gifts and privileges which he had heaped upon Gaveston. The chief of these malcontents was Sir Andrew Hartcla, who only the year previous had intercepted and defeated the Earl of Lancaster while he was upon his retreat to Scotland. For this good service Hartcla was made Earl of Carlisle; but no sooner had he reached this elevation than he appears to have assumed the place of the fallen Lancaster by organizing a conspiracy of the English nobles against their sovereign and opening a communication with the King of Scots. This plot, however, was detected at the commencement of 1323, and Hartcla was arrested and tried for treason. It was proved against him that he had had an interview with Robert Bruce, that he had bound himself by writing and oath to maintain the latter and his heirs in the right and possession of the entire kingdom of Scotland, and that the king and earl had mutually agreed that each should select six persons for the establishment of peace and regulation of affairs between the two kingdoms. It was also proved that Hartcla had pledged himself to resist all who might oppose the execution of this engagement, and had induced others to swear to its observance. He was sentenced to die the death of a traitor with all its revolting circumstances, which were minutely fulfilled. He was degraded from his high rank by having his sword plucked from his side and his gilded spurs hacked from his heels by the cleaver of the executioner. He was beheaded; his heart, bowels, and entrails were torn out and burned, and their ashes thrown to the winds, that they might engender no further conspiracies; and his head was set upon London Bridge, and his four quarters exposed at Carlisle, Newcastle, York, and Salisbury.[2]

This mysterious plot, many of the particulars of which were not published, appears to have alarmed the King of England, and made him think of a peace with Scotland in good earnest.

Not only some of his principal nobles, as the trial had shown, were ready to effect this measure even though himself should be the sacrifice, but the Bishops of Bath, Lincoln, and Wells had participated in their purpose. To promote these pacific intentions, also, Henry de Sully, lately the prisoner and now the grateful friend of Bruce, added his kind offices. A thirteen-years' truce—as near an approach to a perpetual peace as could yet exist between the two countries—was accordingly ratified, Edward on this occasion recognizing Bruce as King of Scotland, an acknowledgment which he had hitherto avoided. But even yet he could not refrain from that mean intrigue and double-dealing which form the chief weapons of the cowardly and the weak; and therefore while he was negotiating with the Scottish king in apparent sincerity and good faith, he was also tampering with the pope and instigating him to publish and ratify in complete form the sentence of excommunication against Bruce and all his adherents. But Scotland was once more resuming the ascendency, and it did not suit the papal interests to give mortal offence to such a kingdom, provided England could still be retained in its allegiance. Happily also for the pontiff's perplexity the tidings of the truce arrived at Avignon, which furnished him with the means of reply. It was his duty, he said, to promote, and still more to enforce a truce, with which the requests of the King of England were incompatible. Edward had also represented the Scottish prelates as fomenters of the contumacy and rebellion of the people, and had therefore demanded that no Scotchman should be admitted to a bishopric in Scotland; but to this the pope answered that such a measure would wholly deprive the country of its spiritual pastors, as by the truce just established no Englishman could receive admission into Scotland.[3]

Ever since the liberties of his country had been recovered it had been the anxious desire of Bruce to be reconciled to the church, and to this the necessity was now added of counteracting the insidious designs of Edward. A fitting envoy was to be selected for the mission, one who could not only confront the emissaries of England, but outmanœuvre, confute, and persuade the whole conclave, and bring them to the point of absolution. Had it been to carry a defiance on the point of a spear to any court in Christendom he had paladins enough; but in the present instance a very different messenger was needed, and such a one as few of even the most refined royal councils could furnish. Fortunately, however, in his nephew, Thomas Ran-

---

[1] Barbour; Fordun.
[2] Murimuth; *Fœd. Ang.*; Walsingham.
[3] *Fœd. Ang.*

dolph, once the hot rash knight of Strathdon and afterwards the prudent and successful leader, he had now the calm, lynx-eyed, persuasive statesman, whom the Italian subtleties of ecclesiastical diplomacy could neither overcome nor elude. Moray accordingly repaired to Avignon upon his mission; and in the pope's own account of the interview, which he afterwards wrote to Edward II., we recognize in the hitherto rough and belligerent Scot a very model and *beau ideal* for modern negotiators and peacemakers. Randolph commenced his approach as if the visit had merely concerned his own affairs: he had made a vow, he said, to repair as a crusader to the Holy Land, but could not accomplish it without the papal sanction and dispensations, which he had now come to Avignon for the purpose of obtaining. To this the pope replied that such sanction could not be given to an individual merely, who could render no effectual service there; and that an excommunicated person could not further his own salvation by going to Palestine; but if he (Randolph) should do his utmost to establish peace between England and Scotland his demand would afterwards be favourably received. This was well, and the earl advanced a step farther: the pope had talked of peace, but a reconciliation with the church must precede it; and Randolph, after stating that an embassy would soon be sent from Scotland to Avignon for that purpose, he requested that his holiness would grant a safe-conduct for the journey through the intermediate territories. The proposal was cunningly made, for had the pontiff complied it would have appeared as if he had yielded to necessity, and solicited the promised embassy from the excommunicated parties like a suppliant instead of awaiting it as an offended sovereign and judge. He therefore declared that he could not under existing circumstances grant formal letters of safe-conduct; still, however, he would issue requisatorial letters addressed to all the princes for the safe conduct of the ambassadors through the different territories on their way. In this manner, although the home-thrust of the wily Scot was parried, it grazed deeply and made his victory more nigh and certain. He then produced a tempting offer in a commission from his uncle: it was to the effect that the King of Scots, hearing of the crusade which the French king was contemplating, would willingly accompany it; and that if the expedition did not take place he would, nevertheless, himself repair in person to the Holy Land, or send his nephew, the Earl of Moray, in his stead. The promised aid of so renowned a warrior as Bruce in an object which the church had so much at heart, and his offer to serve under the banner of France, must have been gratifying to the other, both as a pope and a Frenchman, coming though it did from an excommunicated man and unrecognized sovereign; and therefore he answered it gently, and with a view to the removal of obstacles. It would not be decent or expedient, he said, to receive Robert Bruce as a crusader, either alone or in union with the King of France, until he should be reconciled to the church, and had concluded a peace with England.

Having thus adroitly prepared the way for the main object of his mission Randolph now proceeded with caution to unfold it, not, however, in the form of an official condition, but as an amicable suggestion of his own. The pontiff was eager for peace and reconciliation both spiritual and political; he (Randolph) was equally anxious to secure it; but he felt that he could not labour in the good work without the pope's effectual aid. The difficulty that lay in the way was the recognition of Bruce's royal title; and as long as this was withheld it was certain, from past experience, that every proposal of peace would be rejected at the very outset and returned unopened. He therefore hinted the necessity of his uncle being addressed as king, in which case the overtures to the necessary reunion to the church and peace with England would be certain to meet with instant and cordial attention. The pope agreed in this opinion and consented to give Bruce the title of KING.

It was by such smooth and winding paths that Thomas Randolph reached the mark which seemed otherwise unattainable, and procured the desired concession from the highest as well as most impracticable of all authorities. As for the pope, he seemed to awaken from a dream. The hyperborean had thrown dust into his eyes he knew not how, and infallibility had been pledged too far to retreat. It had bestowed upon Bruce the title of king, and therefore a king he must henceforth be, let his enemies say what they might. But, worse than all, it had conferred that sacred stamp upon an excommunicated man, and that, too, not by its own free grace, but the advice and instigation of another. The bewildered pontiff wrote to the King of England an account of the interview, and his letter was a laboured apology. He said, that though he had bestowed the title of King on Robert Bruce, that would neither strengthen his claim nor impair that of Edward. It had been done for the sake of peace and reconciliation, otherwise the bull for the attainment of these important objects would never have been received in Scotland. He therefore entreats his beloved son of England patiently to suffer him to write to the said Bruce under that kingly designation. He added that Randolph had made no other proposals subversive of the interests of Edward or England, and that had he done so, they would have been instantly rejected. But the English king, obtuse though he was, met these arguments with a sharp reply. He declared that the concession was dishonourable to the church, and injurious to the interests of England; and that the Scots would think that when the pope had given the title he meant to acknowledge the right also. He also sarcastically reminded his holiness of his own maxim lately acted upon against Scotland itself when it best suited his purposes—that no alteration ought to be made in the condition of the parties while the truce continued.[1]

After his success at Avignon Randolph in his diplomatic capacity repaired to the court of France, and renewed the ancient league between that country and Scotland. During the course of these negotiations a son was born to the Scottish king at Dunfermline, 5th March, 1323-24, who afterwards reigned as David II. This happy event diffused gladness over the whole nation as the promise of a direct male succession to the throne.

For some time after this period no event of special importance occurred; the truce between the two kingdoms was observed on either side, and negotiations were continued to convert it into a lasting peace. The proposals, however, of the Scots to that effect, if truly related by an English historian,[2] were connected with conditions of too exorbitant a nature to be complied with; for they not only demanded a full recognition of the independence of Scotland, and the restoration of the chair of Scone upon which their kings had been crowned, but the restitution of certain manors in England which had belonged to the King of Scots, and the cession of all the north of England as far as the city of York. That no peace as yet was sincerely intended on either side was evident, not only from the character of these demands, but the continued attempts of Edward to stir up the papal court against Scotland, and have the excommunication against both king and people continued. Another suspicious indication of his hostile purposes was his recalling of Edward Baliol, the son and heir of John, from Normandy to the court of England. During the progress of these silent undercurrents Sir Andrew Moray of Bothwell, the companion in arms and colleague of Sir William Wallace, married Christina, the sister of King Robert, and widow of Sir Christopher Seton. But during the same year (1326) this accession to the royal family of Scotland was more than counterbalanced by the death of Bruce's son-in-law, Walter the Steward. His career, though short, had been so full of promise, especially in his gallant defence of Berwick, that the highest hopes were entertained of him, so that his premature death was bewailed as a national calamity.

CHAPTER X.

REIGN OF ROBERT BRUCE—CONCLUSION (1326-1329).

Deposition and death of Edward II.—He is succeeded by Edward III.—Formidable muster of Edward III. against Scotland—The Scots invade England—Their array, equipments, and mode of subsistence—They elude their enemies and avoid a battle—Distresses of the English army—Their fruitless attempts to bring the Scots to action—Midnight attack of Douglas upon the English camp—The Scots effect their retreat into Scotland—Singular condition of their encampment—Peace at last established between Scotland and England—Its conditions—Discontent of the English with the treaty—Secluded life of Bruce at Cardross—His last illness—His dying charge to carry his heart to Palestine—His instructions for the defence of Scotland—His death—Discovery of his remains five centuries afterwards—Sir James Douglas departs with the king's heart from Scotland—He lands in Spain to fight against the Moors—His death in battle—His character.

The next event during the present period of a public nature was of vital importance to Scotland; it was the deposition of Edward II. from the throne he had disgraced and the rule which he was so unfit to exercise. His whole reign had been a series of crimes, and of blunders, which, in a sovereign, are often of worse effect than crimes. In his youth he had been an undutiful son and mean ignoble prince; in his more matured age he had been an impolitic king and cowardly and most inefficient warrior; and every succeeding year only showed how unfit he was to profit either by counsel or experience. Above all, his excessive favouritism, first for

[1] *Fœdera Anglia*, iv. 28.   [2] Malmsbury.

Gaveston and afterwards for the Despencers; his oppressive imposts, which he squandered in riotous living or lavished upon his minions; and the disastrous termination of all his military enterprises, so offensive to a brave high-spirited people and so injurious to their past renown,—had confirmed against him the hatred and contempt both of lords and commons. His cup was filled, and domestic hostility was the last drop that made it overflow. His queen raised the standard against him on her return from France, to which she had retired disgusted with the predominance of the Despencers; her train speedily swelled into an army; and Edward, universally abandoned, was deposed without a dissentient voice, thrown into prison, and finally murdered under such circumstances of atrocious cruelty that his fellest enemies were compelled to pity him. Bruce, indeed, might well have done so, as through these gross errors of the English sovereign the victories of Edward I. had been negatived, the liberties of Scotland recovered, and the military reputation of its people raised to the highest point of renown among the chivalry of Europe. It was almost certain that a worse or more luckless king could scarcely be raised to the throne of England; and that whatever ruler might succeed, the battle for Scottish freedom would have to be renewed, and under different auspices. It is possible that these contingencies occurred to the reflective mind of Bruce when he resolved to resume the war with England. Its new king, Edward III., was but a stripling not more than sixteen years old, and the land was under the government of Queen Isabella and her worthless paramour Mortimer, who was as obnoxious to the English nobility as the favourites of the former king whom they had sent to the gibbet. It was during such a tempting period of minority and misrule that the Scottish liberator resolved to crown the good work which he had so successfully commenced by compelling an equal and honourable peace for his country at the sword-point. While the opportunity also was so favourable for a fresh war with England, Bruce had sufficient cause for aggression in the conduct of the English regency; for although they avowed their desire for a permanent peace, and ratified in the name of their young king the truce that had been confirmed with his father, their commissioners were empowered to treat only with the noblemen and leading personages of Scotland, as if its throne had been still unoccupied and its king a mere pretender or usurper.

In what manner the truce was broken by the Scots and their purposes of invasion announced does not clearly appear, but it was of such an unequivocal character that the English were prompt in their preparations to meet it. An order was issued in the name of Edward III. for the whole military array of the kingdom to join him at Newcastle on the 30th of May (1327). The Cinque ports and maritime towns were commanded to supply their naval contingents, and an admiral was appointed whose charge extended from the river Thames along the whole south and west coast of England. Forty-three cities and towns were ordered to send as many men as they could, each provided with a horse of thirty or forty shillings value; while the northern counties were commanded to send their whole array, both horse and foot, of serviceable men between the ages of sixteen and sixty, under the severest penalties for disobedience. Even those who were too old to fight were required to find a substitute. And formidable though these preparations were from the plentiful resources of England, they were still deemed not enough without foreign aid; and accordingly a large body of heavy-armed Flemish cavalry was hired at a great expense, under the command of Count John of Hainault, and another from various continental states, under John of Quatremars. The whole army, when assembled, amounted to 62,000 soldiers. Of these 8000 were knights and squires, covered, both men and horse, with complete armour; and 15,000 were cavalry of lighter appointments; the infantry consisted of 15,000 ordinary feudal foot soldiers and 24,000 archers.[1]

Against this immense force the Scots contented themselves with mustering not more than 20,000 cavalry and 3000 knights and squires who were completely armed. Not only in numbers but also in weapons and military appointments this Scottish force was so greatly inferior to the English that their attempt to wage war against such an enemy would have appeared the extremity of military rashness or despair. But they crossed the Border full of confidence and hope, and were the first to open the campaign. It is fortunate that on this occasion they had Froissart for their historian; and his description of their equipments and mode of warfare, while it fully justifies their audacity, throws a most interesting light upon that chivalrous and stirring period. None were on foot but the camp-followers; they brought no carriages with them to encumber their march; they did not even furnish themselves with the ordinary provisions, lacking which no other army would have thought of moving; even pots and pans for the purposes of cooking such food as they might gather on the hostile soil

---

[1] Froissart; *Fœd. Ang.* iv.

were left behind them as superfluities. Instead of these each man carried under the flaps of his saddle a broad piece of metal, and behind the saddle a little bag of oatmeal; and "when they have eaten too much of the sodden flesh and their stomach appears weak and empty, they place this plate over the fire, mix with water their oatmeal, and when the plate is heated they put a little of the paste upon it and make a thin cake, like a cracknel or biscuit, which they eat to warm their stomachs."[1] As for sheep and hares, these were in such plenty upon the good pastures of England that we are told they collected more than they knew what to do with; and in cooking the flesh they boiled it in the animal's skin, which, on being flayed off and suspended by four stakes over the fire, with a little water in it, served the purposes of a cauldron. The horses which these invaders used were small light Galloways, not intended for the shock of battle, but for convenience and rapidity of movement; so hardy that they could march from twenty to twenty-four miles a day without halting, and so abstemious that, like their riders, they could find sustenance on any common, and only needed to be turned loose at the end of a day's journey. An army that could thus move and subsist, if skilfully commanded, must have been invincible in mountain or Border warfare; and although their antagonists might have crushed them with a single onset in the open field, there was no likelihood that the wary Scots would yield them an opportunity which they could so easily avoid. Bruce, who was now enfeebled by the disease of which he finally died, was unable to accompany them; but his place was worthily supplied by his two brave captains and pupils, Randolph and Sir James Douglas, the first of whom was now almost his equal in military skill and prudence, and the latter in personal prowess and chivalrous daring. Even the danger that might have accrued from placing two rivals so eager for renown and so emulous of each other's deeds in a common command, was not in this case to be apprehended; for there was the same agreement between them as there is between the head that plans the gallant deed and the right arm that achieves it. Much, indeed, in the liberation of Scotland was owing to this generous harmony of the noble pair, whose great motive of action was to set their country free, and whose rivalry was mainly expressed by mutual co-operation and aid.

The young King of England, full of warlike ardour and impatient to signalize the commencement of his reign by deeds of victory and conquest, joined his army at York, and directed its march to the Scottish border. But on reaching Durham he found that his nimble adversaries had anticipated his movements by crossing the Tyne and commencing their wonted ravages; and he was soon apprised of their neighbourhood by wasted districts and burning villages. Guided by the numerous pillars of smoke and the dismal light of the flames, the English marched in fighting order in quest of their enemies for the purpose of giving them battle; but although they saw abundance of melancholy tokens to convince them that the Scots were scarcely more than five miles off, they could neither reach them nor obtain certain knowledge of their whereabouts. Everything, indeed, was now against the English: their formidable but unwieldy array was ill-fitted for marching and countermarching; and although upon their own soil, they were strangers to the wild mountains and dangerous defiles of Northumberland, while the Scots moved as lightly as the wind, and were as conversant with the geography of these profitable districts as with that of their own country. After three days of fruitless search through a region of smouldering fires and ashes the English, weary with hunger, marching, and sleeplessness, resolved to cross the Tyne, and there await the Scottish army on its homeward return, when it would be laden with plunder and least prepared for resistance. Hoping thus to bring all to the issue of battle, for which they were so well prepared, they reached the river by a hasty march at nightfall, and encamped on the Scottish side of the banks. Each soldier, according to orders, had only brought with him a single loaf, which was tied behind his saddle, but it was so wetted with the sweat of his horse as to be unfit to eat; the horses themselves, after a ride of twenty miles, had neither oats nor any kind of forage; and while the rain poured in torrents the army bivouacked upon the cold wet ground without fires, without provisions, and ignorant on account of the darkness of what particular place they occupied. Their only consolation was the hope that on the morning their nimble adversaries would return to Scotland, and thus fall into the trap that had been laid for them. But at morning no Scots appeared, and they felt that their only chance was to continue in their encampment until their antagonists presented themselves of their own accord. They had cut down the brushwood, of which they made temporary huts; but from day to day the heavy rain continued, from which they could find no shelter; they could obtain no wood for firing but what was soaked and useless; all their saddles and horse-girths were

---

[1] Froissart, book i. c. 17.

rotted, and the greater part of the cavalry dismounted. Provisions also were extremely scanty, as might be expected from a region over which a Scottish army had swept; and although they sent out foraging parties in every direction the food thus obtained was so scanty that it only produced a general scramble followed by fierce contention. Thus the English and their foreign allies remained, says Froissart, "for three days and three nights without bread, wine, candle, oats, or any other forage; and they were afterwards for four days obliged to buy badly-baked bread at the price of sixpence the loaf, which was not worth more than a penny, and a gallon of wine for six groats scarcely worth sixpence." After seven days of this self-inflicted penance, during which no enemy appeared, such a mutinous murmur arose in the camp that Edward III. and his counsellors found it necessary to change their quarters and adopt more active operations. An order was issued for the whole army to be in readiness on the following day to recross the river and go in search of the invaders. A proclamation was also made that whosoever should bring certain intelligence of where the Scots were to the king should have £100 a year in land, and receive knighthood from the hand of Edward himself.

The English army repassed the Tyne, which they did with considerable loss, as the waters were swollen by the late rain, while fifteen or sixteen knights and squires, allured by the late proclamation, went off in different directions over the country in quest of their ubiquitous and invisible foes. One of these squires, whose name was Thomas de Rokeby, returned on the fourth day, and at full gallop, with welcome tidings: he had stumbled upon the Scottish army only a few miles distant, and been brought before their chiefs, who had waited in order for battle seven days while the English were encamped on the opposite side of the Tyne. Thus each army had been ignorant of the other's locality, although so nigh each other—a strange contrast, if true, to the usual military precautions adopted in the warfare of every civilized country. They now gladly learned from Rokeby himself of the approach of the English army, and dismissed him without ransom that he might inform his king where they were to be found. Edward was rejoiced at the report; and, guided by the now knighted Sir Thomas de Rokeby, he commenced his march and was soon in sight of the Scots. But the spectacle brought him little comfort, as they were so strongly posted that they could not be assailed with safety, being drawn up on the slope of a hill, with their flanks defended by rugged rocks, having the rapid river Wear in their front, the waters of which were swollen by the late rains and full of large stones, while the ground beyond it, and nearest the Scots, would give too little room to the English ranks even should they cross the river. The English manœuvred in the hope of drawing the enemy from their strong position, and approached so near that the knights of both armies could read the cognizances of each other's shields; but the Scots remained as moveless as the dark gray rocks by which their front and flanks were protected. Edward then endeavoured to tempt them into an open field by arguments drawn from the book of chivalry; and he sent heralds with the offer of retiring back on the morrow, so as to give them an opportunity of crossing the river and forming in order of battle on the open plain. But at this message of the gallant young tyro the Scottish veteran commanders only laughed. "Go and tell your king," they answered, "that we will not do what he requires of us. It is known to him and his barons that we are in his kingdom, and that we have burned and pillaged wherever we have passed. If this displeases him, let him come and amend it, for here we will tarry as long as we list." Perceiving that they had wise and wary foes to deal with, the English resolved to starve them out by a blockade. They accordingly established themselves on the position they already occupied, but in great discomfort, having little food and no fuel, while the cavalry had neither litter nor forage for their horses, nor even halters to secure them, so that they were obliged to hold them by the bridles. On seeing that the English had made a permanent lodgment opposite their own encampment the Scottish soldiers retired to their huts, after placing strong guards on their advantageous position; and as if they had resolved that their enemies should have no rest, even though their bed was nothing but the cold, drenched, miry soil, they made "about midnight such a blasting and noise with their horns that it seemed as if all the great devils from hell had come there." On the following morning the jaded English arrayed themselves for battle; but still this relief was denied them, for the Scots would not stir from their defences. It seemed hopeless also to starve them out of their place of strength; for although they had neither bread, wine, nor salt, the Scots made light of these wants on account of the cattle they had plundered, and their bags of oatmeal. For three days the armies thus confronted each other, the English only able to reach their opponents by parties of skirmishers that occasionally crossed the river, but with little or no advantage, while by night they were kept awake and in constant alarm by the hideous trumpeting of cows' horns that bellowed from the opposite side. But on the fourth morning, when they rose to resume their weary leaguer, the Scottish encampment was empty—its thousands had utterly disappeared

but it was soon discovered that they had only removed to a still stronger position a short way off, where their movements were concealed by a wood upon the side of a mountain, while they were still protected by the river in front. The English army had no resource but a correspondent movement, and they marched accordingly to a place called Stanhope Park opposite the new Scottish encampment, with the Wear still between them. They there drew up and offered battle; but the Scots, as before, would not quit their impregnable encampment, while their enemies saw that it would be too hazardous to cross the river and attack them on their own ground.

While the two armies thus contended in a warfare of quick and sudden movements, in which the English, though the stronger party, had the worst of it, they soon also found themselves exposed to worse midnight *réveilles* than those of the sleep-dispelling horn-music. Sir James Douglas, impatient for action, resolved to vary the monotony of the campaign with one of those daring exploits by which he had so often paralysed his enemies and succeeded against every obstacle—it was nothing less than to capture or slay the young King of England in the midst of his embattled myriads. He knew also that such a desperate deed might be successful, as the English were now accustomed to midnight alarms and were too weary to keep a careful watch. Accordingly, on the first night of the new encamping, having discovered a convenient ford higher up the river, he crossed it with five hundred horse,[1] and making a circuit by an unfrequented path he came upon the rear of the English army. Approaching their outposts and pretending to be an English officer going the usual rounds, while he exclaimed, "Ha, St. George! have we no watch here?" he passed onward unsuspected until he came near the royal tent, when he suddenly sounded his terrible onset, with the cry, "A Douglas! a Douglas! English thieves, ye shall all die!" The guards of the royal pavilion fought and fell in defence of their master; the uproar rang through the whole camp and brought the startled English together in crowds; but still shouting his war-cry and spurring his horse through the throng, Sir James reached the king's tent and cut asunder several of the cords with his sword. The future conqueror of France was almost within reach of his blood-stained brand, and might have there ended his career but for the interposition of his faithful attendants and chaplain, who fell, while Edward himself had time to escape. Douglas then sounded his slughorn to call his men together, and withdrew them in safety with little loss, although 300 of the enemy had fallen in this singular camisade. On returning to the Scottish encampment Randolph inquired how he had fared, to whom he briefly answered, "Sir, we have drawn blood." It was the answer of disappointment. The renown of such a gallant deed could not console him for its failure.

On the day after this attack a Scottish knight was taken prisoner and carried before Edward and his lords, and on being questioned he confessed that the whole Scottish army had been ordered to hold themselves in readiness that night to follow the banner of Douglas; but on being further interrogated he professed his utter ignorance of the intentions of the Scottish leaders. It was instantly concluded that the success of the previous evening had emboldened the Scots for a fresh trial, in which their whole force would be employed instead of a band of skirmishers. To prepare, accordingly, for this midnight battle the English army at evening was drawn up in three divisions, all on foot and in full order for encounter; strong guards were placed on their outposts and numerous fires were lighted, that they might see the coming of their assailants when they approached. But in the opposite camp preparations of a different nature were going on which these precautions of the English only more effectually concealed. The Scots, indeed, lighted their watch-fires and kept up their wonted serenade and shouting; but these were only parting salutations to an enemy whom they meant to disappoint. They had inflicted fearful havoc on Northumberland; they had exhausted one of the best-appointed armies of England, and drained her treasury for its support; and now, laden with spoil as well as crowned with the distinction of having baffled such a powerful enemy, they were returning to their own country unharmed and unchecked. It was for this movement that the Douglas banner was to be unfurled. Their departure was signalized by all that skill which had marked their advance and their subsequent movements. Rank after rank was withdrawn without noise or observation. Behind was a bog two miles in length which defended their rear and could not be passed by the English cavalry; but this they safely crossed with their horses and booty on hurdles which they had prepared for the purpose, of oziers and boughs of trees, that were laid like bridges over the

---

[1] Barbour. With only two hundred according to Froissart. In a question of numbers on such a chivalrous occasion the testimony of the Scottish poet is more likely to be the correct one.

water-runs and taken up when the troops had passed over the bog, that the English, if they pursued, might not make use of them. A retreat like this from an army of thrice their numbers, embattled within a few roods of them, and holding them as it seemed at their mercy, had all the honour and more than the usual benefits of a signal victory.

Of this retreat in the meantime the English were utterly ignorant, and during the whole night they remained in arms and ready for the expected onset, trusting to requite with one destructive blow the annoyance and disgrace of the whole campaign. It was only when morning was about to dawn that they learned from two Scottish trumpeters whom their patrols had taken prisoners that the whole army had decamped at midnight, and were already five miles on their march homeward. But this tale seemed too wonderful for belief; and fearing that this might be a stratagem of their enemies to allure them across the river, they remained in their ranks until daylight, when they saw with astonishment that the late busy encampment was once more a naked and silent hillside. Even yet the Scots might be in ambush not far off; and scouts were sent across the Wear, who soon returned with tidings that their foes had gone indeed. On exploring the Scottish camp a strange spectacle was presented. More than 500 carcasses of large cattle were lying there which the Scots had killed as too cumbrous for their retreat and too good to be restored to their owners; 300 caldrons of ox-hides with the hair outside, and hung over fires with water and meat ready for boiling; about 1000 wooden spits with meat on them to be roasted; and 10,000 pairs of old worn-out shoes made of undressed leather. It was an inventory worthy of a Hunnish or Tartar camp—the larder of one of those armies that moved like a wind or a locust-cloud, and laughed to scorn the cumbrous preparations of civilized warfare either to resist or pursue them. In addition to these relics the scouts, as we are informed, found five English prisoners stripped and tied to trees, some of them with their legs broken, whom they untied and dismissed.[1] When he saw that the enemy who had braved him with impunity during eighteen days could be reached no longer, and that his first campaign, which promised nothing less than a fresh conquest of Scotland, had ended not only in heavy loss but utter mockery, the young English king burst into tears of rage and shame. His only remedy was that which, in modern times, is often found in a bulletin; and he accordingly announced to his parliament that he had marched against the Scots with a large army; that he had inclosed and shut them up as closely as possible at Stanhope Park; but that they had stolen away by night like conquered fugitives, while several of them had been slain in the pursuit.[2] He led back his army to York, but in such evil plight that the splendid chivalry of Hainault, Brabant, and Flanders were reduced to march on foot, their horses having died or become unserviceable, while the English cavalry were in no better condition. In the meantime the Scots continued their homeward march in triumph, enriched with plunder, and on their way they were met by another Scottish army of 10,000 men coming to their aid, under the command of the Earls of March and Angus, bringing with them also a plentiful convoy of provisions. The work upon which they were sent being completed, the united armies returned to Scotland on the 9th of August (1327), where they were gladly welcomed by the king, who congratulated them on having inflicted such damage upon the enemy and suffered so little loss.[3]

It was now full time that the pride of England should take counsel of her prudence. The whole course of the late warfare had been a series of losses and disasters to the English; and the last inroad had shown that, so far from being able to reconquer Scotland, it would be much if they could still retain unbroken the integrity of their own kingdom. Their king also was still an unexperienced minor held in thraldom by the queen-mother and her worthless paramour Mortimer, who ruled everything and marred what they ruled; while, on the other hand, Bruce, Randolph, and Douglas, by whom Scotland had been raised from the dust to such high pre-eminence, were incontestably the best generals of the age, and as wise in counsel as they were able and fortunate in battle. But to relinquish the triumphs of Edward I., the memory of which was only the more endeared to them by their late reverses—to recognize the Scots as their equals who had so lately been their tributaries, and were now their rebellious bondmen—this, the head and front of whatever peaceful treaty would be proposed, the English

---

[1] Froissart. As they were all sent away, it is to be hoped that the fractured legs were nothing worse than chafed by a struggle to get free; and that the phrase of a "broken shin," used by Shakspere in this sense, was also current in the days of Froissart. If the Scots had wished effectually to prevent the escape of their prisoners and thus secure their retreat without tidings being carried to the enemy's camp, it is not to be supposed that they would have lamed only two or three of the prisoners instead of the whole party. This part of the narrative, which has sometimes been quoted as a proof of the savage spirit and gratuitous cruelty of the Scots, is open to more than one question of sceptical doubt and hesitation.

[2] *Fœdera Anglic*, iv. 301.   [3] Barbour, b. xix.

were still unwilling to concede. To overcome this reluctance Robert Bruce appointed a fresh invasion of England; and as he enjoyed an interval of relief from his deadly malady he resolved to head it in person. A very few weeks, therefore, after the return of the last expedition, it was repeated, but on this occasion in greater force than before, as every Scotsman able to bear arms was enrolled for the enterprise. They entered England by the eastern marches in three divisions. One of these, under the command of Bruce himself, laid siege to the castle of Norham; the second, headed by Douglas and Randolph, besieged the castle of Alnwick; while the third was commissioned to lay waste the open country of Northumberland.[1] These formidable demonstrations had their full effect. Tenders of peace were held out by England herself, and commissioners were sent to the Scottish camp to negotiate the terms, which, when finally adjusted, were as full and ample as the Scots themselves could expect. And first of all was recognized the entire freedom and independence of Scotland and the sovereignty of its king, as a preliminary of treaty, in the following words:—

"Edward by the grace of God King of England, Lord of Ireland, and Duke of Aquitain, &c.: Whereas the superiority over the kingdom of Scotland, obtained by certain of our predecessors and pertaining to us, hath occasioned many bitter wars, to the great injury and affliction of both kingdoms of England and Scotland;—Therefore, by these our letters patent, we will and grant, for us, our heirs and successors, by the common consent and assent of the prelates, earls, barons, and community of our kingdom, in our parliament assembled, That the kingdom of Scotland, according to its just boundaries, as these were in the reign of the lately deceased Alexander of good memory, shall remain free and entire for ever to the magnificent Prince Robert, by the grace of God, illustrious King of Scotland, our very dear friend and confederate, and to his heirs and successors, without any subjection, servitude, reclamation, or demand whatsoever; and we hereby renounce and discharge all right which is or has been claimed by us or our ancestors in the kingdom of Scotland, to the aforesaid king and his heirs and successors: And, for us, our heirs and successors, we entirely and altogether disclaim all obligations, conventions, and covenants whatsoever, that may have been entered into with our predecessors at any time relative to the subjection of Scotland or its inhabitants, by any of the kings or inhabitants whomsoever of the said kingdom of Scotland, whether clerical or laical. And if any letters, charters, muniments, or instruments of any kind shall be hereafter discovered, respecting the execution of any such obligations, covenants, and conventions, we will that they shall be considered as broken, useless, void, null, and of no effect, value, or avail whatever. And for the full, peaceable, and faithful observance of all and singular of these premises, in all time hereafter, we give full power and special mandate by our letters patent to our beloved and faithful cousin, Henry de Percy, and to William de Souch, or either of them, to swear upon our soul to the performance hereof. Given at York on the 1st of March, 1328."[2]

The other articles of this treaty of peace, so honourable to Scotland, were the following:—To confirm the unity between the two kingdoms, David, the only son and heir of Robert Bruce, was to espouse Joanna, the sister of the King of England, to whom the Scottish king was to assign a jointure of £2000 yearly in land of that value; and should the princess die before the marriage was accomplished, King Edward or his successors was to have the privilege of providing another bride for David from the blood royal of England, who should enjoy the same dowry. The two kings, with their heirs and successors, were to be good friends and faithful allies, and each to assist the other, saving the alliance between the King of Scots and the King of France; and, in the event of a war against the English by Ireland, or against the Scots by the Isle of Man or the other Scottish islands, neither of these kings was to aid the enemies of the other. All writings, obligations, instruments, and other muniments relative to the subjection of the people or land of Scotland to the King of England, which were annulled and abrogated by the latter, and all other instruments and privileges relative to the freedom of Scotland, were to be faithfully delivered up to the Scottish king as soon as they could be found. The King of England also engaged to give faithful aid in having the processes in the court of Rome and elsewhere against the King of Scots, his kingdom and subjects, clergy and laity, recalled and annulled with all their consequences. On the other hand, the King of Scotland, his prelates and nobles, engaged to pay to the King of England £20,000 sterling in three years at three terms of payment at Tweedmouth; and in case of failure, to submit themselves to the jurisdiction of the papal chamber, but no execution to be issued until two months after each respec-

---

[1] Fœdera; Barbour.

[2] Rymer's *Fœdera* in Ker's *Life of Bruce*, vol. ii. p. 446; Fordun; Tytler's *History of Scotland*, vol. i. p. 363.

tive term of payment. It was finally agreed that the laws of the marches should be faithfully observed on either side. Either because it was considered to belong to the muniments that were to be restored according to the treaty, or by a separate clause which was not publicly announced in England, it was agreed that the sacred marble of Scone on which the kings of Scotland had been crowned, but which Edward I. had carried away as the proudest trophy of his conquest, was to be restored to its old resting-place and home.[1]

In this manner the conquest of Scotland by Edward I., the long war of thirty-two years' duration, and all the losses and sufferings it entailed on England, had vanished like an air-built city of ancient romance at the touch of the enchanter's wand or the utterance of a few words of conjuration. And what had been gained? At first sight *nothing*, for the two kingdoms were only replaced in their original condition, but weakened and exhausted by the struggle. But for the great result we must carry our eye forward to future centuries, and mark how the polity and the national character of Britain at large were nursed and matured by this terrible and seemingly unnatural conflict. Thus regarded these contentions of vainglory, and ambition, and hate, which to a narrow misanthropy appear so contemptible and so undeserving of record, became of paramount import, as the sources from which the two nations derived their heroic love of independence and their energy and skill to maintain it. But the men of that age were neither seers nor sages, and therefore the English people at large were indignant, and with some show of good reason, at a peace which surrendered at once all their past advantages as well as future hopes; and while one party thought that the queen and Mortimer had sacrificed the nation to retain their own usurped dominion, others more extravagantly alleged that they had been purchased with Scottish gold. This feeling broke out into a dangerous riot in London when the Scottish coronation stone was about to be removed from Westminster for its transference to Scone, and the populace retained it by force. In their regard for it as a token of conquest it is evident that they had no fear of its prophetic legend before their eyes, or that its original owners should ever have rule in London. But after-events consoled the Scots for its detention. Even in Scotland, also, the people do not seem to have been fully reconciled to the treaty, by which their long career of victory was suddenly arrested, and the rich resources of English plunder protected from their aggressions; and, in derision of the marriage by which this concord of the two nations was to be cemented, they distinguished the Princess Joanna by the nickname of Make-peace. This royal lady, who was only seven years old, attended by her mother, the Earl of Mortimer, and the Bishop of Lincoln, High-chancellor of England, arrived at Berwick, where she was received by her princely bridegroom, as yet only in his fifth year; and the marriage was celebrated in the presence of Randolph and Douglas, the representatives of their sovereign, on the 12th of July (1328), with great magnificence, and amidst the congratulations of both English and Scots. On this happy occasion the bride had brought with her what was of higher account than rich jewels and ornaments: these were the Ragman Roll so degrading to Scotland, by which its nobles had signed away the independence of the kingdom, and the national muniments and records which Edward I. had carried with him to England, but which were to be restored according to the terms of the late treaty. Although now sore-sick, and enfeebled with a malady that was soon to end fatally, King Robert left his quiet seclusion at Cardross and repaired to Edinburgh, that he might welcome his young daughter-in-law and witness with his own eyes this promise of lasting peace, of which the union of these children was the substantial symbol and type; and having contemplated this happy close of his sufferings and toils with a grateful *nunc dimittis* he returned to his home and his sick-bed, that he might enter into his rest.

There is a melancholy but pleasing interest in contemplating the last days of such a hero. As yet only fifty-five years old, and possessed originally of a frame of iron and a strength surpassing that of the ordinary sons of men, the privations and sufferings of his early career, and the cares and anxieties which accompanied even his triumphs, had brought on premature old age, as well as a fatal disease, which his physicians, who could neither understand nor cure it, were pleased to call a *leprosy*. When he found himself no longer fit for active life he committed the management of affairs to Randolph and Douglas, and retired to a humble dwelling at Cardross, near Dumbarton, on the shore of the Firth of Clyde, where he chiefly spent the last two years of his life. Here, besides planning for his lieutenants those warlike operations which he could no longer superintend in person, he devoted himself to the peaceful pursuits of fishing, boat-building, and hawking. Even the favourite animal which formed the pet of his old age was in keeping with his character, for it was a tame lion; and his care in maintaining the royal beast

---

[1] *Parliamentary Records of Scotland*, I. 85.

is attested by the expense of its provender, recorded in his chamberlain's rolls. Mindful, also, of his days of wandering and hunger, he was the bountiful friend of the poor, as is testified not only by the charities he founded, but his numerous doles of provisions to the poor, who were regularly supplied at his gate. As his simple cottage or fortalice, which chroniclers have aggrandized into the Palace of Cardross, because it was a royal residence, must have been a frequent place of resort to the friends of his youth, as well as of pilgrimage to the distant worshippers of his renown and worth, the open-hearted hospitality of his home is also attested by the copious stores of provisions which are noted down in the same household register. During the last half year of his life he was a widower, his queen Elizabeth having died while he was employed in the siege of Norham; and this bereavement, combined with the thought that his son and heir David was still a child, and that his grandson Robert, who was next in succession, was a boy only ten years old, must have made the peace with England doubly welcome to his royal and paternal heart.

And then came the closing sunset of this day of brightness which had thus lingered upon the mountain tops of the land it had gladdened, and after which there was to be a night of such darkness, and sorrow, and disaster. Robert Bruce was dying, and his iron-nerved warriors were like children weeping around a father's deathbed. But who could venture upon its description after the living pictures of Barbour and Froissart? Even for the hundredth time that of the latter, who writes like an eye-witness with his tears but newly dried, will bear a full quotation:—

"King Robert of Scotland, who had been a very valiant knight, waxed old, and was attacked with so severe an illness, that he saw his end was approaching; he therefore summoned together all the chiefs and barons in whom he most confided, and after having told them that he should never get the better of this sickness, he commanded them, upon their honour and loyalty, to keep and preserve faithfully and entire the kingdom for his son David, and obey him and crown him king when he was of a proper age.

"He after that called to him the gallant lord James Douglas, and said to him in presence of the others, 'My dear friend, Lord James Douglas, you know that I have had much to do, and have suffered many troubles during the time I have lived, to support the rights of my crown: at the time that I was most occupied, I made a vow, the non-accomplishment of which gives me much uneasiness—I vowed, that if I could finish my wars in such a manner, that I might have quiet to govern peaceably, I would go and make war against the enemies of our Lord Jesus Christ and the adversaries of the Christian faith. To this point my heart has always leaned; but our Lord was not willing, and gave me so much to do in my lifetime, and this last expedition has lasted so long, followed by this heavy sickness, that since my body cannot accomplish what my heart wishes, I will send my heart in the stead of my body to fulfil my vow. And, as I do not know any one knight so gallant or enterprising, or better formed to complete my intentions than yourself, I beg and entreat of you, dear and special friend, as earnestly as I can, that you would have the goodness to undertake this expedition for the love of me, and to acquit my soul to our Lord and Saviour; for I have that opinion of your nobleness and loyalty, that if you undertake it, it cannot fail of success— and I shall die more contented; but it must be executed as follows:—

"'I will, that as soon as I shall be dead, you take my heart from my body and have it well embalmed; and you will also take as much money from my treasury as will appear to you sufficient to perform your journey, as well as for all those whom you may choose to take with you in your train; you will then deposit your charge at the Holy Sepulchre of our Lord, where he was buried, since my body cannot go there. You will not be sparing of expense—and provide yourself with such company and such things as may be suitable to your rank—and wherever you pass, you will let it be known, that you bear the heart of King Robert of Scotland, which you are carrying beyond seas by his command, since his body cannot go thither.'

"All those present began bewailing bitterly; and when the Lord James could speak, he said, 'Gallant and noble king, I return you a hundred thousand thanks for the high honour you do me, and for the valuable and dear treasure with which you intrust me; and I will most willingly do all that you command me with the utmost loyalty in my power; never doubt it, however I may feel myself unworthy of such a high distinction.' The king replied, 'Gallant knight, I thank you—you promise it me then?' 'Certainly, sir, most willingly,' answered the knight. He then gave his promise upon his knighthood.

"The king said, 'Thanks be to God! for I shall now die in peace, since I know that the most valiant and accomplished knight of my kingdom will perform that for me which I am unable to do for myself."[1]

---

[1] The account of Barbour agrees in the main with that of

Many have been at a loss to account for this dying request, by which Scotland would be deprived of one of its best and bravest leaders, and that too at a time when his services would be most required. According to modern reckoning it was inconsistent with the well-known wisdom and prudence of Bruce to send a warrior like Douglas upon such a useless pilgrimage; and they have endeavoured to discover more kingly and secular motives for the commission than the superstitious feelings of the age. But Bruce was a warrior, not a theologian; and while in the former character he was the best of his day, in the latter he was neither more learned nor wiser than his contemporaries, who believed in the infallibility of the church, and received its teaching without examination or scruple. It was usual also for sovereigns of the period in their dying hours to look wistfully to the land of redemption and miracles, and to regret that their occupations had prevented them from visiting the Holy Sepulchre either as penitent pilgrims or as warlike champions and deliverers. And in Bruce's case this longing had a tenfold urgency. For he had murdered a man within the sacred girth of the sanctuary and defiled the altar with his blood; and for this, the deadliest of crimes, he had been visited with the heaviest curse of the church, which still lay upon him unremoved. That curse, indeed, he had braved through years of battle and the triumphs of success, and with the hope that it might yet be repealed. But the chance of reconciliation had never arrived, and now that he was upon his death-bed the gates of heaven were still closed, and in a few hours he would knock at them in vain! All this he must have sadly and tremblingly believed unless he was an Albigeois or an atheist, and we well know that he was neither. One chance, however, remained for him—the chance of those who, "dying, put on the weeds of Dominick." Were but his heart carried to Palestine and buried beside the tomb of the Redeemer, the sanctity of such a grave and the merit of such a pilgrimage would disarm the sentence of the church and absolve him from his guilt. Here, then, was a motive sufficient of itself to account for his eagerness to intrust Douglas with the charge. The dying king was also anxious that the purpose of the mission should be announced in every land through which it passed. In this way he could best proclaim to Rome itself and to Christendom at large what, perhaps, from his past independence they had often called in question—the depth of his repentance and the sincerity of his Christian faith.

Besides these cares for his own spiritual wel-

Froissart, and its touching simplicity will excuse its length as a quotation:—

He said, "Lordings, swa it is gayn
With me, that thar is noucht bot ane
That is the dede, withowtyn drede,
That ilk man mon thole off nede.
And I thank God that has me sent
Space in this lyve me to repent.
For throuch me, and my werraying,
Off blud has bene rycht gret spilling;
Quhar mony sakless men war slayn,
Tharfor this sekues, and this payn,
I tak in thank for my trespass.
And myn hart flebyt sckyrly was,
Quhen I wes in prosperité,
Off my synnys to saufyt be,
To trawaill upon Goddis fayis.
And seu he now me tyll him tayis,
Swa that the body may na wyss
Fulfill that the hart gan dewyss;
I wald the hart war thyddir sent,
Quharin consawyt wes that cutent.
Tharfor I pray yow euirilk ane,
That ye amang yow chess me ane,
That be honest, wyse, and wycht,
And off hys hand a nobyll knycht,
Ou Goddis fayis my hart to ber,
Quhen saule and corss dissenerytt wer.
For I wald it war worthily
Brocht thar; son God will noucht that I
Have power thiddyrwart to ga."—
Than war thair harts all sa wa,
That nane mycht hald hym from greting.
He bad tham leve thair sorrowing,
For it, he said, mycht not releve;
And mycht thaim rycht gretly eugreve.
And prayit thaim in hy to do
The thing that thai war chargyt to.

Than wene that furth in drery mode.
Amang thaim thai thoucht it gode,
That the worthy Lord off Dowglas

Best schapyn for that trawaill was.
And quhen the King hard that thai swa
Had ordanyt hym bys hart to ta,
That he mast yarnyt suld it haff;
He said, "So God hymselff me saiff!
I haid me rycht welle payit that ye
Haff chosyn hym: for hys bounté,
And hys worschip, sot my yaruyng,
Ay sen I thoucht to do this thing,
That it with hym thar suld ber.
And sen ye all assentyt ner,
It is the mar likand to me.
Lat se now quhat thartill sayis he."
And quhen the gud Lord off Dowglas
Wyst that thing thus spokyn was,
He come and kuelyt to the King,
And on this wyss maid hym thanking.
"I thank yow grotly, Lord," said he,
"Off mony largess, and gret bounté,
That ye haff done me felayss,
Sen fyrst I come to your seruice.
Bot our all thing I make thanking
That ye sa dyng and worthy thing,
As your hart, that culumyuyt wes
Off all bounté, and all prowes,
Will that in my yemsall tak.
For yow, Sir, I will blythly mak
This trawaill, giff God will me gif
Laysar and space swa lang to lyff."

The King hym thankyt tendrely.
Than wes mane in that company
That thai na wepyt for pité.
Thair cher anoyis wes to se.

fare Bruce was anxious to the last for the welfare of Scotland; and it was either at this interview or about the same period that he delivered those injunctions for the future defence of the kingdom which have been called "Good King Robert's Testament." In their battles he counselled that the Scots should fight on foot; that they should intrench themselves among their mountains, morasses, and woods, instead of stone walls and bulwarks; and that their offensive weapons should be the bow, the spear, and the battle-axe. When they were invaded they were to remove their provisions, drive away all their cattle, and lay waste the country, so that the enemy, finding themselves surrounded by a desert, should be compelled to a hasty retreat. They were also to give the invaders no rest, but to keep their encampment awake with noise and continual alarms. It was the most effectual defence of Scotland, of which he had made full and successful proof; and we have seen in the recent campaign of Randolph and Douglas into Northumberland how successful this plan could be even for aggressive warfare upon the English Borders, where the rugged scenery resembled that of Scotland. As long as they adhered to these simple rules the Scots in after periods were able to battle their numerous and well appointed enemies, and it was only when their pride or impatience hurried them into the unequal conflict that their armies were quelled and their liberties imperilled.[1]

Bruce died at Cardross on the 7th of June, 1329. The father of the land had thus passed away, and from castle to hovel there was weeping and sorrow over every Scottish hearth. The poet-biographer of the hero, who describes the universal wail, gives an affecting account of the lamentations of those brave knights who had thus lost their best leader as well as brightest example and ornament. "Alas!" they cried, "he that was all our defence, all our comfort, our wisdom, and our governance, is thus brought to an end. His nobleness and his prowess made all that were with him so brave that they could not be subdued while they saw him in presence before them. Alas! what shall we do or say? for while he lived we were dreaded by our neighbours and renowned in many a far country, and all because of him!"

According to the royal wish the king's heart was taken out, and the body, after having been covered with cloth of gold and lapped in lead, was interred in the abbey church of Dunfermline, at that time a venerable edifice built by Malcolm Canmore and his pious queen Margaret. A monument of marble, profusely ornamented with gilding, which had been made at Paris by the orders of Bruce himself during his last illness, was erected over his grave. But with the lapse of time both church and monument went to decay, and though a new building was erected it likewise followed the fate of its predecessor, so that the erection of a third church was deemed necessary. But amidst these changes the resting-place of Scotland's preserver had so completely faded from public memory that the precise locality could no longer be ascertained. This, however, was accomplished on the 17th of February, 1818, when on clearing away some of the ancient ruins the workmen came to a vault which was ascertained to be the long-hidden tomb of Robert Bruce; and a subsequent exploration, which was conducted with much of the solemnity and sympathy of the original interment, revealed the dry skeleton of what had once been the victor of Bannockburn. It indicated a man of great physical strength who had been six feet in height, while the strong square nether jaw was such as usually betokens a spirit of unbending resolution; the jaw-bone also bore the traces of a deep wound that had probably been inflicted in battle. The breast-bone of the skeleton was found to have been sawn asunder, and in this rude fashion only the skill of the age could effect the extraction of the heart.[2]

And the career of that heart, so adventurous while it lived, was still to be in peril and conflict. Douglas having procured a safe-conduct from Edward III. for his journey to the Holy Land, to aid the Christians against the Paynims, set sail as soon as the season permitted, having

---

[1] These rules were afterwards reduced into the following leonine verses:—

"Scotica sit guerra pedites, mons, mossica terra:
Silvæ pro muris sint, arcus et hasta, securis.
Per loca stricta greges muniontur. Plana per ignes
Sic inflammentur, ut ab hostibus evacuentur.
Insidiæ vigiles sint, noctu vociferantes.
Sic male turbati redient velut ense fugati
Hostes pro certo; Sic Rege docente Roberto."

Of these lines the following old Scottish version has been preserved by Hearne in his edition of Fordun:—

"On fut suld be all Scottis weire,
Be hyll and moss thainnself to weire,
Lat wod for wallis be; bow, and spier,
And battle-axe, their fechting gear.
That enuymeis do thaim na dreire,
In strait placis gar keip all stoire,
And birnen the planen land thaim befoire,
Thanan sall they pass away in haist
Quhen that thai find nathing hot waist;
With wyllos and wakenen of the nycht
And mekil noyse made on hycht;
Thanen shall thai turnen with gret affrai
As thai were chasit with swerd away.
This is the counsall and intent
Of gud King Robert's testament."

[2] A full account of the discovery and exploration has been given in the 2d vol. of the *Archæologia Scotica*.

the heart of his beloved friend and master inclosed in a silver casket and suspended by a chain from his neck. He was accompanied by eight knights and twenty-six esquires, with a numerous military retinue; and on reaching Sluys in Flanders he remained at that port twelve days, but without landing, waiting for such bold adventurers as might be willing to join him in his warlike pilgrimage. He lived, however, on board in kingly state; kept a magnificent table to which all of fitting rank were made welcome, and served from vessels of gold and silver, with two sorts of wine and two sorts of spices, while the neighbouring shores resounded with the regal music of drums and trumpets that waited upon his banquets.[1] While he abode at the port of Sluys he learned that Alphonso XI., King of Castile and Leon, was at war with Osmyn, the Moorish sovereign of Granada; and finding that no crusade was in preparation for Palestine, Douglas resolved to encounter the infidels upon the soil of Spain, as this warfare for the faith was an essential part of his vow. On arriving at Seville he was received by Alphonso with welcome and offered bountiful supplies of treasure, horses, and armour; but Sir James refused these offers, and declared that he had only halted in his pilgrimage to fight against the Moors for the welfare of his soul. Among the many knights of foreign lands who had repaired to the Christian court of Castile to combat, like himself, with the unbelievers, were several from England, who honoured his worth and frequented his society like friends and brothers; for the generous spirit of chivalry and the common interest of a holy war could suspend for the time every meaner subject of contention. Of the strangers from foreign countries was one who had so often fought against the Saracens that his face was "hewn," as Barbour expresses it, with the scars of many wounds, of which he seems to have been not a little vain. One day this knight, having expressed his astonishment that the countenance of such a famed warrior as Douglas should be smooth and unscarred, Sir James modestly replied, "Thank God, I had always hands to guard my head!" It was a covert rebuke of the other's want of skill in the art of defence, and the "good knights who were by," we are told, "praised the answer greatly."

The Moors of Granada were soon in the field, and Douglas with his Scottish band occupied a conspicuous place in the front rank of the Christian army. But he had now a different enemy to deal with than those he had been used to encounter: instead of maintaining a stubborn stand-up fight to the last, and only quitting the field when they could hold it no longer, the light-armed Moorish chivalry, like the Parthians of old, trusted more to a retreat than an advance, and were most to be dreaded when they seemed to be in full flight. Douglas charged as he was wont, bearing down all before him; the enemy withdrew as if routed, and hurried on by the ardour of pursuit, the unsuspecting Scot was soon enveloped by the wily foe, who had thus withdrawn him from the support of the Spaniards. Although accompanied only by ten of his followers, Douglas, who had been accustomed to such straits, resolved to cut his way through the throng; and, unfastening the casket which he always carried with him from his neck, he threw it among the thickest of the enemy, exclaiming, "Pass before us in battle, gallant heart, as thou wert wont to do; Douglas will follow thee or die!" He fought until he reached this glorious mark, and there he fell; most of his companions were slain with him; and after the battle his body was found stretched beside the casket, which he seemed to guard even in death. Both were brought home by the survivors, and while the heart was buried in the Abbey of Melrose, the remains of Sir James were interred in the burying-place of his ancestors in the church of Douglas.

Such was the romantic death of one of the most romantic knights as well as able leaders of his day. He had fought seventy battles, and in fifty-three had been victorious.[2] The English, who had so often felt his prowess, called him the "Black Douglas;" but by his countrymen, to whom he was endeared by his gentleness, kindness, and unbounded liberality, as well as valour, he was entitled "the good Lord James." Learned beyond the scanty scholarship of his contemporaries, "sweet and debonair" in his bearing, and perfect in every chivalrous accomplishment, he presents to us the fair ideal of knighthood; his unswerving devotedness to his sovereign through every stage of trial, when so many proved faint or false, was the perfection of loyalty; and his generous conduct to Randolph, and the firm friendship he retained for him to the last, shows how superior he was to that envy and jealousy which are usually so predominant in military rivalry. His achievements as a leader, and the success with which they were crowned, are sufficient also to attest that his skill and prudence were equal to his daring, and were permitted to regulate the most adventurous of his attempts. In personal appearance his complexion was gray or dark; his hair black; his body was lean and large-

---

[1] Froissart, book i. c. 20. [2] Fordun, xiii. c. 21.

boned with broad shoulders, and his limbs well proportioned. Among his friends he was gentle, mild, and agreeable of aspect; but those who saw it in battle seemed to see another countenance altogether, so terrible was the change. It is also added, that although he somewhat lisped in his speech, yet what in others would have been a defect, was in him wonderfully becoming, on account, no doubt, of his high renown and martial demeanour. In this description, which Barbour received from those who had known the brave Scottish hero, we have a full portraiture of him who was indeed "the Douglas tender and true" beyond all that ever bore the name. Two such deaths as those of Bruce and the good Lord James were ominous of future losses and disasters to Scotland, which succeeding events but too well verified.

CHAPTER XI.

HISTORY OF RELIGION (1286-1329).

Jealousy of the Scots for their religious liberty—Influence of this spirit on the national character and history—Restrictions imposed by the civil rulers on the power of the clergy—Remonstrance of the pope against these restrictions—Enumeration of them in the papal bull—The married clergy of Scotland—Conduct of the Scottish prelates during the war for independence—Their secret embassy to Rome—The pope's interference with Edward I. on their behalf—His claim upon Scotland as a fief of the Roman see—Indignant rejection of his interference and claim by Edward—The pope's return to the cause of the stronger party—Hopelessness for the national church in Bruce's championship of the kingdom—His successful resistance to the demands of the pope—Recovery of the Scottish church through his successes—Able and energetic letter of the Scots to the pope—Its bold and independent spirit—Its influence in altering the conduct of Rome in their favour—Continuing success of the Scottish church—Increasing influence and wealth of the clergy—Account of Lamberton, Bishop of St. Andrews.

In the history of religion during a preceding period we had occasion to advert to the independent spirit manifested by the Church of Scotland even against the popes themselves, and to the manner in which it was exhibited. But while the churchmen were thus watching the advances of pontifical despotism with a wary eye, and ready to confront it at every aggressive approach, they were themselves watched in turn and circumscribed by the laity, who were as impatient of a priestly as the clergy were of a papal yoke. This double system of check and countercheck, which makes the history of the Scottish church so perplexing an anomaly at this early stage, and which has made so many inquirers pass it over as too obscure to be intelligible, is yet of vital moment. It constituted an important element in the formation of that hardy national character, by which Scotland was to be fitted for her future destination. It prepared her for that terrible strife which awaited her, wherein whole centuries of trial were to be encountered and overcome. And when the victory was won, and her political liberty secured, it had nerved and fitted her for that further conflict which was to succeed—even that war for religious liberty which she was to maintain against the despotism of the Stuarts, and in which she was as bold, self-sacrificing, and successful, as in her wars against the Plantagenets. These considerations give an importance to facts which would otherwise be scarcely worth narrating: they may also apologize for the repetition of facts which have been previously mentioned in the civil portion of the narrative.

Of this twofold watchfulness, so jealous for the preservation of liberty both against priest and pontiff, and so annoying to the papal conclave, a singular proof was afforded in the middle of the thirteenth century. Alexander III. was still in his early minority; but, warned by recent events, his guardians, in administering the affairs of the kingdom, had vigorously checked every encroachment of the clerical upon the civil authority. Such opposition was not to be endured from one petty kingdom when all the rest had proved so acquiescent, or from a clique of nobles who merely acted by a delegated authority; and in 1251 Innocent IV., the reigning pontiff, roused himself to vindicate the rights of the church, which had been violated by the injuries inflicted on the Scottish priesthood. A cry of the Scottish church, it was stated in the preamble of a bull to that effect, had entered into the ears of the Father of Christendom, complaining that the ministers of Alexander III. were availing themselves of the minority and tender years of their young sovereign to invade ecclesiastical liberty, "which they who violate, break the strength of princes wherein the Catholic faith flourishes, and whereby the dignity of kings is rightly led." Innocent therefore gives commission to the Bishops of Lincoln, Worcester, and Lichfield to inquire into the nature of these alleged abuses, with full power to punish the offenders. It is supposed that the bull, though drawn out, may not have been transmitted, as no notice of its execution appears in history. But it is also not unlikely that it reached its destination, and that the English prelates were not very anxious to carry it into effect.[1] From past events, indeed, we can judge how such an inquest was likely to have been received in Scotland. The bull itself is written in a very angry strain, and from it we learn that the guardians of the young sovereign had been guilty of the following enormities:—

1. When the Scottish bishops pronounced sentence of excommunication, interdict, or suspension against offenders for their contumacy or crimes, they had been required by letters in the king's name to revoke the sentence under penalty of confiscation—a punishment which had actually been inflicted upon several of their number.

2. In questions relating to the property and possessions of the church, priests, notwithstanding the privileges of their order, had been compelled to appear in civil courts, where sometimes they were deprived of their possessions by the awards of these incompetent judges.

3. Those possessions which had been given in perpetuity to the church by laymen, burdened only with the condition of military service and bearing a share in public aids, were held to be laic fees, and treated accordingly.

4. On the evidence of laymen who were hostile to the clergy, and ready to perjure themselves, the royal counsellors had narrowed the ancient boundaries of ecclesiastical possessions.

5. Concerning the right of patronage, which, in spiritual matters, is only subject to ecclesiastical jurisdiction, these rulers have issued orders in the name of the king, commanding questions of patronage to be tried in the civil court.

6. In like manner, although the observance of oaths pertains to spiritual matters, they have prohibited ecclesiastical censures for enforcing their observance.

7. They have prohibited ecclesiastical punishments dealt in the form of a pecuniary fine.

8. They have abolished the exaction of several small tithes.

9. They have diminished the privileges of the married clergy.

10. They have refused to allow causes to be tried by papal delegates.

"These are grave offences," it is stated in the bull, "and can no longer be passed over through concealment, or left unpunished, without being guilty of sin." But the exposure and the punishment would have been a difficult task; for it is added that many of the Scottish clergy themselves had co-operated with the lay rulers in encouraging these offences. It is apparent from this papal specification that the chief care of the Scottish statesmen had been to withstand those growing usurpations of the clergy which had become so prevalent in every other part of Europe; that their efforts had been successful; and that they had been aided in their attempts by an influential portion of the priesthood, who were either too careless or too conscientious to make common cause with their less moderate brethren. But what shall we say of the *married* clergy, in whose behalf the pontiff had shown such astounding solicitude? Such men were already reckoned monstrosities in the church; and even in Scotland, where the law of clerical celibacy had been latest in entering, the wives of these priests were branded by the church statutes with the odious name of concubines. Strong, therefore, must have been the rebellion in the Scottish church which compelled the pope to have recourse to such allies. But who were these *clerici uxorati?* A careful attention to the words in which they are described justifies the suspicion that they were no other than the old Culdees, who, having conformed to the period of holding Easter and to the form of the tonsure, had as yet conformed in nothing else, and were still too numerous and influential to be lightly provoked or thrown aside.[2] So late as the close of the thirteenth century they had still been so powerful as almost to exclude William Lamberton from being elected Bishop of St. Andrews;[3] and it was not until after that period, that they ceased to appear as a distinct body in the Scottish church.

In the troubled events and changes that succeeded the death of Alexander III. we find the Scottish prelates taking an active part, but it was rather as politicians or even as warriors than recluse churchmen or dispensers of religious offices. This was nothing less than a necessity of their position according to the usages of the times. A brief notice of a few of

---

[1] A copy of this bull was first published by Sir David Dalrymple in the Appendix to *Annals of Scotland*, vol. i. no. iv.

[2] The words in which the married priests were specified in the bull are the following:—"Clerici vero uxorati ejusdem regni, qui clericalem deferentes tonsuram clericali gaudere solent privelegio, et cum bonis suis sub ecclesiasticæ protectionis manere præsidio ab antiquo, solito immunitatis beneficiis exuuntur, et sub nova rediguntur onera servitutis."

[3] Spottiswood, p. 51.

these appearances will in some measure show the spirit in which they acted amidst the selfish and sudden shiftings of the period. Of the six guardians who were chosen to preside over the realm during the interregnum two were bishops. The ready interference of Edward I. as arbiter among the competitors, for the purpose of reducing Scotland to his own rule, was chiefly owing to the intrigues and counsel of William Fraser, Bishop of St. Andrews. On the other hand when Bruce, Baliol, the Scottish regents, and most of the powerful nobles swore fealty to the English king in 1291, previous to the decision of the claims of the competitors, the only Scottish prelate who joined them in this unnational deed of vassalage was Mark, Bishop of Sodor. But as a counterpart to this magnanimity we find that five years afterwards, when Edward had apparently crushed the liberties of Scotland by his victory of Dunbar, the bishops in his line of march through Scotland joined the nobles in submitting to the conqueror and swearing themselves his liegemen. For this act, and to secure their further obedience, Edward granted to the Scottish bishops the privilege of bequeathing their effects by will—a valuable boon, as previous to this period their property when they died had reverted to the sovereign. When Wallace raised the standard of liberty and was joined by several influential persons, one of these was Robert Wishart, Bishop of Glasgow. But his faith was of the same wavering kind as the rest, and in the hour of trial he joined them in their apostasy, for which the Scottish champion pillaged the bishop's house and led his sons into captivity.[1]

When Scotland was reduced to the last extremity by the defeat of Wallace and dispersion of his followers the Scottish church shared in all the calamities that befell the devoted kingdom. The Bishop of St. Andrews was in France a voluntary exile. Wishart, Bishop of Glasgow, and Maurice, Bishop of the Isles, were prisoners in England. The other churchmen who had manifested any sympathy for the cause of their country's independence were harassed by the oppressions of the victors. In this state of things, and seeing no other source of help, the unfortunate priests applied secretly to Rome by a deputation of three of their number. The arguments of these suppliants prevailed with the conclave, being backed, as an English historian[2] alleges, with money, which could purchase everything at Rome; but how, in their sore straits, they could have found money for the purpose it is not easy to conjecture. The only guerdon, indeed, that they could offer was a promise of the gratitude of their church, and a more compliant spirit in its rulers for the time to come. This, indeed, is probable, from the assertion of Edward that these envoys had suggested the strange mode of the papal interference in behalf of Scotland, and the arguments with which it was enforced. The pontiff, Boniface VIII., now brought forward his memorable claim; it was that Scotland belonged not to England but to the see of Rome, because it had been miraculously converted to Christianity by the bones of St. Andrew! By similar statements he might have extended his claim to every kingdom in Christendom. As might be expected, the proud and passionate Edward was indignant at the claim, and the command with which it was accompanied to desist from his hostile aggressions upon the property of the Holy See. But should he have any pretensions to the whole or a part of Scotland he was desired to send his proctors to Rome within six months, when the cause should be tried by the pope in person and decided according to justice.[3] We can easily conjecture, notwithstanding such a promise, what the decision would have been. But Edward I. was a very different character from John his grandfather, and he rejected the demand with scorn. Still it was necessary to show causes for his refusal, and accordingly every muniment was ransacked for historical or traditionary proofs to show that Scotland had been of old a feudatory of England, and still owed it subjection and fealty. The progress of this singular controversy between the king and the pope, and the extravagant statements with which Edward fortified his claim, have been detailed in a preceding chapter. His reply was enforced by another from the English parliament, in which they declared their sovereigns to be the rightful liege lords of Scotland, their purpose to maintain their king's authority over it to the uttermost, and their firm resolve that he should send no commissioners to Rome to answer upon such a question. In this way a strong political motive could reverse the conduct of two proud kingdoms towards him who claimed to be heaven's vicegerent; and while Scotland seemed to be on the eve of abjuring her past obduracy and becoming his obedient vassal, England had rebelled and was defying him to his teeth. With king and parliament thus combined against him Boniface must have felt that there was little chance of influencing England, and that the rebellion of such a rich province of the Roman see could never be com-

---

[1] Fœdera; Scotichron.; Lord Hailes; Spottiswood.
[2] Walsingham.

[3] Fœdera, II. 844.

pensated by the submission of such a poor and profitless country as Scotland. It was not by such policy that the popedom could attain the rule of every kingdom and the control of every treasury. The pontiff accordingly made haste to repair his blunder. He rated the unfortunate Wishart for having encouraged the Scots to rebel against such a pious king as Edward, by which he had made himself odious both to God and man; and he exhorted the trembling prelate to repent and seek to obtain forgiveness.[1] In the same strain he wrote to the Scottish bishops commanding them to labour for the promotion of the public peace, and threatening them with severe censures if they refused.[2] Such was the requital which Scotland obtained for her lowly submission to Rome, such her experience of its justice and immutable integrity. The lesson was not forgot, and time ripened it into action.

It was thus that, when Scotland had lost the services of her best champion and was lying helpless beneath the foot of the oppressor, the head of the church had also turned against her and even menaced her resistance with excommunication. Nor were matters more promising for the Scottish church when Bruce assumed the place of the murdered Wallace in the high work of national deliverance, for he commenced the attempt with such a deed of sacrilegious murder as was certain to array every Christian community against him. He was, moreover, visited with the awful ban by which he was cast forth as a withered branch; and all who aided or accompanied him were declared in like manner to be accursed. Rome had now a cause of hostility against Scotland in which not only Christendom at large would sympathize, but by which the favour of England could be completely propitiated. But although the cause of Edward was thus consecrated into a holy war, as being waged against outcasts who were no better than Saracens and infidels, the Scottish hierarchy were not to be driven from their patriotism; and among the best supporters of the excommunicated Bruce were Lamberton, Bishop of St. Andrews, Wishart, Bishop of Glasgow, David Moray, Bishop of Moray, and the Abbot of Scone. Long years of trial followed in which we search in vain for any record of the Scottish church, whether as acting or suffering. But in 1317, after the triumph of Bannockburn, it again emerges into notice, and on this occasion through its struggle against the ascendency of Rome. Edward II., quelled by his late defeat, and hopeless of reducing Scotland by the usual form of warfare, had betaken himself to the pope; and at his request John XXII. issued a bull commanding a truce between England and Scotland for two years under penalty of excommunication, and sent two cardinals to enforce its observance. But although Bruce listened patiently to these pacific proposals, he refused to open the pope's sealed letters because they were not addressed to him with the title of KING, and would not agree to a truce without the consent of his parliament. In this way the bold asserter of Scottish independence vindicated his own religious rights and those of his country against the usurpations of the popedom. But still more decisive was the treatment of the sacred bulls and missives themselves, and the messenger who carried them, when the cardinals endeavoured, through their furtive introduction into Scotland, to compel the truce, which would only have been profitable for England. The unfortunate messenger, the father-guardian of a Minorite monastery, on his way to Berwick, was waylaid by an armed band, robbed of his bulls and other papers, and was left naked on the road.

In the following year (A.D. 1318), when the continuing successes of Bruce enabled him to add the duties of a legislator to those of a warrior, a parliament was assembled at which several laws were enacted for the protection of the kingdom and preservation of public order. On this occasion the rights and privileges of the church were first of all taken into account and confirmed anew in all their former integrity, and all encroachments upon or spoliations of its property and goods were strictly prohibited. Churchmen were also prohibited from carrying money out of the kingdom without the royal permission—a necessary check upon those purchasers of church preferments and privileges which now formed the chief traffic of Rome. All that the conclave in the meantime could inflict upon Scotland was the threat of excommunication; but of this the Scots seem to have made little account and to have passed it over in silence.

At length, in 1320, when the recovery of independence appeared certain, it was time to speak out. A national letter was to be drawn up and sent to the pope, not for the purpose of expressing contrition and craving forgiveness, but to justify what they had done, and indicate their future proceedings. This memorable document was written in the name of the earls, lords, barons, freeholders, and the whole community of Scotland, with the exception of the churchmen, who, on this occasion, could scarcely subscribe to such a cartel, and who therefore decorously stepped aside, although they no doubt looked on with deep unbreathing attention and hearty sympathy. The letter itself, which is

---
[1] *Fœdera*, II. 904.   [2] Ibid. 905.

given in full by our old historian,[1] is worthy of heedful notice. In the commencement its writers were careful to show that they were not a nation of yesterday, or worthy of being treated with scorn; in proof of which they referred to the ancient gests and histories in which their deeds were recorded. Their ancestry was derived from Greece and Egypt. Their fathers had migrated to Spain, and there settled for ages, the fiercest and strongest nations having been unable to dispossess or subdue them. Twelve hundred years after the exodus of the Israelites from the land of bondage, the Scots again migrated from Spain to the land in which they now dwelt, and there they had maintained their occupation against Norwegians, Danes, and Englishmen by whom they had been successively assailed, and yet had maintained their freedom throughout, as ancient histories testified. During this period one hundred and thirteen kings of their own blood without foreign admixture had reigned over them. Their conversion as a nation to Christianity, too, was of an early and honoured date, for it had been effected by the ministry of St. Andrew himself, that gentlest brother of the blessed St. Peter, who had chosen from thenceforth to be their patron saint. We may smile as we please at such apocryphal statements, and wonder that they could have been addressed to such a learned college as that of Rome. But these statements formed part of the veritable history of the age: the Italians could not impugn them, the English feared they might be true, and the Scots had proudly resisted and bravely died in the animating belief of their veracity.

After this preamble came the pith of their application, which was made in the spirit of a people proud of their claims, and confident that they were worthy of being heard. "Taking all these things," they added, "into account, and regarding both kings and people as the flock of the brother of the blessed Saint Peter, your predecessors endowed them with many favours and privileges, so that under their protection our nation flourished in peace and freedom; until that powerful king of England, the father of him that now is, under the pretext of unity and alliance, hostilely invaded us while the kingdom was without a head, the people fearing neither fraud nor injury, and being at that time unpractised in war. The injuries, slaughters, and deeds of violence, the plunderings, conflagrations, imprisoning of prelates, burning of monasteries, spoiling and slaying of religious men, and other enormities which he inflicted upon the said people, sparing neither age, degree, nor sex, no man could tell or fully understand, unless he had learned them by experience. From which innumerable evils we have been freed, through the favour of Him who, after wounding, cureth and maketh whole, by that most able prince, our lord and sovereign Robert. He, like another Maccabeus or Joshua, endured toils and trials, privations and dangers with a cheerful heart, that he might deliver his people and inheritance from the hand of the enemy; and him, also, divine ordination, our own laws and usages which we are resolved to maintain to the death, the law of succession, and the due assent and consent of all of us, have made our chief and king. To him by whom deliverance has been wrought to our nation, and for the protection of our liberty, we do adhere; and on account of his rights and deserts we shall continue to adhere to him in all things. But should he desist from his enterprise, and be inclined to subject us or the kingdom to the King of England or the English, and become the subverter of his own and our rights, then, him also we shall immediately strive to expel, and will choose for us another king, who may be better fitted to protect us: for, as long as a hundred of us remain alive, we will never in any case submit to the dominion of England. It is not for riches, glory, or distinction that we fight, but only for freedom, which no good man will forego except with life itself.

"Hence it is, reverend father and lord, that, bowing the knees of our hearts, we entreat your holiness with all the urgency of prayer, that as the earthly vicegerent of Him who is no respecter of persons, and who makes no distinction between Jew and Greek, Scot and Englishman, you would look with paternal eyes upon the afflictions brought upon ourselves and upon the church of God by the English and the King of England, whose own possessions ought to suffice him, seeing England was formerly wont to be enough for seven or more kings. Deign to admonish and exhort him, that he would allow us, Scotsmen, who dwell in a poor remote country, and who seek nothing but what is our own, to remain undisturbed. To obtain this quiet we are willing to grant to him whatever we can concede, respect being had to our national rights. It concerns you, holy father, to do this, who see how the cruelty of the Pagans rages against Christians for the chastisement of their sins, and how the boundaries of Christendom are becoming daily more contracted. You can also perceive how much it would derogate from your renown in future records if (which heaven forbid) the church in any portion of it should be obscured, or give cause for reproach, under your administration.

---

[1] *Scotichronicon*, lib. xiii. 1, 2, 3.

"Let this consideration rouse the Christian princes, who, assigning groundless causes, pretend that they cannot go to the defence of the Holy Sepulchre, from the wars which they have to maintain against their neighbours. A more veritable cause of this unwillingness is, that in subduing their weaker neighbours they find that they have a more immediate profit, with less trouble and resistance. He knows who knows all things how gladly our aforesaid lord and king and ourselves would go thither, if the English king would consent to let us go in peace: and this we now declare and testify to the vicar of Christ and the whole Christian world. But should your holiness give too credulous an ear to the reports of the English, and refuse to credit our sincerity or to desist from favouring them to our destruction, we do believe that to you will be imputed by the Most High the destruction of bodies, the perdition of souls, and all the other mischiefs that may ensue whether on our part or theirs.

"Prepared like dutiful children to yield to you all obedience as the vicar of God himself, we commit our cause to the protection of the supreme Sovereign and Judge; casting our cares upon him, and firmly trusting that he will inspire us with valour, and bring our enemies to nought."

It will be seen at once that this application, simple and even rude though in many points it may appear, was yet a masterpiece of diplomacy. Every argument, whether political or religious, every threat that could deter or promise that might persuade, was brought forward in due place, and with admirable concatenation, to win a favourable verdict from such an arbiter as the pope. It is impossible, too, not to admire its independent spirit, so much in contrast to the appeals of other nations addressed to the papal conclave. It will be seen, also, that among the offered inducements was the promise of a Scottish crusade for the recovery of the Holy Sepulchre. That this promise on the part of the heroic Bruce, unlike that of so many other sovereigns of the age, was made in full sincerity, there can be no doubt; it was his favourite wish during life; and the impossibility of its fulfilment was the chief theme of his dying regrets, when he ordered his heart to be conveyed to the sacred tomb. The pope was moved, and the result was that he sent to Edward II. recommending him to desist from warring against Scotland. So well, too, had the pontiff been schooled by this lesson, that in desiring the cessation of the war, he speaks of it in the very words of the manifesto, where it mentioned "the destruction of bodies, the perdition of souls, and all the other mischiefs that might ensue from it."[1] On further occasions, also, he continued to manifest a gracious relenting towards Scotland and its king. Their cause, indeed, was in the ascendent, at every step they were now successful, and it did not suit the papal policy to commit itself against what might yet prove the winning side. This altered mood towards the stiff-necked and rebellious Scots, although chary in its manifestations from fear of alienating England, seems to have been confirmed by Randolph's memorable embassy to the court of Rome, and it continued till the close of Bruce's reign, when the peace of Northampton made such hesitation no longer necessary; for, by one article of the treaty, the King of England was pledged to employ his mediation in obtaining from the papal court a revocation of all spiritual processes against Scotland and its excommunicated sovereign.

Such is the scanty, though not unimportant history of the Scottish church during this eventful period. It was a period of military struggle and political change, in which no national church could well have a separate record, and where most of its movements were but auxiliary to those great secular proceedings in which the national existence itself was at stake. But that the clergy were steadily advancing in influence, and still more in wealth, even in spite of such untoward circumstances, is evident from the example of one of the most eminent of their order—Lamberton, Bishop of St. Andrews. He held his office for the long period of thirty years; and although, at the commencement of his political career, he veered, like the other men of mark, from the cause of his country to that of England, and again from the English to the patriotic side, he was yet an able and influential supporter of the cause of Bruce, for which he suffered a long imprisonment in England, and was not released till the death of Edward I. He died while the treaty of Northampton was pending. He erected the costly abbey buildings of St. Andrews, and made them his usual residence. One of his servants, astonished at his liberality, asked him, "Why do you lay out such great sums for the monastery, and neglect to build for yourself?" "I hope, before I die, to build more than my successors shall well maintain," was the bishop's confident answer. The promise was fully performed, for, besides repairing his palace of St. Andrews, he built mansions at Monimail, Torry, Dairsie, Inchmurdach, Kettins, and other places, for himself and his successors. This inordinate love of ecclesiastical architecture, which was so greatly in contrast to the poverty of the country,

---

[1] *Fœdera*, t. iii. p. 847.

appears to have become a passion with our early Scottish prelates, and was no doubt inspired by those splendid religious edifices which were already so numerous in Scotland. Besides these spirited undertakings, Lamberton finished the cathedral church of St. Andrews, which had been many years in building, and dedicated it with great solemnity in 1318.[1]

CHAPTER XII.

HISTORY OF SOCIETY (1286-1329).

Condition of Scotland at the commencement of this period—Questionable value of its prosperity—Its sudden interruption—Condition of the country for resistance at the commencement of the war with England—Its artificial defences—Castles and fortresses—Description of the baronial castles—Modes of siege and resistance—Natural defences of the country—Mountains and fastnesses—Woods and forests of Scotland—Military condition of the people—Chivalry—Its introduction and improvement—Armour and equipments of the Scottish knights of this period—Weapons of the common soldiers—Their mode of fighting—Warlike priests of the period—Political state of Scotland—Establishment of the law of royal succession—Revenues of the Scottish kings, and whence derived—Administration of justice—Scottish justiciaries—Royalties and regalities—Multiplication of regalities and their dangerous tendency—First establishment of Scottish parliaments—Causes of the introduction of the popular element—Representatives of burghs—State of Scottish commerce—Its depression from the war with England—Efforts of the English kings to close the foreign ports against it—Coinage of Scotland—Its value in labour and produce—Agriculture of Scotland—Its scantiness—Impediments to the cultivation of the soil—Resources of the people from agriculture, pasturage, and fisheries—Tenure of land in Scotland—State of the free peasantry—Of the slaves and bondmen of the soil—Games and sports of the people—Minstrelsy—Popular ballads—Eminent men—John Duns Scotus—John Bassol.

The reign of Alexander III. appears to have been the happiest era in ancient Scottish history. It was a period in which the spirit of national improvement, now wakened into life, had achieved in a few years a whole century of progress. The kingly authority was establishing its pre-eminence over the rude chieftainship by which it had been rivalled. The law of royal succession, hitherto such a fruitful source of contention, was now so distinctly understood and so cordially recognized that the throne itself was occupied as peacefully as any ordinary patrimony. And although as yet there was no regular parliament by which the wishes of the people could be expressed and their interests maintained, the sovereign authority in all important public measures seems to have been exercised chiefly with the advice and assistance of the nobility, whose power acted as a counterpoise and a check upon the despotic tendencies of monarchical rule. The Teutonic races also—Norwegian, Saxon, Norman, and Flemish—intruders into a land which they were only beginning to claim as their home, and whose right of occupancy rested only on strength to keep what their courage had won, were from that very necessity combining themselves into one people and acting together with a harmony and cordiality which contrasted with their discordance in other countries, and especially in England. While the political condition of the kingdom was thus so greatly advanced, the industrial arts were exhibiting a similar improvement. As we have already seen, commerce was calling forth the active enterprise, and manufactures the ingenuity of the people; and amidst this new stir of occupation it was natural that there should be "wealth of ale and bread, of wine and wax, of game and glee." But was this progress too quick, this exuberance too premature to be lasting? Was it necessary that Scotland should acquire that iron endurance of constitution and invincible persistency of character which have so singularly fitted her for her national mission by an ordeal which few nations could have survived? These are questions which will occur to the reflective, and an answer in the affirmative can scarcely be withheld. It was not a mere random accident that threw Scotland so rudely back and compelled it to commence a new career.

This terrible conflict for independence—this breast-to-breast grapple for life itself as well as liberty, which was to last not for a generation or two but for whole centuries—having thus commenced in earnest, the condition of Scotland for such a furnace of trial, and its primary

---

[1] *Scotichron.*; Spottiswood's *History of the Church of Scotland*, p. 54.

effects upon the people at the commencement, become the chief subjects of consideration at the present period of our history.

In commencing such a survey we begin with the artificial defences of the country — the castles, forts, and ramparts which every people erect for defence against invasion, or even as restraints against internal commotion. But here, unfortunately, we meet with little else than half-forgotten sites or mere fragments of ruins, instead of solid buildings or falling edifices. Even of our time-honoured castles little else than the name remains, while the building itself is of a later date. The stern but wise policy of Bruce, which in the first case decreed the demolition of these edifices, and the barbarism of modern times which has swept away their vestiges, have made an inquiry into this subject both difficult and uncertain. But a country of such stately monasteries could not be without strong castles, were it merely to protect them; and the same skill which sufficed to erect the abbey of Melrose was sufficient for the construction of a fortress. The Scoto-Normans and Saxons also, who needed such defences in a land that was not their own, and who were regarded as intruders, were not likely to forget the strong habitations which they had occupied in England nor willing to dispense with similar shelter. Thus castle-building must have gone on from the period of Malcolm Canmore, and the fortresses of England have served as their models. And that such protections were not few we learn from an incidental notice that during the earlier part of the reign of Alexander III. the northern coast of Scotland was well defended from invasion by castles of stone, and that these were put in a state of defence when the coming of Haco was apprehended.

Taking the baronial castles of England under the reign of King John as the type of those that existed in Scotland during the earlier part of the thirteenth century, we can in some measure imagine their appearance and their fitness for defence. The site was chosen with respect to difficulty of access, and every advantage, whether of land or water, was carefully taken into account. Hence the picturesque position which, in such a country as Scotland, many of these strongholds occupied, although beauty was the last quality thought of in their erection; and a castle whose towers and battlements were built so high as to surmount the danger of escalade necessarily formed one of the most striking features of the landscape. Where the sea or a lake was not at hand to guard the approach to the outer wall, a ditch or moat was made for the purpose. When this had been crossed by the besiegers the main gate was to be entered; and this was made a trying task, as instead of being level with the ground it was elevated by steps to a considerable height above it, and secured in its only approach by a drawbridge that was raised by those within. But even when this gate was won, it and the tower with which it was connected could be destroyed by the defenders; and the assailants were opposed by a second and stronger portal that was closed against them by a heavy portcullis, which descended through a groove in the solid wall. If the enemy sought to shun the multiplied difficulties of the main gate, they could find no other entrance except a small sally-port which was under the drawbridge, but so high that it could only be reached by escalade, and so narrow that only one man could enter at a time. When these outworks were successively won the main building was still capable of holding out; for its entrances were rendered difficult by steep narrow stairs where a single soldier could hold a whole troop at bay, and defended by strong doors of oak that were clamped and riveted with iron. In addition to these means for a stout and successful resistance, the main building and its approaches were provided with blind passages to mislead the enemy, which, when forced, presented at their extremity nothing but a solid wall. There were also towers and arches for the same purpose, being apparently of light structure, but which, when assailed, were found to be absolute rocks of solid masonry and the strongest parts of the building. The means of the besieged to annoy their assailants at every step were also proportioned to the number and strength of their defences. Instead of windows the walls were plentifully provided with loopholes, from behind which the garrison, sheltered by the peculiar structure of these openings, could gall the advancing enemy with showers of stones and arrows, and at every change of movement the assailants were subject to front and flank discharges of the same kind from the ramparts. Within the covered ways, also, there were openings in the roof for pouring down boiling water or molten lead and pitch.[1] That such castles should so often have been taken and retaken might appear surprising, did we not know that the courage of the assailant is generally of a more active and enterprising character than that of the assailed; that no enterprise has as yet been found too difficult for human daring; and that wherever the mason can climb with his tools the soldier can ascend with his weapons.

While such were the means of security and

---

[1] Of the descriptions of ancient castles one of the fullest and best is that of Edward King in *Archæologia*, vol. iv. p. 365, from which these brief notices have been chiefly taken.

defence, it was necessary that the lord of the castle should also have within its walls the means of maintaining his almost regal state and living in comfort. While, therefore, the first and second stories of the great or main tower were loopholed and occupied by his military retainers, the third or upper story, which was lighted by Gothic windows, formed the residence of the baron. Here he had space enough to accommodate his guests, who in those early days of simple life could be content with incredibly narrow quarters and beds of the most primitive material. Here he had his armoury, in which, at any sudden alarm, himself, his friends, and chief officers could be speedily harnessed from head to heel. And here, above all, was the great hall or state apartment in which he presided in full grandeur either as lord of the revel or feudal superior and justiciary of the district. It generally occupied nearly the whole length and breadth of the main tower; its roof was of carved oak; and at either end of the apartment was a large recess which served as a fireplace, having a semicircular stone seat behind the fire. In the upper part of the building was contained the artillery of the castle—the war-wolfs, mangonels, and ballistæ, which, in case of need, could quickly be hoisted up and planted upon the battlements. The store for holding provisions and the dungeon for prisoners were generally in the lowest and strongest part of the building.

In laying regular siege to such fortresses the means adopted were such as necessity and military skill have suggested in every age and country. The garrison was plied with volleys of stones and arrows to facilitate the advance of the storming party upon the fosse, outer wall, and drawbridge. A large beam of wood that served the purpose of a battering-ram kept up an incessant play upon the wall until a breach was effected. A testudo of strong boards covered with hides was often wheeled up to the walls, under shelter of which the assailants worked with shovel and pickaxe to undermine the solid masonry that could not otherwise be shaken. A more laborious process, when these means were ineffectual, was to erect movable wooden towers that overtopped the walls, manned with archers and slingers, and provided with a drawbridge that could be let down upon the battlements as soon as the volleys of missiles had cleared them of their defenders. Sometimes a pile of dry branches was heaped up and kindled at the foot of a wall or tower, that the smoke might bewilder the garrison and the flame crack the solid masonry or set fire to the building. If the castle was surrounded by a stream or lake, dams were built to let the waters accumulate so as to flood the besieged and compel them to yield.

Such were the principal structures for defence at the commencement of the war of independence, varying, of course, in degree from the stately pile of the powerful noble to the humble fortalice of the knight or squire. But of a higher and still more ample description, both for accommodation and resistance, must have been the royal castles, of which there were not less than twenty-three when they were delivered into the hands of Edward I. as arbiter of the royal succession. These had been erected for the protection of the Border against England, for the maintenance of order among the more unsettled districts, or as barriers against the invasions of the predatory clans of the Highlands. But in the war which followed Bruce quickly perceived that the English, from their greater resources and higher skill in fortification, were able to convert these into most formidable chains and bridles of the national liberty; and therefore as often as he could retake them he doomed them to ruin without scruple. The same disinterestedness animated his heroic friend, the good Lord James Douglas, who repeatedly razed his own paternal home as readily as he would have demolished a Northumbrian castle. The surest defences of Scotland from henceforth were to be sought among its natural ramparts, and the battle for freedom was to be fought among its rocks and morasses, its mountains, dells, and valleys—those places where Liberty is contented with a bower or a cave when the land can no longer afford her a settled home.

In every age until the present a mountainous country has proved the best of safeguards against a richer and more powerful enemy; and it has only been in modern times, when strategy seems to have reached its culminating point, that the hours of a stronghold's resistance can be calculated with mathematical certainty, and the defenders of a mountain be more effectually marked off by a cannonade or turned by a countermarch. Of the military advantages afforded by the Scottish mountains, and the alacrity with which they were manned by their bold defenders, the history of the period abounds in instances. Aware of the advantages of such a position, the English seldom cared to attack an army so posted; and their chief effort, therefore, was to allure it into the plain, where their own superiority in arms, discipline, numbers, and cavalry gave them every chance of victory. Of all the generals of his day Bruce seems to have been the only one who not merely understood the art of making such a defence available, but of rendering it useless to the enemy when they endeavoured to turn it against himself. It was in this last particular that his military excellence appears so transcendant as to place him in that front rank of men, of whom each nation has seldom more than one representative. Of the facts illustrative of this peculiar superiority we have only to allude to the signal defeat which he inflicted upon the Lord of Lorn among his own steep mountain passes at Dalry near Tyndrum, and his victory over Edward II. in his almost inaccessible post near Biland. But not only the sides and summits of the Scottish mountains were excellent points of defence, but also their bases, where those valleys which are now drained and well-cultivated fields were at that early period nothing but mosses and swamps, and an army having one of these in front or flank could scarcely be assailed by cavalry. Even to the English infantry an advance through such an intrenchment was full of peril, honey-combed as the ground was with quaking bog and hidden water-spring, which nothing but a thorough acquaintanceship with the locality could avoid. An assailing army, however superior, could scarcely struggle through such obstacles with impunity, even though they had guides to lead them, when they had such an enemy as Wallace or Bruce watching their advance and ready to receive them.

Among the natural defences of a country not the least important are its woods and forests. In these the military musters can be made in silence and secrecy. They furnish those places of ambushment in which a band can lurk undetected until the moment of onset. In the event of a defeat they afford shelters and rallying points for the vanquished which the pursuers are compelled to respect. In reading the history of Scotland the frequent mention of its numerous forests, and the military uses to which they were turned, as well as the stirring exploits of adventure and battle by which they were signalized, form a strange contrast to the aspect of the country in modern times, when its want of trees had become proverbial. But no historical fact is more certain than that Scotland was well wooded at those early periods, and that it abounded in forests of large extent. Many remains, indeed, of that vast Caledonian Forest, whose dark and apparently boundless depths arrested the career of the Roman legions, were still in existence to try the courage of the English invaders. Of these the forests of Ettrick, Selkirk, Jedburgh, Melrose, Boyne, and Forres, so often mentioned in the annals of this period, formed but a small portion of a chain that seems to have stretched over the whole extent of the kingdom. There was, indeed, too much wood for a people that needed sustenance as well as shelter; and there was no William the Conqueror or William Rufus to arrest the progress of demolition in behalf of the wolf, the wild boar, and the wild ox that herded in its deep recesses. Farms were to be cleared for ploughing or pasturage; trees were to be felled for fuel or building; and amidst such urgent wants, the diminution of a forest would go on with the ruthlessness of a confirmed habit, and with greater rapidity than the need strictly warranted. The English, too, when they invaded the country, or established themselves in any wooded district, were eager to destroy those shelters, from which they were exposed to continual attacks. Thus, in a single inroad into Scotland conducted by the Duke of Lancaster, we are told by the historian Knighton that 80,000 English hatchets were employed in the work of clearance. The continued burning of the Scottish towns, also, at each fresh invasion, and the task of rebuilding them, made the nearest wood be regarded as a quarry, from which materials could be obtained on the easiest terms. These circumstances are enough to show that the destruction of timber was likely to be a process both speedy and complete; and that the time would come when this superfluity would be less regretted than the absolute dearth that was sure to follow. But such a consideration was too prophetic for the Scots of the thirteenth century; and Edward I. and his successors were made to feel that their greatest obstacles to a complete Scottish conquest lay in these vast well-sheltered recesses, which contained an enemy that could not be reached, as well as dangers that might not be safely defied.

Scotland having thus so many defensible points that the whole land was a natural fortress, the military appointments of the people themselves come next to be considered. And here that "cheap defence of nations"—chivalry, and chivalry in reference to the knighthood of Scotland, demands its due priority of notice. This institution appears to have been utterly unknown among the Celtic nations, and to have been introduced into Europe by the Teutonic tribes, who, under the various names of Saxon, Dane, and Norman, continued to improve it, until from a rude form it expanded into a magnificent system, when it became the governing spirit of the middle ages and the great arbiter of the fate of nations. Among the Anglo-Saxons before the Norman conquest of England we find that the institution of chivalry essentially partook of a religious character; the young warrior was dubbed, not by a layman, but a priest; and being thus honoured, he was bound to obey the church and advance its interests as the highest of knightly duties. But the Norman conquerors, by whom this Saxon form of chivalry was quickly supplanted, were so profane as to laugh to scorn the idea of a priest-made knight, and would only receive the distinction from a layman of high military fame and rank. It was in this secular character that chivalry was probably brought into Scotland, and by those discontented Norman adventurers who quitted the service of William the Conqueror for that of Malcolm Canmore. From the Bayeux Tapestry and the figures upon early seals we can form some idea of the appearance and warlike habiliments of these fathers and founders of our Scottish chivalry. The new Norman comer, who entered the gates of Dunfermline, and rode through its narrow, hovel-covered streets towards the palace in quest of something better than mere protection and a home, was a personage worth looking at. He brought with him nothing but a skilful eye, a strong arm, and a fearless heart—but he knew that with these alone his countrymen in every quarter of Europe were winning their way to princely honours and possessions. Upon his head is a cone-shaped helmet, having an outward-sloping bar in front, called the nasal, but as yet with no cheek-pieces to cover the rest of the face. His body and legs are protected by a hauberk composed of steel rings set up edgeways and stitched upon a stiff leather garment resembling a modern surtout or overcoat, and reaching below the knee. From the neck of his hauberk hangs a sort of tippet or cowl, also of ring-covered leather; and this, when he is about to enter into battle, he can hook up over the chin and fasten to the nasal in front, so that nothing of his face will be visible but the eyes, that flash with the joy of combat or the hope of victory. His shield, which usually hangs from his neck, except in close hand-to-hand combat, when it can be quickly transferred to the left arm, is of the form of a kite or pear; his sword, that rattles against his ring armour, is of great breadth in the blade next the hilt; and at the head of his long lance, which he holds proudly upright, is a gay streamer, probably intended at first only for ornament, or to frighten an enemy's horse by its fluttering, but which has now become the owner's personal cognizance, as well as the symbol of his knightly rank. How soon that little streamer will become a broad banner to attest its lordship over a hundred hills! The gate of the palace closes upon the stranger, and his proud armed step is welcomed from the throne of which he is to become an ornament and protector.

Such were the earliest equipments of knighthood in Scotland; and it must be confessed that they were both scanty and rude, as compared with those of chivalry in its prime. But in Scotland as in England there was quickly manifested the desire of a gayer, easier, and more protective panoply, as well as more numerous weapons of offence. These stages of improvement, however, were so numerous, that instead of particularizing them we can only give their results, as they were manifested at the commencement of the war. A Scottish knight of the Wallace and Bruce period, instead of a stiff hauberk of leather covered with rings, was now protected by a flexible garment of chain-work, in which the links were interwoven and connected together like the meshes of a net; and this was properly the coat of mail (French *maille*, Latin *macula*) so often mentioned in our early histories. The hands that had hitherto been unprotected were now guarded by a prolongation of the hauberk sleeves as far as the tips of the fingers; and the conical helmet, that had passed into the barrel shape, and been furnished with its ventagil or vizor of steel bars to guard the face, was settling into a still more graceful form by being rounded at the top. The legs and feet were also protected by coverings of the same kind of mail that enveloped the body. But the superiority of plate armour over yielding chain-work in guarding against blows that could crush as well as pierce was beginning to be felt; and at the commencement of the present period defences of this kind were used as caps to guard the shoulders and knees, and sometimes also in the form of greaves to protect the legs. This improvement was so acceptable, that at the close of this period the English knights—and, we may presume, those of Scotland also—were armed half in plate and half in mail. It was not long after that knights and men-at-arms were covered with plate armour from head to heel, the chain-work being only retained in small portions, where flexibility of joint was most needed, or where the wearer wished to be fenced with the double protection of a mail as well as plate covering. Over this panoply was worn a surcoat made of cloth or linen, sometimes much shorter before than behind; and as this mantle was a distinction of knighthood and noble rank, as well as the cognizance by which the wearer could be known, locked up as he otherwise was in a complete inclosure of steel, it was embroidered with those figures by which he could be recognized, and which afterwards constituted the heraldic distinctions of his family. It was not long, also, until what might be called the foppery of knighthood required that the surcoat, especially at tournaments and princely festivals, should be made of silk and richly adorned with embroidery of gold. The chief offensive weapons of knighthood during this period, besides the sword and lance, were the anelace, which was a strong broad dagger tapering to a fine point; the estoc, which was a short stabbing sword; the mace, which requires no description; and the battle-axe. This last weapon, with which Bruce dealt such a signal blow on the helmet of De Bohun at Bannockburn, became a favourite weapon with the Scottish knights, who, according to the testimony of Froissart, could wield it with one as well as both hands, and with such dexterity as to baffle the more agile movements of an antagonist's sword.

In speaking of the equipments of a knight for battle it would be unpardonable to omit his horse, as it was the companion of his warlike adventures and the original badge of his superiority over the mere rabblement of foot-soldiers, while as yet they were nothing better than a mob. Before the war of independence commenced the Scottish knights, although greatly fewer in numbers, seem to have been as well mounted as those of England. A charge of the Scottish cavalry, headed by Prince Henry, rent the English ranks asunder like a cobweb and almost won the battle of the Standard; and at the battle of Largs the Scottish knights were mounted on Spanish horses completely barbed and of great value. This mention of barbed steeds introduces another peculiarity in the knightly equipments of the period. In the closing of a charge or the confusion of a melee it was evident that the chief danger must fall upon the unfortunate steed, and that when it was struck down the heavily-armed rider had the chance of being useless or a prisoner. The horse, therefore, was now cased in armour as well as the knight, having a sort of helmet called a chamfron to defend its head and face, and a covering of steel plates or chain-work to defend the chest and flanks. A horse in this warlike trim was said to be barded or barbed. Man and steed, thus equally harnessed and ready to break through the opposing ranks like an iron statue set in motion by the touch of the magician, must have looked the very perfection of warlike improvement. And yet this was little else than the panoply worn by the Parthian cavalry more than a thousand years earlier, when they brought the Roman legions under Crassus to an unwonted pause at the fatal battle of Carrhæ. But after the victory of the Scots at Largs we hear little more of their troops of mailed horsemen, and for this silence sufficient causes can be assigned. The ruinous invasions of Edward I. and the poverty they occasioned put an end to the costly importation of foreign horses, so that the Scots had to content themselves with their own small-sized Galloways, which were excellent for nimble conveyance but altogether unfit for the shock of battle. Their war for liberty was chiefly of a defensive character, and therefore to be maintained among their own mountains and morasses, where cavalry was generally useless; and when they carried their retaliations into England they relied more upon the nimbleness of their movements and the excellence of their encampments than pitched battles on the open plain. The Scottish knights and nobles, indeed, retained their large-boned heavily-armed war-horses, to cope in battle with the knights of England, or for the purposes of show or a tournament; but in other respects they seem to have contented themselves with a hobin or light horse for the march, and to have fought on foot like the rest.

Of the weapons of the common soldiers a brief notice will suffice, as this is a department which has been forestalled in the account of the battles of the period. The invasion of Edward I. and his establishment of garrisons over the country must have been accompanied by the entire or partial disarming of the natives, and at the commencement of the campaigns of Wallace we find no such mention of military equipments as the earlier Scottish armies had possessed under the leading of their sovereigns. Of defensive armour they had almost none, while their chief offensive weapon was the long spear—a weapon easily made, and only requiring a stout heart and vigorous arm to wield with effect. Of necessity, therefore, they became peculiarly a nation of spearmen fitted for defensive warfare; and an array so armed, whether gathered into a compact phalanx or divided into schiltrons, could only hope to oppose the terrible onsets of the English cavalry by standing unflinchingly shoulder to shoulder and receiving the charge upon a bristling rampart of steel points. And how bravely and successfully this was generally done the history of these wars sufficiently testifies. When the country, however, became more settled Bruce, who saw the necessity of defensive armour for the complete equipment of an effective soldier, directed his cares to this subject; and from his ordinance of arms, published A.D. 1319,[1] we learn how the different classes of his subjects were expected to be armed at this period of his reign. Every gentleman who had land to the value of £10, or movable property to the same amount, was to provide himself for military service with a hacqueton, a steel helmet, gloves of plate, and a sword and spear. Every one who held land or property of a less amount was to have an iron jack, an iron

---

[1] *Cartular. Aberbroth.* p. 295.

head-piece, and gloves of plate. Of the lowest class of soldiers no man was to be without a spear, or a bow and a sheaf of arrows. Had these enactments been complied with to the letter, and for subsequent periods, a Scottish army would not only have been better fenced against the deadly cloth-yard shaft of England, but able in some measure to requite it in kind. But where the choice lay between a spear which could be easily handled, and a bow that required the apprenticeship of half a lifetime, the former was certain to be generally preferred; and therefore during the present period we hear almost nothing of the effective services of the Scottish archery.

In a sketch of the state of society during this warlike period one class of brave and very influential combatants must not be omitted. These were the prelates and high church dignitaries of Scotland. If we are offended at finding these ministers of peace careering, lance in rest, we must also take into account the age and the occasion. Throughout Europe the Crusades had inspired the clergy with such belligerent tastes as were not likely to be soon relinquished; and every country at this period could boast of its valiant bishops, whose favourite seat was a war-saddle and whose most cogent argument was a lance-thrust. The least unscrupulous, indeed, in this portentous array of soldier-priests, that extended over several ages, was the Bishop of Beauvais, the dreaded antagonist of Cœur de Lion himself, who in the latter part of his military career showed such respect for the canon law as to wield no weapon but a massive club, with which he could brain his antagonists without the sin of blood-shedding. And with few of these was the temptation to battle so strong or the cause so justifiable as in the case of the Scottish hierarchy. Nursed in civil commotions where mere self-defence obliged every one to be a soldier, and having lands and possessions which in such a rude age the sanctions of religion alone could not fully guard, every bishop and abbot, in common with the lay lords, had his armiger and scutifer, his men-at-arms and tenants of military service. In such a state the invasion of Edward I., and the national bondage that menaced all right and possession, whether secular or sacred, roused them from their retirements and summoned them to the field as to a holy war in which they might freely participate. In this manner Wishart, Bishop of Glasgow, joined Sir William Wallace. Thus Lamberton, Bishop of St. Andrews, became an active partisan of Bruce, as did also the Abbot of Scone. These three eminent church dignitaries did not scruple to wear harness under their rochets, and when taken prisoners by the English it was in knightly panoply. We have also noticed how readily Sinclair, Bruce's own bishop, started to the onset against the invaders at Donibristle, as if it had been a fit portion of his sacred calling. It would be ungenerous to inquire how learning was prosecuted or its interests advanced under such priestly guardianship. It was not to be expected of these mailed hands that they should transcribe the pages of the ancient classics or turn over the leaves of Augustine or Chrysostom.

In passing from the military to the political condition of Scotland during this period our notices must be both brief and unsatisfactory. What, indeed, can be predicated of any country during so short a time, in which a minority, an interregnum, a usurpation, an anarchy, and finally a regular rule succeed each other in such restless rapidity; and above all, where an arbitrary conqueror could not only tamper with the old national institutions, but blot out their very memory at pleasure? In such a strait we can only glean and gather the few relics that have survived, and attempt from these to form a shadowy outline rather than a life-expressing picture.

The law of royal succession, formerly so fruitful a source of family contest and national change in Scotland, had now been adapted to the usages of Europe and had received the full concurrence of the Scots. This they fully showed at a time when urgent circumstances would have most tempted them to set it aside. At the death of Alexander III. there was no lack of brave and powerful nobles collaterally descended from the royal family; but in preference to these the Scots recognized for their sovereign Margaret of Norway, child, female, and foreigner though she was, because she was Alexander's grand-daughter. In like manner, when Bruce succeeded to the permanent occupation of the throne, his claim was founded neither upon his superior power nor yet upon the fact that he had made Scotland a free kingdom, but upon his being nearest of kin to the royal family after the more direct claims of Baliol and Comyn had been extinguished. With this recognition of the law of royal succession as it prevailed in other countries the same feudalism naturally sprang up which was established throughout Europe at large, and with which a king could no more dispense than Charlemagne with his nine peers or Arthur with his knights of the Round Table.

The royal revenues for the maintenance of his court and authority which Alexander III. enjoyed, and to which Bruce and his descendants succeeded, were derived from various sources, the principal of which were the following:—The rents and produce of royal lands and manors. The customs levied on agricultural produce under the name of *can* or *kain*. The customs on exported wool, woolfels, and hides; on foreign trade and shipping, and on articles of native manufacture. The escheats of estates that fell to the crown by forfeiture or failure in succession. The wardship and marriage of heirs who were under the guardianship of the crown. The presents or benevolences which every great tenant of the crown was required to pay on important royal occasions, such as a coronation, the king's marriage, the marriage of one of his sons or daughters, &c. The state which the Anglo-Scottish sovereigns had maintained from these sources of revenue has been described in a former chapter. Their progressive increase, growing as they must have done with the wealth of the country, had enabled Alexander III. to exhibit an amount of regal splendour which none of his predecessors had reached. This was opportunely done when he repaired to London to attend the coronation of Edward I., for he bestowed such a rich and popular largesse as must have dazzled the crowd and given them a high idea of the riches of a Scottish king. On this occasion he and his attendants dismounted from their richly-caparisoned foreign steeds and turned them loose among the throng as prizes to whoever could catch them. This example was so infectious that the English nobles followed it, and thus the populace were unexpectedly regaled gratis with a horse-lottery full of rich prizes.[1] When Bruce had restored the kingdom to its former independence one of his first cares was to re-establish the royal revenue, which had suffered great waste and alienation during the previous anarchy; and this task, we can well imagine, he found as difficult and far more ungracious than the rigorous military campaigns in which his endurance had been put to the test. Indeed it is not unlikely that his measures to this effect were among those unrecorded causes by which the latter part of his reign was troubled through the discontents of his nobles, whose usurpation of crown lands was thus defeated.

In the system established for the administration of justice at the commencement of this period our knowledge is still imperfect. The patriarchal rule, which prevailed in Scotland even after the accession of the Anglian dynasty, when the king was the dispenser of justice as well as its legislator, could only be practicable in a rude and early age; and the picture of David I., as given by an English historian,[2] sitting on certain days at his palace gate, like an ancient patriarch, to give judgment to all who repaired to him, does not appear to have been repeated by any of his successors. As the kingdom became larger and more populous all that royalty could effect was to make a progress over the country, to ascertain that its delegates were rightly discharging their duty—to judge the judges themselves and punish their delinquencies or shortcomings. Such were the annual journeys which Alexander III. was in the habit of making; and they indicated a state of society still unsettled, and requiring a careful guardianship. Before the death of this king it is supposed that law was administered by two great judges, one called *Justiciarius Scotiæ*, whose charge comprised the whole of Scotland beyond the Forth; and the other, *Justiciarius Loudoniæ*, whose authority extended over the whole of the country south of the two firths. But, besides these, there is occasionally mentioned a third magistrate, called the *Justiciarius ex parte boreali aquæ de Forth*, whose jurisdiction and office cannot be distinctly ascertained. On the subjugation of Scotland Edward I. endeavoured to assimilate the forms of its jurisprudence to those of England by a more minute subdivision of the country and the appointment of more justiciars; but the plan, however excellent in itself, was thrown off by the people, with the other tokens of national vassalage, as soon as they had recovered their liberty. When the framework of government was reconstructed by Robert Bruce, five justiciars appear to have been appointed as supreme judges of Scotland.[3]

By these great officers acting under the king, the recognized head of national law and justice, cases of litigation were tried and conclusive awards delivered. And yet they and their deputies were not the sole judges of the kingdom, but only of those portions of it which were comprised under the title of royalty, and as such subjected to the government of the king and judges of his own appointing. But, besides the royalty, there were numerous regalities scattered over the kingdom, originally crown grants bestowed upon the nobles or the church, and which enjoyed the right of self-government attached to them. At what time they obtained this formidable right is uncertain; but it appears in the first instance to have been conceded to the clergy, who established in consequence an exclusive jurisdiction over their own territories. So tempting a privilege was soon claimed in like manner by the nobility, who were too powerful to be refused; and thus each baron was enabled to erect his court and

---

[1] Knighton, p. 2461.   [2] Ethelred.   [3] Tytler's *History of Scotland*.

appoint his judge over his own domain, who decided in cases even of life and death irrespective both of kings and royal justiciars. In this way the authority of the sovereign was curtailed in extent and rivalled in power by every fresh crown grant; and these regalities continued to grow and multiply to an extent that threatened the royalty itself with final absorption. The evil was too strong to be cured, and the utmost that Bruce could attempt was its abatement. He therefore divided the immense estates that had lapsed to the crown by the treason or death of their owners into smaller baronies, which he bestowed upon his deserving followers, with the old rights of regality attached to them. But the new occupants were not the less eager to manifest their superiority and enjoy their power, because the means were so limited; and accordingly every little baron who held his land by this tenure was ready to erect his court, hold his trials, and exercise the full power of *fossa et furca*, although his dwelling might be but a single tower surrounded by a ditch, his territory a mile or two of heath, and his military array a dozen of jackmen. It was the lofty titles and high immunities of these barons, contrasted with their poverty and limited holdings, that afterwards so greatly puzzled the higher nobility of England, and formed such a tempting opportunity for bribery on the part of the English kings, when they found that Scotland could not be won or quieted by force. The immense political evils that accrued from this unfortunate multiplication of kinglings will be fully apparent in the subsequent stages of Scottish history.

Previous to the death of Alexander III. we find no distinct proof of a parliament properly so called having existed in Scotland. In great political emergencies, of which already there had been not a few, the Scottish kings had been wont to take counsel with the chief men of the nation—with the nobles in whose hands were the military resources, and with the higher clergy who were supposed to represent the intelligence and integrity of the country at large—and their decision, whatever it might be, had the force and effect of law, and was obeyed without disputation. Not only were the people unrepresented, but they do not seem to have felt the omission of a third estate in the national council as a grievance. Even the parliament which sat at Brigham in 1289, for the settlement of the most important difficulty which had as yet occurred in Scotland, consisted, besides the five regents, of nothing more than ten bishops, twelve earls, twenty-three abbots, eleven priors, and forty-eight barons; and these magnates, who negotiated with Edward I. under the title of the "Community of Scotland," were received and acknowledged by him as such. But events were now at hand which made the recognition of the people at large a matter of imperious necessity. A war for national liberty was to be fought, and the people who were to supply the strength and sinews of the battle must have some voice in the national council. How otherwise could their inclination be expressed or their concurrence secured? It is from this war, therefore, although we cannot ascertain at what precise point of it, that we find the commons beginning to be represented in the Scottish parliament. Because the origin of the change commences during this period, it has been often taken for granted that Edward I., the Justinian of England, was the author of this important improvement, and that therefore he may be excused for many of those permanent evils which his ambition entailed upon Scotland. But it would be strange if he had thus sought to give liberty to a people whom he was toiling to crush and enslave. Besides that the pressure of a general calamity and the necessity of a combined effort would naturally induce, and even compel the voice of the people to be admitted into the council of national deliberation, all the interests of Edward in the subjugation of Scotland were decidedly hostile to such an enfranchisement. It was from the people, headed by their favourite leaders, that the opposition first arose; and it was by them that his attempts were defeated. Was it likely, then, that so crafty a politician would so strengthen the popular element and give it a voice in the council, where it was certain to oppose him, more especially when a majority of lords and prelates were already on his side? It was only, therefore, when his tyranny began to display itself in treating the crowned Baliol as a vassal, and Scotland as a conquered province, that we first hear of the meeting of a parliament having its third estate—men who represented, as we are further told, the communities of the villages (or burghs) of the kingdom of Scotland.[1] The acts of this parliament were in full keeping with that popular element which had been infused into it. The Englishmen who had begun to settle in the country were banished out of Scotland. The estates of Edward's adherents in the country were confiscated. An immediate war with England was resolved on. The alliance with France, the enemy of England, was to be renewed and drawn more closely by a royal marriage.[2] From this date to the end of the period, as often as the succession of national difficulties required a parliament to be called, we always find the

---

[1] Rymer's *Fœdera*; *Scotichron.*   [2] *Scotichron.*

majores populi, the representatives of the burghs, forming an essential portion of the meeting.

As we have seen in a former chapter the commerce of Scotland at the death of Alexander III. had rapidly risen in importance and extent; and had the war with England not occurred, it is probable that the two nations would have maintained a rivalry of mercantile enterprise which would have redounded to the welfare of both. Nor was it merely the mercantile enterprise of towns or of the laity by which the resources of the country were called forth, its traffic enlarged, and its wealth increased. The clergy had also brought their influence and superior intelligence into such a profitable competition; and, however secular or selfish their aim might be, it is certain that they benefited the country, while they enriched their own community. The earliest of those privileged mercantile communities in Scotland, called gilds, were chiefly composed of monks. Every monastery that could command the advantage of water conveyance had generally a ship. Besides their cultivation of home produce for internal trade or exportation, the clergy were also careful to promote the fisheries, so abundant a source of national profit, which they were among the earliest to turn to the best account. It was not therefore to be wondered at if they soon became rich beyond the other communities, and turned their wealth into the profitable channels of banking and money-lending. In the old cartularies, from which the foregoing indications can be largely collected, we find that the wealthy monasteries were ready to accommodate with money loans, for which they exacted large profits and concessions. But upon this prosperous active mercantile career both of priest and layman there was laid a sudden and violent arrest, after which the nation was rudely thrown back into its former poverty. The mediæval wealth and grandeur of Berwick, that second Alexandria, its sudden capture, and speedy reduction into a mere military station and fortress—these melancholy changes only typified that Scottish commerce of which it was the great emporium. As soon as a momentary breathing interval had been found in consequence of his first successes, Sir William Wallace, now governor of the kingdom, directed his great natural sagacity and foresight to the restoration of the national commerce as the true source of the national strength and the best promise of its future stability; and one of his first negotiations was with the commercial towns of the Continent for the re-establishment of commercial interests between them and his own country. But the storm of war succeeded in greater violence than before, and in its course, not only his wise patriotic plan, but the very memory of it was swept away.

The history, indeed, of Scottish commerce during the greater part of this period is little else than an account of the efforts of the King of England for its impoverishment and utter extinction. And this, too, after he had previously used its resources for his own benefit. Thus when he was about to invade Wales, Edward I., among his other expedients for the supply of his army, ordered fish to be purchased on the west coast of Scotland, which were to be conveyed to Chester; and among these were specified a hundred barrels of sturgeons of Aberdeen, this town having already been noted for its excellence in curing fish. In like manner, when he invaded Scotland, Galloway supplied him with abundance of horses for draught and carriage. The attempts of Edward II. to tear up the commerce of Scotland by the roots were marked with peculiar vindictiveness. He saddled the letters of safe-conduct granted to the Flemish merchants, with the condition that the Scots should not be permitted to purchase arms or provisions in Flanders—a condition, however, to which Robert, Earl of Flanders, would by no means consent. He answered that he had proclaimed throughout his dominions that the Scots were rebels to the English king, and had prohibited his subjects from aiding them in their rebellion. But from remote ages, he added, Flanders had been dependent upon its commerce, and was open to traffickers from every quarter; and, therefore, neither the Scots nor any other people could be excluded from the Flemish markets, but should rather be protected from all oppression, while they carried on their trade honestly and without fraud.[1] The traffic between Flanders and Scotland was therefore continued to Edward's great discontent, and eight years afterwards (A.D. 1313) he renewed his appeal. He complained to the earl that the subjects of the latter still traded with the Scots and supplied them with arms, as well as provisions and other necessaries; and during the same year he again wrote, declaring that thirteen Flemish ships had lately conveyed arms and victual into Scotland. It was probably in consequence of receiving no redress that Edward II. soon after ordered all the Flemish vessels in the English ports to be arrested.[2] But the Flemings quickly discovered that in sympathizing with the weaker country they had consulted their true interests and benefited themselves. When Edward, as he was bound by treaty, had prepared to aid the King of France in subduing Flanders, he found that in conse-

---

[1] *Fœdera*, v. p. 963.   [2] Ibid. v. iii. 386, 403, 419.

quence of the Scottish wars, and especially the invasion of Ireland by Edward Bruce, he could not send his whole fleet against the Flemings, as he otherwise would have done, but only a part of it. As Bruce in his difficulties was obliged to apply for aid wherever it was likely to be found, he entered into negotiations with Genoa, two citizens of which had engaged to supply him with shipping, provisions, and military stores. But the letters to that effect were intercepted by Edward II., who complained of the bargain to the Genoese government, and demanded the punishment of the two citizens as a warning to those who presumed to traffic with his greatest enemy. And soon after he hired and obtained five vessels from that republic to be employed against Bruce and his adherents.[1]

As the successes of the Scottish arms continued to increase, and the establishment of Scottish independence to become more certain, the King of England became more earnest than ever to shut up the Scots to their own scanty resources, for they still continued to be supplied by their traffic on the Continent with those warlike stores of which they stood most in need. The fact, also, that the Scots and their king had been visited with excommunication and interdict enabled Edward to urge his appeal with a new argument. He accordingly represented to Robert of Flanders that all dealings with a people who were accursed by the church would not only be impolitic but dangerous and damnable, and consequently to be avoided by all good Christians. He therefore besought the earl, for the welfare of his soul, to shun from thenceforth any traffic with the Scots, lest he should become a partaker in the curse and punishment of such godless customers according to the tenor of the papal sentence. He also transmitted the same pious warning to the Duke of Brabant and to the magistrates of Bruges, Damm, Nieuport, Dunkirk, Ypres, and Mechlin. But although this was the most formidable of all his applications, the bold independent spirit of these mercantile communities had already learned to value aright even the papal thunder and to hold it in defiance. He of Flanders accordingly replied as before, that his ports were open to the whole world, and that merchants from whatever quarter could not be excluded without involving his country in ruin. Before this he had also embittered his refusal by designating Robert Bruce "King of the Scots," although Edward claimed them as his own subjects. The Duke of Bretagne in general terms professed his ignorance of any such intercourse between his people and the Scots, and declared that he had prohibited it. The magistrates of Mechlin, in their reply to Edward, complained of the evils they had sustained from the Scots at sea, and promised that none of their ships should ever be allowed to touch at their coasts, unless compelled by stress of weather. The answers of Bruges and Ypres were more sturdy and decisive, the latter only engaging to advise their merchants to have no further dealings with the Scots.[2] From the foregoing statements the restricted limits of Scottish commerce with foreign countries at this time, as also the commodities in which it dealt, will be distinctly understood. They also present a gratifying picture of the sympathy, generosity, and independent spirit of these small mercantile states, as contrasted with the chivalrous pride and pretensions of the more powerful communities, that either kept aloof from aiding the Scots or joined with their oppressors.

Of the coinage of Scotland, a subject so important in mercantile history, we have not as yet spoken. As far as can be discovered from old specimens, it was still wholly of silver; and from the same authorities we learn that it had no earlier origin than the reign of Alexander I. These specimens are chiefly silver pennies, but one of the improvements of Alexander III. was to coin pieces of two pennies in value. In weight, form, and fineness the Scottish money was the same as that of England and bore the same value; the temptations to fraudulent clipping and diminishing of the coin were alike in both countries, and in both the same expedients were adopted to prevent such a ruinous practice. The chief of these was to prolong the arms of the cross stamped in the centre to the edge of the coin and surround it with a border of small beads—a weak device against a dexterous clipper. It was an idea also common to Scotland and England in these rude stages of financial experience that the wealth of a country could be increased by lightening the coinage; and thus, while Edward I. decreed that a pound of silver, which hitherto had produced two hundred and forty pennies, should be coined into two hundred and forty-three—a trifling profit for such a dangerous precedent—Robert Bruce, whose necessities were still more urgent, went a considerable step beyond him by causing a pound of silver to be coined into two hundred and fifty-two pennies.[3] An evil thus commenced was certain to be repeated, but this repetition did not occur until after the close of the present period. As the Scottish coinage at this time consisted wholly of silver, it was divided into

---

[1] *Fœdera*, v. iii. 604.

[2] *Fœdera*, v. iii. 769, 770, 766, 765, 771.
[3] M'Pherson's *Annals of Commerce*, i. p. 466.

groats, half-groats, and pennies, the last coin being easily split at the indentations of its cross into halves and quarters to serve as small change in retail purchases.

But it would be of little use to speak of the coinage of this period without referring to the substantialities of which it was the symbol. In common parlance what would a penny fetch? what was its proportion to the labour or commodity for which it was given in payment? Of this we have a tolerably distinct idea from the chamberlain accounts, in which the expenses of the royal household are minuted. We there find a chalder of wheat sold for a mark, that is 13s. 6d., or 160 pennies. A chalder of rye was sold for four shillings. A boll of oatmeal varied from twenty pence to two shillings. From this average, however, we find the prices shifting with a mutability unknown in modern markets. Passing from grain to animal food, we find a cow sold for five shillings, an ox for six shillings and eightpence, a sheep for tenpence, a sow for a shilling, and a hen for a penny. In looking at the disbursements for the payment of labour we find that the hire of workmen was sufficiently liberal. A barrowman or carrier of lime for a building received from fourteen pence to two shillings a week. A carpenter was paid three pence a day with his provisions. A mason received for his year's wages six pounds thirteen shillings and four pence, while a smith or armourer—a far more important workman in these warlike times—had twelve pounds. To these workmen in the service of the king such sums were paid as, compared with the price of provisions, give a favourable specimen of the rate of wages at the close of this period, and with which, as we have seen, the necessaries of life could be abundantly procured.

At the first outburst of the Scottish war for independence, when every hand that could wield spade or hoe was required for the use of sword and spear, our notices of the agriculture of the country must be still more unsatisfactory than those of its commerce. The encouragement given to the cultivation of the soil by Alexander III. and his predecessors through the establishment of monasteries and royal manors over the kingdom, and the concession of favourable leases and tenures, through which such abundance had grown during the last of these reigns, was abruptly terminated. The ploughshare of war, that can convert the most fruitful Eden into a wilderness, was to pass through the land in every direction and predominate as its principal tillage. An uncleared field was now to be prized beyond a cultivated one, as affording a better chance for ambush or battle; and whoever sowed the harvest had to labour under the dispiriting conviction that he knew not by whom it should be reaped. And yet, not only the inhabitants had to be supported, but also the English garrisons that were quartered over the country. Stern necessity and compulsion alone could now continue those labours of the husbandman that had lately been such a cheerful service, and the produce that was raised must feed the oppressor before the owner could partake of it. From incidental notices of these wars we find that oats already formed the principal grain of the people. The garrisons, indeed, had to be fed with supplies from England independently of purchase or plunder; but they appear to have used large quantities of malt for ale, which was made from the oats of the country. From the same sources we find that wheat, rye, barley, beans, and pease were also raised, and that much of the wheaten bread used by the invading armies of Edward I. was from Scottish grain that was ground in English mills. Still all this limited produce must have fallen very short of the demand, and the famine with which the Scots were learning to defend their country must often have been felt as keenly by themselves as by the enemy. In an extreme case, as we have seen in the career of Wallace, a large army composed of the male population of Scotland from sixteen years old to sixty crossed the Border immediately after their scanty harvest had been gathered in, and quartered themselves in England when their own country could not have sustained them, and there were able to revel for weeks in an abundance to which they had long been strangers. The lesson thus learned was often repeated in after periods, until the Scottish invaders learned to regard the northern counties as their granaries, which they might empty as often as they could reach them. During the precarious intervals of truce, when the country was chiefly shut up within its own resources, the following incidental notices, in addition to those already given, are derived from the cartularies of the period. In agricultural labour ploughing was chiefly performed by oxen, while horses were employed in the cart. Cows formed the principal standard of agricultural value, as sheep had done in earlier communities, and were used in the payment of dues and forfeitures. In the more cultivated districts ten cows were the proportion assigned for keeping to each plough. Black cattle were also reared in abundance, in consequence of their easy maintenance and the large tracts of common pasturage that were still uninclosed. The resources of the dairy were also understood, and cheese is frequently mentioned among the food of the inhabitants.

But in such a state of strife, change, and

uncertainty, it was to be expected that the Scots should find the resources of pasturage more eligible than those of agriculture; and accordingly they depended more upon their flocks, that could be removed into fastnesses or under cover at the enemy's approach, than upon their cornfields, that were so liable to be trampled down or plundered. Besides the large herds of horses, therefore, that were allowed to run at large until they were needed for a warlike inroad, droves of oxen and swine and flocks of sheep and goats formed the chief subsistence of the Scots. In this shifting and precarious life, which, in fact, was a compulsory return to their original barbarism, it was well for the people that they had the produce of their seas, lakes, and rivers to depend upon as well as their pasture-lands; and accordingly every kind of fresh and salt water fish appears to have been used more fully than ever. Not only the supply but the means of using it were also within their reach, as before this period *stell fisheries* or stationary establishments had been set up on the shores and estuaries, as well as *yairs* or machines of wattle within the stream of the principal rivers.

In looking at the condition of the bulk of the Scottish people, we can well perceive that it was for national rather than personal freedom that they fought so bravely and successfully. It was also unfortunate for them that this war for national independence only riveted those links of feudal subjection which their Scoto-Saxon kings had forged, as well as made the chain be more willingly endured. But what could otherwise have been than that in so great a danger the people should have clung all the more closely to their natural leaders, and that the great champions of the war should have won for themselves the gratitude as well as the submission of the commons? The division of the whole community into the rulers and the ruled, the master and the serf, was now completed, and the classes into which the latter were divided may be briefly enumerated. The first and highest in the scale were the tenants of the crown, the church, or the barons. These were the free farmers who paid rent, and might therefore select their residence and landlord according to their own good pleasure. But a part, if not the principal part of their rent, consisted in military service; and therefore in the event of war they were bound to follow the banner under which they held, armed according to their degree, and furnished with forty days' provisions. This service, indeed, must have been light enough where the landlord was a bishop or abbot; but it was different under the lay barons, who were almost constantly at war with each other if not with the English. It is possible, indeed, that this enviable class of *liberii firmarii*, as they were called, was more numerous than is generally thought, as in those days four or five acres of cultivated ground were enough to constitute a farm. But lower than these half-free rent-payers was a class comprising, it is to be feared, the greater part of the population, who under such names as *nativi, servi, villani, homines fugitivi, bondi, mancipii*, were in reality the slaves or serfs of Scotland. Instead of having the choice of a master they belonged to the owner of the land, and were sold or transferred with it like cattle or beasts of burden; and if they moved beyond bounds they could be hunted back like stray sheep and punished for their trespass. Even their children also and the descendants of their children were stamped at their birth with the same indelible brand of slavery, and were the exclusive property of the soil, or rather of him who possessed it, so that their genealogies were carefully preserved that each landlord might be able to identify his property through every succeeding generation. And thus the serf, however high he might rise by worth or office, remained a bondman still unless he was liberated by favour or purchase.

Although the "gamyn and gle" with which the land was so jovial during the golden age of Alexander III. was so mournfully silenced at his death, it was arrested, not extinguished; and when better days returned with the victories of Bruce we can easily imagine that those who mourned the loss of friends were equally ready to rejoice in their own deliverance. But what were the games, the sports, and pastimes in which the long-suppressed national gladness found its utterance? Of this, unfortunately, we have no record, and our knowledge on the subject can be nothing but conjecture. Of minstrels and female dancers, of posturers, tumblers, and buffoons there had been previously no lack in Scotland, so that they sometimes accompanied the army; but in the present period, when the war had assumed such a stern and dangerous character, their uses in military expeditions were apparently no longer in demand. Music is equally the voice of a people whether in sorrow or joy; but here, again, the condition of the early music and musical instruments of Scotland is both an obscure and a controversial subject, which all the antiquarianism of the present day has been unable to settle. It has been conjectured that at this early period, and even for a long time previous, the Scots used three musical instruments—the harp, the tabor, and the bagpipe. Their performances, however, must have been limited to festive or peaceful occasions, as in the wars of the Scots at this time we hear of nothing but the cow-horns with which they were wont to drive sleep from the enemy's camp or keep it all night in alarm.

But whatever popular amusements may have been kept in abeyance by the severity of the common pressure upon the national spirit, it is certain that minstrels and minstrelsy would lose none of their popular favour. It is chiefly in such an age, and under such trials, that poetry is kindled into its highest ardour, and is most welcomed, whether in the form of the rude ballad or the matured Iliad. And of the minstrels of Scotland both at and after the commencement of these wars, we have a few incidental notices. During the progress of Edward I. through the country he was welcomed to the towns by minstrels and singers; and when David was married to Joanna of England both Scottish and English minstrels attended at the marriage. Indeed, it appears, that while the palace and even the baronial hall were incomplete without their musical retainers, the towns had also their minstrels, whose ditties would serve them in lieu both of histories and newspapers. It is not difficult to guess what must have been the popular themes of these bards during such a season of stir, and strife, and national interest. They could be little else than the war with England and the gallant deeds of their brave patriots: above all, they must have recorded the wonderful exploits of Wallace, whose valour was so matchless, and whose short life was so full of incident. This we can easily believe, without the following testimony of Winton—

"Of his gud dedis, and manhad
Gret Gestis, I hard say, ar made;
Bot sa mony, I trow noucht
As he intil hys dayis wrocht.
Quha all hys dedis olf prys wald dyte,
Hym worthyd a gret buk to wryte."

It was doubtless from these popular ballads that Henry the Minstrel collected the main incidents of his *Wallace*, although he professed to derive them from the Latin history of Blair, the hero's chaplain—just as Ariosto, a short time after, in his *Orlando Furioso*, quoted the history of Archbishop Turpin as his authority for the romantic exploits of Charlemagne and his Paladins. But what has become of these rude, yet, doubtless, heart-stirring popular ballads, which would now be so valuable to the Scottish historian after undergoing the usual process of winnowing? The monks, the only men of the pen, who were careful to perpetuate their own Latin doggerel, would not condescend to transcribe the lays of the olden minstrels; and therefore they have passed away—passed so utterly, that even of the poetical triumphs of Bannockburn nothing remains but a single stanza, and that, too, preserved not by a Scottish writer, but the English chronicler of St. Albans.[1]

The present period, however, of the history of Scotland, although so largely occupied with political troubles and military achievements, was not wholly without its learned men, who obtained a European reputation irrespective of their country and its turbulent incidents. This was the era of John of Dunse, better known among the learned men of his day as Duns Scotus. So high was his reputation that the honour of his birth was claimed by England and Ireland, as well as Scotland; but after all that has been written, it is generally allowed that he was a native of Dunse in Berwickshire, where he was born in the latter part of the thirteenth century. An accident decided that he who might have been nothing better than a stout Border spearman should become one of the profoundest metaphysicians and ablest disputants in Europe. While very young, and tending his father's sheep, two Franciscan friars of the town of Dumfries happened to enter into conversation with him, and were so much astonished at the precocious intelligence of the boy, that they resolved to secure him for the church; and with this view they prevailed with his parents to send him to their monastery, where in due time he became a Franciscan friar. Among the Scottish prisoners carried off by Edward I. was John of Dunse and twelve of his brethren; but after enduring captivity for some time he obtained his freedom, upon which he repaired to Merton College, Oxford, where he enjoyed those opportunities of study which he could not have obtained in Scotland. Here he became so distinguished for his attainments in philosophy, mathematics, and theology, that in 1301 he was appointed professor of divinity, and his lectures on the *Sentences* of Peter Lombard obtained such popularity that thirty thousand students are said to have been attracted to Oxford by the fame of his eloquence. These lectures which have been printed fill six folio volumes. In 1304 he went to Paris by order of his monastic superior to defend the doctrine of the immaculate conception; and this he did with such eloquence and success, that a stranger present is said to have exclaimed, "This must either be

---

[1] The single stanza referred to is the following:—
Maydens of Englonde, sore may ye morne,
For ye have lost your lemmans at Bannocksborne,
                With hovelogh;
What wenyth the kinge of Englonde
To have got Scotland,
                With rombelogh.

an angel from heaven, a devil from hell, or John Duns Scotus!" After he had scattered the two hundred objections of his opponents, and triumphantly closed the intellectual tournament, he was rewarded with a professorship in the theological schools of Paris, and the title of the "Subtle Doctor," and had the honour of founding a sect called the Scotists, in opposition to his rival Thomas Aquinas, the "Angelical Doctor," who established the sect of the Thomists. The opinions of these two mighty champions who divided Christendom between them, it would now be a waste of time to state, even if they could be delivered in a form that would be intelligible to the present age. In 1308, when his fame had reached the height, Duns Scotus was invited to Cologne to found a university and defend the doctrine of the immaculate conception; but in a few months his career was terminated by a stroke of apoplexy, when he had reached his forty-fourth, or according to others, only his thirty-fourth year. That he was a man of immense talents, notwithstanding their useless range according to modern estimation, was evinced by the veneration with which his memory continued to be cherished by the brightest intellects of the church, and by the care with which his whole works were collected and republished at Lyons so late as 1639, although they filled twelve folio volumes.[1]

Another distinguished Scotchman of this period was John Bassol, the contemporary and pupil of Duns Scotus, under whom he studied at Oxford, and whom he accompanied to Paris in 1304. Although far inferior to his illustrious master, the latter prized him so highly, that he was wont to say, "If only John Bassol be present I have audience enough." Having entered the order of Minorite friars Bassol was sent by its superior to Rheims, where he taught philosophy for seven years, after which he settled at Mechlin in Brabant, where he lectured on theology during twenty-five years, and died in 1347. As he was of high account among the intellectual men of the age he also received his honorary title, which was that of the "Most Methodical Doctor," on account of his accurate distinctions and precise systematic arrangement, and his works, consisting of his lectures on the *Four Books of Sentences*, and essays in philosophy and medicine, were published in a single folio at Paris in 1517.[2]

Such were the eminent intellectual men whom Scotland at this time produced—men who owed their education to England and France, and their renown to Europe at large, while their own country could neither understand their excellence nor be benefited by their labours. And yet they did not live wholly in vain for their native land, which was distinguished even by the mere accident of their birth, and which shared in the renown that for a long period was attached to their names. In such men as Duns Scotus and Bassol that Scottish metaphysical spirit gave its first manifestations which was afterwards to be so identified with the intellectual character of the country when its great awakening had commenced in earnest.

---

[1] Chambers' *Lives of Eminent Scotchmen*.

[2] Mackenzie's *Scotch Writers*.

SOME WORKS PUBLISHED BY

BLACKIE & SON, Limited,

LONDON, GLASGOW, EDINBURGH, AND DUBLIN.

A LIBRARY IN ITSELF.

THE POPULAR ENCYCLOPEDIA.
NEW ISSUE, REVISED.

A GENERAL DICTIONARY OF ARTS, SCIENCES, LITERATURE, BIOGRAPHY, AND HISTORY.

EDITED BY

CHARLES ANNANDALE, M.A., LL.D.,
Editor of Ogilvie's "Imperial Dictionary of the English Language."

Profusely illustrated with Engravings.

To be completed in Fourteen handsome Volumes, super-royal 8vo, bound in rich cloth, red edges, at 12s. each.

The POPULAR ENCYCLOPEDIA is a perfect library in itself, superseding, practically, the necessity of having recourse to a large number of books on different topics, and furnishing, at moderate cost, a complete body of information on all subjects.

In its survey of human knowledge it will compare in point of fulness of detail with the best works of its size, while in its clear concise style, and in its avoidance of technicalities, the needs of the general reader have been constantly consulted.

It is a Universal Gazetteer.	It is a Dictionary of Philosophy.
It is a Universal History.	It is a Dictionary of Theology.
It is a Biographical Dictionary.	It is a Dictionary of the Fine Arts.
It is a Commercial Dictionary.	It is a Dictionary of the Practical Arts and Handicrafts
It is a Dictionary of Political Theories and Facts.	
It is a Dictionary of the Sciences.	It is a Dictionary of General Information.

This work has been aptly called a Conversations-Lexicon, since in it a man has the clue to all topics of interest and conversation in all professions, trades, and walks of life, and is enabled by it to equip himself to play a many-sided and intelligent part in the world.

It is A BOOK FOR THE HOUSEHOLD, being of value and interest to all its members, old and young alike. It is in itself a liberal education, and, indeed, the best POPULAR EDUCATOR, and it will be found of the highest service to the younger members of families in the prosecution of their studies, and especially in the preparation of their written exercises.

It abounds with pictorial illustrations, many printed in colours, which extend to above 200 pages of Engravings, including over 2000 separate figures. In addition, there is a series of coloured Maps, forming a valuable accompaniment to the geographical and historical articles.

NEW EDITION—REVISED AND GREATLY AUGMENTED.

BLACKIE'S
COMPREHENSIVE HISTORY OF ENGLAND.

CIVIL AND MILITARY, RELIGIOUS, INTELLECTUAL, AND SOCIAL.

FROM THE EARLIEST PERIOD TO THE PRESENT TIME.

ILLUSTRATED BY ABOVE ELEVEN HUNDRED ENGRAVINGS IN THE TEXT, AND SIXTY-FIVE FINELY ENGRAVED PLATES.

BESIDES THE NUMEROUS ILLUSTRATIONS PRINTED IN THE TEXT, EACH PART WILL CONTAIN TWO OR THREE SEPARATE PAGE ENGRAVINGS, ILLUSTRATING IMPORTANT HISTORICAL EVENTS, PORTRAITS OF SOVEREIGNS, &c.

The work will be completed in 26 parts, 2s. each; or 8 divisional-volumes, super-royal 8vo, handsomely bound in cloth, price 8s. 6d. each.

There is no man imbued with even the smallest spark of patriotism who does not desire to know the story of his country, and the career of those remarkable men who, in bygone years, helped to mould the people into a nation, and to build up those two most marvellous fabrics of modern times, The British Empire and The British Constitution. The tale is a wondrous one: fascinating as a romance; full of chivalrous exploits, and of high and lofty example for every condition of life.

THE COMPREHENSIVE HISTORY OF ENGLAND in telling this story will command the appreciative interest of the general reader, and become not only a useful book of reference but an entertaining and instructive work for the family.

A COMPLETE HISTORY OF THE ENGLISH PEOPLE.—Not only political, naval, and military, but also civil, religious, industrial, agricultural, and mercantile, presenting picturesque descriptions of the aspects of the various classes of society in successive periods; concise accounts of the progress of commerce, industries, and manufactures; and of the results arising from inventions and discoveries; sketches of the advance of literature and the fine arts; and the spread of general enlightenment.

ELEVEN HUNDRED ENGRAVINGS.—The Eleven Hundred Engravings, printed in the text, have been carefully prepared, with a view to the real elucidation of the History. They comprise Illustrations of the Dwellings, the Shipping, the Armour, Dress, Manners and Customs, and Utensils of our Ancestors at various periods; Views of Historical Sites, Buildings, and Monuments; Maps and Plans of Battles, Battlefields, Forts, Towns, &c.; Portraits and Statues of Illustrious Persons.

NEW AND REVISED EDITION.

The Casquet of Literature:

A SELECTION IN PROSE AND POETRY from the works of the best Authors. Edited, with Biographical and Literary Notes, by CHARLES GIBBON, Author of "Robin Gray", and revised by Miss MARY CHRISTIE. To be published in 6 volumes, bound in cloth, gilt elegant, with olivine edges, price 7s. 6d. per volume; also in 18 parts, price 2s. each.

The CASQUET OF LITERATURE will contain more than 1000 characteristic Selections from the writings of the most popular authors, accompanied by about 400 Biographical and Literary Notes. The stress of modern life leaves scanty leisure for recreation, yet in the evenings when the fireside is the only comfortable place, one needs something to refresh the jaded spirits, and obliterate for the time the worries of the day. For these purposes, what better than a good, breezy, entertaining book? Practically a guide to the best English literature, illustrated by a series of exquisite drawings.

600 of the greatest writers in the English tongue will be represented, including Tennyson, Browning, George Eliot, Addison, R. Louis Stevenson, S. R. Crockett, Ruskin, Andrew Lang, Douglas Jerrold, Mark Twain, J. M. Barrie, Anthony Hope. In fact, a book in which the reader is provided with the best work of poets, novelists, essayists, humorists, storytellers, and artists. Material for desultory reading—the most delightful of all—of a lifetime. A casquet of inexhaustible treasure, inasmuch as beautiful thoughts and exquisite, like diamonds, never lose their brilliance or charm.

Blackie & Son's Publications.

DESCRIPTIVE ATLAS OF THE WORLD
AND GENERAL GEOGRAPHY.

COMPRISING
ABOVE ONE HUNDRED CAREFULLY EXECUTED MAPS; A DETAILED DESCRIPTION OF THE WORLD, PROFUSELY ILLUSTRATED; AND A COPIOUS INDEX OF PLACES.

PREPARED UNDER THE SUPERVISION OF
W. G. BLACKIE, Ph.D., LL.D.,
Fellow of the Royal Geographical Societies, London and Edinburgh.

To be completed in 12 divisions at 5s. each, forming a handsome volume, 16 inches × 12 inches.

The ATLAS will consist of sixty-four sheets of Maps, comprising seventy-five numbered maps and above thirty inset maps, making in all above ONE HUNDRED MAPS beautifully printed in colours, prepared from the most recent and most authoritative materials available.

While the older countries of the world will all be fully shown, special prominence will be given to Great Britain and its world-wide possessions, and also to the regions recently opened up by the enterprise of adventurous travellers.

Two of the maps are worthy of special notice. The Commercial Chart of the World, showing existing and available fields of commerce; and The British Empire at one view, showing all the possessions at home and abroad, drawn to one scale, and thereby enabling their relative size to be clearly appreciated.

The GENERAL GEOGRAPHY which accompanies the maps forms a very important section of the work. It supplies information geographical, historical, statistical, commercial, and descriptive, of the countries and regions of the world, and has been prepared from recent and authoritative sources. Its pages are enriched by a series of Pictorial Illustrations, consisting of striking views of natural scenery, remarkable edifices, town and river scenes, and picturesque groups of natives, and of animal life.

As a useful adjunct both to the Maps and the General Geography there will be given a Pronouncing Vocabulary of Geographical Names. In addition to this, an Extensive Index of Places will form a very useful section of the work.

To be completed in 14 parts, super-royal 8vo, at 2s. each; or in 4 divisions, stiff paper cover, at 7s. each, forming one handsome volume; or in 4 divisions, cloth, at 9s. each.

The Household Physician:

A FAMILY GUIDE TO THE PRESERVATION OF HEALTH AND TO THE DOMESTIC TREATMENT OF AILMENTS AND DISEASE. By J. M'GREGOR-ROBERTSON, M.B., C.M. (Hon.). With an Introduction by Professor M'KENDRICK, M.D., LL.D., F.R.S., Glasgow University. Illustrated by about 400 figures in the text, and a series of 19 Engraved Plates, many of them printed in colours.

This work is written in the simplest possible language, and includes full information on the conditions of health, and on the ordinary means, as regards food, clothing, exercise, &c., by which health may be maintained in the infant as well as in the full-grown person.

The book treats of the human body in health, and the various changes produced by disease. On Hygiene, or the conditions of health as regards food, drink, clothing, exercise, &c., and the rules to be observed for the promotion of health, both of individuals and communities. An explanation of the nature and mode of action of drugs and other remedial agents. On methods of dealing with Accidents and Emergencies, and on various ailments requiring surgical treatment. Also a chapter on Sick-nursing, and an Appendix containing recipes for Invalid Cookery and medical Prescriptions.

In 15 parts, super-royal 8vo, 2s. each; or 4 vols., cloth elegant, burnished edges, 9s. 6d. each.

NEW EDITION, Continued to 1890.

Gladstone and His Contemporaries:

Sixty Years of Social and Political Progress. By THOMAS ARCHER, F.R.H.S., Author of "Pictures and Royal Portraits," &c. Illustrated by a series of 34 authentic and beautifully executed Portraits.

"*This work is not so much a biography of Mr. Gladstone as a political History of England during his lifetime. It is a book which has evidently been compiled with no ordinary pains and care, and with a praiseworthy desire to be impartial.*"—Daily News.

"*It is probably true that the biographical form of history is the best in dealing with times within the memory of men yet living. The life of a man, prominent in affairs during a particular period, may be taken as a central point round which matters of more general history group themselves.*"—Standard.

THE HENRY IRVING SHAKESPEARE.—SUBSCRIPTION EDITION.

The Works of Shakespeare.
EDITED BY
HENRY IRVING AND FRANK A. MARSHALL.

With a General Introduction and Life of Shakespeare by Professor EDWARD DOWDEN, and nearly six hundred illustrations from designs by GORDON BROWNE and other Artists. To be completed in 25 parts, super-royal 8vo, 3s. each; or 8 volumes, cloth elegant, 10s. 6d. each, with gilt edges, 11s. 6d. each.

The universal popularity of the works of our GREAT DRAMATIST has induced the publishers to issue a sumptuous edition, of such comprehensive excellence that it is fitted at once to meet the requirements of the general reader, the lover of fine books, and the student of Shakespeare. This important edition in many respects has never been surpassed.

*** Every subscriber for this edition of Shakespeare's Works will be presented, on the completion of his copy of the book, with an impression of the admirable PORTRAIT OF HENRY IRVING AS HAMLET, from the painting by EDWIN LONG, R.A., executed in Photogravure in the most finished manner by Boussod Valadon et Cie. (Goupil), of Paris. The size of the engraved surface is 19¼ × 13¾ inches, and with margin suitable for framing 27 × 20 inches.

"*On the care with which the text itself of the plays has been prepared we have nothing but praise to bestow.* . . . *The general result of this care and labour is, however, so good that we must congratulate all concerned in it; and in particular we must congratulate the publishers of the work on one especial feature which could hardly fail to ensure its success as a popular edition—it is profusely illustrated by Mr. Gordon Browne, whose charming designs, executed in facsimile, give it an artistic value superior, in our judgment, to any illustrated edition of Shakespeare with which we are acquainted.*"—The Athenæum.

"*This handsomely printed edition aims at being popular and practical. Add to these advantages Mr. Gordon Browne's illustrations, and enough has been said to recommend an edition which will win public recognition by its unique and serviceable qualities.*"—The Spectator.

In 17 parts, extra demy 8vo, at 2s. each; or 5 volumes, cloth elegant, gilt edges, at 8s. 6d. each.

NEW PICTORIAL EDITION.

The Works of Robert Burns,

With a series of Authentic Pictorial Illustrations, Marginal Glossary, numerous Notes, and Appendixes. Also the Life of Burns by J. G. LOCKHART, and Essays on the Genius, Character, and Writings of Burns, by THOMAS CARLYLE and PROFESSOR WILSON. Edited by CHARLES ANNANDALE, M.A., LL.D., editor of the "Imperial Dictionary", &c.

In this edition of Burns his writings are presented in two sections, the one containing the poetry, the other the prose. Marginal explanations of Scottish words accompany each piece that requires such aid, enabling anyone at a glance to apprehend the meaning of even the most difficult passages.

The Pictorial Illustrations, which consist of Fifty-six beautiful Landscapes and Portraits, engraved on steel in the most finished manner, form a very distinctive feature of this edition. The Landscapes embrace the principal scenes identified with the Life and Writings of the Poet, and are from pictures painted by D. O. HILL, R.S.A.

Altogether in no other edition is so much light thrown from all points of view upon Burns the poet and Burns the man, and it may therefore be said to be complete in the best sense of the word.

In 18 parts, super-royal 4to, at 2s. each; in 6 divisions at 6s. each; and also in 2 volumes, large 4to, elegantly bound in cloth, gilt edges, price 24s. each.

The Natural History of Animals

(CLASS MAMMALIA—ANIMALS WHICH SUCKLE THEIR YOUNG), In Word and Picture. By CARL VOGT, Professor of Natural History, Geneva, and FRIEDRICH SPECHT, Stuttgart. Translated and Edited by GEO. C. CHISHOLM, M.A., B.Sc. Illustrated by above 300 fine Engravings on wood.

This account of the animals comprised in the class Mammalia has a decidedly popular character—not through lack of scientific value, but because the author presents the facts in an attractive form, and studies to smooth the path of those who can give only their leisure hours to learning the results of scientific research. The author's style is above all things clear, simple, and direct, and where occasion offers, lively and animated.

The artist has portrayed in the most spirited manner the animals as they appear in the varied circumstances of real life, in quest of their prey, caressing their young ones, or sporting with their fellows. The engravings have been executed in the most careful and finished manner, under Mr. Specht's own direction.

Blackie & Son's Publications.

In 19 parts, 2s. each; or 6 divisional-volumes, super-royal 8vo, cloth elegant, 8s. 6d. each.

A History of the Scottish People

From the Earliest to the Latest Times. By Rev. THOMAS THOMSON and CHARLES ANNANDALE, M.A., LL.D. With 40 Original Designs by W. H. MARGETSON, ALFRED PEARSE, WALTER PAGET, GORDON BROWNE, and other eminent artists.

It is a full and detailed History of Scotland from the Earliest Times to the Latest.
It is a History of the Scottish People, their manners, customs, and modes of living at the various successive periods.
It is a History of Religion and Ecclesiastical Affairs in Scotland.
It is a History of Scotland's progress in Commerce, Industry, Arts, Science, and Literature.

In 14 parts, 2s. each; or 4 vols., super-royal 8vo, cloth elegant, 8s. 6d. each.

The Cabinet of Irish Literature.

A Selection from the Works of the chief Poets, Orators, and Prose Writers of Ireland. Edited, with biographical sketches and literary notices, by CHARLES A. READ, F.R.H.S., author of "Tales and Stories of Irish Life," "Stories from the Ancient Classics," &c. Illustrated by a series of 32 admirable Portraits in mesochrome, specially prepared for this work.

The Publishers aim in this Work to supply a standard work in which the genius, the fire, the pathos, the humour, and the eloquence of Irish Literature are adequately represented. The specimens selected, which are arranged chronologically from the earliest to the present time, will both present a historical view of Irish Literature, and enable the reader to judge of the individual style and particular merit of each author, while to those not critically disposed the infinite variety presented in this convenient collective form will afford both instruction and amusement.

In 12 parts, demy 8vo, 2s. each; and 4 half-vols., cloth elegant, 7s. 6d. each; or gilt edges, at 8s. 6d. each.

The Poets and Poetry of Scotland:

FROM THE EARLIEST TO THE PRESENT TIME. Comprising Characteristic Selections from the works of the more Noteworthy Scottish Poets, with Biographical and Critical Notices. By JAMES GRANT WILSON. Illustrated by Portraits.

In the preparation of this Work the first object has been to present, not a collection of the ballads or songs, or the writings of the poets of any particular district of the country, but a comprehensive view of the poetry of Scotland in all its forms from the earliest to the present time. Besides original contributions and poems by living authors, the Work will contain poems, hitherto unpublished, by ROBERT BURNS, WILLIAM TENNANT, Mrs. GRANT of Laggan, JAMES HYSLOP, HENRY SCOTT RIDDELL, JOHN LEYDEN, WILLIAM MILLER, and others.
The Illustrations will consist of Twenty-four life-like Portraits, engraved on steel in the most finished manner.

In 15 parts, 2s. each; or two handsome vols., super-royal 8vo, cloth, 36s.

The Works of the Ettrick Shepherd,

IN POETRY AND PROSE. Centenary Edition. With a Biographical Memoir by the Rev. THOMAS THOMSON. Illustrated by Forty-four fine Engravings on steel, from Original Drawings by D. O. Hill, R.S.A., K. Halsewelle, A.R.S.A., W. Small, and J. Lawson.

Hogg's Works comprise *Tales in Prose*, illustrative of Border history and superstitions. They comprise likewise Poems of great imaginative power and descriptive beauty; Ballads full of humour and touches of tender pathos; and Songs which, besides being universally popular when first made public, are still cherished as among the finest productions of our native lyric muse.

"*Certainly we may now recognize him as the only one of Burns' followers who deserves to be named in the same breath.*"—Press.

To be completed in four half-volumes, super-royal 8vo, at 12s. 6d. each; or in
twelve parts at 3s. 6d. each.

The Steam Engine:

A TREATISE ON STEAM ENGINES AND BOILERS. Comprising the Principles and Practice of the Combustion of Fuel, the Economical Generation of Steam, the Construction of Steam Boilers; and the Principles, Construction, and Performance of Steam Engines—Stationary, Portable, Locomotive, and Marine, exemplified in Engines and Boilers of Recent Date. By DANIEL KINNEAR CLARK, M.Inst.C.E., M.I.M.E.; Author of "Railway Machinery"; "A Manual of Rules, Tables, and Data for Mechanical Engineers"; &c. &c. Illustrated by above 1300 Figures in the Text, and a Series of Folding Plates drawn to Scale.

This work provides a comprehensive, accurate, and clearly written text-book, fully abreast of all the recent developments in the principles and practice of the Steam Engine.

Written in full view of the great advances of modern times, it expounds the principles and describes the practice exemplified in the construction and use of Steam Engines and Boilers, in all their varieties.

In 20 parts, 2s. each; or 5 divisions, royal 4to, 8s. each; or one vol., cloth, gilt edges, 42s.

Suggestions in Design;

A comprehensive series of Original Sketches in various Styles of Ornament, arranged for application in the Decorative and Constructive Arts, comprising 102 plates, containing more than 1100 distinct and separate "suggestions", by JOHN LEIGHTON, F.S.A. To which is added descriptive and historical letterpress, with above 200 explanatory engravings, by JAMES KELLAWAY COLLING, F.R.I.B.A.

These suggestions are throughout *original*, designed in the spirit, and with the proper art feeling of the various styles to which they severally belong, and are the accumulated result of long and arduous studies, extending over many years of investigation and thought.

This work will be found to be eminently suited to the wants of nearly every one who has occasion for decoration in whatever form;—to the worker in stone, wood, metal, ivory, glass, and leather—to the house-painter, decorator, &c. &c.

In 20 parts, super-royal quarto, 2s. each; or 8 divisions, 5s. each.

The Carpenter and Joiner's Assistant.

By JAMES NEWLANDS, late Borough Engineer of Liverpool. *New and Improved Edition.* Being a Comprehensive Treatise on the selection, preparation, and strength of Materials, and the mechanical principles of Framing, with their applications in Carpentry, Joinery, and Hand Railing; also, a complete treatise on Lines; and an Illustrated Glossary of Terms used in Architecture and Building. Illustrated by above One Hundred Engraved Plates, containing above Nine Hundred Figures; and above Seven Hundred Geometric, Constructive, and Descriptive Figures interspersed throughout the text.

"*We know of no treatise on Carpentry and Joinery which at all approaches this in merit. . . . We strongly urge our practical mechanics to obtain and study it.*"—Mechanic's Magazine.

In 24 parts, demy 4to, at 2s. each; or in 6 volumes, artistically bound in cloth extra,
with olivine edges, at 10s. each.

The Works of Shakspeare,

Revised from the best Authorities; with a Memoir and Essay on his Genius by BRYAN W. PROCTER (Barry Cornwall), Annotations and Introductory Remarks on the Plays by Distinguished Writers, and numerous Illustrative Engravings from Designs by KENNY MEADOWS and T. H. NICHOLSON.

The most distinctive, as well as the most attractive feature of this edition of the Works of Shakspeare consists in the pictorial illustrations with which it is so copiously enriched. These are upwards of 750 in number, and bring most vividly before the reader the scenes and incidents occurring in the different plays.

By far the greater number are by the well-known artist KENNY MEADOWS, and so important are these illustrations that the edition of which they form a part has been appropriately named the *Kenny Meadows Shakspeare*.

Each play is accompanied by an original introduction, and explanatory notes from the pens of various writers distinguished for their critical acumen and their wide knowledge and high appreciation of Shakspeare's writings. Altogether this work will be found not unworthy of him who "was not of an age, but for all time".

Blackie & Son's Publications. 7

In 12 parts, small 4to size, price 2s. each; or 4 volumes, cloth elegant, gilt edges, 9s. each.

Our Sovereign Lady Queen Victoria:

HER LIFE AND JUBILEE. By THOMAS ARCHER, F.R.H.S., Author of "Pictures and Royal Portraits"; "Fifty Years of Social and Political Progress"; &c. Illustrated by a series of 28 highly-finished Etchings.

It is believed that for the multitudes of men and women who regard the Queen with a sentiment that may be spoken of as that of personal regard and affection, no more fitting memorial can be provided than a complete and worthy Life of our Sovereign Lady—a "Life" such as that which is here announced. The narrative presents a biographical rather than a historical record: a record, faithful, interesting, and well illustrated, of the Royal Family and of the Queen as Sovereign Lady rather than as Sovereign Ruler.

The ILLUSTRATIONS consist of a series of twenty-eight highly-finished etchings, including portraits of Her Majesty, the late Prince Consort, and all the members of their Family; also scenes and events in which the Queen has personally taken part.

In 23 parts at 2s. 6d. each; also 2 vols., cloth extra, gilt edges, price 35s. each.

Pictures and Royal Portraits,

ILLUSTRATIVE OF ENGLISH AND SCOTTISH HISTORY, from the Introduction of Christianity to the Present Time. This Work will comprise a Series of 69 Magnificent Plates engraved on steel in the most finished manner, with descriptive Historical Sketches, by THOMAS ARCHER. Printed on fine medium quarto paper, forming 2 elegant volumes, cloth extra, gilt edges, with richly ornamented boards.

"Pictures and Royal Portraits" will present a series of line engravings of historical designs, beautifully executed in steel, and produced in a new and attractive style, which imparts to them the appearance of highly-finished drawings in sepia. The series will include faithful reproductions of important paintings by some of the most eminent historical painters of the present century.

To be completed in 15 parts, folio (size 16¼ × 11¼ inches), price 5s. each.

The Practical Decorator and Ornamentist.

For the use of ARCHITECTS, PAINTERS, DECORATORS, and DESIGNERS. Containing one hundred Plates in colours and gold. With Descriptive Notices, and an Introductory Essay on Artistic and Practical Decoration. By GEORGE ASHDOWN AUDSLEY, LL.D., F.R.L.B.A., and MAURICE ASHDOWN AUDSLEY, Architect.

The highly practical and useful character of this important Work will at once commend it to those interested in decorative art, to whom it is more immediately addressed.

It will be found useful to the Modeller, the Plasterer, the Stone Carver, the Wood Carver, the Fret Cutter, the Inlayer, the Cabinetmaker, the Potter, the Engraver, the Lithographer, the House Painter, the Architect, the Interior Decorator, and, indeed, to every workman who has anything to do with ornament and design. To the student in drawing and ornamental design it presents a wide field of suggestive study.

Fourth Edition. Large 8vo (1000 pp.), cloth, 16s., or half-morocco, 20s.

A Manual of Rules, Tables, and Data

FOR MECHANICAL ENGINEERS, based on the most recent investigations. By DANIEL KINNEAR CLARK, author of "Railway Machinery", &c. &c. Illustrated with numerous Diagrams.

This book comprises the leading rules and data, with numerous tables, of constant use in calculations and estimates relating to Practical Mechanics:—presented in a reliable, clear, and handy form, with an extent of range and completeness of detail that has not been attempted hitherto. This (the fourth) edition has been carefully revised, and in its preparation advantage has been taken of many suggestions made by those using the former editions.

"*Mr. Clark writes with great clearness, and he has a great power of condensing and summarizing facts, and he has thus been enabled to embody in his volume a collection of data relating to mechanical engineering, such as has certainly never before been brought together. We regard the book as one which no mechanical engineer in regular practice can afford to be without.*"—Engineering

To be completed in 21 parts, super-royal 8vo, 2s. each; or in 6 volumes, cloth extra, 9s. 6d. each.

NEW ISSUE.

The Imperial Bible-Dictionary,

HISTORICAL, BIOGRAPHICAL, GEOGRAPHICAL, AND DOCTRINAL. Edited by Rev. PATRICK FAIRBAIRN, D.D., author of "Typology of Scripture"; &c. With Introductions by the Right Rev. J. C. RYLE, D.D., Lord Bishop of Liverpool, and Rev. C. H. WALLER, M.A. Illustrated by about seven hundred Engravings.

This Edition will be augmented by an interesting discussion on the subject of INSPIRATION, by the Rev. C. H. WALLER, Principal of the London College of Divinity. To this is prefixed a luminous introduction on the same subject by the Right Rev. JOHN CHARLES RYLE, Lord Bishop of Liverpool.

The Work takes up in alphabetical order all the subjects which enter into the contents of the Bible, while the several books of which the Bible is composed in every case receive careful and attentive consideration. In the treatment of the different topics, full advantage is taken of the materials which modern criticism and research have accumulated.

The Pictorial Illustrations include representations of the plants and animals mentioned in Scripture, notable scenes and places, manners of social life, and the manifold productions of human skill. In addition to these illustrations, a Series of Views engraved on steel in the most finished manner, accompany the work.

New Issue, to be completed in 6 half-volumes, imperial 8vo, cloth extra, 9s. 6d. each.

The Whole Works of John Bunyan,

Accurately reprinted from the Author's own editions. Collated and edited, with an introduction to each treatise, numerous illustrative and explanatory notes, and a memoir of Bunyan, by GEORGE OFFOR. Illustrated by engravings on steel and on wood.

Among the Illustrative Engravings will be found the Portrait of Bunyan after Sadler; and a careful copy of the interesting Portrait by R. White, now in the British Museum; Views of Bedford, and Prison on Bedford Bridge; of Bunyan's Cottage, the Market-house and Church, Elstow; and of Bunyan's Tomb in Bunhill Fields. Also, a Series of beautiful Illustrations of *The Pilgrim* from Stothard's elegant designs; with Facsimiles of Bunyan's Writing, and of the earliest wood-cut illustrations to *The Pilgrim*, and to the *Life of Badman*.

All the excellencies of this much admired and highly valued edition of Bunyan's Whole Works (of which over twenty thousand copies have been sold) are retained, the work being simply reprinted with occasional improvements in typography.

Eleven vols., post 8vo, cloth, red edges, 3s. 6d. each; or in handsome case, £2, 1s.

Commentary on the New Testament,

Explanatory and Practical. With *Questions* for Bible-classes and Sunday-schools. By ALBERT BARNES. Edited by the Rev. ROBERT FREW, D.D. With numerous additional Notes, and an extensive series of beautiful Engravings and Maps, not in any other edition.

Shortly before his decease the Author completed a revision of his Notes on the New Testament, to the end of the Acts of the Apostles, the only section of the New Testament respecting the exposition and illustration of which modern research had accumulated new and important materials.

In making this new issue the first three volumes have been re-set so as to embody the author's latest corrections and additions, and they are now presented for the first time to readers in this country. This issue will consequently be the most complete and perfect of any published in Great Britain.

In royal 4to, cloth, gilt edges, 30s.

Family Worship:

A Series of Devotional Services for every Morning and Evening throughout the Year, adapted to the purposes of Domestic Worship; Prayers for Particular Occasions, and Prayers suitable for Children, &c. By above TWO HUNDRED EVANGELICAL MINISTERS. Illustrated by Twenty-six fine Engravings on steel. New and Improved Edition.

The work comprises 732 Services, adapted to be used in the family, being a service for *every* MORNING *and* EVENING throughout the year, with Special Services for the Morning and Evening of New-year's Day. Each Service is composed of Praise, Prayer, and Scriptural Exposition. Thus it points out a suitable psalm or hymn to be sung; next it refers to a portion of Scripture to be read from the Bible itself, and adds some brief explanatory and practical remarks; and the whole closes with a plain and earnest Prayer.

LONDON: BLACKIE & SON, LIMITED; GLASGOW AND EDINBURGH.

www.ingramcontent.com/pod-product-compliance
Lightning Source LLC
Chambersburg PA
CBHW030734230426
43667CB00007B/704